The Lender of Last Resort

Quite simply, a lender of last resort is an institution willing to extend credit when no one else will. The lender of last resort serves to protect depositors, prevent widespread panic withdrawal, and otherwise avoid damage to the economy caused by the collapse of an institution.

This book, edited by two of the world's leading financial historians, collects together classic and modern research on the lender of last resort. As such it represents an authoritative, comprehensive account of the history of the concept and practice of this topic. With a wide variety of contributions the book offers a full analysis which will be of great use to students and academics of financial history as well as financial institutions themselves.

Forrest H. Capie is Professor of Economic History at Cass Business School, City University, London, UK.

Geoffrey E. Wood is Professor of Economics at Cass Business School, City University, London, UK.

Routledge International Studies in Money and Banking

Private Banking in Europe
Lynn Bicker

Bank Deregulation and Monetary Order
George Selgin

Money in Islam
A study in Islamic political economy
Masudul Alam Choudhury

The Future of European Financial Centres
Kirsten Bindemann

Payment Systems in Global Perspective
Maxwell J. Fry, Isaak Kilato, Sandra Roger, Krzysztof Senderowicz, David Sheppard, Francisco Solis and John Trundle

What is Money?
John Smithin

Finance
A characteristics approach
Edited by David Blake

Organisational Change and Retail Finance
An ethnographic perspective
Richard Harper, Dave Randall and Mark Rouncefield

The History of the Bundesbank
Lessons for the European Central Bank
Jakob de Haan

The Euro
A challenge and opportunity for financial markets
Published on behalf of *Société Universitaire Européenne de Recherches Financières (SUERF)*
Edited by Michael Artis, Axel Weber and Elizabeth Hennessy

The Lender of Last Resort

Forrest H. Capie and Geoffrey E. Wood

Routledge
Taylor & Francis Group

LONDON AND NEW YORK

First published 2007
by Routledge
2 & 4 Park Square, Milton Park, Abingdon, Oxon OX14 4RN

Simultaneously published in the USA and Canada
by Routledge
270 Madison Ave, New York, NY 10016

Routledge is an imprint of the Taylor & Francis Group, an informa company

Transferred to Digital Printing 2008

© 2007 Forrest H. Capie and Geoffrey E. Wood

Typeset in Times NR by
RefineCatch Limited, Bungay, Suffolk

British Library Cataloguing in Publication Data
A catalogue record for this book is available from the British Library

Library of Congress Cataloging in Publication Data
CIP data has been applied for

ISBN10: 0–415–32333–9 (hbk)
ISBN10: 0–203–32758–6 (ebk)
ISBN10: 0–415–46495–1 (pbk)

ISBN13: 978–0–415–32333–8 (hbk)
ISBN13: 978–0–203–32758–6 (ebk)
ISBN13: 978–0–415–46495–6 (pbk)

Contents

Acknowledgements

The authors and publishers would like to thank the following for granting permission to reproduce material in this work:

The British Academy for permission to reproduce 'Emergence of the Bank of England as Mature Central Bank' by Forrest Capie in *The Political Economy of British Historical Experience, 1688–1914* (2002).

The Journal of Economic Perspectives and Stanley Fischer for permission to reproduce 'On The Need for a Lender of Last Resort' (Vol. 13, No. 4, Fall 1999, pp. 83–104).

Every effort has been made to contact copyright holders for their permission to reprint material in this book. The publishers would be grateful to hear from any copyright holder who is not here acknowledged and will undertake to rectify any errors or omissions in future editions of this book.

Introduction

As the type of organisation that was by the early twentieth century, and arguably earlier, recognised as a central bank emerged, it was defined by two key functions. These were the conduct of interest rate operations so as to maintain whichever monetary regime had been chosen; and acting as the custodian of the financial system, helping the system (although not necessarily individual members of it) to withstand shocks. Although it is certainly not necessary to justify in times of contemporary relevance the re-publication of the papers in these volumes – every paper is important with regard to the stability function of central banks – it must be observed that a recent development in central banking has focussed attention, rather sharply, on that function. The recent development which has done this is its having become more and more common for central banks to be made 'independent' of government. This 'independence' has taken two main forms. One, rather unusual, is that accorded to the European Central Bank. That bank has been given the task of maintaining price stability in the Euro area, but left to decide for itself what price stability means in practical terms. The other form is that given to the Reserve Bank of New Zealand, and, in almost identical terms, to the Bank of England. Both these institutions were given a target for the rate of inflation, which they were required to hit.

They were also given another responsibility, however – that of maintaining what is termed in the Bank of England Act of 1998 financial stability. All the papers reprinted in this volume bear on the second issue, and are in particular concerned with what a central bank need do, and when, to maintain that stability. In this introduction we aim to provide a context for these papers. To do so we first summarise the key points in current discussions of the meaning of financial stability, and of how to attain it. Then we turn to the papers reprinted here, noting the lines of argument they open up. The introduction then concludes by very briefly relating these papers to current discussions.

It is, however, useful to open this introduction by dispelling the notion that one of the objectives usually nowadays assigned to central banks, price stability, is clear cut, while financial stability is rather woolly. The truth is that neither is easy to define, although both are important.

What is price stability?

Price stability has nowhere been defined as constancy of a particular index of prices. Rather, where a precise definition has been given, or, in the case of the ECB, chosen, it is for a low (by recent standards) rate of inflation, measured in terms of a particular price index. Both the chosen rate and the chosen index can be contentious.

First the rate. The ECB is sometimes accused of choosing a rate that is too low. Now, how can a rate above zero be too low? There are two possible, answers. The first of these rests on the now widely, but regrettably not universally, acknowledged fallacy that a little inflation is good for growth. The second of these is rather better founded in principle; we have no views on its practical significance. Goods change. Quality changes, in many cases improves, and how can this be allowed for if, for example, the price of the goods does not change? The answer is obvious in principle; assume that the price has fallen. By how much is not easy to decide, however. But on these grounds it can legitimately be argued that a small annual rate of price level increase corresponds to constant purchasing power over an unchanging bundle of goods of unchanging quality.

Neither is the choice of index clear cut. This was illustrated in the UK recently, when the Chancellor of the Exchequer announced (in 2003) that the inflation target to be aimed for by the Bank of England would cease to be the well-known and thoroughly familiar RPI, and become the narrower, and unfamiliar, HICP. Substantial criticism greeted the change, commenting on the difficulty of explaining policy henceforward, the difficulty of hitting a relatively novel index with only a short run of data available, and, important to note in this context, whether that index represented UK prices as well as the RPI did.

The then Chairman of the Federal Reserve, Alan Greenspan, remarked some years ago that price stability was when no-one worried about changes in the value of money in their decisions; that is exactly what is intended by asking central banks to maintain price stability, but the above brief discussion illustrates how difficult it is to formalise that idea.

Financial stability

One might paraphrase Alan Greenspan's above remark to define financial stability. One can see when a country has a stable financial system, but it is not so easy to make clear exactly what that means.

A helpful way of thinking about a part of the problem is to define stability as the absence of crisis. That of course needs a definition of crisis. Happily, one is to hand. One which has become classic was provided by Anna Schwartz in 1986.

A financial crisis is fuelled by fears that means of payment will be unobtainable at any price and, in a fractional reserve banking system, leads to a scramble for high-powered money. ... In a futile attempt to restore reserves, the banks may call in loans, refuse to roll over existing loans, or resort to selling assets. No financial crisis has occurred in the United States since 1933, and none has occurred in the United Kingdom since 1866.

Schwartz, 1986, p. 11; this vol. p. 245

But there is more to financial stability than the absence of crisis. Suppose one has been able to balance a pencil on its point. It might not be falling over, but it is hardly stable, for the slightest push would topple it. In other words, before a system can be described as stable it must not just be free of current crises, but must have stabilising mechanisms such that when it is hit by some shock, the shock is dampened, and dies out rather than spreading through the system. Only then can the system be described as genuinely stable.

What can the central bank do to provide such a mechanism? Do its responsibilities extend to that? The answer is that they certainly do, and the mechanism was invented some two hundred years ago. The mechanism is the Lender of Last Resort. What is that, and why was it invented, when, and by whom?

The lender of last resort

The classic role of lender of last resort can best be illustrated by reference to a financial crisis. Schwartz's definition of a financial crisis, given above, is in a line which runs back to Henry Thornton and to his Paper Credit of 1802. It focuses on the banking system, and is concerned with the possibility that a bank failure would lead to a scramble for cash, which in turn can cause more bank failures, lead to a sharp contraction in the money stock, and then in turn to recession, perhaps even to depression. That chain of events is certainly not unknown; it is a brief sketch of what happened in the Great Depression in the United States. The chain can be broken by the central bank acting as lender of last resort – that is, providing cash to the system so as to match the sudden, panic-driven, demand for it. Indeed, were it believed that the central bank would act in that way, there might be no panic driven surges in the demand for cash. When urging the Bank of England to commit itself always to supply cash in the event of a banking panic, Walter Bagehot argued along just those lines:

> What is wanted and what is necessary to stop a panic is to diffuse the impression that though money may be dear, still money is to be had. If people could really be convinced that they would have money ... most likely they would cease to run in such a herd-like way for money

Bagehot, 1873, pp. 64–65

The Bank of England learned to behave in that fashion and there were no crises after 1866. The Federal Reserve learned the lesson in the Great Depression and there were no crises after that. Serious problems in banking might appear, such as the Savings and Loans episode in the US in the 1980s. But these were certainly not crises in the sense of Schwartz and their effects did not spread to the banking system as a whole.

Yet the importance of that role has in recent years been downplayed. Capital markets today are said to be so much more widely developed than they were in the nineteenth century that any solvent firm can get liquidity if needed, and significant flights to cash are no longer likely. That is not true. For example, if a computer failure meant that the entire liquidity of the system were stuck in one place, there would be a sudden shortage of liquidity, just as in a classic banking panic. Classic lender of last resort action – the injection of liquidity to meet a sudden temporary increase in demand for it – can still be necessary.

But should that 'classic' role be extended? Some have argued that being a 'crisis manager' is part of that role. Should central banks try to forestall events which could otherwise very well require them to act as classic lender of last resort, or might be imperfectly resolvable even with such action?

This may well be the way that the Federal Reserve viewed its role in engineering the rescue of Long-Term Capital Management (LCTM) in 1998. By preventing the collapse of LTCM, the Federal Reserve saw itself forestalling problems, possibly substantial, at several large banks. But there is actually a much more persuasive justification than that for the Federal Reserve action (Edwards, 1999). In the LTCM episode the institutional mechanism for resolving LTCM in an orderly liquidation did not exist. Usually bankruptcy law provides for an automatic stay of the firm's assets. This prevents individual creditors from disposing of assets under their control and thus gaining an advantage over other creditors. LTCM's situation was different, and very special, because of its huge derivatives position. Derivatives contracts had statutory exception to the automatic stay provisions of the US bankruptcy code. Derivatives contracts had clauses that give the counterparties the right to terminate the contract in the event of a default of any kind by a counterparty. Further, in the event of such default and termination, counterparties had the right to liquidate any of the defaulting counterparties' assets that they have in their control, *even if the assets are not directly related to the derivatives contracts in question.* Thus, default by LTCM on any of its obligations would surely have triggered a 'run' by its derivatives counterparties. The Federal Reserve in effect inserted itself as a 'trustee-in-bankruptcy' where the law did not provide for one, and thus prevented the financial market turmoil that could have emerged from a legal lacuna.

There may, therefore, be a role for central banks in acting as crisis managers when the institutional mechanism or legal procedures are not in place for there to be an orderly liquidation of an institution. Such circumstances may not be as unusual as one might on the basis of past experience expect, in view of the rapid liberalisation of financial markets around the world and the growing internationalisation of financial transactions. There are bound to be situations where the laws in one country conflict with those in another, and where the legal ambiguities are such that the liquidation of a financial transaction or institution may prove to be more difficult and time consuming than expected, rather than as quick and orderly as is desirable.

But note that such expansion of the role is intended to promote stability of monetary conditions. It is a new way, necessary because laws have not been adapted adequately to changes in financial markets, to achieve a long-established goal.

Do asset prices matter?

Some scholars and practitioners argue that not only is lender of last resort still important, but it is so important that it should encompass not only banking system stability, but also the stabilisation of asset markets. Should central banks concern themselves with stabilising them?

It would surely not be thought prudent if central banks started to use monetary policy to control house prices. More generally, if there were a boom in asset prices based on a rational assessment of improved future prospects, we would not want it stopped. And if it really were irrational, could monetary policy stop it? This is not to suggest central banks should not monitor asset prices for any information they may give about the future behaviour of the economy. And of course it would be legitimate to intervene if the problem were a sudden shortage of liquidity. Indeed, that is a traditional central banking role. It was carried out well by, for example, the US Federal Reserve in 1987, when it injected liquidity when trading was drying up for lack of it; and then withdrew it before it had any undesired inflationary consequences.

That recommendation may suggest an asymmetric response to asset price fluctuations – ignore booms, but provide liquidity if trading dries up for lack of it during a price slump. This is how the US Federal Reserve has behaved in some episodes (October 1987, as noted above, and also October 1988, and 2001); and it has been criticised for doing so. There have been two criticisms. First is the claim that it has led to the 'Greenspan Put' – the claim that in effect the Fed is underpinning the market. This would seem a little unfair, for the aim of the policy is to facilitate trading rather than stabilise prices. (The first may of course contribute to the second – or not.) Discussing that criticism would be a diversion from our subject now, but discussing the other criticism is not.

Some maintain that when asset price rises become 'unsustainable' they generate a probability of a sharp reversal. Central banks should worry about 'bubbles' because of the risk of subsequent 'bursts'. There must surely be doubts about that advice. First, the evidence that asset price crashes cause, precipitate, or predict recessions is not compelling (Wood, 2000). Second, any harmful consequences for the banking system that might occur following the collapse are prevented by liquidity injection if needed. Third, the record of central banks when tightening money because they are worried about a 'bubble' is not encouraging; on more than one occasion their doing so has produced a sharp downturn in the real economy. All in all, the conclusion on balance seems to be that the preferable policy – perhaps only because it is the lesser of two evils – is to let asset price booms run their course but ensure that there is sufficient liquidity in any ensuing price crash.[1]

Should institutions be propped up?

Some writers have broadened the definition of financial stability well beyond that implied by the absence of a crisis, to that of maintaining institutions in operation (see for example Crockett, 2003). The argument for the importance of institutions can in part be traced to Bernanke's (1983) work on the Great Depression in the USA, and in part to the 'too big to fail' doctrine. Bernanke argued that the depth and length of the Great Depression could not be explained by the monetary contraction alone. It was, he suggested, also due in part to the the number of banks which failed leading to the absence of 'channels of transmission' of credit from lenders to borrowers. This reduced investment and hence prolonged the recession. A puzzle with this is why the failed banks were not taken over, and run by new management with new shareholders; that, after all, is what often has happened in more recent years when a bank has failed. The explanation may well be that so many banks were failing, and so deep was the recession, that there was too much uncertainty for such take-over activity. It is therefore not clear that the results Bernanke found can support concern with institutions in times less extreme than the Great Depression.

Can any bank be too big or too important to fail? Certainly in the nineteenth century, the answer would have been no, as is well illustrated by the failure of Overend and Gurney. The consequences of that firm's failure were contained by classic lender of last resort action. In this context it is necessary only to note the vast (relative) size of that financial institution – by balance sheet ten times bigger than the next biggest. That historical episode does not help the 'too big to fail' doctrine.

Be that as it may, it is useful to consider what can be meant by 'fail'. Two aspects of the word must be clarified. The first is to note that in general large, well diversified, banks do not just collapse suddenly. Rather they decline, losing market share and perhaps shrinking absolutely as well as relatively. Thus so long as banks are allowed to grow and diversify, the problem we are discussing is unlikely to be common.

But although difficult, it is possible for a large bank, or group of banks which comprises a substantial part of a country's banking system, to get in

---

1   This conclusion is forcefully and elegantly argued in Trichet (2003).

difficulties quickly. Where there are such failures there can be a role for the central bank, a role properly described as crisis manager rather than as lender of last resort.

The central bank could act as an honest broker, finding a firm in the private sector willing to take over and run the failed institution, buying it for a token sum, injecting new capital, and supplying competent management. (That was exactly how the Bank of England behaved when Barings failed in 1995, and close to how it acted when Barings failed in 1890.) If such a buyer can not be found sufficiently promptly to keep the institution running, and if it is important that it be kept running without even a brief pause, then the central bank can organise public sector purchase and capital provision, and run the organisation until a private sector buyer can be found or a gradual run-down can take place.

The troubled institution (or set of institutions) is allowed to 'fail', in the sense that shareholders lose wealth and the management jobs; but the business is kept running rather than immediately liquidated. This leaves unsettled what should happen to depositors. Should they lose also? The answer surely must be that they should be protected to the extent of whatever deposit protection was in place before the failure, and no further; otherwise, what was the point of the deposit protection scheme?

Now, it is necessary to pause at this point and look back at the nineteenth century. After all, as observed above, when Overend and Gurney failed in 1866, it was huge relative to the rest of the system – bigger by that comparison than any bank today. No problems occurred as a consequence of not keeping it running; what short-lived problems there were resulted from the Bank of England being tardy in acting as lender of last resort. Why did no problems result from the bank's closure? One can conjecture that this was a result of the network of bank interdependencies being less extensive than now; but that is only conjecture, for no work has been done to test that conjecture. Indeed, and casting doubt on that conjecture, Overend's was extensively connected with other banks through its very large bill book. Accordingly, therefore, while the case for keeping an institution running (as described above) seems persuasive, it lacks the strong empirical backing that would be provided by demonstration of what has changed between 1866 and now to make such action necessary.

Another argument advanced for bailing out insolvent banks is that in a time of crisis it is difficult to tell an illiquid from an insolvent bank. Accordingly, a central bank should simply decide whether or not it wishes to lend to a bank, and not concern itself with the bank's solvency. Bagehot's advice was to the contrary; in a crisis, 'advances should be made on all good banking securities and as largely as the public ask for them' (p 70). This advice, Goodhart (1999) observed, was '. . . to distinguish, in part, between those loans on which the central bank might expect, with some considerable probability to make a loss (bad bills and collateral) and those on which little, or no, loss should eventuate' (1999, p. 351). That is surely right. But Bagehot's advice was also intended to serve another purpose. Showing that there is nothing new in the insolvency/illiquidity argument, one finds it tackled with his characteristic lucidity by Hawtrey (1932):

> In the evolution of the Bank of England as the lender of last resort, we have seen how at the beginning it was inclined to ration credit by refusing all applications in excess of a quota, but later on its restriction took the form of limiting the kind of security it would take. It is not ordinarily possible to examine in detail the entire assets of an applicant for a loan. Demonstration of solvency therefore cannot be made an express condition of the loan, at any rate at a time when the need for cash has become urgent. But the furnishing of security makes scrutiny of the general solvency of the borrower unnecessary. The secured debt being covered by assets more than equivalent to it, there is less need to enquire whether the remainder of the borrower's assets will be sufficient to cover the remainder of his debts.
>
> pp. 126–127; this vol. p. 190

Financial benefits of monetary stability

What is the connection between financial and monetary stability? How should we expect long-term price predictability to affect financial stability? We should not expect price stability to deliver perfect financial stability as a by-product, but it should certainly make it easier to attain. For it both reduces rate volatility at every point in the yield curve[2] and facilitates assessment of credit and interest rate risk. Does the evidence support this conjecture? We can look at evidence from the years of the gold standard to see.

It is a little difficult to make direct and straightforward comparisons between the gold standard era and the present day, for the behaviour of prices then was somewhat different from now. The trend was flatter; indeed, in Britain (and in most of the world) prices drifted down from 1870 to the mid-1890s, and drifted up thereafter until 1914. On average over the period, the price level ended up essentially steady; this is quite different from now, when the price level rises steadily, albeit more slowly than it has done in the recent past. The short term, too, is different, for prices sometimes rose and fell quite sharply year by year during the reign of the Gold Standard.

Britain and the USA had very similar price experience, but very different financial stability experience. In the gold standard period the British banking system was very stable, while that of the USA experienced a stream of failures. Why? Two factors were crucial – the lender of last resort and the difference between good and bad regulation. Britain had in the Bank of England an

---

2 It has this effect all along the yield curve because policy rates are stable at the short end, and long-term rates are not pushed around by changing inflation expectations.

effective lender of last resort from 1866. This provided stability in the banking system; hence the absence of crises thereafter. The USA, in contrast, did not have a central bank until 1914, and even then it did not act consistently as a lender of last resort until after the Great Depression. That is well known. What is also well known, but perhaps less often noted in this context, is the effect regulation has on banking structure. In Britain banks were allowed to merge, and to diversify both geographically and by activity. In the USA, in contrast, geographical diversification was restricted, and unit banking close to being the norm. The system was thus failure prone, and failures were common. Two points follow. First, while financial stability benefits from price stability, other factors matter. Second, we have a clear demonstration that regulation can impede financial stability. Regulation needs to be designed carefully. A more recent example of the same point is provided by Japan. In the aftermath of the collapse of asset prices there, the Japanese banking system was very weak and so in turn was the Japanese economy. This resulted because the banks had been allowed to count the appreciated assets in their capital – so when asset prices collapsed, so did their capital. So much for current context: it is now time to turn to the material in these volumes. This review is in three sections; classics, moderns and what we term 'internationalists'.

Classic texts

Section One contains some of the classic texts on the lender of last resort. These texts show that from an early date there was a clear appreciation of the nature of and the true role of the lender of last resort. This is particularly interesting for the fact that the banking system in the late eighteenth century was wholly different from that of the late nineteenth and mid-twentieth centuries. And yet the form of the lender of last resort proposed and used remained the same. Francis Baring's use of the term (dernier resort) at the end of the eighteenth century is both well known and often quoted. Very soon after Baring wrote his 'Observations' and 'Further observations' (in the same year as the 'Observations' and in answer to his critics), Henry Thornton set out with great clarity exactly how a central bank should behave in the normal course of business, and then when a crisis blew up. He covered all the important issues; even today it is difficult to improve on his contribution over much of the subject area. The essence of central banking for Thornton was:

> to limit the amount of paper issued ... to let it vibrate only within certain limits; ... to allow of some special, though temporary, enquiries in the event of any extra ordinary alarm or difficulty; ... This seems to be the true policy of the directors of an institution circumstanced like that of the Bank of England. To suffer the solicitations of merchants, or the wishes of government, to determine the measure of bank issues, is unquestionably to adopt a very false principle of conduct.
>
> Thornton (1802) p. 259

Thomas Joplin was equally clear (though for a number of reasons less influential) in particular on what was needed in the 1825 crisis. A particularly vivid account of that crisis is contained in the chapter reprinted from E.M. Forster's biography of Marianne Thornton, Henry Thornton's oldest daughter. At his instigation she wrote a series of letters to Hannah Moore, detailing the sequence of events during the 1825 crisis, as described to her every evening by her father. These letters, written in the course of the crisis, are as close as it is possible to come to a description of that crisis in Henry Thornton's own words.

From the 1840s onwards Bagehot was the great expounder of the kind of views originally developed by Henry Thornton and Joplin. Following the legislation of 1844 and the 1847 crisis he wrote:

> It is a great defect of a purely metallic circulation that the quantity of it cannot be readily suited to any sudden demand; . . . Now as paper money can be supplied in unlimited quantities, however sudden the demand may be, it does not appear to us that there is any objection on principle of sudden issues of paper money to meet sudden and large extensions of demand. . . . (Such a policy) should only be used in rare and exceptional circumstances.
>
> Bagehot in Stevas vol 9, p. 267

Bagehot was only twenty-one years old when he wrote that. He went on to refine his ideas over the next quarter century, culminating in the publication of *Lombard Street*, in 1873.

Thomas Tooke was the most prominent and important member of the Banking School. His work on the *History of Prices* (with Newmarch) was his principal claim to fame. But he was a major figure in the debates of the second quarter of the nineteenth century and we include here his evidence to the Select Committee on Commercial Distress in 1848. In particular, for the role of the lender of last resort, he saw problems in the 1844 legislation that separated the Banking Department and the Issue Department.

The delightful Gibbs–Price correspondence of the 1870s could have been included on the grounds of entertainment alone; but it is useful for the way in which it examines many of the basic issues, and brings out the need for regular repetition of the doctrine. In the twentieth century Ralph Hawtrey (1932) obliged with another lucid statement, notable in particular for its treatment of the insolvency/illiquidity issue. A few years later (1940) Charles Rist, coming with a slightly different perspective, provided another splendid treatment that placed the nineteenth century classics in better perspective and illustrated the themes with reference to France and the Banque de France. Yet discussion of the subject refuses to go away, as is evidenced in the sample of articles in the next section, some of which appeared only recently.

The moderns

The position that emerged on the lender of last resort was by the end of the nineteenth century clear cut and essentially unanimous. There were the reservations of Thomson Hankey, that a lender of last resort would promote moral hazard, but apart from those there was acceptance of the views first articulated by Thornton in 1802. This agreement persisted into the 1930s, when as noted above they were restated with great clarity by Hawtrey, and to 1940 with Rist.

Hesitations and qualifications started to emerge later in the twentieth century, and, indeed, continued into the twenty-first. What may be termed the classical position is restated in this section ('Moderns') in the opening paper, a famous study by Anna Schwartz. She emphasised that the focus of concern should be the stability of the banking system, not of an individual institution, and that episodes which damaged that system, 'real crises' in her terminology, should be distinguished from 'pseudo crises', such as losses of wealth and exchange rate falls. Challenges to this position take three forms. Some maintain that there should be concern with individual institutions – that some can be 'too big to fail'. Some argue that there should be concern with the financial system generally, encompassing not just institutions other than banks but also asset prices. Some maintain that what has been described as the 'classical position' is in part at least a misunderstanding of what Bagehot, for example, intended. There were also attempts to argue that there should be an 'international lender of last resort'; that subject is examined briefly next.

In his paper 'Myths about the Lender of Last Resort', Charles Goodhart criticised some beliefs which he saw to be false, or alternatively (and sometimes also) based on a misreading of history. He also argued that the lender of last resort role should be somewhat different from that urged by the then contemporary defenders of what they viewed as the classical position. He directs attention in particular to the very limited ability of national central banks to absorb losses. Further, he argues that *only* lending to individual institutions should be regarded as a lender of last resort operation, on the grounds that more general lending is hard, indeed usually impossible, to distinguish from normal open market operations. This is a fascinating and in some respects contentious paper, which opens up a wide range of issues.

Some writers worried about moral hazard, an issue which Goodhart maintains is often over-emphasised. Both Hirsch and Kindleberger are concerned about this, the former suggesting that it was more readily avoided in conditions such as those which prevailed when Bagehot was writing, when banking was more of a club whose members by and large knew and abided by the unwritten rules. Kindleberger was exercised about the implications for taxpayers in general if lender of last resort were extended much beyond the classical practice.

Indeed, a large part of the recent discussion on the subject has been concerned with how far the lender of last resort can be pushed without impairing incentives to efficiency and prudence, and how far it needs to be pushed to preserve the stability of the financial system. There is a tension between preserving the stability of the system so that its behaviour does not threaten the economy at large, and at the same time preserving market discipline and allowing the system to change as new entrants, new methods, and new firms appear. Much of the modern discussion is concerned with trying to resolve this tension.

Capie, in his paper examining how the Bank of England evolved from being a bank distinct from others only in its close and privileged relationship with government to being a fully-fledged central bank, considers these matters. He concludes that the classical position is sound; experience shows that failures, even failures of big banks, need trouble neither the banking nor financial systems, nor the economy at large, so long as monetary stability is maintained. This discussion is, however, carefully embedded in the historical context in which the events leading to that conclusion took place, and a challenge on the grounds that a changed context requires changed methods could still be made. Some of the papers reprinted here raise that possibility, but no-one has as yet pursued it rigorously.

The importance of institutional context to this subject is emphasised also in the papers by Humphrey and by Bordo. The former ends up resoundingly supporting the classical position, as vigorously articulated by Schwartz in modern times. Bordo reviews a range of possibilities, including the 'free banking' view that a central bank with its associated lender of last resort function is both unnecessary and undesirable. He concludes by rejecting both free banking and proposals to broaden the lender of last resort role, albeit adding a rider on the desirability of branch banking.

International

In recent times financial crises appear to have increased in scale and in frequency even if the definition has become increasingly loose and is sometimes extended to cover almost any disturbance in the money, financial, or foreign-exchange markets. Solutions too have abounded and frequent reference has been made to the possibility of an international lender of last resort and of the International Monetary Fund or some such body being the international equivalent to the central bank as the lender of last resort. We believe that a close reading of most of the contributions in Section Two is at odds with this. A proper understanding of what the lender of last resort is, and what makes it possible for most central banks to be such lenders, rules out the possibility of an international equivalent. It is essentially the fact that modern central banks are the sole issuers of their respective currencies that allows them to be and indeed obliges them to be lenders of last resort in their domestic economies. They and they alone are in a position to provide to the market the liquidity that is needed. They must acquire a reputation for good behaviour first though and then learn how to both inject and extract extra liquidity as required. In the international economy there is no international money and hence no possible provider of that kind of international liquidity. All the problems of moral hazard and so on therefore appear when any attempt at replicating the process is made.

Nevertheless, when as distinguished an economist as Stanley Fischer writes of the need for such a lender and proposes that the IMF can fulfil the role there are clearly grounds for discussion. This is what Section III provides. We include a brilliant piece by Hugh Rockoff in this section not because it speaks directly to the question. It could just as easily have appeared in Section II elucidating Bagehot's contribution. But Rockoff does touch on the idea, one that has appeared quite often, that the Bank of England was the international lender of last resort when the gold standard was in its heyday in the closing decades of the nineteenth century. (The idea also has parallels in the discussion of monetary unions when the gold standard is sometimes said to be an illustration of a monetary union.) This is certainly worth considering though we think it would be subject to many of the criticisms that Calomiris and Schwartz make in more general terms in relation to the possibility for such an institution at the present time. Calomiris argues that the use of IMF assistance in crises in the 1980s and 1990s was not only improper but a danger to the stability of international finance. The IMF has been engaged in these episodes – essentially in bail-outs – obviously using taxpayers' money. This is the antithesis of true lender of last resort action. Schwartz attacks Fischer's proposals for the IMF directly. And she makes the point that although when capital markets are limited or repressed there may be a case for an international lender (though the case is not made for there being one in a crisis) that was not the case in the 1980s and 1990s.

Conclusion

As could be seen from the review of contemporary debates with which this introduction opened, while there are substantial areas of agreement over what a central bank need do to preserve financial stability, there remain significant areas of dispute also. The papers reprinted in this volume need no justification in terms of contemporary relevance to support their reprinting; every one illuminates, and in some cases influenced, an important aspect of central banking practice. But by showing the evolution of central banks' financial stability responsibilities and actions, and the context in which that evolution took place, they will indubitably inform current debate, and may well advance it.

References

Bagehot, Walter (1873) *Lombard Street*. John Murray, London.

Bernanke, Ben (1983) 'Non monetary effects of the financial crises in the propagation of the Great Depression' *American Economic Review*, Vol 73, No 3 (June) pp. 257–276.

Crockett, Andrew (2003) 'Strengthening financial stability' in *The Regulation of Financial Markets*, ed. P. Booth and D. Currie, IEA, London.

Edwards, Franklin (1999) 'Hedge funds and the collapse of long term capital management' *Journal of Economic Perspectives*, Vol 13, Spring pp. 189–210.

Goodhart, Charles (1999) 'Some myths about the lender of last resort' *International Finance* Vol 2, No 3 (November) pp. 339–360.

Hawtrey, Ralph (1932) *The Art of Central Banking*. Longman, Green and Co, London.

Seabourne, T. (1986) 'The summer of 1914' in *Financial Crises and the World Banking System*. Macmillan, London. Ed. Forrest Capie and Geoffrey Wood (1986, op cit).

Schwartz, Anna J. (1986) 'Real and pseudo financial crises' in *Financial Crises and the World Banking System*, ed. Capie and Wood op. cit.

Thornton, Henry (1802) 'An enquiry into the nature and effects of the paper credit of Great Britain'.

Trichet, Jean-Claude (2003) 'Asset price bubbles and their implications for monetary policy and financial stability' in *Asset Price Bubbles: The Implications for Monetary, Regulatory, and International Policies*, ed. W. C. Hunter, G. G. Kaufman and M. Pomerleano, MIT Press, Chicago.

Wood, Geoffrey (2000) 'The lender of last resort reconsidered' *Journal of Financial Services Research*, Vol 18, no 2/3 (December) pp. 203–228.

Section One

The classics

1 Observations on the establishment of the Bank of England

And on the paper circulation of the country

Sir Francis Baring, Bart

Observations, &c.

The sudden changes, and even convulsions, which circulation and commercial credit have experienced since the commencement of the year 1793, will serve as an apology, I trust, for an endeavour to draw the public attention to measures of foresight and precaution.

Circulation, as the word implies, must have a pivot or centre on which the whole can turn; and that centre, as far as relates to the island of Great-Britain, is the Bank of England; whose paper or notes represent that object, for every useful or beneficial purpose.

The prosperity which this country has enjoyed, the wealth and resources which it possesses, having been attributed, in a great degree, to the establishment of the Bank, (although, in truth, much more has been owing to its constitution) some individuals, for the sake of relieving their own distress, and to furnish the means for wild speculations, have made a great noise about the circulating medium; endeavouring to inculcate an idea, that if so much trade and prosperity attached to the amount of Bank Notes formerly in circulation, the issue of Bank Notes ought to be increased at present, in proportion to the actual extended trade of the country.

Their object was, not to multiply Bank Notes for the purpose of general circulation, nor for the use of the public, but solely to increase commercial discounts; under cover of which they expected their purpose would have been answered. They therefore founded an alarm as to the want of a circulating medium; and, as the term was not generally understood, whilst it held forth an expectation of relief to pecuniary distress, so many joined in the cry as to create serious apprehensions in the minds of the sober impartial part of the community. Any thing may become a circulating medium; paper is as good a representative sign as gold, and in many instances it is better, – because it is more easy to manage and to transfer; but then it must be understood, that with a correct knowledge of the basis on which such paper is founded, it enjoys the most perfect confidence: in which case, the only difference consists in such paper being the circulating medium for the country where it issues; whilst gold or silver are the circulating mediums in every part of the world – for both are no more than representative signs.

If there were more gold than was wanted, confidence in it, as a representative sign, would slacken, and it would no longer become a circulating medium: If Bank Notes were augmented, so as to be sold at a discount, confidence would vanish, and those Notes be no longer a circulating medium.

It would be desirable, for the purpose of probing this question to the bottom, to ascertain what proportion the issue of Bank Notes has borne to the gradual increase of the Commerce of the Country, although the disclosure would not be prudent in other respects: but I cannot think it possible for the one to require an augmentation of the other in an equal degree; and it remains to be proved that the amount of Bank Notes, before the war, did increase in proportion to the increased trade of the country, before the necessity can be admitted for an augmentation to the circulating medium, in consequence of the large addition to our trade during the war, although such addition is accidental and temporary.

If it shall be urged that such a discussion is become unnecessary, for that no such clamor exists at present; I must answer, that it is impossible to understand the principles upon which the Bank of England is established, the nature of its public and private interest, and more particularly to appreciate the real situation of the country in respect to the paper circulation, without entering into some details and explanations with regard to past occurrences; and I must further request, that my readers will always recollect, that the Bank never did absorb the whole of any operations or circulations: the Bank must be confidered solely as the centre or pivot, for the purpose of enabling every part of the machine to move in perfect order; sometimes by furnishing an addition to the powers necessary to enable that machine to perform its functions, and at others, by receiving back those powers which are superfluous; and although such a position must confequently be limited, yet its importance to the general welfare evinces a necessity of preserving to the Bank a capacity of acting with effect, and without delay, in both those cases.

The operations of the Bank may be considered under three distinct heads:

The first and most important relates to the GENERAL CIRCULATION OF THE COUNTRY.

The second – ITS TRANSACTIONS WITH GOVERNMENT BY LOANS, PAYMENT OF DIVIDENDS, &c.

The third – COMMERCIAL DISCOUNTS.

If it shall ever become a question to sacrifice a part to save the rest, I can have no doubt but that the general circulation of the country ought to have a decided preference; and if ever the Bank shall be reduced to that dilemma, and that the administration of their affairs shall then be correct and pure, their solidity will rest on a rock beyond the possibility of being shaken. We have already experienced the facility with which Government can liquidate a part of their loans; and they could discharge the whole, if necessary, without producing any convulsion in the country. I do not know the amount of the bills discounted by the Bank for commercial purposes nominally; but when the state of their affairs was laid before Parliament, the amount could not have been large; at least it must have borne a small proportion to the commerce and solid circulation of the country; but if the amount of paper discounted for fictitious and stock-jobbing purposes shall be deducted therefrom, the remainder will bear a very small proportion indeed to the whole; – and therefore the commerce of the country would not receive a fatal blow if the Bank should decline discounts altogether, unless it was done abruptly; especially, as it would not be difficult to provide resources for the solid part of the commerce of the country in the case of such an event: – but, as we have experienced a capacity on the part of the public to discharge their loans without much difficulty, if the Bank could be liberated from their commercial discounts in case of need, with equal facility, their notes would then become really and *bona fide* the representation of coin or bullion.

These subjects are no doubt gloomy, and I may be blamed for having mentioned them; but whilst we are disposed to adopt half measures, every thing may be apprehended; and therefore it is right to look forward, to point out the consequences, and at the same time to suggest such means as occur to prevent, or alleviate, those which are pregnant with danger. In this respect it is proper to consider what would be the result if the Bank were annihilated, in consequence of confidence in their paper being destroyed.

The convulsion would no doubt be great, the difficulty and distress incalculable, but the country would not be ruined. The existence of the Bank depends no doubt on that of the country, but the reverse is by no means the cafe. If the fall of the Bank should be owing to the misconduct of its Directors, the calamity would be great; however, in a short space of time, a remedy or substitute might be found, to answer many very substantial purposes. But if its miscarriage should arise from the operations or interference of Government, confidence must vanish, and its restoration in any shape or form become impracticable.

Very few foreigners have understood the principles on which the Bank is established; they have always considered their Notes as Government paper, and the experience they have had of the practice of Governments in every country, induced them to suppose that when gold was refused on the presentation of the Notes, the Bank and the country were equally ruined. They could not distinguish between paper issued for the sole purpose of circulation, limited in its amount, and under the authority and responsibility of a corporate body, absolutely independent, – and that paper which Government could issue *ad libitum*, bearing an interest, which rendered it an object for persons to purchase as a productive investment of their capitals; – they were very much astonished to find the total amount of Notes in circulation to be so small, compared with the commerce and wealth of the country; and equally so, that after all, Bank Notes continued to circulate at par. Those opinions, however, did not prevail at home, for the knowledge of the sources from whence those Notes issued, namely, deposits of bullion, loans to Government, and commercial discounts, together with the confidence reposed in the Directors, from the manner in which they represented the consequences of those pernicious measures which were then pursuing, – and the resistance they finally made to the expectations of the Minister, when the case absolutely required it, – induced the public to place sufficient reliance in them, under such conduct, and with such responsibility; the more so, as the personal attachment of a very large majority of the Court of Directors to the present Administration was well known, and for whom the powers of the Bank had been stretched in a certain degree.

From long experience, the Directors of the Bank must understand correctly the amount to which their Notes can circulate without depreciation or discount; and although they acted very wisely at the awful moment to issue a larger sum than usual, yet the event has proved, that they have conducted themselves with equal judgment, by not extending their issues beyond what the currency of the country requires, and can support.

It was from a combination of these, and some other circumstances, not necessary to be mentioned at present, but more particularly from a confidence in the conduct of the Directors, as a corporate body, that they would maintain and preserve the independence of the Bank in their transactions with Government, notwithstanding the partial influence which now and then prevailed, – that their Notes continued to circulate at par, with the same facility and convenience to the public as before, and that confidence was restored to a degree much beyond what could have been expected; whilst, however, the slur must remain, and never can be effaced.

As the circulation of the Bank of England, although the most important, doth not form the largest part of that of the country in general, it becomes necessary to take a more comprehensive view of the subject, in order to entertain a correct opinion of the whole. The establishment of Country Banks is of modern date, and within my recollection; but I believe there was no material convulsion, with regard to circulation, from the Rebellion, until that which happened by the failure of the Air Bank, in the year 1772. This failure was accompanied with others of great extent at the same time in Holland; – but as it was evidently a partial, and not a general convulsion, the Bank of England acted very wisely, by affording even a liberal support to those houses whose solidity was unquestionable, leaving others which were rotten, to fall; and as they were swept away, confidence was gradually restored. The next check to commercial credit arose from the failure of a circulation established between Lancashire and London, well known in the courts of law by the case of Gibson v. Johnson, which has been so often tried; but, although the amount was large, it moved in so narrow a line, that it produced no general effect on the country. What happened in the beginning of 1793 was, however, very different: far beyond any thing which preceded, or has followed it, in magnitude, it pervaded, more or less, every part or place in both islands, and affected every description of property. The last, and most important event, in one respect, is that which compelled the Bank of England to suspend their payments.

During the interval between the failure of the Air Bank, and the distress of 1793, a very material change had taken place in regard to the general circulation: Banks had been established in almost every town, and even in villages, throughout the country; and in the larger towns rival establishments were formed. These produced a most important, and whilst it was secure, a beneficial change to the country, by increasing its circulation: but unfortunately the principles on which those Banks were usually established, were insecure, in their being compelled at all times to invest or employ the deposit left in their hands, and thereby rendering themselves incapable of facing a sudden storm, or, as it is called, answering a run upon them, which, from natural events, must, in a course of time, arise. A Banker in London never allows interest to his customers, and can afford to reserve a proportion of his deposits, to enable him to answer sudden demands, or a run on his house; as he thereby sustains no real loss, but only diminishes the amount of his profit. The country Banker is in a very different situation, for he allows interest on deposits, and therefore he cannot afford to suffer even a small sum to remain dormant and unproductive; for every 100l. which he suffers to remain in that predicament, is a loss of the interest which he pays to his customer, and which interest he must get reimbursed (by investing the money) before he can realise any profit for himself. Thus it will appear, that whilst the circulation was greatly increased, and its beneficial effects enjoyed, by the commerce, manufactures, agriculture, &c. of the country, it was founded on the most insecure principle, and liable to almost instantaneous convulsion, by unforeseen, and even trifling circumstances. This might be promoted, more or less, by the practice of particular establishments; for if Country Banks, whose principals are men of large unquestionable property, should fail, the contagion will immediately spread, and the consequences are incalculable. Thus, for instance, in the beginning of the year 1793, and of the present year, the Banks of Newcastle stopt payment, whilst those of Exeter and the West of England stood their ground. The partners in the Banks of Newcastle were far more opulent, but their private fortunes being invested, could not be realised in time to answer a run on their Banks. Their Notes allowed interest to commence some months after date, and were then payable on demand; by which means they had not an hour to prepare for their discharge. The Banks at Exeter issued notes payable twenty days after sight, with interest to commence from the date of the Note, and to cease on the day of acceptance. There can be no doubt but the practice of the Banks at Newcastle is more lucrative, whilst it must for ever be liable to a return of what has happened. The twenty days received at Exeter furnishes ample time to communicate with London, and receive every degree of assistance which may be required. It is therefore most earnestly to be wished, that a law should pass, to prevent Country Banks from issuing Notes payable on demand, as they never can be in a situation to pay without some notice; and the country ought to be protected against those convulsions which have arisen, and will continue to arise from such a practice.

Another circumstance contributed very materially to produce the distress of 1793, which was the sudden, unexpected declaration of war. That dreadful calamity is usually preceded by some indication which enables the commercial and monied men to make preparation. On this occasion, the short notice rendered the least degree of general preparation impossible, and which may be ascertained by the prices of stocks in the preceding month of October, and various collateral circumstances. The foreign market was either shut, or rendered more difficult of access to the merchant; of course he could not purchase from the manufacturer; and an important variation in the rate of exchange on the Continent, furnished a pretence to foreigners to withhold their remittances from both. The manufacturers in their distress applied to the Bankers in the country for relief; but as the want of money became general, and that want increased gradually by a general alarm, the country Banks required the repayment of old debts, being utterly incapable of increasing them, and which of course brought their own situation to the test.

In this predicament the country at large could have no other resource but London; and, after having exhausted the Bankers, that resource finally terminated in the Bank of England. In the mean while, the alarm in the country continued to increase; confidence in their Banks vanished; every creditor was clamorous for payment, which he insisted should be made in gold, and which was complied with, until the Bankers in London were exhausted. At first the Bank accommodated themselves to the circumstances, and furnished large supplies; but unfortunately the Directors caught the panic; their nerves could not support the daily and constant demand for guineas; and for the purpose of checking that demand, they curtailed their discounts to a point never before experienced, and which placed every part of the commerce of the country in a considerable degree of danger. This dreadful convulsion (for it really was so at the time) was occasioned by the erroneous principle upon which country Banks are established, and that principle operated upon in the manner I have described. I can readily believe, that under all circumstances it might then have been right for the Bank to lessen the amount of their discounts, or to lessen the amount of the accommodation which individuals had been accustomed to receive, but then it ought to have been gradual; their determination, and the extent to which it was carried, came like an electrical shock.

In such cases the Bank are not an intermediate body, or power; there is no resource on their refusal, for they are the *dernier resort*. The laws against usury effectually destroy every other means of relief in this country, whilst experience has proved, at Hamburgh, at Amsterdam, and other places, that the most effectual mode of keeping the rate of interest low, is to leave it free from every restriction. But this point has been very fully discussed by Mr Bentham, in a small tract, entitled 'A Defence of Usury,' which has never been answered, because in truth it is unanswerable. As the determination of the Bank was founded upon the demand which came from every quarter of the country for guineas, I must beg leave to add some remarks on that subject. I do not mean to offer those remarks for the information of the Directors, as they are no doubt well informed on the subject; nor do I pretend to arraign their conduct, as circumstances may have existed to justify their proceedings, although it may be improper to disclose them publicly. I can reason only upon what is generally known, and upon those principles in which I am persuaded the Directors will agree.

For the present purpose, it may be sufficient to confine the considerations, as to the cause of the demand for guineas, to three heads:

First, As a Medium of Remittance to foreign parts, to supply the want of Bills of Exchange.

Second, For the purpose of Hoarding in the country, from a want of confidence in the Government, and in the circulating paper.

Thirdly, To enable Country Banks to discharge their demands, whilst confidence in the Government, and in the Bank of England remained entire and perfect.

The first is the most dangerous, as being the most injurious to the country; every measure ought to be taken to palliate or prevent it, prohibitions or bankruptcy excepted; but it is inevitable, if we shall continue for a long time to have more to pay to foreigners than we receive from them; or, in other words, if the Balance of Trade is against us.

The Second is the only circumstance which can in any measure justify the late bankruptcy; but I wish to reserve this point for future consideration.

The Third ought to be viewed, not with perfect indifference, but with a disposition on the part of the Bank to supply almost their last guinea; as they cannot be sent abroad, but must return again to their own coffers, as proved to be the cafe in the year 1793.

It was notorious, at the time, that large quantities of gold and silver were received from France; of course none could be sent thither.

The following calculation will serve for Amsterdam, viz.

100 guineas cost, with freight, insurance and charges,...............£106 13 0
Sold at f12 each, is f1200, agio 100½ per cent. is banco
f1193, II, and at the average exchange of 386 from
January to March 1793, is £103 6 9
Loss £3 6 3

The price of guineas at Amsterdam was invariably f12, from January to the 12th April, 1793; but guineas were hardly ever in sufficient quantity in Holland to become an object of trade, until the British troops landed in February, 1793.

The calculation for Hamburgh appears still more unfavourable.

100 guineas cost, with charges.. £106 13 0

They contain, in ducat gold, at Hamburg, 225 ducats, at
96½ banco per ducat, is marks banco 1357, at the aver-
age exchange of 35, 3 .... £102 10 6
Loss £4 2 6

The price of 96½ is the par for a ducat, which was about the average price
for January, February, and March, 1793.

In this situation of the foreign exchange, it was impossible that the coin of
the country could have been exported: individuals will not act contrary to
their own interest, which operates in such cases more effectually than acts of
parliament; and is in reality the only wise restriction which ought to exist, in
a country so much dependent on its trade. Individuals must pay freight,
insurance, brokerage, and some small expences, in addition to the loss on the
price; so that no impartial person can entertain apprehensions for a moment,
under such circumstances. The export of foreign gold and silver ought
always to be free, and the Bank ought to supply the demand, whenever it
shall arise; under a certainty that the export will produce a beneficial effect
on the course of exchange, and thereby ensure its return, (provided the balance of trade is in our favor) with additional profit. The coin of the country
may, however, be in a different situation; but on this subject I will not enter,
as it will require a volume to discuss. If the balance is against us, whether
arising from our trade, or as the result of subsidies paid to foreign powers,
that balance must be paid in gold or silver; and if there is not sufficient
foreign bullion in the country for the purpose, guineas must and will be sent,
or Bank Notes will be reduced to an enormous discount: it is in vain to
prohibit what cannot be hindered; the severest law will only tend to throw
that profit into the pocket of the smuggler, which would otherwise belong to
the fair trader.

I must distinguish, however, between that drain which is the result of a
balance against the country, and forced operations for temporary purposes,
which Government, with the aid of the Bank of England, can more or less
prevent. Thus for instance, at the commencement of the French revolution,
the Comptroller-General endeavoured to draw silver from hence, and from
other places, to serve temporary purposes at Paris, which the Minister
stopped. If his object was to benefit this country, or to distress the finances of
France, he ought to have encouraged and promoted such operations; or,
which would have been most effectual, he ought to have remained a silent
spectator. Such was the state of the exchange at the time, that each operation
cost 12½ per cent. and as those operations could have been performed four,
five, perhaps six times in the course of a year, the benefit to this country, and
the loss to France, could only have been limited by the extent of the powers of
the latter; and which must in time be exhausted, when 100l. Sent from hence
in silver shall be found to return in two, or at most in three months, with an
addition of 12l. 10s. for profit. Such operations would have produced a real
effect without the aid of acts of parliament, or the hand of power; whilst the

wild and ignorant speculations on the consequences of the assignats and mandats of France, have vanished in smoke.

I trust that I have said enough to prove, that in the beginning of the year 1793, when the foreign exchanges were favorable, and that no disposition existed in the country to hoard, from a confidence in the Bank of England; whatever may have been the demand for guineas, they could not be sent out of the kingdom, but must return to the place from whence they came.

If any doubt shall exist on the subject, I should desire to produce an indirect, but collateral proof, in the novel and very extraordinary measure which was brought forward at the time, to relieve the public distress; I mean the Commercial Exchequer Bills for five millions sterling, voted by parliament for the purpose; a measure which was attended with complete success. This success, however, has served unfortunately for a precedent to introduce a similar measure as a job, or for partial purposes. At this time the distress was universal in England, Scotland, and Ireland; the capital felt it in an equal degree; and the Bank must have participated; for nothing short of real distress could justify their conduct towards the country at large, and the cordiality with which they concurred, in having recourse to so extraordinary a measure for the purpose of general relief. Those Exchequer Bills were voted for the use of the general circulation; and the Commissioners were active and anxious to disperse them in every quarter to which they could be applied with security and effect. The event proved that their endeavours fully answered the intention of the legislature; for in a space of time scarcely credible, confidence was completely restored, money became plentiful, and the commission was terminated with a profit to the public, after every expence had been defrayed.

A most unexpected discovery, however, was the result of this extraordinary measure; namely, the very extensive and important effects which may be produced from a cause comparatively trifling. The circulations from the Air Bank, and from Holland, in 1772, were very large. Those from Lancashire, mentioned before, were, I think, to the amount of about two millions; but it was now found that the universal distress in which every part of the three kingdoms was involved, and even the Bank of England itself, could be completely and effectually relieved by so small a sum as two millions one hundred thousand pounds sterling; which was about the amount of the Exchequer Bills issued on this important occasion. A single drop of oil (and the sum of two million one hundred thousand pounds, when compared with the property and circulation of the country, is no more than a drop) withheld from the main spring or pivot on which a great machine turns, will disorder the whole. It must be evident that the Bank of England, in its relative position with respect to the country is, what I have described before, a pivot or centre, on which the general circulation depends; and however important in that respect, may be removed or substituted, without entailing the certain, positive destruction of the country.

These delicate subjects require investigation at a period when the frenzy of temporary distress will catch at every straw for relief: it has been urged with a degree of plausibility, 'Why not enable the Bank, by means of an adequate additional capital, to supply every demand which shall arise from commercial distress, and to face every storm?' or, 'Why not establish new and rival Banks for those purposes?'

To the first I answer, the Proprietors of Bank Stock will never consent to take upon themselves the expence and risk of increasing their capital, only because great and unforseen distress has arisen to the public in the beginning of 1793 and of 1797. They will ask, how could such additional capital be employed, and what profit would it produce in the years 1794, 1795, and 1796? Nor can the public expect such exertions on the part of the proprietors, when the subject comes to be thoroughly explained: especially as the public may at all times relieve the commerce, by reducing the amount of their loans at the Bank, and their floating securities in the market. I beg however to be understood, that I am not an advocate for making too great sacrifices to what is called commercial discounts; because I know, that under such pretence, much of the accommodation furnished by the Bank, has been absorbed occasionally by stock-jobbers, and improper speculations.

The second question requires some explanation; and although a part of what I shall have to say belongs more properly to the bankruptcy, yet I will bring the whole into one point of view, for the purpose of preserving the subject entire, and also to avoid repetition.

An honorable Baronet, (Sir William Pulteney) in a very able and ingenious speech, at the close of the last session of parliament, urged the propriety and facility of establishing a rival Bank, in case the Bank of England could not reassume their payments on a fixed day. I do not mean on this occasion to attempt to answer his speech, but solely to point out those obstacles, which, under the present circumstances, in my humble opinion can not be surmounted. I must confess that I do not consider the Bank refusing to recommence their payments on any fixed day, to be sufficient ground for a forfeiture of their charter. An enquiry must first be made into the cause of such refusal; and, if it shall be found that Government has been the real cause of their bankruptcy, however culpable the Directors may appear in the eyes of their constituents, yet the company are neither criminal nor culpable; and in such a case it would be the heighth of injustice for the public to deprive them of their charter, – provided the Proprietors of Bank Stock do not, by approving of the conduct of their Directors, make it their own.

Suppose, however, that a rival establishment should be permitted; common justice requires, that the debt due from the public to the company should be first discharged. It amounts to near twelve millions, and is lent to the public at an interest of 3 per cent. per annum, being 360,000l. If the Proprietors, on receiving payment of their capital, shall invest the same in the 3 per cent. consols, it would amount to twenty-four millions of capital, producing annually 720,000l. The Proprietors probably would not make any very serious objections to such an arrangement; but I doubt whether the public would feel disposed to pay so enormously for an experiment only, or that the Chancellor of the Exchequer would be very much pleased with an addition of 360,000l. annual taxes, to the amount of what the current service of the year requires.

But whether the present Bank remains or retires, no new establishment can be suffered to enter the lists, unless upon terms equally advantageous to the public, and with powers capable of performing equal service. It is therefore fair to ask from whence, or by what means, is such a combination to be formed? Can it be supposed that a real capital of twelve millions can be raised, in the first instance, when it is known that the whole must be lent to Government at an interest of 3 per cent. per annum, thereby reducing the value of their capital, at the market price, six millions sterling at one stroke? and I confess that it is beyond my skill in arithmetic to calculate the possibility of profit under such circumstances. I do not deny that subscribers may be found, of which we have an instance in the Air Bank, if the managers of the new establishment will promise an accommodation of 200l. for every 100l. Subscribed; namely, 100l. to make good the subscription, and the same sum for other purposes; in such case, indeed, there is no doubt but that subscribers will appear in abundance.

It is proper for me to mention further, that I differed essentially in opinion from the Honorable Baronet, in the principle for which he contended. The difficulty arose from a want of coin or bullion: paper was already too abundant, and measures had been adopted to reduce the quantity, which were proceeding gradually and with success. The old Bank could augment its paper *ad infinitum*, if that was the object; but the country was smarting under its pressure, and called for a reduction. A new establishment could not add one single guinea to those in circulation, (and the distress arose solely from the want of guineas) but could only increase the difficulty, and add fuel to the flame, by an emission of more paper; which must by degrees have led to a second bankruptcy, before it was possible to surmount the consequences of the first.

To the charter of the Bank of England this country is indebted in a high degree for the prosperity she has enjoyed; and to a clause in that charter, which prohibits any other establishments of a similar description, we may look as to a shield, to protect us against projects, such as those of the South Sea, the Mississippi, the Air Bank, &c. &c. It ought to prove a decisive answer to every new plan, for an increase of paper by means of a new Bank, that the Bank of England can, and must, issue to the full extent which the circulation of the country can support with safety; for their charter obliges them, and it is their interest to do so. If an addition is made by the means of a new establishment, the paper of one, perhaps of both Banks, must suffer a depreciation, and cannot circulate at par.

Paper, as a circulating medium, is more than convenient; for in these enlightened times it is necessary, and even indispensable. The difficulty arises from the consequences which result from the two extremes: in the case of too great an excess, depreciation, distress and convulsion must follow; but, if too much curtailed, the exertion and industry of the country is chilled, or palfied, and its growing prosperity thereby prevented. The Bank of England, from their central position, are most fortunately placed to form a correct judgment on this subject, and the amount of their Notes in circulation will constitute a perfect barometer, resulting from long experience and practice.

The tranquillity, confidence, and general prosperity which succeeded the first six months of the year 1793, and continued for those of 1794, 1795, and part of 1796, was wonderful: during those periods it frequently happened that money could not be employed at an interest of 4 per cent. per annum. I have very little doubt about the causes which produced this happy effect, but their discussion is unnecessary for the present: it is sufficient only to observe, that money became scarce towards the end of 1796, and that the Bank stopt payment in the beginning of 1797.

This very sudden transition from plenty to scarcity, from scarcity to distress, and from distress to bankruptcy, could arise from no common cause: – indeed all convulsions in the circulation and commerce of every country must originate in the operations of government, the plans of ministers, or in the mistaken views and erroneous measures of those possessing the power of influencing credit and circulation; for they are not otherwise susceptible of convulsion; and if left to themselves, they will find their own level, and flow in one uniform stream. The famous answer of the merchants of France, to the minister of Louis the XIVth, is often quoted, and its truth universally acknowledged, 'Let *us* alone.' It is in the mouth of every minister, but with a slight alteration, 'Let *me* alone;' by which means it is used as a ladder to private ambition, or for some great political operation; in both which cases the commerce and the country equally suffer. There is no doubt but that the prosperity of the country is in a great measure owing to its flourishing trade; but deep reflection will carry conviction to a strong mind, that the commerce of every country will flourish the more, as it is preserved separate and distinct from ministerial plans of political arrangement. Every attempt to blend these endangers the respectability and character of the nation. How much more dignified should we have appeared, for instance, in the eyes of Europe, if, in the conduct of the present war, the most prominent feature had not been a pursuit of plunder.

When the French party was prevalent in Holland, in the year 1787, the ambassador, (at the suggestion of the leaders of the party) offered to the merchants, to make any alterations for the purpose of introducing further commercial advantages into the treaty between the two countries. Such alterations would, no doubt, have furnished materials for many fine declamatory speeches; but the merchants were too wise to be so easily caught, – their answer was, 'Let the treaty alone.'

My object, in making these remarks, and which may be considered as a digression from the subject, is to state distinctly, that whenever the hand of power interferes in the circulation or commerce of the country, it always proves injurious, and sometimes destructive.

For the last six months of the year 1793, the whole of 1794, and until the close of 1795, money was as plentiful as in time of peace; but some slight appearances begun then to arise, which were very much increased in the spring of 1796. In former wars it had been the practice of ministers to form a combination of the most respectable monied men, to contract for the loan for the year; under an opinion, that as they possessed the powers, they would support and carry through the engagements they had undertaken to perform. On this occasion a set of gentlemen were selected by the minister, who did not possess those powers; as they had recourse to circulations, operations on foreign places, and other expedients, to enable them to make good their payments; which produced some effect on the course of exchange, but still more on the rate of interest in the country, which was soon pushed beyond what is allowed by law to be received; as the merchants, manufacturers, &c. can pay no more than 5 per cent. per annum, and as money was not to be obtained at that rate in the market, they were driven once more to the Bank as a *dernier resort*. In the mean while the calm and confidence which had reigned so long within the walls of the Bank, was materially disturbed, in consequence of the increased amount of foreign subsidies, and remittances to the continent, for the public account: these had increased beyond the capacity of the current circulating paper to supply, and therefore could not be melted down in the course of the year, by means of the balance of trade; but must be liquidated with gold and silver alone. How far those operations were conducted with common skill and judgment, I will not attempt to discuss, but shall confine myself solely to the effects they have produced. At first, and indeed for many months, the Bank acted in such a manner as to satisfy the public, and to keep the country quiet; but the demand for guineas must have been enormous: this will soon be understood from the following calculation of the profit to be obtained on exporting them to Hamburgh, in the months of January, February, and March, 1796.

The price of Gold abroad had advanced to 99¾ per ducat, which for 100 guineas makes 1402–12 marks banco, and at the average exchange of those months 32–3 is...£115 9 9
Deduct the cost as before...£106 13 0

  Profit.. £8 16 9

But as this was the highest price, it may be proper to quote the average of each month in 1796.

	Exchange in London	Price of Gold in Hamburgh	Produces on Exchange	Profit
In January	31–8	97½	34–2	7½
February	32–8	99⅝	34–10	6½
March	31–11	99	34–8½	8⅜

With such documents in the possession of every foreign Merchant, there is no occasion to ask a question either of the Minister or of the Bank: there must exist some forced unusual operation, by which the country was drained of its bullion, and of its coin, beyond a possibility of continuing for any length of time; and this drain was in a great degree the Imperial Loan, aided by some other collateral circumstances.

As the public attention was particularly drawn to the Imperial Loan at the time, and as it formed the prominent feature in the remonstrances from the Bank, it has been considered as the sole cause of the general embarrassment. I wish therefore to explain, that it was the magnitude of the sum, not the description of service, which created the difficulty. It must be indifferent to the country, if bullion is exported, to what service it shall be applied; but it is of infinite importance, whether the magnitude of the sum shall exceed, or fall short, of the balance of trade. Whether money so exported shall be applied to the payment of the British troops in Germany, for the foreign expenditure of fleets in the Mediterranean or Lisbon, or whether it shall be for an Imperial Loan, or foreign subsidies, is exactly the same to the country; for whilst the balance of trade is favorable, the money must return.

I do not mean to insinuate that foreign loans, or that foreign expenditures, are subjects of indifference to the country; they are no doubt clear unequivo- cal losses, which the calamity of war has produced; but my endeavour is, to distinguish correctly the effect which they produce on the general circulating coin, when they exceed, or when they fall short of the balance of trade. It is no doubt most ardently to be wished, that there should be no occasion for the exportation of bullion; or in other words, that there should be perpetual peace; but during war, one of the most essential services which commerce can render for the aid and assistance of the public, is to furnish from that treasure which the balance of trade has contributed to accumulate during peace, the gold and silver which the exertions and exigencies of the state shall require for their operations abroad during the war. It is by such means alone, that the political and commercial powers have formed a combination of strength both for offensive and defensive operations, which has astonished Europe; although from the lavish profuse manner in which they have been applied, they have not always produced their proper effect.

It was, therefore, not the nature or description of service, which rendered the Imperial Loan so injurious; but so many drains on the bullion of the country existed previous thereto, and at the time, that the addition of such an enormous sum produced the most pernicious consequences. The alarm of the Bank, and their remonstrances, were well founded; and their situation, if such operations had continued, was pregnant with real danger. They had strug- gled, however, through the year 1796, and must finally have surmounted this difficulty, as any further Imperial Loan had been abandoned, and the foreign exchange was turning in favor of the country, when an event happened which was decisive on the fate of the Bank.

After what has been mentioned, it may be expected that the amount of the guineas in their possession must have been reduced to a low ebb, when the landing of a handful of French troops created an instantaneous general alarm, and occasioned a demand for money, to which neither gold nor silver in bullion could be applied, as nothing would be accepted but the circulating coin of the country. Persons of almost every description caught the alarm; tradesmen, mechanics, and particularly women and farmers, (to whom I am ashamed to add many of a superior class and rank) all wanted guineas, for the sole purpose of hoarding. In the year 1793, when confidence in the Notes of Country Banks, and in every other description of paper had vanished, those of the Bank of England circulated with the utmost freedom, and without the slightest hesitation or doubt. But on this occasion Bank Notes at first were considered almost as waste paper, so that it was impossible to satisfy the timid and ignorant with any other payment but guineas.

If this event had happened before the Bank had been drained for foreign services, it might have produced a temporary effect only, which they could have faced by means of their usual deposits, under a persuasion that the cause would soon be removed, on finding that the attempt on the part of the French was not supported. But it came at a moment when their stock of guineas was already too low, and rendered the calamitous measure to which they adverted, in my opinion, indispensable. The demand for guineas ceased, no doubt; not because the desire of obtaining them had abated, but because the Bankers and Merchants united firmly to support the Bank in their refusal to issue guineas, and to accept of their Notes instead thereof, as a circulating medium. The cause of the calamity originated in those drains which had previously existed, to supply the foreign loans, and foreign services, on behalf of Government, and which had never been properly combined with the capacity which the country possessed to supply them; but what produced the crisis was, the landing of the French troops.

The timidity which appeared in many very sensible men, on that occasion, surprised me much: they must know the impossibility of obtaining a sum in guineas, in any degree proportionable to their property; as every person had an equal right to be supplied, and would hoard as well as themselves. Whatever sum they could obtain (as property, from its nature, cannot be entirely converted, but is more or less fixed and immoveable) would serve only for a short time, when their general property must serve at last, for a purpose to which it is equally applicable from the first; namely, that of exchange or barter. If the French could possibly land with an irresistable force; if the Bank of England was annihilated; if the public debt followed, accompanied with general confusion and convulsion, some order of things must either continue to exist, or soon be re-established: we know from authority more than human, what followed even a state of chaos. The circulating paper cannot be entirely destroyed; it must in every event preserve a certain value: in the first place, it must liquidate, and at par, a large mass of engagements by a mutual exchange, as those who hold a large sum in paper have generally a large sum to pay: the balance which results, after such liquidation, will stand, however, in a very different predicament, and depends altogether on circumstances, but appears in such numerous intricate points of view, as to render a discussion impossible; excepting only that I cannot consider those balances, even viewing them in their worst light, as of no value.

Property must always exist under every government, and cannot be annihilated; its nominal value will vary considerably; but its comparative value, although it may be affected for a time by accidental circumstances, will in the end be more or less the same. The comparative advantage, therefore, of any one description over another, in cases of public convulsion, is at least very dubious, and opens a wide field for opinion. It depends, at the same time, upon the magnitude or value of such property: my argument applies chiefly to that which is considerable, for a small amount will admit of managements of which even a few thousand pounds are not susceptible. The depreciation or annihilation of property, is however a very different question; for in case of convulsion or general calamity, all must, or ought to suffer; many, or perhaps most, will endeavour to escape; but perhaps this is neither to the credit of their head or their heart. I must however add, that whatever may be their intention, they cannot succeed except in a certain degree. To explain my ideas more fully, on the subjects of paper and of property, I will beg leave to state the probabilities of an investment to the amount of ten thousand pounds, in the case of an invasion, or even conquest of the country, by a foreign enemy, with a view to the security of the individual; and for that purpose I will compare what I conceive to be two opposite extremes; I mean wheat or corn, with Bank of England Notes. The sum of ten thousand pounds, vested in corn, will form a mass of considerable bulk, and cannot escape the knowledge of the neighbourhood; it will no doubt preserve its comparative value more than any other article, because it is indispensable; but in this superiority consists its disadvantage or danger: for what relates to the neighbourhood, they will pay for their purchases by an exchange of goods or labour, as far as their capacity will permit, by a transfer of debts to a certain extent; and as the exchange and the transfer cannot suffice for the whole amount, they may perhaps offer in payment for what remains the circulating medium of the time; for persons in such situations cannot be possessed of gold or silver. If the proprietor accepts such payment, all objections against the circulating medium vanishes; but as it is probable the wealthy proprietor or farmer will refuse, the neighbourhood will not starve, with the means of subsistence in view; and then the common proverb may be literally verified, that hunger will break through stone walls. With regard to invaders, or suppose even that they are conquerors, they would demand corn as well as money; and their requisitions would be more irresistable for corn, which cannot be concealed, than for articles which are less bulky and more easily kept from notice: these circumstances are independent of fire, and depreciation of quality. If it shall be said, that the objections are against the mass, or amount, and not to the article, I must answer, that the effect will be the same, whether corn is withheld by one or by twenty persons. Its being withheld produces the consequences; in the first place against the large masses, but finally against all; and the same argument will apply against holding a stock of any article of superior use or necessity for the public, in cases of convulsion and danger.

The circumstances which would attend the Notes of the Bank of England do not require so much detail. Under every situation of calamity, convulsion, or invasion, most of the gold and silver would disappear, and something must be substituted. In such a predicament what substitute can equal the paper of the Bank of England? the extent being so moderate, compared to the circulation of the country, and issuing totally independent of the Government. It would even be for the interest of an invading enemy to support a Bank so established; for by destroying it they would deprive themselves of the mean of drawing any advantage for a long period from a conquest. When the French took possession of Amsterdam, they were wise enough not to touch the Bank; and Bank money at Amsterdam is worth much more since that invasion, than it was before. I am therefore disposed to think it possible, that even in such an event as is now stated by way of supposition, paper of this description, instead of being the worst, would prove the best security in which property could be invested. At all events, a wheat stack may be consumed by fire, and the whole of the capital lost; but something must attach, in my opinion, to a Bank Note in the worst of times, so long as the independence of the Bank on Government shall be preserved, and that their paper in circulation doth not much exceed its present amount.

If I have explained my meaning, and am founded in my arguments, it will appear that convulsion will not operate partially, but generally upon property; and that the precipitancy with which one description of property is rejected, in preference to another, is not likely to produce the desired effect; but that all or most will have their comparative value. Perhaps it may illustrate this point still more, by observing, that if my neighbour, who is worth 50,000l. Shall be reduced to 25,000l. whilst my fortune of 10,000l. is reduced to 500l. and that the fortune of every person is reduced in the same proportion, our comparative situations will be the same, and we should enjoy the comforts and luxuries of life in the same degree. In short property of every description, land, corn, paper, & c. &c. all must suffer under a general convulsion; a part, more or less of each, will no doubt be lost; but a part of each must also remain.

If I entertain a favorable opinion of the paper of the Bank of England, it is natural that I should wish to see every endeavour used to strengthen the general confidence, and to protect it against the possibility of depreciation; and although I am persuaded that in case of absolute necessity the country could exist and prosper without the Bank; yet, so long as it can be maintained, and enjoy a well-founded confidence, the prosperity of the country will increase far more rapidly and extensively; at the same time, the ease and accommodation which accompany it must contribute very much to internal tranquillity.

Independent of mismanagement, the Bank may suffer from the following causes:

Convulsions in Country Banks, and country circulation, by which
means too great and sudden a demand may arise, similar to that of 1793.

An invasion by the enemy producing general alarm.

Too large an export to the Continent of its bullion or coin, for foreign
subsidies or services.

An improper influence of Government.

There are, no doubt, other circumstances of less importance, which either
by direct or indirect means will produce an effect on the Bank, but they are
not applicable to the present moment, or they would require too much detail
to investigate and explain; and at all events they cannot apply to shake the
confidence due to the Bank.

The first and third points have been already explained, and a remedy in
part only has been proposed for the first. When the bankruptcy took place,
and which I have no doubt was brought to a crisis by the trifling and con-
temptible circumstance already mentioned, the legislature thought proper to
screen the Government, who were the cause, in consequence of the previous
drains on the country for foreign services; and the Bank, who were the
defaulters, by making Bank Notes a legal tender as far as related to themselves. But the blameless suffering public were deprived of such a shield; those
Notes were not a legal tender between individuals, who were given to understand, that if they were compelled to have recourse to a court of law, by
means of sophistry and quibbling, they should have – not relief – but
something which was never distinctly explained, as it never was correctly
understood. Confidence in the Bank, however, has supplied the want of legal
protection; and it may now be asked, what detriment or inconvenience could
have arisen, if the Notes had been made a legal tender for all? It is a miserable
subterfuge to suppose, that by such an arrangement the disgrace could be
palliated, or the word bankruptcy be evaded. In all great movements, whether
in mechanics or governments, or even in the intercourse of nations, the more
simple, general, and intelligible the principle, the greater is the power, and the
more certain is the effect. On such an occasion, it ought to have been one
common cause, of Government, Bank, and people; there could have been but
one opinion, as there was but one interest. The distinction was unjust and
invidious, whilst the event has proved that it was wholly unnecessary.

The situation of the Bank is now totally altered; in consequence of the very
high course of exchange with Hamburgh, which has produced a prodigious
influx of gold and silver, whilst the panic has subsided, and confidence is
generally restored. In this predicament, it merits serious consideration what
ought to be done in regard to the act of parliament which will soon expire.
Whether it should be suffered to expire? Whether it shall be renewed? Or,
whether it shall be continued with alterations? And from the most mature
consideration I am capable of giving to the subject, I am induced to prefer the
last, namely, that Bank Notes should be made a legal tender generally, during
the present war, under restrictions which I shall mention hereafter.

My chief reason is, that credit ought never to be subject to convulsions; a change even from good to better ought not to be made, until there is almost a certainty of maintaining and preserving it in that position; for a retrogade motion in public credit is productive of consequences which are incalculable. With this principle in view, I am averse to the Bank re-assuming their payments generally during the war, whilst there is a possibility of their being obliged to suspend them again.

We have experienced the consequences of the landing of only 1200 French; and an enemy will avail themselves of every circumstance which can produce an alarm. I have read and conversed with foreigners at many different periods of my life, on the subject of invasion; and although young men will recommend and hazard every thing for the chance of personal fame; yet I have been always impressed with an idea, that the judgment of the sober-minded, and particularly the scientific experienced men, always had two objects in view, namely, the possibility of success; but in case of miscarriage, the dangerous effect an attempt might produce on the Bank of England, in consequence of spreading a general alarm. And admitting always the impossibility of making a serious impression on the country, it is an object of real importance to guard against the confusion (in pecuniary concerns) which must result from the attempt, unless the Bank shall be protected in the manner I have proposed. It is in vain to treat the consequences of an alarm as chimerical, when so many descriptions of persons possess property which exceeds in value the total amount of the circulating coin of the country. For instance, the farmers, who have grown rich by the war, and hold more circulating paper than any other description of persons, and which consists, in a great degree, of the Notes of the Country Banks at present: but the farmers have been distinguished for taking the lead in cases of alarm. It is unnecessary to enumerate, or to enter into further details, as every well-informed person must be capable of judging on this point.

We have also found by experience, that no inconvenience can arise to individuals, or the public; for every person can procure with ease, as much gold coin as he wants to supply every common purpose. At the same time a power to withhold need not prevent the Bank from issuing as much coin as may be wanted, although it ought not to be issued with too liberal a hand, from the certainty of its being hoarded for a time, on the appearance of the most trifling alarm.

If this principle is adopted, and the conduct of the Directors shall be pure and correct, I am satisfied that it will promote confidence, as it must also increase the security of their Notes. But as the Directors are men, and of course fallible, it will be dangerous in the extreme to trust them with such power, without some efficient check and controul. They may, for the advantage of the proprietors, increase their circulating paper without bounds. Or, they may, under the influence of the minister, enter into loans or engagements beyond what the general security and safety can justify. These objects can only be attained by limiting the amount to which the company shall be permitted to issue their Notes; and which, as observed before, ought not much to exceed the amount of what is at present in circulation. The precise sum, and the regulations which are requisite, must be the result of mature consideration, and of practical knowledge; and which will not be difficult to arrange, if the principle shall be admitted.

I am aware of all the objections which can be urged against the making paper of any description a legal tender; and I should have been forward in opposition to every such plan or proposal, if the Bank had not already stopped payment. But whilst we have suffered the disgrace, no serious bad consequences have arisen; yet, if the same disgrace shall happen a second time, we may not be equally fortunate with regard to the consequences. I desire, however, to be understood, that I do not recommend Government paper of any description as a circulating medium; between that, and the paper of a corporate, independent, responsible Company, there is a wide difference, a long interval indeed.

The Exchequer Bills of Government never can circulate, and never will be taken as a medium, because the public never can rely on the amount being confined within proper bounds. So long as they are paid, or can be absorbed in the revenue, soon after they become due, they are of use to the Executive Government, and a benefit to the public. But when the amount exceeds the means of liquidation, they become a dead weight, and clog every channel of the general circulation in such a manner as to compel the Minister to reduce them once more within proper bounds. If this were not the case, Exchequer Bills and Assignats would be synonimous terms, and ultimately experience the same fate. The Assignats issued originally under a plan and promise for their gradual extinction, but when it was found that they continued to issue, to an amount far beyond what was extinguished, the discount bore a proportion to that amount, and finally swallowed up the principal.

I never could understand the reason for the clamor that was raised, and the philippics that were pronounced in this country against assignats. We were induced to suppose, from what we heard and read, that the destruction of assignats in France was necessary for the salvation of Europe. I confess that it always appeared to me those advocates totally mistook their object, which I presume was, to distress France by every possible means. They ought (I mean upon their principles) to have used every endeavour to encourage and support the assignats in France; because they would thereby have entailed an enormous debt on the country, for which taxes must have been imposed, soon or late, to defray the interest. What a situation the two countries would have been in, if peace could have been made, leaving the assignats in existence, with a discount of seventy or eighty per cent? thereby intailing upon the country the necessity of imposing taxes sufficient to pay the interest, and of course augmenting the price of labour in a proportionable degree. At present the debt of France is trifling, and the taxes, when peace comes, will scarcely affect the price of labour; whilst our own taxes, for the purpose of defraying the interest alone, will amount to full thirty shillings for every head; and which for every labourer, who generally pays for many others besides himself, cannot be less than three or four times that sum. It may be very easily said, that the French would at all events have availed themselves of a spunge at the close of the war; but experience authorises me to reply, that Republics are distinguished for preserving their faith towards the public creditor; and the conduct of the French on this occasion will justify it, for they made long, unremitting exertions, to support the credit of their assignats, thro' various administrations of moderantism and terror; nor did they abandon them, until every struggle had been made, and that there was a decided incapacity in the country to pay or to circulate. I know very well, that the magnitude of the public debt is not decisive on the fate of any country, but the price of labor is the leading prominent feature, where so much depends on foreign commerce for the support of that debt. At this moment no judgment can be formed, as we must conclude the war before any comparison can be made of our relative situations. The prospect is no doubt gloomy in the extreme, and the change may be aggravated from the extent of our present trade, which is temporary, and cannot, by any contrivance, be preserved after peace.

Amongst many other expedients to promote the circulation of assignats in France, when they bore a large discount; one was, to fix the price of provisions, and every article at which the seller should be compelled to receive those assignats in payment, and which was called the law of the maximum. So long as the real discount on the assignats bore a tolerable proportion to the maximum price fixed on the provisions, all went on smooth and well; but when the discount advanced, the provisions disappeared, and which was chief cause of the distress and famine which prevailed in that country.

The same fate will infallibly attend all government paper, or paper of any description, whether Exchequer Bills, or Bank Notes, which may be issued beyond a capacity in the circulation of the country, to receive at par. Not even the terror of Robespierre could induce the farmers or graziers to sell corn and meat at the nominal price of the assignats: in a very short time, notwithstanding the dread of the guillotine, two prices were established by universal practice, the one for money, the other for assignats; the interval, however, had been dreadful, having produced real distress and famine.

I think it will be superflous to add more, for the purpose of explaining the difference between government paper, which may be issued *ad libitum*, and that of the Bank of England; as a justification of the opinion I entertain, that the latter (under satisfactory restrictions) may be made a legal tender during the war, or at least under the present existing circumstances. It will not be sufficient however to say with Sir Thomas More, (on a very different occasion) *crede quod habes et habes*. The grounds on which confidence can be expected to rest must be fully explained, perfectly understood, and prove equally and generally satisfactory.

I have therefore to propose, that the principle on which Country Banks are established, should be taken into consideration; for the purpose of preventing, as far as the nature of the case will permit, such convulsions as happened to commercial credit and the circulation of the country in the year 1793.

That with a view to guard against a return of the shock, which happened in the beginning of the present year 1797, the Notes of the Bank of England should be made a legal tender during the war, or for such a period as shall be deemed most proper, under certain regulations and restrictions.

But if the legislature shall repose so much confidence in the Bank; or even if the present act of parliament shall be continued, the Bank should be restrained and limited in the amount for which their Notes shall be issued, as a security to the public with regard to the private interest of the Bank, and also to prevent their becoming, either directly or indirectly, the means of introducing Government paper as the circulating medium of the country.

Further observations

In consequence of my late publication, I have had the opportunity of receiving opinions which are entitled to the highest respect; and I therefore hope that I shall be excused for making a few additional Observations. These Observations were intended to follow the Second Edition, as a Postscript; but as the Bank and the Minister came forward with their plans sooner than I expected, I withdrew the Postscript until I could understand the nature and extent of the measures proposed. They are now fully explained; and as they fail in my humble opinion, by not providing against two material points, which I conceive to be necessary for the preservation of the internal tranquillity of the country, and for the security of the public against the misconduct of the Bank in certain cases; by not making Bank Notes a general legal tender, with regard to the first point; and by not limiting the amount or extent to which the Bank shall be suffered to issue their Notes, in regard to the second object; I shall forbear to offer these additional Observations in the usual mode of publication, but content myself with circulating them to those persons who I think may be disposed to consider the question in a private and deliberate manner; trusting that no disturbance or convulsion will happen to affect the paper circulation of the country; in which case any further regulation will be unnecessary. On the other hand, I shall rest satisfied in the discharge of what I conceive to be a duty I owe to the public, in explaining the true principle or basis on which the paper circulation rests, and the means by which it could have been secured against any temporary storm, or attack from within, or from without.

The material points which I have endeavoured to discuss in my former publication are:

Regulations with regard to Country Banks.
To make the Notes of the Bank of England a legal tender.
To render the Bank, as a Corporate Body, independent of Ministers.

And finally, to limit the amount, beyond which the Notes of the Bank shall not be suffered to circulate.

I have heard no objection against what I have mentioned with regard to Country Banks, except that the observations may be much extended; of which I was aware, as I know that every establishment must have some local circumstances attach to it; but it would be unjust to form a hasty decision in the capital, upon Banks in the country, without further information, and a more deliberate discussion.

A very small part of the circulation of Country Banks, consists of Notes payable on demand, and without interest: the danger arises from their Notes or running accounts on which interest is allowed. If the subject shall ever be seriously considered, with a view to legal restrictions, it is probable that Notes without interest may be suffered to continue as at present; not only because the comparative amount is small, but also for the convenience of the country circulation, which must not be impeded, and which cannot be substituted by the small Notes of the Bank of of England. When pecuniary operations amount to hundreds and thousands, Notes for pounds are proper, and answer the purpose of transferring debts from one person to another, in cases where gold would be inconvenient and troublesome; but, when it relates to the few guineas which are used in daily or hourly payments, and carried in every man's pocket, Bank Notes for pounds are inconvenient, whilst those of the Country Banks, for guineas, are totally the reverse; and thus the Notes of a Banker in an obscure village will always receive a decided preference in its neighbourhood.

But whilst I find every opinion concurs with mine, to preserve the independence of the Bank, and to limit the extent of their circulation, so long as they receive that protection from the law, of which individuals are deprived; yet many entertain doubts, and some are averse to making Bank Notes a general legal tender.

The gentlemen of the profession of the law are, with a very few exceptions, against making them a legal tender; at which I am not surprised; for the mind of every theorist must revolt at the idea. My opinion is founded upon personal knowledge and experience, as it will be seen in page 73 that I have reprobated the principle, which nothing but absolute necessity can justify. The question, however, is not, Whether we shall do that which in itself is most desirable and right? for something stronger than opinion has already decided the point: but, Whether the public are disposed, from motives of prudence and foresight, to take the only effectual measures to prevent a return of those convulsions to circulation and commercial credit, which *may* possibly arise from the circumstances I have already described?

With regard to commercial opinions, or those who entertain doubts, but who are few in number, I will beg leave to observe, that our object is precisely the same. If my proposal to make Bank Notes a legal tender for a time, limiting the amount, is not a better security for the public against abuse and danger, than to suffer the Bank to remain with an exclusive protection, and a power to issue their Notes to an unlimited amount; either my arguments have been misunderstood, or they are of no avail.

The mischief is already done, and a partial remedy has been applied, but a physician will be deemed unskilful and negligent, who, in the progress of a cure, does not take effectual means to guard against a relapse. It is difficult in the extreme to combat opinions which the present generation has received with their milk from the breast; the more so, as those opinions are just and well founded. If we really possessed the power and capacity of acting upon those principles, all would be well: but we are unfortunately deprived of those means, and in the midst of events and circumstances which are unprecedented in history, and beyond the powers of the human mind to fathom, we ought not to hesitate about a word, or a name, but to seize the substance wherever it can be found, and not to hazard the security of the country, by grasping at a shadow. I therefore repeat that in my humble opinion, to make Bank Notes a legal tender, limiting their amount, is much more safe, and more likely to secure the tranquillity of the country, than to suffer the Bank to remain as at present, with an exclusive protection, and a power to issue those Notes to an unlimited amount.

It is said, that an association of the Merchants and Bankers in London has been found sufficient to stamp a currency and confidence in Bank Notes, for the purpose of giving them a general circulation: this is true with regard to the metropolis, more particularly as the measure was accompanied with large and liberal discounts from the Bank of England at the time. But we must inquire into the situation of the country establishments in the months of February and March, many of which were tottering on the brink of ruin, whilst the Bankers in London, in consequence of the association, were put completely at their ease. They will tell you, that the Bank of England Notes were refused on many occasions by their customers; and that, instead of accommodation, ease, or advantage, they have experienced great difficulty, and a considerable diminution in the amount of their deposits. In short, the metropolis enjoyed on that occasion, a preference or advantage over the country at large, which is precisely the reverse of what ought to have been the case.

Such an association, which was composed of men of the most respectable characters and upright intentions, did all that could be done on the occasion, and merited the thanks of the public; but their resolution was founded on some knowledge of the amount, or nearly the amount, of Bank Notes in circulation: and an opinion that the Directors would maintain their independence. But, if the Directors should increase the amount of their Notes beyond a capacity in the public to receive them at par, either for the private interest of the Bank, or under the influence of Ministers, whatever resolution the members of that association may make to receive them at par, the public at large will appreciate those Notes according to circumstances, and attach a rate of discount, in proportion to the excess beyond what is a reasonable and proper amount.

When the Country Banks were distressed in the year 1793, they were supplied with guineas to enable them to discharge their demands, which were received, and understood. In February and March 1797, they could offer no other substitute in discharge for their own Notes, but those of the Bank of England, which were often refused, and their solidity often questioned, in consequence of the exclusive protection which the Bank enjoyed; and those difficulties were increased by the inconvenience arising from their Notes being made payable in pounds, and not in guineas. I know that such objections do not apply to Bankers in London, who have experienced ease and accommodation, instead of embarrassment: but they are serious evils with regard to the internal tranquillity of the country, and it must be remembered, that if the value of Bank Notes should fall below par, it is more likely to originate from the Grazier and Butcher refusing to receive paper for meat, or the Farmer and Baker for bread, than from any reluctance on the part of Bankers in London, whose rapid circulations will not afford them sufficient time to reflect, or to brood over the circumstances of a gloomy moment, whether well or ill-founded; more particularly, as their interest and convenience will induce them to support to the last moment, the value of paper, in which a proportion of their deposits must always be invested.

I therefore see no reason to alter the opinion I have entertained, and which has been strengthened by those who understand the subject much better than myself. But, as it has been determined, that Bank Notes shall *not* become a legal tender, I must express my regret that the Bank are *not* limited with regard to the amount of their Notes, so long as they enjoy any legal protection to screen them from payment. If the Bank shall reassume their payments, restrictions of any description would become totally unnecessary; but, under the present regulations, circumstances *may* arise to place the circulation of the country in a great degree of danger, and which it has been my endeavor to prevent and to secure.

I cannot conclude without acknowledging that some respectable persons have objected to the term of bankruptcy, which I have used in the preceding publication; and I freely confess that I should have been very forward to have apologised for my error, if I could satisfy myself that I had committed one on the occasion. My views were altogether prospective, and precautionary; it was therefore incumbent on me to describe the past distinctly, and not to overstep the truth; for, by whatever word, or in whatever manner, the event shall be described, I trust that I shall be believed when I assert, that I had no other motive in pointing out the danger we had escaped, but to call forth the attention of the public, to adopt measures for the purpose of preventing its return. Perhaps those who object, are not aware that the case is new, and without a precedent; of course, that no word, conformable to its common use and acceptation, can be correctly applied; for those who have suggested the words 'failure, suspension,' (which are the same) or 'insolvency,' should be apprised, that the Bank were *not* insolvent, nor could I be satisfied to describe an event which must stand conspicuous in the history of this country, as a 'failure,' when I have heard a lady use the same word in attempting to thread her needle. A state of insolvency is correctly understood, and is irretrievable; that of bankruptcy is more indefinite, for there are many instances where they are not insolvent, and which are ascertained by the commission of bankruptcy being superceded. I apprehend the name attaches more to a legal form of proceeding, than to a correct definition of real capacity or incapacity of the party to fulfil his engagements: and the reason why insolvent persons are anxious to prefer a deed of trust to a commission of bankruptcy, is, for the purpose of avoiding the disgrace which would thereby be published to the world. In the present instance, concealment was impossible. The Bank was not insolvent, they had more than failed, and had passed beyond the line of bankruptcy; for they had received from the legislature an exclusive protection, to the prejudice of their creditors, who were thereby left without an option; and who, in every other instance, may use their own discretion, in consenting to a deed of trust, in taking out a commission of bankruptcy, or, in arresting the person of their unfortunate debtor. Under such circumstances therefore, I humbly presume the word will not be deemed too strong, to mark the very bitter pill which the public has been forced to swallow.

FINIS.

2 Of country banks – their advantages and disadvantages

Henry Thornton

The country banks in Great Britain appear to have amounted, in the year 1797, to three hundred and fifty-three. By a numeration taken in 1799, they appear to have been three hundred and sixty-six. By a third numeration taken in 1800, they were three hundred and eighty-six.* It seems, therefore, that no material addition to their number has arisen in these three years.

A great increase of country banks took place during the time which intervened between the American and the present war, and chiefly in the latter part of it; a period during which the trade, the agriculture, and the population of the country must have advanced very considerably. The circumstances of so many of our country banks having originated at such a time, affords a presumption that they are consequences and tokens of the prosperity, rather than indications of the declining state of the country. No banks have arisen in France during the period of its troubles, though several attempts to erect them have been made. It was with difficulty that any banks supported themselves in America during the war; but after the establishment of peace, banks were instituted in most of the American states. They seem naturally to belong to all commercial countries; but are more particularly likely to be multiplied in a state like ours, in which the mercantile transactions are extended, the population is great, and the expenditure of individuals considerable; and where also a principal bank exists, which, through the necessity imposed on it by its situation, undertakes the task of providing a constant reservoir of gold accessible to every smaller banking establishment. The creation of the large bank operates as a premium on the institution of the smaller.

A description of the origin of one of our smaller country banks may elucidate the subject before us. In every town, and in many villages, there existed, antecedently to the creation of what were afterwards termed banks, some trader, manufacturer, or shopkeeper, who acted, in many respects, as a

---

* This statement of the number of country banks is taken from three printed accounts of them, the first of which may not have been very accurate, but may be presumed to state them at too low rather than too high a number. The two later enumerations were made in a more careful manner.

banker to the neighbourhood. The shopkeeper, for example, being in the habit of drawing bills on London, and of remitting bills thither, for the purposes of his own trade, and receiving also much money at his shop, would occasionally give gold to his customers, taking in return their bills on the metropolis, which were mixed with his other bills, and sent to his London correspondent.

Persons who were not customers being also found to want either money for bills, or bills for money, the shopkeeper was led to charge something for his trouble on accommodating them: and the trade of taking and drawing bills being thus rendered profitable, it became an object to encrease it. For the sake of drawing custom to his house, the shopkeeper, having as yet possibly little or no view to the issuing of bank notes, printed 'The Bank' over his door, and engraved these words on the checks on which he drew his bills.

It may be assumed, also, to have been not uncommon, before country banks were established, for the principal shopkeeper in a town to take at interest some of the money of his neighbours, on the condition, however, that he should not be required to pay it back without some notice. The money thus deposited with him, or borrowed by him (it is difficult to say which term is the more proper), might either be thrown into his trade, or employed in discounting bills soon to become due; but the latter would evidently be the more safe and prudent way of investing it.

All these parts of the banking business arose out of the situation and circumstances of the country; and existed in many places before the name of banker was assumed.

The practice of issuing country bank notes, that is to say, notes payable to the bearer on demand, may, undoubtedly, be considered as a separate branch of business. These notes, however, have been shown to be not so very different in their nature from other paper as is commonly imagined.

For the sake of more particularly proving this point, let us advert to the nature of interest notes, a species of paper which some country banks have issued to a great extent. Even the shopkeeper, it was lately observed, would take sums at interest. For each of these sums, especially if he became a banker, he would give out his note, in which would be expressed the sum lent or deposited, the rate of interest upon it, and the time which was to intervene before payment could be demanded. This note would be transferable to any third person. There would, however, be some impediments to its circulation. The interest must be calculated as often as it should change hands. Some of the persons to whom it was offered might not be disposed to accept it as a payment, especially if it had a long time to run. Although these notes might circulate, they would circulate heavily. In order to promote their circulation, and thus encrease the whole number of issuable notes, the banker would be inclined to lessen the time within which they should be payable; and he would find that, in proportion as he adopted this practice, a lower rate of interest on the notes would suffice to induce persons to take them. Notes carrying no interest would circulate, if due within a short time, better than notes bearing interest which should be due at a very distant period. But the only notes which would circulate freely would be those which should be payable, or at least paid, without any notice. Some banks wishing, on the one hand, to encourage the circulation of their paper, and, on the other, to avoid the inconvenience of a strict obligation to pay without notice have issued notes payable after a certain time, and yet have been in the regular practice of giving money for them whenever payment was demanded, and have taken no discount for the accommodation.

Thus, then, the shorter the notice is, the greater is the currency of the note; and, in proportion, therefore, as the circumstances of a country render it more safe for the banks to shorten their notice, in the same proportion it may be expected that notes to the bearer on demand will be issued, and gold displaced.

Some speculative persons have imagined, that the practice pursued by bankers of emitting notes payable on demand is founded on an altogether vicious and unwarrantable principle, inasmuch as such paper is issued with a view to a profit which is to be obtained only by lending out part of the sum necessary for the payment. A number of promises, it is said, are thus made, which the banker has evidently placed it out of his power to perform, supposing the fulfilment of them all to be required at the same time, an event by no means impossible. This objection implies that the banker ought not, after receiving the deposits left with him by his customers, to lend out part of the sum necessary for the payment of these deposits; for he is much bound to discharge demands for deposits without notice, as to pay without notice all his notes. The Bank of England, the London banker, the country banker, the merchant, and also the individual of every class, proceed, in respect to all their promises to pay money, not on any principle of moral certainty, but on that of reasonable and sufficient probability. The objection to bank notes, *as such*, if pushed to that extent to which, if it is at all just, it might be carried, would apply to all verbal promises to pay money, and, indeed, to almost all promises whatever; for there is scarcely any class of these for the performance of which a *perfectly sure* provision is always made at the time of giving the promise. The objection implies, therefore, that men ought to be prohibited from acting in their commercial concerns according to that rule of sufficient probability by which all the other affairs of human life are conducted*.

It is completely understood by the holders of notes, as well as by the

---

* In some of the democratic pamphlets of the present day, bank notes of every kind are spoken of not merely as liable to be carried to excess, or to be issued by irresponsible persons, or as producing particular evils, but as radically and incurably vicious; they are considered in the light of a complete fraud upon the public, which is practised by the rich, and connived at by the government; and the very issue of them has been stigmatized as equivalent to the crime of forgery. The resemblance of bank notes to other paper, and the resemblance of a promise on paper to any other promise, have been here touched upon with a view of exposing the absurdity of those doctrines.

customers of banks, that instant payment is provided for only a part of that sum which may, by possibility, be demanded; and the banker, therefore, seems fully justified if he makes such provision as the general and known usage of others in the same profession (for he is supposed, by those who trust him, to follow this usage), and a prudent regard to all the circumstances of his own case teach him to consider as sufficient.

The practice of issuing notes payable to bearer on demand became very common a few years antecedent to the present war, when various circumstances united to encourage this part of the country banker's employment. Confidence was then high, the number of traders in the country had been greatly multiplied, the income and expenditure of individuals were much increased, and every branch, therefore, of the banking business had naturally enlarged itself. Some addition had been made to the number of London bankers; and a few of these took forward and active measures to encourage the formation even of very small banks in the country, with a view to the benefit expected from a connection with them. In many of our great towns a fair opening was afforded for the erection of additional banks. These new establishments having taken place, various country traders, who had before made use of their own correspondents in London, fell into the practice of transacting their business with the metropolis through the medium of the country banker with whom they kept their cash. The country banker drew largely on a London banker on the account of the country traders, and the London banker was willing to execute the extensive country business which he thus acquired, in consideration of a much lower commission than had before been paid by the several country traders to their separate correspondents in London, who had been, for the most part, London merchants. The reduction of the rate of commission arose from two causes: first, from the new security which was afforded to the transactions between the town and the country, by the interposition of the credit of rich and responsible country banks; and, secondly, from the transfer to one house of that labour of keeping accounts, writing letters, and receiving and paying bills, which had, before, been divided among many. The risk and trouble being diminished, a proportionate abatement in the rate of commission could be afforded.

The multiplication even of country banks, purposing to deal chiefly in bills, would tend, in many ways, to produce an encreased issue of notes on demand. Some deposit of gold would be kept by banks of every class, with the view of satisfying the demands of their customers; and the stock, maintained for this purpose, would would form a part of the necessary provision for the payment of notes payable on demand, and it would, therefore, become an encouragement to the issue of them. The multiplication of deposits of gold through the country would, moreover, furnish, in many cases, more prompt means of obtaining gold on any sudden emergency; since one country bank might often procure a supply from a neighbouring one, especially if a good understanding on this subject should subsist between them. The establishment of mail coaches afforded, at the same time, a more cheap and ready method than before, of bringing gold from London, as well as of transmitting thither any superfluity of it which might arise in the country. In proportion to the facility of obtaining gold, the unproductive stock of it kept in hand might be reduced; or, if the same stock should be maintained, the issue of notes payable on demand would be less hazardous. Indeed, a few old and respectable country banks had long been in the habit of emitting much paper of this sort, and had seldom experienced any inconvenience from doing it. The new ones, therefore, many of which were not at all inferior in property to the old, were led into the practice partly by example.

The circumstances which chiefly operated in procuring currency to the new circulating paper, was that participation of the benefit resulting from it which was enjoyed by the customers of the country banker; for he lent among them the capital which was acquired by the issue of his paper, and they became his instruments in sending it into circulation, by accepting it as a ready-money payment in return for bills discounted. In consideration of their obligations to the banker, and of the interest which they had in his stability, they were also forward, on most occasions, in the support of his credit. Such appear to have been the chief circumstances which led to that great encrease of our country banks, and to that substitution of paper in the place of gold, which have been, for some years past, so much the subject of complaint.

In order to assist the reader in judging whether a preponderance of good or of evil results from our numerous country banks, an endeavour shall now be made to enumerate the principal benefits as well as inconveniences of them.

That country banks have, in a variety of respects, been highly advantageous, can scarcely admit of a doubt. They have afforded an accommodation to many descriptions of persons; but more especially to those who are engaged in commerce. They may be regarded as an effect of that division of labour which naturally takes place in every opulent country. The receipts and the payments of money are now no longer conducted at home, even by the middling trader, but are become a separate branch of business in the hands of bankers. It was to be expected that they to whom this employment has been transferred would find means of abridging labour, and of sparing the use of coin, the most expensive circulating medium. By their skill in attaining these objects, they transact an important portion of the business of the trader at an expense far inferior to that which he must incur were he to conduct it by his own clerks; and they derive a profit to themselves, which, no less than the saving to the customer, may be regarded as clear gain to the kingdom.

Country banks are also useful by furnishing to many persons the means of laying out at interest, and in a safe manner, such money as they may have to spare. Those banks, in particular, which give interest notes for very small sums, afford to the middling and to the lower class of people an encouragement to begin to lay up property, and thus to make provision for the time of sickness or old age. Country banks also furnish a very convenient method of distributing to one class of men the superfluity of another. All who have money to spare know where they can place it, without expence or loss of time, not only in security, but often with pecuniary advantage: and all commercial persons of credit understand in what quarter they can obtain such sums, in the way of loan, as their circumstances will fairly warrant them in borrowing. While country banks thus render a benefit of the first magnitude to fair and prudent commerce, they are important barriers against rash speculation, though not unfrequently they are loudly accused of favouring it. However some few banks may have subjected themselves to this charge, banks in general, and particularly those which have been long established, take care to lend the sums which have been deposited in their hands, not to the imprudent speculator, or to the spendthrift, by whom they are in danger of suffering loss, but to those who, being known to possess some wealth and to manage their concerns with prudence, give proof that they are likely to repay the loan. Borrowers of this class are not apt to enter into very large and perilous undertakings; for they are unwilling to risk the loss of their own capital. Bankers, especially men of eminence, feel a special motive to circumspection, in addition to that which operates with other lenders. The banker always lends under an impression that, if he places in anyone a boundless or immoderate confidence, the imprudence will necessarily be known, in case the borrower should fail, as the affairs of every bankrupt are laid open to the body of creditors; and that his rashness is, therefore, liable to become the subject of conversation among his customers. Indiscretion of this kind, even if the particular instance be of no prominent magnitude, may thus prove an occasion of injuring the character and credit of the banking house, and of lessening the general profits of the business.

The banker also enjoys, from the nature of his situation, very superior means of distinguishing the careful trader from him who is improvident. The bill transactions of the neighbourhood pass under his view: the knowledge, thus obtained, aids his judgment; and confidence may, therefore, be measured out by him more nearly than by another person, in the proportion in which ground for it exists. Through the creation of banks, the appreciation of the credit of numberless persons engaged in commerce has become a science; and to the height to which this science is now carried in Great Britain we are in no small degree indebted for the flourishing state of our internal commerce, for the general reputation of our merchants abroad, and for the preference which in that respect they enjoy over the traders of all other nations. It is certainly the interest, and, I believe, it is also the general practice, of banks to limit not only the loan which any one trader shall obtain from themselves, but the total amount also, as far as they are able, of the sum which the same person shall borrow in different places; at the same time, reciprocally to communicate intelligence for their mutual assistance; and, above all, to discourage bills of accommodation. While the transactions of the surrounding traders are thus subject to the view of the country banks, those of the country banks themselves come under the eye of their respective correspondents, the London bankers; and, in some measure, likewise, of the Bank of England. The Bank of England restricts, according to its discretion, the credit given to the London banker. Thus a system of checks is established, which, though certainly very imperfect, answers many important purposes, and, in particular, opposes many impediments to wild speculation.

Country banks, also, as well as the Bank of England, have been highly beneficial, by adding, through the issue of their paper, to the productive capital of the country*. By this accession our manufactures, unquestionably, have been very much extended, our foreign trade has enlarged itself, and the landed interest of the country has had a share of the benefit. The common charge which is brought against country banks, of having raised up a fictious capital in the country, admits of the following answer. They have substituted, it is true, much paper in the place of gold: but the gold which has gone abroad has brought back, as Dr Smith observes, valuable commodities in return. The guinea spared from circulation has contributed to bring home the timber which has been used in building, the iron or the steel which has been instrumental to the purposes of machinery, and the cotton and the wool which the hand of the manufacturer has worked up. The paper has thus given to the country a *bonâ fide* capital which has been exactly equal to the gold which it has caused to go abroad; and this additional capital has contributed, just like any other part of the national stock to give life to industry.

It has lately been objected to paper credit, that, by supplying the farmers with large loans, it has enabled them to keep back their corn from the market, and enhance the price. It is true, that farmers, both in the last and many preceding years, may have obtained larger loans than they would have procured if no country bank notes had existed. The capital so furnished to the farmers may possibly have induced some of them, at certain times, to keep in hand a larger quantity of grain than they would otherwise have found it convenient to hold. We know, however, that the general stock of grain in the autumn of 1800 was particularly low. Since, therefore, but a small part of the capital of the farmers, whether borrowed or their own, was then vested in grain, the principal share would probably be laid out on their land, and would encrease its produce; for, unquestionably, the value of a crop obtained from a

---

* Dr. Smith remarks, that it is not by augmenting the capital of the country, but by rendering a greater part of that capital active and productive than would otherwise be so, that the most judicious operations of banking can increase the industry of the country. 'Dead stock,' he observes, 'is converted into active and productive stock.' Whether the introduction of the use of paper is spoken of as turning dead and unproductive stock into stock which is active and productive, or as *adding* to the stock of the country, is much the same thing. The less the stock of gold is, the greater will be the stock of other kinds; and if a less stock of gold will, through the aid of paper, equally well perform the work of a larger stock, it may be fairly said that the use of paper furnishes even *additional* stock to the country. Thus, for example, the use of a new sort of machinery which costs less in the erection than that which was employed before, and which just as effectually does the work required, since it enables the owner to have always more goods in the course of manufacture, while he has exactly the same means of manufacturing them, might not improperly be described as adding to the stock of the country.

farm depends chiefly on the sum employed in cultivation and improvement. Country bank notes have thus added to the general supply of grain; and, by doing so, have contributed to prevent a rise in its price: they have, probably, in this manner, afforded much more than a compensation for any temporary advance in price to which they may have given occasion by enabling farmers to keep a larger quantity in hand. The very possession of a large quantity in hand is to be considered as, in general, a benefit rather than a disadvantage; for it is our chief security against scarcity, and, consequently, also against dearness. To the want of a large surplus stock at the end of the years 1799 and 1800 is to be ascribed, in a great degree, the subsequent high price of provisions. The tendency, therefore, of country bank paper to encrease generally the stock of grain in the hands of the farmer is to be ranked among the advantages of country banks. The tendency to encrease it at the particular time of actual scarcity, is to be classed among the evils which they produce; and it is an inconsiderable evil, which is inseparable from a great and extensive good. To those who are disposed to magnify this occasional evil, it may be further observed, that the farmer is enabled to enlarge his stock by the encrease of his own as well as of the general wealth, much more, no doubt, than by the share which he obtains of that particular part of the new capital of the kingdom which is created through the substitution of country bank notes for gold; only a portion, therefore, of the mischief complained of is to be referred to country bank notes. It is principally to be ascribed to the growing riches and prosperity both of the farmers and other inhabitants of the country.

It is no small additional recommendation of the use of our paper, that the public draws a large yearly revenue from the tax imposed on bills and notes. If paper credit did not exist, a sum equal to that which is thus raised must be supplied by taxes either burthening the industry, or paid out of the property of the people. The public has, since the late additional tax, become a very considerable sharer in the profits of the country bankers' business.

Since, therefore, a paper medium has served the purposes which have been described, and has been, generally speaking, quite as convenient an instrument in settling accounts as the gold which it has displaced, the presumption in favour of its utility seems to be very great; and, if it could be added, that no other effects than those which have as yet been stated have arisen or are likely to arise from it, the advantage of it would be beyond dispute. To reproach it with being a merely fictitious thing, because it possesses not the intrinsic value of gold, is to quarrel with it on account of that quality which is the very ground of its merit. Its merit consists in the circumstance of its costing almost nothing. By means of a very cheap article the country has been, for some years, transacting its money concerns, in which a very expensive material had previously been employed. If this were the whole question, the substitution of paper for gold would be as much to be approved as the introduction of any other efficacious and very cheap instrument in the place of a dear one. It would stand on the same footing with the substitution, for example, of cast iron for wrought iron or steel; of water carriage for land carriage; of a steam engine for the labour of men and horses; and might claim a high rank among that multitude of ingenious and economical contrivances to be found among us, by the aid of which we have attained to the present unrivalled state of our manufactures and commerce.

Some very solid objections, however, may be urged against the system of banking in the country.

The first which I shall mention, is, the tendency of country banks to produce, occasionally, that general failure of paper credit, and with it that derangement and suspension of commerce, as well as intermission of manufacturing labour, which have been already spoken of.

Country bank notes, and especially the smaller ones, circulate, in a great measure, among people out of trade, and pass occasionally into the hands of persons of the lower class; a great proportion, therefore, of the holders of them, have few means of judging of the comparative credit of the several issuers, and are commonly almost as ready to take the paper of any one house calling itself a bank as that of another. A certain degree of currency being thus given to inferior paper, even the man who doubts the ultimate solvency of the issuer is disposed to take it; for the time during which he intends to detain it is very short, and his responsibility will cease almost as soon as he shall have parted with it*. Moreover, the amount of each note is so small, that the risk seems also, on that account, insignificant. The notes of the greater and of the smaller country banks, thus obtaining, in ordinary times, a nearly similar currency, they naturally fall at a season of alarm into almost equal discredit. If any one bank fails, a general run upon the neighbouring ones is apt to take place, which if not checked in the beginning by a pouring into the circulation a large quantity of gold, leads to very extensive mischief. Many country bankers, during a period of danger, prescribe to themselves a principle of more than ordinary reserve in the issue of their notes, because they consider these as the more vulnerable part of their credit. They know, that if the character of their house should be brought into question, through the fears or even the caprice of any of those strangers into whose hands their circulating paper passes, some distrust may be excited among their customers, the effect of which may be a sudden demand for the payment of large deposits. The amount, therefore, of the country bank notes circulating in the kingdom is liable to great fluctuation. The country banker, in case of an alarm, turns a part of the government securities, bills of exchange, or other

---

* I apprehend that, supposing a country bank to fail, the holder of one of its notes, who should have parted with it in sufficient time to afford to the next holder an opportunity of applying for the discharge of it before the day of failure, could not be called upon for the payment of the value of it. The responsibility therefore, of him who has been the holder of a country bank note commonly ceases in about one or two days after it has been parted with. That of the holder of a bill continues till after the bill is due, namely, for a period, perhaps, of one or two months.

property which he has in London, into Bank of England notes, and those notes into money; and thus discharges many of his own circulating notes, as well as enlarges the fund of gold in his coffers. The Bank of England has, therefore, to supply these occasional wants of the country banker; and, in order to be fully prepared to do this, it has, ordinarily, to keep a quantity of gold equal to that of the notes liable to be extinguished, as well as a quantity which shall satisfy the other extraordinary demands which may be made at the same season of consternation either by banking houses, or by individuals. Thus the country banker by no means bears his own burthen, while the Bank of England sustains a burthen which is not its own, and which we may naturally suppose that it does not very cheerfully endure*.

The national bank, indeed, may fairly be called upon, in consideration of the benefits enjoyed through its monopoly, to submit to a considerable expence in supplying gold for the country; but there must be some bounds to the claims which can equitably be made upon it: and, in estimating the benefit arising to the kingdom from the use of country bank notes, we have either to deduct the loss which the Bank of England incurs by maintaining an additional supply of gold sufficient to answer the demands which they occasion, or else we have to take into consideration the risk which the bank incurs by only keeping a fund of gold which is somewhat inadequate. The country banks may, perhaps, cause the bank in some measure to encrease its general fund of gold, though not to hold so much of this unproductive article as to afford a security equal to that which the bank would enjoy if no country bank notes existed.

It is obvious, that the additional capital given to the kingdom through the use of country bank notes must not be measured by the amount of those notes, but that a deduction must be made of the sum kept in gold in the coffers of the issuers, as their provision for the occasional payments to which their bank paper subjects them. The other deduction, which has been spoken of, is of the same nature. It is a second deduction, which must be made on account of a similar, and, perhaps, no less considerable provision for the payment of country bank notes, which is rendered necessary to be kept in the coffers of the Bank of England. In other words, the capital given to the country, through the use of country bank notes, is only equal (and it was so stated in speaking of that subject) to the amount of the gold which they cause to be exported.

---

*   At the time of the distress of 1793, some great and opulent country banks applied to the Bank of England for aid, in the shape of discount, which was refused on account of their not offering approved London securities: some immediate and important failures were the consequence. The Bank of England was indisposed to extend its aid to houses in the country. The event, however, shewed that the relief of the country was necessary to the solvency of the metropolis. A sense of the unfairness of the burthen cast on the bank by the large and sudden demands of the banking establishments in the country, probably contributed to produce an unwillingness to grant them relief.

I shall endeavour here to explain more particularly than has yet been done, some of those circumstances which cause a great diminution of country bank notes to bring distress on London, and to end in a general failure of commercial credit.

In a former chapter it was observed, that when that alarm among the common people, which produces an unwillingness to take country bank paper, and an eagerness for gold has risen to a considerable height, some distrust is apt to be excited among the higher class of traders; and that any great want of confidence in this quarter produces an encreased demand for that article, which is, among London bankers and merchants, in much the same credit as gold; I mean Bank of England notes, and which forms, at all times, the only circulating medium of the metropolis in all the larger transactions of its commerce. This more than usual demand for Bank of England notes the bank is at such a time particularly unwilling to satisfy, for reasons which I shall endeavour fully to detail. The reader will have been prepared to enter into them by the observations on the subject of the bank, introduced towards the close of the chapter which treated of that institution.

First, the bank may be supposed to be unwilling to satisfy that somewhat *encreased* demand for its notes which a season of consternation is apt to produce, because it is not unlikely to partake, in some degree, in the general alarm, especially since it must necessarily be supposed to have already suffered, and to be still experiencing a formidable reduction of the quantity of its gold. The natural operation of even this general sort of fear must be to incline it to contract its affairs, and to diminish rather than enlarge its notes.

But it must also be recollected, that the bank has necessarily been led already to encrease its loans in the same degree in which its gold has been reduced, provided it has maintained in circulation the accustomed quantity of notes. This point was explained in the chapter on the subject of the bank. The directors, therefore, must seem to themselves to act with extraordinary liberality towards those who apply to them for discounts, if they only go as far as to maintain the usual, or nearly the usual, quantity of notes. The liberality inlending which they must exercise, if, when the gold is low, they even augment their paper, must be very extended indeed.

In order to render this subject more clear, let us suppose that an extra demand on the Bank of England for three millions of gold has been made through the extinction of the paper of country banks, and through the slower circulation and hoarding of gold which have attended the general alarm. Let us assume, also, that the bank, during the time of its supplying this gold, has thought proper to reduce its notes one million. It will, in that case, have necessarily encreased its loans two millions. Let us further assume, as we not very unreasonably may, that the two millions of additional loans have been afforded, not to the government, who owe a large and standing sum to the bank (suppose eight or ten millions besides the bank capital), but exclusively to the merchants; and let the total amount of loans antecedently afforded to the merchants be reckoned at four millions. The bank, in this case, will have raised its discounts to the merchants from four millions to six; that is, it will have encreased them one half, even though it has diminished its notes one million. This extension of the accustomed accommodation to the mercantile world must appear to call for the thanks of that body, rather than to leave any room for complaint; and yet it is plain from reasoning, and, I believe, it might be also proved from experience, that it will not ease the pressure. The difficulties in London, notwithstanding this additional loan of *two* millions to the merchants will be somewhat encreased; for a sum in gold, amounting to *three* millions, has been drawn from the bank by the London agents of the country bankers and traders, and has been sent by those agents into the country. London, therefore, has furnished for the country circulation three millions of gold; and it has done this by getting discounted at the bank two additional millions of bills, for which it has received two of the millions of gold, and by sparing one million of its circulating notes as a means of obtaining the other million. This reduction of the usual quantity of notes is borne by the metropolis with peculiar difficulty at a time of general alarm. However liberally, therefore, the bankers and merchants may acknowledge themselves to have been already relieved by the bank, they will repeat, and will even urge more than ever, their application for discounts.

It may be observed, with a view to the further elucidation of this part of our subject, that both the bank, and they who borrow of it, are naturally led to fix their attention rather on the amount of the loans furnished than on that of the notes in circulation. The bank is used to allow to each borrower a sum bearing some proportion to his supposed credit; but seldom or never exceeding a certain amount. It is true, the various borrowers do not always in an equal degree avail themselves of their power of raising money at the bank; and, therefore, a material enlargement of the sum total of the bank loans may take place at a moment of difficulty, through the encreased use which some of the richer merchants then make of their credit, as well as through the creation of a few new borrowers at the bank. The directors also, in particular cases, may suffer their rule to be relaxed. The circumstance, however, of the general principle on which the bank ordinarily, and, indeed, naturally proceeds, being that of a limitation of the amount of each of its loans to individuals, must tend, as I conceive to place something like a general limit to the total sum lent. It must conduce to prevent the fluctuation in the bank loans from keeping pace with the variation in the necessities of the public, and must contribute to produce a reduction of notes at that season of extraordinary distrust, when the state of the metropolis, as was more fully remarked in a former part of this Work, calls rather for their encrease.

That the borrowers at the bank are likely to pay no attention to the subject of the total quantity of notes in circulation, is easily shewn. They have, indeed, no means of knowing their amount. They can only judge of the liberality of the bank by the extent of its loans; and of this they form an imperfect estimate by the sum which they or their connexions have been able to obtain. Scarcely any one reflects, that there may be a large encrease of the general loans of the bank, as well as possibly an extension of each loan to individuals, while there is a diminution of the number of bank notes; and that the amount of the notes, not that of the loans, is the object on which the eye should be fixed, in order to judge of the facility of effecting the payments of the metropolis.

It was remarked, in a former chapter, that the bank, at the time antecedent to the suspension of its cash payments, having diminished the sum lent by it to government, and enlarged, though not in an equal degree, that furnished to the merchants, the pressure on the merchants was not relieved, as was expected, by the encreased loan afforded them, but even grew more severe. It was also shewn, that this could not fail to be the case, since the bank notes necessary for effecting the current payments of the metropolis were then diminished, and since the additional loans afforded to the merchants only in part compensated for the new pressure which was created in the general money market of the kingdom, by the circumstance of the government being obliged to become a great borrower in that market. Whenever the bank materially lessens its paper, similar pressure is likely to be felt. Neither the transfer of the bank loans from the government to the merchants, nor even a large encrease of its loans, when that encrease is not carried so far as is necessary to the maintenance of the accustomed, or nearly the accustomed, quantity of bank paper, can prevent, as I apprehend, distress in the metropolis; and this distress soon communicates itself to all parts of the kingdom. The short explanation of the subject is this. Many country bank notes having disappeared, a quantity of gold is called for, which is so much new capital suddenly needed in the country. The only place in which any supply of gold exists is the Bank of England. Moreover, the only quarter from whence the loan of the new capital, under all the circumstances of the case, can come, is also the Bank of England; for the gold in the bank is the only dead or sleeping stock in the kingdom which is convertible into the new active capital which is wanted. The bank, therefore, must *lend* the gold which it furnishes; it must lend, that is to say, to some individuals a sum equal to the gold which other individuals have taken from it: otherwise it does not relieve the country.

If it should be asked, Why does not the bank in such case demand something intrinsically valuable, instead of contenting itself with mere paper in return? – the answer is, first, that if the bank were to receive goods in exchange for its gold, or, in other words, were to purchase goods, it would have afterwards to sell them; and it would then become a trading company, which it is forbid to be by its charter: it is allowed to traffic only in bullion. The answer is, secondly, that if it were to take goods as a mere security, and to detain them as such, it would then prevent their passing into consumption with the desirable expedition. By proceeding on either of these plans, it would also involve itself in a degree of trouble which would not be very consistent with the management of the business of a banking company*. It may be answered, thirdly, that the bills which the bank discounts, are, generally speaking, so safe, that the security either of goods, or stocks, or land, none of which are received in pledge by the directors, may be considered as nearly superfluous. A very small proportion of the five per cent. discount, gained upon the bills turned into ready money at the bank, has compensated, as I believe, for the whole of the loss upon them, even in the years of the greatest commercial failures which have yet been known.

The observations which have now been made sufficiently shew what is the nature of that evil of which we are speaking. It is an evil which ought to be charged not to any fault in the mercantile body, but to the defects of the banking system. It is a privation which the merchants occasionally experience of a considerable part of that circulating medium which custom has rendered essential to the punctual fulfilment of their engagements. In good times, the country banks furnish this necessary article, which they are enabled to do through the confidence of the people in general; but when an alarm arises, the country banks cease to give it out, the people refusing what they had before received; and the Bank of England, the only body by whose interposition the distress can be relieved, is somewhat unwilling to exercise all the necessary liberality, for the reasons which have been so fully mentioned. The merchants are some of the chief sufferers, and they are generally, also, loaded with no inconsiderable share of censure; but the public, the country banks, and the Bank of England, may more properly divide the blame.

The mischief produced by a general failure of paper credit is very considerable. How much such a failure interrupts trade and manufacturing industry, and, therefore, ultimately also tends to carry gold out of the country, has been already stated at large. It also causes a great, though merely temporary, fall in the market price of many sorts of property; and thus inflicts a partial and very heavy loss on some traders, and throws extraordinary gain into the hands of others; into the hands, I mean, of those who happen to have superior powers of purchasing at the moment of difficulty. By giving to all banking, as well as mercantile, transactions the appearance of perilous undertakings, it deters men of large property, and of a cautious temper, from following the profession of bankers and merchants. It creates no small uneasiness of mind, even among traders who surmount the difficulties of the moment. Above all, it reduces many respectable, prudent, and, ultimately, very solvent persons to the mortifying necessity of stopping payment; thus obliging them to share in that discredit, in which, it is much to be desired, that traders of an opposite character only should be involved. If, indeed, we

* Of the parliamentary loan of exchequer bills in 1793, which was directed to be granted on the security either of sufficient bondsmen, or of a deposit of goods, only a small proportion was taken on the latter principle, on account of the great obstruction to the sale of goods, which was thought to arise from warehousing them on the account of the commissioners appointed by parliament. It has been already remarked, that no part of the sum lent was lost.

suppose, as we necessarily must, that, on account of the multitude of failures which happen at the same time, the discredit of them is much diminished, then another evil is produced, which, in a commercial country, is very great. Acts of insolvency, leaving less stigma on the character, become not so much dreaded as might be wished. The case of some, who bring difficulties on themselves, being almost unavoidably confounded with that of persons whose affairs have been involved through the entanglement of paper credit, to stop payment is considered too much as a misfortune or accident, and too little as a fault; and thus a principal incentive to punctuality in mercantile payments is weakened, and an important check to adventurous speculation is in some measure lost.

The observations which have been made will, however, shew that the tendency of country bank paper to produce a general failure of paper credit, is an evil which may be expected to diminish; for, first, if the Bank of England, in future seasons of alarm, should be disposed to extend its discounts in a greater degree than heretofore, then the threatened calamity may be averted through the generosity of that institution*. If, secondly, the country bankers should be taught (as, in some degree, unquestionably they must), by the difficulties which they have experienced, to provide themselves with a larger quantity of that sort of property which is quickly convertible into Bank of England notes, and, therefore, also, into gold, then the country bankers will have in their own hands a greater power of checking the progress of an alarm. Still, indeed, their resource will be the gold which is in the bank. The encreased promptitude, however, with which the greater convertibility of their funds will enable them to possess themselves of a part of the bank treasure, will render a smaller supply of it sufficient; and this smaller supply may be expected to be furnished, without difficulty, either by means of such a trifling addition to the bank loans as the bank will not refuse, or by sparing the necessary sum from the paper circulation of the metropolis, which, if commercial confidence is not impaired, will always admit of some slight and temporary reduction. The Bank of England will itself profit by the circumstance of its gold becoming more accessible to the country banks; for the untoward event of a general failure of paper credit will thus be rendered less probable, and, therefore, a smaller stock of gold will be an equally sufficient provision for the extraordinary demands at home to which the bank will be

---

* It is by no means intended to imply, that it would become the Bank of England to relieve every distress which the rashness of country banks may bring upon them: the bank, by doing this, might encourage their improvidence. There seems to be a medium at which a public bank should aim in granting aid to inferior establishments, and which it must often find very difficult to be observed. The relief should neither be so prompt and liberal as to exempt those who misconduct their business from all the natural consequences of their fault, nor so scanty and slow as deeply to involve the general interests. These interests, nevertheless, are sure to be pleaded by every distressed person whose affairs are large, however indifferent or even ruinous may be their state.

subject. Or if, thirdly, those among whom country bank notes circulate should learn to be less variable as to the confidence placed by them in country paper, or even to appreciate more justly the several degrees of credit due to the notes of different houses, then the evil which was before supposed to be obviated by the liberality of the Bank of England, or by the prudence of the country banker, will abate through the growth of confidence and the diffusion of commercial knowledge among the public. It seems likely that by each of these means, though especially in the second mode which was mentioned, the tendency of country bank notes to produce an occasional failure of commercial credit will be diminished. In time past, the mischief has been suffered to grow till it appeared too formidable to be encountered; and this has happened partly in consequence of our wanting that knowledge and experience which we now possess.

Another evil attending the present banking system in the country is the following.

The multiplication of country banks issuing small notes to bearer on demand, by occasioning a great and permanent diminution in our circulating coin, serves to encrease the danger, lest the standard by which the value of our paper is intended to be at all times regulated should occasionally not be maintained.

The evils of a great depreciation of paper currency are considerable. In proportion as the article which forms the current payment for goods drops in value, the current price of goods rises. If the labourer receives only the same nominal wages as before the depreciation took place, he is underpaid. Antecedent pecuniary contracts, though nominally, and, perhaps, legally fulfilled, are not performed with due equity. It is true, that the general stock of wealth in the country may remain nearly the same; and it is possible that the circulating paper may be restored to its full value when the period of the particular difficulty shall have passed by. Some degree, however, of unfairness and inequality will, in the mean time, have been produced, and much pressure may have been felt by the lower classes of people, whose wages are seldom raised until some time after the occasion for a rise has begun to exist.

In those countries in which the government is the chief banker or issuer of notes, a temptation arises, on the occasion of every public pressure, either to lessen the quantity of precious metal contained in the chief current coin, as one of the means of detaining it in the country, or to allow paper to pass at a considerable and professed discount, which is another mode of preventing the coin from being exported. These are evils from which we consider ourselves as happily secured by the established principles of good faith which prevail in Great Britain. Those principles, however, should, perhaps, lead us even to place ourselves at a distance from that temptation to depreciate coin, or to permit a discount on paper, to which so many other countries have yielded. The possession, in ordinary times, of a very considerable quantity of gold, either in the bank or in general circulation, or both, seems necessary for our complete security in this respect. The substitution of country bank notes for gold tends to lessen that security. The evil of them is not that they create any false and merely ideal riches, or that they do any constant prejudice to the country. They enable the trader to vest a capital in merchandize, which, without them, he would not possess, and thereby add to the annual income of the nation. In their immediate effect, therefore, they are beneficial; but they leave us more exposed to an occasional evil, against which it is prudent to guard, provided we can accomplish that purpose without too great a sacrifice of present advantages, It seems, on this account, as well as on some others, very undesirable to render permanent the temporary law passed some years since, and subsequently renewed, for the purpose of permitting the issue of English notes under five pounds. When it shall have expired, the power of re-enacting it, which we shall possess, will be a valuable resource. If, moreover, any measure can be devised, which, by encreasing the public confidence in good paper, will lessen the danger of a general failure of paper credit, and of a run upon the bank for gold, and which, also, by obstructing the issue of five and ten pound notes by smaller and less respectable banks, will somewhat extend the use of coin, on the whole, it will have a twofold argument to recommend it*.

The reader will observe, that even our circulating gold coin has here been considered in the light of a provision against an unfavourable balance of trade with foreign countries, and, therefore, as exportable. Part of our coin will, in fact, always be exported when the balance is very unfavourable, and the exportation, under such circumstances, is beneficial to the country. We are apt to think that it is the interchange of the usual gold coin for paper at home which alone maintains the value of our paper; and we are partly, on this account, much more anxious to detain our gold at home, than we are to discharge by means of it an unfavourable balance of trade, and thereby to improve our exchange with foreign countries. I apprehend, however, that an unfavourable course of exchange, which the export of our gold would cure, will, in many cases, tend much more to depreciate our paper, and to produce a rise in the nominal price of articles, than the want of the usual interchange of gold for paper at home. Our coin itself, as has been already remarked, when paper is depreciated, passes not for what the gold in it is worth, but at the paper price; though this is not generally observed to be the case. It is the maintenance of our general exchanges, or, in other words, it is the agreement of the mint price with the bullion price of gold which seems to be the true proof that the circulating paper is not depreciated.

---

* Various objections, however, occur against almost every parliamentary measure for the regulation of country banks. Dr. Smith is of opinion, that a law prohibiting the issue of small notes is alone a sufficient remedy for the evils attending these institutions, and that the danger arising from banks is lessened by the multiplication of them. It is the object of this Work not so much to canvass any question respecting the particular means of regulating paper credit, as to lay down some general principles concerning it.

3   The Birchin Lane Bank

E. M. Forster

Midway in this amiable decade of the twenties there was an appalling financial crisis. It exploded suddenly.

The Bank which provided most of the family fortune had had a fairly prosperous career since its establishment in 1773. It had first functioned as Marlar, Lascelles, Pell and Down. When Marianne's father entered it in 1784 it changed its name to Down, Thornton and Free. At his death in 1815 it had passed out of Thornton control. Young Henry longed to join it, but he was only fifteen and nothing could be done.

By the time he was twenty-five the situation had altered. His claims were now considerable. He had had a successful career at Cambridge, he had served three years to learn his job, he was well thought of by his Uncle Samuel Thornton, by his Thornton cousins, by his Melville cousins, and by others connected with the profession of his choice, he had the integrity, the intelligence, the industry, the business acumen that might be expected from his father's son. Early in 1825 he became an active partner.

The Bank had again changed its name. It was now styled Pole, Thornton, Free, Down and Scott, or, more compendiously, Pole, Thornton and Co. It was said to be yielding £40,000 a year, and was regarded as one of the most stable and most extensive Banking Houses in London. Sir Peter Pole was the leading partner; an elderly gentleman who lived in the country. The active partner was Peter Free, and it was his incompetence – according to Marianne – which had been responsible for worries and shortages at the time of her father's death. On the surface all was now serene. Young Henry must have stepped aboard the family ship with confidence and pride, and with the expectation of a calm voyage. He never suspected that before the end of the year the ship would founder, and nearly wreck Battersea Rise too.

The letters from Marianne to Hannah More, describing the catastrophe, are the most considerable she ever wrote. Besides being vivid and documentary, they show financial insight. The causes of the disaster may have lain deeper than she or even her brother realised, but she thoroughly grasped such facts as she knew. The fruits of her early education become evident. The little girl who had been talked to by her papa about Paper Credit and had helped him to do his accounts reveals herself at twenty-eight as a woman of business.

I will print the letters in full from my own copies of them. They have already been published in a shortened form in the *Three Banks Review* for June, 1951.

Battersea Rise
7th December 1825

Private and Confidential

Dearest Mrs H. M.,

I am so delighted that Henry has desired me to tell you some late events which have occupied all my thoughts and time, and which I know will interest you almost as much. He thinks that you may have heard some rumours which he knows are flying about Bristol and many other places, that Pole Thornton & Co. are about to break, and as it may be some pleasure to you to be able to say on the contrary they are in higher credit than ever I am to tell you all the story, only if you please it is all in confidence – for where no report has reached people, it is much better they should hear no contradiction.

Well then I am afraid I must begin with the beginning of the story, tho' I don't like going so far back. Ten years ago I think you knew that Peter Free contrived by his speculations nearly to ruin us, Down and himself. Sir P. Pole, however, an immensely rich man, came in, and since then the profits have been immense, and the House going on apparently most prosperously. Three years ago Henry began to serve his time there, merely to *learn the trade*, under the understanding that when the Partnership dissolved, which it did last Midsummer, he was to come in. He met with some opposition from Pole – who is a mere sleeping partner and did not like his share being diminished by Henry receiving some of the profits – and from Free who did not like being watched. However, for very shame's sake they admitted him. As soon as he was there, and let into their secrets, he found that Down and Scott were perfect cyphers, Pole never came near them, Free governed supremely, and he was not satisfied with many parts of his proceedings. There was a spirit of speculation, a love of concealing what he did, *making the best* of a story, which to Henry was intolerable, and they have had some lively disputes about things; on one occasion Henry set off in the night, and brought up Pole from Hampshire, to interfere by nine the next morning, because he could not make Free give up a plan which he did not think strictly honourable and *therefore* not prudent.

That there were these disputes was rather known, and made people think Free had been worse than he really was. There is just now a great pressure in the mercantile world, in consequence of the breaking of so many of these scheming Stock Company Bubbles, and Free had been inexcusably imprudent in not keeping more cash in the House, but relying on that credit in them which never had been shaken, and which would enable them to borrow whenever they pleased; he had really run things so near, that Henry had often remonstrated, especially as Pole's property is much of it in land, and cannot be turned into money the minute it is wanted. He was not however particularly uneasy till last Thursday and Friday, when there seemed to be something like a run upon them, and a difficulty in borrowing money which they had never felt before.

On Saturday however – that dreadful Saturday I shall never forget – the run increased to a frightful degree, everybody came in to take *out* their balance, no one brought any in; one old steady customer, who had usually £30,000 there, drew it out without, as is usual, giving any warning, and in order to pay it the House was left literally empty. Henry went out to endeavour to borrow but people made shuffling excuses – some said they would go and fetch some, and never returned – in short both he and Mr Free returned unsuccessful. Such a moment of peril completely turned Free's head; he insisted on proclaiming themselves Bankrupts at once, and raved and self-accused himself, and in short quite lost his powers of action.

Old Scott cried like a child of five years old, but could suggest nothing, Pole and Down were both out of Town. Henry saw it all lay upon him. Had he believed the House was really insolvent he said he would have stopped instantly sooner than have involved a human being any farther, but he was sure the money was theirs only they could not get at it, and he resolved to fight it out to the last minute, tho' what he endured, knowing that if any *large* Bill was presented they *must* stop – he says he never shall forget.

They shut up always at five. At four, he ordered the balance for the day to be struck, and found that during the next hour they would have to pay thirty-three thousand, and they should receive only twelve thousand. This was certain destruction, and he walked out, resolved to try one last resource.

There had always been such a jealousy between their House and Smith's (the Carrington Smiths I mean) that Free had often observed that morning how pleased they would be to hear they had broken, but John Smith had been an early friend of the Sykes', and particularly kind to Henry, and to him he resolved to go – but not according to Banker's etiquette, as if he did not care whether he gave it him or not – but he told him honestly he believed they must break, and he could hardly expect him to lend it, but yet if he could get them on till five, it would be an inexpressible relief. John Smith asked if he could give his word of honour that all was safe, that is, that the House was solvent, Henry said he could. Well! then he said they should have everything they could spare, which was not quite enough tho', for they had been hard-pressed themselves that day, but he went back with Henry to watch the event.

Two people had chanced to pay *in* some money whilst Henry had been absent, this, with what he had borrowed exactly met the demand upon them – but never, he says shall he forget watching the clock to see when five would strike, and end their immediate terror – or whether any one would come in for any more payments. The clock did strike at last, and they were safe for the moment, but as Henry heard the door locked, and the shutters put up, he felt they would not open again at that dear House, which every association led him to love so dearly.

I suppose there was something in the sight of so youthful a pilot weathering such a storm, which interested John Smith and one or two old-stagers, who had seen his father act just like him in olden time, and they told him that the openness and the firmness with which he had acted, made them very desirous to see whether nothing could be done. No private assistance could save them, for in proportion to their immense credit in general would be the run now, but John Smith declared if Henry would make a statement of the accounts and prove their solvency, he would apply to the Bank of England for them. Henry had little hope from this, for the Bank had never been known to do such a thing in the annals of Banking, but willing to save them if possible, he proceeded, with as much composure as he would open my work-box this moment, to break open Free's, Pole's and Down's desks to procure the books. He told them afterwards, they had left him alone in extreme danger, and he must resort to extreme measures; he next sent off expresses for his Uncle Thornton and Sir P. Pole, and put four confidential clerks to a thorough examination of the state of their affairs. In the meantime the Smiths worked for him like post horses in running after all the Bank of England Directors, and appointing a meeting the next morning at 8 o'clock.

Near one in the morning Henry returned home. I had been a little anxious about him, and had been sitting up for him, but, hearing his usual calm voice tell Nurse to get him some tea, I was just getting into bed when she came to say he wanted me to make it for him. I ran to him, and found him perfectly white and bloodless with the anxiety and the exertion he had gone through, but so quiet and composed, I could scarcely believe it when he told me they must be proclaimed Bankrupts Monday morning, but not to mind it for no one would lose anything by it; but he was certain the House was solvent, and he had rather break at once than go through such another day. He said they were very kind to him in the City, but here *could* be no hope from the Bank; he was more sorry for the ruin it would occasion, as they reckoned that thirty-eight country Banks would fail in consequence. That it was owing partly to Free's folly in locking up the money partly to the pressure of the times, but help or hope he thought there was none. He next proceeded to do two or three things which almost broke my heart. He paid me and Nurse two or three pounds he owed us, for he said he shouldn't feel any was his own by Monday.

He then told me that one of his young Cambridge friends came to open an account with them that day; he dared not tell him they should stop by night, he *could* not take the money, and feel it would be impossible to get it again in three hours, so he put it into his purse instead of into the account, and brought it home. He and I sat up most of the remainder of the night, for sleep was out of the question. I am sorry to say I behaved much the worst of the two, for the thought of their breaking was very intolerable to me. I had indeed suffered much greater trials, but they seemed to come direct from Heaven and *must* be borne; this, being through more second causes, I could not make up my mind, as he did, to the disgrace and the confusion which it would occasion. At six when we, that is Nurse and I (for we never can help telling Nurse anything), saw him off again, he desired me to say nothing to my sisters, or any one else of their difficulties, and I had to get through Sunday as well as I might.

Fortunately ours is rather an active Sunday, and what with schools and Church, tho' very miserable, I had not time to realise it to my mind till the quiet of the evening. My sisters in high spirits were preparing a good scold for Henry when he came in for being out all Sunday for the first time in his life, and I felt he would return to say all was over. But when he did come, and I opened the Hall door for him, he whispered to me 'we are all afloat again', ran up to his room, tired out, and threw himself on the bed; he then told me the marvellous tale of their preservation, but wishing to keep himself out of the foreground, I never rightly understood it, till I heard it from a friend of his who was with him. It seems he first got the accounts from the Banking House, made poor Scott wipe his eyes sufficiently to go with him, wrote to advise Free to keep quiet, and went off to John Smith's where he met all the Bank of England Directors who were in Town, and some of the principal Bankers in the City. John Smith began by saying that the failure of this House would occasion so much ruin that he should really regard it as a national misfortune, and also that what he had seen of the conduct of one of the Partners at a crisis of extreme peril, had convinced him that, could it be saved for the moment, it might be well managed in future; he then turned to Henry and said, 'I think you give your word the House is solvent?' Henry said he could. 'Then,' says John Smith to the Directors, 'your money is safe.' Henry then proceeded to tell them he had brought the Books, those precious things which no Banker will ever let another catch a glimpse of, and which he begged they would examine thoroughly; he trusted Sir Peter Pole would soon be there, who could give him an exact statement of his property – but he believed the House not only to be *sound* but after paying everything to be worth a good deal of money. 'Well then,' said the Governor and Deputy Governor of the Bank, 'you shall have four hundred thousand pounds by eight tomorrow morning, which will I think float you.' Henry said he could scarcely believe what he heard.

Then Sir P. Pole, Uncle Sam, and Free came in, the former in a dreadful fright, Uncle Sam ditto, Free with an affectation of carelessness and unconcern. They had a most thorough examination of the affairs, during which the Governor said he saw the business had been a most profitable one. 'Yes,' says Henry, 'but', looking at Free, 'it has been grossly mismanaged.'

'That shall be provided for' and they proceeded to arrange that this enormous sum which they lent was to be watched by three of their number from accounts sent in not by Pole, Free, Scott or Down, the Partners who have been there for twenty years, but by 'Mr Henry Thornton', who entered it five months ago. Can you believe it? I really hardly can. They were all to give the most ample security for the money, and it was settled that Free should go out, and Henry choose another Partner who should work with him. But Sir P. Pole's nerves have been so shaken that he seems anxious to be off, as he has now a very handsome fortune left, tho' Free has wickedly injured the enormous one with which he came in. So Henry begs he will decamp and means to get a fresh Partner, just as rich and rather more wise. So Down and Scott are left, one of them foolish, the other old and failing, and these Bank of England Directors advised Henry to give them both an annuity to keep away, rather than to come there, and to be content with one working, and one paying Partner – both of his own choosing.

It still appears to me magic that when we only looked forward to his rising in years to come, he is at once placed at the head of one of the first, in some respects the very first, Banking House in Town. He was off again in the dark on Monday morning to the Bank of England, where he found the Governor and Deputy Governor who for the sake of secrecy had no clerks there, and they began counting out the Bills for him. 'I hope this won't overset you my young man', said one of them, 'to see the Governor and Deputy Governor of the Bank acting as your two clerks.' He went back to the Banking House £400,000 richer than he left it on Saturday. For the first hour there was a little run, but the rumours that the Bank of England had taken them under its Wing soon spread, and people brought back money as fast as they had taken it out on Saturday, and by night they were so full of cash that they might have done without assistance.

On Wednesday, the Country Banks who had only then heard of it, made a little breeze, but so slight Henry said he 'rather liked it', and from being near stopping, no House in the City is considered so safe, and indeed it never really was so safe as now that it is backed by the Bank of England itself.

So ends this fearful tale, and from the deepest sorrow, we are all at once the happiest of the happy. To me a special Providence seems to watch over those walls. Those same qualities of high honour, strict principle, and fearless integrity which once built it up, have now saved it from falling, and may they ever do so.

Sir Robert exclaimed to Henry 'I only trust you will have grace to keep you humble, for indeed it is enough to spoil you.' I am not so much afraid of that, he takes it so quietly, and says that his character could have done nothing, if it had not been for Pole's money, and assures me the Bank *must* have assisted them, because it knew that some of their late arrangements had increased the present pressure. But that he may now have his head so filled with business as to have time for nothing else is very possible, and I trust that he may remember 'this is not our rest'.

> Ever, my dearest Mrs H. M.,
> Your affectionate,
> Marianne Thornton

The opening of the next letter is puzzling. The 'worst anticipations' had not been realised and this is admitted as the letter proceeds.

> Battersea Rise
> 12th December 1825 (Monday)

Dearest Mrs H. M.,

I little thought when I closed my last happy letter to you how soon it would all be reversed – and that a few hours would realize our worst anticipations. On Thursday and Friday the new Partnership was all but formed, they had one man of great property in it, but it was necessary to have another who had ready money at command, and at such a time of commercial distress this was not easy to discover. I believe however that one day more would have accomplished it, when on Saturday morning there was another tremendous crash among the Country Banks which produced such a sensation that Henry said whoever else entered the new Partnership, he would not, for he foresaw only ruin on all sides from the general want of confidence which ensued; this of course produced another run upon them, but of a very different nature to the one before. Then Henry had been all alone and unfriended till he went to John Smith uncertain of his reception – now he was surrounded by Bank of England Directors, and all the principal Bankers of London, whose magnificent offers of support are hardly to be credited, but Henry calmly settled that on the whole it would be best to stop payment.

If he had borrowed more money it would have only been to lend to Country Banks, who might all have stopped tomorrow. He felt sure that the House was solvent. This too was the only way of getting rid of Free's old embarrassments, and tho' it is hard upon Pole, since he chose to come into the House on those terms, he *must* now pay them all, and in short they went on till the usual hour of shutting up, and then wrote round to their Country Banks that they meant to stop payment on Monday morning – this notice being considered a handsome thing.

I was dining out, quite unconscious of the events of the morning, at a large dinner party, when I received a note, which tho' very guarded convinced me of what had happened, and said that Henry wished me to come to him at his cousins, the Melvilles, in that street, so I persuaded Sir Robert directly to let me go there. I found John and Eliza Thornton in loud distress about it, the Melvilles almost as bad, Henry exactly as calm as usual, assuring us it was the best ending if we would but think so; he said that a new Partnership formed in such haste might have led to great inconveniences, that he could not feel responsible for mismanagement in this concern, in which he has only had any power for the last five months, and that the kindness he had met with during the short and stormy part of his reign was enough to keep up his spirits. He drove me home in his gig that night, and almost talked me over to his belief till I found the poor girls at home waiting in high spirits to know who was to be the new Partner, and when they heard the termination of it all they were miserable indeed.

However, by today we are beginning to look up again. That Henry's career in the City is but just beginning I firmly believe, and whatever may be the close, he will be a greater and a better man as long as he lives for these events. The marvellous way in which the City grandees speak of him, and the unmeasured confidence they have reposed in him, proves it; indeed he said in his quiet way yesterday, 'You have no idea, Marianne, what a great man breaking makes of me, I have had all these first-rate people trailing after me as if I had been Secretary of State. I always loved the character of a City Merchant and Banker, and it is delightful to see how they unite the powers of a man of business with the romantic effects of the heroes of fairy tales. I said the other day John Smith appeared to me like a beneficent genius in a fairy tale, he not only promised impossibilities, but he was always performing them.' If any exertion of money, of talent, of time could have saved that House, it would have been done, but Free's mismanagement extends through a long series of years, during which he had been left to his own speculations, first and last. Henry says he thinks he must have run through nearly half a million. He would however have gone on much longer if this state of things in the City had not brought things to a point. The examination last week shewed the House was solvent, but had no large surplus, and therefore if their Country Banks broke, it might, had they continued, have all dwindled away. The accounts are so enormous and so complicated, that it will be difficult for the present to be quite sure how matters will turn out, it will partly depend on how the Country Bankers stand it – but at present Henry seems quite satisfied that every one will be paid in full, and Sir Peter have a wreck left, 'enough to make a man happy'.

Henry we think must be safe, while any of Sir P.'s remains. *We* are quite safe, I mean we Girls, you will be pleased to hear, and many other little things which might have plagued him are nicely settled. The Bible Society and Missionary Society money which was kept there was all drawn out, and indeed owing to the immense assistance of the Bank they have scarcely a London creditor to whom they owe £1,000, except that same wealthy personage, the Bank, who may afford to wait for her money and has good security for every farthing of it. The Governor of the Bank was standing by Henry during the run on Saturday, and said 'if you had brought this all on yourself I should say I was sorry for you, but that you were behaving very well now; but since none of it is your doing, I can only tell you this is just the scene to make a man of you, and I can't be sorry for you after all.'

The young Smiths have been working for Henry like so many clerks – more than one night last week they sent Henry home to bed, and long after he was asleep, John Abel, his Cambridge friend, was sitting up, and running over London for him, resolved to save his House if it were possible. Another man, in spite of Henry's warning, would leave his balance in to shew the world what confidence he had that the House was solvent. One thing pleased me much, that Henry walked off on Saturday to call upon poor disgraced Free, because he thought it kinder than letting him hear it through a clerk, and to enquire how Mrs. F. bore it. Free only told him 'it was a confounded bore' that the House had stopped, but seemed very little touched with the recollection that it was his own performance. As to the other Partners they were inconceivably supine, and I hear they mean to give poor Henry the winding up of the affairs. They say this is a good thing for him, for that it keeps him in the way of advancement; but still it might be a pleasanter employment.

We find it quite impossible however to be very unhappy whilst he is amongst us – he says 'if I had behaved like a rogue and ruined myself besides, you could but be so miserable; *now* I do think my character is rather the higher, and I believe the money is safe, so where is the use of being unhappy?'

> Ever, dearest Mrs H. M.,
> Your affectionate,
> Marianne Thornton

In spite of the goodwill and help offered by other Bankers, winding up the affairs of Pole, Thornton & Co. was not easy. In the meantime Henry Thornton was asked to join the banking house of Williams & Co.

[Fragment]

December 29, 1825

... There have been ten thousand difficulties in the way, his capital locked up in Pole's House, his name can't appear now for some weeks, as he is not clear of his old affairs, but his City friends have one and all come forward to help him in every possible way. Alexander Baring says there are two things he hates – an abolitionist and a saint – and yet he can't help liking that young Thronton, in proof of which he very carelessly yesterday offered him £200,000 to begin with, if they were likely to want it. Henry says he never had so much command of money as since he has not been worth a shilling, and wonders how it happens. Pole's affairs are decided: they will pay everybody, and have a hundred thousand left, but Henry is obliged to let his capital go in the first instance to be repaid hereafter.

In the midst of these anxieties, we have had some of a different kind, in hearing Watson read prayers for the first time in Clapham Church on Xmas Day; and he preached on Monday a little quiet sermon when there was no one but his sisters and cousins to hear him. There was something fearfully nervous in seeing him in *that* pulpit, but he was so composed himself, and though I say it that should not say it preached so well that I could not feel anxious to the end. Gibbs, our clerk, said as he came down 'he has done excellently well, but then I take the greatest delight in him because I saw him christened, and have seen him at church most Sundays since'. Nurse said she turned so red she was sure everybody would know she was his Nurse, 'but to be sure he did read so beautiful!' We don't mean him to preach on a Sunday for a year at least, but he is doing the occasional and reading prayers duty for Dr Dealtry for a week or two, which is a great pleasure to us. Goodbye, dearest Mrs H. M. for I have many letters to write.

Ever your affectionate
Marianne Thornton

The old *Times* has announced that one of Pole's partners is to join Williams, a young man who is supposed to have strong connections in the dissenting interest! This, Henry says, is very hard when he has generally found time to slip off to prayers at St Paul's on Wednesdays and Fridays during all these troubles: it is so quiet and refreshing there.

Battersea Rise, January [1st or 2nd]
1826

Already my dearest Mrs H. More I believe we may congratulate ourselves on Henry being again afloat, and on Monday next his new Bank opens, with every prospect of being as like the old House as possible in the days of its glory. I can hardly yet believe that so few days should elapse between the downfall and the rising, but I feel so convinced now that he is a *cork*, that the deeper he is plunged into the water the more quickly he reappears, or to speak more like a Christian, that gracious Providence which we know always watches over us, has in this instance made plain those ways which are sometimes hid in darkness for years.

You will be surprised when you hear that it is perfectly obvious that even the stoppage of the old affair was the greatest blessing that could have happened to us – had it gone on we might have been *all* involved in the ruin and a hundred others. But as you tell me you like my long stories, you shall hear this one, for it is curious to trace the little causes from which come great events.

You perhaps saw the failure of Williams Bank, a very large one, the day after ours. It fell in our train for the Houses had always been much connected in the habit of lending each other assistance, but though the property in it was enormous it had been badly managed and they could not get at it when they wanted it. There was a young man in the House much in Henry's case, on whom the chief labour had devolved, while the rich sleeper kept out of the way. On the House stopping they went immediately to Henry to say they meant to go on again, for they were still worth enormous sums, and to ask if he would join them and become their managing Partner – he rather laughed at it, and said he supposed as two negatives made an affirmative, two deficiencies made a surplus, as the only explanation of their asking a *failed* man to join them.

However, about ten days ago, Cunningham who is their brother-in-law came down with a proposal to Henry to unite the ruins of his House with theirs, the old Partners of Williams going out, and leaving it to him and to his young friend Charles Williams to manage it, if they could find another monied man to join them, which would be needful to give the thing stability, and this he hoped he had done. It seemed all delightful when their *rich man* proved to be not worth as much as was expected, and Cunningham and Charles Williams arrived here one eventful Monday night to say their wits were exhausted to find a Partner, and they feared they must the next day give themselves in as Bankrupts, twenty four hours only remained in which to discover a man worth £300,000 and willing to risk it in these troublous times at a day's notice with two young men who had nothing to offer but the ruins of their respective Houses.

The case seemed desperate – so much so that even Ladies were allowed to meddle in it. Long shall I remember the anxious faces round the fire during the many hours of the night we spent in discussing every person likely and unlikely who could be applied to. Mr Williams with a large sheet of paper taking down the names which our ready wit supplied by hundreds – but some were fools, some were knaves, some worth nothing, some speculative, and the prudent Henry sat there, as we said, to object to every being who was named, but as the burnt child dreads the fire, he said he had rather be reduced to want at once than connect himself with people on whom he could not rely. But people had been so terrified with the late events, that to find one of sufficiently strong nerves who was yet a prudent man seemed impossible. 'We won't give it up tho' said Mr Cunningham, 'Henry reminds me of the Man in the Parable who fell among thieves who wounded him leaving him half dead – if we behave like Priests and Levites, we shall bitterly repent it one day. It is the difference between ten thousand a year to him or nothing, for if he does not set up directly, people's sympathies will be over, and it will be useless to attempt it six months hence.'

Among the last resources somebody mentioned our neighbour at Broomfield, Mr Deacon, late Partner of the Barings, who made £19,000 a year, and retired from business some years – and it was thought he might know of some one – and to pursue the same connection two of my sisters were to be off as soon as it was light to besiege the bedside of Mrs. Staniforth, a sister of the Barings to know whether her brothers would take it in hand. So when we met at breakfast, a disconsolate, pale-faced lot – things already looked better. Mrs. Staniforth thought of an excellent young Baring who she thought would do, and had sent off to her brother. Mr Williams had routed out Deacon, who to our amaze confessed that time had been very heavy on his hands ever since he had quitted business – that he had a large family growing up, he had a regard for Henry, and in short that he thought he should like it. They gave him 24 hours, by which time he consented if the accounts proved as satisfactory as was stated. He and Henry have rummaged over them like two cats after mice, and being thoroughly satisfied, it was yesterday settled that young Williams, Deacon and Henry and John Melville, whom Henry has brought in, start on Monday – and the young Baring who is now in Hope's House in Amsterdam comes in after a few weeks.

Henry has slipped in Melville, who was to have been one of his Partners if he had raised his old House, because he had been a thoroughly good man of business for some years, and has behaved to Henry lately with all the affection and zeal of the most anxious brother. It is the greatest comfort to know that these are all *good* men, so whatever else happens there will be no iniquity to mourn over as in the last case, and they are such a prudent lot that I was telling Nurse I don't think a Bill will ever get signed, they will look it over so long first. Such the end of a Drama, that in the 5th Act is a marriage – and so the end of ours is a resuming of payments, which has indeed taken place today, and a happier person I have seldom seen than Henry, after fourteen hours of intense work, but so pleasant he says, people pouring in with all their congratulations and their accounts – so that in spite of the numbers, who having wanted to pay their Christmas bills drew out of the House small sums – the number of new friends who paid in left them with a much larger sum than they had in the morning when they opened. Sir Peter Pole who has behaved very well up to this day, was at last touched with a little human feeling of envy at seeing Henry so soon afloat, and showed it by going into a violent passion at some of the Clerks following Henry to his new House. Henry says he let him rave on till he was quite tired, and then asked him whether the Clerks were not free agents, and might not choose what master they would serve, etc. etc. and would you believe it! the old man at length came round, and ended in giving him leave to take the remaining ones.

Old Scott, tho rather late, is turning out a Christian and is exerting himself in Henry's favour to obtain his old customers; Henry said to one of the principal ones who had followed him, 'And, Sir, and if you do not see that we do business in an exactly opposite way to the old House I hope you will leave us immediately.' Deacon, who is one of the best of men and a strongish Calvinist, says that there must be some mysterious leading of Providence that induced him to enter business when he had so long left it; and I for my part do not go far to find it, for I think the setting up Henry again one of the most providential events that ever fell to the lot of Man.

That he should have had the power of choosing four Partners out of six and be set afloat so instantly is so remarkable that I can only compare it to your 'turn' of the carpet; we really saw the wrong side only for one minute, and before we could begin to wonder what it meant, we saw the reverse.

It is very naughty of me to tell you Banking events, and this is one which if you please you must keep quiet, for it is very important that it should not be known. But two days before they opened, they discovered that it was absolutely necessary they should have a very large supply of sovereigns in their House for their country Banks, but such is the scarcity of gold now in London that they could not by any means obtain as much as they wished. The Partners were in despair, and separated in the evening, fearing this difficulty would prevent their opening on Monday: but Henry called Melville aside and told him he saw one resource, to get into a post chaise instantly, go during the night to Brighton where John Smith was, knock him up, persuade him to return to town with him, go with Alexander Baring to Rothschild, and these two Princes of the City might, they thought, induce the Jew King of City, Rothschild, to give them the money, for he, probably, was the only man in England who *could* help them having it is suspected, been hoarding up sovereigns for exportation for some time.

Henry did the deed, found Mr J. Smith, whose kindness is beyond all praise, quite willing to return with him, and by dint of a little persuasion and exhortation the Jew was induced to bring out his gold, first charging 2½ commission, then saying he did it out of public spirit, and lastly begging they would never tell it or he would be besieged night and day. However Henry and the sovereigns were in William's House before hardly any one knew he had been further than home during the night.

In the midst of all this our thoughts have been differently occupied by a very different theme. Dearest Mrs Grant was attacked by an illness yesterday from which Pennington does not give any hope that she will recover. She has been in Charles' arms ever since, surrounded by her other children. She the only calm and collected one of the group, aware and almost rejoicing in her danger, and still – even to the last – retaining her accustomed character of comforter to the mourners and the weeping. Nothing can be more sweet and serene than this almost translation to a better world – for indeed she seemed to cling to this only by her affections, and they are chiefly centred in those who have gone before her. It reminds me only of that expression 'the peace that passeth understanding' and that is surely hers, and will continue hers now for ever.

I must conclude with once more thanking you for your delightful little bit today. I wish you and Nurse could talk over Free, she says 'mere hanging is too good for him'. Perhaps it is, but poor creature, he is suffering far more from the loss of everything, and no domestic happiness or peace of conscience to support him with it.

Ever your affect. Marianne Thornton.

I forgot to say that Henry's new partners told him in the handsomest way that though his name could not appear as yet, they considered his share as beginning from today.

It will be noticed that Sir Robert Inglis scarcely comes into the exciting story. It is the triumph of youth. Henry Sykes Thornton, at the age of twenty-five, stands forth as the Head of the Family, surrounded by his rejoicing and adoring sisters. It was a great moment, the greatest in their combined lives. He must have felt that he was master at last in the House of his Father, and that though the girls might be technically Inglis wards they would look to him and take their orders from him in future. At the moment of his triumph perhaps was born to him the wish, the hope, that none of them would ever marry. And perhaps from this moment his nose – the prominent rather predatory nose that turns portraits of him into caricatures – began to assert itself at the expense of his softer features.

A cheerful letter from Lucy to Marianne shows him and his partners happily enthroned at Birchin Lane, and dispensing hospitality to their womenfolk.

> We spent a pleasant day at the Banking House, and the Partners who were present did all in their power to make up for the absent. Mrs C. Williams and Harriet with 2 children were there when we arrived. Harriet enjoyed herself extremely . . . The upstairs room was so cool and fresh that we quite enjoyed it after the drive; the luncheon was rather like a Harrow one, only so orderly and gentleman like and the ice was much praised. They have no manservants to wait, but the maids brought the dishes into the room, and Henry and Charles Williams carved, talked, carried spoons, ice, plates &ct to their company. Melville sat at one end of the table. C. Williams regretted Labouchere's absence every 10 minutes and said how angry he would be at this taking place in his absence. Harriet kept looking at the maid's dress as they appeared at the door, laughing and whispering across the table – wondering which of the partners had told them to trim up their caps. They were very nice looking. She also told us that before we came one of them had offered to show her to the W.C. and wondered whether it was her own idea: she was very Harriet Melvillish indeed. Then we went all over the premises and saw their underground fireproof place &ct &ct. Henry went with us to see the Monument, but I had 'Emma' with me in the carriage and sat with her. They went to the top.

The Bank that underwent these vicissitudes still flourishes on its original site: Williams Deacon's Bank Limited, 20 Birchin Lane EC3.

4 Case for parliamentary inquiry, into the circumstances of The Panic

In a letter to Thomas Gisborne, Esq., MP

T. Joplin

Case, &c.

The great Panic of 1825 was caused by the Bank of England contracting its issues to the extent of three millions and a half, in the short space of six months, and was suddenly arrested by its re-extending them to twice that amount, in as many days. This latter was one of the boldest and most success-ful measures of a financial character ever adopted, and was the theme of grateful and universal praise, voluntarily tendered to the Bank, but also claimed by the Government of that day for itself. The chief credit of the transaction however, was neither due to the Bank nor the Government, but to the writer of the following pages, from whom it emanated, as by subsequent disclosures he is now enabled to show.

In this pamphlet, evidence is afforded of these particulars with a view to substantiate a claim for a fuller inquiry. It was written two or three years ago, upon notice of a motion by Mr Gisborne, for a committee to investigate the subject; but the motion has for different reasons been hitherto postponed. It however is presumed that the time has now arrived, or is very fast approaching, when it has a better chance of being attended to.

To Thos. Gisborne, Esq., MP

Dear Sir,

There are but few motions of greater importance than the one you have declared it your intention to make, for a Committee to inquire into the circumstances of the memorable Panic which took place at the close of 1825. If a plague were to occur, and to baffle every ordinary remedy until the community were on the eve of universal desolation, – and if *suddenly* the contagion should be stopped by the adoption of a bold and novel course of practice – the first duty of the conservators of the public health would be, to ascertain the nature and powers of the salutary specific which had been applied, in order that thereafter it might be safely and effectually resorted to, to check the progress, and prevent the recurrence of similar calamities. Collateral with this, it would be incumbent upon them, as a bare matter of justice, to inquire at whose suggestion the remedy had been adopted, to which the Nation was indebted for its preservation, and officially to notice the fact as creating an individual claim upon the national gratitude.

It is not presuming too much when I say, that something of the same kind ought to have been done, both on public and private grounds, after our rapid and unexpected recovery from the Panic. The country, however, were so absorbed in joy for having escaped its worst, and seemingly inevitable consequences, that all idea of such a crisis returning, was banished from their minds, and the important principles, to which our salvation was owing, remain to this day far from sufficiently established or understood.

The Committee for which it is your intention to move, will analyze, elucidate, and establish them, so that in future emergencies they may be applied with precision and effect; and parliament it is to be hoped, will not refuse the investigation, if it be only to ensure the safe exercise of that great and irresponsible power with which the Bank has been intrusted. The possibility that it may lead to justice being eventually done to an humble individual like myself, cannot, I am confident, indispose any one against it.

As what may be called the secret history of the Panic may not be universally known, I will beg leave briefly to detail the circumstances of it; and I take the liberty of doing so in a personal address to yourself, with the assurance that the incidental use of your name will give a weight to the narrative, which I cannot expect it to derive from my own.

It is well known that the influx of gold when the exchanges are much in our favour, causes an inconvenient redundancy of capital in the money market of London, and a reflux the reverse; that is, when gold is imported into London to any considerable extent, capital becomes plentiful amongst bankers and others, and they have more than a usual amount to lend. This reduces the rate of interest, raises the prices of public and other securities, and enables the bankers, bill-brokers and others to accommodate the commercial classes with loans of money for longer periods, and on more favourable terms than usual. On the other hand, when gold comes to be exported to any extent, money becomes scarce, bankers and others have not so much to lend as before, the rate of interest rises, the prices of public securities fall, and the accommodation previously afforded to the commercial classes is suddenly withdrawn, by which great distress and inconvenience are generally occasioned. Neither of these effects are natural. When gold is imported, it is received in payment for our manufactures exported, and adds nothing to the capital of the manufacturer in payment for whose goods it is received. If he receives one hundred pounds in money for one hundred pounds' worth of goods, he is not a richer man than before, with the exception of the profit made upon his goods; and in the aggregate, the chief part of this profit goes to his support. Ninety-nine times out of a hundred also, the money thus received is required for the purposes of his trade. He does not send it up to London from Yorkshire or Manchester or wherever he may reside, to employ it in the funds, or to lend it to the merchants of London. He requires it at home, to replace the goods he has sold, by manufacturing more. On the other hand, when gold is exported, it consists of money paid for foreign produce by the English consumers of it; and if the wine annually consumed by a family in Cheshire, be this year paid for in gold to the foreign producers of it, the money for this purpose is neither obtained from the London banker nor the funds, but from their annual income; and there ought to be no reason whatever, that the money thus taken out of circulation in Cheshire, and sent to Portugal or France, should have any effect in producing a scarcity of capital in London. Such, however, is the case, and it arises from a defect in our system of currency, which renders the administration of the London circulation, by the Directors of the Bank of England, one of peculiar difficulty and embarrassment. I shall not, however, trouble you with the inquiry, how this strange and mischievous anomaly is produced. It is sufficient for my purpose, to state the fact, which though generally incomprehensible, is yet perfectly familiar.

An enormous influx of gold took place from 1819 to 1824, with the usual consequences, a great super-abundance of money, and a very low rate of interest. This gave rise to numerous speculations of a new and adventurous character, as well as a general enlargement of legitimate trade to a great extent on borrowed capital. The Bank might have anticipated that such an overwhelming influx would eventually be followed by a re-action, and that of a very fatal character; for however inconvenient a superabundance of capital may frequently prove to those who have it to lend, an unexpected scarcity and withdrawal of it from the commercial community, by whom it has been borrowed, is a matter of much more dangerous consequence. Now the Bank entertained an opinion, which was likewise general, that they had the power of almost immediately checking the reflux of gold by a contraction of their issues; but as this produces, to a greater or less extent, an immediate suspension of commercial and manufacturing operations, as well as a fall in prices, whenever they use this power, except in a very gradual manner, the result is most mischievous. It ought therefore to be exercised with great foresight, delicacy, and judgment. When, however, the Bank had found, in November, 1824, that a reflux had set in, they did not commence the usual steps they adopt to counteract it; and it was not until the latter end of April 1825, when six millions and a half of their treasure had left them, that they began to contract their issues.

Then, however, they did it with an unsparing hand, and effected in six months, what ought not to have been done, if done at all, in less than two years. A pressure, proportionately severe, was the consequence; which was aggravated by the violent absorption of the circulation, peculiar at such periods to our currency, and threatened the most serious consequences.

From November 1824 to September 1825, they had lost more than ten millions of their treasure, and had little more than three millions left; and as the only means of preventing their ultimately stopping payment themselves, they conceived they must effect a still sharper contraction. As might be expected, therefore, the commercial world presented every appearance of drifting speedily to inevitable destruction.

By the middle of November, the shadow of the approaching storm was upon us. It was yet to burst – but the gloom was palpable. The coming confusion, as usual, was first visible in the leaves of the public press; and on the 23d, the *Times*, one of its most influential organs, took the earliest public cognizance of it. I will trouble you with an extract from that able journal, as it conveys, more forcibly than I can, the embarrassment of the period, and the popular views concerning it.

'It is said that a degree of difficulty exists in obtaining commercial discounts, which has not been equalled for several years past. That the immediate cause is the extreme caution of the Bank of England, who, seeing a decline in the exchanges, are apprehensive of a fresh exportation of gold, and therefore contract the issues of their bank notes with more timidity than, perhaps, the urgency of the case demands, &c. That the distress thereby occasioned, would exceed the belief of persons not familiar with the subject: and there is reason for suspecting the attention of Ministers to be, at the present moment, seriously occupied with the aforesaid scarcity of money; its causes, and, perhaps, its remedies; and that, finally, as the result of the discussion between Ministers and the Bank, the Government must reduce its debt to the Bank; or that the latter establishment will not be able to fulfil the important functions of a discount Bank, so as to carry the trade of the country through the approaching crisis. Such is the substance of our City Bulletin of yesterday, representing, we believe, with much fidelity, the opinions, but with still more exactness conveying, indirectly, the wishes of commercial men, that, by some means or other, the Bank should be, at once, enabled and induced to extend its accommodation, in the shape of discount to the public.

'To begin with the latter part of the subject; our own most hearty and earnest prayer to the Bank Directors would be, that no consideration should induce them to extend their discounts, if the condition of the commercial world be truly described in the statements we have just now given.'

On the following day the *Times* intimated the fact that the Governor and Deputy Governor of the Bank, had, at their own request, held a conference with the Chancellor of the Exchequer; and that the principal object of it was, to require of the Ministers, as early as possible, a repayment of part of the advances which they had made on deposits of Exchequer Bills.

The conference with the Chancellor of the Exchequer led to nothing conclusive. The business, the *Times* informs us, was deferred until the arrival of Lord Liverpool in town on the succeeding Monday; but not the slightest hope was held out that the application of the Bank would be entertained. It was stated to be the opinion of the Chancellor of the Exchequer – and the statement was sanctioned and confirmed by the conduct pursued after Lord Liverpool did arrive – that the *evil would work its own cure;* and that, in any case, he was not aware that assistance could be given to the Bank by the Government.

In short, all the assistance afforded by the Government to the Bank at this critical period may be said to have been compressed into a figure of speech – they thought that 'the evil would work its own cure.' That it would be best to let the fire burn itself out!

The Bank, as subsequently appeared, should have retraced the steps which had led to the evil. They should have re-extended their issues, until the excessive pressure at least was removed; for it was not so much the magnitude, as the suddenness and *character* of their operations, which had produced it. But so far from doing this, we find that, ten days after, their circulation had actually been contracted from 17,594,301*l.* to 17,497,299*l.*

The immediate cause of these difficulties was not then, if it be at present, generally understood. They were commonly attributed to over-trading and wild speculations; the scarcity of money which existed was imputed to vast amounts supposed to be sunk in visionary undertakings; and the discredit and want of confidence it was presumed would merely extend to those houses who were implicated in them. Hence it was the opinion, that while those who had speculated so rashly would suffer, the sound and sober part of the commercial community would remain uninjured – an opinion so plausible, that we cannot wonder at its being entertained. But what said Mr Baring afterwards? 'A panic had seized the Public. Men would not part with their money on any terms, nor for any security. Persons of undoubted wealth and real capital were seen walking about the streets of London, not knowing whether they should be able to meet their engagements the next day.' Nor can we be surprised that a panic seized the public, when the Bank had set the example, by refusing the accommodation necessary to save the country, for the purpose, a justifiable one no doubt, of saving themselves. Can we be surprised that men would not part with their money, when the Bank dared not? When the king's ship consults its own safety, is it not to be expected that a convoy of merchantmen will do the same? The panic began in the Bank parlour; and when the garrison shut themselves up in the citadel, it was only natural that the citizens should abandon all idea of mutual assistance in the struggle for individual preservation.

Every day, however, the crisis grew more imminent. On the 29th of November, it was announced in London, that Sir William Elford's bank at Plymouth had been brought to a stop, and that additional embarrassment had been created in the city, from the alarming demand for money which this failure had occasioned. The Country Bankers, of course, began to prepare against a similar fate, and to call upon the money market of London for supplies. Still not only were the Government and the Directors decidedly opposed to any fresh creation of circulating medium by the Bank, but the Press deprecated it in the strongest terms, and the public themselves coincided with the policy which they espoused. '*The main good of the nation*,' said the *Times*, 'requires that the experiment should work. * * * As for relief from the King's Government, the ministers know very well the causes of the evil, and the extent of it, and its natural and appropriate remedies; and we venture to forewarn the men of paper that no such help as they are seeking will be contributed by the State. An inundation of bank notes has aimed at overflowing the real capital of the kingdom. Lord Liverpool, therefore, will think a long time before he does any thing to *countenance that original mischief under the pretence of curing it.*' The same sentiments were enforced by another influential organ of public opinion. 'That the Bank, at present,' said the Morning Chronicle on the 28th, 'has only the alternative of limiting its discounts, or becoming insolvent, we can believe;' and on the day following, 'the Country Banks can only weather the storm, in any quarter, by the greatest exertions; and frequent must be the applications for relief, directly and through indirect channels, to the Bank. But the Bank has to choose between its own insolvency, and the insolvency of these imprudent speculations, and as *it is quite impossible, in the present state of things, for the Bank, with any regard for its own safety, to stretch out a friendly hand to them*, the consequences may easily be foreseen.'

The mischiefs apprehended from an increase of issues were these – first, that it might drive the exchanges still further against the country, and, by thus continuing the drain upon the Bank for gold, finally compel it to stop payment; and secondly, that when any issues that might be made were again withdrawn, as eventually they must be, we should revert to the same situation of difficulty as before. It would be postpoining the evil day, not averting it, and create the original mischief, as the *Times* observed, under the pretence of curing it. With these views it is difficult to conceive how the Directors, in the conscientious discharge of their trust, could act otherwise than they did. Personally, as merchants, they were deeply interested in adopting any course by which the pressure could have been removed; and when the press arrayed itself on the side of principle – for the press only advocated a line of conduct, as before observed, acknowledged on all hands to be right – it might not be without some misgivings as to the firmness of the Directors in doing their duty under the peculiar circumstances in which they were individually placed. In questioning the policy therefore which the Bank adopted, it is but justice to give the Directors full credit for the integrity by which their conduct was animated. But to resume our narrative.

One Country Bank went after another; the panic reached the London Banks; two or three of the weakest fell at once; and thus matters daily grew worse and worse until Monday morning, the 12th of December, when it was announced that Pole, Thornton, and Co., one of the oldest and largest Banking firms in the metropolis, had stopped payment.

That this would be the case was communicated to the Bankers in Lombard-Street on Saturday night: and some of them called upon the Governor of the Bank, as also upon Ministers, on Sunday, to impress upon them, that if, at that moment, such a House, which was drawn upon by no less than forty-seven Country Banks, were allowed to stop, a run would take place upon every Bank in London, as well as upon every Bank in the country, and a panic would inevitably take place, the consequences of which it would be impossible to foresee. The house, however, was allowed to stop, and a dreadful run immediately took place; a panic seized upon the public, such as had never been witnessed before; everybody was begging for money – money – money – but money was hardly on any condition to be had. 'It was not the character of the security,' observes the *Times*, 'that was considered: but the impossibility of procuring money at all.' The next day (*Tuesday*) was still worse. It was ushered in by the announcement that Williams, Burgess, and Co., another equally large Banking house, as also two or three more, had been brought to a stand; and the panic became universal, and threatened to be irresistible.

It was idle to dream of satisfying the clamorous and voracious demands of the public with any thing but money. Nothing but a plentiful supply of Bank issues could meet the exigency; and this could hardly now be afforded by the ordinary means of discounting bills. All bills were more or less in discredit; and, moreover, the amount of money required was such, that the time which would have been occupied in advancing it upon such securities, would have rendered the relief by discounting, too tardy for the emergency which had arisen. And this again was supposing that the parties in want of the relief had such securities to offer; whereas it was only the *City* Merchants and Bankers who held such bills as the Bank professes to discount, and money was wanted now by Bankers in every part of the Metropolis, and would quickly be by Bankers in every part of the country.

The proper way for the Bank at this conjuncture to give relief, was by bills or loans on government securities. These were the securities, in which the Bankers, generally speaking, held the funds, with which they were provided to encounter such an emergency; and, as they had become unsaleable, their only resource was to procure advances upon them. A hundred thousand pounds, moreover, could be as easily valued in them, and handed over, as a hundred pound bill. In order therefore, to afford the assistance required, and with the promptitude that was called for, the Bank must not only have enlarged its issues, against the judgment of the Government, against the opinion of the public, and against their own conviction; but they must have done so upon a species of securities, inconsistent with the principles upon which their business had always been conducted.

We cannot, therefore, be surprised that the Bank, notwithstanding the events of the Monday, and the growing embarrassment of the Tuesday, resolutely persevered in holding back. On the latter day, many attempts were made to induce them to lend on stock, but without avail. We appeared, therefore, on the eve of an unavoidable convulsion. Another day lost in passive suffering, and the ruin seemed sure and irretrievable. The panic, which had hitherto been confined to London, but of which the elements had already been spread in the country, by the next post, would roll back upon the metropolis, like a torrent swollen from a thousand sources. 'The question,' says a Bank Director, 'had become, not who would fall, but who could stand?' when the Bank suddenly stepped forth, and saved the kingdom from impending desolation, by one of those unexpected movements, by which the fate of a nation is sometimes determined in the chances of war, but seldom in the accidents of its civil condition.

After having doggedly refused the accommodation required, up to the moment of closing their doors on *Tuesday afternoon*, they opened the next day with a liberality that knew no bounds, and disdained all risks. In the course of *Wednesday* they began, sudden as a new thought, not only to increase their discounts, but to purchase Exchequer bills, and make advances upon stock. The day following, they did the same, lending without reserve on any good security, and even, in many instances, taking the security, without wasting much time in examining its validity. All restriction upon their issues, was now out of the question. The only consideration was, how they could issue fast enough. The sovereigns they gave out by weight, to save the interruption of counting, and handed over their notes as fast as they could be told; until, in four days, they had neither a sovereign nor a note to go on with. On Saturday night they could not give any kind of change for fifteen of their own thousand pound notes.

The rapidity with which they enlarged their issues, when they once set about it, has no parallel in their history. From November the 19th, to December the 3d, their issues remained nearly at a stand; from December the 3d, to December the 10th, they only varied from 17,477,290*l.* to 18,037,960*l.*; but on Saturday, December the 17th, they amounted to 23,942,810*l.*, and on the 24th of that month, were swelled to 25,611,800*l.* Including their issues of gold, they must have distributed nearly ten additional millions of currency in the short space of eleven days, seven of which would be issued in the first four. The following is a weekly account of their issues of paper, from the first Saturday in September to the last in December,

			£
1825.–Saturday,	*September* 3	. . .	19,028,060
Ditto	*October* 1	. . .	18,536,550
Ditto	*November* 5	. . .	18,497,400
Ditto	12	. . .	18,031,860
Ditto	19	. . .	17,594,280
Ditto	26	. . .	17,464,880
Ditto	*December* 3	. . .	17,477,290
Ditto	10	. . .	18,037,960
Ditto	17	. . .	23,942,810
Ditto	24	. . .	25,611,800
Ditto	31	. . .	25,709,410

A measure so sudden and unexpected, so opposed to the general practice of the Bank, and carried to such an extreme in the teeth of their own prejudices and of public opinion, it is not probable that they would have undertaken on their own single responsibility. The *Times*, on the subsequent Friday (the 16th), adverted to a rumour of the Government having recommended the Bank to purchase a few Exchequer bills; and seemed to think such an act of interference too curious to be true. But it *was* true; and the only curious part of the story is, that up to the *Tuesday afternoon*, their recommendation went no further. There was much assertion and contradiction at the time, as to whether and when the Government interposed its advice. Mr Huskisson declared, that the Bank had acted throughout with the countenance and concurrence of the Government, which decides the fact that the Government sanctioned the sudden change which the Bank adopted on the *Wednesday*. At the same time it is demonstrable from subsequent disclosures, that this change was not meditated, either by the Government or the Bank, until after the hours of business on the *Tuesday*. In the Appendix to the Report of the Bank Charter Committee, we find the following conclusive minute.

'At a Court of the Directors at the Bank, *Tuesday December* 13*th*, 1825, the Governor laid before the Court the following note from the First Lord of the Treasury and the Chancellor of the Exchequer, *viz.*

'In order *to relieve the present distress in the money market*, the First Lord of the Treasury and the Chancellor of the Exchequer, are prepared to give immediate directions for the purchase of 300,000*l.* Exchequer Bills, in addition to the 200,000*l.* which they understand the Bank directed to be purchased yesterday.

'If it should be thought, however, more advisable that the whole 500,000*l.* should be purchased by the Bank on their own account, the First Lord of the Treasury and the Chancellor of the Exchequer, will be prepared, if the Bank should require it, immediately to redeem the same.

Signed,   { Liverpool.
          { Frederick John Robinson.

Treasury Chambers, December 13*th*, 1825

'Resolved,
'That the Governor be authorised to order the purchase of Exchequer Bills to the amount of 500,000*l.* upon the conditions specified therein.'

Without explanation, which the transaction does not bear upon the face of it, it is difficult to conceive how the purchase of 500,000*l.* worth of Exchequer Bills by the Government, could afford relief to the money market, even to that limited extent; for the question naturally arises, where did the Government get the money? They do not keep bank notes in the Exchequer. The place of deposit for the money of Government is the Bank of England. This purchase of Exchequer Bills by the Government must therefore have been made by a cheque upon the Bank, the providing for the payment of which must have limited the advances of the Bank to the public in some other way, to an equal extent; so that nothing would be gained. Assuming it, however, to have afforded the amount of relief proposed:

It is clear from this document, that a purchase of 500,000*l.* of Exchequer Bills was on *Tuesday* the utmost relief contemplated, from which it is evident that the measures pursued on *Wednesday* had not then entered into the views of the Government or the Bank. Nor were the public at all prepared for the change. To the last moment it was deprecated by the press; though, no sooner was the experiment adopted, than they gave it their approbation and support. The question now is, what produced it? – That it neither originated with the Bank, nor with the Government, I think is obvious; for even after adopting it, they were not aware of the amazing effect it was calculated to work. At the very moment they were venturing upon it (*on the Wednesday*), the Bank applied to the Government for a restriction; the Government on the other hand, advised the Bank to stop on its own responsibility, and to give notice of resuming payment in February; and 'the Bank,' says the Deputy Governor in his evidence, 'not being clear that it could do so,' refused to implicate itself in any such pledge. When people pursue measures of their own, they know what they are about, and have made a calculation at least of the result to be expected. On the contrary, when they adopt the system of another, the operation and tendency of which they do not clearly comprehend, they can never wait coolly and confidently for the result. The Bank and the Government were manifestly in this latter situation. Where, then, are we to look for the source of the successful policy which they followed? It must either have been an inspiration from above, or a suggestion of earthly origin; and as there is no necessity to suppose a miracle, where a natural cause, adequate to the effect, is at hand, I venture to presume that it may be accounted for as follows: –

The Directors, as I have before remarked, apprehended that an increase of their issues would turn the exchanges against us, and lead to a demand for gold, which might ultimately bring the Bank to a stoppage. The same opinion was entertained by the public generally. *It was not perceived that a demand for money in ordinary times, and a demand for it in periods of panic, are diametrically different.* The one demand is for money to be *put into* circulation; the other, for money to be *taken out* of it. A person, who wishes to have the command of a hundred pounds, places it with his banker. When the banker falls into discredit, he takes it from him, *not to spend*, but to keep in idle security at home, until he sees whether the banker will stand. Money, thus required, is not required for circulation, but to be hoarded; and the moment that confidence is restored, it will be returned to the banker again. This distinction did not strike the Government, the Bank, or the public; and therefore it was not observed, that a demand for money, arising from panic, might be supplied with safety; that the money advanced would not enter into consumptive circulation, so as to effect the exchanges, by elevating prices, but would spontaneously return on the recovery of credit.

Simple as this view of the matter may appear *now*, it struck, as before remarked, no one else at the time. Convinced, however, of its correctness, and that it was in my power, if I could command attention, to redeem the country from a capital and mischievous error, I sent the following to the *Courier* (the official organ of the government), on the *Tuesday morning,* and the editor made it his leading article for that day.

Tuesday Evening, *December* 13*th*

'There never was, perhaps, less real cause for commercial embarrassment than at the present moment; and no doubt can possibly be entertained that the actual distress in the money market arises in part from obstructed circulation, produced by want of confidence, and in part from the great supplies of sovereigns and Bank of England notes, which have been sent down to the Country Banks, in all parts of the kingdom, amounting, probably, in the aggregate, to many millions. There are between five and six hundred country bankers in England, exclusively of Scotland; and there is little doubt that every one of them has thought it necessary to increase his stock of gold and Bank of England notes to a greater or less extent, and the whole of this supply has been taken out of the money market of London.

'The best possible proof that the present difficulties are the mere result of want of confidence, is the fact, that there are no such difficulties where this want of confidence does not exist. By our accounts from Scotland, we find that there, all is tranquil. Money has been more in demand of late, but this appears to be rather a beneficial result than otherwise. People are making more money in their respective trades, and are willing to give a better interest for it. Bankers, consequently, are not only enabled to charge a higher interest for the money they lend, but also to give a higher interest for money deposited with them, which they have lately commenced doing. The same is taking place not only in Ireland, but in those parts of England where there is no want of confidence. As soon, therefore, as confidence is restored, the distress will be at an end. This, however, in the mean time, may be very much relieved by the Bank of England, who, with perfect safety, might issue notes to the extent of those either withdrawn from circulation by individuals, or sent into the country. In so doing, they would not add to the circulation, but only supply a vacuum in it; and the moment confidence returns, they may withdraw the whole amount of notes thus issued to meet the present emergency.

'In the state of the money market, the Directors have a very easy test by which to regulate their issues. So long as the pressure is unnatural (of which they will be able to form a tolerable judgment) the demand must be unnatural, and may be supplied without any increase to the quantity of money, which would otherwise have been in actual circulation. On the other hand, when confidence is restored, the Directors will perceive, by the depreciated value of money in the market, the period when the money hoarded and supplied to the Country Bankers is beginning to find its way back into the circulation of London, and this, of course, will be the proper time for withdrawing their surplus issues.

'We have reason to believe that this policy is actually pursued by the Bank to a considerable extent. They are, no doubt, increasing their issues.* But considering the pressure in the money market, we conceive they might go considerably further with perfect safety. The Bank, indeed, is, in a great measure, bound to administer the relief necessary upon such occasions. It is certainly a defect in our present system of currency, that it is liable to be contracted by a touch, or frightened, as it were, out of circulation by the mere breath of opinion. But this, perhaps, is in some measure caused by the charter of the Bank itself; and it is bound to supply the deficiencies caused by such alarms, when they occur.

'We believe also, the Bank need not fear that any issue of their notes could turn the exchanges against the country, until long after confidence was restored, even if those issues were carried to a comparative excess. Adam Smith has somewhere likened an excess of circulation to too much water put in a vessel, which, consequently, runs over; and we perceive that many of our contemporaries imagine that the Bank have the power of turning the exchanges in our favour, or against us, by merely putting their notes into circulation, and taking them out again. The issues of the Bank, however, could only affect the exchanges, through the medium of an elevation or depression of prices increasing or diminishing the amount of our exports or imports, which must be an operation of many months; and we feel some degree of confidence, therefore, that the Bank, for a temporary purpose, might increase its issues with less reserve than has been sometimes supposed necessary.'

The next (Wednesday) morning, the Bank instantly and vigorously adopted the policy recommended and explained in that article; and having once induced them to commence a bold but judicious operation, the great matter was, to inspire them with courage to proceed with it. The finessing between the Bank and the Government on the Wednesday – their higgling for a suspension, but diplomatising to throw the blame upon each other – shews that they wanted no little fortifying in the resolution they had taken; and I therefore continued to address myself daily to the same subject in the same manner, until every danger and doubt had subsided. It is only, however, to the two following articles that I shall more particularly call your attention, for the sake of illustrating the principles to be investigated. The first was

---

* They had enlarged their discounts by increased issues of gold, but the probability is, that they had not increased their issues of paper.

intended more effectually to dissipate the apprehension of the Bank, that the
exchanges would be affected by the expansion of their issues; and the next
to enforce the prudence of a prompt and sufficient supply, by proving the
facility with which the surplus issues would be withdrawn when the crisis
was over.

The exchanges would not be effected by an enlargement of issues

Wednesday Evening, *December* 14*th*

'The resolution of the Bank to increase their rate of interest to five per
cent. is perfectly justifiable at the present moment; but whether the real
value of money will justify the change, after confidence is restored, they
will discover by experience. No objection, however, can possibly be made
to the change, under existing circumstances, if the Bank will but supply
the dreadful vacuum, which want of confidence has caused, and continues
to cause, in the circulation.

'That the Directors have every disposition to do this, we are well
assured; and the question, we believe, with them is, how far they can do it
with safety. The danger they naturally apprehend is, that, by an excess of
issues, they may turn the exchanges against the country, and create a
demand for gold which they cannot supply.

'If the present demand for money were a natural one, we have no
doubt that, in the course of twelve months, an increase of issues might
have that effect. The money issued would be employed in increasing the
stocks of the merchant, and the employment of the manufacturer; by
which means the general consumption would be increased, and a corresponding elevation of prices would follow. This would increase the foreign
demand for our manufactures, and of course diminish our exports, on
the one hand; while, on the other, an additional consumption would
take place in foreign commodities, as well as in our own, and increase our
imports. Thus our exports being diminished, and our imports being
increased, gold would be demanded of the Bank, with which to pay the
difference. It is quite idle to suppose that the issues of the Bank can affect
the exchanges, or the exportation and importation of gold, except by a
process similar to this. Money comes into the country, or goes out of it,
in actual payment for commodities which have been previously exported
or imported; and before the exchanges can be effected, an alteration in
our exports or imports must take place.

'The simple question, therefore, for the Bank Directors to ask themselves, is this: Does the present excessive scarcity of money arise from a
demand for capital, to be immediately employed in commercial, manufacturing, or other speculations, by which consumption will be generated
and increased? If it do not arise from this cause, the demand may
be supplied by an increase of issues, on the part of the Bank, with
perfect security; and we may safely say, never was the commercial and

manufacturing world more innocent of any intention to increase their operations than at this moment.

'The present scarcity of money is the mere result of alarm and want of confidence; and as the demand has been a sudden one, so ought the supply to be. A judicious and adequate relief afforded by the Bank, at the present moment, would, we are persuaded, restore confidence in a few weeks.

'We do not, by any means, wish to be understood as proposing that the Bank should make advances to bankers, without adequate security. But if a banking house be pressed, or has a run upon it, and wishes for assistance, we do think, provided the security offered be sufficient, that the description of such security ought not to be considered too scrupulously. By meeting the present difficulties in a manner at once judicious and decisive, we are persuaded, that it is in the power of the Bank to end them with perfect safety to itself; and we trust that the Directors will not, from a misplaced caution, which, in point of fact, would, at this moment, be the greatest rashness, allow the present temporary but alarming pressure for money, and want of confidence to be increased.'

Prompt supply of notes required, which supply may be afterwards withdrawn without danger

Thursday Evening, *December 15th*

'A Meeting took place at the Mansion-House yesterday, to consider the present alarming state of public credit. Of the proceedings at this Meeting we gave some account in a second and third edition of our paper of yesterday; and for more detailed particulars, we refer our readers to our columns of this day. At this meeting it was stated that Sir P. Pole and Co. have a surplus of one hundred and seventy thousand pounds, after the payment of all claims upon them, besides the large landed property of Sir Peter Pole, and about one hundred thousand pounds the private property of the other partners of the House; and that Williams and Burgess have property sufficient to pay forty shillings in the pound. We have little doubt, also, that the other Houses that have since stopped payment, are equally competent to pay all claims upon them.

'When we thus perceive the perfect solvency of the two Houses above-mentioned, we cannot but consider it a most unfortunate circumstance, that they were allowed to come to a stand, at such a time, for want of proper assistance. It might, with certainty, have been anticipated, that the stoppage of two such houses would produce all the consequences that have ensued. There are times when rules and precedents cannot be broken; others, when they cannot be adhered to with safety; and it is extremely probable, that if the Bank had done on Saturday, what they have done both yesterday and to-day, (Wednesday and Thursday), namely, advanced upon other securities than bills, these houses would not have stopped payment, and confidence by this time, instead of being almost destroyed, would have been nearly restored.

'Neither the amount of the advances which the Bank may have made, nor the securities they may have accepted, will now, we understand, meet the exigency, and further extension must take place in both these respects. It is a mere waste of time and words to talk of restoring confidence at the present moment with any thing but money. The case is not one to be met by palliatives. If a sufficient supply of money be not afforded by the Bank, the only source whence it can be supplied, we should fear to trace what, in our opinion must be the consequences.

'When we press this upon the consideration of the Directors, we do it, with a perfect conviction, that they may afford the relief required with safety. So soon as confidence is restored, we are persuaded that nearly the whole of the extra advances made by the Bank, will be returned upon it without any effort of its own.

'The individuals who now draw their money from their bankers and keep it at home, will replace it again in their hands, and the Country Bankers will reduce their stocks of Bank of England notes and gold to their original amount, by returning to their agents, in London, the extra supplies which they have lately received. By this means the London Bankers will be overstocked with money; be enabled to pay off any debts they may have contracted with the Bank of England; and, instead of applying to the Bank for discounts, they will on the contrary discount freely themselves. When this is the case, the Bank Directors are well aware that their issues will contract without any effort on their part.

'We do not mean, however, to say that the Bank need trust to their surplus issues – put forth to meet the present exigency, being thus returned upon them; though, we are of opinion, if they continue to charge five per cent. interest, that this will be the case. We merely advert to this, to shew the ease with which they may, at any rate, be withdrawn at the proper period.

'If the Bank recal their additional issues when the alarm is over, and before matters have been so long settled as to give time for their being applied in commercial, manufacturing, or other speculations, they may be increased without any inconvenience. It is a perfectly sound operation to make a temporary addition to the circulation, equal to the emergency, at such a period as the present, to be withdrawn again, without hesitation, when the crisis is over. Every reflecting person will agree with us on this point; but even those who do not, and who contend that such a temporary advance is an evil, must admit, that it is a much less evil than that which it would remedy. It, however, would not be an evil. When want of confidence prevails, twice the amount of currency becomes necessary to conduct the same operations, at the same scale of prices as before, and nothing can be more legitimate, than to supply such extra demand for currency while it lasts.'

As before stated, other articles were written to the same effect, but it is unnecessary to quote them. Now, considering all the circumstances of the case – considering *what* the Bank did, and *how*, and *when* they did it – considering that up to the close of business on the *Tuesday*, up to the very moment of the publication of the first of these articles, the Bank and the Government had no idea of any further relief than the purchase of half a million of Exchequer Bills – that their first and immediate step *after* its publication, was to follow implicitly the course it suggested, though opposed to the policy to which they were in some degree pledged by so long persisting in it, though contrary to all the ordinary rules of their business, and repugnant to the hitherto expressed opinions of the Ministers of their own body, and of the public; considering, moreover, that their doubts and fears did not subside, even after they had committed themselves to the experiment; until the second article, which was calculated to allay their apprehensions from the exchanges, had made its appearance on Wednesday: – considering these remarkable coincidences and consequences, and that, amidst the confusion of all parties urging the Bank on to the gulph of universal bankruptcy, mine was the only voice (if I may use the expression) to call upon it to retrace its steps; no reasonable man will deny but that there is something more than presumptive evidence, for attributing to these articles the adoption and prosecution of the measure, by which the country was saved from commercial, and perhaps from civil desolation.

There are some people so peculiarly fortunate, as to achieve success by means which would be the ruin of others. In this case the Bank, the original cause of all the mischief which had ensued, as matters turned out reaped nothing but praise for what they had done. Ministers took the Directors by the hand in mutual congratulation; Parliament applauded them; and the country was grateful beyond expression. No event in the history of the Bank, ever won for its Directors so large a meed of public favour, or raised their reputation so high in public estimation as managers of the currency. Panegyric was unsparingly lavished upon them from all quarters. Nor did it appear to me to argue badly for the principles and feelings of ministers, that they set the example in these expressions of gratitude, and were disposed rather to overrate than undervalue the merit of the Bank.

I could not *then* publicly avow myself the author of those articles. In sending articles to newspapers – which has always on my part been done gratuitously – secresy as regards the public, is one of the conditions implied. In the present instance this was more especially necessary, as the articles were supposed to have been furnished by the Government itself to its usual organ of communication; an impression, which no government paper would wish to be impaired. But from the liberal and handsome manner in which the Ministers had behaved to the Bank, it was not unreasonable to imagine that if informed who was the author of these articles, they could not fail, though of course in a more private manner, to notice in some way the service he had rendered: for no one can desire so undefined a body as the public to receive important benefits at his hands without some kind of acknowledgment. I however thought it advisable to feel my way cautiously; and I induced Sir Thomas Lethbridge, to mention to the Chancellor of the Exchequer, in the first place, that the articles in question were mine, and hear what he had to say upon the subject. In doing this, Sir Thomas perceived, from his expression and manner, that the intelligence was not without interest; but his acknowledgment extended no further than that he was not before aware who had written them. If there was nothing to encourage me in this, there was nothing the reverse; and I should have taken other steps, had not a fact come to my knowledge which deterred me.

On sending Mr Mudford, (the editor of the Courier) a short article for the Monday or Tuesday, after the week of the Panic, I mentioned to him in a note, not intended for publication and marked *private*, the fact, that the Bank of England had been so close run on the preceding Saturday night, as to be unable to change either in paper or gold fifteen of its own thousand pound notes. The Panic was over in London, but was still raging in the country. The Country Banks were pressing as much as ever upon the Bank of England for supplies; and as the Mint, working day and night, could not coin more than 100,000 sovereigns in twenty-four hours, it was possible that the Bank might not be able to meet all the demands upon it with the promptitude required. Such being the case, it was perhaps not unwise to prepare the people in the country for some tardiness or short stoppage on the part of the Bank, by a notice, given in an unconsequential manner, of its being so closely pressed for time; and Mr Mudford ventured to insert the fact I had communicated to him. The Panic being over in London, no harm could well arise from this; and, if it did no other good, it might have furnished such of the Country Bankers, who were too closely pressed, with an excuse for not being better supplied with change. I think he acted with judgment, and certainly with the best intentions, in making the fact known to the public. Lord Liverpool, however, thought otherwise. He saw danger in it, as in everything else; and had the fact contradicted. No harm resulted from the statement, and it was well that none resulted from the denial. Nevertheless he was pleased, like most people who are frightened, to fall into a passion with the unfortunate editor, and went so far as to meditate his ruin, by insisting on his dismissal. Nor was it a mere expression of displeasure, conveyed to the proprietors, which might have been intended as a warning for greater discretion in future. He actually went so far as to provide another editor for the paper himself; and would certainly have effected his purpose, had it not been for the inflexible remoustrances of Mr Canning. This conduct to say the least of it was very extraordinary. A member of his own government, and a great authority in such matters, Mr Huskisson, spoke of the deliverance which had been effected in the following terms: 'of this Panic, no man could tell what might have been the consequences, if the Bank had not stepped in, and, by their timely and liberal interference *saved the country from destruction.*' He also remarked, 'if the difficulties which existed in the money market a short time since, had continued for only eight and forty hours longer, he believed the effect would have been to put a stop to all dealings between man and man, except by means of barter. It had very truly been observed, that the Bank, by their prompt and efficacious assistance, had put an end to the Panic, and averted the ruin which threatened all the Banking Establishments in London, and, through them, the Banking Establishments and monied men all over the country. The conduct of the Bank had been most praiseworthy, and had, in a great degree, *saved the community from a general convulsion*. He would take upon himself to say, that the Bank, throughout their prompt and efficacious, and public spirited conduct, had had the countenance, advice, and *particular recommendation of the First Lord of the Treasury*, and his Right Honorable Friend the Chancellor of the Exchequer to assist them.*'

Hansard's Debates, vol. 14, *p.*

'Now when the service rendered through the medium of the Courier in bringing about this great deliverance is considered, – a service which Lord Liverpool was unable to perform himself, although not unwilling to share the credit of it, – his proceeding against the editor appears almost incredible. It was, however, such as I have stated it to be, and I of course declined taking any further steps respecting myself in the matter. But as the present time is more favourable; as no necessity for secresy with respect to these articles any longer exist; as there is no statute of limitation against the reward of public services, and as I have obtained the requisite evidence, I trust it will not be thought improper to call public attention to the subject.

'If the suggestion had been merely accidental, the public were equally benefited by it, and ought not to undervalue it on that account. But such views are rarely accidental: for though they may appear simple, and produced without effort, the principles which lead to them are generally the result of much previous labour and reflection. This was my case. I was then publicly engaged – both theoretically and practically – in the subject of which this recommendation formed a branch. Now whatever may be thought of the law of patents in other respects, no objection can be urged against the *rationale* of insuring to every man some of the fruits of his own labour. This is a debt which Society owes to every one of its members; and, where from the peculiarity of the case, it cannot be discharged in the ordinary manner, it is the duty, and usually the practice, of the legislature to step forward, and bestow that reward upon the discover, which he has no means of securing to himself. In mechanical inventions men find their reward in the profits accruing from them: but there are discoveries from which no particular benefit can result to the individual, though of immense advantage to the public at large. In such cases the public, or rather those

---

* Lord Liverpool and Mr Robinson. Now Lord Ripon.

who administer the public affairs, are justly bound to make some acknowledgment; and, if the facts which I have stated can neither be confuted nor
explained away, I think that it will not be denied that I stand in some such
relation to the country, for having chalked out a path, by which it escaped
the most tremendous convulsion which ever threatened its commercial
prosperity.

'Should however, the Committee discover that justice remains to be done
to me, or to anybody else, this will be only one of the minor incidents of the
investigation. The grand result to be obtained is, a sure and satisfactory
knowledge of the principles, upon which the Bank, in such situations
should act in regulating their issues – a knowledge which it may be doubted
whether the Bank Directors have yet fully attained. This appears to me
to have been rendered sufficiently obvious in the evidence given by the
Directors, before the Bank Charter Committee of 1832. There is much
curious and important matter in that evidence, but the Committee made no
report; and seeing that anything but the right conclusions were likely to be
drawn from it, I ventured to take the liberty of making a few observations
upon it myself,* from which I beg leave with reference to the point in
question, to make an extract or two.

'We must observe in the first place, that one of the advantages which may
be adduced as a set-off against the many evils of a paper currency such as
ours, is the facility with which it may be expanded upon extraordinary
occasions when wanted. A striking example of this was exhibited during
the great panic of 1825. The usual demand for money then experienced,
was not for the purpose of additional circulation. It was to supply a
vacuum in the circulation, which the fears of the timid for the safety of the
Banks had caused. People were led to withdraw their deposits, and to
demand payment of the country Bank notes in gold, or the notes of the
Bank of England, not for circulation, but to lock the money up in their
strong boxes at home, until their confidence in the Banks they dealt with
had revived. In meeting this demand by an increase of issues, the Bank did
not add to the practical circulation, they only supplied the want of it which
the panic had caused: and they were enabled to increase their issues to the
extent of eight or ten millions on securities, not only with the greatest
advantage at the time, but without any subsequent inconvenience being
experienced on the withdrawal of this large sum.

'The value of such events in the hands of those who endeavour to turn
the experience of the past to the benefit of the future, is not of course
confined to the immediate practical good experienced. It could not but

---

*   I did this by way of preface or introduction to a *digest of the evidence* which I took upon me
the labour of preparing for *Messrs. Ridgeway and Sons*. I have not, and never had any
personal interest in the publication. I may, therefore, perhaps, be allowed to recommend it as
a useful book of reference: the materials in the original report though exceedingly valuable,
being presented in so confused a mass as to render them nearly useless.

be obvious, that what required eight or ten millions in December, might perhaps have been prevented by one or two millions at an earlier period. But at all events it was clear, that a demand for money not wanted for circulation might be supplied over and above the regular amount of issues, and withdrawn at the proper period without any inconvenience, and consequently that such demands in future ought to be met by a prompt and adequate supply of the amount of additional circulation which might be called for.

'Now the demand experienced by the Bank, in May 1832, was clearly of this description. During the ministerial interregnum of that month, when the King sent to the Duke of Wellington to form a Tory administration, the public, in order to embarrass the embryo government, and defeat the attempt to form it, made a run upon the Bank of England for gold to the amount of two millions. This demand was for money to be withdrawn from circulation; and the Directors were aware that the circulation was proportionately contracted. Mr Ward observes, (Question 22073) – "There has been a diminution of nearly two millions sterling in consequence, and I do not hesitate to say, the public is suffering very considerable inconvenience from the circumstance; but I do not know how to alter it." And they did not alter it. But their experience had, or ought to have taught them, that the proper mode of altering it was to re-issue the notes on securities until the gold returned, and this it was obviously their duty to do.

'Politically speaking, the course they pursued was in the minds of the parties by whom the gold was demanded, most desirable. It was giving the wished for effect to the objects they had in view, which were evidently to cause embarrassment and alarm.

'But the Bank have nothing to do with politics. They have a discretionary power given them, to be exercised not for political objects, but for the protection of the circulation against derangement; and they ought, in order to discourage such attempts in future, to have taught the public, by re-issuing their notes as fast as they were brought in, that no sinister effect whatever would be produced on the circulation by any such means. If the public were thoroughly satisfied that a political panic would do no harm to any, but to the parties who were the cause of it, such measures would never be resorted to for political purposes, and such panics would never be repeated.

'The Bank, however, took a different view of their duty, and imagined they were acting in strict accordance with it, in contracting their issues; for they seem to take credit to themselves for the line of conduct they adopted. Mr Ward's explanation of the transaction is curious, and is as follows:

'(22073). 'Do you hold the opinion to be a correct one, that the Bank should conduct itself in its issues, with reference to the state of foreign exchanges and the bullion market? – *Ans.* Certainly; I do not think there is one person in the Bank of England that denies it, or is disposed to act in opposition to it; but over and over again I have been responsible myself for violating it, when some extraordinary case has arisen, and I think I can hardly state a more extraordinary case than what has arisen at the present moment. Since the month of March a most enormous amount of gold has found its way into the country, probably as great as ever found its way in a corresponding period of time. My reasoning would be, that the public ought to have the benefit of that, by an increased circulation. That is the effect that would have been produced, if nothing but the king's gold currency existed. At the present moment the Bank of England notes are at a lower point than they have been for some years; they are at 16,600,000*l.* Then a person would tell me, that in pursuing that course, *I violate the very principle I contend for: and the fact is so:* but I cannot help it, for the solution of the question comes thus; – when his Majesty thought proper to send for the Duke of Wellington, portions of the people chose to come to the Bank, and to take coin for their notes. There has been a diminution of nearly 2,000,000*l.* sterling in consequence of that, and I do not hesitate to say the public is suffering very considerable inconvenience from the circumstance; but I do not know how to alter it. My business was, that the public should have a supply when they demanded it, and they had a right to demand it.'

'The question, however, is not whether the public should have the gold, but whether the Bank, as conservators of the currency, ought to have allowed it to be deranged by such a cause, more especially as they could have prevented it without any practical inconvenience. But the curious part of the affair is the admission of Mr Ward, that they violated their own principles on that occasion. Their stated principle, as we have seen, is, that their issues, and consequently the issues of the whole country, shall be regulated by the foreign exchanges. But their practical rule of business is that the state of exchanges shall be indicated by the actual demand for gold, which they term the action of the public. If a person come and demand gold, they infer as a general rule, and as a general rule the inference is correct, that if he does not want it for small change, he wants it for exportation, and *vice versá.*

'But here it was known that the gold called for was not wanted for exportation, and that the currency of the whole country, as well as the money market, would be deranged by the unusual demand. Yet they felt themselves compelled to adhere to their rule, and did so, though they at the same time violated their principles.

'But, as Mr Ward says, they have over and over violated their principles in the same way; and though it is not specifically stated, yet we are left to infer that in 1828, when Mr O'Connell caused a panic in Ireland, which produced, it seems, a demand upon the Bank for 1,000,000*l.* of gold, he deranged the English circulation as well as the Irish, and produced a certain degree of embarrassment here as well as in Ireland; and that the Emperor of Russia, when he made war upon the Turks, and obtained a million of money from this country to assist him in his operations (which he did at a period when our currency was deficient, and the exchanges in our favour, 2134), did, in fact, make every Englishman, as well as the Turks, suffer from the effects of his campaign.

'This is probable, though not distinctly stated. But if there could be any doubt upon the subject, it is removed by Mr Palmer.

' "If the drain," Mr Palmer is asked (2416), "of bullion from abroad proceeded, in your opinion, decidedly from political discredit there, not indicated by the exchange being below par, and not to be traced to an over issue of paper in this country, would you contract the circulation under those circumstances? *Answer.* The public would contract the circulation, if bullion were required for exportation, by returning the notes of the Bank."

'That is to say, they would not break their rule, however obvious it might be that the demand for gold was a foreign one, arising out of events abroad which had no connexion with our currency.' – *Digest of Evidence before the Bank Charter Committee.*

It is, in short, clear, not only from the above observations, but generally from their evidence before the Committee, that the Directors have not deduced those principles from the Panic, which its history ought to have established, and by which they ought to govern themselves under similar circumstances; and that, consequently, unless the subject receive some such investigation as proposed, no great reliance can be placed upon their turning the experience it has afforded to the proper account at the proper time.

But were it otherwise, when we consider the changeable nature of the Bank Direction, and the important trust imposed in it, it is not right that a proceeding of such consequence should be left in that state of mysterious obscurity in which it is now involved. Every new Director, at least, will be in the dark, and no one should be allowed to take upon himself an office of such vital interest to the nation, without every opportunity being afforded him of acquiring the general principles on which its administration should be based. In every view, therefore, a proper investigation of the subject is desirable, and I am willing to hope will not be denied.

I am, Dear Sir,
Your most obedient Servant,
Thomas Joplin.

Postscript

The object of the foregoing pamphlet, as will have been observed, is to exhibit the grounds on which the House of Commons ought to grant a committee, to investigate into the history and circumstances of the panic of 1825: which grounds may be thus recapitulated.

First – That such an inquiry is demanded, by justice and fair dealing to an individual. It is generally admitted that the country was saved from a general prostration of credit, which must have produced the most fatal consequences, by a sudden and very unprecedented operation of the Bank of England, attended by the most happy results. The lapse of time has enabled the writer to collect the evidences requisite to establish the fact, that the country is indebted to him for originating this important measure, and not to the Bank of England, as has been hitherto supposed. Now although the present House of Commons have set their faces against the public favour being misapplied, confidence is entertained that this will not extend to the denial of justice for services that have been actually performed; and still less to permitting the strong to bear away the credit which may be due to the weak.

Secondly – The inquiry may be recommended on economical grounds. Supposing a nobleman had obtained a valuable property by a happy discovery, communicated to him through his solicitors or other agents, whom he continually employed, and whom he paid at a very high rate, which he was desirous to reduce. Now should it be shewn to him by very conclusive evidence that this discovery was not made by his agents, but by a humble labourer on the estate, who would be amply repaid by a comparatively trifling compensation; would it be wise in him to disregard the claim of this poor man, and give to his agents a credit to which they were not entitled; licensing them thereby to make charges, which, under the weight of obligation he admitted himself to be under to them, he could not resist? Yet if the House of Commons do not grant this inquiry, they will voluntarily place the country in a similar predicament, and allow the Bank to enjoy a credit, which it is clear from all experience, will somehow or other, be acknowledged to it fifty fold.

Thirdly – The inquiry is called for on still higher grounds; namely, that of management. Supposing, to illustrate the case by another allegory, a person was ill of a distemper; that his physician was unable to prescribe a sufficient remedy until he was upon the point of death; and that he was so fortunate at this extremity as suddenly to restore him to perfect health by a very novel and successful course of treatment, applied in his case for the first time. It would be natural for him under these circumstances, to be very grateful to his physician; to think highly of his skill, so happily exerted; to feel greater confidence in him than before; and to resolve the more implicitly to trust to him in future. But supposing it should be shewn as highly probable that he was altogether mistaken, and that the mismanagement of the physician was the true cause of his illness; that his cure was adopted at the suggestion of others, little or no credit being due to the physician for it; he would obviously institute some inquiries to ascertain whether such were the case or not, ere he placed the implicit confidence in him in future, he was disposed to do. Now the nation is precisely in this situation with the Bank of England. It places a most important trust in the hands of the Directors, and it has yet to ascertain whether the history of the panic supplies a proof of their skill, or a proof of their want of it, in the administration of this trust; and consequently, whether it furnishes grounds for increased confidence in them, or reasons for placing some limitation upon the amount hitherto reposed.

Fourthly – An inquiry is demanded with reference to the principles, which an examination into the origin of the panic, is calculated to develop. It was caused as we have seen, by the Bank contracting its issues three millions and a half in six months, which it was induced to do by the state of the exchanges. It may also be shewn, that one or two heavy pressures in the money market which have subsequently occurred, were produced by similar operations. Now there is reason to believe that these pressures are unnatural; that they are peculiar to our currency; that they are the result of a defect in it; and that they would not exist under a more correct system. Hence it becomes vitally important, either with reference to the management of the present defective system, by which the evils of it may be mitigated, or with a view to adopting measures for its improvement, that the history of the panic should be inquired into, that persons be examined capable of throwing light upon it, and that the subject be thoroughly investigated.

Fifthly – An inquiry is equally demanded with reference to the important principle involved in the measure by which the panic was arrested. We have seen, that while it was caused by a contraction of three millions and a half of paper in six months, it was cured by re-issuing twice that amount in as many days, without any evil consequences having resulted from its subsequent withdrawal. We have seen also, that under circumstances similar in principle, though not in their details, the Directors had lost sight of those principles by which they were governed, at the memorable period in question; and that there is reason to believe that their system of management has not been improved by the experience which the panic afforded. It, consequently, is important with reference to the recurrence of such pressures in future, that the principles by which they may be obviated or remedied, should be clearly ascertained by Parliament; and the more especially, as the Direction of the Bank of England is an ever-changing body, and no dependence can, with any safety, be placed upon any system of management by such a body, which is not based on principles well established and generally understood.

Finally – Inquiry is thus demanded as a matter of justice – it is demanded on the ground of economy, – it is demanded with a view to ascertain whether the History of the Panic ought to create confidence, or distrust in the management of the Bank, – it is demanded with a view to ascertain whether Panics are not the consequence of a defect in our currency, – and it is demanded with a view to the development of the principle by which Panics ought to be dealt with in future. There is, however, another reason, which would render such an investigation extremely useful. The present low prices of agricultural produce are attributed, and with almost obvious truth, to a restricted currency. One of the remedies proposed for this, and generally conceived to be the most effectual, is an alteration of the standard; that is – to coin, three sovereigns, say, into four, or four into five; and by this means diminish the value of the sovereign, and enlarge the currency, by increasing the number in circulation. Our currency being chiefly paper, is, however not capable of this transformation. If the standard were altered, it would have to be met on the part of the Bankers, by a corresponding increase of issues. Hence, the question arises, might not such an increase be made without such alteration? But so long as we voluntarily shut ourselves out from any thing like an investigation of the principles, upon which our currency dilates and contracts, we shall be perfectly unable to answer this, or any such question. Now while the proposed inquiry, would refer only to one period of its contraction and dilation, and would be limited in its immediate object, to the comparatively unimportant question, of who suggested the measure by which the Panic was arrested: it could not fail, if well conducted, to throw light upon the system generally, and be the means of opening the way to further information, respecting the difficult subject to which the public attention is so strongly called by the situation of the farming interest.

5   Selection from *Lombard Street*

Walter Bagehot

Chapter II

A General view of Lombard Street

I

The objects which you see in Lombard Street, and in that money world which is grouped about it, are the Bank of England, the Private Banks, the Joint Stock Banks, and the bill brokers. But before describing each of these separately we must look at what all have in common, and at the relation of each to the others.

'The distinctive function of the banker, –' says Ricardo, 'begins as soon as he uses the money of *others*;' as long as he uses his own money he is only a capitalist. Accordingly all the banks in Lombard Street (and bill brokers are for this purpose only a kind of bankers) hold much money belonging to other people on running account and on deposit. In continental language, Lombard Street is an organisation of credit, and we are to see if it is a good or bad organisation in its kind, or if, as is most likely, it turn out to be mixed, what are its merits and what are its defects?

The main point on which one system of credit differs from another is 'soundness.' Credit means that a certain confidence is given, and a certain trust reposed. Is that trust justified? and is that confidence wise? These are the cardinal questions. To put it more simply – credit is a set of promises to pay; will those promises be kept? Especially in banking, where the 'liabilities', or promises to pay, are so large, and the time at which to pay them, if exacted, is so short, an instant capacity to meet engagements is the cardinal excellence.

All that a banker wants to pay his creditors is a sufficient supply of the *legal tender* of the country, no matter what that legal tender may be. Different countries differ in their laws of legal tender, but for the primary purposes of banking these systems are not material. A good system of currency will benefit the country, and a bad system will hurt it. Indirectly, bankers will be benefited or injured with the country in which they live; but practically, and for the purposes of their daily life, they have no need to think, and never do think, on theories of currency. They look at the matter simply. They say – 'I am under an obligation to pay such and such sums of legal currency; how much have I in my till, or have I at once under my command, of that currency?' In America, for example, it is quite enough for a banker to hold 'greenbacks,' though the value of these changes as the Government chooses to enlarge or contract the issue. But a practical New York banker has no need to think of the goodness or badness of this system at all; he need only keep enough 'greenbacks' to pay all probable demands, and then he is fairly safe from the risk of failure.

By the law of England the legal tenders are gold and silver coin (the last for small amounts only), and Bank of England notes. But the number of our attainable bank notes is not, like American 'greenbacks,' dependent on the will of the State; it is limited by the provisions of the Act of 1844. That Act separates the Bank of England into two halves. The Issue Department only issues notes, and can only issue 15,000,000*l.* on Government securities; for all the rest it must have bullion deposited. Take, for example, an account, which may be considered an average specimen of those of the last few years – that for the last week of 1869:

An account pursuant to the Act 7th and 8th Victoria, cap. 32, for the week ending on Wednesday, the 29th day of December, 1869.

Issue Department.

	£		£
Notes issued	33,288,640	Government debt . .	11,015,100
		Other securities . .	3,984,900
		Gold coin and bullion	18,288,640
		Silver bullion . .	—
	33,288,640		33,288,640

Banking Department.

	£		£
Proprietors' capital	14,553,000	Government securities	13,811,953
Rest	3,103,301	Other securities . .	19,781,988
Public deposits, including		Notes	10,389,690
Exchequer, Savings' Banks,		Gold and silver coin	907,982
Commissioners of			
National Debt, and			
dividend accounts . . .	8,585,215		
Other deposits	18,204,607		
Seven-day and other bills . . .	445,490		
	44,891,613		44,891,613

GEO. FORBES, *Chief Cashier.*

Dated the 30th December, 1869.

There are here 15,000,000*l.* bank notes issued on securities, and 18,288,640*l.* represented by bullion. The Bank of England has no power by law to increase the currency in any other manner. It holds the stipulated amount of securities, and for all the rest it must have bullion. This is the 'cast iron' system – the 'hard and fast' line which the opponents of the Act say ruins us, and which the partisans of the Act say saves us. But I have nothing to do with its expediency here. All which is to my purpose is that our paper 'legal tender,' our bank notes, can only be obtained in this manner. If, therefore, an English banker retains a sum of Bank of England notes or coin in due proportion to his liabilities, he has a sufficient amount of the legal tender of this country, and he need not think of anything more.

But here a distinction must be made. It is to be observed that properly speaking we should not include in the 'reserve' of a bank 'legal tenders,' or cash, which the bank keeps to transact its daily business. That is as much a part of its daily stock-in-trade as its desks or offices; or at any rate, whatever words we may choose to use, we must carefully distinguish between this cash in the till which is wanted every day, and the *safety*-fund, as we may call it, the special reserve held by the bank to meet extraordinary and unfrequent demands.

What then, subject to this preliminary explanation, is the amount of legal tender held by our bankers against their liabilities? The answer is remarkable, and is the key to our whole system. It may be broadly said that no bank in London or out of it holds any considerable sum in hard cash or legal tender (above what is wanted for its daily business) except the Banking Department of the Bank of England. That department had on the 29th day of December, 1869, liabilities as follows:

	£
Public deposits	8,585,000
Private deposits	18,205,000
Seven-day and other bills	445,000
Total	27,235,000

and a cash reserve of 11,297,000*l.* And this is all the cash reserve, we must carefully remember, which, under the law, the Banking Department of the Bank of England, as we cumbrously call it – the Bank of England for banking purposes – possesses. That department can no more multiply or manufacture bank notes than any other bank can multiply them. At that particular day the Bank of England had only 11,297,000*l.* in its till against liabilities of nearly three times the amount. It had 'Consols' and other securities which it could offer for sale no doubt, and which, if sold, would augment its supply of bank notes – and the relation of such securities to real cash will be discussed presently; but of real cash the Bank of England for *this* purpose – the banking bank – had then so much and no more.

And we may well think this a great deal, if we examine the position of other banks. No other bank holds any amount of substantial importance in its own till beyond what is wanted for daily purposes. All London banks keep their principal reserve on deposit at the Banking Department of the Bank of England. This is by far the easiest and safest place for them to use. The Bank of England thus has the responsibility of taking care of it. The same reasons which make it desirable for a private person to keep a banker make it also desirable for every banker, as respects his reserve, to bank with another banker if he safely can. The custody of very large sums in solid cash entails much care, and some cost; everyone wishes to shift these upon others if he can do so without suffering. Accordingly, the other bankers of London, having perfect confidence in the Bank of England, get that bank to keep their reserve for them.

The London bill brokers do much the same. Indeed, they are only a special sort of bankers who allow daily interest on deposits, and who for most of their money give security. But we have no concern now with these differences of detail. The bill brokers lend most of their money, and deposit the remnant either with the Bank of England or some London banker. That London banker lends what he chooses of it, the rest he leaves at the Bank of England. You always come back to the Bank of England at last.

But those who keep immense sums with a banker gain a convenience at the expense of a danger. They are liable to lose them if the bank fail. As all other bankers keep their banking reserve at the Bank of England, they are liable to fail if it fails. They are dependent on the management of the Bank of England in a day of difficulty and at a crisis for the spare money they keep to meet that difficulty and crisis. And in this there is certainly considerable risk. Three times 'Peel's Act' has been suspended because the Banking Department was empty. Before the Act was broken –

			£
In 1847, the Banking Department was reduced to			1,994,000
1857	"	"	1,462,000
1866	"	"	3,000,000

In fact, in none of those years could the Banking Department of the Bank of England have survived if the law had not been broken.

Nor must it be fancied that this danger is unreal, artificial, and created by law. There is a risk of our thinking so, because we hear that the danger can be cured by breaking an Act; but substantially the same danger existed before the Act. In 1825, when only coin was a legal tender, and when there was only one department in the Bank, the Bank had reduced its reserve to 1,027,000*l.*, and was within an ace of stopping payment.

But the danger to the depositing banks is not the sole or the principal consequence of this mode of keeping the London reserve. The main effect is to cause the reserve to be much smaller in proportion to the liabilities than it would otherwise be. The reserve of the London bankers being on deposit in the Bank of England, the Bank always lends a principal part of it. Suppose, a favourable supposition, that the Banking Department holds more than two-fifths of its liabilities in cash – that it lends three-fifths of its deposits and retains in reserve only two-fifths. If then the aggregate of the bankers' deposited reserve be 5,000,000*l.*, 3,000,000*l.* of it will be lent by the Banking Department, and 2,000,000*l.* will be kept in the till. In consequence, that 2,000,000*l.* is all which is really held in actual cash as against the liabilities of the depositing banks. If Lombard Street were on a sudden thrown into liquidation, and made to pay as much as it could on the spot, that 2,000,000*l.* would be all which the Bank of England could pay to the depositing banks, and consequently all, besides the small cash in the till, which those banks could on a sudden pay to the persons who have deposited with them.

We see then that the banking reserve of the Bank of England – some 10,000,000*l.* on an average of years now, and formerly much less – is all which is held against the liabilities of Lombard Street; and if that were all, we might well be amazed at the immense development of our credit system – in plain English, at the immense amount of our debts payable on demand, and the smallness of the sum of actual money which we keep to pay them if demanded. But there is more to come. Lombard Street is not only a place requiring to keep a reserve, it is itself a place where reserves are kept. All country bankers keep their reserve in London. They only retain in each country town the minimum of cash necessary to the transaction of the current business of that country town. Long experience has told them to a nicety how much this is, and they do not waste capital and lose profit by keeping more idle. They send the money to London, invest a part of it in securities, and keep the rest with the London bankers and the bill brokers. The habit of Scotch and Irish bankers is much the same. All their spare money is in London, and is invested as all other London money now is; and, therefore, the reserve in the Banking Department of the Bank of England is the banking reserve not only of the Bank of England, but of all London – and not only of all London, but of all England, Ireland, and Scotland too.

Of late there has been a still further increase in our liabilities. Since the Franco-German war, we may be said to keep the European reserve also. Deposit Banking is indeed so small on the continent, that no large reserve need be held on account of it. A reserve of the same sort which is needed in England and Scotland is not needed abroad. But all great communities have at times to pay large sums in cash, and of that cash a great store must be kept somewhere. Formerly there were two such stores in Europe; one was the Bank of France, and the other the Bank of England. But since the suspension of specie payments by the Bank of France, its use as a reservoir of specie is at an end. No one can draw a cheque on it and be sure of getting gold or silver for that cheque. Accordingly the whole liability for such international payments in cash is thrown on the Bank of England. No doubt foreigners cannot take from us *our own* money; they must send here value in some shape or other for all they take away. But they need not send 'cash;' they may send good bills and discount them in Lombard Street and take away any part of the produce, or all the produce, in bullion. It is only putting the same point in other words to say that all exchange operations are centering more and more in London. Formerly for many purposes Paris was a European settling-house, but now it has ceased to be so. The note of the Bank of France has not indeed been depreciated enough to disorder ordinary transactions. But any depreciation, however small – even the liability to depreciation without its reality – is enough to disorder exchange transactions. They are calculated to such an extremity of fineness that the change of a decimal may be fatal, and may turn a profit into a loss. Accordingly London has become the sole great settling-house of exchange transactions in Europe, instead of being formerly one of two. And this pre-eminence London will probably maintain, for it is a natural pre-eminence. The number of mercantile bills drawn upon London incalcul-ably surpasses those drawn on any other European city; London is the place which receives more than any other place, and pays more than any other place, and therefore it is the natural 'clearing-house.' The pre-eminence of Paris partly arose from a distribution of political power, which is already disturbed; but that of London depends on the regular course of commerce, which is singularly stable and hard to change.

Now that London is the clearing-house to foreign countries, London has a new liability to foreign countries. At whatever place many people have to make payments, at that place those people must keep money. A large deposit of foreign money in London is now necessary for the business of the world. During the immense payments from France to Germany, the sum *in transitu* – the sum in London – has perhaps been unusually large. But it will ordinarily be very great. The present political circumstances no doubt will soon change. We shall soon hold in Lombard Street far less of the money of foreign governments; but we shall hold more and more of the money of private persons; for the deposit at a clearing-house necessary to settle the balance of commerce must tend to increase as that commerce itself increases.

And this foreign deposit is evidently of a delicate and peculiar nature. It depends on the good opinion of foreigners, and that opinion may diminish or may change into a bad opinion. After the panic of 1866, especially after the suspension of Peel's Act (which many foreigners confound with a suspension of cash payments), a large amount of foreign money was withdrawn from London. And we may reasonably presume that in proportion as we augment the deposits of cash by foreigners in London, we augment both the chances and the disasters of a 'run' upon England.

And if that run should happen, the bullion to meet it must be taken from the Bank. There is no other large store in the country. The great exchange dealers may have a little for their own purposes, but they have no store worth mentioning in comparison with this. If a foreign creditor is so kind as to wait his time and buy the bullion as it comes into the country, he may be paid without troubling the Bank or distressing the Money Market. The German Government has recently been so kind; it was in no respect afraid. But a creditor who takes fright will not wait, and if he wants bullion in a hurry he must come to the Bank of England.

In consequence all our credit system depends on the Bank of England for its security. On the wisdom of the directors of that one joint-stock company, it depends whether *England shall be solvent or insolvent*. This may seem too strong, but it is not. All banks depend on the Bank of England, and all merchants depend on some banker. If a merchant have 10,000*l.* at his banker's, and wants to pay it to some one in Germany, he will not be able to pay it unless his banker can pay him, and the banker will not be able to pay if the Bank of England should be in difficulties and cannot produce his 'reserve.'

The directors of the Bank are, therefore, in fact, if not in name, trustees for the public, to keep a banking reserve on their behalf; and it would naturally be expected either that they distinctly recognised this duty and engaged to perform it, or that their own self-interest was so strong in the matter that no engagement was needed. But so far from there being a distinct undertaking on the part of the Bank directors to perform this duty, many of them would scarcely acknowledge it, and some altogether deny it. Mr Hankey, one of the most careful and most experienced of them, says in his book on the Bank of England, the best account of the practice and working of the Bank which anywhere exists – 'I do not intend here to enter at any length on the subject of the general management of the Bank, meaning the Banking Department, as the principle upon which the business is conducted does not differ, as far as I am aware, from that of any well-conducted bank in London.' But, as anyone can see by the published figures, the Banking Department of the Bank of England keeps as a great reserve in bank notes and coin between 30 and 50 per cent. of its liabilities, and the other banks only keep in bank notes and coin the bare minimum they need to open shop with. And such a constant difference indicates, I conceive, that the two are *not* managed on the same principle.

The practice of the Bank has, as we all know, been much and greatly improved. They do not now manage like the other banks in Lombard Street. They keep an altogether different kind and quantity of reserve; but though the practice is mended the theory is not. There has never been a distinct resolution passed by the directors of the Bank of England, and communicated by them to the public, stating, even in the most general manner, how much reserve they mean to keep or how much they do not mean, or by what principle in this important matter they will be guided.

The position of the Bank directors is indeed most singular. On the one side a great city opinion – a great national opinion, I may say, for the nation has learnt much from many panics – requires the directors to keep a large reserve. The newspapers, on behalf of the nation, are always warning the directors to keep it, and watching that they do keep it; but, on the other hand, another less visible but equally constant pressure pushes the directors in exactly the reverse way, and inclines them to diminish the reserve.

This is the natural desire of all directors to make a good dividend for their shareholders. The more money lying idle the less, *cætcris paribus*, is the dividend; the less the money lying idle the greater is the dividend. And at almost every meeting of the proprietors of the Bank of England, there is a conversation on this subject. Some proprietor says that he does not see why so much money is kept idle, and hints that the dividend ought to be more.

Indeed, it cannot be wondered at that the Bank proprietors do not quite like their position. Theirs is the oldest bank in the City, but their profits do not increase, while those of other banks most rapidly increase. In 1844, the dividend on the stock of the Bank of England was 7 per cent, and the price of the stock itself 212; the dividend now is 9 per cent, and the price of the stock 232. But in the same time the shares of the London and Westminster Bank, in spite of an addition of 100 per cent. to the capital, have risen from 27 to 66, and the dividend from 6 per cent. to 20 per cent. That the Bank proprietors should not like to see other companies getting richer than their company is only natural.

Some part of the lowness of the Bank dividend, and of the consequent small value of Bank stock, is undoubtedly caused by the magnitude of the Bank capital; but much of it is also due to the great amount of unproductive cash – of cash which yields no interest – that the Banking Department of the Bank of England keeps lying idle. If we compare the London and Westminster Bank – which is the first of the joint-stock banks in the public estimation and known to be very cautiously and carefully managed – with the Bank of England, we shall see the difference at once. The London and Westminster has only 13 per cent. of its liabilities lying idle. The Banking Department of the Bank of England has over 40 per cent. So great a difference in the management must cause, and does cause, a great difference in the profits. Inevitably the shareholders of the Bank of England will dislike this great difference; more or less, they will always urge their directors to diminish (as far as possible) the unproductive reserve, and to augment as far as possible their own dividend.

In most banks there would be a wholesome dread restraining the desire of the shareholders to reduce the reserve; they would fear to impair the credit of the bank. But, fortunately or unfortunately, no one has any fear about the Bank of England. The English world at least believes that it will not, almost that it *cannot*, fail. Three times since 1844 the Banking Department has received assistance, and would have failed without it. In 1825, the entire concern almost suspended payment; in 1797, it actually did so. But still there is a faith in the Bank, contrary to experience, and despising evidence. No doubt in every one of these years the condition of the Bank, divided or undivided, was in a certain sense most sound; it could *ultimately* have paid all its creditors all it owed, and returned to its shareholders all their own capital. But ultimate payment is not what the creditors of a bank want; they want present, not postponed, payment: they want to be repaid according to agreement: the contract was that they should be paid on demand, and if they are not paid on demand they may be ruined. And that instant payment, in the years I speak of, the Bank of England certainly could not have made. But no one in London ever dreams of questioning the credit of the Bank, and the Bank never dreams that its own credit is in danger. Somehow everybody feels the Bank is sure to come right. In 1797, when it had scarcely any money left, the Government said not only that it need not pay away what remained, but that it *must* not. The 'effect of letters of licence' to break Peel's Act has confirmed the popular conviction that the Government is close behind the Bank, and will help it when wanted. Neither the Bank nor the Banking Department have ever had an idea of being put 'into liquidation;' most men would think as soon of 'winding-up' the English nation.

Since, then, the Bank of England, as a bank, is exempted from the perpetual apprehension that makes other bankers keep a large reserve – the apprehension of discredit – it would seem particularly necessary that its managers should be themselves specially interested in keeping that reserve, and specially competent to keep it. But I need not say that the Bank directors have not their personal fortune at stake in the management of the Bank. They are rich City merchants, and their stake in the Bank is trifling in comparison with the rest of their wealth. If the Bank *were* wound up, most of them would hardly in their income feel the difference. And what is more, the Bank directors are not trained bankers; they were not bred to the trade, and do not in general give the main power of their minds to it. They are merchants, most of whose time and most of whose real mind are occupied in making money in their own business and for themselves.

It might be expected that as this great public duty was cast upon the Banking Department of the Bank, the principal statesmen (if not Parliament itself) would have enjoined on them to perform it. But no distinct resolution of Parliament has ever enjoined it; scarcely any stray word of any influential statesman. And, on the contrary, there is a whole *catena* of authorities, beginning with Sir Robert Peel and ending with Mr Lowe, which say that the Banking Department of the Bank of England is only a Bank like any other bank – a Company like other companies; that in this capacity it has no peculiar position, and no public duties at all. Nine-tenths of English statesmen, if they were asked as to the management of the Banking Department of the Bank of England, would reply that it was no business of theirs, or of Parliament at all: that the Banking Department alone must look to it.

The result is that we have placed the exclusive custody of our entire banking reserve in the hands of a single board of directors not particularly trained for the duty, – who might be called 'amateurs,' – who have no particular interest above other people in keeping it undiminished – who acknowledge no obligation to keep it undiminished – who have never been told by any great statesman or public authority that they are so to keep it or that they have anything to do with it – who are named by and are agents for a proprietary which would have a greater income if it *was* diminished, – who do not fear, and who need not fear, ruin, even if it were all gone and wasted.

That such an arrangements is strange must be plain; but its strangeness can only be comprehended when we know what the custody of a national banking reserve means, and how delicate and difficult it is.

II

Such a reserve as we have seen is kept to meet sudden and unexpected demands. If the bankers of a country are asked for much more than is commonly wanted, then this reserve must be resorted to. What, then, are these extra demands? and how is this extra reserve to be used? Speaking broadly, these extra demands are of two kinds – one from abroad to meet foreign payments requisite to pay large and unusual foreign debts; and the other from at home to meet sudden apprehension or panic arising in any manner, rational or irrational.

No country has ever been so exposed as England to a foreign demand on its banking reserve, not only because at present England is a large borrower from foreign nations, but also (and much more) because no nation has ever had a foreign trade of such magnitude, in such varied objects, or so ramified through the world. The ordinary foreign trade of a country requires no cash; the exports on one side balance the imports on the other. But a sudden trade of import – like the import of foreign corn after a bad harvest – or (what is much less common, though there are cases of it) the cessation of any great export – causes a balance to become due, which must be paid in cash.

Now, the only source from which large sums of cash can be withdrawn in countries where banking is at all developed, is a 'bank reserve.' In England especially, except a few sums of no very considerable amount held by bullion dealers in the course of their business, there are no sums worth mentioning in cash out of the banks; an ordinary person could hardly pay a serious sum without going to some bank, even if he spent a month in trying. All persons who wish to pay a large sum in cash trench of necessity on the banking reserve. But, then, what is 'cash?' Within a country the action of a government can settle the quantity, and therefore the value, of its currency; but outside its own country, no government can do so. Bullion is the 'cash' of international trade; paper currencies are of no use there, and coins pass only as they contain more or less bullion.

When, then, the legal tender of a country is purely metallic, all that is necessary is that banks should keep a sufficient store of that 'legal tender.' But when the 'legal tender' is partly metal and partly paper, it is necessary that the paper 'legal tender' – the bank note – should be convertible into bullion. And here I should pass my limits, and enter on the theory of Peel's Act, if I began to discuss the conditions of convertibility. I deal only with the primary pre-requisite of effectual foreign payments – a sufficient supply of the local legal tender: with the afterstep – the change of the local legal tender into the universally acceptable commodity – I cannot deal.

What I have to deal with is, for the present, ample enough. The Bank of England must keep a reserve of 'legal tender' to be used for foreign payments if itself fit, and to be used in obtaining bullion if itself unfit. And foreign payments are sometimes very large, and often very sudden. The 'cotton drain,' as it is called – the drain to the East to pay for Indian cotton during the American Civil War – took many millions from this country for a series of years. A bad harvest must take millions in a single year. In order to find such great sums, the Bank of England requires the steady use of an effectual instrument.

That instrument is the elevation of the rate of interest. If the interest of money be raised, it is proved by experience that money *does* come to Lombard Street, and theory shows that it *ought* to come. To fully explain the matter I must go deep into the theory of the exchanges, but the general notion is plain enough. Loanable capital, like every other commodity, comes where there is most to be made of it. Continental bankers and others instantly send great sums here, as soon as the rate of interest shows that it can be done profitably. While English credit is good, a rise of the value of money in Lombard Street immediately by a banking operation brings money to Lombard Street. And there is also a slower mercantile operation. The rise in the rate of discount acts immediately on the trade of this country. Prices fall here; in consequence imports are diminished, exports are increased, and, therefore, there is more likelihood of a balance in bullion coming to this country after the rise in the rate than there was before.

Whatever persons – one bank or many banks – in any country hold the banking reserve of that country, ought at the very beginning of an unfavourable foreign exchange at once to raise the rate of interest, so as to prevent their reserve from being diminished farther, and so as to replenish it by imports of bullion.

This duty, up to about the year 1860, the Bank of England did not perform at all, as I shall show farther on. A more miserable history can hardly be found than that of the attempts of the Bank – if indeed they can be called attempts – to keep a reserve and to manage a foreign drain between the year 1819 (when cash payments were resumed by the Bank, and when our modern Money Market may be said to begin) and the year 1857. The panic of that year for the first time taught the Bank directors wisdom, and converted them to sound principles. The present policy of the Bank is an infinite improvement on the policy before 1857: the two must not be for an instant confounded; but nevertheless, as I shall hereafter show, the present policy is now still most defective, and much discussion and much effort will be wanted before that policy becomes what it ought to be.

A domestic drain is very different. Such a drain arises from a disturbance of credit within the country, and the difficulty of dealing with it is the greater, because it is often caused, or at least often enhanced, by a foreign drain. Times without number the public have been alarmed mainly because they saw that the banking reserve was already low, and that it was daily getting lower. The two maladies – an external drain and an internal – often attack the Money Market at once. What, then, ought to be done?

In opposition to what might be at first sight supposed, the best way for the bank or banks who have the custody of the bank reserve to deal with a drain arising from internal discredit, is to lend freely. The first instinct of everyone is the contrary. There being a large demand on a fund which you want to preserve, the most obvious way to preserve it is to hoard it – to get in as much as you can, and to let nothing go out which you can help. But every banker knows that this is not the way to diminish discredit. This discredit means, 'an opinion that you have not got any money,' and to dissipate that opinion, you must, if possible, show that you have money: you must employ it for the public benefit in order that the public may know that you have it. The time for economy and for accumulation is before. A good banker will have accumulated in ordinary times the reserve he is to make use of in extraordinary times.

Ordinarily discredit does not at first settle on any particular bank, still less does it at first concentrate itself on the bank or banks holding the principal cash reserve. These banks are almost sure to be those in best credit, or they would not be in that position, and, having the reserve, they are likely to look stronger and seem stronger than any others. At first, incipient panic amounts to a kind of vague conversation: Is A. B. as good as he used to be? Has not C. D. lost money? and a thousand such questions. A hundred people are talked about, and a thousand think – 'Am I talked about, or am I not?' 'Is my credit as good as it used to be, or is it less?' And every day, as a panic grows, this floating suspicion becomes both more intense and more diffused; it attacks more persons, and attacks them all more virulently than at first. All men of experience, therefore, try to 'strengthen themselves' as it is called, in the early stage of a panic; they borrow money while they can; they come to their banker and offer bills for discount, which commonly they would not have offered for days or weeks to come. And if the merchant be a regular customer, a banker does not like to refuse, because if he does he will be said, or may be said, to be in want of money, and so may attract the panic to himself. Not only merchants but all persons under pecuniary liabilities – present or imminent – feel this wish to 'strengthen themselves,' and in proportion to those liabilities. Especially is this the case with what may be called the auxiliary dealers in credit. Under any system of banking there will always group themselves about the main bank or banks (in which is kept the reserve) a crowd of smaller money dealers, who watch the minutiæ of bills, look into special securities which busy bankers have not time for, and so gain a livelihood. As business grows, the number of such subsidiary persons augments. The various modes in which money may be lent have each their peculiarities, and persons who devote themselves to one only lend in that way more safely, and therefore more cheaply. In time of panic, these subordinate dealers in money will always come to the principal dealers. In ordinary times, the intercourse between the two is probably close enough. The little dealer is probably in the habit of pledging his 'securities' to the larger dealer at a rate less than he has himself charged, and of running into the market to lend again. His time and brains are his principal capital, and he wants to be always using them. But in times of incipient panic, the minor money dealer always becomes alarmed. His credit is never very established or very wide; he always fears that he may be the person on whom current suspicion will fasten, and often he is so. Accordingly he asks the larger dealer for advances. A number of such persons ask all the large dealers – those who have the money – the holders of the reserve. And then the plain problem before the great dealers comes to be – 'How shall we best protect ourselves? No doubt the immediate advance to these second-class dealers is annoying, but may not the refusal of it even be dangerous? A panic grows by what it feeds on; if it devours these second-class men, shall we, the first-class, be safe?'

A panic, in a word, is a species of neuralgia, and according to the rules of science you must not starve it. The holders of the cash reserve must be ready not only to keep it for their own liabilities, but to advance it most freely for the liabilities of others. They must lend to merchants, to minor bankers, to 'this man and that man,' whenever the security is good. In wild periods of alarm, one failure makes many, and the best way to prevent the derivative failures is to arrest the primary failure which causes them. The way in which the panic of 1825 was stopped by advancing money has been described in so broad and graphic a way that the passage has become classical. We lent it,' said Mr Harman, on behalf of the Bank of England, 'by every possible means and in modes we had never adopted before; we took in stock on security, we purchased Exchequer bills, we made advances on Exchequer bills, we not only discounted outright, but we made advances on the deposit of bills of exchange to an immense amount, in short, by every possible means consistent with the safety of the Bank, and we were not on some occasions over nice. Seeing the dreadful state in which the public were, we rendered every assistance in our power.' After a day or two of this treatment, the entire panic subsided, and the 'City' was quite calm.

The problem of managing a panic must not be thought of as mainly a 'banking' problem. It is primarily a mercantile one. All merchants are under liabilities; they have bills to meet soon, and they can only pay those bills by discounting bills on other merchants. In other words, all merchants are dependent on borrowing money, and large merchants are dependent on borrowing much money. At the slightest symptom of panic many merchants want to borrow more than usual; they think they will supply themselves with the means of meeting their bills while those means are still forthcoming. If the bankers gratify the merchants, they must lend largely just when they like it least: if they do not gratify them, there is a panic.

On the surface there seems a great inconsistency in all this. First, you establish in some bank or banks a certain reserve; you make of it or them a kind of ultimate treasury, where the last shilling of the country is deposited and kept. And then you go on to say that this final treasury is also to be the last lending-house; that out of it unbounded, or at any rate immense, advances are to be made when no one else lends. This seems like saying – first, that the reserve should be kept, and then that it should not be kept. But there is no puzzle in the matter. The ultimate banking reserve of a country (by whomsoever kept) is not kept out of show, but for certain essential purposes, and one of those purposes is the meeting a demand for cash caused by an alarm within the country. It is not unreasonable that our ultimate treasure in particular cases should be lent; on the contrary, we keep that treasure for the very reason that in particular cases it should be lent.

When reduced to abstract principle, the subject comes to this. An 'alarm' is an opinion that the money of certain persons will not pay their creditors when those creditors want to be paid. If possible, that alarm is best met by enabling those persons to pay their creditors to the very moment. For this purpose only a little money is wanted. If that alarm is not so met, it aggravates into a panic, which is an opinion that most people, or very many people, will not pay their creditors; and this too can only be met by enabling all those persons to pay what they owe, which takes a great deal of money. No one has enough money, or anything like enough, but the holders of the bank reserve.

Not that the help so given by the banks holding that reserve necessarily diminishes it. Very commonly the panic extends as far, or almost as far, as the bank or banks which hold the reserve, but does not touch it or them at all. In this case it is enough if the dominant bank or banks, so to speak, pledge their credit for those who want it. Under our present system it is often quite enough that a merchant or a banker gets the advance made to him put to his credit in the books of the Bank of England; he may never draw a cheque on it, or, if he does, that cheque may come in again to the credit of some other customer who lets it remain on his account. An increase of loans at such times is often an increase of the liabilities of the bank, not a diminution of its reserve. Just so before 1844, an issue of notes, as in 1825, to quell a panic entirely internal did not diminish the bullion reserve. The notes went out, but they did not return. They were issued as loans to the public, but the public wanted no more; they never presented them for payment; they never asked that sovereigns should be given for them. But the acceptance of a great liability during an augmenting alarm, though not as bad as an equal advance of cash, is the thing next worst. At any moment the cash *may* be demanded. Supposing the panic to grow, it *will* be demanded, and the reserve will be lessened accordingly.

No doubt all precautions may, in the end, be unavailing. 'On extraordinary occasions says Ricardo, 'a general panic may seize the country, when everyone becomes desirous of possessing himself of the precious metals as the most convenient mode of realising or concealing his property, – against such panic banks have no security *on any system*.' The bank or banks which hold the reserve may last a little longer than the others; but if apprehension pass a certain bound, they must perish too. The use of credit is, that it enables debtors to use a certain part of the money their creditors have lent them. If all those creditors demand all that money at once, they cannot have it, for that which their debtors have used, is for the time employed, and not to be obtained. With the advantages of credit we must take the disadvantages too; but to lessen them as much as we can, we must keep a great store of ready money always available, and advance out of it very freely in periods of panic, and in times of incipient alarm.

The management of the Money Market is the more difficult, because, as has been said, periods of internal panic and external demand for bullion commonly occur together. The foreign drain empties the Bank till, and that emptiness, and the resulting rise in the rate of discount, tend to frighten the market. The holders of the reserve have, therefore, to treat two opposite maladies at once – one requiring stringent remedies, and especially a rapid rise in the rate of interest; and the other an alleviative treatment with large and ready loans.

Before we had much specific experience, it was not easy to prescribe for this compound disease; but now we know how to deal with it. We must look first to the foreign drain, and raise the rate of interest as high as may be necessary. Unless you can stop the foreign export, you cannot allay the domestic alarm. The Bank will get poorer and poorer, and its poverty will protract or renew the apprehension. And at the rate of interest so raised, the holders – one or more – of the final Bank reserve must lend freely. Very large loans at very high rates are the best remedy for the worst malady of the Money Market when a foreign drain is added to a domestic drain. Any notion that money is not to be had, or that it may not be had at any price, only raises alarm to panic, and enhances panic to madness. But though the rule is clear, the greatest delicacy, the finest and best skilled judgment, are needed to deal at once with such great and contrary evils.

And great as is the delicacy of such a problem in all countries, it is far greater in England now than it was or is elsewhere. The strain thrown by a panic on the final Bank reserve is proportional to the magnitude of a country's commerce, and to the number and size of the dependent banks – banks, that is, holding no cash reserve – that are grouped around the central bank or banks. And in both respects our system causes a stupendous strain. The magnitude of our commerce, and the number and magnitude of the banks which depend on the Bank of England, are undeniable. There are very many more persons under great liabilities than there are, or ever were, anywhere else. At the commencement of every panic, all persons under such liabilities try to supply themselves with the means of meeting those liabilities while they can. This causes a great demand for new loans. And so far from being able to meet it, the bankers who do not keep an extra reserve at that time borrow largely, or do not renew large loans – very likely do both.

London bankers, other than the Bank of England, effect this in several ways. First, they have probably discounted bills to a large amount for the bill brokers, and if these bills are paid, they decline discounting any others to replace them. The directors of the London and Westminster Bank had, in the panic of 1857, discounted millions of such bills, and they justly said that if those bills were paid they would have an amount of cash far more than sufficient for any demand.* But how were those bills to be paid? Someone

---

* See Note B at the end of the volume.

else must lend the money to pay them. The mercantile community could not on a sudden bear to lose so large a sum of borrowed money; they have been used to rely on it, and they could not carry on their business without it. Least of all could they bear it at the beginning of a panic, when everybody wants more money than usual. Speaking broadly, those bills can only be paid by the discount of other bills. When the bills (suppose) of a Manchester warehouseman which he gave to the manufacturer become due, he cannot, as a rule, pay for them at once in cash; he has bought on credit, and he has sold on credit. He is but a middleman. To pay his own bill to the maker of the goods, he must discount the bills he has received from the shopkeepers to whom he has sold the goods; but if there is a sudden cessation in the means of discount, he will not be able to discount them. All our mercantile community must obtain new loans to pay old debts. If some one else did not pour into the market the money which the banks like the London and Westminster Bank take out of it, the bills held by the London and Westminster Bank could not be paid.

Who, then, is to pour in the new money? Certainly not the bill brokers. They have been used to re-discount with such banks as the London and Westminster millions of bills, and if they see that they are not likely to be able to re-discount those bills, they instantly protect themselves and do not discount them. Their business does not allow them to keep much cash unemployed. They give interest for all the money deposited with them – an interest often nearly approaching the interest they can charge; as they can only keep a small reserve a panic tells on them more quickly than on anyone else. They stop their discounts, or much diminish their discounts, immediately. There is no new money to be had from them, and the only place at which they can have it is the Bank of England.

There is even a simpler case: the banker who is uncertain of his credit, and wants to increase his cash, may have money on deposit at the bill brokers'. If he wants to replenish his reserve, he may ask for it, suppose, just when the alarm is beginning. But if a great number of persons do this very suddenly, the bill brokers will not at once be able to pay without borrowing. They have excellent bills in their case, but these will not be due for some days; and the demand from the more or less alarmed bankers is for payment at once and to-day. Accordingly the bill broker takes refuge at the Bank of England – the only place where at such a moment new money is to be had.

The case is just the same if the banker wants to sell Consols, or to call in money lent on Consols. These he reckons as part of his reserve. And in ordinary times nothing can be better. According to the saying, you 'can sell Consols on a Sunday.' In a time of no alarm, or in any alarm affecting that particular banker only, he can rely on such reserve without misgiving. But not so in a general panic. Then, if he wants to sell 500,000*l.* worth of Consols, he will not find 500,000*l.* of fresh money ready to come into the market. All ordinary bankers are wanting to sell, or thinking they may have to sell. The only resource is the Bank of England. In a great panic, Consols cannot be sold unless the Bank of England will advance to the buyer, and no buyer can obtain advances on Consols at such a time unless the Bank of England will lend to him.

The case is worst if the alarm is not confined to the great towns, but is diffused through the country. As a rule, country bankers only keep so much barren cash as is necessary for their common business. All the rest they leave at the bill brokers', or at the interest-giving banks, or invest in Consols and such securities. But in a panic they come to London and want this money And it is only from the Bank of England that they can get it, for all the rest of London want their money for themselves.

If we remember that the liabilities of Lombard Street payable on demand are far larger than those of any like market, and that the liabilities of the country are greater still, we can conceive the magnitude of the pressure on the Bank of England when both Lombard Street and the country suddenly and at once come upon it for aid. No other bank was ever exposed to a demand so formidable, for none ever before kept the banking reserve for such a nation as the English.

The mode in which the Bank of England meets this great responsibility is very curious. It unquestionably does make enormous advances in every panic –

		£		£
In 1847 the loans on 'private securities' increased	from	18,963,000	to	20,409,000
1857 ditto	ditto	20,404,000	to	31,350,000
1866 ditto	ditto	18,507,000	to	33,447,000

But, on the other hand, as we have seen, though the Bank, more or less, does its duty, it does not distinctly acknowledge that it is its duty. We are apt to be solemnly told that the Banking Department of the Bank of England is only a bank like other banks – that it has no peculiar duty in times of panic – that it then is to look to itself alone, as other banks look. And there is this excuse for the Bank. Hitherto questions of banking have been so little discussed in comparison with questions of currency, that the duty of the Bank in time of panic has been put on a wrong ground.

It is imagined that because bank notes are a legal tender, the Bank has some peculiar duty to help other people. But bank notes are only a legal tender at the Issue Department, not at the Banking Department, and the accidental combination of the two departments in the same building gives the Banking Department no aid in meeting a panic. If the Issue Department were at Somerset House, and if it issued Government notes there, the position of the Banking Department under the present law would be exactly what it is now. No doubt, formerly the Bank of England could issue what it pleased, but that historical reminiscence makes it no stronger now that it can no longer so issue. We must deal with what is, not with what was.

And a still worse argument is also used. It is said that because the Bank of

England keeps the 'State account' and is the Government banker, it is a sort of 'public institution,' and ought to help everybody. But the custody of the taxes which have been collected and which wait to be expended is a duty quite apart from panics. The Government money may chance to be much or little when the panic comes. There is no relation or connection between the two. And the State, in getting the Bank to keep what money it may chance to have, or in borrowing of it what money it may chance to want, does not hire it to stop a panic or much help it if it tries.

The real reason has not been distinctly seen. As has been already said – but on account of its importance and perhaps its novelty it is worth saying again – whatever bank or banks keep the ultimate banking reserve of the country must lend that reserve most freely in time of apprehension, for that is one of the characteristic uses of the bank reserve, and the mode in which it attains one of the main ends for which it is kept. Whether rightly or wrongly, at present and in fact the Bank of England keeps our ultimate bank reserve, and therefore they must use it in this manner.

And though the Bank of England certainly do make great advances in time of panic, yet as they do not do so on any distinct principle they naturally do it hesitatingly, reluctantly, and with misgiving. In 1847, even in 1866 – the latest panic, and the one in which on the whole the Bank acted the best – there was nevertheless an instant when it was believed the Bank would not advance on Consols, or at least hesitated to advance on them. The moment this was reported in the City and telegraphed to the country, it made the panic indefinitely worse. In fact, to make large advances in this faltering way is to incur the evil of making them without obtaining the advantage. What is wanted and what is necessary to stop a panic is to diffuse the impression that, though money may be dear, still money is to be had. If people could be really convinced that they could have money if they wait a day or two, and that utter ruin is not coming, most likely they would cease to run in such a mad way for money. Either shut the Bank at once, and say it will not lend more than it commonly lends, or lend freely, boldly, and so that the public may feel you mean to go on lending. To lend a great deal, and yet not give the public confidence that you will lend sufficiently and effectually, is the worst of all policies; but it is the policy now pursued.

In truth, the Bank do not lend from the motives which should make a bank lend. The holders of the Bank reserve ought to lend at once and most freely in an incipient panic, because they fear destruction in the panic. They ought not to do it to serve others; they ought to do it to serve themselves. They ought to know that this bold policy is the only safe one, and for that reason they ought to choose it. But the Bank directors are not afraid. Even at the last moment they say that 'whatever happens to the community they can preserve themselves.' Both in 1847 and 1857 (I believe also in 1866, though there is no printed evidence of it) the Bank directors contended that the Banking Department was quite safe though its reserve was nearly all gone, and that it could strengthen itself by selling securities and by refusing to discount. But this is a complete dream. The Bank of England could not sell 'securities,' for in an extreme panic there is no one else to buy securities. The Bank cannot stay still and wait till its bills are paid, and so fill its coffers, for unless it discounts equivalent bills, the bills which it has already discounted will not be paid. When the reserve in the ultimate bank or banks – those keeping the reserve – runs low, it cannot be augmented by the same means that other and dependent banks commonly adopt to maintain their reserve, for the dependent banks trust that at such moments the ultimate banks will be discounting more than usual and lending more than usual. But ultimate banks have no similar rear-guard to rely upon.

I shall have failed in my purpose if I have not proved that the system of entrusting all our reserve to a single board, like that of the Bank directors, is very anomalous; that it is very dangerous; that its bad consequences, though much felt, have not been fully seen; that they have been obscured by traditional arguments and hidden in the dust of ancient controversies.

But it will be said – What would be better? What other system could there be? We are so accustomed to a system of banking, dependent for its cardinal function on a single bank, that we can hardly conceive of any other. But the natural system – that which would have sprung up if Government had let banking alone – is that of many banks of equal or not altogether unequal size. In all other trades competition brings the traders to a rough approximate equality. In cotton spinning, no single firm far and permanently outstrips the others. There is no tendency to a monarchy in the cotton world; nor, where banking has been left free, is there any tendency to a monarchy in banking either. In Manchester, in Liverpool, and all through England, we have a great number of banks, each with a business more or less good, but we have no single bank with any sort of predominance; nor is there any such bank in Scotland. In the new world of Joint Stock Banks outside the Bank of England, we see much the same phenomenon. One or more get for a time a better business than the others, but no single bank permanently obtains an unquestioned predominance. None of them gets so much before the others that the others voluntarily place their reserves in its keeping. A republic with many competitors of a size or sizes suitable to the business, is the constitution of every trade if left to itself, and of banking as much as any other. A monarchy in any trade is a sign of some anomalous advantage, and of some intervention from without.

I shall be at once asked – Do you propose a revolution? Do you propose to abandon the one-reserve system, and create a new a many-reserve system? My plain answer is that I do not propose it. I know it would be childish. Credit in business is like loyalty in Government. You must take what you can find of it, and work with it if possible. A theorist may easily map out a scheme of Government in which Queen Victoria could be dispensed with. He may make a theory that, since we admit and we know that the House of Commons is the real sovereign, any other sovereign is superfluous; but for practical purposes, it is not even worth while to examine these arguments.

Queen Victoria is loyally obeyed – without doubt, and without reasoning – by millions of human beings. If those millions began to argue, it would not be easy to persuade them to obey Queen Victoria, or anything else. Effectual arguments to convince the people who need convincing are wanting. Just so, an immense system of credit, founded on the Bank of England as its pivot and its basis, now exists. The English people, and foreigners too, trust it implicitly. Every banker knows that if he has to *prove* that he is worthy of credit, however good may be his arguments, in fact his credit is gone: but what we have requires no proof. The whole rests on an instinctive confidence generated by use and years. Nothing would persuade the English people to abolish the Bank of England; and if some calamity swept it away, generations must elapse before at all the same trust would be placed in any other equivalent. A many-reserve system, if some miracle should put it down in Lombard Street, would seem monstrous there. Nobody would understand it, or confide in it. Credit is a power which may grow, but cannot be constructed. Those who live under a great and firm system of credit must consider that if they break up that one they will never see another, for it will take years upon years to make a successor to it.

On this account, I do not suggest that we should return to a natural or many-reserve system of banking. I should only incur useless ridicule if I did suggest it. Nor can I propose that we should adopt the simple and straightforward expedient by which the French have extricated themselves from the same difficulty. In France all banking rests on the Bank of France, even more than in England all rests on the Bank of England. The Bank of France keeps the final banking reserve, and it keeps the currency reserve too. But the State does not trust such a function to a board of merchants, named by shareholders. The nation itself – the executive Government – names the governor and deputy-governor of the Bank of France. These officers have, indeed, beside them a council of '*regents*,' or directors, named by the shareholders. But they need not attend to that council unless they think fit; they are appointed to watch over the national interest, and, in so doing, they may disregard the murmurs of the '*regents*' if they like. And in theory, there is much to be said for this plan. The keeping the single banking reserve being a national function, it is at least plausible to argue that Government should choose the functionaries. No doubt such a political intervention is contrary to the sound economical doctrine that 'banking is a trade, and only a trade.' But Government forgot that doctrine when, by privileges and monopolies, it made a single bank predominant over all others, and established the one-reserve system. As that system exists, a logical Frenchman consistently enough argues that the State should watch and manage it. But no such plan would answer in England. We have not been trained to care for logical sequence in our institutions, or rather we have been trained not to care for it. And the practical result for which we do care would in this case be bad. The governor of the Bank would be a high Parliamentary official, perhaps in the Cabinet, and would change as chance majorities and the strength of parties decide. A trade peculiarly requiring consistency and special attainment would be managed by a shifting and untrained ruler. In fact, the whole plan would seem to an Englishman of business palpably absurd; he would not consider it, he would not think it worth considering. That it works fairly well in France, and that there are specious arguments of theory for it, would not be sufficient to his mind.

All such changes being out of the question, I can propose only three remedies.

First. There should be a clear understanding between the Bank and the public that, since the Bank hold our ultimate banking reserve, they will recognise and act on the obligations which this implies; – that they will replenish it in times of foreign demand as fully, and lend it in times of internal panic as freely and readily, as plain principles of banking require.

This looks very different from the French plan, but it is not so different in reality. In England we can often effect, by the indirect compulsion of opinion, what other countries must effect by the direct compulsion of Government. We can do so in this case. The Bank directors now fear public opinion exceedingly; probably no kind of persons are so sensitive to newspaper criticism. And this is very natural. Our statesmen, it is true, are much more blamed, but they have generally served a long apprenticeship to sharp criticism. If they still care for it (and some do after years of experience much more than the world thinks), they care less for it than at first, and have come to regard it as an unavoidable and incessant irritant, of which they shall never be rid. But a Bank director undergoes no similar training and hardening. His functions at the Bank fill a very small part of his time; all the rest of his life (unless he be in Parliament) is spent in retired and mercantile industry. He is not subjected to keen and public criticism, and is not taught to bear it. Especially when once in his life be becomes, by rotation, governor, he is most anxious that the two years of office shall 'go off well.' He is apt to be irritated even by objections to the principles on which he acts, and cannot bear with equanimity censure which is pointed and personal. At present I am not sure if this sensitiveness is beneficial. As the exact position of the Bank of England in the Money Market is indistinctly seen, there is no standard to which a Bank governor can appeal. He is always in fear that 'something may be said;' but not quite knowing on what side that 'something' may be, his fear is but an indifferent guide to him. But if the cardinal doctrine were accepted, if it were acknowledged that the Bank is charged with the custody of our sole banking reserve, and is bound to deal with it according to admitted principles, then a governor of the Bank could look to those principles. He would know which way criticism was coming. If he was guided by the code, he would have a plain defence. And then we may be sure that old men of business would not deviate from the code. At present the Board of Directors are a sort of *semi*-trustees for the nation. I would have them real trustees, and with a good trust deed.

Secondly. The government of the Bank should be improved in a manner to be explained. We should diminish the 'amateur' element: we should augment the trained banking element; and we should ensure more constancy in the administration.

Thirdly. As these two suggestions are designed to make the Bank as strong as possible, we should look at the rest of our banking system, and try to reduce the demands on the Bank as much as we can. The central machinery being inevitably frail, we should carefully and as much as possible diminish the strain upon it.

But to explain these proposals, and to gain a full understanding of many arguments that have been used, we must look more in detail at the component parts of Lombard Street, and at the curious set of causes which have made it assume its present singular structure.

Chapter VII

A more exact account of the mode in which the Bank of England has discharged its duty of retaining a good bank reserve, and of administering it effectually

The preceding chapters have in some degree enabled us to appreciate the importance of the duties which the Bank of England is bound to discharge as to its banking reserve.

If we ask how the Bank of England has discharged this great responsibility, we shall be struck by three things: *first*, as has been said before, the Bank has never by any corporate act or authorised utterance acknowledged the duty, and some of its directors deny it; *second* (what is even more remarkable), no resolution of Parliament, no report of any Committee of Parliament (as far as I know), no remembered speech of a responsible statesman, has assigned or enforced that duty on the Bank; *third* (what is more remarkable still), the distinct teaching of our highest authorities has often been that no public duty of any kind is imposed on the Banking Department of the Bank; that, for banking purposes, it is only a joint stock bank like any other bank; that its managers should look only to the interest of the proprietors and their dividend; that they are to manage as the London and Westminster Bank or the Union Bank manages.

At first, it seems exceedingly strange that so important a responsibility should be unimposed, unacknowledged, and denied; but the explanation is this. We are living amid the vestiges of old controversies, and we speak their language, though we are dealing with different thoughts and different facts. For more than fifty years – from 1793 down to 1844 – there was a keen controversy as to the public duties of the Bank. It was said to be the 'manager' of the paper currency, and on that account many expected much good from it; others said it did great harm; others again that it could do neither good nor harm. But for the whole period there was an incessant and fierce discussion. That discussion was terminated by the Act of 1844. By that Act the currency manages itself; the entire working is automatic. The Bank of England plainly does not manage – cannot even be said to manage – the currency any more. And naturally, but rashly, the only reason upon which a public responsibility used to be assigned to the Bank having now clearly come to an end, it was inferred by many that the Bank had no responsibility.

The complete uncertainty as to the degree of responsibility acknowledged by the Bank of England is best illustrated by what has been said by the Bank directors themselves as to the panic of 1866. The panic of that year, it will be remembered, happened, contrary to precedent, in the spring, and at the next meeting of the Court of Bank proprietors – the September meeting – there was a very remarkable discussion, which I give at length below,* and of which all that is most material was thus described in the 'Economist': –

'The great importance of the late meeting of the proprietors of the Bank of England.

'The late meeting of the proprietors of the Bank of England has a very unusual importance. There can be no effectual inquiry now into the history of the late crisis. A Parliamentary committee next year would, unless something strange occur in the interval, be a great waste of time. Men of business have keen sensations but short memories, and they will care no more next February for the events of last May than they now care for the events of October 1864. A *proforma* inquiry, on which no real mind is spent, and which everyone knows will lead to nothing, is far worse than no inquiry at all. Under these circumstances the official statements of the Governor of the Bank are the only authentic expositions we shall have of the policy of the Bank directors, whether as respects the past or the future. And when we examine the proceedings with care, we shall find that they contain matter of the gravest import.

'This meeting may be considered to admit and recognise the fact that the Bank of England keeps the sole banking reserve of the country. We do not now mix up this matter with the country circulation, or the question whether there should be many issuers of notes or only one. We speak not of the currency reserve, but of the banking reserve – the reserve held against deposits, and not the reserve held against notes. We have often insisted in these columns that the Bank of England does keep the sole real reserve – the sole considerable unoccupied mass of cash in the country; but there has been no universal agreement about it. Great authorities have been unwilling to admit it. They have not, indeed, formally and explicitly contended against it. If they had, they must have pointed out some other great store of unused cash besides that at the Bank, and they could not find such store. But they

---

* See Note D in the Appendix.

have attempted distinctions; – have said that the doctrine that the Bank of England keeps the sole banking reserve of the country was "not a good way of putting it," was exaggerated, and was calculated to mislead.

'But the late meeting is a complete admission that such is the fact. The Governor of the Bank said:

> A great strain has within the last few months been put upon the resources of this house, and of the whole banking community of London; and I think I am entitled to say that not only this house, but the entire banking body, acquitted themselves most honourably and creditably throughout that very trying period. Banking is a very peculiar business, and it depends so much upon credit that the least blast of suspicion is sufficient to sweep away, as it were, the harvest of a whole year. But the manner in which the banking establishments generally in London met the demands made upon them during the greater portion of the past half-year affords a most satisfactory proof of the soundness of the principles on which their business is conducted. This house exerted itself to the utmost – and exerted itself most successfully – to meet the crisis. We did not flinch from our post. When the storm came upon us, on the morning on which it became known that the house of Overend and Co. had failed, we were in as sound and healthy a position as any banking establishment could hold, and on that day and throughout the succeeding week we made advances which would hardly be credited. I do not believe that anyone would have thought of predicting, even at the shortest period beforehand, the greatness of those advances. It was not unnatural that in this state of things a certain degree of alarm should have taken possession of the public mind, and that those who required accommodation from the Bank should have gone to the Chancellor of the Exchequer and requested the Government to empower us to issue notes beyond the statutory amount, if we should think that such a measure was desirable. But we had to act before we could receive any such power, and before the Chancellor of the Exchequer was perhaps out of his bed we had advanced one-half of our reserves, which were certainly thus reduced to an amount which we could not witness without regret. But we would not flinch from the duty which we conceived was imposed upon us of supporting the banking community, and I am not aware that any legitimate application made for assistance to this house was refused. Every gentleman who came here with adequate security was liberally dealt with; and if accommodation could not be afforded to the full extent which was demanded, no one who offered proper security failed to obtain relief from this house.

'Now this is distinctly saying that the other banks of the country need not keep any such banking reserve – any such sum of actual cash – of real sovereigns and bank notes, as will help them through a sudden panic. It acknowledges a "duty" on the part of the Bank of England to "support the banking community," to make the reserve of the Bank of England do for them as well as for itself.

'In our judgment this language is most just, and the Governor of the Bank could scarcely have done a greater public service than by using language so businesslike and so distinct. Let us know precisely who is to keep the banking reserve. If the joint stock banks and the private banks and the country banks are to keep their share, let us determine on that; Mr Gladstone appeared not long since to say in Parliament that it ought to be so. But at any rate there should be no doubt whose duty it is. Upon grounds which we have often stated, we believe that the anomaly of one bank keeping the sole banking reserve is so fixed in our system that we cannot change it if we would. The great evil to be feared was an indistinct conception of the fact, and that is now avoided.

'The importance of these declarations by the Bank is greater, because after the panic of 1857 the Bank did not hold exactly the same language. A person who loves concise expressions said lately "that Overends broke the Bank in 1866 because it went, and in 1857 because it was not let go." We need not too precisely examine such language; the element of truth in it is very plain – the great advances made to Overends were a principal event in the panic of 1857; the bill brokers were then very much what the bankers were lately – they were the borrowers who wanted sudden and incalculable advances. But the bill brokers were told not to expect the like again. But Alderman Salomons, on the part of the London bankers, said, "he wished to take that opportunity of stating that he believed nothing could be more satisfactory to the managers and shareholders of joint stock banks than the testimony which the Governor of the Bank of England had that day borne to the sound and honourable manner in which their business was conducted. It was manifestly desirable that the joint stock banks and the banking interest generally should work in harmony with the Bank of England; and he sincerely thanked the Governor of the Bank for the kindly manner in which he had alluded to the mode in which the joint stock banks had met the late monetary crisis." The Bank of England agrees to give other banks the requisite assistance in case of need, and the other banks agree to ask for it.

'Secondly. The Bank agrees, in fact, if not in name, to make unlimited advances on proper security to anyone who applies for it. On the present occasion 45,000,000*l.* was so advanced in three months. And the Bank do not say to the mercantile community, or to the bankers, "Do not come to us again. We helped you once. But do not look upon it as a precedent. We will not help you again." On the contrary, the evident and intended implication is that under like circumstances the Bank would act again as it has now acted.'

This article was much disliked by many of the Bank directors, and especially by some whose opinion is of great authority. They thought that the 'Economist' drew 'rash deductions' from a speech which was in itself 'open to some objection' – which was, like all such speeches, defective in theoretical precision, and which was at best only the expression of an opinion by the Governor of that day, which had not been authorised by the Court of Directors, which could not bind the Bank. However, the article had at least this use, that it brought out the facts. All the directors would have felt a difficulty in commenting upon, or limiting, or in differing from, a speech of a Governor from the chair. But there was no difficulty or delicacy in attacking the 'Economist.' Accordingly Mr Hankey, one of the most experienced Bank directors, not long after, took occasion to observe:

'The "Economist" newspaper has put forth what in my opinion is the most mischievous doctrine ever broached in the monetary or banking world in this country; viz. that it is the proper function of the Bank of England to keep money available at all times to supply the demands of bankers who have rendered their own assets unavailable. Until such a doctrine is repudiated by the banking interest, the difficulty of pursuing any sound principle of banking in London will be always very great. But I do not believe that such a doctrine as that bankers are justified in relying on the Bank of England to assist them in time of need is generally held by the bankers in London.

'I consider it to be the undoubted duty of the Bank of England to hold its banking deposits (reserving generally about one-third in cash) in the most available securities; and in the event of a sudden pressure in the Money Market, by whatever circumstance it may be caused, to bear its full share of a drain on its resources. I am ready to admit, however, that a general opinion has long prevailed that the Bank of England ought to be prepared to do much more than this, though I confess my surprise at finding an advocate for such an opinion in the "Economist."* If it were practicable for the Bank to retain money unemployed to meet such an emergency, it would be a very unwise thing to do so. But I contend that it is quite impracticable, and, if it were possible, it would be most inexpedient; and I can only express my regret that the Bank, from a desire to do everything in its power to afford general assistance in times of banking or commercial distress, should ever have acted in a way to encourage such an opinion. The more the conduct of the affairs of the Bank is made to assimilate to the conduct of every other well-managed bank in the United Kingdom, the better for the Bank, and the better for the community at large.'

I am scarcely a judge, but I do not think Mr Hankey replies to the 'Economist' very conclusively.

---

* Vide *Economist* of September 22, 1866.

First – He should have observed that the question is not as to what ought to be, but as to what is. The 'Economist' did not say that the system of a single bank reserve was a good system, but that it was the system which existed, and which must be worked, as you could not change it.

Secondly – Mr Hankey should have shown 'some other store of unused cash' except the reserve in the Banking Department of the Bank of England out of which advances in time of panic could be made. These advances are necessary, and must be made by some one. The 'reserves' of London bankers are not such store; they are *used* cash, not unused; they are part of the bank deposits, and lent as such.

Thirdly – Mr Hankey should have observed that we know by the published figures that the joint stock banks of London do not keep one-third, or anything like one-third, of their liabilities in 'cash' – even meaning by 'cash' a deposit at the Bank of England. One-third of the deposits in joint stock banks, not to speak of the private banks, would be 30,000,000*l*; and the private deposits of the Bank of England are 18,000,000*l* According to his own statement, there is a conspicuous contrast. The joint stock banks, and the private banks, no doubt, too, keep one sort of reserve, and the Bank of England a different kind of reserve altogether. Mr Hankey says that the two ought to be managed on the same principle; but if so, he should have said whether he would assimilate the practice of the Bank of England to that of the other banks, or that of the other banks to the practice of the Bank of England.

Fourthly – Mr Hankey should have observed that, as has been explained, in most panics, the principal use of a 'banking reserve' is not to advance to bankers; the largest amount is almost always advanced to the mercantile public and to bill brokers. But the point is, that by our system all extra pressure is thrown upon the Bank of England. In the worst part of the crisis of 1866, 50,000*l*. 'fresh money' could not be borrowed even on the best security – even on Consols – except at the Bank of England. There was no other lender to new borrowers.

But my object now is not to revive a past controversy, but to show in what an unsatisfactory and uncertain condition that controversy has left a most important subject. Mr Hankey's is the last explanation we have had of the policy of the Bank. He is a very experienced and attentive director, and I think expresses, more or less, the opinions of other directors. And what do we find? Setting aside and saying nothing about the remarkable speech of the Governor in 1866, which at least (according to the interpretation of the 'Economist') was clear and excellent, Mr Hankey leaves us in doubt altogether as to what will be the policy of the Bank of England in the next panic, and as to what amount of aid the public may then expect from it. His words are too vague. No one can tell what a 'fair share' means; still less can we tell what other people at some future time will say it means. Theory suggests, and experience proves, that in a panic the holders of the ultimate Bank reserve (whether one bank or many) should lend to all that bring good securities quickly, freely, and readily. By that policy they allay a panic; by every other policy they intensify it. The public have a right to know whether the Bank of England – the holders of our ultimate bank reserve – acknowledge this duty, and are ready to perform it. But this is now very uncertain.

If we refer to history, and examine what in fact has been the conduct of the Bank directors, we find that they have acted exactly as persons of their type, character, and position might have been expected to act. They are a board of plain, sensible, prosperous English merchants; and they have both done and left undone what such a board might have been expected to do and not to do. Nobody could expect great attainments in economical science from such a board; laborious study is for the most part foreign to the habits of English merchants. Nor could we expect original views on banking, for banking is a special trade, and English merchants, as a body, have had no experience in it. A 'board' can scarcely ever make improvements, for the policy of a board is determined by the opinions of the most numerous class of its members – its average members – and these are never prepared for sudden improvements. A board of upright and sensible merchants will always act according to what it considers 'safe' principles – that is, according to the *received* maxims of the mercantile world then and there – and in this manner the directors of the Bank of England have acted nearly uniformly.

Their strength and their weakness were curiously exemplified at the time when they had the most power. After the suspension of cash payments in 1797, the directors of the Bank of England could issue what notes they liked. There was no check, these notes could not come back upon the Bank for payment; there was a great temptation to extravagant issue, and no present penalty upon it. But the directors of the Bank withstood the temptation; they did not issue their inconvertible notes extravagantly. And the proof is, that for more than ten years after the suspension of cash payments the Bank paper was undepreciated, and circulated at no discount in comparison with gold. Though the Bank directors of that day at last fell into errors, yet on the whole they acted with singular judgment and moderation. But when, in 1810, they came to be examined as to their reasons, they gave answers that have become almost classical by their nonsense. Mr Pearse, the Governor of the Bank, said:

In considering this subject, with reference to the manner in which bank notes are issued, resulting from the applications made for discounts to supply the necessary want of bank notes, by which their issue in amount is so controlled that it can never amount to an excess, I cannot see how the amount of bank notes issued can operate upon the price of bullion, or the state of the exchanges; and therefore I am individually of opinion that the price of bullion, or the state of the exchanges, can never be a reason for lessening the amount of bank notes to be issued, always understanding the control which I have already described.

Is the Governor of the Bank of the same opinion which has now been expressed by the Deputy-Governor?

> Mr Whitmore – I am so much of the same opinion, that I never think it necessary to advert to the price of gold, or the state of the exchange, on the days on which we make our advances.
>
> Do you advert to these two circumstances with a view to regulate the general amount of your advances? – I do not advert to it with a view to our general advances, conceiving it not to bear upon the question.

And Mr Harman, another Bank director, expressed his opinion in these terms:

> I must very materially alter my opinions before I can suppose that the exchanges will be influenced by any modifications of our paper currency.

Very few persons perhaps could have managed to commit so many blunders in so few words.

But it is no disgrace at all to the Bank directors of that day to have committed these blunders. They spoke according to the best mercantile opinion of England. The City of London and the House of Commons both approved of what they said; those who dissented were said to be abstract thinkers and unpractical men. The Bank directors adopted the ordinary opinions, and pursued the usual practice of their time. It was this 'routine' that caused their moderation. They believed that so long as they issued 'notes' only at 5 per cent, and only on the discount of good bills, those notes could not be depreciated. And as the number of 'good' bills – bills which sound merchants know to be good – does not rapidly increase, and as the market rate of interest was often less than 5 per cent, these checks on over-issue were very effective. They failed in time, and the theory upon which they were defended was nonsense; but for a time their operation was powerful and excellent.

Unluckily, in the management of the matter before us – the management of the Bank reserve – the directors of the Bank of England were neither acquainted with right principles, nor were they protected by a judicious routine. They could not be expected themselves to discover such principles. The abstract thinking of the world is never to be expected from persons in high places; the administration of first-rate current transactions is a most engrossing business, and those charged with them are usually but little inclined to think on points of theory, even when such thinking most nearly concerns those transactions. No doubt when men's own fortunes are at stake, the instinct of the trader does somehow anticipate the conclusions of the closet. But a board has no instincts when it is not getting an income for its members, and when it is only discharging a duty of office. During the suspension of cash payments – a suspension which lasted twenty-two years – all traditions as to a cash reserve had died away. After 1819 the Bank directors had to discharge the duty of keeping a banking reserve, and (as the law then stood) a currency reserve also, without the guidance either of keen interests, or good principles, or wise traditions.

Under such circumstances, the Bank directors inevitably made mistakes of the gravest magnitude. The first time of trial came in 1825. In that year the Bank directors allowed their stock of bullion to fall in the most alarming manner:

		£
On Dec. 24, 1824, the coin and bullion in the Bank was......		10,721,000
On Dec. 25, 1825, it was reduced to		1,260,000

– and the consequence was a panic so tremendous that its results are well remembered after nearly fifty years. In the next period of extreme trial – in 1837–9 – the Bank was compelled to draw for 2,000,000*l.* on the Bank of France; and even after that aid the directors permitted their bullion, which was still the currency reserve as well as the banking reserve, to be reduced to 2,404,000*l.* a great alarm pervaded society, and generated an eager controversy, out of which ultimately emerged the Act of 1844. The next trial came in 1847, and then the Bank permitted its banking reserve (which the law had now distinctly separated) to fall to 1,176,000*l.*; and so intense was the alarm, that the executive Government issued a letter of licence, permitting the Bank, if necessary, to break the new law, and, if necessary, to borrow from the currency reserve, which was full, in aid of the banking reserve, which was empty. Till 1857 there was an unusual calm in the Money Market, but in the autumn of that year the Bank directors let the banking reserve, which even in October was far too small, fall thus:

	£
Oct. 10..................	4,024,000
″ 17..................	3,217,000
″ 24..................	3,485,000
″ 31..................	2,258,000
Nov. 6..................	2,155,000
″ 13..................	957,000

And then a letter of licence like that of 1847 was not only issued, but used. The Ministry of the day authorised the Bank to borrow from the currency reserve in aid of the banking reserve, and the Bank of England did so borrow several hundred pounds till the end of the month of November. A more miserable catalogue than that of the failures of the Bank of England to keep a good banking reserve in all the seasons of trouble between 1825 and 1857 is scarcely to be found in history.

But since 1857 there has been a great improvement. By painful events and incessant discussions, men of business have now been trained to see that a large banking reserve is necessary, and to understand that, in the curious constitution of the English banking world, the Bank of England is the only body which could effectually keep it. They have never acknowledged the duty; some of them, as we have seen, deny the duty; still they have to a considerable extent begun to perform the duty. The Bank directors, being experienced and able men of business, comprehended this like other men of business. Since 1857 they have always kept, I do not say a sufficient banking reserve, but a fair and creditable banking reserve, and one altogether different from any which they kept before. At one period the Bank directors even went farther: they made a distinct step in advance of the public intelligence; they adopted a particular mode of raising the rate of interest, which is far more efficient than any other mode. Mr Goschen observes, in his book on the Exchanges:

> 'Between the rates in London and Paris, the expense of sending gold to and fro having been reduced to a minimum between the two cities, the difference can never be very great; but it must not be forgotten that – the interest being taken at a percentage calculated per annum, and the probable profit having, when an operation in three-month bills is contemplated, to be divided by four, whereas the percentage of expense has to be wholly borne by the one transaction – a very slight expense becomes a great impediment. If the cost is only $\frac{1}{2}$ per cent, there must be a profit of 2 per cent. in the rate of interest, or $\frac{1}{2}$ per cent. on three months, before any advantage commences; and thus, supposing the Paris capitalists calculate that they may send their gold over to England for $\frac{1}{2}$ per cent. expense, and chance their being so favoured by the Exchanges as to be able to draw it back without any cost at all, there must nevertheless be an excess of more than 2 per cent. in the London rate of interest over that in Paris, before the operation of sending gold over from France, merely for the sake of the higher interest, will pay.'

Accordingly, Mr Goschen recommended that the Bank of England should, as a rule, raise their rate by steps of 1 per cent. at a time when the object of the rise was to affect the 'foreign Exchanges.' And the Bank of England, from 1860 onward, have acted upon that principle. Before that time they used to raise their rate almost always by steps of $\frac{1}{2}$ per cent, and there was nothing in the general state of mercantile opinion to compel them to change their policy. The change was, on the contrary, most unpopular. On this occasion, and, as far as I know, on this occasion alone, the Bank of England made an excellent alteration of their policy, which was not exacted by contemporary opinion, and which was in advance of it.

The beneficial results of the improved policy of the Bank were palpable and speedy. We were enabled by it to sustain the great drain of silver from Europe to India to pay for Indian cotton in the years between 1862–1865. In the autumn of 1864 there was especial danger; but, by a rapid and able use of their new policy, the Bank of England maintained an adequate reserve, and preserved the country from calamities which, if we had looked only to precedent, would have seemed inevitable. All the causes which produced the panic of 1857 were in action in 1864 – the drain of silver in 1864 and the preceding year was beyond comparison greater than in 1857 and the years before it – and yet in 1864 there was no panic. The Bank of England was almost immediately rewarded for its adoption of right principles by finding that those principles, at a severe crisis, preserved public credit.

In 1866 undoubtedly a panic occurred, but I do not think that the Bank of England can be blamed for it. They had in their till an exceedingly good reserve according to the estimate of that time – a sufficient reserve, in all probability, to have coped with the crises of 1847 and 1857. The suspension of Overend and Gurney – the most trusted private firm in England – caused an alarm, in suddenness and magnitude, without example. What was the effect of the Act of 1844 on the panic of 1866 is a question on which opinion will be long divided; but I think it will be generally agreed that, acting under the provisions of that law, the directors of the Bank of England had in their Banking Department in that year a fairly large reserve – quite as large a reserve as anyone expected them to keep – to meet unexpected and painful contingencies.

From 1866 to 1870 there was almost an unbroken calm on the Money Market. The Bank of England had no difficulties to cope with; there was no opportunity for much discretion. The Money Market took care of itself. But in 1870 the Bank of France suspended specie payments, and from that time a new era begins. The demands on this market for bullion have been greater, and have been more incessant, than they ever were before, for this is now the only bullion market. This has made it necessary for the Bank of England to hold a much larger banking reserve than was ever before required, and to be much more watchful than in former times lest that banking reserve should on a sudden be dangerously diminished. The forces are greater and quicker than they used to be, and a firmer protection and a surer solicitude are necessary. But I do not think the Bank of England is sufficiently aware of this. All the governing body of the Bank certainly are not aware of it. The same eminent director to whom I have before referred, Mr Hankey, published in the 'Times' an elaborate letter, saying again that one-third of the liabilities were, even in these altered times, a sufficient reserve for the Banking Department of the Bank of England, and that it was no part of the business of the Bank to keep a supply of 'bullion for exportation,' which was exactly the most mischievous doctrine that could be maintained when the Banking Department of the Bank of England had become the only great repository in Europe where gold could at once be obtained, and when, therefore, a far greater store of bullion ought to be kept than at any former period.

And besides this defect of the present time, there are some chronic faults in the policy of the Bank of England, which arise, as will be presently explained, from grave defects in its form of government.

There is almost always some hesitation when a Governor begins to reign. He is the Prime Minister of the Bank Cabinet; and when so important a functionary changes, naturally much else changes too. If the Governor be weak, this kind of vacillation and hesitation continues throughout his term of office. The usual defect then is, that the Bank of England does not raise the rate of interest sufficiently quickly. It does raise it; in the end it takes the alarm, but it does not take the alarm sufficiently soon. A cautious man, in a new office, does not like strong measures. Bank Governors are generally cautious men; they are taken from a most cautious class; in consequence they are very apt to temporise and delay. But almost always the delay in creating a stringency only makes a greater stringency inevitable. The effect of a timid policy has been to let the gold out of the Bank, and that gold *must* be recovered. It would really have been far easier to have maintained the reserve by timely measures than to have replenished it by delayed measures; but new Governors rarely see this.

Secondly. Those defects are apt, in part, or as a whole, to be continued throughout the reign of a weak Governor. The objection to a decided policy, and the indisposition to a timely action, which are excusable in one whose influence is beginning, and whose reign is new, is continued through the whole reign of one to whom those defects are natural, and who exhibits those defects in all his affairs.

Thirdly. This defect is enhanced, because, as has so often been said, there is now no adequate rule recognised in the management of the banking reserve. Mr Weguelin, the last Bank Governor who has been examined, said that it was sufficient for the Bank to keep from one-fourth to one-third of its banking liabilities as a reserve. But no one now would ever be content if the banking reserve were near to one-fourth of its liabilities. Mr Hankey, as I have shown, considers 'about a third' as the proportion of reserve to liability at which the Bank should aim; but he does not say whether he regards a third as the minimum below which the reserve in the Banking Department should never be, or as a fair average, about which the reserve may fluctuate, sometimes being greater, or at others less.

In a future chapter I shall endeavour to show that one-third of its banking liabilities is at present by no means an adequate reserve for the Banking Department – that it is not even a proper minimum, far less a fair average; and I shall allege what seem to me good reasons for thinking that, unless the Bank aim by a different method at a higher standard, its own position may hereafter be perilous, and the public may be exposed to disaster.

II

But, as has been explained, the Bank of England is bound, according to our system, not only to keep a good reserve against a time of panic, but to use that reserve effectually when that time of panic comes. The keepers of the banking reserve, whether one or many, are obliged then to use that reserve for their own safety. If they permit all other forms of credit to perish, their own will perish immediately, and in consequence.

As to the Bank of England, however, this is denied. It is alleged that the Bank of England can keep aloof in a panic; that it can, if it will, let other banks and trades fail; that, if it chooses, it can stand alone, and survive intact while all else perishes around it. On various occasions, most influential persons, both in the government of the Bank and out of it, have said that such was their opinion. And we must at once see whether this opinion is true or false, for it is absurd to attempt to estimate the conduct of the Bank of England during panics before we know what the precise position of the Bank in a panic really is.

The holders of this opinion in its most extreme form say that in a panic the Bank of England can stay its hand at any time; that, though it has advanced much, it may refuse to advance more; that, though the reserve may have been reduced by such advances, it may refuse to lessen it still further; that it can refuse to make any further discounts; that the bills which it has discounted will become due; that it can refill its reserve by the payment of those bills; that it can sell stock or other securities, and so replenish its reserve still further. But in this form the notion scarcely merits serious refutation. If the Bank reserve has once become low, there are, in a panic, no ineans of raising it again. Money parted with at such a time is very hard to get back; those who have taken it will not let it go – not, at least, unless they are sure of getting other money in its place. And at such instant the recovery of money is as hard for the Bank of England as for anyone else, probably even harder. The difficulty is this: if the Bank decline to discount, the holders of the bills previously discounted cannot pay. As has been shown, trade in England is largely carried on with borrowed money. If you propose greatly to reduce that amount, you will cause many failures unless you can pour in from elsewhere some equivalent amount of new money. But in a panic there is no new money to be had; everybody who has it clings to it, and will not part with it. Especially what has been advanced to merchants cannot easily be recovered; they are under immense liabilities, and they will not give back a penny which they imagine that even possibly they may need to discharge those liabilities. And bankers are in even greater terror. In a panic they will not discount a host of new bills; they are engrossed with their own liabilities and those of their own customers, and do not care for those of others. The notion that the Bank of England can stop discounting in a panic, and so obtain fresh money, is a delusion. It can stop discounting, of course, at pleasure. But if it does, it will get in no new money; its bill case will daily be more and more packed with bills 'returned unpaid.'

The sale of stock, too, by the Bank of England in the middle of a panic is impossible. The Bank at such a time is the only lender on stock, and it is only by loans from a bank that large purchases, at such a moment, can be made. Unless the Bank of England lend, no stock will be bought. There is not in the country any large sum of unused ready money ready to buy it. The only unused sum is the reserve in the Banking Department of the Bank of England: if, therefore, in a panic that Department itself attempt to sell stock, the failure would be ridiculous. It would hardly be able to sell any at all. Probably it would not sell fifty pounds' worth. The idea that the Bank can, during a panic, replenish its reserve in this or in any other manner when that reserve has once been allowed to become empty, or nearly empty, is too absurd to be steadily maintained, though I fear that it is not yet wholly abandoned.

The second and more reasonable conception of the independence of the Bank of England is, however, this: – It may be said, and it is said, that if the Bank of England stop at the beginning of a panic, if it refuse to advance a shilling more than usual, if it begin the battle with a good banking reserve, and do not diminish it by extra loans, the Bank of England is sure to be safe. But this form of the opinion, though more reasonable and moderate, is not, therefore, more true. The panic of 1866 is the best instance to test it. As everyone knows, that panic began quite suddenly, on the fall of 'Overends.' Just before, the Bank had 5,812,000*l*. in its reserve; in fact, it advanced 13,000,000*l*. of new money in the next few days, and its reserve went down to nothing, and the Government had to help. But if the Bank had not made these advances, could it have kept its reserve?

Certainly it could not. It could not have retained its own deposits. A large part of these are the deposits of bankers, and they would not consent to help the Bank of England in a policy of isolation. They would not agree to suspend payments themselves, and permit the Bank of England to survive, and get all their business. They would withdraw their deposits from the Bank; they would not assist it to stand erect amid their ruin. But even if this were not so, even if the banks were willing to keep their deposits at the Bank while it was not lending, they would soon find that they could not do it. They are only able to keep those deposits at the Bank by the aid of the Clearing-house system, and if a panic were to pass a certain height, that system, which rests on confidence, would be destroyed by terror.

The common course of business is this. A B having to receive 50,000*l*. from C D takes C D's cheque on a banker crossed, as it is called, and, therefore, only payable to another banker. He pays that cheque to his own credit with his own banker, who presents it to the banker on whom it is drawn, and if good it is an item between them in the general clearing or settlement of the afternoon. But this is evidently a very refined machinery, which a panic will be apt to destroy. At the first stage A B may say to his debtor C D, 'I cannot take your cheque, I must have bank notes.' If it is a debt on securities, he will be very apt to say this. The usual practice – credit being good – is for the creditor to take the debtor's cheque, and to give up the securities. But if the 'securities' really secure him in a time of difficulty, he will not like to give them up, and take a bit of paper – a mere cheque, which may be paid or not paid. He will say to his debtor, 'I can only give you your securities if you will give me bank notes.' And if he does say so, the debtor must go to his bank, and draw out the 50,000*l*. if he has it. But if this were done on a large scale, the bank's 'cash in house' would soon be gone; as the Clearing-house was gradually superseded it would have to trench on its deposit at the Bank of England; and then the bankers would have to pay so much over the counter that they would be unable to keep much money at the Bank, even if they wished. They would soon be obliged to draw out every shilling.

The diminished use of the Clearing-house, in consequence of the panic, would intensify that panic. By far the greater part of the bargains of the country in moneyed securities is settled on the Stock Exchange twice a month, and the number of securities then given up for mere cheques, and the number of cheques then passing at the Clearing-house, are enormous. If that system collapse, the number of failures would be incalculable, and each failure would add to the discredit that caused the collapse.

The non-banking customers of the Bank of England would be discredited as well as other people; their cheques would not be taken any more than those of others; they would have to draw out bank notes, and the Bank reserve would not be enough for a tithe of such payments.

The matter would come shortly to this: a great number of brokers and dealers are under obligations to pay immense sums, and in common times they obtain these sums by the transfer of certain securities. If, as we said just now, No. 1 has borrowed 50,000*l.* of No. 2 on Exchequer bills, he, for the most part, cannot pay No. 2 till he has sold or pledged those bills to some one else. But till he has the bills he cannot pledge or sell them; and if No. 2 will not give them up till he gets his money, No. 1 will be ruined, because he cannot pay it. And if No. 2 has No. 3 to pay, as is very likely, he may be ruined because of No. 1's default, and No. 4 only on account of No. 3's default; and so on without end. On settling day, without the Clearing-house, there would be a mass of failures, and a bundle of securities. The effect of these failures would be a general run on all bankers, and on the Bank of England particularly.

It may indeed be said that the money thus taken from the Banking Department of the Bank of England would return there immediately; that the public who borrowed it would not know where else to deposit it; that it would be taken out in the morning, and put back in the evening. But, in the first place, this argument assumes that the Banking Department would have enough money to pay the demands on it; and this is a mistake: the Banking Department would not have a hundredth part of the necessary funds. And in the second, a great panic which deranged the Clearing-house would soon be diffused all through the country. The money therefore taken from the Bank of England could not be soon returned to the Bank; it would not come back on the evening of the day on which it was taken out, or for many days; it would be distributed through the length and breadth of the country, wherever there were bankers, wherever there was trade, wherever there were liabilities, wherever there was terror.

And even in London, so immense a panic would soon impair the credit of the Banking Department of the Bank of England. That department has no great *prestige*. It was only created in 1844, and it has failed three times since.

The world would imagine that what has happened before will happen again; and when they have got money, they will not deposit it at an establishment which may not be able to repay it. This did not happen in former panics, because the case we are considering never arose. The Bank was helping the public, and, more or less confidently, it was believed that the Government would help the Bank. But if the policy be relinquished which formerly assuaged alarm, that alarm will be protracted and enhanced, till it touch the Banking Department of the Bank itself.

I do not imagine that it would touch the Issue Department. I think that the public would be quite satisfied if they obtained bank notes. Generally nothing is gained by holding the notes of a bank instead of depositing them at a bank. But in the Bank of England there is a great difference: their notes are *legal tender*. Whoever holds them can always pay his debts, and, except for foreign payments, he could want no more. The rush would be for bank notes; those that could be obtained would be carried north, south, east, and west, and, as there would not be enough for all the country, the Banking Department would soon pay away all it had.

Nothing, therefore, can be more certain than that the Bank of England has in this respect no peculiar privilege; that it is simply in the position of a Bank keeping the banking reserve of the country; that it must in time of panic do what all other similar banks must do; that in time of panic it must advance freely and vigorously to the public out of the reserve.

And with the Bank of England, as with other banks in the same case, these advances, if they are to be made at all, should be made so as, if possible, to obtain the object for which they are made. The end is to stay the panic; and the advances should, if possible, stay the panic. And for this purpose there are two rules: – First. That these loans should only be made at a very high rate of interest. This will operate as a heavy fine on unreasonable timidity, and will prevent the greatest number of applications by persons who do not require it. The rate should be raised early in the panic, so that the fine may be paid early; that no one may borrow out of idle precaution without paying well for it; that the banking reserve may be protected as far as possible.

Secondly. That at this rate these advances should be made on all good banking securities, and as largely as the public ask for them. The reason is plain. The object is to stay alarm, and nothing, therefore, should be done to cause alarm. But the way to cause alarm is to refuse some one who has good security to offer. The news of this will spread in an instant through all the Money Market at a moment of terror; no one can say exactly who carries it, but in half an hour it will be carried on all sides, and will intensify the terror everywhere. No advances indeed need be made by which the Bank will ultimately lose. The amount of bad business in commercial countries is an infinitesimally small fraction of the whole business. That in a panic the bank, or banks, holding the ultimate reserve should refuse bad bills or bad securities will not make the panic really worse; the 'unsound' people are a feeble minority, and they are afraid even to look frightened for fear their unsoundness may be detected. The great majority, the majority to be protected, are the 'sound' people, the people who have good security to offer. If it is known that the Bank of England is freely advancing on what in ordinary times is reckoned a good security – on what is then commonly pledged and easily convertible – the alarm of the solvent merchants and bankers will be stayed. But if securities, really good and usually convertible, are refused by the Bank, the alarm will not abate, the other loans made will fail in obtaining their end, and the panic will become worse and worse.

It may be said that the reserve in the Banking Department will not be enough for all such loans. If that be so, the Banking Department must fail. But lending is, nevertheless, its best expedient. This is the method of making its money go the farthest, and of enabling it to get through the panic if anything will so enable it. Making no loans, as we have seen, will ruin it; making large loans and stopping, as we have also seen, will ruin it. The only safe plan for the Bank is the brave plan, to lend in a panic on every kind of current security, or every sort on which money is ordinarily and usually lent. This policy may not save the Bank; but if it do not, nothing will save it.

If we examine the manner in which the Bank of England has fulfilled these duties, we shall find, as we found before, that the true principle has never been grasped; that the policy has been inconsistent; that, though the policy has much improved, there still remain important particulars in which it might be better than it is.

The first panic of which it is necessary here to speak is that of 1825: I hardly think we should derive much instruction from those of 1793 and 1797; the world has changed too much since; and during the long period of inconvertible currency from 1797 to 1819, the problems to be solved were altogether different from our present ones. In the panic of 1825, the Bank of England at first acted as unwisely as it was possible to act. By every means it tried to restrict its advances. The reserve being very small, it endeavoured to protect that reserve by lending as little as possible. The result was a period of frantic and almost inconceivable violence; scarcely anyone knew whom to trust; credit was almost suspended; the country was, as Mr Huskisson expressed it, within twenty-four hours of a state of barter. Applications for assistance were made to the Government; but though it was well known that the Government refused to act, there was not, as far as I know, until lately any authentic narrative of the real facts. In the 'Correspondence' of the Duke of Wellington, of all places in the world, there is a full account of them. The Duke was then on a mission at St. Petersburg, and Sir R. Peel wrote to him a letter of which the following is a part:

We have been placed in a very unpleasant predicament on the other question – the issue of Exchequer Bills by Government. The feeling of the City, of many of our friends, of some of the Opposition, was decidedly in favour of the issue of Exchequer Bills to relieve the merchants and manufacturers.

It was said in favour of the issue, that the same measure had been tried and succeeded in 1793 and 1811. Our friends whispered about that we were acting quite in a different manner from that in which Mr Pitt did act, and would have acted had he been alive.

We felt satisfied that, however plausible were the reasons urged in favour of the issue of Exchequer Bills, yet that the measure was a dangerous one, and ought to be resisted by the Government.

There are thirty millions of Exchequer Bills outstanding. The purchases lately made by the Bank can hardly maintain them at par. If there were a new issue to such an amount as that contemplated – viz. five millions – there would be a great danger that the whole mass of Exchequer Bills would be at a discount, and would be paid into the revenue. If the new Exchequer Bills were to be issued at a different rate of interest from the outstanding ones – say bearing an interest of five per cent. – the old ones would be immediately at a great discount unless the interest were raised. If the interest were raised, the charge on the revenue would be of course proportionate to the increase of rate of interest. We found that the Bank had the power to lend money on deposit of goods. As our issue of Exchequer Bills would have been useless unless the Bank cashed them, as therefore the intervention of the Bank was in any event absolutely necessary, and as its intervention would be chiefly useful by the effect which it would have in increasing the circulating medium, we advised the Bank to take the whole affair into their own hands at once, to issue their notes on the security of goods, instead of issuing them on Exchequer Bills, such bills being themselves issued on that security.

They reluctantly consented, and rescued us from a very embarrassing predicament.'

The success of the Bank of England on this occasion was owing to its complete adoption of right principles. The Bank adopted these principles very late; but when it adopted them it adopted them completely. According to the official statement which I quoted before, 'we,' that is, the Bank directors, 'lend money by every possible means, and in modes which we had never adopted before; we took in stock on security, we purchased Exchequer Bills, we made advances on Exchequer Bills, we not only discounted outright, but we made advances on deposits of bills of Exchange to an immense amount – in short, by every possible means consistent with the safety of the Bank.' And for the complete and courageous adoption of this policy at the last moment the directors of the Bank of England at that time deserve great praise, for the subject was then less understood even than it is now; but the directors of the Bank deserve also severe censure, for previously choosing a contrary policy; for being reluctant to adopt the new one; and for at last adopting it only at the request of, and upon a joint responsibility with, the Executive Government.

After 1825 there was not again a real panic in the Money Market till 1847. Both of the crises of 1837 and 1839 were severe, but neither terminated in a panic: both were arrested before the alarm reached its final intensity; in neither, therefore, could the policy of the Bank at the last stage of fear be tested.

In the three panics since 1844 – in 1847, 1857, and 1866 – the policy of the Bank has been more or less affected by the Act of 1844, and I cannot therefore discuss it fully within the limits which I have prescribed for myself. I can only state two things: First, that the directors of the Bank above all things maintain that they have not been in the earlier stage of panic prevented by the Act of 1844 from making any advances which they would otherwise have then made. Secondly, that in the last stage of panic, the Act of 1844 has been already suspended, rightly or wrongly, on these occasions; that no similar occasion has ever yet occurred in which it has not been suspended; and that, rightly or wrongly, the world confidently expects and relies that in all similar cases it will be suspended again. Whatever theory may prescribe, the logic of facts seems peremptory so far. And these principles taken together amount to saying that, by the doctrine of the directors, the Bank of England ought, as far as they can, to manage a panic with the Act of 1844, pretty much as they would manage one without it – in the early stage of the panic because then they are not fettered, and in the latter because then the fetter has been removed.

We can therefore estimate the policy of the Bank of England in the three panics which have happened since the Act of 1844, without inquiring into the effect of the Act itself. It is certain that in all of these panics the Bank has made very large advances indeed. It is certain, too, that in all of them the Bank has been quicker than it was in 1825; that in all of them it has less hesitated to use its banking reserve in making the advances which it is one principal object of maintaining that reserve to make, and to make at once. But there is still a considerable evil. No one knows on what kind of securities the Bank of England will at such periods make the advances which it is necessary to make.

As we have seen, principle requires that such advances, if made at all for the purpose of curing panic, should be made in the manner most likely to cure that panic. And for this purpose, they should be made on everything which in common times is good 'banking security.' The evil is that, owing to terror, what is commonly good security has ceased to be so; and the true policy is so to use the banking reserve that if possible the temporary evil may be stayed, and the common course of business be restored. And this can only be effected by advancing on all good banking securities.

Unfortunately, the Bank of England do not take this course. The Discount Office is open for the discount of good bills, and makes immense advances accordingly. The Bank also advances on Consols and India securities, though there was, in the crisis of 1866, believed to be for a moment a hesitation in so doing. But these are only a small part of the securities on which money in ordinary times can be readily obtained, and by which its repayment is fully secured. Railway debenture stock is as good a security as a commercial bill, and many people, of whom I own I am one, think it safer than India stock; on the whole, a great railway is, we think, less liable to unforeseen accidents than the strange Empire of India. But I doubt if the Bank of England in a panic would advance on railway debenture stock; at any rate no one has any authorised reason for saying that it would. And there are many other such securities.

The *amount* of the advance is the main consideration for the Bank of England, and not the nature of the security on which the advance is made, always assuming the security to be good. An idea prevails (as I believe) at the Bank of England that they ought not to advance during a panic on any kind of security on which they do not commonly advance. But if bankers for the most part do advance on such security in common times, and if that security is indisputably good, the ordinary practice of the Bank of England is immaterial. In ordinary times the Bank is only one of many lenders, whereas in a panic it is the sole lender; and we want, as far as we can, to bring back the unusual state of a time of panic to the common state of ordinary times.

In common opinion there is always great uncertainty as to the conduct of the Bank: the Bank has never laid down any clear and sound policy on the subject. As we have seen, some of its directors (like Mr Hankey) advocate an erroneous policy. The public is never sure what policy will be adopted at the most important moment: it is not sure what amount of advance will be made, or on what security it will be made. The best palliative to a panic is a confidence in the adequate amount of the Bank reserve, and in the efficient use of that reserve. And until we have on this point a clear understanding with the Bank of England, both our liability to crises and our terror at crises will always be greater than they would otherwise be.

6 Correspondence between Henry Hucks Gibbs, Esq. and Professor Bonamy Price

On the Reserve of the Bank of England

Henry Hucks Gibbs and Bonamy Price

Correspondence

Woodend, Witley, Godalming,
July 19, 1877.

My Dear Gibbs,

Let me call your particular attention to a statement in the *Economist* of July 14, at the end of long tables on rates of interest. It contains this – for me most memorable – sentence:

> The entire thought and language of the last generation regarding what was called in most vague and misleading language, "the regulation of the currency, or the control of the circulation by the Bank of England" (meaning by currency and circulation, the amount of Bank of England notes in the hands of the public), has become obsolete.' This is from the pen of Palgrave, no doubt. What will Grenfell say to it? I have had to say this in the Press for many years; and I have been called heretic, theorist, unpractical, unreal, and excommunicated; and lo! I am told everybody now is of my opinion. Not quite yet, Mr Palgrave, I should say; but it is fast being accomplished. Overstone and all the City erected and preached up the Bank Charter Act as the controller of the circulation, and thereby the creator of steady interest and trade, and the averter of panics. I had to cry, Bosh! and was put away as an unpractical fellow, who knew nothing about it. The talk about the Bank Act has been for the most part nonsense. From the very first, I wrote that it had done two things: it had given a safe Bank of England note, – and, secondly, decreed the ultimate extinction in England of private notes. It did nothing more. And now Palgrave testifies that 'the uniform testimony of the actual facts over a long series of years has convinced everyone that the only control which the Bank of England can exert over credit, markets, and prices, is by changes in the rate of interest.

So much for the circulation theory. There remains the Bank rate and its principle, on which I am still reckoned a heretic of the most abominable order. I must have it out with you some day. The next generation will undoubtedly pronounce me right. There's conceit, you will say: no, it isn't, but conviction of truth.

My little book, 'Currency and Banking,' sums up all I ever said on the Bank Act.

Yours very sincerely,
B. Price

Aldenham House
July 29, 1877

My Dear Price,

I have no doubt you *are* a heretic, and probably an incorrigible one – most people *are* in some point or other – but I don't discover in your letter before me any theses deserving excommunication.

Palgrave's language, though true, is itself misleading. It would lead one to think that some people supposed the Bank of England did still regulate the currency. It used to do so before '44. Since then it has no more intelligent regulating power than the 'governor' of a steam-engine, which controls, indeed, the speed, but has no will of its own, but only that of the engineer who devised it.

It is quite true that many wise men said many foolish things about the real regulator of the currency – the Bank Charter Act. They expected it to cure panics, and perhaps stomach-aches; to create steady interest, and perhaps infuse wisdom into fools. It does none of these things (except giving a substitute for wisdom – control – to fallible Bank Directors).

What it does do is exactly what is expressed by you. It gives a safe note, and has digged a pit for all notes other than the one national currency. They have not all fallen into it as yet, but their feet are that way turned, and the hill down which they go is steep.

I say the Bank Act is the regulator of the currency; by which I mean – not that it prescribes what notes are to be in the hands of the public (that the need of the public prescribes), but how they are to get into those hands, and what sort they are to be of.

The Bank of England has but one weapon, the rate, wherewith they defend their own position, and make those who want to borrow money pay a little more for it, inducing, by the rise of interest, the foreigners to minister to the provisions of the Act of '44, and send more note-producing gold into our coffers.

Very truly yours,
Henry H. Gibbs

2, Norham Gardens, Oxford,
November 5, 1877

My Dear Gibbs, –

You may well suppose that the present position of the Money Market attracts my keenest attention. I am anxious to make one remark to you.

The Bank rate is at 5; the out-door rate from 3½ to 4. If (I do not say that it is, on that point. I have no information) the Bank's object is to attract gold from abroad to increase its Reserve, how can that be done now by merely raising the rate?

The prevalent view has always been that a raised rate draws funds from abroad to the English market, which yields a better interest than the foreign ones. These funds, not being a result of trade, come into England in the form of gold.

But, these funds will now come to a 3½ per cent. interest, not to 5; they must go into the general market. The Bank might take up these funds at 5, if so minded; very little likely to do so, I should imagine. If it does not, then I am wholly unable to conceive how the raised rate could bring in funds from abroad to the English Money Market. A new explanation must be devised; but no one in England will endure less than you that it should come from any other source than facts. It won't come from 'wool!'

I need hardly say that I am prying into no secrets; nor making any remarks on the aims and conduct of the Bank of England. I speak as an outsider, and I seek to be spoken to only as an outsider.

Yours very sincerely,
B. Price

Aldenham House
November 8, 1877

My Dear Price,

You are quite right, of course. It is the *market* rate which governs the flow of gold into the country: *not* the rate at which we, the Bank of England, are content to lend our own money.

We cannot and never could govern the outside rate so far as to raise it to an arbitrary level of our own. We could bring it down, indeed, till we were tired of being drained, but we couldn't make borrowers take other folks' money – or our own, for that matter – at a higher rate than they choose. When they do choose to have our money, and take it faster than we like, we *might* need to raise our rate to protect our Reserve, which is only so far affected by such an action on the part of the public, that it bears a less proportion to the liabilities, and especially to that portion of them which is in the hands of the bankers: but if the public takes that money in order to buy gold to send abroad, we *must* raise our rate; and if we begin in time and move fast enough we effect two objects – we make the taking our gold more difficult (though not impossible) by making the price to the purchaser abroad greater, and thus *check* the diminution of our Reserve: and, which is more important and more cogent, we induce foreigners to send their gold here to gain higher interest than they do at home, and so both replenish our Reserve, and, by acting on the exchanges, check in another way the demand for gold.

Now this is not 'wool,' but it is coals–coals to Newcastle when written to you: and you will say, what is the use of it? What has this to do with a rate of 5% when the rate out-of-doors is 4, and when people don't want to borrow your money, and don't seem to care to take your gold?

Well! I don't think I should have cared to raise our rate to 5 last week if it had been at 4 or 4¼; but our Reserve was low – our liabilities high – and especially those liabilities which were most disposable. There was every prospect (and so it turned out) of a further reduction of the Reserve, by the natural ebb of notes countrywards and of gold to Scotland, *which unfailingly takes place at this time*; and *if* a foreign drain of gold should have taken place, our Reserve would have really been brought to a *quasi* dangerous point, and the *currency*, of which the Old Lady is the guardian, unduly contracted.

'If a drain should take place! Do you raise your rate on an *if*?' No; but when the storm signals are up, we take in a reef – and there they were.

In America the exchange was at a point which would take gold or securities. They were taking securities as it happens, but that might cease any day – and it *has* ceased. The French Exchange was weak and weakening, and gold seemed like to go; and Germany's action is inscrutable and was threatening. So this was no time for the Bank of England to lower its rate.

They meant one simple thing by it. Not to attract gold to this country – but to say 'we haven't got too much in our till, considering the actual home power of call upon us, and the possible foreign demand upon us, and we won't lend our money at less than 5 (which, when it becomes a real acting rate, will tend to check exports and allure imports), you others may do as you like.'

I said on last page the action of America as to securities had ceased. Why, then, don't they take gold. They *do*. They are now enquiring for eagles. But that does not trouble us for two reasons – 1st. because, as to Scotland and the country, ebb will presently turn to a flow; and 2nd, because there is no longer that disposable capital afloat which makes the public independent of us; and if a demand for gold should now arise, our rate would become a real acting rate, and the market rate would approximate to it as nearly as it ever ought.

You see public writers now tell us we of the Bank of England have no longer the power we had to command and control the market. I doubt if we ever had it, but what we had we have. I astonished one of my colleagues once, when the bankers' balances were very low, by telling him that he could not then pay £100,000 without the necessity of application to us for a loan (on the part of somebody), and so he would have found it to be if he thought it out.

And so our rate is a real power; and as to export of gold, it is so also. So long as the bankers have *with us* more in balance *than what is necessary for them to work with*, they can of course buy gold and export it, whatever the rate of discount in the Bank; but we, of course, know by practice how far they can go; and, when they can go no farther, our rate is an all-controlling engine. Nor are we powerless while they have a surplus balance with us, for of course a timely disposal of some of our Consols or other securities takes the spare money off the market, and makes the Banker of Bankers ('*Shah-in-Shah*') the real arbiter.

I wonder if I have made all this intelligible. If not, *mea culpa*, and we will have it out *vivâ voce*. I think I shall be in Oxford on Saturday, 24th, and Sunday, and will come and see you if I can.

> Believe me,
> Always truly yours,
> Henry H. Gibbs

> 2, Norham Gardens, Oxford
> *November* 10, 1877

My Dear Gibbs,

I am so deeply obliged to you. I do love and admire your style of writing so keenly, – you are so clear, so precise, so to the point, so real, and hence so powerful. Whether I may or may not agree with you is a different matter: but one can always put one's finger on the very spot which raises the quarrel, and that is everything. Your letter is full of instruction for me, which will grow the oftener I read it, and so will my thanks.

One detail first. To be Banker of the Bankers has always seemed to me a very dangerous position. It is a bad banking account, for the decisive reason that the banker must be most uncertain as to what will happen to it. Accounts are of the right sort in proportion as the banker understands the general character of his depositors' operations. The account of the banks reaches the bad extreme, because it is so hard to estimate the forces which act upon their movements: my conception of the Bank of England is that it practises the best banking in the world – save and except that account. It is one on which you must feel very uncomfortable at times: and I suspect tells in no slight degree on the alterations of the Bank rate. However, that's the Bank's affair.

There is, I fear and I heartily grieve to say it, some difference of view between us on a cardinal point: so I pass on to it at once, for it lies at the root of the whole discussion. You regard the state of the Reserve, the quantity of the gold in hand, as the pivot of the Bank's action: I do not. Let me say first – The Bank is no more concerned with the Bank note circulation till it gets down to 15 millions than I am. That is the affair of the Issue Department, which is no part of the Bank. Nor, as I hold, is there any truth or importance in the fluctuations of the circulation.

The article I referred to in the *Economist* called the language about the circulation obsolete. It is not obsolete, certainly: but that it is empty of all reality I have long known. The gigantic trade of England at home is not worked by bank notes: and if they were really searce, more cheques would be used, and that would be all.

To come, then, to the point: why all this commotion about the Bank's Reserve, about its gold? The last return gives a Reserve of upwards of 9 millions: now tell me specifically what harm would arise if it stood at 5? Do not talk of feelings of alarm, excitement in the money market, or the like! These are children of the imagination, belief in the all-mighty necessity of gold. But say what distinct harm would happen if, in quiet times, money abundant, borrowers scanty, confidence in the solveney of the Bank adamantine, no panic, no danger of a run, 4 millions went away to buy corn, bringing your Reserve to 5? That is what I want to know. I see none.

Nay more: what, if owing to exceptional causes, unconnected with any commercial pressure, the Bank's Reserve ran down to less than a million, or even to zero – what then? specifically, what then? If it gave bills payable, say, at a month, every one would take them, as they did certified cheques at New York – cheques which the banks drawn upon did not pay, but which were guaranteed by the collective banks; but – no injury to any one. Granted that the Bank must find the gold: there would be plenty to be had in France. Expensive! Yes, but expense is not danger or ruin, or stoppage of trade, or anything else of that kind.

Lastly – and crushingly!! The Bank Directors themselves do not believe in the gold theory. They shew their contempt for it in crises. The only reason I have ever heard given for a Reserve is security against inability to pay debts. Well, this danger is most violent in panies. How did the Directors behave in 1866? Their Reserve fell fast – very fast. Did they keep their funds as they were paid in, and so strengthen their Reserve? Not a bit of it. They did just the very contrary, they lent away with all their might, amidst the applause of the city – Bagehot!! included. They ran up their loans in a month from 18¼ millions to 33½, their Reserve going down to below a million. Where was their feeling of danger in a trumpery Reserve?

But enough for now. We do not exactly know about ourselves for the 24th: if we are free, I hope you will dine with us.

Yours very sincerely,

B. Price

Aldenham House
November 11, 1877

My Dear Price,

Thank you for your letter – in two volumes. I divide it so, because the subjects of the two sheets are various though the same, and the first can be dispatched in a short *excursus*, a sort of Sabbath-day's journey into the realms of Banking; the latter demands some thought, and probably some more paper. Yet here is an answer to a bit of it, too: if I am in Oxford on the 24th (which is becoming doubtful), and if you are disengaged (which is already doubtful), I shall be very glad to dine with you.

You would not write what you do about the Banker of the Bankers if you had ever sat in a certain chair in Threadneedle Street; and if the ghost of Bagehot ever gets you made permanent Governor of the Bank of England, you will not have sat in it three weeks before you will see that next to the Government account, the account of the collective bankers is the most certain and the most intelligible. Sometimes a weak-kneed brother cries out, 'Oh! look at the Bankers; their account makes me feel very uncomfortable! They might do the-Lord-knows-what, any day!' But such an one has not seen and touched the daily working of the account. It never gave me any uneasiness. I contemplated it like Mr Olivier, but with better reason, with a light heart. Take this formula and you will see that the 'Bankers' Account' has no danger in it to a Governor of the most ordinary care. We know of the bankers, better than of any account in our books, what is the minimum balance wherewith they can live. They must have x on their account (a quantity unknown to all but us), and $x-y$ therefore never appears. But if $x + y$ is seen, then we know that y must remain untouched and uninvested; must, in fact, form an addition to our *Reserve*.

x is ours for profit *if we like to use it*, but y is ours only for safe custody. Where is the danger?

On the other hand, the possession of that account is of the greatest value to us, as affording us the most perfect and accurate measure of how far the public can at all act independently of us.

The Bankers (I may say in parenthesis) have their own x and y too.

In a former letter of mine I said that I entirely concurred with you and the *Economist* in reprobating the idea of our regulating the currency; and if in my last I spoke of the Bank as guardian of the currency, I mean it only in the sense of the control exercised by the 'governor' of a steam-engine. The Issue Department is automatic, and works with the precision and regularity of the said governor, and the Bank, as a bank in the Lombard Street sense, has no more active interference in it than 'the sweet little cherub who sits up aloft' has with the life of poor Jack.

But the Issue Department has a very active effect on the Banking Department, for under the law it affects the amount of disposable funds for the payment of its creditors and for lending to those who need.

But I am getting towards vol. 2, so I will shut up.

Ever yours sincerely,
Henry H. Gibbs

2, Norham Gardens, Oxford
November 13, 1877

My Dear Gibbs,

You have silenced me on the first volume; for you know, and I don't. I am surprised that you can say that the big account is the one you best understand; but I do not for a moment challenge your assertion, even though some of your colleagues poured out wailings in the Press not so very long ago.

Doubt is over on my side. There will be dinner here at 7.30 on the 24th, whether you come or not; but pray do, if you can.

Yours very sincerely,
B. Price

Aldenham House
November 16, 1877

My Dear Price,

I am pleased with your commendations of my style – *Laudari a laudato*, you know. You write so well yourself, that your praise is better than other men's praise. Now I shall answer your letter in the intervals of business, *i.e.* when I am not eating or shooting or idling or sleeping, and, therefore, though I begin it now I daresay you won't get it for a day or two.

First, to thank you for yours of the 13th, and to say that I don't know that 'the Bankers' account is one which we can *best* understand,' but that up to a certain point (x), their normal balance, we can infallibly understand it: (y), their abnormal balance, is an element of doubt which an unwise Governor can misunderstand if he likes: but he must be *very* unwise – unwise to the nth.

Now for your vol. 2 and a little bit out of vol. 1.

1. You don't consider 'the Reserve to be the necessary pivot of the Bank's action.'

2. The Bank you say 'is no more concerned with the Note circulation up to a certain point, than you are. The Issue Department is no part of the Bank.'

In this last I concur; but, as I shall presently point out, your arguments show me that you don't fully realise it: your faith and works don't correspond.

As to (1): What do you mean by the 'Bank's action'? Action in what? By your coupling the sentence with No. 2, I almost think you mean its action as bearing on the circulation of notes: if so, I agree, and I suppose we all agree with you.

Yet I regard the Reserve as the pivot of the *Bank's* action, nevertheless.

When I mean *Bank*, I'll say *Bank*; and when Issue Department, I'll call it *Issue*.

And now for *Bank*. If the Reserve is not to be the pivot of its action, what *is?*

What *is* the Reserve of a Bank? or to go further back, What is a Bank?

A, B and C, and the other 22 letters of the alphabet, place £1,000 each in the hands of Z, who they know has got a certain number of thousands of his own, and is an honest man besides. He makes his gain out of the interest of their money, and does them the service of paying their bills, collecting their bills, and giving them their money as they ask for it.

Z, so set up in trade, is a *Bank*.

Now Z, besides being honest, is prudent, and therefore, instead of lending *all* the money of his fellow letters – to Alpha, Beta, Gamma, Aleph, Beth, Gimel, and all the other letters of sundry nationalities, usurers of more or less honesty and solvency, who should pay him that interest which is his gain – he lays up some of it in a napkin, that he may have to give to the owners as they need it. That napkin contains his Reserve. He in the parable put *all* his lord's money in his napkin, which was bad banking; but it would be worse banking for Z, who has many lords, whose coming is continual, and whose requirements are only limited by their possessions in his hands, if he lent *all* his money to the usurers and could not get it back when it was wanted. The question for him to consider is *what* he may prudently lend: in other words, *how much he must necessarily keep in Reserve*. That is, and must be, the 'Pivot of his action:' for if not, and he leaves his Reserve out of consideration, down comes N or M one day and asks for his money; but the Hebrews Mem or Nun have got it, and it can't be got at; and where is Z, and where is his credit?

But to leave parables. You ask me to 'tell you specifically what harm would happen if the Bank Reserve were down to five millions,' and afterwards you say 'to less than a million, to zero!' 'What need one?'

Well, we will suppose the Reserve of unemployed deposits to have fallen to two millions, and the '*y*' of my former letter to be, as it often is, that and more than that; it is obvious that if it pleased the Bankers, the Bank would be at any moment declared unable to meet its engagements! The Old Lady would not be *insolvent*, it is true – her capital is a guarantee against that; but she would stop payment!

Now you don't seriously mean that that is a catastrophe which – not to say a Governor of the Bank – but anybody in England, can contemplate with an easy mind!

But you quote New York banks and their certified cheques, or rather 'certificates of deposits.' Well, even if the loss of credit to those banks is to be considered as nothing, what are we to say for the hapless depositor who had to content himself with certified cheques which were only worth 80 in the 100?

What is to happen at such a time to the Public Deposits? To the owners of Private Deposits? I have supposed the *Bankers* withdrawing their surplus and swamping the Bank; but you never see one vulture by himself. The whole flock of depositor-vultures would be all at once on the decaying carease; a mere scramble – everybody getting what he could, and none getting enough to satisfy his hunger. It would be a general famine – a general breakdown of commerce – everbody failing around. Neighbour's fare!

I have known such a thing in Lima where once or twice everybody did stop payment, except one or two houses who had more cash in their own chests than their liabilities amounted to. That was all very well. It was in the main only a temporary absence of circulating medium. The Peruvians liked it, but I share the English prejudice in favour of solvency.

Of course I am writing under the supposition that the law of '44 is maintained. A cure, worse than the disease, can be found, when the patient has gone far to ruin his health. You can flood the whole city and country with promises to pay, which can't be fulfilled – and all *cui bono?* I'll come to the *cui bono* presently; but remember I am dealing with the *Bank*, and not the *Issue*. At such a time, Government empowers Issue to make more notes, and Bank gets hold of them against securities.

But in my opinion the thing you suppose is impossible. It will happen at Latter Lammas, and not before.

It *cannot* be that, 'in a quiet time – money abundant, borrowers scanty – confidence in the solvency of the Bank adamantine – no panic – no danger of a run,' our Reserve would ever go to the point you speak of.

Don't forget that *Bank* accounts are published. It was a great folly so to enact. *Issue* accounts should be. *Bank* should not, but they *are*.

Well, then, I will follow you for a moment. The Bankers draw 'y' from their accounts. That does not affect us in the least, if, as is possible, it only goes on to the Public or other Private Deposits. But if it goes to send away gold? There are only two things that can permanently affect our Reserve: the export of gold, or the hoarding of notes. The latter *pre-supposes* panic, and may be dismissed. Temporary efflux of gold and notes into the provinces is regular and tidal, and may also be disregarded in the argument. Suppose then 'y' is all used for export of gold. In my former letter I showed you that we then obtain the complete command of the market: so then either the demand for gold ceases, or else it continues. If it ceases, *cadit quæstio*; for our Reserve no longer falls. If it continues, money abounds no longer, borrowers are frequent, times are the reverse of quiet, and the conditions which I quote from your letter have ceased to exist. How do we meet this? We gradually raise our rate: we take in our reefs to meet the coming storm.

But if we neglect to do so, and serve out our notes to all who with the exchanges falling naturally export gold, without doing that which alone rectifies exchange, *i.e.* raising our price for accommodation, then our Reserve falls in earnest; and, as it falls, so demand increases. 'No panic!' did you say? There never *ought* to be a panic, and I may almost say it is always through the unwisdom of the managers of the ultimate Reserve of the kingdom if there *is*. But, in the case I have described, a panic would come in the twinkling of an eye, and with it wide-spread ruin and distress of trade. No one knows when *panic-point* is reached. *Crises* come and pass without hurting any one, if only the *gubernator* sits watchfully at the helm; but a panic comes like a flash of lightning, and *then* the storm must pass as it best may. See 1866, which you quote triumphantly, but *not* "crushingly.' Let the galled jade wince – my withers are unwrung. I was not Governor in 1866! Nor do I blame him who was. The matter was not then so well understood as it is now. When the panic once began they were powerless, for the notes were hoarded; and no rate will stop that. The Government letter authorized *Issue* to make notes, and ordered *Bank* to charge 10 per cent. for their loan, and time cured the panic; brought peace, but not life to the killed and health to the wounded. What was done could not be the deliberate act of the Directors, but was the act of the Governor taking his decision on the spot in a matter which admitted of no delay, and acting, with the advice of such as he could summon, as he thought for the best. He did not err in lending, but in lending without raising the rate and shortening the period of the loans. There has been as severe a crisis since his time, but it did not reach panic-point, and was never in danger of doing so. The rate was raised in due time, and went on being raised, till the effect was produced; all applauding, and the very victims not complaining.

Now I say *cui bono* should one let one's Reserve fall and put it out of our power *cuique suum tribuere?* Is it that we should not raise the rate of money? Why, the rate of discount hurts nobody! Calculate 5 per cent. for six weeks on £100: no one is ruined by that! Besides, when a panic once comes, 10 per cent. gets charged after all.

Now I have written enough; but here is a text for a new sermon, on a fourth sheet! 'Granted that the Bank must find the gold: there would be plenty to be had in France. Expensive! Yes, but expense is not ruin.'

'*Suo sibi gladio hune jugulo!*' 'The Issue Department is no part of the Bank.' 'What has the Bank – the great Deposit-compelling, Reserve-conserving Bank – to do with finding gold for notes. Its sole *duty* is to pay its Deposits in the legal tender of the country, – gold if it likes, and has it, – but notes, notes, notes, are all it needs to find. *Issue*, indeed, must pay gold for those notes on demand; *i.e.* after 15 millions, it must issue no notes if it has not gold; and if its gold were drained away, if such a time could arise, or rather before its gold was drained away, it would have to call in notes, by the sale of its securities.

But what has the *Issue* – the automatic *Issue* – to do with finding gold? A steam-engine does not go to fetch its own coals! That is the business of the cambist or merchant, – of anyone rather than the Bank of England, whether *Issue* or *Bank* proper.

But supposing it were the Bank's business. You say: 'Plenty to be had in France. Expensive! Yes, but expense is not ruin.'

Now *think* over this. Tell me with what substance the Bank would pay for the gold you suppose it should buy. Follow the steps of a falling Reserve and a failing credit, reaching even to my old Mistress in Threadneedle Street, and then set to work to fetch the gold from France. Don't say 'of

course it can be done,' but describe the operation – tell me step by step *how* it's done.

There is only one way; and if we don't walk straight in it, a time might come when one might have to scramble through many thorny thickets, and flounder through many dangerous bogs, before one could find oneself again in that smooth and easy way!

If the gold is being withdrawn from our coffers, and that Reserve with which we pay our debts is falling too low for safety, *Bank* must charge more for its loans, the market value of money rises, and gold flows in instead of flowing out. The Reserve must be kept up, *quand même*.

Cui bono are we to leave the pleasant, though slightly uphill path marked by a rising rate of discount, only to struggle into it again later on, with toil and sorrow?

Is there anything more to say? I trow not! You are already tired out. Never mind, I must have one growl more at a remark of yours.

'If Bank notes were really scarce, more cheques would be used, and that would be all.'

Now a cheque is an order to pay Bank notes, and represents Bank notes in a way somewhat analogous to that in which notes represent gold. People know they will get gold for their Bank of England notes, and they hope they will get notes, if they want them, for a cheque.

I think it probable that many notes might be spared if more cheques were used: it is certain that if cheques and clearing houses were spread all over the country the 'Notes with the Public' would be normally fewer. Time may still breed, as it has for a long time been breeding, more economy in this matter. But it is not when confidence is failing that people are willing to take cheques instead of notes, – to take what they *hope* is as good as gold instead of what they *know* is as good as gold.

But I doubt whether notes are *ever* scarce in the sense in which you mean it. The public never has, and never had, a note less than it wanted. One only Pilgarlic feels a scarcity of notes – the Reserve of the Bank. The 'Notes with the Public' are larger (*cæteris puribus*) in times of panic than at other times. Accommodation is diminished; but it is not notes that are in defect, but credit.

I remain sincerely yours,
Henry H. Gibbs

I have read my letter again, and add that, where I say in the third sheet [p. 135] that a temporary efflux 'may be disregarded,' it is only in the argument that it may be so. If the Reserve were already low, and the exchange adverse, *i.e.* were falling, we should need to raise the rate of discount more promptly than if the tide from Scotland, &c., were setting hitherward.

Norham Gardens, Oxford
November 27, 1877

My Dear Gibbs,

So many thanks for your long letter. It is very good of you to give me such an outpouring.

The issue between us is not quite clear, for you are but imperfectly acquainted with my general view. I must refer you to my little book, 'Currency and Banking,' published by King & Co. The *Spectator*, which has a great economist for editor, said that it saw no answer to it.

One impression your letter has made on my mind, that my first belief that the account of the banks is a bad account, was about right, at least for the country. Anyhow, that account must not be mixed up with the question of the general position of the Bank of England and its Reserve and rate. If this great fuss and anxiety about the Reserve come from this account, and the trade of the whole country has to suffer from complications arising from this source, then the public would be warranted in asking your Directors to give up that account. You have colleagues to whom this opinion would not be unwelcome. To make the Bank the sole depositary of the country's gold, and then to argue away and act upon that idea, is a most mischievous thing. The Bank, whose banking is adamantine and known to be so, is mixed up with other bodies, of which the world knows little, and which are always susceptible of being suspected; and this is a situation, I conceive, full of harm, both in thought and practice. The Bank of England ought to stand alone, left to its own true nature: much mist would then be cleared away.

I have ever preached the importance of a Reserve for a bank, with the same explanation that you give: but – and here is the rub – I do not attach the same significance that you, and city articles, and the universal conventional talk, ascribe to fluctuations in that Reserve: there is no truth or reality in it for me. It is a purely got up rule – propounded by city oracles, who are emphatically practical men, that is men who claim to know; just as the propounders of the Mercantile Theory did before Adam Smith, and do not condescend to give reasons. I beg to say that I do not look upon you as one of these 'practical men:' quite the reverse: you do give reasons, and that is the reason why it is so agreeable and instructive to me to have talk with you.

The grand formula is this: 'Gold has gone away, up with the rate: gold has come in, down with it.' I repudiate that formula absolutely; and I think its consequences – not to the bankers who profit by it, but to the whole trading community – to be very mischievous. And the formula does the further harm, that it blinds the eyes of everybody to the real forces in the banking market, the supply and demand of purchasing power, which again depends on the state of the national wealth.

I fear you have not exactly apprehended my line of argument.

Two positions must be carefully distinguished:

(1) Ordinary banking tranquillity.
(2) Crises and panics – approaching, or come already.

My remarks on the first cannot be met by arguments on the second position. If you tell me that a crisis is on the point of coming on, I can understand and accept action for the Reserve. This is a very critical point in the discussion.

The question I raised was this – say that the Reserve is 10 millions – that the Bank has not the account of the banks – that times are thoroughly quiet – and that 5 millions have gone away rather quickly, to pay for corn, or other importations; what is the harm?

With all respect, I submit that you have given no answer to that question, and therefore not met my charge that the gold movements are a false, irrational and, in a very real sense, *un*-banking principle of regulating the rate of discount. I say, that the rate of discount is the price of the day's market, or the state of supply and demand of what the banks are agents of, and not makers, or real owners, purchasing power – that power not being gold or money. Arguments derived from the possible insolvency of the Bank have no force or truth here, unless that insolvency is pleaded as being probable, or even possible.

Now, I go further. I take up the case of a crisis and panic: when the danger may be said to be on. What is it that in an extreme case might happen? The Bank might have no gold, might be insolvent. You say, 'That would be a catastrophe.' A thing very undesirable, Yes: because the public mind is poisoned with all this absurd theory about gold. However, gold is demanded, and there is none. Ought all England to be convulsed with horror, every trader stand aghast, as if a forty days' rain had destroyed all the corn in the fields? Nothing of the kind. Supposing that the banking of the Bank is the sound thing it always has been. If every creditor asked every banker for his deposit in gold to-morrow at 10 o'clock, the thing could not physically be done. Is England ruined, and any creditor, except one who had a foreign debt to pay in gold, the worse, really? You forget that in a panic people ask for money simply from fright. Here 1825 teaches much. There was a great demand for deposits to be paid: but in what? Was it a run on the Bank, from fear of insolvency? Not a jot of it. The Bank's creditors did not want gold or coin, what they wanted was that they should feel their money to be safe: but in what did that safety consist? In notes of the Bank, resting on the solvency alone of what you call the insolvent. There was no gold terror here: no raising of the rate needed solely on the ground of gold.

Still more. At the end of last century the Bank was forbidden by law to pay in gold. Did any harm happen? Not a particle, so long as no excess of notes was issued. Was there a catastrophe? Answer that yourself. Hard, no doubt, upon a few people, who required gold for payments abroad, and couldn't get it with their notes: but is this a public calamity? and couldn't they get it elsewhere, though with possibly some loss? Now, suppose the worst – though as the Bank is fairly run out, an order in Council for such a national establishment is always possible – where, I ask again categorically, would be the harm, it being known that the Bank was perfectly solvent, but only short of a commodity which can ever be demanded in a quantity physically impossible? And that want of supply would last only a day or two: gold could and would be had from some quarter, English or foreign, always – the Bank being, what it is now, an adamantine banker.

And then, as if the gold would never come back: as if it had other important function but to travel, to be current, to run. Money, coin, gold, notes, are merely machinery – cartage: they are not the wealth of a nation, except the metal – a small matter. Other carts could be found. The American certified checks were such carts, and answered under the circum-stances perfectly. When the restriction was put on, the vultures who sought to devour metal were sent empty away. They had to five on pieces of paper: but those pieces of paper were as good, for all purposes, except exportation, as guineas.

But I speak of the Bank of England only: my words are not the same for other banks, but simply because their solvency is never so assured as to be above the reach of distrust. Let them look after their own reserves, each for itself. That is not a national affair.

But please mark very carefully – that I do not advocate that the Bank may be left to come to this position: I am only arguing simply that if things come to the worst, the issue is not in any way disastrous, the Bank being undeniably solvent.

You say: 'I have the English prejudice in favour of solvency.' Right, so have I, as strongly as you have. But I see no reason or pleasure in a rise of 2 or 3 per cent. because, by purchases for corn, 3 or 4 millions have gone abroad in quiet, unruffled times, out of 11 or 12.

You remark, 'When the patient has gone far to ruin his health, Govern-ment empowers Issue to make more notes, and Bank gets hold of them against securities.' Are you really not aware that in the crises of 1847, 1857, and 1866, suspension did absolutely nothing at all – absolutely was as barren of effect as the sea sand, except to a trifling extent in 1857 – and even that little would not have existed if the line of uncovered issues had been drawn, as now, at 15 millions?

You add, 'What you suppose is impossible: it will happen at Latter Lamnas, and not before. It cannot be that "in quiet times, confidence in the solvency of the Bank adamantine,' &c., our Reserve would ever go to the point you speak of.'

That is exactly my case against you: precisely what I say. Then, I repeat, why, why raise the rate, because a couple of millions have gone away? Your remark awards victory to my argument. You cannot answer that *why!* You have not, and without bragging, never will.

'To compel the publication of the Bank's accounts was a blunder, and a mischievous one.' Most true.

I have never raised objection to raising the rate when 'borrowers are frequent and times the reverse of quiet.' Clearly, then, demand has increased against supply: you have a right to the market price. But when you say, 'money abounds no longer,' the word money is city slang – not your own good English. Banks do not deal in money, do not lend it, nor receive it, except to the tune of 3 per cent.

When gold goes out in quiet times, the exchanges only register the fact. They bring no new element into the discussion.

In the paragraph on getting gold extensively from France, I did not speak of 'gold for notes.' So I am not 'jugulated' here. The 'sermon' was not needed, for there was no text.

How get gold from France? It was done, at least negotiated, for 2 millions, some years ago. Will any man say that the Bank could not borrow abroad, for a limited time? And what harm, except expense?

You seem to imply that I would sit with my hands folded when a crisis is really approaching, and the gold ebbing away fast from unsatisfactory causes. Hoist away! then, I cry, like you. But in 1866, when the Reserve was frightfully low, the Bank cried, Lower away! and not the least harm came of it.

I repeat, there was never a panic about the Bank, and, as Sir D. Salomons declared in evidence to the House of Commons, after restriction was repealed its notes never went to a discount.

I never understand the word 'represent' – (it is a darling of your friend, and Macleod, his coach) – and never use it myself on money: but I say that cheques, though 'orders to pay money,' coin or notes, are settled per 100 millions every week, without a shilling passing.

Quite right: the public always has notes enough. I only put an argumentative hypothesis.

Money is mere machinery of exchange, and not nearly used in the same quantities as cheques and bills. Lines in ledgers, clerks in Clearing House, bits of paper, do the work. One might suppose from the way in which city articles write that the world would stick fast, and half the people of England starve, but for gold.

With many apologies for this diffusiveness,

Yours very sincerely,
B. Price

2, Norham Gardens, Oxford
December 24, 1877

My Dear Gibbs,

I have written a short notice of Giffen's new book for the *Contemporary* of January: just look at it. I should like you much to read it.

The long digestion of the big letter does not seem to be completed. I dare say it will never be.

With the very best wishes of the season,

Yours very sincerely,

B. Price

December 19, 1877

My Dear Price,

I have not been able till within the last day or two to fall to at your long letter of the 27th November and now that I sit down to answer it, I find it difficult to do so satisfactorily. Not because I have the slightest doubt on any of the points raised, but because we seem to me to be speaking a different language, and that our divergence is mainly in *words* and not in *sense*.

When there is any material difference it arises from your not being 'a practical man.'

Now it seems to me to be of the first necessity for truly understanding – not the theory of these subjects, but – the conduct of the business to which it relates, that one should be 'a practical man;' not indeed in the sense in which you use it, of a man who says, 'Don't tell *me*! I *know* it is so and so: I have been in it, man and boy, for 50 years, and I must know: I am a practical man!' but I mean a man who, knowing the theory, has personally seen it in practice – who knows not only the theoretic forces, but can take into account the friction of external circumstances which modifies them.

Now your views are really purely theoretical: your theory is right and good, but your practice is defective; your would-be practical examples are not at all *ad rem*. The things which you combat as evils, are either no evils at all, or have no existence except in popular twaddle. You 'make the giants first, and then you kill them.'

One very good thing you said in a former letter: 'You have silenced me,' you said, 'for you know, and I don't.' That is my point: *I know and you don't*. How should you? You are like a man having his 'Cavendish' at his fingers' ends, who sits down to play a rubber without seeing his cards. If you *did* know, you could not have returned to your notion about the 'bankers' account.'

You say (p. 18), 'If this anxiety . . . about the Reserve comes from this account . . . the public would be warranted in asking your Directors to give up that account.' My handwriting is not very good, and I think you were unable to read all my last letters; but I explained in one of them that we had not the slightest anxiety or reason for anxiety about the bankers' balances. However, I will try again. '*That* account.' *What* account? There are 52 of them – all alike and all different. '*Facies non omnibus una, nec diversa tamen.*' On what principle are we to say to Jones, Brown & Co., of Mincing Lane: 'You shall have a drawing account here if you like:' but to Brown,

Jones & Co., of Lombard Street, one of the 52, who ask the same thing: 'You shall not; you're a disturbing force! Be off!' *Vade retro!* You have said twice that some of my colleagues agree with you on this head. I should like to see the man! I never heard a single word from any of them, even the most inexperienced, which in the least degree supports your belief. If you tell me which of them thinks with you on this subject, I will engage to convince *him* in five minutes, because I can shew him figures and facts on the spot: rather, I will cause him to convince himself by seeing that he can give absolutely no reasons at all for his belief; can point out no way at all in which these accounts are prejudicial to the Bank or to the country. Read your letters again, and you will see that you give absolutely none.

You say 'that account must not be mixed up with the question of the general position of the Bank, its Reserve, and rate;' and 'the Bank is mixed up with other bodies . . .' &c.; and 'the Bank ought to stand alone . . .' &c.

Now what *do* you mean by 'mixed up'? Here it is that we speak a different language. There is absolutely no mixing at all. You evidently suppose that the bankers' account exercises some specific and peculiar influence on the Reserve and rate of discount in the Bank of England; and therefore you write afterwards: 'Say that the Reserve is 10 millions, that the Bank has not the account of the banks, that . . .' &c., &c.

Now, you may take it from me that those accounts exercise absolutely no especial disturbing influence that is not exercised by *all* our Deposits, by the merchants' accounts, for instance, and by each particular account among them. They do not differ in kind from any of them. The only peculiarity about them is, that being, if looked at in a lump, our second largest account, being an aggregate of similars, and being, as I have before explained, most invariable in their character, they are, if not more easy to manage than any other class, at least *as* easy. We, of course, *can* know and understand smaller mercantile accounts as well; but they are usually too small to make it worth while to know them as thoroughly as we do these, whether we look at them (the banks) as a class, or as individuals.

Neither does the presence of these deposits in our books have an atom more effect on the country, than that of an equally large aggregate of mercantile accounts. Try and think out for yourself what, if any, beneficial difference to the country there would be if they took them away and placed them elsewhere. You say we ought not to be 'mixed up with other bodies . . . &c. . . . but should stand alone.'

Now a bank that is mixed up with nobody else, in the sense of having no depositors, would, it seems to me, cease to be a bank. Whether these particular depositors, especially the joint-stock part of them, keep their reserves at a point safe for themselves and *their* depositors and shareholders, and for the country, is another question. *Where* they keep them would seem at first sight to affect no one materially, if only it were a safe place, though if they did keep them 'each for himself,' as you say, or placed them elsewhere than as now, it would be no little inconvenience to themselves if not to others.

The fluctuations of the Reserve would be far more frequent and far more violent than now. The fact of the bankers banking with us acts as the balance-wheel to our clock-work.

Now for some of your 'giants,' which I mean to reduce to their original vaporous condition, to drive them into their bottles, and to set the seal of Solomon upon them.

'Fluctuations of the Reserve' [p. 138] Where do you find me, or any one else out of a money-article, attaching importance to them except as taken in conjunction with other circumstances? So that they keep a due proportion to the Deposits – not a numerical proportion, mind you, but a proportion corresponding to the character of those Deposits – so long, that is, as, taking all attendant circumstances into consideration, I have enough to pay my debts when they are due, let it fluctnate every day and all day long.

I don't meet your arguments about tranquillity by arguments founded on panic; nor does any one else who understands the matter; but I say, as I said before: 'In quiet times the Reserve could never get to the point you suppose.' You exult over this saying of mine, and think it proves your point. But you have misapprehended it; it means the converse of what you take it to mean. You had said: 'In quiet times what would be the harm if the Reserve went to two millions?' I said that, unless our Deposits justified so small a Reserve, long before it reached that point the public would see that we had not wherewithal to pay our liabilities when due, and to lend to those who brought securities to us, and quiet times would cease, a reasonable alarm would begin, soon to develop into an unreasonable panic.

Now again you say [p. 139], 'Reserve 10 millions; Bank not having the account of the banks; times quiet; five millions go away to pay for corn; what harm?' And then you say I have not answered that question. Well then, I will! I don't tie myself to precise figures, because they must depend on the character of our remaining deposits; but, taking your question as a general one, my answer is short: *No harm at all!* Who says there is? *Quis vitu-peravit?* Pray don't father upon the Bank of England the follies of others, the slipshod stuff of sciolists, the nonsense of newspapers, the crotchets of Crump! So long as you content yourself with saying that the mass of public writers on the subject don't understand what they are writing about, that they can't criticise the navigation of the ship for want of knowing the ropes, or understanding the chart or the compass, I am with you; but when you imagine that because *they* vent follies, *we* here must needs be guided by their arguments, we part company.

In the case supposed, it may be that we *might* think proper to raise the rate, because it might be that our Reserve would be insufficient; but we should not be led to do so merely because a few millions of gold had gone away.

But we may carry your question further. Take away the merchants' accounts also, and another 2 or 3 millions of gold may safely go; and so on, till, fine by degrees and beautifully less, we dwindle away to nothing. Gold, or rather an insane belief in gold, which you impute to us, is another of your giants, and you hurl many denunciations at me and its other supposed votaries for the misdeeds which you imagine us to commit in our fright at its departure.

Now you are no opponent of the Act of 1844. Your chapter thereanent is a capital one, and, with a few exceptions, I agree with it all. Most of the exceptions are unimportant; but one sentence, as you repeat it in the letter before me, shewing that time has not brought repentance, will receive a cudgelling in the course of this my answer.

But I can't at all understand how, apprehending and applauding that Act as you do, you can believe in the *auri sacra fames* which you charge on the Banking Department of the Bank of England.

Under that law the amount of notes issued varies with the amount of gold; but that is the *law*, and has nought to do with the discretion or practice of the Bank.

The Bank has to look only to having a sufficient amount of notes in reserve, to perform its functions and discharge its liabilities when due, and has nothing at all to do, as a bank, with gold. If its Reserve appears likely to be reduced, from whatever cause, below the point of safety, it asks more for its accommodation, and will not lend except at a higher price, and perhaps also only for a short time. As a matter of fact that rise in price does bring back the gold, and thus the remedy, under the operation of the law, is speedier; but the Bank, as a bank, has nothing to do with that.

You say also [p. 138], 'To make the Bank the sole depositary of the country's gold, and then to argue,' &c. Who made the Bank the depositary of gold? I repeat, the Bank has nothing to do with gold; has none, in deposit or otherwise, except for convenience, and by way of *change*. It can get gold if it wants it, just as other banks, and other Her Majesty's subjects can do, who have notes in their pockets; but that is all.

It is the Issue Department, a wholly different body, which is the depositary of the country's gold; and the Issue Department has neither discretion nor indiscretion, and is much better without them.

Separate the two Departments clearly in your mind, and you will not fall into these fallacies. If they were physically separated, as you recommend, you would then see more clearly where the truth lies. The only object of such physical separation would be the explosion of certain fallacies, but, *pace* Mr Gladstone, popular education is dearly bought at the cost of material inconvenience, and a loss of efficiency. No transfer to Whitehall could make the real separation more absolute than it is.

You say on [p. 139] 'An extreme case might happen . . . The Bank might have no gold; might be insolvent.' How could the non-possession of gold make the Banking Department insolvent? What possible fear is there of the insolvency of the Issue Department? None whatever.

The mischief really is that, as I have intimated, you have never rightly realized *in practice* the total separation of the two Departments; half your letter is incompatible with your having done so.

The Department over which the Governor and Directors have to spend daily thought and care, is, as you rightly say in your book, a bank, like other banks, and has to think only, or almost only, how it is to meet its liabilities when due.

I will come presently to the question of its solvency, my supposed erroneous fears on which point are another of your giants.

What can you mean by suggesting that the Bank might get gold from France? Why should it? What should it do with it? Not pay its depositors, certainly; its notes will do that. And if it does not 'lower away,' as you call it, when it ought to 'hoist,' its notes will not be lacking.

But let us suppose that it did need gold, how should it get it? 'Oh!' you say, 'it can borrow.' No doubt it could; and so could I if I were in temporary difficulties. I could go to some friends and colleagues, and say, 'Pray look over my balance-sheet: you will see that I am perfectly solvent; but my capital is for the moment locked up. Lend me £100,000, or I must stop payment before Christmas.' No doubt, also, that they would do it if they could; but I can tell you I should not eat my breakfast with much appetite that day. Now, *do* you think the Bank of England ought to be liable to drift into the position of having to go cap-in-hand to ask for a loan lest she should stop payment? Would that be much short of a national calamity? You say it *was* done some years back. It was before my time; but I may venture to say that the uselessness of the measure and its indecorum were equal, and were stupendous.

We *did* 'lower away' in 1866, and you think the crisis (and panic) in that year did no harm. So do not I. It did some good, as did all those you mention, by bringing to light the insolvency of insolvent houses; but it was, as they all were, the cause of great loss, and more than loss, to many of the solvent. All crises do so more or less, even that of 1873, when there was no panic; and in all of them the price of accommodation is necessarily forced up to a high point.

But now, tell me, why all this cry about the raising of the rate of discount to protect our Reserve? What is the harm of a bank's saying 'I won't lend you anything under 5%. If you don't like my loan, don't take it. Go elsewhere.' You can't and will never answer that *why*. But if they *do* take it, and if they go on taking while the rate rises to 10, what harm? Specifically and categorically, what barm? Don't give me the answer of some of our instructors in the Press, and tell me of the importance of having no fluctuations in the rate – as if the cost of accommodation were different from the cost of everything else, and were not bound to obey the law of supply and demand. You won't, I am sure, echo the feeble utterances of our newspaper critics who, at such times, bleat about wide-spread distress and ruin, but will tell me in intelligible and precise language, *What harm.*

Ruin! What ruin can be produced by a rise in the rate of discount? If you should think it could, you would show that you mistook one of the effects for the cause. Calculate the debit entry to a man's 'Interest and Discount' account on a loan of £50,000 for a month at an extra 5%, at 5% beyond what he had calculated on, and then bring me the man who has been 'ruined' by a loss (if one may call it loss) of £200 on a transaction of £50,000! No! The man who is ruined is not the man who discounts good bills at 9 or 10%, but the man who has not got the good bills to discount. Ruin comes from failure of *Credit*; and Failure of Credit comes from bad Trading.

To return. You say: 'If you tell me a crisis or a panic is coming on, I can understand and accept your action for the Reserve;' and afterwards you say, 'When demand has increased against supply, you have a right to the market price,' (implying that when there is no such excess we are not entitled to it). Again you say: 'I see no reason or pleasure in a rise of 2 or 3 per cent, because, by purchases of corn, 3 or 4 millions of gold have gone abroad in quiet times, out of 11 or 12.' And again – 'Why, why raise the rate, because a couple of millions have gone away? You can't answer that *why!*'

Well: I answer the two last quotations as the Royal Society ought to have answered Charles the Second: 'We can't tell you why, your Majesty; for the thing is not so.'

I see the millions go with a light heart when only I know that their departure does not, by the operation of the law, put my reserve out of due harmony with the owners of it, my depositors. If I *don't* know this, I don't lend with both hands, and I make my loans more difficult and more costly. 'Ah! but that is only legitimate if a crisis should be approaching,' say you. A crisis is *always* approaching, and only needs carelessness on the subject of a bank's reserve to bring it on: add a little more carelessness, and you have a panic. Don't you believe in '*Venienti occurrere morbo*'? A gentle and gradual rise in the rate meets and checks the disease on its way. Let it alone, and the market rate, when the crisis has really come, is something much more formidable. 'You have a right to it in that case,' you say. We have, I suppose, a right to the *market rate* in any case, but we certainly don't get any other, except in a few trifling instances, as I explained in my former letter, let us raise it how we will. 'Why raise the rate?' you say: 'Why not?' say I; and I should be very glad of a precise answer to *that* question.

With many things that you say in your letter I quite agree; but I don't think that, after reading this letter, you will consider them *ad rem* in our discussion.

Gold, of course, is but a cart, or a pack-horse: I never thought it to be much else. Money, too, is quite properly called by you mere 'Machinery of Exchange.' Cheques, and ledgers, and so forth, do all you say: one must live with one's eyes very close shut not to see it. But American 'Certified Cheques,' as you call them (Deposit Notes they were really called, I think:

Confessions of Insolvency they really were), were by no means the same thing in my mind. They were rickety carts; and let fall one-fifth of the holders' property.

I don't at all agree that suspension of cash payments was or ever is harmless. As long as notes are not in excess no one is hurt: not even the man who wants to pay his foreign creditor in gold; for if notes are not at a discount, and if prices have not risen owing to their superabundance, he can buy gold, if there is any, or buy goods and remit the worth of the gold he needs. But when they *are* in excess (and who is to control them?) and are at a discount, you are merely robbing the creditor class for the benefit of the debtor.

Don't imagine that the evil is confined to the exporter of gold. Prices rise, and every one suffers. Don't I see it before me at this day in Mexico and Perú?

Of course I know all about the events of 1847, 1857, and 1866. But here comes the phrase from your book. Do you really suppose that 'in 1857 the line would not have been overstepped if the line of uncovered issues had been drawn, as now, at 15 millions instead of 14'? Had it been at 20 millions, or at 2, it would not have made the slightest difference. The issue, and consequently the available notes, would not have been more or less by a single £5 note. The only appreciable function of the issue on securities is to put an insignificant sum into the pockets of the nation and of the Bank proprietors. Read my letter to the Chancellor of the Exchequer (enclosed).*

The chapter in your book on 'What is a Bank?' is a capital one; and with its principles and theories I quite agree, and always have agreed; and so I may say do all of us here who have had to manage the Bank. None of those who have not had to do it *dis*agree with them, so far as I know. I protest, therefore, that when you write '*they* hold,' '*they* affirm,' and so on, 'They' must not be held to include the Governors of the Bank of England.

But when you come to principles in action, and to your reading of historical facts, the eleven foot of error sometimes shews itself.

You shew now and then, as I have already said, that you don't fully realize the separation of the two Departments. You talk there also of the Bank's buying gold. I suggest as an amendment, that the Clarendon Press should buy it. It is as much the duty or interest of one body to do it as another.

I wholly dispute the conclusion you draw from the events of 1866. That lending, that 'lowering away,' was, in my opinion, most disastrous. Not the thing itself, but the way in which it was done. Could '66 happen again, which with our present lights it could not, we should not be slack to lend, but we should lend, as we did in the unobserved because undisastrous crisis

---

* *See* Appendix.

of 1873, in such a way as not to bring about the mischievous and futile suspension of the Act of 1844.

By-the-bye, are you not sinning against your own knowledge when you say we lent £800,000 of gold in 1857? That was the popular language. What we lent was paper issued on securities. What a banker deals in is accommodation, and it was accommodation we gave.

This letter will have shewn you also that I consider a part of your page 144 very heretical, and that your American examples are no examples at all; but you probably could only be converted by becoming, in my sense, a 'practical man.' It is a great pity that one so sound in theory should not have been so!

Now for 'Solvency.' If I used the word in one sentence of my former letter, it was for the sake of brevity. It was right enough; for solvency is *paying when due*. But all your arguments are about the sense of *paying on liquidation* – about ultimate solvency. The ultimate solvency of the Bank is of course beyond question, but the solvency in the other sense, whether of the Bank or any other body or person, is by no means so adamantine but that it requires daily care and watchfulness; and in order to ensure it, the Bank at least must maintain such a Reserve as can resist all assaults.

Now the Bank, among other functions and other duties, has this function and this duty: – The function to lend to borrowers who can bring security; the duty to pay its liabilities *when due*. To be able to fulfil both of these, a full Reserve is needed. Some may say – but you won't – Why should they lend? The answer is, that credit is a part of our mercantile system; that many perfectly solvent houses look to pay their own acceptances by the discount of bills; and if that source is suddenly dried up, they can't pay by its means, and if their goods are unsaleable, must stop, and must lose their credit, and their trade.

That they should pay a few pounds more in one quarter of a year hurts them not at all; they have paid a few pounds less in another. It is an average, and a low one. But that they should find themselves unable to borrow at all would be a calamity, and a far-reaching one.

The duty is – to pay its liabilities. What are its liabilities? The return of its depositors' money *on demand*.

If, then, its Reserve is running low, or is likely to run low, there are two ways of meeting this duty:

I.   Diminishing the Deposits.   II. Increasing the Reserve.
I.   By selling securities.   II. By raising the rate.
      Which latter, on the one hand, checks the diminution of the Reserve, and on the other, under the operation of the law of 1844, adds to it.
I.   Our securities are a chest in which we place a portion of our Deposits. When our depositors want them, or we want to return them, we open it; and this is easy enough in quiet times. But when our Reserve comes to the point which you contemplate *avec le cœur léger*, the lock and

hinges are rusty and the chest won't open; never mind whether this is the result of human folly or human wisdom; but it won't. In your favourite crisis of 1866 we could not have sold a million Consols had we wished to do so. Now don't answer, 'Not sell a million Consols! Pooh! Nonsense! The credit and solvency of the State are adamantine! I *know* you could!' That is just what the 'practical man' – in your sense – says. Try the 'practical man' in mine. Make your sale at such a time (nothing more easy with some fall in price), and follow up the transaction till you get the notes into our coffers. *Complete* your sale: there's the rub!

My conclusion is, that both measures, I. and II., to be effective, must be taken in time; that when it is necessary to rectify a disproportion, present or foreseen, between Reserve and Deposits, we cannot wait till the evil is upon us, and that neither you nor any one else has ever given us the slightest reason why we should so wait.

Of that disproportion and that necessity, the only persons who have the faintest means of judging are those who have before them the ever-changing character of the Deposits and the ever-changing condition of the Reserve, viz., the Directors of the Bank of England; and the only lever which they have in the ultimate resort, the only force which can efficiently act on the Reserve, is the rate of discount. *Experto crede!*

Sincerely yours,
Henry H. Gibbs

Dec. 24.

Norham Gardens, Oxford
December 26, 1877

My Dear Gibbs,

What a charming Christmas present you have sent me. I read your letter – not yesterday, for a house full of romping children forbade that, but to-day – with the keenest pleasure, but not without infinite amusement and endless astonishments, as well as the most liberal admiration. My sensations at this moment are of the very pleasantest. In spite of the very clever cuts and thrusts, the dexterous parryings, and all the roar of the combat, I do not feel that a drop of my blood has been drawn. There is no penitence in me – not a grain; but there is very much to explain, to the great risk of boring you, I fear. But I have stood nineteen pages without flinching; and no one knows better than you how to do battle on even terms. So here goes.

'I am not a practical man.' You set up against me as the practical man; 'but not in the sense of "don't tell me, I know it is so and so,"' and yet, a few lines on, you say of yourself, '*I know, and you don't.*' How to find two senses of the word practical in such words is too hard for me. But however that may be, I am credited with good theory, but deficiency in practice. This is a variation of the reproach hurled against me for years and years. All very fine – but a mere theorist; not practical; doesn't know; why trouble ourselves with listening to him; we have other things to do. So it always has been, and always will be, when men not of a profession give words and reasonings to those who belong to it. It is human nature so to do; and you are a man. On the other hand, I, too, am a man; and not always infallible, intelligent, or right. However, your letter summons me to receive corrections of ignorance caused by want of that practical character which alone supplies true knowledge. My answer is, that I have to deal with a marvellous adept in the art of giving just that slight turn to words lying before him as makes him misunderstand either their meaning or their application. Could you establish that I had really asserted some of the thoughts you impute to me, I should feel unbounded amazement at my having contradicted what I knew as well as my A B C, and had ever asserted in a thousand ways.

I will now go through your letter, missing nothing if I can help it.

I understood and took in fully what you said of your feeling about the accounts of the bankers at the Bank. I had not the remotest idea or wish of controverting it. This was a point of detail, and respecting it you had knowledge and I had not. I am very sorry now that I alluded to these accounts, for it has caused you a large amount of unneeded trouble. But you had a strong, pleasurable zest in smiting me: please set that to the credit side. At the time I wrote I remember that I felt there was no real need for making the allusion; what induced me to go on with it was this. I was anxious to discuss the gold theory of the rate on its own merits purely. I knew that from Bagehot downwards every sort of writer had dwelt on the peculiar character of these banks' accounts as a grave element in the case. I wished to eliminate it altogether; to go on with my subject without any reference to this account; and I felt that, if this account disturbed the otherwise natural principle, it had better be given up. I wrote in this sense, and in this sense only. I had no thought of having an opinion of my own on that account. You had satisfied me; and writing to you, I, perhaps, ought to have stood on your stand-point. But the desire to clear away all reference to that account prevailed; so I wrote on; but, I repeat, not to express an opinion on it, much less to controvert your declaration, but solely to clear that element away altogether. I am sorry that it gave you the trouble of preaching to me; but the sermon was not really wanted. I was not resisting 'the practical man, who knew,' the banker who knew all about one of his accounts. Hence I need not enter into your argument; I accept – and did at the time – all you say. I did not use 'a different language' from yours. 'Let us talk about the increase or diminution of gold ruling the rate of discount, and of nothing else,' is what I wished to say.

No doubt, I have said – not that 'any of your colleagues agreed with me,' for I had nothing of my own with which they might agree, but that some of them had spoken of that account as of doubtful desirableness, and had even hinted that the money lodged in it should be kept intact. This state-ment rests on memory, and I will not swear that my memory was accurate, though I believe it to have been so. I do fancy to remember that a few years ago this very account came under public discussion, and that your col-league, Thomson Hankey, expressed what I said. My memory may be deceiving me: but, I know that I speak honestly, and can perfectly afford to be told that I am in error, and that he never uttered anything of the kind. And I know further that I had no decided view of my own as to that account: and that the first time when I had such a decided view was when I learnt your views about it. Mr Hankey, I am sure, wrote a letter in *The Times*, – the date I forget.

'Fluctuations of the Reserve.' You overwhelm me with astonishment: whatever may be the opinions held within the Bank, there is only one opinion before the whole world – that the rate is ruled by the gain or loss of gold to the Bank. This is what I attack. This is my accepted heresy: this my title to be called a theorist: this is what I have denied, fought against, and traversed in every imaginable way. This is why I stand alone on banking. *Every practical man*, every banker, so far as I know, the whole commercial literature, every city article of every newspaper, every city authority that I ever came across – (not you, for the question has never before been raised between us) – every Stock Exchange in and out of England – takes his stand on this doctrine. They never speak of connection with other circum-stances: for with that adjunct the principle perishes. And now you tell me, that not only you, but the Bank Directors, agree with me: you speak of this doctrine in terms yet more contemptuous than mine. Then why have I been left to do the battle alone? Why has not the Bank proclaimed the principle of its practice to a benighted and deluded England? Bagehot's 'Lombard Street' was hailed as a great explainer of these operations. I reviewed it in *Fraser*, and said my mind about it; but the Press would not listen: and not a banker but looked upon me as a theorist. And now my theory is declared to be truth. It is announced that the rate is not ruled by gold alone. That you think so, I am as certain as man can be: that the miscellaneous body called the Directors of the Bank think so, I must venture to doubt. Anyhow, write out aloud what you have written to me privately, and then see the startling commotion which would arise.

You say, that unless 'your Deposits justified a Reserve of 2 millions, long before it reached that point the public would see we had not wherewithal to pay our liabilities.' Exactly; because that public is trained to think safety involved in a much larger Reserve. The rule of gold is the very instructor – the creator of this feeling. Now observe, I have never denied the necessity – a general one – of a reasonably large Reserve: and I do not deny that the Bank Directors are the proper judges of the fitting magnitude of that Reserve. I have preached this doctrine. But it matters infinitely what is the banking education and feelings of the Directors. It is most easy for them to have very wild ideas about this ratio to liabilities. They come out of a commercial community trained to such thoughts. And further – and this is very important – my declamations have never been poured out against the size of the Reserve adopted, against it being normally too large; but against the fluctuations of gold being at once converted into laws for acting on the rate of discount – without any reference to the state and nature of the business going on at the time. This is the giant I have ever tried to kill; and I say that I have killed him, but he won't die! his ghost is as powerful, as fully believed in, as his living form ever was. Still – even under such training and habits of thought – I totally disbelieve that panic would ever arise simply because the Bank Reserve was very low, with no other cause superadded. My ideas of a city panic are radically different from that: so *were* (qr. are) those of the Bank when it ran out its gold so vigorously in 1866.

'No harm at all,' you cry – when 5 millions go away out of 10. Grand! this satisfies all my desires: we are brothers, all other discordances notwithstanding. And if it be really true that your colleagues think like you – and have always thought like you – then *peccari!* in muddling up the Threadneedle Street men with Crump & Co. I should not have put the gold rule into their sacred lips. But with Prince George of Denmark, I exclaim: '*Est-il-possible?*' That page 7 of yours (p. 26) is invaluable to me.

But, pray one question. If ever I write again, may I say that I have reason to believe that the Directors of the Bank of England do not hold the principle of a rate governed by mere fluctuations of gold, and do not act upon it?

You say: 'Under the law of 1844 the amount of notes issued varies with the amount of gold' – most right – 'but that is the *law* and has nought to do with the discretion or practice of the Bank.' Have I ever said in any place that it had?

Clearly, 'the Bank has nothing more to do at all with gold, as a bank,' no more than any other bank. Its business is exclusively with its Reserve – till the circulation descends to 15 millions, which it never does. I am tired of preaching that the Bank gets gold like other mortals with notes. But this surely may happen. Rothschild brings over a million in metal. He takes it to the Bank, as bankers: the Bank sends it across the court to the Issue Department, and gets notes. This is practically to get gold, or tickets which will instantly procure gold from the outer world. But you appear to me not to perceive – yet it can hardly be so – that the notes so procured are in substance gold. For such gold, the real fact that takes place is that the Bank lodges that gold in the vaults of the Issue Department for convenience sake – takes the receipts or tickets away for it. Thus the Reserve is always gold – not actually – but virtually – being to be had by sending across the court for it. As that Reserve may become larger or smaller, the Bank so far has to deal with gold. That gold in the Issue Department – I mean Rothschild's gold – really belongs to you: you hold the tickets for the lumps in the Clock Room.

You bid me 'separate the two Departments clearly in my mind:' I think I do so as firmly as any man in England. I have preached that separation in the Press, to Chambers of Commerce, &c., for many years. Then, you say, I should not 'fall into these fallacies.' What fallacies? I can perceive none. I cared for a transfer of the Issue Department to Somerset House solely as an educational process: for really in currency people – not can't, but – won't understand.

You add on [p. 139], that I 'say an extreme case might happen: the Bank might have no gold, might be insolvent,' and you comment, 'How could the non-possession of gold make the Banking Department insolvent? What possible fear is there of the insolvency of the Issue Department? None whatever!'

I am in a complete haze here: I do not know what you are at. I miss not only your point, but the idea you are speaking about. The Banking Department's Reserve is to guard against insolvency. It consists of tickets or receipts for gold – which is to be had across the court. The Issue Department, we are agreed, is no part of the Bank of England: it belongs to me in principle as much as to you – for I have a £5 note in my pocket. As I said, I am all abroad here: as I fail to see your point. Not often do I do that.

I reply firmly, that I do not see that I have said a single thing inconsistent with the separation of the two Departments. I cannot put a single proposition before my eyes out of your letter, which has a particle of this inconsistency.

I did not mean much by saying that the Bank might on an emergency borrow gold from France. I did not recommend it. I only spoke of it as a possible resource if by any chance its gold was run out, whilst its credit was untainted. The Issue Department could not bring a particle of help: for the hypothesis is that the Reserve is disappearing. You say – 'what should the Bank do with it? – not pay its depositors with it, certainly.' I answer, certainly it would. Its Reserve is gone, and the depositors may be asking for payment: a couple of millions of borrowed foreign gold would be the very thing to give help. Only, I repeat, I spoke of this foreign gold merely in arguing against the fancied possibility of the Bank stopping payment. You are quite right in requiring that the Bank should not be allowed to drift into such a position: but was that position quite impossible in 1866, when, through your vigorous lendings, your Reserve sank to below a million? How, if some mischievous depositors had sent in cheques for a couple of millions?

When I spoke of the panic of 1866 as doing no harm, your great art comes into play. You forget the context. I meant simply that the Bank itself did not come to grief through its dwindled Reserve and its contempt – (as I thought) – of the doctrine that as gold goes out the rate must be raised, whilst all the time it was lending away.

And now comes the tug of war between us. Clearly, you have a perfect right to lend on your own terms; that is indisputable. As a single bank, acting for itself, you had entire liberty to deal with your means at your pleasure: you were accountable only to your shareholders.

But the position was radically changed when you became the chief of a universal confederation of banks, who followed your lead, obeyed your signal, repeated your acts, and presented to the nation the united front of a great host. The nation then acquired a moral right to criticise the principles which guided your action. Banking is one of the most powerful and most valuable instruments of modern trade. Through its agency multitudes of manufacturers and merchants acquire the means for carrying on commerce. Their transactions, to an enormous extent, repose on a reliance on banking funds. The banks thus, collectively, form a great national institution. Now, if this vast collective body assumes as the guide of its daily, even hourly, action a false principle which works infinite harm, it becomes a matter both of scientific interest and of national concern to apply a remedy. I do not say that that remedy shall be interference by edict or law; but I do say that the whole people become summoned to resist that principle, to expose its falsehood, and to stimulate a strong public opinion against its maintenance.

But 'what can be the harm?' This: the rule that the fluctuations of gold shall rule the rate of discount involves this consequence – that these fluctuations, which, if unconnected with other circumstances, may reach 5 millions in your judgment without harm to the Bank or banks, are converted into machinery for sudden and severe rises in the terms of borrowing the aid of banking: and I must repeat what I have always heard traders confess, with even passion, that these rises are acutely felt, perplex traders, inflict severe losses by the largely increased sums paid for accommodation necessary and reckoned upon, and frequently turn legitimate enterprises into positive losses. Ruin is a big word, I admit; but I should not fear to present myself to any Chamber of Commerce, and ask whether a high rate of discount has never brought a trading house to stoppage. And since the fact that the mere departure of gold by itself alone involves no danger to the Bank – the leader of the banks – then it follows that this loss, imposed by the rule on traders, is the offspring of the gain reaped by the banks in working the rate up and down at their fancy. That gain – I will not call it unlawful – so far as it rests on the allegation of a false and unfounded principle – the whole community is deeply interested in resisting. But so far as it is claimed on the avowed ground that the loans can fetch those terms in the open market it is legitimate, but to be met on the part of the sufferers by efforts to overthrow the combination which renders it possible.

You see, then, I admit your *why?* A seller is entitled to what his article will fetch. But if he tries to render the terms endurable by founding them on false doctrine, he is to be encountered by argument, exposure, and, if needs be, by competition. Traders 'do take' the loans; but it is because they have humbugged themselves, or been humbugged by others, with this fine theory about gold, and then they surrender themselves to their fate.

What made you put out the strange inference, that 'when,' as I said, 'demand has increased against supply, you have a right to the market price;' I implied that 'when there is no such excess we are not entitled to it.' Surely, the ordinary cause of a rise of market price is increase of demand against supply: I was not dreaming, as you (the subtle art again) imagine, of a difference of right in two cases.

My *why – why?* – are answered, of course, by the remark that 'the thing is not so.' I had not had the astonishing revelation yet made to me that the Bank Directors do not heed the departure of the gold. Pray, does my friend and occasional correspondent, Harry Grenfell, coincide in this view? Stranger and stranger every hour! How I should like to cross-examine him on the point before you!

'Why *not* raise the rate?' you ask, and you want a 'precise answer to *that* question.' I have given it. If you can get the raised rate, – raise away. But if you succeed, because the public is deluded with a false doctrine, then the public must be educated up to understanding the character of the markets, and the want of foundation for the reason given. But, if you do not act on the false principle, but solely upon your ideas on the then state of the banking, then. I say with you, Why not raise the rate?

When I was in America, they were called 'certified cheques.' But I do not admit that they were 'confessions of insolvency.' They imply, of course, that the money pledged is not at hand. It is the nature of banking that deposits should be lent. If they are all demanded together at 10 o'clock to-morrow morning there is not cash enough in England to face one-tenth of the demand: insolvency for the moment there must be. The certified cheque merely said – your money is safe: but it is impossible to give it to-day.

Now for a fine specimen of logic:-

You 'deny that suspension of cash payments was or ever is harmless.' Then the next sentence shows that 'if notes are not in excess no one is hurt.' Bravo! Surely you were not in the Schools when you wrote that.

Now for a mathematical operation – going off at a tangent:

You write [p. 148], 'Do you really suppose that "in 1857 the line would not have been overstepped if the line of uncovered issues had been drawn at 15 millions, instead of 14." '

Then you comment:

'Had it been at 20 millions, or at 2, it would not have made the slightest difference. The issue, and consequently the available notes, would not have been more or less by a single £5 note.'

Quid ad rem?

I recorded [p. 140] a dry, hard fact – a piece of history.

In 1857, the Act was suspended, and uncovered issues were available.

On stock being taken, it was found that there was some £800,000 of notes out, for which the gold in the Issue Department, required by the Act, was not in store.

Had the line stood at 15 millions, the Act would have been fulfilled. It stood at 14, and the Act was not obeyed by the above sum.

This is not doctrine or opinion, but simply an historical event.

I am very glad to have your letter to Northcote. I go along with you. Only don't use 'fiduciary' – it is too like jargon – say uncovered, that is plain English.

It is most gratifying to me that you like my chapter on banks, and that your colleagues who have had to manage the Bank do not disagree. Then why do not some of you help poor Me out of my isolation? I should instantly cease to be a theorist. I have corresponded at times with three of them – Latham, Thomson Hankey, and Grenfell.

You are warranted in protesting against my speaking of 'they': but then I thought that they agreed with the whole of the Press, and all banking literature.

Again, *'illicit process'* – or rather, the application of the great Art.

I did not praise or censure what was done in 1866: I simply said that in spite of it all no one said the Bank was in danger.

The suspension of the Act of 1844 was certainly 'futile,' a pure nullity: but was it mischievous?

I do not catch exactly what is 'so very heretical' in page 144, and which sentences me to be 'not a practical man.'

In 1825, all that depositors cared for was to get the Bank's – uncovered – notes. When restriction was imposed – no harm. And I am certain that the Bank's signature would suffice in the worst of crises: for, mind, people do not want the money, but the assurance of safety.

Remember, I have not preached – ever – be indifferent to Reserve. But I have argued, that when over-taken, practically you never were in danger. As my dear old friend, Sir David Salomons, told the House of Commons – in the worst days since 1819, the Bank note never was discredited, never went to a discount.

I repeat: I cannot find any specific charge which I have to answer on my imperfect apprehension of – or rather, inconsistency with – the separation of the two Departments of the Bank. I cannot *préciser* to myself out of your letter a single distinct statement of any such inconsistency.

Ergo: since that is the basis of my not being a practical man, – I still subscribe myself to you as

The NOT-Unpractical Man,
Bonamy Price

2, Norham Gardens, Oxford
December 28, 1877

My Dear Gibbs,

I am not sure that I said to you yesterday, that nowhere, in spoken or written words, have I ever pleaded that 'when it is necessary to rectify a disproportion present or foreseen between Reserve and Deposits, you ought to wait till the evil is upon you.' I can never have uttered an opinion in such complete contradiction with all my thoughts. You most rightly say, that 'neither I nor any one else has ever given you the slightest reason why you should so wait.'

Yours sincerely,
B. Price

To shew that when, in a given case, there has been such waiting, no harm has ensued, is something radically different from advising it.

December 31, 1877

My Dear Price,

A happy new year to you, and thanks for your letter of the 26th, which has been on its travels into Herts, before it reached me at my London address.

Pray don't think me arrogant in saying 'I know, and you don't.' The words were yours: not my own. I only accepted them as signifying not that I knew what was right better than you, but that I know the practice – the working; – and that *no* one not engaged in the business can know it so well and so truly as one who is so engaged. The *soi-disant* 'practical man' whom you contemn is an empiric, who justifies his practice by its long duration, and can give, as you say, no reasons for it. The *real* practical man is right in theory (and his theory is yours), but can, and does, give his reasons for his practice in accordance with his theory.

Now let me say that if I have ever, as you think, given an untrue turn to your words, I beg your pardon. I have never intended to do so; but if I have done it, it has been through misunderstanding them and you. How often it has been my fault, and how often yours, I can't say. Once at least, if not twice, it has been mine. I have not the smallest desire to controvert, in this discussion, any error which is not yours. I have not even the least wish for the glory of having the best of the battle. If you have the best, I will gladly admit it, and amend my ways; but where you seem to me to be wrong in your facts, or imperfectly informed as to our practice, I am glad to set you right; and if you have a notion implanted in your mind that we act on one principle, when we know that we don't act on that, but on another, I want to root it out.

'Then why leave me in my isolation?' you say; 'why not proclaim the principle of your practice to a benighted England?' I answer, that it is not our calling to preach in the wilderness the true doctrines of Currency and Banking, and it *is* yours. Our teaching is contained in our practice; and I believe our practice ('errors excepted') will stand any test. True, we *may* have very wild ideas about the ratio of our Reserve to our Deposits; but I don't think anyone can show that we *have*. It was only a dream of

Bagehot's that we ought to maintain continually a certain, large, Reserve (10 or 12 millions, I think he said). *We* have to consider what part of our Deposits can be withdrawn, and to keep such a Reserve as will insure our meeting the demand for such part, be it 2 millions, or 20. No one doubts, of course, that it would be impossible to demand or withdraw them all at ten o'clock to-morrow; and I will add, that while Banking is Banking, and we are a Bank, it will be impossible to withdraw them all in any given time, however long. But I will substitute for the dictum in page [156] – 'It is the nature of Banking that deposits should be lent' – another: 'It is the danger of Banking that deposits should be rashly lent.' Only such should be lent as cannot be peremptorily demanded, and all that *is* lent should be so lent as that what can by any possibility be demanded should be 'at hand' *when* demanded. That is the fundamental principle of good Banking.

However, we need scarcely discuss Reserve, for I entirely agree with your page 4 [p. 152] on the subject: indeed, I agree with the whole of your first sheet, except where you doubt the concurrence of my colleagues. My colleagues, I am sure, agree with me. You have not killed the giant in our minds: he was never born, as far as we were concerned. Slay him where he exists in the minds of the public, and you do good service.

You rejoice on page [153] in what I say about five millions. Good! but be sure that you stick to what I *did* say. That was: 'Reduce our Deposits by $\frac{1}{x}$, and 5 millions out of 10 may go, and welcome.' But it is impossible to tie oneself to a numerical proportion: that would be exceedingly bad banking.

Yes. If ever you write again, you may say 'that the Directors of the Bank of England' (as a body, I know; one and all, I *believe*) 'do not hold the principle of a rate governed by mere fluctuations of gold, and do not act upon it.'

You say: 'Write aloud what you write to me privately, and you will see what a commotion will arise!'

Well; if you like it, and if the Governor thinks well, I will have our correspondence printed (not published), and then we shall know if I am right in my 'one and all.' I shall be much surprised indeed, if Henry Grenfell dissents.

I will try to explain more clearly what I mean. All the world, you tell me, lays down a golden rule – 'Gold, and gold alone, must rule the rate.' How can all the world of practical men be wrong! Well; they are not so *very* wrong. What they *say* is not quite correct; but what the well-informed *mean* by the compendious form of speech which they use is near enough to the truth, though it may lead to erroneous impressions in the minds of both utterers and hearers.

Filling out their sentence, they mean to say 'Every, the slightest, fluctuation of gold affects the Bank Reserve: the state of the Bank Reserve affects the rate of discount; *therefore*, the fluctuations of gold affect the rate of discount.'

So they do, potentially, but not necessarily; nor at all, if their action on the Reserve is not such as to threaten to make it insufficient for our requirements.

That they do not *govern* the rate is as plain as the sun at noon. The question *solvitur ambulando*. The gold goes or comes, and the rate very often stays unmoved. In January of this year, for instance, our bullion decreased by £1,200,000; our rate was 2% and at 2% it remained, and why? The Reserve had remained practically unaltered; and had the Reserve been lessened by the same sum, we could have well afforded, taking our Deposits into the account, to remain as we were.

Certainly, you never said that the dependence of the amount of issue on the fluctuations of bullion was ruled by our discretion and not by the law; and certainly, I never said you did. I only meant by the passage on page 27 to say in other words what I have just now put into the mouths of others: viz., that the influx and efflux of gold do affect the issue, and do so by the operation of law, and not by our will; that the issue being thus expanded or contracted tends to the increase or diminution of our Reserve; that the movements of gold therefore, both actual and foreseen, require the closest care and attention; that those movements *may* be such as to cause us to alter our rate; but that our action in the matter is founded on the state of the thing materially affected – viz., our Reserve – and not on the movements of the bullion, which may or may not have materially affected it.

I don't agree with you that it is the 'love of gold' which leads the 'blind' multitude to fear, when they see our Reserve *lower than is justified by the character of our Deposits*. No explanation is then needed of their just fear. But that which often causes them to be afraid where no fear is, when our Reserve *seems* low but *is* not, is the publication of our Wednesday accounts; a measure fraught with incalculable mischief; a measure which utterly fails to instruct, and never fails to mislead when misleading is possible; for it gives but dry figures, and can give no explanation of the ever-changing character of those figures.

I only recurred to the 'Bankers' Accounts' because you said in your last that you thought that after all you were right in your former doubt that the presence of these accounts in our books was prejudicial to the country, and that if so the country would have a right to ask us to abandon them. I am glad that I have satisfied you.

My Logic is rusty, I admit: but I must say I can't see the fallacy in the passage you quote. I said that 'suspension of cash payments is never harmless;' for it opens the door to the danger of excessive Issue. There is no contradiction in saying that under some circumstances the danger does not walk in.

My History is rusty, too; but I am sure this is the first time I ever read a 'historical *fact*' stated in the tense 'would have been.' However, one historical fact of that kind is as good as another; and here is *my* historical fact in answer to yours – *fact*, you know: not opinion! 'Had the line stood at

15 millions in 1857, the Act would NOT have been fulfilled. The amount of Issue when the crisis set in would have been precisely the same as it actually was at that time; and whatever need there was for a suspension of the Act would still have existed. The only difference would have been that there would have been exactly £1,000,000 less gold in the Issue Department.'

I am sure we must be at cross-purposes as to this; for *my* fact is as certain as sunrise, but the demonstration is too long for this letter. Work out my letter to Northcote, and you can't fail to see it.

I don't like the word 'Fiduciary,' but 'Uncovered' is not quite correct. The 15 millions have no tangible *gold* cover, but they are covered by securities based on the credit of the State.

The suspension of the Act of 1844 is so far mischievous that it disaredits and damages the Act. No such suspension ought ever to be needed.

What seemed to me heresy in page 144 of your book was your statement that the Bank Reserve might be drawn to its last farthing without danger. I see you meant danger to its ultimate solvency, which is true enough.

My reference to your remarks on 1866 were no subtle play of my supposed art: no cleverness of mine, but, I suppose, pure dulness. I simply mistook you: I thought you had meant 'no harm to *any* one.' I fully admit that, as you say, none happened to the Old Lady: but to the commercial world, much.

By-the-bye, you say just above that the great mischief of her drifting into a Reserveless position might have happened to her in 1866; but you point to a wrong source of it. The danger of her being drawn dry by mischievous depositors is more apparent than real. I doubt whether there was at that time – I will not say any single depositor, but – any combination of depositors who could have ventured to draw out half-a-million. The Bankers had the fear of the Clearing House before their eyes; and as for other depositors – a time of crisis is a time when they pay into the Bank, rather than draw out from her. It is then that the adamantine character of our Banking comes into play. At every crisis our Deposits increase largely; and the increase is permanent.

It is the borrower from whom the danger came, and would come: danger, that is, so long as we lent with both hands, and took no means to keep up the stock from which to lend.

I have, I think, cleared off all the small skirmishers in your letter; and now for the main body, with whom is the 'tug of war.' There will be indeed three tugs, but, I hope, short ones.

Tug the first. All your argument in a splendidly written passage in page [154] is based – 1st, on the Bank of England being the Chief of an universal Confederation of Banks; and 2nd, on our assuming as our guide of daily action a certain false principle. I have shewn that in the action of the Bank that false principle has not been our guide for many years, if ever it was, and I will now add that there is no more confederation, actual or virtual, between us and the other banks than there is between me and my tailor.

They deal with us, and I deal with him. I don't, indeed, set him up as in any respect a light to guide my path, and they are sometimes, in some feeble sort, guided by us; but there is no *solidarité* between us. They have, as you know, sometimes used our rate as a convenient point of departure, allowing interest to their depositors at a percentage below it; but nothing obliged them to do so, (and if our rate was too high, no one suffered but their share-holders; if too low, their depositors had no one to blame but themselves,) and they have lately varied it as they thought good. As to their rate of discount, the last six months has probably opened every one's eyes on that matter. The rate charged by any one of them has probably very little relation to that of any particular one of the others, and varies, I dare say, according to the customer and according to the bills offered. To our rate it has no relation at all, except in the way of comparison. No arbitrary rate of the Bank of England can ever lead the market, at least in an upward direction. At the most it is a barometer, pointing to the state of the accommodation market; but even for that purpose, it is, like an ancroid, too much affected by other influences to be quite trustworthy. All I claim is, that its rate may be accepted as a trustworthy index of its own position, and that its Directors may be accepted as the best judges of that position.

At the same time, though I repudiate all responsibility as 'the Chief of a Confederation of Banks' – (we are not even a 'collective body,' except in the mind of any one who chooses to *collect* us) – I quite allow that, as, in one capacity, we are the administrators of the currency, and, in another, the bankers of the nation and managers of the National Debt, the nation has a perfect right to criticise the principles which guide our actions, and indeed to criticise us all round. Only let the criticism be based on knowledge not partial but complete.

Tag the second. I have little doubt that if you presented yourself to any Chamber of Commerce and asked whether a high rate of discount had ever brought a trading house to stoppage, you would get the answer you anticipate, and if you ventured to doubt, you would be told 'of course it is so; every body knows it is so; are we not practical men!' But when you do examine your Chamber of Commerce, – may I be there to see, and to cross-examine! The great majority of your witnesses will not, you will find, have gone to the bottom of the subject. What percentage of men who write or talk on any subject do go to the bottom of it? – and those who will tell you that they or their acquaintances have so suffered, will be found, I think, to have failed, as most people in such circumstances do fail, to put the saddle on the right horse. I will bring him out of the stable for you presently. But you quote 'all traders' against me. Not *all*: I am a trader: a banker, if you please, but a trader first. I borrow sometimes – not often; but when I do, it always happens to be when the rate of discount is exceptionally high. (I wonder if you at all know *why*, – yet that is a horse of the same colour as that of which I just now spoke.) Now, does a 10% cause me *loss?* Certainly not.

It is an abuse of terms to call it *loss*. If the rate were lower, my 'Interest and Discount Account' would certainly look better on the 31st December, but it is the average rate which one has to consider, and, as I told you in my last, the amount to the debit on any such transaction is ridiculously small compared with the magnitude of the transaction itself. It is not a *loss*, but a natural cost of trade. A trader may as well complain of the salaries of his clerks, of the cost of his stationery, or of an increase in the price of his coals for the office-fire.

True: you may take a particular transaction involving the turnover of £50,000, say in a month, and suppose your trader to enter upon it, borrow- ing the whole of the money, and calculating on a gain of £100 on the business: If he finds himself obliged to pay 5% more than he thought to pay for his loan, his *loss* on this wise transaction will be about £100 (sup- posing the rest of his calculation to have been correct); but will any one call that a real *loss?* It is his year's business which shows profit or loss, not an isolated transaction. In no year since 1844, would his business, even if he traded wholly on his borrowed £50,000, discounting his bills at the Bank of England, show a greater debit than £576, for the difference between his expected gain, and the extra amount over 5% paid by him for discount. £7 8*s.* was the highest average in any one year – '64, I think. Now if the 'loss' is £100 in a month at £5%, it will be £576 for a year at the remaining £2 8*s.*%.

But could he not find something more deserving of blame than the rise in the price of accommodation? Had his own unwisdom and rash calcula- tion on the stability of that price nothing to do with the failure of this speculation? Because he is virtuous shall there be no cakes and ale? Because he is imprudent shall the nature of things be changed, and that which varies like all other commodities be fixed immutably for his benefit?

When you do make your appeal to Chambers of Commerce, merchants and traders solvent and insolvent, don't be content with answers in the form of accusations, declamations, denunciations and vague assertions: put them to their *figures:* tell them to show you by *them* how Titius and Caius were brought to ruin, or even to suspension of payment, by their heavy payments for loans! If they answer your questions correctly, they will want no cross-examination from me. You will tell them in reply, 'I see: Titius fell a victim to the prevalent vice of over-trading – his goods were unsaleable, both those which he held on speculation and those he received on consignment; his money was gone and his credit was gone; but his money had been other people's money, not his own; and his credit had been obtained by false pretences. He said there was little harm after all, for *if* his goods ultimately realized their cost, he should pay everybody: but meanwhile Caius, another of the bubbles on the stream of commerce, had held Titius's bills, and had been irretrievably ruined, and others with him. They both *said*, and you say, that they had been brought down by the heavy sums they had had to pay for discount, but those sums have been found on investigation to be but an item in the cost of their business. It is evident now to me that no man was ever ruined, or even suffered severe loss, by having to pay a high rate of discount.'

When a man *is* ruined by his own folly, he always persuades himself that it is somebody else's fault; but it does seem to me strange that he should persuade *you*, even though all the Chambers of Commerce in England, and all the money-articles, should sing the same song.

It does seem to me strange that you should strain at that very small gnat, the rate of discount, and yet swallow such great camels as the monstrous expedient of 'borrowing gold,' or the fatal collapse of commerce involved in your 'certified cheques.'

You are right, by the way, about the immediate effect of borrowing: it could be done, and would supply the *Bank* with notes procurable against it from *Issue*. But it is not the Bank's business; and it would be a disastrous substitution of a difficult and indecorous, for an easy and legitimate, way of replenishing the Bank's Reserve.

Besides: consider what it is. By the hypothesis gold has been, and is, flowing out of the country to balance its indebtedness to other nations, and you ask for gold to be sent hitherward to increase that indebtedness! The stream is flowing rapidly down-hill, and you ask that some of it shall flow up-hill to its source.

So, you think that the banks make their gains by the fluctuations of the rate of discount? Do you know where the Paradise of Bankers is situated? In a country where demand is brisk and constant, and the rate of discount is always 4 per cent! Do you know what the average rate of discount at the Bank of England has been for the last 11 years? – £3 3s. 5d. per cent.!

Tug the third. No doubt you see, and have always advocated, the advantages of separating the two Departments of the Bank; but I must still say that you do not realize the working of that separation. Pages 5–7 of your letter would shew that to any one who had ever had that working under his own eye.

By-the-bye, I wonder whether you ever thought on the *process* of the material separation by transfer to Somerset House (it is not to be done by a 'fiat,") and the course of the subsequent transactions. The inconvenience would be a heavy price to pay for an education, which, if people would but *think*, is supplied now.

Now for your example of the working, on page 38 [153–4], and my answer.

Rothschild does *not* bring a million of metal to the Bank – as bankers: the Bank does *not* send it across the court to the Issue Department and get notes (which, of course, would be, as you say, to get the command of gold): it does *not* lodge that gold in the Issue Department for convenience sake, or for any cause at all; it has not got it to lodge: it does *not* take any 'tickets' away with it; it is entitled to none: and finally – that gold – Rothsehild's gold – does *not* belong to me as banker, for I do *not* hold the tickets for it.

Can you have a more categorical contradiction! What does happen is this.

Rothschild brings a million of metal to the ISSUE DEPARTMENT in Threadneedle Street, exactly as he would do if it were in Somerset House. That Department gives *him* £1,000,000 in notes; and he does with them what seemeth him good. Neither they nor the gold (their substance) ever enter in any way, at this stage, into the banking books of the Bank of England. I, as banker, have no more to do with them or the gold than the Pope has. I, as one of the administrators of the Issue, have a sort of property in them. But the gold belongs to Rothschild: *he* has the tickets for it.

If the Issue Department *were* in Somerset House and under another Governor, the Governor of the Bank of England would have no more knowledge of the coming in of the parcel of gold than the Governor of the Bank of France.

This has been the law and practice since August, 1844; so I hope you really *will* see now that you have not realized the working of the Act. It is never too late to learn.

It is true that the affair does not necessarily travel through all the steps I have mentioned: economy of time and other things demands, and the close contact of the two Departments allows, a more compendious mode of dealing. Rothschild does not *touch* the notes: he either pays them into his account with us, if he is a customer of ours, or to his bankers in Lombard Street. Thus they may come on our banking books, either to swell *his* balance or that of his bankers. But they would do so by a fresh act of deposit, and in no way as a necessary condition of the bringing in of the gold. The bankers may, if they choose, keep them in their own till, or Rothschild may, if he is so minded, paper his dressing-room with them.

The Bank, I repeat, has, as a bank, nothing to do with the substance gold, as a matter of obligation: it can get it, as you and I can, for a £5 note, or for the whole £12,000,000 of its Reserve; for it has the 'tickets' for it, which are, as you say, potentially gold; but it never needs gold, and gold can never be claimed from it.

No; not if the Issue could be and were reduced to 15 millions, would the Bank, as a bank, have anything to do with gold. Such reduction is of course an impossibility, but we may imagine it, nevertheless. The 'Notes with the Public' would be, we will say, £10,000,000, and the Reserve £5,000,000. There would not be an ounce of gold in the Issue Department: that office of the State would be in evil case if it could not provide 5 sovereigns for your £5 note, or if the true Bank, its other self – its sister-self – moved by a spirit of mischief, were to send across the court for gold, which it does not want, in lieu of the 'tickets' which it holds as its Reserve. But the BANK can pay its way in notes, and need never ask, and would never be asked, for gold.

Very truly yours,
Henry H. Gibbs

You say I feel a pleasure in smiting you. There is something in that: one always has a pleasure in dealing a good-humoured blow at an adversary who gives good-humoured blows in return – especially when one has the best of it.

2, Norham Gardens, Oxford
January 5, 1878

My Dear Gibbs,

I cannot sufficiently thank you for your truly delightful letter, which I have just received and read. I am firmly persuaded that we do not differ in substance; no, not even about Rothschild's gold. But more of that anon, when I will go into your letter, I hope not too long.

I write now under particular circumstances. I sent to the press, a little time ago, a little book in MS., entitled, 'Chapters on Practical Political Economy' – you see I stick to it that I am a Practical Economist – and you do not object in a way. The Chapter on Rent is a reprint of a Lecture I gave to the Manchester Statistical Society, when people came down to see a battle go off between Jevons and me, as he had just published a book which contradicted my view. But the battle did not come off.

Well; I do not know why I should have bothered you with all this. A chapter or two was to have been a reprint of a part of my book on Currency and Banking. Paul objected, because it had been a book of their publishing. He has accepted the book, but I must re-cast the Currency Chapters a bit.

Then I told him of your Christmas present of 19 pages. He said, 'Can't we print it as introduction?' I smiled and said, 'That could hardly be done.'

Well, the thought occurs to me: might a very short letter be written to me by you on the general theory and practice of the Bank, as you put it, and with which generally I agree? This is a very vague idea of mine, without bodily parts, but I just lay it before you. Anyhow, I will modify my usual language as to the actual practice of the Bank and its ideas – *Teste Te* – not Grenfell. I really do not ask it: it is a pure raw thought. I have not yet got back the Chapters to go to work on.

You must have been pinching me when you talked of publishing for private circulation such a correspondence as ours. To pelt each other with chaff before the public, that would be really too good.

Yours very sincerely,
B. Price

St. Dunstan's, Regent's Park
January 7, 1878

My Dear Price,

I don't much like the idea of a letter for publication, but I will think about it, and let you know when I come back from Somerset, whither I go to-morrow.

I had no thought of printing, even for private circulation, our correspondence – only I should like my Governors to read it; and I should be glad to learn positively whether or no ail my colleagues do, as I believe (but as you don't believe), agree with me: that is to say, whether my belief and practice is the belief and practice of the 'Bank of England.'

Now, when I praised the excellence of your style, I did not extend my praise to your handwriting, and I am quite sure that if I gave them either your or my specimens of calligraphy, two out of three would leave them unread. So you see it's not by any means for distribution, but merely for the purpose of being read by my colleagues, that I should have some few copies made. I found it very instructive to myself to write the letters to you, and I think to read them may be instructive also to some of my colleagues; therefore Mr Coe shall strike them off, if you don't object.

I think we do agree *substantially* – even about Rothschild's gold. We should agree altogether if – especially about the dangers of a rise of discount – you had not listened too much to the *soi-disant* practical man who howls in the money-article of the day about the hardships it causes to his clients.

> Truly yours,
> Henry H. Gibbs

As to Grenfell. You must not take too much heed even of written words, unless the writer knows the precise point involved. If I had not known what you supposed our practice to be, *I* should have answered the question, 'what affects the rate of discount?' by 'the influx and efflux of gold.' Look at my letter of the 8th November, in which I dare say I implied as much. The fact being that I had no notion that anyone supposed, or thought we supposed, that anything could affect it but the state of our Reserve, and gold being the only thing which, *in ordinary* times, acts *violently* on our Reserve, it is natural enough to speak of that which frequently, though indirectly, affects the rate as that which governs the rate.

> *January* 6, 1878

My Dear Gibbs,

I have never thought that you gave intentionally any misconstruction to my words; but here and there you have misapprehended the bearing which I meant to give them. Nothing can possibly have been fairer in spirit, aye, and, spite of the fun, in words too, than your letters.

1. Yes: it is not your business to preach currency and banking doctrines: you practise them. But you spoke of the folly of the Press in misunderstanding your practice, and the ideas which underlie it. To apprehend you

correctly is of vast importance to all England. An enormous literature of the past and present steadily misrepresents your real thoughts. A literary man who preaches the truth is called a theorist, who knows nothing about the matter. These are the reasons why I asked not to be left in isolation.

I am most grateful for your permission to use your sentence about the Directors of the Bank.

2. I entirely agree – nay, I have never preached otherwise – that it is the exclusive business of the Directors to judge what Reserve is neccessary. Only, I have proclaimed that their guide is the state of their market, of its supply and demand; and not merely of the quantity of their gold and its fluctuations, by themselves alone. I understand you to say the same. An outsider cannot judge what Reserve the Deposits and their quality require. Personally, I believe that there are times when a very small Reserve is perfectly safe, and times when, with the same amount of Deposits, a very large one is called for. But I do not, and cannot know – nor have I ever pretended to know in a single one of my writings. The one urgent point is, that the commercial community should distinetly know that the movements of the gold, *as such*, are not the regulators of the rate of discount.

3. I quote your passage *in integro* ([p. 144], Dec. 19). 'Now again you (*i.e.* I) say, 'Reserve 10 millions; Bauk not having the account of the banks; times quiet; 5 millions go away to pay for corn; what harm?' You say I have not answered that question – then I will. I don't tie myself to precise figures, because they must depend on the character of our remaining Deposits; but, taking your question as a general one, my answer is short: *No harm at all!* Who says there is? *Quis vituperavit?* Pray don't rather upon the Bank of England the follies of others, the slipshod stuff of sciolists, the nonsense of newspapers, the crotchets of Crump.' ... 'In the case supposed, it may be that we *might* think proper to raise the rate, because it might be that our Reserve would be insufficient; but we should not be led to do so merely because a few millions of gold had gone away.'

Exactly; and so say I, and have said, and have been pronounced a heretic and a theorist for saying it.

May I quote – the case supposed, the words, 'no harm at all,' and the last quotation, 'it may be,' &c.

4. I ask – would the departure of 5 millions for so legitimate a purpose as the purchase of corn on a deficient harvest, have 'an action on the Reserve such as to threaten to make it insufficient for our requirements?' In other words, the departure of the gold renders the Reserve smaller over against the Deposits: but assuming, as I do, that the character of the Deposits has not altered, ought the diminished ratio to call for a rise of rate? If you say yes, then all I can say is that I do not see why: but here practice comes in – you are a banker, I am not. Still my reason is not convinced.

Anyhow, here is the capital point. I understand by the 'no harm' distinctly to mean, that the quantity of gold at the Bank – by itself – is no concern of the Bank; that it has no feeling of duty whatever to keep up a central stock for the nation; that all arguments in the Press derived from this source do not touch it; that its one *sole* concern is a proper Reserve for its own banking state, *whether there be much or little gold in the country*; and that, naturally and fittingly, the Directors are the judges of what that Reserve ought to be, with regard to the Bank's Deposits, their quality, the probabilities of their becoming larger or smaller. This I take to be your position – if so, then you and I are entirely at one.

Indeed, your sentence declares this to be your meaning. 'The fluctuations of gold do, potentially, but not necessarily, effect the rate of discount; nor at all, if their action on the Reserve is not such as to threaten to make it insufficient for our requirements; that they do not govern the rate is as plain as the sun at noon.'

5. You are most right; the publication of your Wednesday accounts is outrageous, and the parent of ills incalculable. It was the product of the Overstonian legislation, of people with fanciful and limited ideas, and full of timidity. Traders look to these accounts *faute de mieux*. They have no wit to guide themselves by understanding the commercial position of the day; they take the figures as a rule of thumb, without any knowledge of their relation to the actual position of the Bank; and the result is quackery. But where is the statesman who will have the courage to propose their suppression? More easy to find one who will tell the Russians, – If you come near Constantinople, we go into it.

By the way, with reference to what I wrote to you yesterday, to be allowed to quote, in my new book, from – in page 3 –'Every, the slightest fluctuation . . .' down to the end of page 4, would be invaluable for me, and I am convinced, more so yet for the whole commercial community.

6. 'A historical fact, stated in the tense "would have been." ' As I forget my words, I am in the dark here.

Yes, we must be somehow at 'cross-purposes' about suspension.

My fact is certain. The law said: No gold in store for the first 14 millions of notes issued; for every note-issue beyond these 14 millions, there shall be gold lodged in the Issue Department. In other words: all notes beyond 14 millions must be bought with gold. This is literally the one sole enactment of the law as to the issues of Bank of England notes. Well; there came three suspensions. In 1847 and 1866, on taking account, it was found that though the Bank was empowered to put out unlimited issues, nevertheless, the notes in circulation were covered with gold for every pound above 14 millions. The law was fully, though spontaneously, obeyed. In 1857, there were about £800,000 of notes out for which the prescribed gold did not exist in the Issue Department. If the line to which the uncovered issue might go had stood then, as now, at 15 millions, the law would have been obeyed to the letter.

All this is dry, hard fact, which any of your clerks can verify. What your fact is, I am vexed to say, I do not perceive or know: my dulness, no doubt.

You express it in two sentences: 'Had the line stood at 15 millions, the law would *not* have been fulfilled. The amount of issue when the crisis set in would have been precisely the same as it actually was at that time, and whatever need there was for a suspension would still have existed. The only difference would have been that there would have been exactly £1,000,000 less gold in the Issue Department.'

I have not the faintest notion of what this meaus. The fault, I am sure, is mine.

7. TUG I. – I agree, and have all along held the same. In the *Daily News*, two years ago, I pointed out two money-markets. I was right substantially in the expression; but my explanation shewed what you shew, that each bank acted for itself.

TUG II. – Your comments are great fun. I should uncommonly like to have you to cross-examine the Chambers of Commerce. You know, I should appear *now*, after your letters and the principles you take your stand on, not as an inveigher against the Bank, but, as an appreciator of its sound doctrine and practice. It really would be delicious.

But, you scoff at loss.

ANSWER. – In letter to Sir S. Northcote, I find, 'The extra 2 millions of loanable money – (city slang: it ain't money at all) – kept the Bank rate of discount down for a time, and enabled people temporarily to hold their goods at a less cost to themselves.' Then they might hold the goods at higher cost – which is tantamount to loss, however you may cry down its magnitude.

By the way, all admiration be given to you for that magnificent expression 'holding goods.' There you are in the very realities of banking, as I have so long preached, and alone. How many people are aware that bankers are mere exchangers of goods, as I said in my notice of Giffen in the *Contemporary*; they put goods into different hands: and that is *all* – though the machinery they work is very complex. I do not like the word 'accommodation:' it specifies nothing – only that a favour is done, but what favour it sayeth not.

I have no doubt whatever you are right – that a steady 4% would be the Paradise of Bankers; but do they, and can they, reach such a beatitude in modern trade?

Right, too, again about Somerset House. I never thought of it as a practicable thing; only used it to illustrate the separation – absolute – of the Departments.

TUG III. – Rothschild.

So I have not realized the law and practice of the Act since 1844. It is not too late for me to learn.

Rothschild, then, takes his million of gold to the Issue Department just as if it was in Somersetshire. Let us see.

You tell me a physical fact first. Rothschild does not give you the trouble of the cartage across the court; he directs his porter straight to the Issue

Department. But this is merely a question of who is to be the carter, a mere detail in itself. The gold was sure to go to the Issue Department for notes. The question is, how about them? You write, Rothschild does not touch the notes. 'He pays them into his account with us, if he is a customer of ours.' Exactly so; then they go to your Reserve, as I said, I believe, in my letter; 'or to his bankers in Lombard Street.' 'Then they may come on our banking books.' Exactly, again: you have got them at last.

Then what do I read in the Northcote letter?

'A, B & Co., the buyers of the gold, have paid us in their cheques, diminishing . . . in any case our deposits.'

Precisely, the gold bought for export is at your cost.

Then again – 'The importer of gold would bring it to the Bank.' Why, really, I find my own words here all round.

8. Let me express the very keen pleasure with which I see in the Northcote letter the fundamental principle so thoroughly treated – that the wants of the public alone regulate the quantity of notes in circulation. This principle I had to advocate for years in many writings, against the whole weight of Overstone and all the circulation doctors – parents of the Act of 1844, which they themselves did not understand. And now a writer in the *Economist* tells us that all the thought and language of that past generation is obsolete. This principle is the cardinal ruler of the quantity of all currency, as certain as that the number of hats in use is determined by the number of heads.

In respect of what I wrote yesterday, it occurs to me to lay before you, whether you would write me a letter for the new book, 'protesting' against my imputation on the Bank's practice, or allow me to quote passages – (not the controversial ones) – from these letters.

Yours very sincerely,
B. Price

Oxford
January 7, 1878

My Dear Gibbs,

You will say that I am intolerable; but with a correspondent of such precision and sharp thinking, and such an absence of the jargon which is the malaria of this region, it is hard to leave any important element uninvestigated. So forgive.

I must wish to speak of a detail, but a detail of supreme importance, and which was not touched in my letter of yesterday.

We are agreed on fundamental principles. The Bank must have a Reserve. Its practice is not governed by the fluctuations of the gold taken by themselves alone. The Reserve must be regarded in relation with the Deposits. Five millions of gold may go away to buy corn, in quiet times, without harm: that is, as I understand it, without any need, *so far as the loss of the gold extends*, for a rise of rate. The banking state of the Bank is the grand consideration. The character of the Deposits, as you put it, is the matter to be weighed. In my words, the state of the banking market, the character of its demand and supply, is the capital point.

Now these matters are very complicated, and admit of being judged by very various feelings and ideas. No two bankers may judge the situation alike. You say that the movements of the gold must be closely watched: that is, for me, a very suspicious expression, and brings an unpleasant corrector, possibly, on some of your propositions. The outer world holds that you lay down some abstract rule as to the ratio to be maintained between reserve and liabilities. This is very mechanical indeed, and these believers in gold get what they want – a rate all but directly dependent on the quantity of gold. I do not understand you to mean anything of the kind. You do, of course, estimate the size of the Reserve in conjunction with the liabilities: but you seem to me most clearly to imply that their character tells for much – the mood you may fancy depositors to be in – the present condition of your borrowers, their strength or their weakness, the state of trade, of the harvest, of peace or war, of over-production, of overloaded markets, and numberless other influences – which I sum up in the phrase, the state of the banking market, the conditions of its supply and demand, as of all other markets.

These feelings and appreciations have resulted in the most diverse relations of its Reserve of gold – (for it is gold, though held in its tickets, the notes) – to its liabilities at different periods; and further, in language that I have repeatedly used, in different rates of discount, as you yourself admit, going along with the most different amounts of Reserve. Further, as I have already pointed out, in 1866, the Bank, deliberately, of its own free will, ran up its loans from 18 to 33 millions during a crisis, reducing its Reserve to less than one million. You disapprove of that policy – you have an entire right to your judgment: but you admit that no harm or danger came to the solvency of the Old Lady, and so far that that policy, though mistaken, was compatible with the then banking market, and the Bank's position in it.

Now what I seek to learn from you, is, whether this description is not generally correct, so far as it bears on this specific point, that the amount of the Reserve, its ratio to liabilities, and the movements of the gold, are all capable of very wide variations, in perfect consistency with the Bank's safety. The size of the Reserve is a matter of opinion, to be judged by each Bank Director for himself; but, however mistaken he may be, there is no fixed, arbitrary, mechanical rule, which he is bound to observe as his principle, and which, if he violates, he is ignorant of, and offends against the law of his business. Hence, the banking of the Bank of England is the same, *mutatis mutandis*, as the operations of dealers at Ballinasloe fair – governed by the circumstances of the market at that hour.

I had written so far when your letter came. Really, I am startled at the thought of our rollicking chaff appearing in print. What can readers do but laugh when they see us hitting each other like two wild fellows? However, it may do them good to learn that amidst the absurdest merry-making, the most dismal part of the dismal science can be fathomed.

You make jibes on my calligraphy: but you would be surprised, if you saw any proof sent to me, how perfectly well compositors read it.

Yours very sincerely,
B. Price

January 12, 1878

My Dear Price,

My difficulty about writing you such a letter as you desire for publication, and about your quoting in your book passages from my letters to you, is, that though I fully believe the views I have there expressed to be the views of my colleagues, as well as of myself, I have, of course, no authority to speak for the Bank. But when I have shewn them our correspondence, and made myself sure that they agree with me, I can either write you a letter protesting against the false impression you had received, or else you can quote some passages from what I have already written.

But publication of partial quotations is a dangerous thing. There are many things you might quote of mine which are quite correct and quite harmless, taken with the context, but which look rather startling alone. If you do quote, let me see your proof before publication.

Now, to answer your letters of the 6th and 7th January. Whatever you quote, you must not, as you do in No. 3 of the 6th, give as my words in any hypothesis 'the Bank not having the accounts of the bankers.' I only took your words to that effect for the sake of argument. The absence of those accounts from our books would be so mischievous to the working of the great machine of London commerce, that it would be preposterous to suppose it. What I, and I presume you, meant was 'our Deposits being largely diminished.'

Never mind the laughing which may follow when this correspondence gets into type. It would, perhaps, be indecorous to see in published print a Professor of Political Economy and an Ex-Governor of the Bank belabouring one another with arguments clothed in lively vernacular; but for purely domestic use, *quid vetat?*

No doubt the compositors can read your hand: so can I – fluently; and so I could Greek, when I had once mastered the alphabet!

In answer to your question in No. 4 in the same letter, I can only say, 'I don't know!' The 5 millions might diminish both Reserve and Deposits, and the character of the remaining Deposits might be such as to make the remaining Reserve still amply sufficient; but it is obvious that, if an existing quantity of Reserve, at any given time, was no more than sufficient to meet the requirements of the Bank and the wants of existing depositors, any diminution of the Reserve would make it no longer sufficient, if the character of the Deposits and the state of the market have remained unchanged. If they *had* changed, it might be sufficient.

Probably the makers of the law of '44 may have thought it was desirable to have a store of gold in the country, and, for aught I know, so it may be. But that is their affair, not mine. It is a political rather than a banking question. The Bank has nothing to do with it, and is not, and ought not to be, influenced in its action in the slightest degree by any such supposed necessity.

As to a rise in the rate of discount: if you like to call 'cost' '*loss*,' I have no objection; only I affirm that increased cost of coals is in the same category as increased cost of loans, and that the amount is insignificant.

We shall come to that Paradise of Bankers when pigs, whether of iron, lead, or swine's flesh, are invariable in price, but not till then.

You have not quite apprehended the Bank's action in 1866, nor my objections to it. It was no policy of the Directors that their Reserve should be allowed to fall to a million. They lent as freely as they did, thinking it would *not* be so brought down. Remember loans, as such, don't affect *our* Reserve. Nothing does really, except the taking away of gold, and the hoarding of notes; and hoarding it was which falsified the expectations of the Bank Authorities in 1866. The credit of the Bank didn't suffer, of course; but commerce did. I don't object to their lending what they lent; but to their lending it on terms which, as events shewed, were not the real market terms, nor suited to the exigencies of the case.

At last I can conjecture how it is that we are at cross-purposes as to the suspension of the Act in 1857. You state facts, which, as you truly say, are verifiable; but you add a deduction, in which your 'would have been' comes in: 'if the line . . . had stood then, as now, at 15 millions, the law would have been obeyed.' And then you call fact and deduction together 'hard, dry fact.' But your deduction appeared to me to be the opposite of fact or truth, and the fact *was* as I stated it: the law would *not* have been fulfilled; but I now think you did not mean what I thought you did. My fact will be clear to you if you suppose the line to have been so drawn on January 1, 1854; follow out the process from that point as detailed in my letter to Northcote, and see where the Issue would stand on January 1, 1857.

But I think you must have meant to say, 'If the Government had *then* (when they issued the letter) drawn the line at 15 millions, instead of allowing an unlimited issue . . .' and that would, of course, have been true. Your word 'stood' misled me.

That part of your letter of the 7th, beginning 'now what I seek to learn . . .' states the real case of the Bank quite correctly. The banking state of the Bank is the grand consideration. There is no such abstract rule in our minds as to the ratio between Reserve and Deposits, as you say is supposed.

We know the character of our Deposits, and we know that, being what it is, the amounts both of Deposits and Reserve have to be disclosed to a public necessarily ignorant of that character, and we must take all such circumstances into consideration, and act accordingly.

But don't make any mistake about gold! Gold, or rather its movements, *must* be closely watched; but that phrase need not alarm you or any one. Of course they must be closely watched, because in all times but those of panic, gold is the *only* thing which really affects our Reserve. The efflux and influx of gold do take from or add to our reserve of notes, and therefore the fall and rise of our rate is often consequent upon, but never directly dependent upon, the movements of gold; but gold may flow out and in daily, and not affect our rate one whit.

You say people might think the rate 'all but directly' dependent upon gold. I don't understand 'all but directly.' It is very often *in*directly dependent, as I have laboured to shew; but in that '*in-*' lies the gist of the whole matter.

It is indirectly dependent on other things, too. The state of the borrowing market out-of-doors, – which state may or may not have been influenced by the movements of gold, – naturally affects us. If it approaches very nearly to our rate, and seems as if it would pass it if it could, naturally we go up. If it is much lower than our rate, and our own banking position allows it, naturally we go down. We have power to prevent a rise, because we are such large lenders, but we have none to prevent a fall.

Now I think the end of our long correspondence is, that we are substantially at one upon all the points which we have discussed; but I hope to be at Oxford at the end of the month, and I shall no doubt fall in with you, and we can talk over some details.

Sincerely yours,
Henry H. Gibbs

2, Norham Gardens, Oxford
January 15, 1878

My Dear Gibbs,

The correspondence has given me great pleasure and satisfaction in every way: and I thank you very warmly for the part which you have taken in it.

You do not speak of the printing in this last letter. I presume it is going on: if so, please do not forget what I asked, that I might see proofs of my effusions.

I have not the faintest desire to commit the Bank to any thing, nor to quote their authority for a single thing: that would be a vast deal too much even to think of. But to quote you, as an individual, is a different matter. We are in substantial agreement. We are in strong opposition to the general mass of outside opinion and writing. I am called a heretic and a theorist: you don't think me either. I have one great issue, as an economist, with the commercial literature: and 'substantially' you are on my side. Now to be able to say this in any way – by no means by letter, if you don't like it – would be of immense service to me, and, shall I add, to our cause? I take it that the passage in your letter of December 31st, in which you say: –

'Yes. If ever you write again, you may say that the Directors of the Bank of England do not hold the principle of a rate governed by mere fluctuations of gold, and do not act upon it.' May I add your name to that statement? I understood you to give it, but I should wish, before using it, to have more distinct leave. (Please answer these questions categorically.) And remember, that if you print the correspondence, opinion must ooze out, and with names, too: so that to use your name, to an authorized statement, is not the first act of publicity. My book is in the press – Kegan Paul & Co. – but the printing moves slowly.

At the end of the month, I shall be in London for a little while. I hope we may meet then.

Yours very sincerely,
B. Price

Appendix

London
March 12, 1875

My Dear Sir Stafford,

I think if I put down on paper the way in which the accounts would be worked under the two several conditions of which we were speaking the other day, you will see that, as regards the circulation, the supposed changes would neither contract nor expand it, except for the moment.

Those conditions were –

(1.) The increase, and, (2.) The decrease, of the Fiduciary Issue of Notes.

The Issue of the Bank of England is at present, in round numbers, £35,000,000–£10,000,000 with the Bank, £25,000,000 with the rest of the public, – of which £15,000,000 is on Securities, and £20,000,000 on Bullion. Our Reserve is now £10,000,000.

When there is a demand for Gold for the Continent, it is not the Notes in the hands of the public which are affected, for they increase or diminish according to the requirements of the public for circulation; but it is the Banking Reserve of the Bank of England which is diminished, and it is the Bank which has to see that that Reserve does not reach a point which is unsafe, compared with the amount of its Deposits; which are, I may mention, at this moment £26,000,000.

Let us see what is the operation of the movements of Gold.

I. The Bank working under the existing provisions of the Act of 1844.

Leaving out of the question any amount of Gold which the Bank could supply from the Banking Department (diminishing its Reserve *pro tanto*), and speaking only of that which it would take from the Issue Department, and supposing the demand to have amounted to £1,000,000, the operation would have been this:

A, B, and Co., the buyers of the Gold, have paid us in their cheques, on their own bankers, £1,000,000, diminishing, *pro tanto*, their balance with their bankers, and (unless *we* are their bankers) the general item of Bankers' Balances in our books, and, in any case, our Deposits.

THE BANK has transferred, out of its Banking Reserve of Notes, £1,000,000 into the Issue Department, for cancelment, and has delivered the Bullion, which they represent, to A, B, and Co.

The RESULT is, that the Reserve is lessened by one million, and stands at £9,000,000; and the Deposits by a like amount, and stand at £25,000,000.

But the Notes in the hands of the public, the active paper currency of the country, are in no wise affected. They stand as before, at £25,000,000.

What *may* happen is, that, having regard to the nature of the Deposits, the Bank may (or may not) think the proportion of Reserve to Deposits unsafe, and may raise its rate of discount, until, by attracting Gold from abroad, it redresses the proportion; but it cannot, by so doing, affect in any material degree the Notes in circulation.

In the above instance of the working of the Bank under its present laws, and in the instances which follow, I of course confine myself, when I describe the effect on our accounts, to this operation alone. – The Notes with the Public (and, indeed, every other item) may and will be affected by a legion of other daily transactions; but those transactions are not themselves affected by the movements of Bullion, or by the proportion which the Bullion bears to the total issue of Notes; and, being the same in all three cases, may be disregarded in the comparison of them.

I saw once some words of one of your predecessors to this effect – 'What seems to be the case in practice is, that we are settling balances progressively larger and larger with a Currency which, by banking expedients of all kinds, we contract and do not enlarge. But I should look on all forced and artificial remedies as likely to increase and not to mitigate inconvenience.'

I do not agree with this, about contracting the Currency, for reasons to which I will advert later; but I refer to the words above quoted, as an introduction to an inquiry whether an enlargement of the Fiduciary Issue would not be one of the forced and artificial remedies alluded to, which would increase rather than mitigate inconvenience.

II. Suppose, then, that it were determined to *increase* the Fiduciary Issue by two millions. How would it be done, and what would be the effect? Not, certainly, the keeping one single Note more in the hands of the public, nor the expansion, even potentially, of the Currency of the country in the least degree (though the temporary cheapening of accommodation *might*, possibly, for the moment cause some few more Notes to remain out than would otherwise be the case).

This is what would happen. The Bank would transfer £2,000,000 of its Securities to the Issue Department, receiving in its Banking Department an equal sum in Notes, the Reserve consequently reading £12,000,000.

Some time or other a demand for Gold would come. A million would go, and again another million, without its being necessary or even prudent for the Bank to endeavour to check it; the Reserve again reading, as now, £10,000,000, and being an ample provision for the Deposits of £26,000,000.

What have you done, then? Two things only: you have temporarily altered the relation of the money of the country to commodities by a sudden outpouring of Notes into the Bank Reserve (for the extra two millions of loanable money kept the Bank rate of discount down for a time, and enabled people temporarily to *hold* their goods at a less cost to themselves); and –

You have permanently, though not, indeed, very dangerously, affected the convertibility of the Note. The Issue would still be £35,000,000, but the Gold fund for conversion would be £18,000,000, instead of £20,000,000.

Nor would the Gold ever come back to displace your two extra millions of Securities. Come back, it would; but only in the exact manner, and under the identical conditions, under which it now does – swelling the Bank Reserve, and continuing to do so until a lower rate of discount and adverse exchanges again carried it away.

The Notes with the Public would remain practically unaltered at £25,000,000.

The same would be the case whatever number of millions you added to the Fiduciary Issue. You would do *mischief* by any addition, because you would impair the *reputation* of the Note for convertibility.

But *danger* would only begin when you had reached the point where the proportion of Notes to Gold was so large as to impair the *real* convertibility of the Note.

III. Now, let us reverse the operation, and suppose the Fiduciary Issue to be *diminished* by two millions.

It is quite conceivable (though not likely) that such a course might be taken; as a step to our having, as Hamburgh had, a Note-circulation wholly based on Bullion [there on Silver Bullion]; the Notes being practically only *receipts* – vouchers for the possession by the issuer of so much Bullion, the property of the Note-holder; but I discuss the case here as a parallel to the opposite proposal.

How would it be worked?

Probably a day would be fixed on which the issue on Securities should read £13,000,000 instead of £15,000,000.

The Bank would in the interim have to keep the rate of discount up beyond what would otherwise be necessary, so as gradually to attract Gold from abroad.

The importer of Gold would bring it to the Bank; his banker's balance, and, consequently, our Deposits, would be swollen by the amount; the Gold would go into the Issue Department, and instead of issuing its value in Notes to the Banking Department, the Issue Department would from time to time, and as the operation proceeded, hand back Securities to the Banking Department, until the limit of two millions, or whatever other limit might be fixed, was reached.

The Notes in the hands of the public would not change, or have changed, one iota *owing to this operation*. When it was completed, they would still read £25,000,000.

The Reserve would again be £10,000,000, and the total Issue £35,000,000, neither more nor less; but –

The Fiduciary Issue would be £13,000,000, and the Bullion £22,000,000.

To make the matter clearer, and to meet the exact case suggested by you, I will assume this latter operation to have been continued to the point of extinguishing the Fiduciary Issue altogether, and resting the Notes wholly on Gold.

That is wholly a question of Currency and Convertibility. The question of the supply of the pecuniary needs of the public is wholly a question of Banking, and would not be affected in the remotest degree by a Bullion Currency, or a Currency based wholly on Bullion.

For, supposing such a Currency to exist, and that, consequently, while our Notes issued were, as now, £35,000,000, the Bullion in the Issue Department £35,000,000, a drain of Gold would not (as the foregoing operations show) touch the Notes with the Public; nor would the public be affected by it at all except (*as they are now*) by the lessening of the Banking Reserve, and the consequent scarcity and higher price of accommodation.

Every bar of Gold taken away would follow exactly the same course, and with exactly the same effect, on the public, as it does under the present system, or as it would were the Fiduciary Circulation increased.

I said above, that I did not agree with the statement that 'the Currency was contracted by banking expedients.' No banking expedients – that is, no improvements in the economy of banking – can avail to contract (if by 'contract' we mean *restrict*) the Currency. As well might we say that *one* steam-engine which does the work of *forty* horses contracts the means of locomotion. By employing it, we contract or diminish the *number of locomotives*; but *one* does the work of *forty*; and, in like manner, good economy in banking makes one £5 Note do the work of forty. It diminishes not the power of getting what currency is needed, but the *need* of using so *much*.

In the same way, no banking or legislative expedients can really increase the Currency. They may temporarily, as I have shewn, increase its *bulk*, but only at the cost of proportionally diminishing its effective character.

They may, indeed, increase the *Note*-currency by the issue of £1 Notes, abstracting or setting free, *pro tanto*, Gold from the pockets of the public, but this will in no way alter the quantity of the joint-currency of Gold and Notes.

Whatever amount of circulation commerce wants, commerce will have, – borrowers meanwhile sometimes paying more, sometimes less, for their borrowings, – but the amount being wholly independent of the movements of Bullion.

A proof of this is, that in the last twenty years the Note-circulation in the hands of the public has gradually increased from a maximum of about £20,000,000, to a maximum of £27,000,000; and the fluctuations in this amount take place with the regularity of the tides, obeying the wants of commerce, but wholly unaffected by the exchanges, and the consequent efflux and influx of Bullion.

That the Note-circulation has not been increased infinitely more, to keep pace with the vast increase of our commerce, is the result of those banking expedients to which allusion has been made above.

> I remain,
> My Dear Sir Stafford,
> Sincerely yours,
> Henry H. Gibbs

The Right Hon.
Sir Stafford Northcote, Bart., M.P.

P.S. – When I say above, that Banking Expedients do not 'contact' the circulation, I use a somewhat ambiguous term: I don't mean, of course, that the Bank of England Notes in the hands of the public are not less in amount now than they would be without those expedients. What I mean is, that these expedients do not *limit* the amount, or in any way prevent or affect its indefinite expansion, wherever and so far as such expansion is needed.

If there were none of those Banking Expedients, we should then have an enormous Note-circulation, which would, though very clumsily, fulfil exactly those functions which a small one now does, and with nothing to spare; and then, as now, and precisely as now, neither more nor less, would that circulation expand as the needs of commerce required.

London
March 25, 1875

My Dear Sir Stafford,

Thank you for your note of the 15th, and for the return of my letter. I send it you back, copied out afresh with some few verbal alterations for the sake of greater clearness, and with a P.S. addressed to the first half of your note.

As to the 'doubt' expressed in the second half; – certainly the action you describe would, as you say, add to the amount of Notes with the Public.

I have said that the fluctuations of the Note-circulation have a tidal character – have their ebb, their flow, their spring and neap – which can be calculated with certainty, if not with numerical exactness. The abnormal addition to which you refer, would be like a volcanic wave, and would disturb all ordinary trdal calculations.

It is a PANIC which you describe – a panic which takes the form of Note-boarding; and when that happens, nothing can quench the fire but its burning out, or a cessation of the fear as unreasonable as its beginning, or – a *Deus ex machina.*

But this is a matter rather of Banking than of pure Currency, though the Currency has been disturbed by the disappearance of a certain number of Notes, which have ceased for the time to circulate.

In such a case, a forced and temporary addition to the legal Issue of the Bank of England – an injection of fresh blood, in the shape of an extra million or two of Notes, into the veins of the sinking patient, Commerce – may avail sometimes, by quieting men's minds and supplying their immeidate necessities, to remedy the inconvenience caused by the abnormal demand for Notes, but no permanent addition to the Fiduciary Issue could have any such effect, or indeed, as I have shown, any beneficial effect at all.

You say, in your note, 'if you *cannot* check the drain of Gold by raising the rate of Discount.' But the Bank can *always* check the drain of Gold by that means, when the Gold has to be procured by borrowing from it, and *so* it must always be procured in the last resort. I will say more. The Bank, by acting in time, can always prevent, if not a panic, yet certainly the dangers which lead to a panic. When a panic has once set in, our power is gone.

Sincerely yours,
Henry H. Gibbs

P.S. – I may add a corollary to my long letter of the 12th. It is this:

That the Fiduciary Issue is of no importance whatever to Commerce:

And that the only appreciable profit or advantage springing from that Issue accrues to the Issuer – *i.e.* to the State, which is the real Issuer – and to the Bank, which, as the agent of the State, takes a portion of the profit for its trouble in the administration of the Issue.

London,
May 5, 1875

My Dear Sir Stafford,

I send you the print of my two letters to you, and I have only to add a word of explanation of one term in the first of them.

By 'Notes with the Public' we understand those Notes which are in the hands of other persons than the Bank of England.

Looking at it from an 'Issue Department' point of view, the Notes which *we* hold are as truly 'Notes with the *Public*' as are those held by a man in Berwick-upon-Tweed; for the Bank, in its banking capacity, is one of the Public.

But the distinction is a proper one as made in my letter; because, from a 'Banking Department' point of view, the Notes so held by us form the greatest part of our Reserve; and it is our Reserve only, and not the Notes in the tills of other people, which is acted upon by the Export and Import of Gold.

I remain,
Very truly yours,
Henry H. Gibbs

7 The art of central banking
The lender of last resort

R. G. Hawtrey

A central bank is a banker's bank. It affords to the other banks of the community, the competitive banks, the same facilities as they afford to their customers. The competitive banks make payments to one another by drawing on balances at the central bank, they draw out currency against those balances or pay currency in, as their business may require, and they replenish their balances, when low, by borrowing from the central bank.

These facilities being secured to them, the competitive banks are relieved from responsibility for the provision of currency. They still have to keep their position liquid, but this they can do by maintaining sufficient assets of the kind that can be pledged or rediscounted with the central bank. The exclusive responsibility for seeing that the supply of currency in the community is adequate, and no more than adequate, devolves upon the central bank.

The real reason for that is not, as is sometimes supposed, that the central bank is usually a bank of issue, with the power of creating currency in the form of its own notes. Even if it has no such power and has to dispose of a strictly limited supply of currency, still, so long as it never refuses to lend to any borrower who complies with the customary conditions (provided the customary conditions are not unduly narrow) the competitive banks can always command access to additional supplies of currency.

The Central Bank is the *lender of last resort*. That is the true source of its responsibility for the currency. If there were no right of issue, and the currency were based exclusively on a specie standard (the use of coin as hand to hand currency), the central bank would be absolutely dependent upon its reserves of coin to meet any increased demand for currency. This was approximately the position of the Bank of England in the nineteenth century for, though its notes were legal tender after 1833 (and were practically equivalent to legal tender before), the minimum denomination after 1829 was £5, and, for most of the purposes of hand to hand currency, notes could not fill the place of coin. The consequence was that the joint-stock banks relied on the Bank of England to supply them with gold coin, and the resulting liability was a very real one.

That was the theme of Bagehot's *Lombard Street*. In Bagehot's view, the 'natural' system of banking was that of many banks each keeping its own cash reserve, but the system of a single bank keeping the whole reserve of the country had in fact grown up, and 'you might as well, or better, try to alter the English monarchy and substitute a republic, as to alter the present constitution of the English Money Market, founded on the Bank of England, and substitute for it a system in which each bank shall keep its own reserve.'

The London discount market

The Bank of England was the first central bank, and its evolution was on somewhat different lines from that of later examples. Historically its rediscounting business grew up not so much with other banks as with merchants. In the eighteenth century, the London merchant would ordinarily rely on a private banker to discount his bills. If the amount of bills offered for discount became excessive, and the private bankers were unwilling to take any more, the merchants would come direct to the Bank of England.

This was not a rediscounting system, but it played essentially the same part. The Bank of England stood ready to take bills, and when it took bills it added to its liabilities, which were actually or potentially currency. The bills became the channel through which the community was supplied with additional cash.

The system of passing on the overflow of bills to the Bank of England required for its smooth working the constitution of a *market* in bills. It would frequently happen that some banks had taken all the bills they could afford to take, while others were still short of them. The merchants refused by the former group of banks would not have to come to the Bank of England if only they were aware of the position of the latter group.

The essential function of the bill brokers who created the discount market was to enable any merchant who wanted his bills discounted to find any bank which wanted to discount bills. The result was that only a real excess of bills over what the banks could take was brought to the Bank of England.

In the latter part of the eighteenth century, there was an enormous development of the country banks in England, private note-issuing banks all over the country outside London. These banks were always discounting bills for their customers, and among them many bills on London, as the marketing centre where the merchants were gathered together. A country bank would transmit these bills on London to a London bank which acted as its correspondent, and the latter would get them accepted. The country bank would want to hold some of the bills as a London reserve (either leaving them for safe keeping with the correspondent bank or bringing them home after acceptance). The rest it would want to sell in order to meet current liabilities in London.

The sales of bills on account of country banks contributed materially to extend the operations of the discount market. In the second quarter of the nineteenth century, a further refinement of the system was realised. A bank which found its cash in London exposed to the considerable daily fluctuations incidental to the active accounts of customers engaged in commercial and financial business on a large scale, would either have to lose interest on a relatively large idle reserve or be involved in constant purchases and sales of bills. To avoid the inconvenience of the latter alternative, the practice grew up of lending money at call or short notice to the bill-brokers. The bill-brokers, ceasing to be mere brokers, bought bills and held them on their own account, and paid the banks interest on the money lent at a rate a little below the average yield of the discount on the bills. To the banks it was convenient to call up just so much money as was needed for the day, or to lend just so much as could be spared. And the bill-brokers found that in general when one bank called up money another had more to lend, so that they were not exposed to the inconvenience of frequent purchases and sales of bills. Only when the banks as a whole were short of money did the sums received by the bill-brokers fall short of the sums called up. In that case they had recourse to the Bank of England. When Samuel Gurney gave evidence before the Parliamentary Committee of 1848 (Qn. 1344), it was still a novelty for the bill-brokers to get bills rediscounted by the Bank not as intermediaries but as principals. And, after the crisis of 1857, the Bank tried for a time to restore the earlier practice and exclude them from the rediscounting system. But experience showed that this was impracticable.[1] The organisation of the market was such that the need for rediscounts was inevitably felt primarily by the bill-brokers or 'discount houses' as they are more accurately called, and to ignore them would have been merely to introduce an unnecessary complication. Thus the discount market came to be the regular agency for procuring cash for the banks through rediscounting with the Bank of England.

The Bank of England before 1844

The Bank of England did not easily or willingly assume the responsibilities of the lender of last resort. At the end of the eighteenth century we find it giving accommodation grudgingly.

In the crisis of 1793 the ordinary discounting facilities offered by the Bank were found inadequate. Merchants found themselves burdened with stocks of goods temporarily unsaleable. There were no purchasers on whom bills were to be drawn. The Government intervened by making advances to them, in the form of Exchequer bills, on the security of merchandise. The Bank would not make advances on merchandise, but it would on the Exchequer bills. The effect was much the same as if the Government had guaranteed the advances to the traders. The Government could itself have advanced money only by borrowing the requisite sums from the Bank. The actual procedure employed had the advantage of keeping down the cash advanced by the Bank to a minimum. The merchant who received Exchequer bills felt his position

---

1 See Professor Gregory's Introduction to his *Select Statutes, etc.*, pp. xxxii–xxxiv.

secure; he had the power of raising cash in case of need, and was content to use only so much of that power as his daily business essentially required. The same plan of making advances of Exchequer bills was resorted to again in the crisis of 1811.

The Bank was definitely confronted with the responsibilities of the lender of last resort in December, 1795. The rediscounting system had broken down in 1793 because the embarrassed merchants were not in a position to draw bills. In December, 1795, the bills were forthcoming, but the Bank was exposed to a heavy drain of gold, and feared that the continuance of the customary unrestricted facilities for discount would exhaust its reserve. The directors decided to ration discounts. That is to say, if on any day bills sent for discount exceeded an amount resolved upon, the amount taken from each applicant would be reduced in proportion and the remainder returned to him. This amounted to a partial repudiation of the position of lender of last resort.

There followed the period of the Restriction of Cash payments, 1797–1821. Under inflationary conditions the prevalent rate of commercial profit became disproportionately high. As the Bullion Committee of 1810 pointed out, the usury laws, which limited interest to 5 per cent, had the effect of expanding the demand for discounts under those conditions. And the Bank, being exempted from the obligation to pay specie, felt no need to ration discounts or place any other restriction upon them.

After the return of the currency to parity the inflated profits that had made a 5 per cent. Bank rate count as low passed away, and there ensued a period in which the discounting of commercial bills by the Bank became relatively exceptional, and its principal assets were Exchequer bills and other Government securities.

But at a time of pressure, whether due to exceptional activity or to a shock to credit, the demand on the Bank for discounts immediately revived. The tradition that at such times the Bank should never refuse to accommodate any eligible borrower gradually became established.

That responsibility was not assumed explicitly, or very willingly, by the Bank. The first test of the Bank's lending policy after the resumption of cash payments came in the crisis of 1825. A heavy external drain of gold had left the country short of currency. Extreme credit stringency, and a collapse of commodity prices developed into panic, accompanied by runs on banks. The Bank of England continued to discount bills of the type it was always accustomed to take. But that was not sufficient. There were banks and financial houses that had to meet such heavy withdrawals by depositors that their holdings of bills eligible for discount were quickly exhausted. If they were to be saved, they would have to be enabled to borrow on the security of other assets.

The banks were private partnerships, and their 'capital,' the margin of their assets over their liabilities, was composed simply of the private fortunes of the partners, and would usually include considerable blocks of Government securities. At the height of the panic, on the 14th December, 1825, the Bank of England (acting in close consultation with the Government) suddenly relaxed its usual practice, and made advances upon such securities instead of limiting itself to discounting bills. It does not sound a very tremendous concession. In giving evidence before the Committee of 1832, a Director of the Bank, Jeremiah Harman, gave the impression that the Bank had gone to extreme lengths. It lent money, he said, 'by every possible means and in modes we had never adopted before; we took in stock on security, we purchased Exchequer bills, we made advances on Exchequer bills, we not only discounted outright, but we made advances on the deposit of bills of exchange to an immense amount, in short by every possible means consistent with the safety of the Bank, and we were not on some occasions over nice.'

In reality the advances he instanced were of a highly conservative character. The importance of the change of practice was that it admitted a class of borrowers on irreproachable security, who had nevertheless been barred by the previous limitations. The concession was a real one, and it stayed the panic.

Nevertheless it did not prove sufficient to restore the normal activity of business. By the end of February, 1826, the Ministers were being pressed by the City to relieve the situation by an issue of Exchequer bills, as in 1793 and 1811. But they 'advised the Bank to take the whole affair into their own hands at once, to issue their notes on the security of goods, instead of issuing them on Exchequer bills, such bills being themselves issued on that security.'[2]

Lending on merchandise was a further departure from ordinary practice, especially at a time when panic was passing into depression, and advances were sought just because the merchandise could not be sold. The actual amount of such advances granted by the Bank was not very great, but it is significant that the concession was made at the instance of the Government.

Before the next crisis arose, a new power had been conferred upon the Bank in the exemption of discounts from the usury laws. And in 1839, for the first time, it defended itself against excessive demands for accommodation by raising Bank rate above 5 per cent. It was raised no higher than 6 per cent, but the question of how far the Bank should go in lending did not then become acute.

With the use of Bank rate as an instrument for controlling credit, and so for regulating the monetary situation and the foreign exchanges, we shall deal later on. For the present we are concerned with it only as an expedient for keeping the demands upon the Bank as the lender of last resort within bounds.

2 Quoted by Bagehot from the Duke of Wellington's Despatches. The letter was written by Peel to Wellington on the 3rd March, 1826. Bagehot did not observe that it came long after the first and most important relaxation of the Bank's lending conditions.

The Bank of England, 1844–73

The next phase was initiated by the Bank Charter Act of 1844, separating the Issue Department from the Banking Department and establishing the fixed fiduciary issue. The policy of the Act, as understood by the Bank and stated by the Government to the Select Committee of 1848, was that the Banking Department 'is to be managed in the same way as any other private bank,' except so far as the magnitude of its operations and its position as holder of the Government account placed it in a special position (Questions 2653 and 2845. See *Select Statutes, Documents and Reports relating to British Banking*, by Professor T. E. Gregory, vol. ii., pp. 19, 28).

Logically it would seem to follow that the Bank had no more obligation to lend or rediscount in times of need than 'any other private bank.' The supply of currency in the country was restricted to the coin in circulation together with the strictly limited note issue of the Issue Department. The Banking Department had to compete on equal terms with all other banks for its share of this supply. If there was a shortage, that affected the Banking Department in the same way as the other banks, and it would have to restore the position in the same way as the others by restricting credit, and in the last resort refusing to lend.

So far as the Statute was concerned, there was nothing to contradict this doctrine. In the period of tension that arose in the spring of 1847 and preceded the crisis of that year, the Bank acted accordingly, and limited its discounts, as it had in 1795. When, in October, 1847, tension culminated in crisis, and crisis in panic, the Government once again intervened. In 1825 the reluctance of the Bank to lend had been due to the dwindling of its holding of bullion and specie. When it changed its policy and lent freely, it was taking the risk of the complete exhaustion of the reserve and a renewed suspension of gold payments. In 1847 the reserve in the Banking Department was similarly dwindling. But the reserve in the Banking Department was no more than a legal concept, the offspring of the Act of 1844. The Act ordained that the notes issued should be equal to the fixed fiduciary issue of £14,000,000 *plus* the metallic reserve in the Issue Department. The notes in the Banking Department which composed the reserve were the excess of the issue thus legally defined over the amount of notes actually issued, the 'active circulation.'

The unwillingness of the Bank to lend in 1847 was due not to any insufficiency of gold (for it held more than £8,000,000 of bullion and specie), but to the shrinkage of the legally defined margin. The risk to be run was not of a suspension of gold payments, but of a breach of the law.

Here the Government, in virtue of its constitutional position as possessing the confidence of Parliament, was able to help, for it could promise legislation indemnifying the Bank for breaking the law.

Ministers were faced with a clear issue. By promising the indemnifying legislation they could place the Bank in a position to lend freely. They decided to take this formidable responsibility, and the first example of the famous 'crisis letters' was the result. The letter, signed by the Prime Minister and the Chancellor of the Exchequer, recommended the Directors of the Bank 'to enlarge the amount of their discounts and advances on approved security; but that in order to retain this operation within reasonable limits, a high rate of interest should be charged,' viz. not less than 8 per cent, and the letter promised a bill of indemnity if the law were broken.

The Bank did not ask for this letter. The initiative was taken by the Government. The object of the Government's intervention was to induce the Bank 'to enlarge the amount of their discounts and advances on approved security.' The rediscounting facilities were the root of the matter. The panic was attributed to the Act of 1844 because the limit placed upon the fiduciary issue was the obstacle to free lending by the Bank, and relief was given by suspending the limit. That once done, the panic subsided and it was not found necessary actually to exceed the limit.

On the occasion of the crisis of 1857 the Government again issued a crisis letter on its own initiative, but there had been no actual restriction of discounts and advances by the Bank, and the Governor confessed that he was in reality counting on the letter. The crisis of 1857 originated abroad and was particularly acute in America. It was accompanied by a heavy outflow of gold, and, the metallic reserve of the Bank being reduced substantially lower than in 1847, an actual excess on the fiduciary limit was incurred, and duly condoned by Parliament in a subsequent indemnifying Act.

A third crisis letter was evoked by the crisis of 1866. But on that occasion the Bank took the initiative in approaching the Government. And though they did not expressly ask for the authority to exceed the fiduciary limit, they frankly accepted the responsibility of unstinted lending. 'We have not refused any legitimate application for assistance,' they said in their letter to the Chancellor of the Exchequer.

Bagehot quotes a passage from the speech of the Governor of the Bank to the Court of Proprietors in September, 1866, 'We had to act,' the Governor said, 'before we could receive any such power [to exceed the fiduciary issue], and, before the Chancellor of the Exchequer was perhaps out of his bed, we had advanced one-half of our reserves, which were certainly thus reduced to an amount which we could not witness without regret. But we could not flinch from the duty which we conceived was imposed upon us of supporting the banking community, and I am not aware that any legitimate application made for assistance to this house was refused.'

This statement of policy was the text from which Bagehot preached. The policy had not been undisputed in the interval between 1866 and the year, 1873, when he wrote. The old doctrine that the Banking Department ought to be conducted like any other bank still found influential advocates. But the lucid common sense of *Lombard Street* was itself decisive. Since then the responsibilities of the Banking Department as the lender of last resort have been unequivocally recognised.

Eligible bills and securities

The essential duty of the central bank as the lender of last resort is to make good a shortage of cash among the competitive banks. But that cannot mean that it should lend to *any* bank that needs cash, regardless of the borrowing bank's behaviour or circumstances. Neither a commercial concern nor a public institution could undertake to supply cash to insolvent borrowers. A commercial concern in particular cannot afford to take risks out of proportion to its own capital.

In the evolution of the Bank of England as the lender of last resort, we have seen how at the beginning it was inclined to ration credit by refusing all applications in excess of a quota, but later on its restriction took the form of limiting the kind of security it would take. It is not ordinarily possible to examine in detail the entire assets of an applicant for a loan. Demonstration of solvency therefore cannot be made an express condition of the loan, at any rate at a time when the need for cash has become urgent. But the furnishing of security makes scrutiny of the general solvency of the borrower unnecessary. The secured debt being covered by assets more than equivalent to it, there is less need to enquire whether the remainder of the borrower's assets will be sufficient to cover the remainder of his debts.

A bank, the ordinary deposit liabilities of which are unsecured, ought of course to be readily able to find security for such loans as may be occasionally necessary to make good a casual shortage of cash. So long as nothing more than that is required, the central bank can give adequate facilities by undertaking to rediscount bills of exchange of the most unexceptionable type.

In the eighteenth century the greater part of the lending operations of banks took the form of the discounting of their customers' bills of exchange. A bank which needed cash would raise it by selling bills, and it was to meet this need that the discount market grew up in London. In the early nineteenth century the bills dealt in in the market were predominantly those drawn to finance the internal trade of the country, though bills drawn to finance foreign trade were continually growing in importance. As the practice of financing internal trade by advances and over-drafts grew, the internal bill became a rarity, but such was the development of foreign trade and of acceptances on behalf of foreign clients as well as of the ordinary import bills, that the London discount market became bigger and more active than ever. Bills still formed a sufficient proportion of the banking assets of London to play their traditional part in the rediscounting system.

When a central bank rediscounts a bill, it relies on the credit of the names that appear on the bill. Besides the names of the drawer and the acceptor, there will appear that of the bank which was the first holder and which had sold the bill, and there may be endorsements by intermediate holders. The names will include those of traders and those of bankers. At a time of pressure, when the central bank requires a test of solvency, the endorsement of a banker, which would ordinarily be unquestioned, is no longer conclusive as to the goodness of the bill. For the danger to be guarded against is that the facilities offered by the central bank as the lender of last resort may be abused by banks whose position has become impaired. Their embarrassment usually arises from the embarrassments of their customers. Debts due from traders have become temporarily or perhaps permanently irrecoverable. It is at a time of pressure, when there has been a general decline of commodity prices, that such embarrassments become widespread, and banks which have been prudently conducted according to accepted standards find themselves never-theless in difficulties. Their difficulties will undoubtedly be concealed, so long as concealment is possible. At such a time the central bank, like Descartes's sceptic, must doubt everything.

The need has therefore been felt for some further criterion of the sound-ness of bills to supplement that of the credit of the names upon them. And a code of morality has grown up in the bill market. The virtuous bill is that which is drawn by the seller of goods despatched to a buyer who is himself in a position to sell them without delay. The bank which buys the bill is financing the seller and the buyer for the strictly limited interval required for the transport and disposal of the goods. Provided all goes according to plan, the bill is 'self-liquidating.' And in any case the buyer, on whom or on whose account the bill has been drawn, has in the goods an asset to hold against his liability. (The goods can actually supply a collateral security for the bill so long as bills of lading are attached to it, but the bills of lading have to be detached to permit of the goods being sold before the maturity of the bill.)

By contrast with the self-liquidating commodity bill the finance bill or accommodation bill, which is no more than a device to enable the drawer to borrow temporarily on the credit of the acceptor, is an object of suspicion and condemnation.

It has very commonly been the practice of central banks to favour com-modity bills, and they have sometimes been bound by their statutes to confine their rediscounts to such bills. The discrimination is not entirely without justification. The commodity bill is a normal outcome of commercial business; the reason for its existence is the time necessarily occupied by the transporta-tion and marketing of goods. Any other bill *may* be a signal of distress, or the outcome of some imprudence or vagary. Like all temporary borrowing, it ought to be no more than an anticipation of forthcoming receipts. But in practice forthcoming receipts are apt to be offset by forthcoming liabilities, and it may be that the bill has to be paid at maturity by the proceeds of another temporary borrowing operation.

But if it is legitimate for any business to be financed by a bank advance, it is difficult to give any good reason why it should not as legitimately be financed by a bill. That the bill is marketable and that there are special sanctions for prompt payment at maturity, these are advantages to the lender who discounts it, in virtue of which the borrower obtains more favourable terms than for a bank advance. The special merits of the 'self-liquidating' commodity bill are in reality very dubious. Any bill which is drawn to meet a genuinely temporary need for cash is self-liquidating. And the expectation that commodities can be promptly sold or can be sold without loss is liable to disappointment just as much as any other expectation of forthcoming receipts.

In giving evidence before the U.S. National Monetary Commission in 1910, the then Governor of the Bank of England instanced as legitimate finance bills those '(*a*) representing exchange transactions; (*b*) made to carry stocks of goods or securities; (*c*) made in anticipation of public loans.' These he contrasted with 'accommodation bills pure and simple.'

The real point is that the accommodation bill is a sign of distress. It is not drawn to supply funds for the acquisition of an asset, but to make good a deficiency of cash due to disappointed expectations. And this is precisely the case which throws a special responsibility on the central bank as the lender of last resort.

The commodity bill is a fair-weather security. So long as the central bank only requires suitable machinery for bringing about expansions and contractions of credit for the normal purposes of monetary regulation, it serves very well.

But at moments of discredit, such as occur when a heavy fall of commodity prices has impaired the position of many debtors, the commodity bill has two defects. In the first place, in an unfavourable market it ceases to be self-liquidating; there may be both delay and loss in selling the goods financed by the bill. And secondly, there may be applicants for loans, whose position is ultimately sound and solvent, and who ought to be assisted, but who cannot furnish commodity bills sufficient in amount to cover the loans needed.

That does not mean that finance bills then become a desirable form of security. In fact, there is an obvious danger that a finance bill may be drawn and accepted by people whose credit though reputed good has in reality been weakened. The right course is rather to accept *any* security representing a sufficient amount of wealth to cover the loan with adequate margin, without being too particular in defining the form of the security or even in insisting on its immediate marketability.

The requirements of the central bank as to security react upon the practice of the competitive banks. By limiting its rediscounts in normal times to a class of eligible bills (or promissory notes like the American 'commercial paper') it gives a preferential encouragement to the use of the securities so favoured. Eligible bills will command a relatively low rate of discount. The evil reputation of finance bills has been partly due to their being created for the purpose of masquerading as commodity bills and obtaining the advantages of eligibility.

The central bank can discourage any special class of business, such, for example, as advances for speculation, by letting it be known that it will discriminate against banks undertaking such business. In an emergency, the central bank may have to pass judgment at a moment's notice on the solvency of an applicant for assistance, and the appearance among its assets of items regarded as undesirable may result in its application being barred.

Among the several classes of securities that may be acquired by central banks, Government securities are the subject of sharply conflicting views. On the one hand, they are regarded as the safest and most readily realisable of assets. If a country has a bill market, the bills constituting the Government's floating debt will be the most marketable. And among all the long-term obligations dealt in in the investment market, the most marketable will be those of the Government.

But on the other hand, the acquisition of Government securities by the central bank is regarded as opening the door to inflation. It is usual for the power of the central bank to *lend* to the Government to be carefully circumscribed, and the dividing line between lending direct and buying Government securities in the market may be rather a fine one. The Bank of England and the American Federal Reserve Banks are quite free to buy Government securities (though till the passage of the Glass-Steagall Act in February, 1932, the latter could not use them as backing for their note issue). The Bank of France on the other hand is precluded from acquiring any (apart from its permanent holdings) except when National Defence Notes are offered to it for rediscount.

Inflationary Government finance is a subject to which we shall return at a later stage.

The Bank of England and the note issue

If the essential characteristic of a central bank is its function as the lender of last resort rather than its privilege of note issue, that does not mean that the evolution of the former function has not been intimately associated with that of the latter. It is obvious that a bank which can create currency in an emergency out of nothing has a great advantage, in facing the responsibilities of the lender of last resort, over one which runs the risk of stopping payment if a reserve of specie, which cannot be unlimited, is exhausted.

Till Bank of England notes were made legal tender in 1833, the only exclusive privilege of the Bank in regard to note issue was that, among note-issuing banks, it had a monopoly of the constitution of a joint-stock company. It was this privilege which gave it its pre-eminence. Private banks were limited to six partners, and no six partners could possibly be found whose joint fortunes would come anywhere near rivalling the huge capital of the Bank. The capital of a bank is a guarantee fund against losses, and the magnitude of the bank's operations is limited by prudence to a due proportion of this guarantee fund.

A financial crisis arises in a banking system when the banks find themselves short of money. In general the shortage is experienced in the payments from bank to bank. A bank which lends more freely than its neighbours has to pay debit balances at the clearing house. If its cash reserves are reduced too low, it restricts its lending. If the total cash reserves of the banks are too low, all will restrict lending. Traders who cannot borrow are driven to sell, and forced sales cause a collapse of prices. The collapse of prices involves a depreciation of traders' assets and so there arise the commercial failures and, following upon them, the financial failures characteristic of a crisis.

This was true of the crises of the eighteenth century as well as later. In those days banks were banks of issue, and, side by side with the clearing of cheques,[3] there was a continuous presentation to each bank of those of its notes which the others received in the course of business. The clearing of notes like the clearing of cheques gave rise to liabilities between bank and bank, and in the English banking system of the eighteenth century, such liabilities were ordinarily settled by Bank of England notes or (in the country) by bills on London.

So long as nothing more than the mutual liabilities of banks was involved, a rediscounting system which provided credit at the Bank of England was adequate. But if the shortage of money reached such a pitch that the public had not enough for their daily needs, and the customers of the banks drew out more coin than the banks could spare, bills on London and £10 Bank of England notes would no longer meet the case.

This was what occurred in 1797 after a particularly heavy outflow of gold. The remedy was found in the restriction of cash payments, combined with the issue of £1 and £2 notes by the Bank of England (£5 notes had already appeared in 1795). The country banks were likewise authorised to issue small notes, but the predominance of the Bank of England was such that the Bank of England notes became the staple currency of the country. The country banks were and continued to be subsidiary to London.

It was the position of the Bank of England as the lender of last resort that led to its assuming the responsibility for the currency in 1797. The borrowers needed a medium of payment not between banks but for hand-to-hand circulation, and when the reserve of coin approached exhaustion, notes of small denomination were the only expedient available.

At the time of the crisis of 1825 the Bank of England notes below £5 had been withdrawn, but the legal power of issuing them had not been abrogated. Once again the intensity of the crisis was such that there was a shortage not merely of the means of payment between bank and bank but of the essential hand-to-hand currency. The metallic reserve of the Bank of England was reduced to £1,027,000 (24th December, 1825), and difficulty was experienced in making available so much of this as was in bullion by coining, owing to the limited capacity of the Mint. Succour was forthcoming from some chests of £1 notes, which had been set aside when the small notes had been withdrawn, and since forgotten. There was no legal obstacle to their being issued, and they were sent out to some of the hard-pressed country banks, and served the purpose of currency just as well as gold coin.

---

3   The clearing house was not established till 1773, but of course banks presented cheques and notes to one another.

One consequence of the Act of 1844 which has hardly been sufficiently recognised is that, so long as an adequate proportion of the gold in the Issue Department was kept in the form of coin, it guarded against a shortage of hand-to-hand currency. In the crises of 1847, 1857 and 1866, the demand was for the money market medium, the means of payment between bank and bank. The fiduciary limit once suspended, the Bank's gold might have been so depleted as to cause a shortage of coin. But this never seriously threatened. Only in 1857 was any actual use made of the authority to exceed the fiduciary issue, and even then the real excess never reached a million, nor was the metallic reserve reduced below £6,000,000.

In fact, it was not till 1914 that the experience of 1825 was repeated, and a shortage of hand-to-hand currency threatened. On that occasion the suspension of the fiduciary limit was accompanied by the issue of currency notes of £1 and 10s. The issue of the notes by the Treasury instead of by the Bank of England was a departure from precedent, and the original arrangement by which the notes were advanced by the Treasury to the banks was an encroachment on the function of the Bank of England as the lender of last resort. The acceptance crisis and the moratorium had paralysed the discount market, and the normal procedure, by which the joint-stock banks called money from the discount houses and the discount houses borrowed from the Bank of England, was interrupted. It was contrary to the practice of the joint-stock banks to borrow direct from the Bank of England, and so they were given advances of currency notes by the Treasury. But as soon as the normal rediscounting machinery began to function again, these advances were allowed to drop out, and currency notes were drawn out against deposits at the Bank of England, exactly like Bank of England notes or sovereigns. The note-issuing function reverted naturally to the rediscounting authority though the Treasury continued to be legally responsible for the notes and to be credited with the equivalent of notes issued and debited with those withdrawn.

Bank rate and the foreign exchanges

Because it was the lender of last resort, the Bank of England held the only reserve of bullion and specie in the country. Upon it fell the impact alike of an internal and of an external drain of gold. An internal drain could be met by an emergency issue of small notes, but an external drain allowed no other alternative to an adequate supply of gold except a suspension of gold payments.

Whether the demand for gold were external or internal, gold could only be drawn out against the liabilities of the Bank. When the Bank discounted a bill, it created a deposit, and opened the door to a withdrawal of gold. If its function as lender of last resort compelled it to grant unlimited discounts and to create unlimited deposits, it might be threatened with unlimited withdrawals of gold. If the Bank never refused to lend to eligible borrowers, its position would be impossible, unless the demands upon it could be kept within reasonable limits by some other means than a direct refusal. The requisite instrument was ultimately found in the rate of discount or Bank rate.

The Bank of England was the guardian of the gold standard. It had repudiated that position in 1819, when the Court passed its famous resolution denying the doctrine 'that the Bank had only to reduce its issues to obtain a favourable turn in the exchanges and a consequent influx of the precious metals.' But in that year the currency returned to par, and a few years' experience of an effective gold standard brought the Directors round to the contrary view. In 1827 the resolution of 1819 was rescinded.

The policy of the Bank was expounded to the Parliamentary Committee of 1832 by the Governor, Horsley Palmer. The influence of Ricardo is clearly shown.

> 'By the term excessive issues,' says Palmer (Qn. 925), 'I have intended to refer to such excess as has been exhibited by a state of prices higher than those in other countries, thereby rendering the foreign exchanges unfavourable and causing a return of notes upon the Bank for bullion.'

Asked 'What is the process by which the Bank would calculate upon rectifying the exchange by means of a reduction of its issues' (Qn. 678), he replied:

> The first operation is to increase the value of money; with the increased value of money, there is less facility obtained by the commercial public in the discount of their paper; that naturally tends to limit transactions and to the reduction of prices; the reduction of prices will so far alter our situation with foreign countries, that it will be no longer an object to import, but the advantage will rather be upon the export, the gold and silver will then come back into the country and rectify the contraction that previously existed.

By the 'value of money' was meant, of course, the short-term rate of interest.

So clear a recognition of the use of Bank rate as an instrument for affecting the price level, formulated a hundred years ago, is remarkable. It is all the more so, considering that only very tentative steps had at that period been taken towards the practical application of the system. Bank rate only moved within a very narrow range. It was never reduced below 4 per cent, and the usury laws prevented it from rising above 5.

The Bullion Committee had already pointed out the effects of the limitation to 5 per cent, and Horsley Palmer recurred to the subject, explaining that 'in the event of the foreign exchanges being adverse, the Bank might not only be under the necessity of raising the rate of interest to that maximum, but afterwards, as the only resource left, be compelled to limit the quantity or description of bills to be tendered for discount, either of which last measures would be equally detrimental to the commerce of the country' (Qn. 477). The limitation of the quantity or description of bills would be a dereliction of the Bank's function as the lender of last resort.

So long as Bank rate was confined within the limits of 4 and 5 per cent, the Bank had rather to rely on an open market policy as a method of regulating the exchanges. For long periods the market rate of discount was below 4 per cent, and the Bank's discount business dwindled to very small dimensions. At such times the Bank would buy Exchequer bills or other Government securities to make up the shortage in its earning assets.

On the other hand, if pressure in the money market raised the market rate of discount above 4 per cent, an increasing volume of bills would be brought to the Bank. The rate could be raised to 5 per cent, and if the pressure still persisted and discounts continued to increase, and if the Bank adhered to the practice of refusing no legitimate demand, it could still prevent an expansion of the note issue so long as it could sell Exchequer bills.

At the time of the Committee of 1832 the Bank had evolved a definite policy of keeping the total of its securities approximately unchanged, so that every gain or loss of metallic reserves would mean an equal increase or decrease of its liabilities (note issue and deposits). An importation or exportation of gold would thus be immediately reflected in the Bank's note issue and deposits, whereas a demand for gold coin for internal circulation would leave the total supply of currency in the country unchanged. A favourable or unfavourable exchange would bring its own corrective in perfect accordance with the Ricardian theory. The total of the securities the Bank Directors thought should be so determined that when the currency was 'full' the metallic reserve should be one-third of the Bank's liabilities.

The one-third reserve proportion corresponded to the normal or equilibrium position, and, so long as the fixed holding of securities was adhered to, every departure from it would take the form of a gain or loss of gold, which, it was presumed, could be left to work its effects automatically.

Experience between 1832 and 1840, when the next Parliamentary Committee sat, showed that this policy was not altogether practicable. Contingencies arose from time to time which gave rise to deposits of a special character. It seemed absurd to require all such deposits to be automatically covered by specie, and yet it was difficult to draw the line between those which might legitimately be covered by an addition to the normal holding of securities and those which might not.

But the real test came in 1839, when crisis conditions on the Continent and in America caused a heavy drain of gold. It was found that the policy of keeping the securities to a fixed total was impracticable. Discounts were increasing, and the sale of Exchequer bills merely caused them to increase faster. It was in these circumstances that Bank rate was for the first time raised to 6 per cent, but that was not enough to prevent the securities increasing, and the Bank Directors thought a higher rate inadvisable. The crisis was eventually surmounted by the expedient of establishing credits in Paris and Hamburg, which served to supplement the gold reserve and save it from complete exhaustion.

8   History of monetary and credit theory

From John Law to the present day [1940]

Charles Rist, translated by
Jane Degras

In the second half of the nineteenth century central banks of issue became so important as the *points d'appui* of the chief money markets that it is difficult for us to imagine a time when they did not exist.

But at the end of the eighteenth century, when the first credit theories were being formulated, there was only one bank of issue that acted as a central bank, in the sense in which that term is now used. This was the Bank of England. England alone possessed at that time a real money market in London. The country banks of issue, however important, were all dependent in a greater or less degree on London. The deposit Bank of Amsterdam was not in any respect comparable to the Bank of England. As to France, although Paris was the centre of financial transactions, and bills on Paris were in common use as means of payment, the issue of notes was confined to two or three Paris banks of wholly secondary importance.

Central banks of issue, and consequently theories concerning their functions and operations, really developed in the course of the nineteenth century. The Bank of France, with its large reserves of bullion, and the growing abundance of French capital, made France, in the period between 1850 and 1870, the second financial and money market of the world. Other continental money markets were either too small, or were situated in countries politically too split up to play a part comparable to that of London or Paris. The monetary and banking system of the United States was not centralised, although New York was steadily becoming the financial centre of the country, and bank-notes were of secondary importance only; in that country stock exchange centralisation preceded currency unification. It was therefore in England and France that the classical doctrine of central banks of issue was gradually elaborated; interesting discussions on the same subject also took place in Holland and Belgium.

After 1871 a new and important money market arose, the Berlin market. The Reichsbank immediately entered the front rank of European central banks. Later central banks, occupying in their own countries a position very similar to that of the Banks of France and England, were established or developed in Austria, Italy, Switzerland, the Scandinavian countries and, with the return to the gold standard, in Russia. Their establishment and operation naturally gave rise to serious theoretical discussions in the legislatures and in print. Statesmen and the public in general paid greater and greater attention to the duties and functions of the banks within the national economy, and books on the subject became more and more numerous.

A new impetus was given to these discussions when the United States, after the 1907 crisis, proposed in its turn to establish a central bank (or rather twelve large central banks under unified control). The principle of unifying the great national money markets by the unification of the note issue became as it were an elementary truth in currency policy.

As might have been expected, the war, with the need for money that it implied, and the concentration of national resources which was one of its immediate results, accelerated the movement towards the establishment of central banks, considered less as credit institutions than as instruments of State finance. After 1918 new banks were created, and the functions and influence of the old banks were extended. There was indeed a widespread tendency to attribute to them greater powers of action than they actually possessed; and certain central banks were tempted into efforts to gain international predominance which aroused anxiety in those countries jealous of their financial independence. Since it is often difficult to grasp the real driving forces and the methods used, the public as a whole regard these activities as mysterious, although they are in fact simple enough; they have given rise to such a vast quantity of literature that on this subject as on no other the historian must confine himself to the few most important writers and the main currents of thought only.

As early as 1802 Henry Thornton noted the centralising role of the bank of issue regarded as a 'national' bank. The superiority of his ideas to Ricardo's is striking. In his book Thornton brings forward and in part answers all those questions which even to-day daily confront a bank of issue. Like Tooke, his grasp of these problems gives evidence of a breadth of mind and a practical common sense that are of far greater worth than the strict and narrow logic which Ricardo brought to bear on their solution.

Once the Napoleonic wars were over, England, like France, had a central bank which henceforth fulfilled all the functions that devolve on such an institution. These functions arise less from a preconceived plan than from an organic development out of the note issue monopoly conferred on a bank situated at the chief business centre of a country. There were, it is true, profound differences in the methods of the Bank of England and the Bank of France, the former displaying a more marked tendency to intervene on the market, and greater initiative than the latter. The important parliamentary enquiries which were held whenever the charter of the Bank of England came up for renewal, and the great 1864 enquiry in France, provided opportunities for working out a theory to fit the practice which events had step by step imposed on the central banks. Thus there arose what might be called the classical theory of central banks, summarised in the formula: 'The central bank of issue is the banks' bank.'

From 1871 onwards, with the growing severity of financial and monetary crises (the 1866 crisis which inspired Bagehot's great book gave, as it were, a warning of the difficulties of a prolonged depression), and the rapid expansion of the large commercial banks in England and France (by means of which the unused cash balances of the public were made available on the market instead of remaining split up among numberless private banks), it became increasingly obvious that it was imperative to strengthen the metallic reserves of the great central banks. It was as much a question of checking too frequent variations in the discount rate as of ensuring the convertibility into international currency no longer of bank-notes only, but of all circulating credits in the country. From Bagehot to Hartley Withers we can trace an unceasing effort to inculcate in all minds the idea of a central bank conscious of its responsibilities as the country's supreme gold reserve. This idea found its embodiment in the establishment of the Federal Reserve Banks of the United States; the name alone is a sufficient indication of their character. To Paul Warburg, practical banker and theorist, is due the credit for formulating with incomparable lucidity the principles governing a bank of this kind.

After the war a new current of ideas set in. During hostilities the banks of issue ceased to be credit institutions and became government contractors for paper money. Then came the world crisis, inevitable after the orgies of 'necessity moneys,' as Galiani would have called them, and certain persons, misunderstanding the real origins of the crisis, exaggerating the influence of credit on prices, and overestimating the possibilities of international agreement, urged that the central banks should assume the function of controlling the world price level. Curiously enough, this proposal was, as a rule, made by the same writers and experts who advocated the return to paper money as being more easily 'manageable,' and the abandonment of the only international currency so far known to the world, gold. This current of thought is in fact in harmony with the tendency towards economic nationalism, apparent in so many States to-day; for the central banks of issue, since their normal operations result in the concentration of the country's currency reserves, have potentially become powerful instruments of nationalism in monetary affairs.

In the following pages we shall examine this development of ideas concerning the role of banks of issue.

1. Thornton, first theorist of the central bank

Adam Smith described the working of the Bank of England as if it were an ordinary bank of issue. Nowhere does he allude to its role as a central bank acting as the fulcrum of the entire English money market. Henry Thornton's description of this mechanism is the first of its kind in English economic literature; it was followed later by the famous descriptions given by Bagehot and Withers. The oblivion into which Thornton's book has fallen can only be explained by the popularity gained by Ricardo's ideas after the Napoleonic wars. The recently published American Encyclopedia of the Social Sciences does not even mention his name. Nevertheless his ideas dominated the *Bullion Report* and he was as a man not lacking in distinction. Member of Parliament from 1783 until his death in 1815, and member of the Governing Board of the Bank of England, he followed its policy from close quarters; business man and philanthropist (he assisted Wilberforce in the anti-slavery campaign), and the author of some devotional works, he was one of the small group of economists gathered about William Pitt who exerted so great an influence on the political life of England in the first quarter of the nineteenth century. He favoured a progressive income tax, and paid his own taxes not at the legal rate, but on a higher scale fixed by himself, and more in harmony with what he regarded as fiscal equity.

Thornton lived through two severe banking crises, which occurred in 1793 and 1797; the latter resulting in the suspension of payments in specie. In both cases the crisis was reflected not in a run on the provincial banks for gold, but in an intense demand by these banks for Bank of England notes. Far from credit restriction alleviating the crisis (the remedy prescribed by Adam Smith) it was only the issue of supplementary notes which brought the crisis of 1793 to an end.[1] Four years later, in 1797, the panic assumed such proportions that it was decided to introduce forced currency rather than cut down banking advances, which would have precipitated bankruptcies and brought about a breakdown of trade.

Here are two cases which belied Smith's well-known thesis, according to which a demand for note redemption is certain proof of excessive note issue. To calm the market and avoid a catastrope, it was necessary to issue additional notes to take the place of the Bank of England notes that were being hoarded.

The contradiction between the facts and the theory arises from the character of the Bank of England. It was not an ordinary bank but a 'public' or

---

1   This crisis occurred immediately after the outbreak of war with France; it took the form of suspension of payments by a large number of banks, particularly in Newcastle. The Bank of England restricted its note issue, leaving the country's economy without any safeguard. With credit restricted, there was a certain amount of hoarding of Bank of England notes (cf. Thornton, pp. 48–49). After a meeting of City bankers, the Government decided to alleviate the shortage of currency instruments by issuing Exchequer bills to the value of five million sterling; merchants could obtain these bills against the security of their goods. They could be sold, or used for obtaining credit at the Bank. 'The very expectation of a supply of exchequer bills, that is, of a supply of an article which almost any trader might obtain, and which it was known that he might then sell, and thus turn into bank-notes, and after turning into bank-notes might also convert into guineas, created an idea of general solvency. This expectation cured, in the first instance, the distress of London, and it then lessened the demand for guineas in the country, through that punctuality in effecting the London payments which it produced, and the universal confidence which it thus inspired' (Thornton, pp. 50–51). The panic did in fact subside before even half the authorised issue was taken up.

'national' bank, as Thornton frequently remarked;[2] he may indeed be regarded as the inventor of the term. Private banks depend on the national bank. When they are in difficulties they want its notes, and not gold, for the notes are equivalent to gold. This means that the national bank's duties are different from those of an ordinary bank. Here, for the first time, the classical problem which confronts central banks of issue during a crisis is enunciated in its broadest terms: to what extent shall they restrict credit in order to safeguard their cash position; to what extent shall they expand credit in order to save a financial centre threatened by panic?

The distinguishing characteristic of a 'public' or 'national' bank, the feature in which it differs from private issuing banks, consists in this, that as a rule, and by a natural process of development, it becomes the country's gold reservoir. Thornton was the first to draw attention to this outstanding feature of countries with central banks:

> 'The establishment of a great public bank has a tendency to promote the institution of private banks. The public bank, obliged to provide itself largely with money for its own payments, becomes a reservoir of gold to which private banks may resort with little difficulty, expence, or delay, for the supply of their several necessities.'[3]

The great service that Thornton rendered was to emphasise this special feature of the Bank of England and to shew how it affected the organisation of credit; Adam Smith, with his attention focussed on the Scottish banks, does not mention it; it is true that it was probably not so marked at the time he was writing. Of its effects on credit organisation, two are particularly important:

1. The notes of the central bank take the place of gold. In case of need, or in times of panic, it is these notes which are sought after. They serve the same purpose for the big business men of London as coin does for small traders: if they are agitated, if they fear that they will be short of ready cash to meet their commitments, they hoard their notes, as smaller men hoard coin. This is what happened during the panics of 1793 and 1797. As soon as they were given the means of obtaining bank-notes, the panic subsided. Thus, by meeting note requirements, the demand for coin was arrested.

> 'It also deserves notice, that though the failures had originated in an extraordinary demand for guineas, it was not any supply of gold which effected the cure. That fear of not being able to obtain guineas, which arose in the country, led, in its consequences, to an extraordinary

demand for bank-notes in London; and the want of bank-notes in London became, after a time, the chief evil.'[4]

The same happenings occurred in 1797. Thornton notes moreover that the total note circulation in London never exceeds what is strictly necessary for trade, so great is the economy which time and experience have made possible in the means of payment. Thus any reduction in their quantity, far from improving matters, may create difficulties, aggravate the crisis and encourage rather than stop the hoarding of gold.

'A reduction of them [Bank of England notes] which may seem moderate to men who have not reflected on this subject – a diminution, for instance, of one-third or two-fifths, might, perhaps, be sufficient to produce a very general insolvency in London, of which the effect would be the suspension of confidence, the derangement of commerce, and the stagnation of manufactures throughout the country. Gold, in such case, would unquestionably be hoarded through the great consternation which would be excited; and it would, probably, not again appear until confidence should be restored by the *previous* introduction of some additional or some new paper circulation.'[5]

2. A second result of the establishment of a 'public' or 'national' bank of issue is that private banks, instead of keeping their own gold reserve, rely on the gold reserve of the Bank of England and henceforth only keep either bills on London or Bank of England notes. Private banks of issue acted then in the same way as commercial banks act now. They trust the central bank to ensure their immediate solvency. Adam Smith, Thornton points out, was mistaken in believing that private banks keep their own gold reserve. They do no more than make sure that they have in London the wherewithal on which to draw in case of need.

'The country banker, in case of an alarm, turns a part of the government securities, bills of exchange, or other property which he has in London, into Bank of England notes, and those notes into money, and thus discharges many of his own circulating notes, as well as enlarges the fund of gold in his coffers. The Bank of England has, therefore, to supply these occasional wants of the country banker; and, in order to be fully prepared to do this, it has, ordinarily, to keep a quantity of gold equal to that of the notes liable to be extinguished, as well as a quantity which shall satisfy the other extraordinary demands which may be made at the same season of consternation either by banking houses, or by individuals. Thus the country banker by no means bears his own burthen, while the Bank of England sustains a burthen which is not its own, and which we may naturally suppose that it does not very cheerfully endure.'[6]

Thus London became the centre for payments for the whole country, and in London the means of payment was Bank of England notes. Furthermore, *London became the centre where all payments due to England were made.* Thornton paints that picture of London as the Clearing House of the entire world which so many writers were to describe during the course of the nineteenth century, and which still remains its characteristic feature:

'Bills are drawn on London from every quarter of the Kingdom, and remittances are sent to the metropolis to provide for them, while London draws no bills, or next to none, upon the country. London is, in this respect, to the whole island, in some degree, what the centre of a city is to the suburbs. The traders may dwell in the suburbs, and lodge many goods there, and they may carry on at home a variety of smaller payments, while their chief cash account is with the banker, who fixes his residence among the other bankers, in the heart of the city. London also is become, especially of late, the trading metropolis of Europe, and, indeed, of the whole world; the foreign drafts, on account of merchants living in our outports and other trading towns, and carrying on business there, being made, with scarcely any exceptions, payable in London. The metropolis, moreover, through the extent of its own commerce, and the greatness of its wealth and population, has immense receipts and payments on its own account; and the circumstance of its being the seat of government, and the place where the public dividends are paid, serves to increase its pecuniary transactions. . . . On the punctuality with which the accustomed payments of London are effected, depends, therefore, most essentially the whole commercial credit of Great Britain. The larger London payments are effected exclusively through the paper of the Bank of England; for the superiority of its credit is such, that, by common agreement among the bankers, whose practice, in this respect, almost invariably guides that of other persons, no note of a private house will pass in payment as a paper circulation in London.'[7]

It should be noted in passing that even at that date Bank of England notes were no longer the only means used in London for settling English or continental debts and claims. At that time the bankers had organised the Clearing House among themselves (probably following the example set by the Dutch bankers); it developed very rapidly and the description of it given by Jevons sixty years later has become classical; clearing houses on the English model

6 Cf. pp. 173–174.   7 Cf. pp. 59–60.

were founded throughout Europe and America. The relevant passage in Thornton is as follows:

'The following custom, now prevailing among the bankers within the city of London, may serve to illustrate this observation, and also to shew the strength of the disposition which exists in those who are not the issuers of bank-notes to spare the use both of paper and guineas. It is the practice of each of these bankers to send a clerk, at an agreed hour in the afternoon, to a room provided for their use. Each clerk there exchanges the drafts on other bankers received at his own house, for the drafts on his own house received at the houses of other bankers. The balances of the several bankers are transferred in the same room from one to another, in a manner which it is unnecessary to explain in detail, and the several balances are finally wound up by each clerk into one balance. The difference between the whole sum which each banker has to pay to all other city bankers, and the whole sum which he has to receive of all other city bankers, is, therefore, all that is discharged in bank notes or money; a difference much less in its amount than the *several* differences would be equal to. This device, which serves to spare the use of bank-notes, may suggest the practicability of a great variety of contrivances for sparing the use of gold, to which men having confidence in each other would naturally resort, if we could suppose bank paper to be abolished.'[8]

The originality of Thornton's book, as against the account of the English banking system to be found in Adam Smith, consists in his description of the specific part played by the central bank of issue. Its power, combined with the concentration of the country's commercial business in London, brought about the unification of the English money market, and its notes provided a general means of payment and enabled the country banks to dispense with a gold reserve of their own. But if this system was to work, both the private banks and the bank of issue had to carry out certain obligations. Thornton realises this very clearly; and there is no essential difference between his definition of these obligations and that which was to be given early in the twentieth century.

Private banks must keep in London assets easily convertible into bank-notes. Deposit banks to-day regard this liquidity as essential. Here again we see the similarity between our present-day commercial banks and the private banks of issue of earlier times, and note the identity of the function fulfilled by bank-notes and by current credit accounts.

The duties of the central bank are equally imperative. Its first and chief duty is to maintain exchangeability between paper and gold, and to accumulate

8   Cf. p. 55, footnote.

reserves large enough to meet any sudden domestic and/or foreign demand for gold.

> 'In order to secure that this interchange [of notes for gold] shall at all times take place, it is important that, generally speaking, a considerable fund of gold should be kept in the country, and there is in this kingdom no other depository for it but the Bank of England. This fund should be a provision not only against the common and more trifling fluctuations in the demand for coin, but also against the two following contingencies. First, it should serve to counteract the effects of an unfavourable balance of trade, for this infallibility will sometimes occur, and it is what one or more bad harvest cannot fail to cause. It is also desirable, secondly, that the reserve of gold should be sufficient to meet any extraordinary demand at home, though a demand in this quarter, if it should arise from great and sudden fright, may undoubtedly be so unreasonable and indefinite as to defy all calculation. If, moreover, alarm should ever happen at a period in which the stock of gold should have been reduced by the other great cause of its reduction, namely, that of a call having been recently made for gold to discharge an unfavourable balance of trade, the powers of any bank, however ample its general provision should have been, may easily be supposed to prove insufficient for this double purpose . . . .
>
> 'For this reason, it may be the true policy and duty of the bank to permit, for a time, and to a certain extent, the continuance of that unfavourable exchange, which causes gold to leave the country, and to be drawn out of its own coffers: and it must, in that case, necessarily increase its loans to the same extent to which its gold is diminished. The bank, however, ought generally to be provided with a fund of gold so ample, as to enable it to pursue this line of conduct, with safety to itself, through the period of an unfavourable balance; a period, the duration of which may, to a certain degree, be estimated, though disappointment in a second harvest may cause much error in the calculation.'[9]

Just as he emphasises the duty of the national bank to free the country banks from the necessity of keeping reserves, so Thornton regards it as the duty of a central bank to re-establish equilibrium in the balance of payments without the internal market being disturbed. Far from advocating economy in the use of gold, as Ricardo was to do later, he was in favour of a 'very considerable' quantity of gold being in circulation or at the bank. 'The possession, in ordinary times, of a very considerable quantity of gold, either in the bank or in general circulation, or both, seems necessary for

9 Cf. pp. 71 and 133.

our complete security in this respect.'[10] He is thus the first in a long line of economists who, from Tooke to Withers and Palgrave in England, or Warburg in the United States, were to insist on the necessity for strong gold reserves. He goes even further, and asserts that this reserve can only be guaranteed by a *single* central bank; the arguments which Thornton uses are the same as Warburg was to use when he urged the establishment of a central reserve bank.

> 'It may be apprehended, also, that, if instead of one national bank two or more should be instituted, each having a small capital; each would then exercise a separate judgement; each would trust in some measure to the chance of getting a supply of guineas from the other, and each would allow itself to pursue its own particular interest, instead of taking upon itself the superintendance of general credit, and seeking its own safety through the medium of the safety of the public; unless, indeed, we should suppose such a good understanding to subsist between them as to make them act as if they were one body, and resemble, in many respects, one single institution.
>
> 'The accident of a failure in the means of making the cash payments of a country, though it is one against which there can be no security which is complete, seems, therefore, to be best provided against by the establishment of one principal bank.'[11]

Thornton, of course, does not mean that the country banks of issue should disappear; on the contrary! What he means is that *at London*, the national centre for the country's payments, there should be one single bank of issue, whose functions and duties cannot be compared with those of private banks; this bank, he adds, should not be judged on the same standards, nor, if it is unable to carry out its engagements, criticised in the way in which one would be justified in criticising private banks.

He believed that the bank should keep a strong cash reserve, and (what is no less remarkable, for it was the policy that Tooke was to advocate later) he was in favour of using the discount rate to regulate the volume of credit. He does not, of course, dispute the effect of credit restriction on domestic prices, or deny that it may help to re-establish equilibrium in the balance of trade. On the contrary, he fears that credit restriction may go too far in this direction and prove so drastic a remedy that it aggravates the ailment. As against the over-mechanical theories of Smith, he draws on his practical experience as a banker. His book may be taken as the first reaction of practical bankers against the too doctrinaire or even wholly erroneous conceptions of the

10 *Ibid.*, p. 189.   11 Cf. p. 94.

theorists.[12] In this respect the difference between Thornton and Adam Smith was later paralleled between Tooke and the Ricardians in regard to the Act of 1844.

There is a middle road between the policy advocated by Smith and an unlimited provision of credit – *that of raising the discount rate.*

At the time that Thornton was writing, the usury laws prohibited a higher rate than 5 per cent for commercial loans. These laws applied as much to the Bank of England as to any other institution; it was therefore compelled, when its rate stood at the maximum, to cut down the volume of discounting. This is a method still used to-day by certain banks of issue, but it has great drawbacks. It substitutes the arbitrary choice of the bank for the spontaneous distribution of credits that results when credit is made dearer, and induces banks to demand more than they actually require in fear that they may not get enough for their needs.

Thornton is opposed to this method and urges that the raising of the discount rate alone should be used to ration credit:

'The bank is prohibited, by the state of the law, from demanding even in time of war, an interest of more than 5 per cent, which is the same rate at which it discounts in a period of profound peace. It might, undoubtedly, at all seasons, sufficiently limit its paper by means of the price at which it lends, if the legislature did not interpose an obstacle to the constant adoption of this principle of restriction. . . . At some seasons an interest, perhaps, of 6 per cent per annum, at others of 5 or even 4 per cent may afford that degree of advantage to borrowers which shall be about sufficient to limit, in the due measure, the demand upon the bank for discounts. . . . The interest of the two parties is not the same in this respect. The borrowers, in consequence of that artificial state of things which is produced by the law against usury, obtain their loans too cheap. That which they obtain too cheap they demand in too great quantity. To trust to their moderation and forbearance under such circumstances, is to commit the safety of the bank to the discretion of those who . . . have in this respect an individual interest which is at variance with that of the Bank of England.'[13]

Thornton's views as to the role of a central bank may be summarised as follows: it should maintain exchangeability between notes and gold; it should

---

12 'One object of the present and succeeding chapter will be to shew that, however just may be the principle of Dr. Smith when properly limited and explained, the reduction of the quantity of Bank of England paper is by no means a measure which ought to be resorted to on the occasion of every demand upon the Bank for guineas arising from the high price of bullion, and that such reduction may even aggravate that sort of rise which is caused by an alarm in the country.' *Loc. cit.*, pp. 58–59.

13 *Loc. cit.*, pp. 287–289.

be the central gold reserve both for the internal demand for gold and for payments abroad; to provide against emergencies from either quarter it should build up a strong reserve; in times of crisis it should not suspend credit but merely sell it more dearly by raising its discount rate; it should have a monopoly of the right to issue notes, at least in the capital where, in the nature of things, an overwhelming proportion of the country's payments is made. In these conditions its notes become the usual means of payment and provide the element of elasticity in the currency. The knowledge that they can obtain these notes allows local banks to keep as their reserve assets for which they can easily obtain the notes of the central bank, and compels them to keep the credits they grant (and for which notes are used) within the limits which make it possible for them to maintain solvency by an appeal to the central bank.

Here are all the ideas that Tooke was to develop in his controversy with the Currency School. Here are all the ideas which were to be regarded as the essential of what might be termed the classical theory of banks of issue as it developed in the course of the nineteenth century. They mark a notable advance over the ideas of Adam Smith and bear – particularly in comparison with those of Ricardo, for whom bank-notes were a money similar to metallic currency, differing only in that they cost less to produce – the stamp of realism which is entirely lacking in the theories of the arch doctrinaire.

One last observation, which is of interest mainly in relation to the widespread discussions which have taken place in the last twenty years concerning the method known as open market policy. We have seen that this method is by no means new. Cantillon describes it in detail and Ricardo advocates its use. Thornton, too, defends its use, but with a certain hesitation.

At the time that he was writing, the securities held by the Bank of England consisted more of Treasury bills than of commercial paper. This proportion was reversed during the Napoleonic wars, but on their conclusion the old position was re-established. The Treasury was the Bank of England's biggest client, while the Bank refrained from 'direct' discounting. Thornton notes the 'preference given by the Bank to the Government securities.'[14] He rejects the idea that this may be due to the Bank's dependence on the government and tries to shew that, by discounting Treasury bills, the Bank is merely allowing the other banks to concentrate on commercial discounting, and that, in the absence of the Bank of England, the government's bills would be taken up by the market. We shall soon see what reply Gilbart made to this argument. Here we would note the utter difference between the French and the English attitude towards the note issue. Mollien believed that it was the requirements of commercial discounting which determined the volume of notes issued; in England an entirely different principle was invoked, with which we shall presently deal.

14 *Loc. cit.*, p. 62.

Mollien was working out his plans for reorganising the Bank of France at the same time that Thornton was writing his book. As we have seen, he took his ideas about bank-notes straight from Adam Smith, but there is no doubt whatever that he wanted the Bank of France to become the central bank for that country in the same sense that the Bank of England was for Britain; the position of the Bank of England as a central bank had become even more obvious since the establishment of forced currency.

In the first place, he urged that in Paris the Bank of France alone should have the right to issue notes. It was at his instigation that in 1802 Napoleon agreed to the fusion of the three banks of issue then operating in the capital.[15] On the other hand, he was opposed to a 'general' bank, that is to say to a single bank for the whole of France on the lines of Law's disastrous institution. He took British banking organisation as his ideal: one bank having a monopoly in the capital, and provincial banks connected to it by reciprocal credits. Article 8 of the proposal contained in his second memorandum on banks is extremely significant: 'The Bank of Paris (which under article 5 was to be given a monopoly of the note issue for the Paris district) may open credits with the chief banks of other towns and maintain with them such relations as promote their mutual interests.' In a footnote Mollien adds:

> 'The object of this arrangement is to confer on the Bank of Paris all the advantages of a general bank without exposing it to any of the disadvantages that a general bank as such may suffer or cause.'

He elaborates the idea in another passage: what had been done in London should be done in Paris, neither more nor less:

> 'I regard banks as a great instrument of prosperity, and in the present state of Europe I think that France should become the home of banks, and Paris the home of the greatest bank in the world, because it is the point at which the roads from the capitals of all countries meet and cross. But can a real bank exist in Paris? Nothing of this kind need be created, or even improved upon. . . .'[16]
>
> 'If we recall what London was like in 1694 [i.e. in the year the Bank of England was founded] we have an answer to this question; and the example of what the Bank of London did to strengthen the position of the new government that had been established [he is here drawing a parallel, which the First Consul did not overlook, between Napoleon's position and that of the English government in 1688] and to develop the industrial resources of the country shews, by a hundred and eight years of success, what may be expected from the establishment of a bank in

---

15 Mollien, *Mémoires*, Vol. I, p. 339.   16 Quoted by Ramon, p. 44.

London and in other English towns; advantages which Paris and the cities of France can in their turn appropriate to themselves, and with still greater success.

'The Bank of London is a tried and tested machine, like the spinning mills of Manchester; we have but to copy it, as the mills have been copied, and study with as much care its no doubt more complex mechanism.'[17]

Mollien, a great admirer of England, proposed that the Emperor should set himself the task of making Paris the banking centre of the continent.

II. Triumph of note-issue monopoly and formation of the classic doctrine of the functions of a bank of issue between 1825 and 1870

At the end of the Napoleonic wars the resumption of cash payments in England and the convertibility of notes in France re-established a more normal functioning of the currency systems.

In England there was no banking monopoly except within the area allowed by law to the Bank of England; in France country banks of issue were gradually established, but without much success. In both countries events tended to emphasise the function of the two chartered banks to act as the country's central gold reserve. In England this represented the maintenance of an old tradition, which Thornton had described. In France it was a new but characteristic phenomenon. Bank of France notes became the means chiefly used by the big merchants of Paris in their transactions, while bills on Paris, as we have seen, served this purpose for the rest of the country. In Paris the Bank's notes came to be used more and more instead of coin, and its branches became the reservoirs of coin to which, in case of need, both individuals and other banks of issue could turn for the hard cash they required.

It is not surprising that in these circumstances the banks of issue in both countries should try to obtain a monopoly of the note issue. In London as in Paris a new bank would be bound to prejudice the concentration of reserves. The two banks would either be rivals, which would hamper the operations of both, or they would tacitly co-operate, which would amount in fact to a monopoly. As to the country banks, it was quite natural, as Thornton and Mollien perceived, and as was shewn in the debates of 1840 and 1848 from which we have quoted in Chapter Five, that they should be content to rely on the central bank to keep their position liquid. It is a curious fact that the arguments used in the theoretical discussions for and against a monopoly of the note issue rarely take these realities into account, although they are in fact decisive. The controversies still go on with the aid of general principles, when

17 *Mémoires*, Vol. I, p. 459.

the facts have already imposed the unitary solution on both countries. But the majority of those who take part in them fail to understand the structure and development of the money market. In France the dispute went on long after the legal decision was taken in 1848, and when the issuing monopoly was so deeply rooted in the currency structure of the country that there was no risk of any attempt to break it. The Péreires raised the question again when they took over the Bank of Savoy. To overcome the difficulties placed in their path by the Bank of France, they conceived the idea of competing against it. This was the origin of the *Enquiry into the Fiduciary Currency* which was held between 1864 and 1868, and contains much valuable material on the history of French thought on banking. The most interesting evidence was put in by business men rather than by economists. It shews how small was the number of men who realised that monopoly had become essential, for the public as a whole and the professional economists did not share this opinion.

In England the question was settled by the Peel Act of 1844. The evidence submitted by experts to the commissions appointed in 1832 and 1840, following the crises which shook the country, gives a comprehensive survey of the ideas of the time relating to central banks of issue and to the question of monopoly or plurality. As Professor Gregory has so well said: 'The men of the period did not, as we are inclined to do, take a Central Bank for granted; whilst the paradoxical aspect of the situation lay in the fact that, in spite of indecision on the main point of principle, a Central Bank in the true sense did actually exist.'[18] It is however true to say that from 1832 onwards it was the ideas of Thornton which inspired the action of the Governors of the Bank of England and the legislative measures which they advocated. In his evidence before the 1832 Commission Palmer, one of the Governors of the Bank, argues strongly that the Bank should protect its reserves in order to be able to undertake discounting on a large scale in times of crisis. He adds that to give the required support to the market it should be able to raise its discount rate above the legal maximum of 5 per cent still enforced for commercial loans. Unless it has that power, he says, it will have to ration credit. It will be in a better position to support the market in times of crisis if on the one hand it has a monopoly of the note issue and its administration is independent of the government, and, on the other, if it does not undertake commercial discounting in normal times. Palmer's evidence recapitulates Thornton's arguments. His ideas were those which the Bank applied in 1825, when it allowed its cash reserve to fall to a minimum while it continued to grant credit in order to support the market.

An extract from Palmer's evidence will illustrate the difference in the English and the French attitude towards a note issue. 'My intention was to impress upon the Committee an opinion, that in ordinary times the leading

---

18 Cf. Gregory, *Select Statutes, Documents and Reports, relating to British Banking, 1832–1928*, 2 Vols., London, 1929. Introduction, p. xiv.

functions of the Bank of England have been to furnish, upon a stated principle, an adequate supply of paper money convertible into coin and bullion upon demand, and to act as a bank for safe deposit of public and private money, and in so acting, that it is not deemed to be desirable to attempt to regulate the amount of issues of the Bank in London through commercial discounts.'[19] Herein lies the fundamental difference between the English and the French conception of bank-notes. It is well to bear it in mind to-day.

Two important steps, both inspired by Thornton's ideas, were taken as a result of the 1832 Commission of Enquiry. The first was that the Bank was given power to raise its discount rate above 5 per cent for bills of less than 90 days, that is to say for the very kind of bills which it was asked to rediscount in times of crisis. From then on the power to manipulate their discount rate at their own discretion became a standard feature of all banks of issue.

The second step was to give *legal* currency to Bank of England notes, that is to say to make them as much a legal means of discharging indebtedness as metallic currency itself. This step (which was also copied by almost all issuing banks) was taken with a wholly practical object in view, that of safeguarding the Bank from an internal drain of gold during times of crisis or panic; it made any demand for gold on the part of local banks unnecessary by providing them with the means of legally satisfying the demands either of their depositors, or of the bearers of their notes, without having to obtain gold. From one point of view the consequences of this step were unfortunate, for it created doubts as to the nature of the notes. It strengthened the idea that bank-notes are money in the same sense that coin is money. But bank-notes, whether legal tender or not, derive their value wholly from their convertibility. The holders of the notes always retain the right of converting them into gold if they wish to; notes remain merely circulating credits, and do not lose this character when they are made legal tender. When, in order to protect the cash reserves of the Bank from sudden demands for gold, they were made legal tender, the confusion between notes and money, which was later to take, as it were, concrete form in the 1844 Act, was strengthened. A further step in the same direction was taken, and further confusion created in 1925, when the law which re-established in England the convertibility of notes into gold laid it down that notes could only be exchanged for bullion and not for coin. The idea that the Bank's reserves should be kept for payments abroad – an idea that Thornton had already put forward – was embodied in these two measures, separated by nearly a hundred years.

The Currency School was not satisfied with Bank of England notes being made legal tender, nor probably was the Bank itself; they wanted a monopoly of the note issue. This demand was met by the 1844 Act, which laid it

19 *Ibid.*, p. 14, Sitting of June 5, 1832.

down that private banks of issue were not to increase the number of their notes beyond the point then reached. The arguments adduced at that time by Lord Overstone, the chief protagonist of the Currency Principle, shew that he had failed to understand the course of development taken by the banking system, and the role of central bank filled by the Bank of England. He criticised the private banks for not varying their note issue in accordance with gold movements, which, he said, is the duty of all issuing banks. The private bankers admitted that in fact they had not followed this rule, for the very good reason that they could safeguard their position by holding the credits necessary to obtain Bank of England notes. The position of the deposit banks to-day is exactly the same; they too, like the private banks of earlier times, may create difficulties for the central bank by a too sudden demand for rediscounting facilities, but they consider themselves entitled to rely upon getting them. Lord Overstone's arguments were invalid because they were based on the false assumption that banks of issue create money,[20] but his conclusion (which events themselves tended to bring about without the intervention of the law) was correct. Tooke came to the same conclusion by a wholly different process of argumentation.

It is extremely instructive, having read Loyd's evidence, to turn to Gilbart, the founder of the first large deposit bank and author of a famous treatise on banking. The only bank of issue which does not regulate the volume of its notes according to market needs, says Gilbart in reply to Lord Overstone, is the Bank of England. In fact, in normal times, the Bank of England refrains from discounting commercial paper and purchases government securities. It therefore puts on to the market a greater quantity of notes than is required for the purposes of trade. It is therefore not astonishing if, having forced up the note circulation and kept the discount rate artificially low, it is compelled to push that rate up to excessive heights in order to retain its gold. His statement is extremely interesting, for it shews that the Bank was still pursuing the policy of open market operations described by Cantillon and recommended by Ricardo and which, after the World War, it urged so strongly on the Bank of France, as if it were a wholly new device.

'The country circulation can be issued only in consequence of transactions which have taken place, and to the extent only required by the wants of the district; whereas it is obvious that the Bank of England has the power of increasing the circulation by the purchase of Exchequer bills or

---

20 Cf. on this point the evidence of Samuel Jones Loyd (Lord Overstone) before the 1840 Commission, reprinted on pp. 27–62 of Gregory's *Select Statutes, Documents and Reports*, 1919: 'Issuing paper I always consider as the creation of money, and that is a duty or privilege which I think can be better exercised for the benefit of the Community by one body, acting under the control of the Legislature or Government, than by trusting it to the principle of competition' (p. 49).

stock, or by purchasing bullion,[21] and throwing a mass of notes on the market when the state of trade does not require them.'[22]

In fact, throughout this period, the Bank's policy was to maintain the note circulation at as constant a level as possible by buying Treasury bills when the volume of discounting declined and reselling them when the market brought in a larger volume of discounting.[23] One of the members of the Commission remarked to Gilbart that by buying government securities the Bank set free the capital of those who held the securities and that consequently 'it comes to the same thing, whether the persons applying for discount obtain their discount through those parties whose capital is thus liberated, or whether they make direct application to the Bank of England, and obtain discount,' to which Gilbart rightly replied: 'But you are not warranted in assuming that those notes do go into channels of commerce afterwards; the probability is, that they remain upon the Stock Exchange, and make interest low, and excite speculation.'[24] Gilbart's words were prophetic. When we remember the open market policy pursued by the American Federal Reserve Banks between 1926 and 1929, and its effects in facilitating stock exchange speculation in New York, it is impossible not to admire the accuracy of his judgment. No doubt the Governors of the Bank of England could justify their policy of buying Treasury bills on the ground that thereby they did not enter into competition with the private banks on the discount market; but there was perhaps another reason, the same reason which explains the purchase of securities on the market by the Federal Reserve Banks – that is, the Bank's desire to make profits. That policy is noteworthy in two other respects. In the first place it shews the Bank's confidence in the solvency of the State, in its punctual fulfilment of its obligations. In one of the two memoranda which we have already quoted from so often, Mollien pointed out to Napoleon the unfailing readiness of the Bank of England to act as banker to the State; this, he remarks, is due to the promptitude with which the State for its part carried out all its obligations as debtor to the Bank. Still later, when the 1864 Commission was holding its enquiry, this difference in the financial standing of the State in France and in England was noted by more than one witness, in particular by Baron Alphonse de Rothschild; the unwillingness of the

21 It appears from this passage that Gilbart was also opposed to the purchase of gold by the Bank with the object of expanding the currency, at a time when there was no commercial demand for such an expansion, Gilbart wanted the note issue to be backed entirely by bills of exchange. He forgets that, in order to maintain the interchangeability of notes and gold and to retain contact with the international standard, the Bank must buy gold at a fixed price, or the foreign exchanges will fall.
22 Gilbart's evidence in Gregory, *loc. cit.*, Vol. I, p. 83.
23 Some extremely interesting data on this question are given in Professor Gregory's introduction to the *Select Statutes*, pp. xviii and xix.
24 *Ibid.*, pp. 93 *et seq.*

Governing Board of the Bank of France to meet the State's requests for credit has been an unchanging feature of its history from the day of its establishment; such a state of affairs was unknown in England.

In the second place, the open market policy has a tendency to insulate the national money market by enabling the Bank to exert a direct influence on the market, either by increasing or by diminishing the funds available, apart from any inflow of gold from abroad and from any demand for credit. In the absence of such a policy, the issue of notes (or the creation of current accounts) depends on two factors only: the inflow of gold from abroad, and the extent of the internal demand for credit on the market. In respect to both these factors the Bank remains passive. It issues notes to the amount required. On the other hand an open market policy enables it, should the occasion arise, to increase or to diminish the currency media at the disposal of the market, in order either to offset the tendency towards restriction or expansion that normally follows from gold movements, or to avoid a rise in the discount rate if the market is short of cash, or on the other hand to force the market to raise its rate if the funds available are too abundant. This is what Warburg had in mind when, later, he said that in its open market policy the Bank plays the part not only of anvil but also of hammer. But it is obvious that a bank of issue, when it buys securities on the market in order to offset by the credits that it thus creates the monetary restriction that an outflow of gold normally produces, tends, at least for a time, to detach the national market from the international money market.

Peel's Act, by giving the Bank of England a practical monopoly of the note issue, apparently confirmed its position as the central bank. It recognised its character as the central money reservoir, as the mainstay of the private banks in times of crisis, as the supreme arbiter of credit. On the other hand, and without fully understanding its import, it tended to weaken the Bank's capacity for action as a central bank, by prompting the Banking Department to overlook the necessity for accumulating strong reserves. Lord Overstone, obsessed by the idea of 'economising money' (as Ricardo was in his 1823 Plan), is of the opinion that the Issue Department does not need strong gold reserves, while the Banking Department is, in respect to this problem, in the same position as any other commercial bank.

In short, the establishment of a note monopoly in England weakened rather than strengthened the conception of the central bank as it had been formulated by Thornton and later by Tooke, for both of whom one of the essential features of such a bank was the creation of strong gold reserves. We shall return to this point later on.

In France, during the same period, the idea of a central bank gradually took root among the most farsighted men of the time. Underlying the discussions as to the advantages and disadvantages of a note-issuing monopoly, the idea of the importance to the national economy of a single bank concentrating the country's reserves of metal and supplying the other banks, in times of crisis or panic, with the credits they required, gradually took on a clearer

outline and won an increasing number of adherents. The principle of monopoly itself had gained the field on the day when Napoleon wrote his famous
letter to Mollien, asking him to amalgamate into one, the three banks of
issue then operating in Paris. 'I take up this standpoint: it is easier for the
government and the public to supervise one bank than many; whatever the
economists may say about it, competition cannot serve any useful purpose in
this case.'[25]

In an earlier chapter we have described how a unified note issue gradually
became a necessity as the money market itself was unified. No practical man
of affairs believed that it was possible to revoke the monopoly enjoyed by the
Bank in law and in fact. While Michel Chevalier and Courcelle-Seneuil went
on endlessly discussing the general benefits of competition,[26] a small group
of men, including Adolphe Thiers, Vuitry, President of the Council of State
and author of some excellent works on French financial history, bankers like
d'Eichthal, economists like Wolowski and Léon Faucher, extracted from
events themselves arguments proving that the Bank of France really fulfilled
the functions of a central bank (this is the name used by Léon Faucher), that
is to say of a banks' bank, and that the existence of such an institution had
become vitally necessary to the economic life of the country.

Their ideas are already familiar to us: the bank of issue is the credit reserve
on which the private banks can draw in times of crisis; the concentration at
one point of the country's metal reserves makes it possible to use them, in the
best and quickest way, at whatever point they may be required; the chief
method of protecting this central reserve is the manipulation of the discount
rate. In short, the bank of issue represents the country's monetary reserve for
internal and external payments.

25 Mollien, Vol. I, p. 339.
26 In his evidence Chevalier remarked: 'We should remember that the principle of freedom for
    banks of issue is implicit in the fundamental principle of modern legislation, which is that
    industry is free.' This was the kind of generalisation that appealed to the great rhetorician. He
    forgets that even Adam Smith was in favour of limiting the freedom of banks. Courcelle-
    Seneuil and his followers also appealed to general principles of freedom in their advocacy of
    competition among banks of issue, though in his book he does make an attempt, from which
    Chevalier carefully abstained, to give a theoretical justification of his position. Courcelle-
    Seneuil's argument rests solely on the idea that banks of issue can in no case issue more notes
    than are required for circulation. Consequently they must be acquitted of the charge made
    against them, that they help to provoke crises (cf. p. 229 of his *Traité des Banques*, 1889
    edition). But although he believed that in this he was upholding the position of the Banking
    School, he does in fact, as regards banks of issue, take up the standpoint of the Currency
    School and of Adam Smith, that bank-notes replace coin, and that they can never exceed in
    quantity the coin which *would have been* in circulation if no notes existed. He had not caught
    up with Thornton, who had so clearly exposed Adam Smith's mistake; or with Mollien,
    who knew that notes took the place of discounted commercial paper and were therefore an
    addition to the existing metallic currency. Of course, it never occurred to Courcelle-Seneuil
    that notes are merely a means of putting hard cash into circulation without its being used in
    the physical sense.

Adolphe Thiers was the first to bring these arguments forward, and he did so with exceptional vigour in 1840, in a speech which has become famous, and again in 1864 in his evidence before the Commission of Enquiry into the Banks. Few statesmen have had as clear a grasp of the character and operation of the Bank of France. Since writing his book on John Law, he had never lost interest in currency problems, and he had gained undisputed mastery in handling them. In 1840 he describes in the following words how, in times of crisis, the national bank comes to the rescue of the market:

'Let me say that I think the Bank behaved admirably when, during the crisis, it doubled its discounts. The Bank is accused of keeping reserves equal to the note circulation, but I make bold to say that if it had not performed this service in the time of crisis it would have acted unwisely. ... A bank should be cautious when everybody is offering money, but in times of crisis it should have the courage to supply trade with money. I say that an institution which obeys this precept of being close-fisted during prosperity, and generous during crises, is fulfilling its true function. That was when the Bank demonstrated its great usefulness to the government. There was one thing in which people had not lost confidence when they distrusted everything else, and they proved this by bringing their money to the Bank. This Bank, which seemed to have been instituted for private credit, has become an instrument of public credit and has saved the country.'[27]

If it was to fill this position the Bank had to be free of too rigid control. Its note issue had to be given the necessary elasticity. In his evidence before the 1866 Enquiry into the Fiduciary Note Circulation, Thiers makes a comparison between the Bank of France and the Bank of England, as governed under the Peel Act:

'Mr Peel is a great political and historic figure, for whom I have the greatest respect; but it must be admitted that the Act which he sponsored has met with general disapproval. It was a mistake on his part to fix an absolute limit to the note circulation, and to tie the Bank down to an unvarying proportion between notes in circulation and the reserve of bullion. It is good to keep a certain proportion always in mind, in order to depart from it as little as possible; but to make that proportion compulsory is so excessively cautious as to be imprudent; it has been necessary to suspend this provision three or four times. In France, and practically everywhere, it has been decided that bullion reserves should be kept at one third the note issue. I think that is not a bad figure to have

---

27 Quoted by Ramon, *La Banque de France*, pp. 190–191.

chosen, and it should always be borne in mind, but it is unwise to impose it as absolutely binding. It is bad enough when we get near the figure which denotes exhaustion of the bullion reserve; it is bad enough to have this terrifying vision ahead, without adding the terror of a fixed and absolute limit. When the figure falls below one third, this is and should be a matter of anxiety, but it is not predestined that it will be followed by insolvency. With courage, coolness, and timely action, that may still be averted. Money may flow in again, as it usually does. But to fix a precise and compulsory limit is to create insolvency beforehand, and to declare one-self bankrupt before one has actually reached bankruptcy. Whenever there has been a crisis the Peel Act has filled everybody in London with fear; they have clamoured for its suspension, and immediately it is suspended people calm down and gradually the panic subsides. Mr Peel's very strict Act was the consequence of the mistakes made previously by the banks. There was an outcry against them, and everybody welcomed the severity displayed by Mr Peel. . . . But you cannot resist evil by evil, and I think that in the end the 1844 Act will be abrogated. As far as their management is concerned, I think the Bank of France is the superior; and it is also superior in organisation, for it regards the proportion that it is desirable to maintain between note issue and cash reserve as a principle of prudence and not a compulsory rule.'[28]

This statement was made at a time when deposit banks in France, unlike those in England, were still in their infancy. The concept of the banks' bank which Burdeau was to emphasise in his famous Report of 1892,[29] and Pallain in his reply to the 1910 Commission of Enquiry into the National Currency in the United States, was well understood long before the great commercial banks had covered France with their branches.[30] In 1870 these

---

28 Their's evidence before the 1866 Enquiry; *Report*, Vol. III, pp. 436–437.
29 Burdeau's report is dated June, 1892. It is very concise, and it is a pity that be did not at times elaborate his basic ideas somewhat more fully. Theoretically it does not differ from evidence submitted to the 1864–1868 enquiry. Below we give the statement of M. de Saint-Paul, more detailed than the brief phrase in which Burdeau remarks that 'in times of difficulty private credit institutions have to rely on the Bank to take over a large part of their commercial bills' (p. 38).
30 At the 1864 enquiry M. de Saint-Paul was practically the only witness to refer to the deposit banks and to the function of the Bank of France in relation to them. 'I call your attention to the nature of the repayments which may be demanded. The deposit banks are as follows: The Société Générale de Credit Industriel, the Société de Depôts et Comptes Courants, the Société Générale pour le Développement du Commerce, and five other deposit banks. If the Bank cannot rediscount their bills, these banks would have to close their doors the day a panic started. They have to accept first-class bills, bills which the Bank will never refuse if it is accepting any paper at all; but if there is a crisis, a panic, and the Bank can no longer give cash, it will no longer rediscount even such bills. Then all deposit banks will be endangered.' Vol. I, p. 432.

banks refused the offer of a moratorium, for the rediscounting undertaken by the Bank of France made it unnecessary. On the outbreak of the war in 1914, the Bank of France, forgetting this principle, faintheartedly preferred a moratorium for the deposit banks, with all its disastrous consequences, to rediscounting on a large scale, although that would immediately have put an end to withdrawals by depositors. But the theory about the role of the central bank in times of crisis had been firmly established long before that date.

A further point was made by Vuitry at the 1864 Enquiry; he pointed out that, with the country's metal reserves concentrated, it was possible to send coin to the places where it was at any time most urgently required. The Bank is not merely the supreme reserve of credit; it is also a guarantee that coin or bullion will always be available if required. This essential fact, which was to be used by Warburg in the United States after the 1907 crisis to justify his proposal for the establishment of a central bank, was emphasised by Vuitry (as it had been by d'Eichthal in 1848[31]) in the following words:

'During the session on November 21, 1868, something very curious happened, which attracted little attention from the economists: I refer to the movements of the currency, the currents running in different directions which it follows. The Bank of France has branches all over the country. Some of these branches accumulate currency steadily; from others there is as constant an outflow, and the Bank frequently has to send money to the latter. The cause of such a movement is difficult to find, but the fact is indisputable; there are a certain number of branches in which a balance is achieved after fluctuations in their cash reserves; others, and they are always the same, have to have money sent to them at great cost in order to cover their transactions; in a third category of the Bank's branches the cash reserves accumulate to such an extent that sometimes cash has to be sent to Paris, to the Bank, which then distributes it throughout the country. These movements of the currency arising out of the commercial practices peculiar to different districts, I think it follows that it is inadvisable to have separate privileged institutions for each district, for those whose cash is constantly being drawn out would encounter grave difficulties because of the considerable costs with which they would be burdened, while in the areas where the reserves accumulated the banks, not knowing what to do with them, would choke of surfeit. That is what happened before 1848. The inconveniences of the system have been amply demonstrated by experience.'

---

31 'What are the results of a single currency bank? Far from concentrating resources it divides them equally, distributes capital equally; it takes them from where they are not serving a useful purpose commensurate with the costs and risks, and brings them where they are lacking, where they can be useful' (G. d'Eichthal's speech of February 22, 1848).

The reserves which are concentrated at the Bank are drawn not merely from holdings within the country; gold, of which the Bank is the principal buyer, is also brought in from abroad. Thiers summarised the position in a felicitous phrase: 'The Mint should be the manufacturer of coin; it is the Bank which fills the position of merchant, by obtaining the raw materials which the Mint requires.'[32] That in fact was what the Bank was, the middleman through whom gold imported from abroad was transferred to the Mint. All the witnesses at the 1864 Enquiry agreed in recommending the Bank to buy all the gold offered to it and to do voluntarily what the Bank of England was by law compelled to do, buy the gold at a minimum price[33] so that all the available metal would be brought to it. That is what the Bank decided to do; it was in fact the only practical result of the Enquiry.[34]

From that time, it became a recognised maxim that the normal method by which a central bank protects its reserves, in the event of an outflow to foreign countries, or to prevent excessive credits on the market which might lead to the export of gold, is the raising of the discount rate. On this point unanimity reigned. The words which Bagehot used in his famous *Lombard Street* were accepted by all competent men:

> 'If the interest of money be raised, it is proved by experience that money *does* come to Lombard Street, and theory shows that it *ought* to come. To fully explain the matter I must go deep into the theory of the exchanges, but the general notion is plain enough. Loanable capital, like every other commodity, comes where there is most to be made of it. Continental bankers and others instantly send great sums here, as soon as the rate of interest shows that it can be done profitably. While English credit is good, a rise of the value of money in Lombard Street immediately by a banking operation brings money to Lombard Street. And there is also a slower mercantile operation. The rise in the rate of discount acts immediately on the trade of this country. Prices fall here; in consequence imports are diminished, exports are increased, and, therefore, there is more likelihood of a balance in bullion coming to this country after the rise in the rate than there was before.
>
> 'Whatever persons – one bank or many banks – in any country hold the banking reserve of that country, ought at the very beginning of an unfavourable foreign exchange at once to raise the rate of interest, so as

---

32 *Inquiry*, Vol. III, p. 422.

33 'The Bank of France,' said Alphonse de Rothschild in his evidence in 1864, 'is not compelled to accept gold always, but in fact it does so and has done so for a great many years. In certain circumstances it has bought gold at a premium, but usually it buys it at the Mint rate' (*Inquiry*, pp. 459 *et seq.*).

34 The law passed in 1928 made it compulsory for the Bank to buy gold when offered.

to prevent their reserve from being diminished farther, and so as to replenish it by imports of bullion.

'This duty, up to about the year 1860, the Bank of England did not perform at all, as I shall show farther on.'[35]

Bagehot was not the only one to express this idea; all the witnesses at the 1864. Enquiry were of the same opinion, and when in 1871 a third great bank was established on the continent, the Reichsbank, its entire legal structure was based on the use of the discount rate as the means of protecting the reserve and controlling credit.

There is practical unanimity as to the process by which the discount rate attracts short term foreign funds and eventually causes a fall in the price of stock exchange securities and then of commodities; it is described by Goschen in his *Theory of the Foreign Exchanges* (1861), by Bagehot in *Lombard Street*, by Marshall in his evidence before the 1887 Commission of Enquiry, and earlier by Tooke in his *History of Prices*. The theory which they formulated on this point remained practically unchanged, and was repeated in all standard textbooks and in Léon Say's preface to the French edition of Goschen.[36] It was not challenged until 1928, when Mr Keynes published his *Treatise on Moncy*.[37]

On the other hand, objections to the too frequent variations in the discount rate became more and more numerous at this time, particularly in France; it was suggested in many quarters that the raising of the discount rate should be replaced by other methods which would not expose the market, and trade in general, to the shocks arising from sudden rises and falls. Secondly, great differences of opinion began to emerge as to whether the bank of issue could control the discount rate, or whether it had itself to submit to it. These two elements in the classical theory of central banking require more detailed attention.

As early as 1840 Tooke had criticised the Bank of England for keeping its discount rate too low, in normal times, in order to attract more business. The bank of issue, he says, should always take care to maintain ample reserves, and should not let its rate fall below 4 per cent. By letting it fall too low, it is acting like an ordinary commercial bank which is anxious to attract clients, and it thus allows its reserves to be exhausted, whereas its position as the central bank should make it keep a greater reserve in order to meet possible crises.

At the 1864 enquiry in France many witnesses, of whom most were

---

35 W. Bagehot, *Lombard Street*, London, sixth edition, 1875, pp. 45–47.

36 'There is only one legitimate way of attracting gold from abroad when the exchanges become unfavourable: that is the raising of the discount rate, and this method, with which Mr Goschen deals, amply proves that it cannot be replaced by any other, however ingenious it may appear.' Léon Say's *Preface* to the *Théorie des Changes*.

37 Cf. Chap. XIII, which is given over to this question.

engaged in banking, accused the Bank of France of being too ready to raise its discount rate: it should, they argued, try to protect trade from too frequent and too great increases; it should regard it as one of its principal duties to maintain the utmost possible stability in its discount rate, and to be prepared to lose gold rather than follow, almost automatically, and to the great detriment of French trade, rises in the discount rate on the London market. Such criticism can be traced back to the working of the absurd clause in the Peel Act of 1844 under which the Bank of England was too frequently compelled to raise its discount rate; this naturally had an immediate repercussion on the French market. The argument was put forward with great vehemence by the Péreire brothers,[38] whereas bankers like d'Eichthal thought that the intimate connexion of the two markets in London and Paris made it necessary for the Bank of France to follow movements in the London rate.[39]

The two suggestions made to meet this point were designed to give the Bank of France alternative means of defending itself against changes in the London rate which would not react unfavourably on French trade. The first is no longer of interest except as a curiosity: the Péreire brothers proposed that the capital stock of the Bank of France should be sold and replaced by bullion. Their proposal was rejected at once on the ground that the sale of this stock would withdraw coin, or more probably notes, from the home market, and the Bank would be compelled to increase its discounting to an equal extent, in order to fill the gap in the currency created by this operation. The number of notes would therefore remain the same, or it might be increased, without the Bank having really strengthened its reserves. If, on the other hand, the Bank sought to obtain gold abroad, the foreign markets would be compelled, because of the loss of gold, to raise their discount rate and thus to recapture part of the gold which the Bank had tried to get. In neither case would the gold position of the Bank be strengthened.

The second suggestion is of interest because, although it was at that time rejected by the Bank (as Lord Overstone had rejected it at the Banking Enquiry of 1840 in England), it was, considerably later, adopted. This was the suggestion that the Bank should purchase foreign securities, not as a permanent investment, but in order to be able to use them in a temporary crisis and thus to avoid the disagreeable necessity of raising the discount rate in the event of temporary disequilibrium in the balance of payments. Many of the witnesses (in particular M. Pinard) supported this proposal.

This is in fact one of the methods used under the Gold Exchange Standard. It was employed freely by the Bank of Belgium. Later (in 1906 and 1907) it was adopted by the Bank of France in exceptional circumstances as a measure of assistance to London, and, on a much larger scale in 1927 and 1928, in order

38 Cf. Isaac Péreire's book, *La Banque de France et l'organisation du Crédit en France*, 1864, which resulted in the appointment of the Commission of Enquiry into the currency.
39 Cf. d'Eichthal's remarks on Péreire's evidence.

to avoid embarrassing London by the withdrawals of gold which the Bank of France's extensive deposits in London would have allowed her to make.

In 1864 the object of the proposal was to enable the Bank, if dollars or sterling rose, to supply the market for some time with bills on New York or London, without having to embarrass the money market by raising the discount rate. It was conceived as a way of meeting a temporary difficulty. The same object would have been served by the Bank's keeping a reserve of gold large enough to withstand a drain without taking any defensive measures. Those who supported this suggestion were fully aware that it would not prove effective against a steadily unfavourable balance of trade; in such cases the balance itself would have to be readjusted, which could only be done by changing the movements of capital or commodities.

The opponents of this proposal were chiefly the representatives of the large private money houses, who kept extensive holdings of foreign bills. The evidence of Baron Alfred André and Baron James, de Rothschild is particularly illuminating on this point. At that time, and subsequently, the private houses kept a large portfolio of bills on London, firstly, in order to take advantage of differences, often considerable, in the rate of interest at the two centres, and secondly, to have at their disposal a reliable means of obtaining gold at all times (since Bank of England notes were always convertible into gold) in case the Bank of France, exercising its legal right, chose to give silver instead of gold in exchange for its notes (this practice was condemned by Léon Say in the Preface referred to above). In other words it was London and not Paris which to some extent served as the central bank for the French private banks.

The bills held by the private banks constituted an ever available reserve by which Paris could make certain that on the dates due gold would flow in. The situation was similar to that of London itself, which, by means of its acceptances covering world trade as a whole, was at all times in a position, merely by refusing to renew these credits, to make certain of a substantial access of specie, or to reduce in equal measure the volume of the demands which could be made on it for gold.

The arguments brought forward by the opponents of this measure were twofold: in the first place, if an institution as powerful as the Bank of France were to build up such a portfolio, foreign markets might regard this as a potential danger (and this in fact did happen in 1927 and 1928); secondly, foreign banks of issue, by constituting their own portfolios of bills on France, could easily counteract French policy.

During the course of the enquiry Alphonse de Rothschild outlined another method of influencing the market. This was for the Bank of England to compel the market to raise its discount rate if it differed too widely from the Bank rate. With the government bonds and Treasury bills which it held, it was in a position either to sell them on the market, or to borrow on their security, and thus to withdraw part of their cash reserves from the banks, which would then be compelled to raise their discount rate.

But Baron de Rothschild was careful to add that such action presupposes that the banks regard the government bonds as a perfectly safe investment that would not fluctuate, in short that the financial standing of the State is above all suspicion. He remarked that the financial standing of the French State was not so incontestable that methods of this kind could be used. The central factor in these proposals is the use of open market policy.

All witnesses however were agreed that the raising of the discount rate, the method *par excellence* of protecting cash reserves, should be used only as a last resource. On this point too Thiers merits quotation.

> 'I agree that as a brake, as a means of stopping speculation when it has become a matter for anxiety, the raising of the discount rate can be a good thing in itself, but only on condition that its use is timely, not during a crisis, but beforehand, when it is first anticipated. I admit that it is difficult to act in this way, and that it requires great courage and foresight, for the bank would certainly be attacked for slowing down business. The brake has always been put on too late; facilities having been granted when they should have been refused, they are withdrawn when they should be granted. The raising of the discount rate is not very useful as a brake; it is useful only as a means of preventing our cash reserves from draining away to our neighbours. The situation disclosed by the state of the exchanges shews that in many cases this danger has been illusory. But I repeat that the raising of the discount rate cannot be wholly condemned; it is even legitimate and indispensable if bullion has to be bought. The Bank has sometimes spent as much as 14 million for premium alone in order to get gold, and it is natural that the effect should be felt in the discount market. But it would be better if the Bank of France, instead of raising its rate to 10 per cent, as the English do, were to work within narrower limits, not going below 4 per cent and not rising above 6 per cent or 7 per cent at the most. But it is impossible to be dogmatic on this point; the best advice that can be given is that changes in the rate should be kept as small as possible.'[40]

One further question, which we cannot overlook, was raised at the enquiry. What are the real powers of the central bank as regards discounting? Can it force the market to obey, or does bank rate merely reflect the state of affairs created by the supply of and demand for short-term capital?

According to the Governor of the Bank, M. Rouland, and to M. Thiers, whose evidence on this point is of great interest, the Bank of France does not claim to do more than register the state of the market; it merely affirms a position that already exists. Later, in his famous report, Burdeau writes: 'It would be a mistake to think that the Bank fixes its rate arbitrarily. It can only register the rate for money.'[41]

---

40 Thiers' evidence at the 1866 Enquiry, Vol. II, pp. 439–444.   41 *Report*, p. 34.

Bagehot does not agree with this official theory. He very rightly points out that the Bank, which holds a large part of the resources of the market, is in the position of a merchant with a large stock of non-perishable goods; he can offer a larger or smaller quantity of these goods on the market, and thus make their price vary. This view is obviously more correct than the preceding one, but it should not be forgotten that the power of the Bank is not arbitrary and that very precise limits to its control are fixed by the resources of the market. Any attempt on the part of the Bank to raise the discount rate at a time when the open market has abundant resources at its disposal is bound to be ineffective. Indeed, the gap between what is called the market rate and the official rate is one of the best indexes to the demand and supply position.

But, these reservations made, the powers of a central bank in this respect are far greater than those which the Bank of France and M. Thiers would have us believe. It is enough to remember the influence it can exert on the market by open market operations. Nor should it be forgotten that in France, for example, commercial discounting is usually undertaken by all the banks at a rate slightly above Bank rate, so that in fact the Bank does control the discount rate prevailing throughout the country.

It is true that if the Bank is mistaken in its judgment of the rate to be fixed, the effects immediately produced on external gold movements, on credit operations within the country, or on stock exchange speculation, will compel it to change its policy.

It will be seen that while experts in France were at that time familiar with the essential features of the policy of a central bank of issue, and discussed the pros and cons of the case, to the majority of economists, even those like Courcelle-Seneuil who specialised in banking questions, the idea of a central bank and its functions remained unfamiliar.

III. The bank of issue as the country's supreme gold reserve
From Bagehot to the federal reserve banks of the U.S.A.

Throughout the period we have been discussing the idea of a central bank and the idea of a bank of issue were closely associated in men's minds. It was generally believed that it was because they were banks of issue that the Bank of England and the Bank of France became central banks. That, however, was not in fact the only reason. Another, and more important reason was that these two banks operated in the capital cities of England and of France, where the greatest part of the payments of the country are made; in such centres bankers and business men naturally try to *simplify* methods of payment, and wherever possible to replace payment in coin, with all the attendant difficulties and costs of transport, by less cumbersome methods. In the eighteenth and nineteenth centuries the alternative open to them was to use bank-notes; hence the gold of the country was gradually concentrated in the hands of the bank of issue in the capital. But if, instead of bank-notes, the method employed had been cheques or transfers, central banks would still have grown up. Gold would have been deposited in the most important bank, the bank inspiring the greatest confidence, and its owners would have been credited with a corresponding sum in their bank accounts. A clearing bank instead of a bank of issue might have become (at least in theory, and if bank-notes had not been, historically, the forerunner of cheques) the central bank, concentrating the country's gold reserves.

The distinction between the process of note issue and the function of a central bank became clearer as the use of cheques, settled by a clearing arrangement between the banks, became more widespread. A few shrewd men realised (and stated in books that have become famous) that what was important for a country, if it was to be prepared for internal crises and assured of a supply of international currency for its payments abroad, was in the first place the concentration of its gold in a central reserve which would ensure the best use being made of it. Whether this gold could be drawn on by means of cheques on the central bank or by means of notes was a question of practical convenience, not of principle.

Thus, between 1870 and 1914, there gradually arose the idea that central banks of issue were and should be first and foremost 'central reserve banks.' This was the name adopted by the American banks of issue when they were established in 1913.

In France Vuitry had given an admirable account of the way in which the concentration of gold in a single reserve ensures its rapid despatch to any centre where there is a shortage. He considered this concentration the chief advantage of a single bank of issue; bank-notes were useful to the extent to which they facilitated the concentration of gold.

In England the Act of 1844 and the ideas which inspired it deflected and retarded the natural evolution of ideas. Those who supported the Act thought that, once the administration of the special money represented by bank-notes was determined (which was the work of the Currency Department), the Bank of England, in so far as it was a deposit bank, was no longer in a special position. It was just one deposit bank among many; it had no specific responsibilities or obligations. Like any other business undertaking, it did its duty if it made a profit. Far from desiring the accumulation of a strong reserve, the promoters of the Act, and in particular Lord Overstone,[42] obsessed by the idea of economising money, and disdaining Tooke's precepts, were anxious to have the gold reserve reduced to the minimum.

In a work which is one of the most brilliant and most profound that have ever been written on this subject, Bagehot directed attention to the role of

---

42 'I should have no hesitation whatever in saying, that whatever reserve of bullion has under the existing system been found to be sufficient, would be found to be amply sufficient under the new system proposed; and I should fully anticipate that our experience would soon justify us in reducing that amount.' Cf. Gregory, *Select Statutes*, Vol. I, p. 59.

the banks as the country's supreme reserve, and to the duties which that position involves; in so doing he brought English credit and banking theory back to the road marked out by Thornton and Tooke, from which it had been turned aside by Ricardo.

Bagehot's book was written in 1866, on the occasion of the failure of the house of Overend and Gurney, when the Bank of England was once more compelled to ask for the suspension of the Peel Act in order to save the City of London from disaster. Bagehot seized the opportunity of formulating once more the doctrine that the Bank of England – even if it is regarded merely as a deposit bank – is a central bank with all the responsibilities implied by that position.

The fact that it was necessary, in England, to devote an entire work to defending a principle which was widely recognised by all competent men, economists or financiers, can only be explained by the curious organisation imposed on the Bank of England by the Act of 1844. Bagehot's book can only be understood if that organisation is borne in mind. Whereas in all other countries the cash reserves of the Bank and its unissued note reserve are spoken of as the supreme resource in times of crisis, Bagehot only speaks of *the reserves* of the Banking Department. It is this reserve, he says, which constitutes the country's supreme resource. Bagehot refuses to discuss the merits and demerits of the Peel Act; he takes it as it is, and is not concerned with the issue of notes, but only with the working of the Banking Department. Through its Banking Department, the Bank of England had become the cashier of all the English banks which kept their reserves there. On the other hand the cash reserves of the country banks and deposit banks did not exceed 12 to 15 per cent of their deposit liabilities (the rest being used to grant credits). Thus, apart from the Bank of England's reserves, that is to say the cash reserves of the Banking Department, there were no resources available for meeting any sudden demand for means of payment.

The Banking Department's reserve was made up entirely of the unissued note reserve of the Issue Department, which was prohibited from issuing notes in excess of a certain sum, fixed once and for all, except against new gold. The Banking Department's reserve was thus completely inelastic. It could only be increased by appealing to the government to authorise a supplementary issue.

Bagehot comes to the conclusion that the Bank – more particularly the Banking Department – is not entitled to conduct its business on the lines of an ordinary commercial bank. It should not be satisfied with a reserve of 10 or 12 per cent of its deposit liabilities, which represent the cash reserves of all the English banks. It should maintain a credit margin, that is to say a margin of note issue, which will enable it to meet and withstand any panic. Consequently in normal times it should restrict its discounting and keep a large part of its deposits inactive. It is true that the Bank of England admits this obligation in practice; but in theory it disputes it. Bagehot wants it to be openly and publicly acknowledged, and made the basis of the Bank of England's credit policy.

This is Bagehot's thesis. He was the first to propound the theory of a central bank *in relation to a bank which claims to be nothing but a deposit bank*. In fact his theory is applicable to all banks of issue and, although the Banking Department's reserve is the only one mentioned, to the gold reserve and the issuing powers of all central banks. Similarly, his concern extends beyond a panic at home, to the possibility of a drain from abroad.

> 'Of late there has been a still further increase in our liabilities. Since the Franco-German war, we may be said to keep the European reserve also [America was not yet important]. Deposit banking is indeed so small on the Continent, that no large reserve need be held on account of it. A reserve of the same sort which is needed in England and Scotland is not needed abroad. But all great communities have at times to pay large sums in cash, and of that cash a great store must be kept somewhere. Formerly there were two such stores in Europe, one was the Bank of France, and the other the Bank of England. But since the suspension of specie payments by the Bank of France [the Bank of France had established forced currency during the war of 1870–1871, and it was retained until 1876], its use as a reservoir of specie is at an end. No one can draw a cheque on it and be sure of getting gold or silver for that cheque. Accordingly the whole liability for such international payments in cash is thrown on the Bank of England.'[43]

Having thus indicated the special responsibilities incumbent on the Bank of England, he concludes with a trace of bitterness:

> 'It might be expected that as this great public duty was cast upon the Banking Department of the Bank, the principal statesmen (if not Parliament itself) would have enjoined on them to perform it. But no distinct resolution of Parliament has ever enjoined it; scarcely any stray word of any influential statesman. And, on the contrary, there is a whole *catena* of authorities, beginning with Sir Robert Peel and ending with Mr Lowe [Chancellor of the Exchequer], which say that the Banking Department of the Bank of England is only a Bank like any other bank – a Company like any other companies; that in this capacity it has no peculiar position, and no public duties at all. Nine-tenths of English statesmen, if they were asked as to the management of the Banking Department of the Bank of England, would reply that it was no business of theirs of Parliament at all; that the Banking Department alone must look to it.
>   'The result is that we have placed the exclusive custody of our entire banking reserve in the hands of a single board of directors not particularly

43 *Lombard Street*, pp. 31–32.

trained for the duty – who might be called 'amateurs,' – who have no particular interest above other people in keeping it undiminished – who acknowledge no obligation to keep it undiminished – who have never been told by any great statesman or public authority that they are so to keep it or that they have anything to do with it – who are named by and are agents for a proprietary which would have a greater income if it *was* diminished, – who do not fear, and who need not fear, ruin, even if it were all gone and wasted.

'That such an arrangement is strange must be plain.'[44]

Bagehot concludes that the organisation of the Bank of France is better than that of the Bank of England, and proposes that a permanent vice-governor should be appointed whose duty it would be to keep before the elected governors the special duties and functions of the Bank.

His book – which, after an interval of seventy years, comes, as it were, as a direct sequel to Thornton's – is for economists not merely an eloquent plea in a just cause, but the perfect model of the analysis of a money market. His account of the minute division of labour on the London market, with its deposit banks, its discount brokers, its acceptance houses, and their dependence on the Bank of England, is as interesting to the sociologist as to the economist, as important for the statesman as for the banker.[45]

The problem of strengthening the Bank of England's reserve was not however solved. It was to go on engaging the minds of experts and economists up to the eve of the world war. Twenty years after the publication of *Lombard Street* another crisis occurred in connection with the house of Baring. The Bank of England turned to the Bank of France and the Bank of Russia for assistance in strengthening its reserve and enabling it to issue more notes. This appeal to foreign countries made a deep impression on public opinion. The inadequacy of the gold reserve was commented on by all the important papers. *The Times* wrote that the gold reserve had for a number of years been too small. It suggested that the government should repay its debt to the Bank, which appeared in its balance sheet as capital; the Bank would then 'be in a position to hold a large number of bills of exchange, as the Bank of France does, and could by that means exercise a more effectual command over the discount market, and consequently over the imports and exports of gold;' the article goes on: 'Too large a proportion of the Bank's assets is in the form of fixed investments. If it transacted a much larger discount business it could afford to pay for a larger idle bullion reserve than at present.'[46]

44 *Lombard Street*, pp. 41–42.
45 For an account of the same market to-day see R. J. Truptil's excellent book *British Banks and the London Money Market*, 1936.
46 *The Times*, November 24, 1890, reproduced in Gregory, *Select Statutes*, Vol. 2, p. 193.

Once again it is suggested that the Bank should be reorganised on the lines of the Bank of France, but, the danger having passed, things remained unchanged. The proposal put forward by Lord Goschen, Chancellor of the Exchequer, that notes of small denomination should be issued to strengthen the Bank's reserve was not acted upon; it is an interesting indication of the trend of ideas, and from that time on was constantly under discussion, the more so as the mining of gold in the Transvaal and the consequent increase in the gold holdings of the majority of banks of issue after 1890 greatly strengthened the world monetary position, and made the acquisition of a large reserve an achievement coveted by all countries.

In Germany and France imports of gold were encouraged. Although long term international loans were made from Paris, the French balance of payments shewed a substantial bullion import each year. The only country where, notwithstanding the increase in the world's gold, the Bank's reserve remained more or less stationary, was England. The position was curious, since London was the chief gold market, and the volume of international credits granted by the English banks was far greater than that made by any other banking system in the world. Criticism arose from all sides. Clare pointed out[47] that the Bank of England's reserve served not only the English money market, but, in times of widespread crisis, the entire world. Inglis Palgrave[48] drew attention to the anomaly of a reserve growing steadily smaller in relation to the obligations not merely of the Bank of England itself, but of all the banks in the United Kingdom, and to the impossibility, in such conditions, of keeping the discount rate as stable in London as it was on the chief foreign markets. He urges the banks to come to an understanding about the maintenance of adequate reserves. Shortly before the war he returns to the same point in an article in the *Bankers' Magazine* for 1912, in which he compares the amount of gold acquired by the Bank of England with that acquired by other continental banks, and shews how inadequate it is.

It was, however, the 1907 crisis which brought home the weakness of the London market's reserves in relation to its international liabilities. A sudden loss of confidence led to enormous withdrawals from the banks in New York and throughout the United States. In the absence of a central bank where the American banks could rediscount their bills, the American market was for a short time in a state of bankruptcy. Gold stood at a premium over cheques and even over notes. This premium served to attract gold from Europe, and London was called on to provide the gold. London in its turn was unable to cope with the sudden demand; the discount rate was raised to attract gold from the continent. The Bank of France sent gold to the Bank of England and agreed to rediscount English bills.

---

47 *A Money Market Primer*, 1891, pp. 112–113.
48 I. Palgrave, *Bank Rate and the Money Market*, 1903.

These events provided a further demonstration of the necessity of having strong gold reserves at the central banks, and the advisability of establishing a central bank where no such institution existed. In England the occasion called forth Hartley Withers' *Meaning of Money* (1909) a worthy sequel to Bagehot's masterpiece, and in the United States it led somewhat later to the establishment of the Federal Reserve Banks, and to an enormous output of literature on banking questions.

In his really great book which, after a lapse of forty years, carries on Bagehot's penetrating analysis of the London money market, Withers brings home the contrast between the Bank of England's gold reserve and the enormous liabilities of the banks, emphasising the weakness of the first in relation to the second. He is disturbed not so much by the Bank of England's responsibilities in regard to the home market, as by its obligations abroad, which had become much greater since Bagehot's days as a result of the increase in the volume of international loans.

Withers then examines the various proposals made for strengthening the Bank's reserves: the creation of a special Treasury reserve to guarantee the deposits of the savings banks; repayment in gold of the state debt to the Bank of England; the issue of one pound notes against gold; the creation of a special reserve by the banks to be held by the Bank. He concludes that all these methods amount to no more than taking gold out of one pocket and putting it in another.

The Bank's reserves might also be strengthened by its keeping the gold imported into England, but that would mean a high discount rate, and a high discount rate means credit restriction. The desired object might perhaps be attained by making all the important banks publish a weekly return, shewing the proportion maintained by each between its reserves and its advances. The publication of these figures would necessarily reveal any tendency to grant excessive credits, and the banks would consequently practise greater caution; 'its immediate effect would be the blotting out of a certain amount of credit which ought not to be in existence.' The result, it must be admitted, would not be startling.[49]

The most important outcome of the 1907 crisis was the establishment of the Federal Reserve Banks in the United States, and the unequalled clarity with which on this occasion the concept of a central bank emerged. For the first time in the history of economic thought the concept of a central bank was linked up, not with the issue of notes, but with the concentration of the country's gold reserves. In England and France the spontaneous development of the money market had made of the bank of issue the country's gold reserve; from now on this is regarded as the purpose for which a central bank exists, the issue of notes being merely *one* of the methods that a central bank may use to fulfil its main function.

---

49 *Meaning of Money*, p. 280.

The evolution of ideas along these lines is particularly noticeable in the writings of Paul Warburg, an American banker of German origin, who from 1907 on took an active part in the campaign for an American central reserve bank. In articles and speeches he explained with truly admirable lucidity and comprehensiveness the role and functions of central banks of issue; at the same time he helped to draft bills for submission to Congress; the law establishing the Federal Reserve Banks was finally passed in 1913. In these articles and speeches, which were published in two volumes in 1930,[50] the role and functions of a central bank are formulated with the matured elaboration gradually achieved by a century of experience.

The essential ideas may be briefly summarised as follows:

1.   The violent crisis experienced in the United States in 1907, which shook the whole of Europe, was the result not of a shortage of gold in the United States, for the bullion reserves of the banks were in themselves equal to if not greater than the reserves of all the European banks put together, but of the dissipation of these reserves among a very large number of banks. Since gold was scattered in this way, the banks, when the panic started, all hoarded gold, and thus brought about both a shortage of gold and a prolonged crisis. 'The net result of our system is that immense amounts of gold and currency are wastefully locked up, and that, in spite of our immense gold treasure, which is four times as large as that of England, and notwithstanding our enormous *per capita* circulation of thirty-five dollars, we suffer almost annually from acute scarcity of money.'[51]

In one passage he makes a striking comparison between the position in the United States in regard to the gold reserve, and an Eastern town where each household is given a few buckets of water for protection against fire at a moment when a violent storm is about to break. If the United States had had a central reserve on which all banks could have drawn by rediscounting their bills, the panic would not have spread and the crisis would have been avoided.[52]

Burgess makes another illuminating comparison in his *Federal Reserve System*. He says that the system under which it is necessary for each American bank to keep its own reserve brings about a position similar to that which would exist in a town where every taxi rank is compelled to keep three or four taxis in readiness all the time; for the town as a whole there would be an enormous waste of taxis. It might be claimed for such a system that it guaranteed the services of taxis whenever required, but in fact its introduction would greatly diminish the supply of taxis in relation to the demand.

---

50 *The Federal Reserve System its Origin and Growth. Reflections and Recollections* by Paul Warburg.
51 *Ibid.*, Vol. II, pp. 55–56.   52 *Ibid.*, Vol. II, p. 125.

Warburg is of the opinion, held earlier by Thiers, Vuitry and d'Eichthal, that the main purpose served by a bank of issue is the concentration of reserves; this was achieved by its having a monopoly of the note issue;

2.   The issue of notes is a secondary function of central banks. Notes, says Warburg, represent an 'auxiliary' reserve, an addition to the main reserve which consists of gold. The object to be kept in mind in the organisation of a banking system is less the issue of notes, and the conditions of their issue, than the centralisation of reserves.[53] Thus the idea of a *reserve bank* clearly takes precedence over the earlier idea of a bank of issue;

3.   Once a central reserve is formed, it is essential that the subsidiary banks should at all times be able to obtain credits at the central bank for which, should the need arise, they can get gold. The necessity to draw on these credits in gold will arise less frequently when the banks themselves are in a position to supply their clients, in the form of notes, with claims convertible into gold at the central bank.

Europeans did not find it difficult to grasp this concept, which had been clearly explained by Thornton; it was not so readily comprehensible to Americans, for they were not accustomed to the use of internal bills of exchange; merchants obtained funds from their bankers by giving them promissory notes, which it was difficult for an issuing bank to rediscount. These notes were held by the banks against advances, but they did not represent assets that could be always and easily realised. In the United States the banks' loanable funds were employed largely in forward operations on the New York Stock Exchange, so that the surplus funds of the country, instead of being used in trade, were employed to finance stock exchange speculation.[54] Warburg also makes great efforts to convince the Americans of the usefulness of a rediscounting system which would ensure the safety of the funds used for financing commercial bills and provide merchants with a constant reservoir of short term capital;

4.   In his vivid account of the rediscounting system operated by European central banks, the advantages of which he constantly brings to the attention of American bankers, Warburg takes the Reichsbank and the Bank of France, not the Bank of England, as the model on which the system which he advocates should be based.

Without directly criticising the Bank of England, he makes it clear that he is no admirer of its hybrid and complicated organisation; he is, however, explicit in his praise of the English deposit banks which are, in his opinion, the best commercial banks in the world;

---

53 *The Federal Reserve System, its Origin and Growth*, Vol. I, pp. 123–128.

54 Apparently this still holds good; writing in 1937 Mr M. Palyi says: 'The introduction of the Federal Reserve System did not succeed at all in altering this characteristic feature of the American money market: the extraordinary concentration of surplus liuqid funds in the field of financing security speculation.' *The Chicago Credit Market*, p. 83.

5.   In regard, however, to direct intervention on the market by the purchase of relatively short term government securities, Warburg supports the Bank of England; the majority of continental banks have always rejected this method as dangerous; both in his draft constitution for the Federal Reserve Banks, and in his articles, Warburg explicitly favours this practice; he also advocates the purchase of international bills; he hopes that New York will become as important a centre for such operations as London.

In advocating the adoption of this twofold method he uses a striking phrase: 'The bank of issue,' he says, 'should be able to act both as anvil and hammer.' That is to say, in providing the money market with funds, it should at times assume a passive role, awaiting the demands for rediscounting that come to it as and when the market requires funds, and at times take the initiative by itself entering the market, either to increase the funds available on the market, or to diminish them, by the purchase or sale of government securities.

At first the primary object of the purchase of government securities in periods of stagnation, when the commercial bill holdings of the bank of issue tend to decline, was to enable the Federal Reserve Banks to earn some income (since the Government paid interest on these securities) during the lean years. It was only later that this method was employed as a means of maintaining business activity by making fresh funds available whenever the withdrawl of gold by foreign holders, by compelling the bank to raise its discount rate, might have caused a setback.

This open market policy, when conducted on a large scale, means that the bank of issue's judgment as to the *real* needs of the money market takes the place of ordinary gold movements as the controlling agency on that market. The dubious results achieved by this policy on the American money market are well enough known. We have already shewn that it tends to isolate the different money markets, since the bond established between them by gold movements is no longer effective. Furthermore, it deprives the national money market of the one effective check that can correct an exaggerated rise in relation to other markets, that is, the withdrawal of bullion.

It was not until after the war that the full consequences of this policy became apparent. The central banks of issue had departed further and further from the position of distributors of gold among the world's money markets, and had become purely national instruments for the creation of money. This change represents the last stage in the development of ideas relating to central banks.

At the time when Warburg was writing, that is to say in the period following the 1907 crisis, the dominant idea, as we said at the beginning, was that of the central bank acting as the country's gold reserve; and it was on these lines that the Federal Reserve Banks were organised. From the moment of their establishment they were taken as the model *par excellence* of the central bank, and the new banks of issue in different countries were founded on the same principle and usually bore the same name.

Thus the concept of the central bank, originating in the functioning of the Bank of England at the end of the eighteenth century, taken up by the continent, and for a time obscured in England by the disastrous ideas introduced by Ricardo, found its fulfilment in the United States in the early years of the twentieth century. It was elucidated in a comprehensive and brilliant fashion by a banker with a thorough knowledge of European banking practice. The theory of central banks might then appear to have been definitely established; it was however at this moment that a wider ambition was expressed. A few hardy spirits, shaken by the 1930 crisis, wished to give a new function to central banks, that of regulating world prices.

IV. Banks of issue and price stabilisation

In the years which followed the war it occurred to certain economists that banks of issue might be entrusted with the task of stabilising prices; an attempt should be made on an international scale to keep the volume of loans within the limits commensurate with the price level that it was desired to maintain.

The banks of issue themselves shewed no disposition to take up the proposal. In the United States (still haunted by memories of the severe crisis of 1922) a Senate Committee was set up in 1928 to investigate the question whether the Federal Reserve Banks should adopt as part of their policy the stabilisation of prices. The most eminent authorities consulted, including Benjamin Strong, Governor of the New York Federal Reserve Bank, were emphatically opposed to the suggestion; they believed that a central bank of issue should in no circumstances assume such a responsibility.[55]

More imaginative men, like Mr Hawtrey (in his *Art of Central Banking*) and Mr Keynes (in the last chapters of his *Treatise on Money*) proposed that a joint effort should be made by the central banks of issue to achieve, by deliberate credit policy, the object which Benjamin Strong thought it impossible to reach.

> 'If the central banks of the world, acting in concert, aim at stabilising the wealth value of their currency units and therefore of gold ... the gold standard would be maintained, but gold would be tied to the currency units, instead of the currency units to gold.'[56]

In another passage Hawtrey puts it this way:

---

55 Cf. *Hearings before the Committee on Banking and Currency: House of Representatives.* 69th Congress. Washington, 1927, 2 vols.
56 Hawtrey, *The Art of Central Banking*, p. 194.

'The central banks are the source of the world's supply of money. It is their essential duty to adjust the supply to the world's needs. The supply of money is made dependent on the supply of gold, but the relation between the two is determined by the central banks and legislatures. The legislatures limit the freedom of the central banks. The residue of freedom remaining to the central banks was quite sufficient to enable them to prevent the depression and crisis of the past three years. That it was not so used was the result partly of divided responsibility and partly of a want of far-sightedness.'[57]

The idea of regulating the price level by the restriction or expansion of credit has attracted a great number of people. It has, of course, always been recognised that a bank of issue, if its intervention is *timely* (the entire difficulty lies in that one small word) can prevent a crisis from being extremely severe; the restriction of credit serves as a warning and checks the violence of a speculative boom. What is new in the recent suggestions is the proposal, firstly, that such action should be taken simultaneously on all markets, and, secondly, that while credit restriction should be employed to mitigate an impending crisis, *credit expansion* should be used to maintain a given price level, or to overcome a prolonged depression.

Nobody will deny that in *certain clearly defined circumstances* the co-operation of the chief central banks could mitigate certain price fluctuations, particularly those which arise from excessive credit. But to contend that by such action it is possible to maintain a given price level over a long period seems to the present writer to rest on a failure to discriminate between the action of credit, which can only cure the ills created by credit, and the action of the fundamental and permanent factors which determine long term price movements.

This confusion touches the very concept of credit and of money. It requires a brief examination here, although in a theoretical work of this kind it is, of course, impossible to examine the wholly practical and ever changing problem of co-operation between the great issuing banks.

The real question at issue is the extent to which credit can affect prices; it is one which in the last few years has been the occasion of a great deal of subtle and complex discussions on the interaction of saving and credit. It is the same problem, in slightly different guise, as the one that Tooke examined when dealing with the relations between short term price fluctuations and what he called *general* price movements.

The central banks are asked to increase the credits they grant, or to make it possible for the commercial banks to increase their credits, in order that world prices may be maintained at a certain level. We think that this proposal rests on a delusion. They are asked to bring about the result that would be

57 *Ibid.*, pp. 245–246.

brought about by inconvertible paper money (assuming that this paper money did not depreciate because of lack of confidence).

What can the central bank do? They can only make *advances*, and short term advances at that. These advances are necessarily *repayable*. The additional purchasing power put into circulation by the banks is to be returned to them (if not wholly then at least in large part) in the future, and indeed in the near future, unless it is assumed that the banks of issue no longer regard it as their duty to grant *credit*, but to create definitive purchasing power.

How can the purchasing power which they lend be returned? Only by deductions from the final income of those to whom the credit was granted. In other words, *if credits are repayable* (and it cannot be assumed that they are not) they take the place of sums which, though not in existence at the moment, *have to be deducted a little later from the final income of those who enjoyed the credits*. This means that the present increase in expenditure (with the action on the price level that it involves) will subsequently be offset by a diminution of the expenditure that *would have* been made if there were no credits to be repaid; and this diminution tends to lower prices.

Three examples may be given to make this clear.

If the advances made by the banks are purely commercial advances intended for the purchase of commodities already in existence, the anticipated sale of which will automatically provide funds, it is obvious that the advances are repaid from the gross proceeds of the sale, which are part of the normal income of the community.

If the advances represent loans to provide working capital, the problem is more complicated, for in this instance the advance made by the bank takes for the time being the place of *long term savings* which have not yet been accumulated. When a bank lends an industrialist the funds to pay for the labour and raw materials which he requires, it replaces by a bank credit a sum which as a rule the business man should have saved, before starting the undertaking, out of income, and which should have provided him with his working capital. The bank lends him these savings in advance. It follows that in subsequent years the business man, in order to repay his obligations to the bank, and to regain 'the freedom of his treasury' will have to deduct *from his net income*, that is from his profits, savings *equal to the entire loan made to him by the bank*. Thus the *present* demand for goods is increased at the cost of a *reduction in the demand for goods and services exactly equal to the advance originally made by the bank*, this reduction being made at a later period. Unless it is contended that the banks need pay no heed to their *credit margin*, and that they can prolong their loans indefinitely, the initial action on the price level *will be offset by an exactly equivalent action in the opposite direction* in the period following the advance.

This argument is even stronger when the banks grant credits, not to provide working capital, but for investment, that is to say when they render their funds immobile by granting long term loans with short term capital. The history of every crisis demonstrates that it is impossible to maintain the price level by bank credit.

But, it will be asked, do not bank loans themselves create the income with which they can later on be repaid? Nothing of the kind! It is true that bank loans create incomes (wages and profits) which increase the general demand for goods and consequently the *gross* income devoted to their production. But these loans (which represent, at least in the two last examples, anticipated savings) can only be repaid out of *actual savings*, that is to say with funds deducted from the net proceeds of industry. Now there is no reason to believe that in the usual term for which a bank credit is granted, savings will increase by a sum equal to the advance. On the contrary, the advance is as a rule greater than the sum usually saved in the same period. Consequently the demand for goods in the period following the advance will be smaller than it *would have been* if the advance had not been made. That will exert downward pressure on prices.

Thus, the rise of prices resulting from the granting of loans is subsequently offset by the deductions that have to be made from net income to meet the repayment of the loans.

This process is entirely different from that set in motion by the issue of paper money – except of course when a State decides to redeem the paper money, that is to say to start deliberately the process of deflation, which is automatically set going in the case of bank credits.

The only way in which the pressure exerted on prices by the repayment of bank advances can be counteracted is by an inflow of gold; *this increases the banks' credit margin*, and thus enables them either to grant further credits, or to put up with delays in the repayment of loans without suffering any ill effects.

This being so, it seems to the present writer wholly mistaken to believe that a world price level can for any length of time be maintained by means of credits granted by the central banks, or through the banking system in general.

If the discussion of this problem is to serve any useful purpose, it must be based upon a thoroughly clear understanding of the way in which credit and savings affect income. This is not the place in which to discuss this process, which has in recent years exercised the ingenuity of many economists. This question is part of the general problem of savings and crises, which lies outside the field covered by a general history of credit theories, and requires separate investigation. But I would say that the way in which this problem has in recent years been treated has often been far from satisfactory. The mechanism of saving is complex. Its effects vary according to whether the savings are made out of consumption or out of increased income (consumption, in the latter case, shewing no decline); whether they are made in a country where population is stationary or growing; whether they are invested entirely at home, or partly in other countries, etc., etc. The majority of economists who have studied the effects of saving on the national economy have not taken these possible alternatives into account. They have examined the effects of saving as though it were a simple phenomenon, whose consequences in regard to consumption and production develop in strict accordance with a single uniform pattern. Nothing is further from the truth. What we unquestionably know is that savings, in so far as they are used to increase agricultural or industrial productivity, tend to bring world prices down. There is no reason to believe that this profound and permanent effect can be counteracted by credit expansion. On the other hand an increase in gold output (provided, of course, that Governments do not sterilise the new gold) and the issue of paper money can be relied on (though the two have very different results) to bring about a rise in prices or to check a fall.[58]

58 It is impossible to mention all the writers who in the last few years have, with greater or less success, tackled this problem. A complete bibliography, as well as a notable analysis and examination of the different theories put forward, is to be found in Gottfried von Haberler's *Prosperity and Depression* (Geneva, 1937). For the theory of savings the reader will find M. Divisia's *L'Epargne et la Richesse Collective* (Paris, 1928) particularly useful.

Modern articles with a domestic focus

9 Real and pseudo-financial crises

Anna J. Schwartz

A widely held belief in the United States and the world financial community is that the default of major debtors – whether companies or municipalities or sovereign countries could lead to bank failures that would precipitate a financial crisis. The remedy proposed by those propagating this view is that major debtors therefore must be rescued from the threat of bankruptcy to avert the projected dire consequences for banks and for the stability of the financial system. I shall argue that (a) a debtor whose affairs have been mismanaged should be liquidated or reorganised under new management; (b) default by major debtors need not result in bank failures; (c) if defaults do result in bank failures, so long as the security of the private sector's deposits is assured, no financial crisis will ensue. The bugaboo of financial crisis has been created to divert attention from the true remedies that the present financial situation demands.

A financial crisis is fuelled by fears that means of payment will be unobtainable at any price and, in a fractional-reserve banking system, leads to a scramble for high-powered money. It is precipitated by actions of the public that suddenly squeeze the reserves of the banking system. In a futile attempt to restore reserves, the banks may call loans, refuse to roll over existing loans, or resort to selling assets. Such a sequence of events is to be distinguished from what happens during a disinflation or a deflation. A deflation or a disinflation is a consequence of restricted growth of bank reserves but it is not precipitated by the public's behaviour. The essence of a financial crisis is that it is short-lived, ending with a slackening of the public's demand for additional currency. A disinflation or a deflation may be long drawn out. Nominal wealth may decline, real debts may rise, but these are not financial crises.[1]

No financial crisis has occurred in the United States since 1933, and none has occurred in the United Kingdom since 1866. All the phenomena of recent years that have been characterised as financial crisis – a decline in asset prices of equity stocks, real estate, commodities; depreciation of the exchange value of a national currency; financial distress of a large non-financial firm, a large municipality, a financial industry, or sovereign debtors – are pseudo-financial crises.[2]

A real financial crisis occurs only when institutions do not exist, when authorities are unschooled in the practices that preclude such a development, and when the private sector has reason to doubt the dependability of preventive arrangements. Institutional changes introduced since 1933 in the United States and since 1866 in the United Kingdom and the private sector's familiarity with and confidence in the responses of institutions and authorities assure that concern with financial crises is misplaced. What should be the object of concern with respect to the proposals to deal with pseudo-financial crises is the perpetuation of policies that promote inflation and waste of economic resources.

The first section reviews the last real financial crisis in England and notes developments at later dates when a financial crisis did not occur in England but did in the United States. The second section tries to account for the record in the two countries. The third section examines the link that Kindleberger (1978) attempts to establish between manias and financial crises from 1720 to 1975. Finally, the fourth section questions the emphasis currently given to financial distress as the trigger for financial crises and shows that it is based on a misinterpretation of the development of past real financial crises. It is not financial distress that triggers a crisis. The failure of authorities or institutions to respond in a predictable way to ward off a crisis and the private sector's uncertainty about the response are the triggers of a real financial crisis.

England's last real financial crisis in 1866 and later dates when none occurred there but did occur in the United States

I begin by reviewing the circumstances that led to a financial crisis in England in 1866 and then turn to developments in 1873, 1890, 1907, 1914, and 1931 – dates when real financial crises might have but did not occur in England. I also refer to the experience of the United States at these dates leaving for the next section reference to its experience in 1884, when a financial crisis was averted and in 1893, when it was not. In that section, I try to show why the record changed after 1866 in England, and why it was variable in the United States.

1866

The onset of the financial crisis in 1866 may be traced to the collapse in January of a firm of contractors, Watson, Overend & Company, and two other companies, the Contract Corporation and the Joint Stock Discount Company, with which the first had ties. These three drew on paper issued to one another and discounted with Overend, Gurney & Company, among others. Overend, Gurney in earlier years had been a solid conservative partnership, one of the pillars of the City. About 1860, a younger generation then in charge of the business became less circumspect in its lending operations, accepting equity interests for unrepayable loans extended to ironworks and shipping companies. Losses led to a decision to incorporate with the possibility of turning over a new leaf. The new company was launched in 1865 just after the conclusion of the US Civil War, when there was every reason to anticipate a strong revival of demand for British exports, but the new company did not live long enough to benefit from it. The failures noted above in January 1866 were followed by additional ones in March and April, but again those were firms of marginal significance. However, when on 10 May Overend, Gurney shut down, the market was shaken. The next day panic broke loose.

1873

Twice during the year financial crises were said to have occurred but only the second time was the characterisation accurate. The first occasion, centred on the Continent, began on 9 May with a sharp decline in prices on the Vienna Stock Exchange. The price decline spread to Germany, Switzerland, and Italy, affecting assets like real estate, building, railways, and iron and steel ventures that had been in great favour. Contraction and liquidation followed but no disruption of payments. In England, the only reflection of events abroad was a series of increases in the Bank rate over a four-week period, followed by stepwise reductions over the succeeding ten weeks.

The real financial crisis, centred on the United States, had its beginnings on 8 September when the New York Warehouse & Security Company, organised to lend on grain and produce but involved in railway loans, failed. Five days later, Kenyon, Cox & Company, a stock brokerage firm that had endorsed the paper of another railroad, also failed. A depressed railroad bond market had led these railroads to obtain temporary financing; with the loans about to fall due, neither the lenders nor borrowers were prepared to pay up. The failures were marginal firms, but on 18 and 19 September two leading firms were suspended. Jay Cooke & Company (failure followed the suspension) and Fisk & Hatch (resumed but failed in 1884). At the same time runs began on two small banks, and on 20 September, on a larger New York bank. Panic selling on the New York Stock Exchange led to the closing of the market for ten days. Currency went to a premium as the New York and interior banks restricted payment in greenbacks. By 22 October, the currency was obtainable virtually at par.

Gold was exported to the United States on 25 September by the Bank of England, exports from other central banks as well continuing until the end of October. Bank rate rose. Since investors in England and Germany were holders of American securities, the stock market crash in New York had reverberations. A sharp sell-off on the London Stock Exchange on 6 November led to a rise in Bank rate to 9 per cent the next day, but the payment system was not impaired.

1890

Two monetary disturbances occurred, one in New York, the other in London. Prices on the New York Stock Exchange in November had been falling, partly due to selling by English investors, in order 'to carry the load of investments of a less desirable description' (Sprague, 1910, p. 132) in South America. On 11 November, the failure of Decker, Howell & Company was announced, involving the Bank of North America. The next day a stock brokerage firm failed and another bank closed. On 15 November, the failure of Baring Brothers in London was cabled to New York and stock prices fell. The following week several firms failed but panic did not develop.

In England, the imminence of failure by Baring Brothers, owing to imprudent investments in the Argentine, became known to the Bank of England on 8 November. In addition to underwriting South American securities, Barings had a large short-term banking business and considerable liabilities on deposit account. The actions undertaken by the Bank of England and a syndicate of bankers, to be discussed in the following section, prevented a crisis.

1907

London was exposed to a series of disturbances from abroad in October, beginning with a stock market decline in New York. The London and Amsterdam stock markets registered sympathetic declines in the prices of American railway securities, but the main disturbance began during the week of 14 October when five banks that were members of the New York Clearing House and three outside banks required assistance from a group of Clearing House banks. These eight banks were controlled through stock ownership on margin by a few men of no great financial standing, who used the banks to further speculation in the stocks of copper-mining companies. A decline in the price of those stocks alarmed depositors who started runs. Order seemed to have been restored by Monday 21 October, when the Knickerbocker Trust Company, the third largest trust company in New York, began to experience unfavourable clearing balances because the president had connections with one of the men in control of the banks that were in difficulty. The former's resignation did not allay distrust. On 22 October a run on Knickerbocker forced it to suspend business. The next day, a run began on the second largest trust company, and the day following on still another trust company. Assistance was given to these two companies, but by that time alarm had spread to the rest of the country. Restriction of payments by the banks followed and currency went to a premium over deposits.

Despite the repercussions from abroad, no financial crisis developed in London. Three increases in Bank rate from 31 October to 7 November sufficed to replenish gold exported to New York during the crisis there. No bank failures occurred, although voluntary company liquidations were abnormally high in 1908, presumably because of the level interest rates reached in 1908 (Clapham, 1945, II, p. 393).

1914

The problems that arose with heightened war fears in Europe were not dissimilar to those that characterised earlier peacetime episodes of threats to the dependability of the credit and payments system. What was different was the range of financial markets – long-term capital, short-term credit, foreign exchange, and gold markets – affected in both England and the United States.

In the summer of 1914, New York, as usual, was in debt to London on short-term account, dependent for its supply of sterling exchange on the proceeds of commercial bills accepted in London and bought on a daily basis by the London discount market. The disruption of remittances from European clients of English accepting houses to cover maturing bills led, on 27 July, to a cessation in London of discounting of foreign bills. At the same time, heavy liquidation of foreign-held securities was in process on the London and New York stock markets, the proceeds of sales in New York, on London's instructions, to be remitted abroad. New York banks without sterling exchange could remit only in gold, draining reserves. Moreover, the New York banks could not count on the proceeds of the sales to provide bank accommodation for domestic purchasers of the securities. For the London clearing banks, their main liquid assets – bills, loans to the bill market, and loans to the Stock Exchange – ceased to be liquid. Both London and New York closed the stock markets on 31 July. A countrywide panic both in England and the United States threatened.[3]

1931

Britain's abandonment of the gold standard on 20 September has been described as a crisis, as have all the subsequent devaluations of the pound and more recently of the dollar. The overvaluation of sterling reflected in weakness in the current account in fact was corrected by the decision to stop selling gold at a fixed price. As Moggridge has noted (1982, pp. 181–2), the many repercussions of Britain's suspension of convertibility included the decision of others to follow in her wake; elsewhere the imposition of exchange controls, tariffs, and trade controls; a traditional tightening of monetary policy in the United States in response to an external drain of gold followed by a massive wave of bank failures; and further deflation not only in the United States but in all countries that remained on gold. The so-called crisis does not refer to the situation in other countries. Indeed, there was no crisis internally, except for Bank of England, Treasury, and other officials involved in negotiating credits for the Bank before the event and scheduling meetings on what to do next as reserves dwindled. As the text of the press notice announcing the decision stated, 'There will be no interruption of ordinary banking business. The banks will be open as usual for the convenience of their customers; and there is no reason why sterling transactions should be affected in any way' (Sayers, 1976, 264). Schumpeter commented, '[I]n England there was neither panic nor – precisely owing to the way in which the thing had been done or, if the reader prefer, had come about – loss of "confidence", but rather a sigh of relief' (Schumpeter, 1939, 956).

When did a real financial crisis occur?

I begin the answer to the question by citing Bagehot's analysis with respect to 1866, the last real financial crisis in England (Bagehot, 1873, repr. 1902, pp. 64–5):

> And though the Bank of England certainly do make great advances in time of panic, yet as they do not do so on any distinct principle, they naturally do it hesitatingly, reluctantly, and with misgiving. In 1847, even in 1866 – the latest panic, and the one in which on the whole the Bank acted the best – there was nevertheless an instant when it was believed the Bank would not advance on Consols, or at least hesitated to advance on them. The moment this was reported in the City and telegraphed to the country, it made the panic indefinitely worse. In fact, to make large advances in this faltering way is to incur the evil of making them without obtaining the advantage. What is wanted and what is necessary to stop a panic is to diffuse the impression, that though money may be dear, still money is to be had. If people could be really convinced that they could have money if they wait a day or two, and that utter ruin is not coming, most likely they would cease to run in such a mad way for money. Either shut the Bank at once, and say it will not lend more than it commonly lends, or lend freely, boldly, and so that the public may feel you mean to go on lending. To lend a great deal, and yet not give the public confidence that you will lend sufficiently and effectually, is the worst of all policies; but it is the policy now pursued.

Bagehot thus stressed the importance of predictable action by the monetary authority to prevent a panic; failing that, a bank holiday was the course to follow. In 1866, the Bank's actions were hesitant so the public was not convinced that there was no reason to panic. H. H. Gibbs, Governor of the Bank, 1875–7, referred to the 1866 crisis as 'its only real blunder in his experience', because, instead of lending freely at an appropriately high rate, as Bagehot advised, 'it erred in lending at too low a rate before the crisis turned into panic' (Pressnell, 1968, p. 188). Although in 1873, when Bagehot wrote he still regarded the Bank's behaviour in 1866 as undependable, Gibbs did not blame the then Governor since 'the matter was not as well understood as it is now', noting that the Bank had done the right thing in 1873, when the underlying situation was just as troublesome as in 1866.[4]

The United States, by contrast, experienced a real financial crisis in 1873 because no institutional framework was immediately available to deal with the surge of demand for high-powered money by the public and banks. Belatedly, the crisis was alleviated by the issue against collateral of clearing-house loan certificates for use in the settlement of clearing balances and by US Treasury redemption with greenbacks of outstanding government debt.[5]

During the next two decades both England and the United States were spared the experience of financial crisis in circumstances that might have been breeding grounds for it. The impact of the failure of the City of Glasgow Bank in 1878 was sufficiently great to suggest to some observers that suspension of the Act of 1844 was required (Pressnell, 1968, p. 189), but it was not.[6]

In May 1884, the failure of a Wall Street brokerage firm involving a bank whose president was a partner in the brokerage firm was followed by the suspension of several other banks. However, a phenomenal rise in money market rates brought in an inflow of foreign capital and the supply of funds was further expanded by prompt issue of clearing-house loan certificates. The suspended banks were thereby enabled to resume. Sprague commented (1910, pp. 113–15):

> It will be seen that the steps taken to allay alarm were immediate and effective. . . . The success which crowned the efforts of the banks in dealing with the crisis affords convincing evidence that if clearing-house loan certificates are to be issued at all, they should be issued at the beginning of a disturbance. Local runs on the banks did not become severe, because announcement was made that assistance would be granted at the moment when the disasters which might have weakened general confidence became known to the public.[7]

The final episode of the two decades under consideration, when financial crisis did not occur either in England or the United States, was occasioned by the troubles of Baring Brothers in 1890. In the United States, Sprague noted (1910, p. 142) that it was 'the prompt action taken by the clearing-house authorities', by issuing loan certificates to meet the needs of particular banks experiencing runs, that prevented 'the spread of panic'. Sprague summarised (p. 144) 'one of two specifics for the proper treatment of a panic – the continuance of loans to solvent borrowers. A second equally important specific is the prompt payment by the banks of every demand by depositors for cash'. In England, the principal device the Bank of England adopted to prevent a crisis – it also borrowed gold from France and bought it from Russia – was to advance sums to meet Barings' immediate maturing liabilities, with the guarantee of a syndicate of bankers to make good any loss sustained by the Bank in liquidiating Barings over a period of years.[8] No loss was sustained by the Bank and no call on the guarantors was needed. Presnell concludes: 'The news of the guarantee allowed knowledge of Barings' troubles to spread beyond the inner circles without causing panic; indeed, anxiety lifted' (1968, p. 207).[9]

For two decades after 1873 clearing houses and the US Treasury took actions that neutralised monetary disturbances so that crisis conditions did not develop. Why did similar actions in 1893 and 1907 not have comparable effects? No simple explanation is at hand to account for the occurrence of financial crisis in the United States in 1893. It is easier to account for the crisis in 1907.

Two features of the situation in 1893 that differed from earlier experience may be noted: fears that silver advocates would succeed in forcing the country off gold first had to be put to rest, and only subsequently did the condition of the banks as a result of mercantile failures excite independent concern. At that point the clearing houses issued loan certificates. Sprague reports (1910, p. 173), 'Serious strain had been met boldly and successfully', but that was not to be the end of the episode. A second wave of distrust of banks spread over the west and south with consequent withdrawals of cash reserves from New York banks. Thereupon the Erie Railroad went into receivership and the stock market suffered the worst decline of the year. Bank suspensions followed in the east as well as in the south and west. Starting with banks in New York, banks throughout the country partly restricted cash payments, sending currency to a premium. The restriction, which lasted from 3 August to 2 September, came six weeks after the issue of clearing-house loan certificates and when gold was arriving from Europe.

Why did the issue of loan certificates not cut short the episode? One suggestion is that some banks did not avail themselves of the opportunity to obtain the certificates and therefore were unable to offset the shrinkage of their reserves (Noyes, 1894, p. 22). In addition, individual banks with the bulk of bankers' deposits had reserve deficiencies even though aggregate reserves of the banks were adequate. The suggestion that best conforms to the view I am presenting is that as early as July (Noyes, 1894, p. 25) rumours of refusal of banks to convert deposits into cash incited the financial crisis. A misinformed public can nullify the beneficial effects of actions designed to avert panic.

In 1907, the explanation for the occurrence of crisis appears straightforward. Assistance to troubled trust companies was granted slowly and without dramatic effect. The runs on the trust companies depleted the currency holdings of the New York Clearing House banks which were also shipping currency to interior banks and paying it out over their counters to their own frightened depositors. Although the Treasury helped by depositing currency with these banks, New York was threatened with panic, loans were obtainable only with great difficulty, and stock market prices collapsed. Sprague argued that at this point the clearing-house banks should have issued loan certificates to enable banks to extend loans more freely to borrowers and also to prevent the weakening of particular banks with unfavourable clearing-house balances. In his view, the banks did not do so due to their mistaken belief that an issue of clearing-house loan certificates would cause restriction (Sprague, pp. 257–8, 272–3). While local runs in New York subsided, alarm spread throughout the country. Loss of confidence was displayed less by the public than by country banks. They demanded currency for the funds on deposit or on call in New York. Belatedly, the New York Clearing House issued loan certificates and immediately restricted the convertibility of deposits into currency. Countrywide restriction followed. In 1907, the right actions were taken too late to be effective.[10]

The wartime features of the 1914 episode make it not wholly comparable to earlier cases of threatened crises that were averted. Yet to cope with the problems that rose in the summer of 1914, some of the methods relied on in peacetime episodes were applied. Foremost was the provision of emergency currency issues, in the United States, both clearing-house loan certificates and Aldrich – Vreeland currency (issued by groups of banks under the Act of 1908 establishing the National Monetary Commission), and in England, Treasury Currency Notes, which soon displaced gold coin. Initially, in the United States, concern was directed to limiting shipments of gold, but that became otiose: with the reopening of the sterling acceptance market in London, the belligerents' growing demand for exports, and the balance of trade turning strongly in favour of the United States. In England, initially Bank rate was lifted to 10 per cent, the level at which it had stood on the suspension of the Act of 1844 on three previous dates. This time no suspension was needed, and Bank rate was lowered to 5 per cent within the week to remain unchanged for the duration.

The additional measures taken to restore the channels of international and domestic financial activity were basically government subsidies (to the export trade in the United States in the form of war risk insurance) or government guarantees against loss (to the banking system in England). The guarantees in England led to the termination of an extended August Bank Holiday and of moratoria on the payment of bills making possible the renewal of availability of acceptance credits in London. A protracted closing of the stock markets in both New York and London was ultimately ended.

Britain's decision to suspend convertibility into gold in September 1931, as I noted earlier, does not qualify as a financial crisis. Real financial crises *par excellence* were experienced by the United States from 1930 to 1933. The lender-of-last-resort was responsible for a series of crises that intensified over time because it did not recognise the need to provide liquidity to the fractional reserve banking system that was confronted with surges of repeated runs. A multiple contraction of deposits was enforced by the inability of the banks to acquire adequate amounts of high-powered money. By March 1933 the entire financial system was prostrate.

The reasons may now be summarised, accounting for financial crises that did or did not occur in the past. In both cases the setting is one in which the financial distress of certain firms became known to market participants, raising alarm as creditors became concerned about the value of their claims not only on those firms but also firms previously in sound condition. Banks that were creditors of the firms in distress became targets of suspicion by their depositors. When monetary authorities failed to demonstrate readiness at the beginning of such a disturbance to meet all demands of sound debtors for loans and of depositors for cash, a financial crisis occurred. A financial crisis *per contra* could be averted by timely predictable signals to market participants of institutional readiness to make available an augmented supply of funds. The sources of the funds supplied might have been inflows from abroad – attracted by higher domestic than foreign interest rates – or emergency issues of domestic currency. The readiness was all. Knowledge of the availability of the supply was sufficient to allay alarm, so that the funds were never drawn on. In a few instances, orderly liquidation of the firms in distress, with a guarantee against loss by the liquidator, isolated the problem so that it did not spread to other firms and averted a financial crisis in this way.

A breakdown of the payments system has not occurred in the last century and more in England – ignoring the 1914 episode – and in the last half-century in the United States. The lesson has been learned that the financial distress of the few must not be permitted to become a financial crisis for all. Individual debtors fail but their difficulties do not become wide-spread and undermine creditors in general. Bad banks fail, or more likely are reorganised under new management or merged with a good bank, but if a run on a bank occurs – it is said to have occurred on the Banco Ambrosiano in the recent scandal in Italy – it is not permitted to cumulate into a banking panic. In the United States, federal deposit insurance attempts to remove the problem of a loss of confidence in the ability of banks to convert deposits into currency and thus to eliminate the reason for bank runs, but, as the experience of other countries proves, such insurance is not essential. Not only are authorities better educated. So also is the public. As its experience has grown with the institutional arrangements that prevent disruption of the payments system, its behaviour contributes to the dependability of the system.

Manias, panics, crashes

The preceding sections have focused on the relation between financial distress of firms with perceived significant market presence and the historical incidence of financial crises. In this section the focus shifts to the validity of the identification of manias with financial crises (Kindleberger, 1978).

For Kindleberger, manias, panics, and crashes are three phases of the same process. During manias, investors shift from money to real or financial assets. During panics, they try to shift from real or financial assets to money. Crashes are the denouement of the process, with the collapse of prices of whatever was eagerly acquired during the mania – 'commodities, houses, buildings, land, stocks, bonds' (1978, p. 5). He takes for granted that manias occur during cyclical expansions and the panic phases at peaks, while disclaiming that every business expansion leads 'inevitably to mania and panic. But the pattern occurs sufficiently frequently and with sufficient uniformity' (p. 5). Finally, he regards the manias, panics, and crashes that he discusses as financial crises per se.

In current economic analysis, the word 'bubble' has supplanted the pejorative 'mania'. In the definition proposed by Flood and Garber (1982, p. 275). 'The possibility of . . . a price bubble exists when the expected rate of market price change is an important factor determining current market price.' No reference is made to cyclical conditions in the definition. In my view, bubbles may arise independently of the economy's cyclical stage, although business expansion may foster them. No one has systematically examined all the cases, so the ones associated with particular cycle movements have had the lion's share of attention. Kindleberger's assertion that, according to a monetarist view, 'mania and panic would both be avoided if only the supply of money were stabilized at some fixed quantity, or at a regular growing level' (pp. 5–6) does not accord with my monetarist view. Bubbles, like bankruptcies, would occur even if the money stock were free of destabilising cyclical swings. The Florida land boom of 1925–6 and the gold price bubble of 1979–80 were created by opportunities those markets appeared to offer rather than the pattern of monetary growth.

A basic fact concerning bubbles is that they leave eager investors in sure-fire, get-rich schemes at the take-off considerably poorer at the landing. The loss of wealth attendant on misguided, unprofitable, voluntary investment decisions is, of course, not confined to bubbles. Bankruptcy proceedings are a daily occurrence in economic life. Willingness to spend may be reduced and previously glowing expectations may be replaced by uncertainty. But loss of wealth is not synonymous with a financial crisis.

At the stock market peak in 1929, the total value of all shares listed on the New York Stock Exchange was about $200 billion. The decline in October is estimated at nearly $15 1/2 billion, so many investors undoubtedly were poorer. Yet no financial crisis occurred following the great crash. The reason is that prompt and effective action by the New York Federal Reserve Bank provided additional reserves to the New York banks through open market purchases. Kindleberger acknowledges that the crash did not 'lead to a money market panic . . . or to runs on banks, probably because of the effective action of the New York Federal Reserve in pumping funds into the market' (p. 113), but still classifies the crash as a financial crisis apparently because it 'spread liquidation to other asset markets, such as commodities, and seized up credit to strike a hard blow at output' (p. 113). Any deflation would thus qualify as a financial crisis.

In a perceptive comment on bubbles, Wood (1983) has noted that they concern markets 'where quantities traded have varied little, while there have been enormous variations in price. They are interesting, but the fate of nations seldom depends on them'.

Kindleberger provides a tabulation in an appendix to his book that lists some three dozen financial crisis during two and a half centuries, characterising each one by the subject of the mania, how it was financed, dates of the peak and crash, and a final entry identifying the lender-of-last-resort. It is the final entry that motivates Kindleberger's study. He argues the importance of a lender-of-last-resort 'who comes to the rescue and provides the public good of stability that the private market is unable to produce for itself' (p. 4).[11] Yet he does not discriminate between episodes in which successful action was taken to prevent the development of a crisis and episodes in which no action was taken or the action was unsuccessful.[12]

Despite his designation of all episodes as financial crises without differentiation of those where the 'rescue' provided stability, even Kindleberger notes that there has been a dwindling of the number and a lessening of the severity of domestic financial crises since 1866 in Britain and since 1929 in the United States and on the Continent. He considers three possible explanations: (i) the decline of usury laws, making it possible for interest rates to be raised sufficiently to limit manias; (ii) the shunning of manias by markets that had learned from experience; (iii) the calming of anxieties owing to the known existence of a lender-of-last-resort. He dismisses the first two out of hand, but his position on the third is ambiguous. Nor is it clear why at this point he cites Minsky's reference (1977) to 'near panics' in 1966, 1969–70, and 1974–5, and 'incipient crises' in 1974 (p. 218).

The record on domestic financial crises may thus be reassuring to Kindleberger, but his current concern is the greater frequency now than in the nineteenth century of foreign exchange crises. The solution he suggests is an international lender-of-last-resort.[13] The recent analytical literature on bubbles also encompasses runs on a currency that is fixed in price in terms of at least one other currency and runs under flexible exchange rates (Flood and Garber, 1982). The underlying assumption that a run on a currency is a crisis seems to me untenable. The market will sell off an overvalued currency under fixed or floating exchange rates and will shift to an undervalued currency. If authorities resist the market's evaluation, it may be costly for them, but the problem facing the currency is more fundamental: the economic policies that are responsible for the currency's plight are the heart of the matter. If there is a crisis, it resides in the failure to adjust those policies.

I conclude that manias, panics, and crashes reduce wealth. They are not *per se* financial crises unless the shift from tangible or financial assets to money leads to a run on banks. A lender-of-last-resort can forestall such a development, so I agree with Kindleberger that there is an important role for such an entity, although I do not subscribe to the notion that only a public authority has in the past filled or can at present fill that role.

Financial distress versus financial crises

In my lexicon, the events since the mid-1960s that have been termed 'financial crises' or 'threats of a financial crisis' have been pseudofinancial crises.

Essentially the response to each of these events (to be noted in what follows) has been a form of bail-out, for which the justification was that the action averted a crisis. Since no financial crisis would in fact have been experienced had a bail-out not been undertaken, the events were pseudo-financial crises. Moreover, the policies adopted were economically inefficient or inflationary in effect.

The first event to be considered here was the failure of the Penn Central Railroad in June 1970. The Federal Reserve was concerned lest the company's default on its $200 million commercial paper borrowings would jeopardise that market. The Fed assumed that lenders would not discriminate between a troubled issuer and other perfectly sound issuers. The scenario envisaged by the Fed was that the latter would need to pay off their commercial paper because of generalised distrust of the instrument. Accordingly, the banks were informed that the discount window was 'wide open' (Maisel, 1973, p. 9) if they needed funds to make loans to customers unable to roll over commercial paper. In addition, to enable banks to bid freely for funds in the open market, the Fed suspended interest rate ceilings on 30 to 89-day large denomination certificates of deposit – an action that was desirable in its own right. Maisel concludes that the Fed's actions averted a panic (p. 4). However, if there were commercial paper issuers that faced difficulties, as Carron notes (1982, p. 398), it was not owing to the condition of the market as such but to 'conditions peculiar to those firms' (Chrysler Financial and Commercial Credit among others). The verdict of the 1971 *Economic Report of the President* (p. 69) was that no 'genuine liquidity crisis existed in mid-1970'.

Events in 1973–4 centred on bank failures in the United Kingdom, West Germany, the United States, and Switzerland that were thought to threaten the international financial order. Hirsch (1977, p. 248), who believes that co-operation to achieve 'collective intermediate goods' of bank stability is technically easier to organise 'in a small group of like minded individuals and institutions than in an open group' (p. 249) – a view reminiscent of de Cecco's – describes what happened in Britain when 'fringe banks', bank new-comers, experienced difficulties in December 1973. A deterioration of the market value of real estate investments of these banks led to deposit withdrawals and the switching of new deposits to established banks. To save depositors of the fringe banks from losses, the four-member oligopoly of deposit banks had to commit resources to that end. Hirsch interprets the action taken by the established banks as in their self-interest by removing a source of competition. Whatever the motivation of the established banks, their collective action bespeaks an understanding that the failure of individual banks must not be allowed to contract the aggregate money stock.

Two views have been presented with respect to the actions taken by the Federal Reserve when Franklin National Bank announced, in May 1974, that it had lost heavily in forward transactions in the foreign exchange market. The Federal Reserve initially announced that it would advance whatever funds Franklin needed, so long as it remained solvent, the loans ultimately reaching a maximum of $1.75 billion in early October. At that point the bank was merged with another institution and the FDIC assumed the Federal Reserve's loan.

One view (Carron, 1982, p.400) is that the preconditions of a genuine financial crisis existed, as evidenced by the fact that corporations paid premiums on their borrowings that reflected risks perceived in the banking system rather than in their own positions. The preconditions were, however, mitigated both because markets remained orderly with no lack of confidence on the part of investors and the central bank intervened effectively. An opposite view is that the immediate impact of Franklin's failure was erased by a Federal Reserve bail-out that led market participants to believe that no bank failures would be tolerated and that encouraged 'banks to become more reckless than ever' (Wojnilower, 1980, pp. 298–9). It was not only the losses in the foreign exchange market that the Franklin case revealed. The aftermath of its failure also disclosed the near-bankruptcy of real estate affiliates many banks owned. The affiliates had financed construction with short-term funds and invested in real estate and mortgages whose value declined when interest rates rose. Selling off real estate at distress prices further compromised the position of the affiliates, so that they experienced problems in selling their paper.

The perception of increased risk in lending to banks raised the cost of funds for them. Does this justify a bail-out or concern that a financial crisis was imminent?

Banking difficulties in Europe in 1974 that arose because of losses sustained in the foreign exchange market were apparently met without bail-outs. The Bundesbank announced the liquidation of Bankhaus I.D. Herstatt. Neither Westdeutsche Landesbank Girozentral of West Germany nor Union Bank of Switzerland was mortally wounded by its losses.

It was not banking difficulties but financial distress of two large real sector firms – Lockheed Corporation (1971) and Chrysler Corporation (1979) – and a municipality – New York City (1975) – that also provided occasions for a prognosis of a threat of financial crisis. In each case federal government legislation was enacted to guarantee private loans to these entities. The object was to avoid bankruptcy. Though Penn Central Railroad had filed for bankruptcy and subsequently restructured its operations to become an efficient firm, the view that has since come to prevail is that bankruptcy proceedings by themselves will create a financial crisis. The loan guarantees thus serve to mask the inefficient use of resources that had produced financial distress. It is true that some restructuring of claims on and operations of the entities was required as a condition of the guarantees, but it is not clear why reorganisation under bankruptcy proceedings would have precipitated a financial crisis. Again, the underlying assumptions seems to be that markets cannot discriminate between a firm or municipality in financial distress and others in sound condition. The inefficient are sustained in their misuse of resources because of the imagined hardship that would be imposed on the efficient.

Another class of events that is said to raise the prospect of domestic financial crisis is still impending – the impairment of the ability of many sovereign countries to make scheduled payments on their outstanding bank loans. Short-term loans extended to governments and to private borrowers abroad in some cases appear to be beyond their prospective capacity to repay. Acknowledgement of default on outstanding loans would require write-downs that would reduce capital of the banks involved and that would undoubtedly raise the cost to them of funds obtained in the open market. This course has been rejected on the ground that confidence in the stability of the banking system would be shaken. The alternative chosen has been the subterfuge that all the loans will be repaid, with the banks exhorted to provide an increase in lending sufficient to enable delinquent borrowers to maintain interest payments and to reschedule principal. In addition, the goal of stable non-inflationary monetary growth has been sacrificed as part of the effort to resolve the international debt problem. It is taken for granted that, if the policy of papering over the true economic prospects of the borrowing countries ultimately fails, standing in the wings will be the authorities ready to bail out the lenders. The costs of renewed inflation will then be dismissed as an unfortunate side effect.

Real financial crises need not occur because there is a well-understood solution to the problem: assure that deposits can be converted at will into currency whatever the difficulties banks encounter. The solution does not preclude failure of mismanaged banks. Recent discussion of moral hazard in relation to real financial crises would be more apt in relation to pseudo-financial crises. They provide the rationale for bail-outs and shoring up inefficiency. Pseudo-financial crises in recent years have generated expectations 'that no monetary authority will allow any key financial actor to fail' (Wojnilower, 1980, p. 299). Political authority seems well embarked in the direction of not allowing any key non-financial actor to fail, and of encouraging inflationary actions by domestic monetary authorities and international agencies in the cause of pseudo-financial crises.

Notes

1 The example of the deflation in 1920–1 in the United States may be cited. Bank reserves declined from $2.8 billion in April 1920 to $2.4 billion in August 1921. Wholesale prices (on the base 1926) fell from a peak of 167 in May 1920 to a trough of 91 January 1922. An index of liabilities of business failures rose from a trough of 6.0 in January 1920 to a peak of 71.2 in February 1922. Although 506 banks suspended business in 1921, there was no financial crisis. The deposit-currency and the deposit-reserve ratios in August 1921 were higher than in April 1920.

2 Financial distress defines the condition of an individual, a non-financial firm or an individual bank, or an industry that has assets with realisable value in money that is less than the amount of its indebetedness.

3 De Cecco (1975) argues that no problem would have arisen, had not the joint stock banks arbitrarily begun a credit squeeze in the middle of July, recalling loans they had made to bill brokers, and refusing to finance foreign clients of the accepting houses who usually borrowed in London to meet their maturing bills that the London houses had accepted. Stock Exchange dealers who worked on loans from foreign banks dumped their stocks to be able to return borrowed money, compelling the joint stock banks to call for extra margin from customers with Lombard loans, since the value of the collateral had declined. De Cecco says that the banks assumed a crisis of confidence on the part of the public would occur but in fact it did not happen. Therefore the banks engineered a crisis of confidence by refusing to pay out gold to the public and themselves drawing on the Bank's gold. The motive for the banks' behaviour, according to de Cecco, was to 'substitute themselves in lucrative international business' and 'exclude traditional intermediaries from their functions', though they wanted only 'to threaten them with the possibility of . . . death, in order to have them rescued *in extremis* and to paralyse their future action' (p. 149).

 According to Sayers (1, p. 70), it was sales of internationally traded securities on European stock exchanges that initiated the credit squeeze in London. He also notes that the joint stock banks' refusal to pay out gold before the August Bank Holiday may be interpreted in a more favourable light than de Cecco presents (I, p. 72).

4 De Cecco (1975, pp. 80–2) dismisses Bagehot's analysis. According to de Cecco, the Bank deliberately sought the fall of Overend, Gurney because 'they were encroaching upon the very branch of business on which the Bank throve: the discounting of bills from all over the country. . . . So conflict between the two giants seemed inevitable, particularly as their business had become very similar in nature' (p. 80). 'The Bank watched its rival fall without making any attempt to come to its rescue; on the contrary, it implemented a six-month "dear money" policy specifically to make Gurney's fall inevitable. Only after its rival had gone under did the Bank go to the market's rescue by extending unlimited assistance to anybody needing it, to allay the panic induced by Gurney's failure (p. 82).

 If de Cecco is right, the Bank was culpable because it deliberately ignored 'what was well understood', but the evidence does not support de Cecco's opinion that by 1866 the Bank understood what needed to be done in a timely way to prevent a crisis.

5 In Austria, in 1873, the main response to the stock market decline which was followed by a large number of insolvencies and bankruptcies was the suspension of the Banking Act of 1862 to 'assist the mobilization of central bank funds in case a liquidity shortage should make itself felt' (März, 1982, p. 188). No shortage occurred. Six months later, a consortium of banking houses and the central bank rescued from collapse the Bodencredit–Anstalt, an issuer of mortgage bonds with credit standing abroad equal to that of Austrian treasury certificates. The firm had been involved in 'risky stock-exchange operations' (p. 189).

6 *The Economist*, 5 October 1878 (Gregory, 1929, II, pp. 289–90), commented on the bank's failure: 'There was no run, or any semblance of run; there was no local discredit. . . . The fact that the other Scottish banks are willing to take up the notes of the City of Glasgow Banks appears to support the belief that all the liabilities of the bank will be met in full. The danger of discrediting the circulation may, however, have had some influence on the other banks in determining their action in this matter.'

7 Pressnell (1982, p. 152) reports the actions taken in Ceylon, when the Oriental Banking Corporation, a major international bank with many branches in Southeast Asia and in Australia, collapsed in May 1884. The colony's governor

guaranteed the bank's substantial note issues and the other banks imported silver rupees from India. A financial crisis was averted.

8 A similar device had apparently been used by the Bank of France in 1889. Pressnell (1968, p. 205) cites a French historian as crediting France with helping England in 'two ways in 1890: with gold and by her example'. The example refers to the use of a collective guarantee by French banks in support of the Bank of France. A certain Comptoir d'Escompte, in 1889, experienced a run as the result of unwise loans it had made to a company that speculated in copper. The Bank provided the Comptoir with funds to reimburse its depositors and creditors and then liquidated it.

9 According to de Cecco (1975, p. 92), because of the Bank of England's rivalry with the joint stock banks, only merchant bankers were first asked to underwrite the guarantee, and the joint stock banks only later. He concludes that the Baring crisis 'proved to be the swan song of the power of the Bank of England and of the merchant banks. Barings were prevented from going down and taking other houses with them; but this was made possible only by a series of expedients – all traditional instruments of policy had been abandoned' (p. 95).
Pressnell deplores the device of the guarantee as 'not central banking', as well as loss of the opportunity the Barings' situation created to advance reform of the Act of 1844, and more particularly the need for larger banking and larger gold reserves.

10 Bonelli's article (1982, pp. 51–65) on the '1907 financial crisis in Italy' should be retitled 'the 1907 financial crisis that did not occur in Italy'. He defines the crisis as a prolonged decline in prices of shares that brought one of the largest mixed banks close to suspension. It did not happen because the Banca d'Italia, the largest of the three issuing banks, initiated and co-ordinated 'anticrisis measures' (p. 51). 'It began to provide liquidity in all directions by means of discounts and advances . . . it also announced that its reserves were increasing, that it could issue money without any difficulty, and that it could even count on the government's readiness to take any extraordinary measures that might become necessary (to wit, removal of the ceiling established by law as regards the volume of circulation not enjoying full metallic coverage)' (p. 58).

11 Kindleberger cites no evidence in support of the proposition that the private market is unable to serve as the lender-of-the-last-resort. The clearing houses at times undertook that function under the National Banking System in the United States.

12 An oddity is that the tabulation includes an entry for 1819 in England. The listing for that episode is 'none' under 'crisis', and 'none needed' under 'lender-of-last-resort'.

13 I share the view expressed by Griffiths (1983) that the proposal should be rejected. The grounds for rejection that he cites relate to the role of banks and international debt. They also apply to foreign exchange markets.

References

Bagehot, W. (1873) *Lombard Street*. Repr. 1902 (New York: Scribner's).

Bonelli, F. (1982) 'The 1907 financial crisis in Italy: a peculiar case of the lender of last resort in action', in Kindleberger, C. P. (ed.) *Financial Crises: Theory, History, Policy* (Cambridge: Cambridge University Press).

Carron, A. S. (1982) 'Financial crises: recent experience in US and international markets', *Brookings Papers on Economic Activity* (2): 395–422.

Clapham, Sir. (1945) *The Bank of England: A History*. Vol. II, 1797–1914 (New York: Macmillan).

de Cecco, M. (1975) *Money and Empire: The International Gold Standard, 1890–1914* (Totowa, NJ: Rowman and Littlefield).

Economic Report of the President, (1971) (Washington, DC: US Government Printing Office).

Flood, R. P. and Garber, P. M. (1982) 'Bubbles, runs, and gold monetization', in Wachtel, P. (ed.) *Crises in the Economic and Financial Structure* (Lexington, Mass: Heath).

Gregory, T. E. (ed.) (1929) *Select Statutes, Documents and Reports Relating to British Banking, 1832–1928*. Vol. II, 1847–1928 (London: Humphrey Milford).

Griffiths, B. (1983) 'Banking in crisis', *Policy Review* 25 (Summer): 28–35.

Hirsch, F. (1977) 'The Bagehot problem'. *The Manchester School of Economic and Social Studies* 46 (September): 241–55.

Kindleberger, C. P. (1978) *Manias, Panics, and Crashes: A History of Financial Crises* (New York: Basic Books).

Maisel, S. J. (1973) *Managing the Dollar* (New York: Norton).

März, E. (1982) 'Comment', in Kindleberger, C. P. (ed.) *Financial Crises Theory, History, Policy* (Cambridge: Cambridge University Press).

Minsky, H. P. (1977) 'A theory of systematic fragility', in Altman, E. I. and Sametz, A. W. (eds) *Financial Crises: Institutions and Markets in a Fragile Financial Environment* (New York: Wiley).

Moggridge, D. E. (1982) 'Policy in the crises of 1920 and 1929', in Kindleberger, C. P. (ed.) *Financial Crises: Theory, History, Policy* (Cambridge: Cambridge University Press).

Noyes, A. D. (1894) 'The banks and the panic of 1893', *Political Science Quarterly* 9 (March): 12–30.

Pressnell, L. S. (1968) 'Gold reserves, banking reserves, and the Baring crisis of 1890', in Whittlesey, C. R. and Wilson, J. S. G. (eds) *Essays in Money and Banking in Honour of R. S. Sayers* (Oxford: Clarendon Press).

Pressnell, L. S. (1982) 'The sterling system and financial crises before 1914', in Kindleberger, C. P. (ed.) *Financial Crises: Theory, History, Policy* (Cambridge: Cambridge University Press).

Sayers, R. S. (1976) *The Bank of England, 1891–1944*, 3 vols. (Cambridge: Cambridge University Press).

Schumpeter, J. A. (1939) *Business Cycles*. 2 vols. (New York: McGraw-Hill).

Sprague, O. M. W. (1910) *History of Crises under the National Banking System*. National Monetary Commission (Washington, DC: US Government Printing Office).

Wojnilower, A. M. (1980) 'The central role of credit crunches in recent financial history', *Brookings Papers on Economic Activity* (2): 277–326.

Wood, G. E. (1983) Review of *Crises in the Economic and Financial Structure*, Wachtel, P. (ed.) *The Banker* (June): 266–7.

10 Lender of last resort

The concept in history

Thomas M. Humphrey[*]

Averting banking panics and crises is the job of the central bank. As lender of last resort (LLR), it has the responsibility of preventing panic-induced collapses of the money stock. Traditionally, it has discharged this responsibility by making emergency loans of high-powered money to sound but temporarily illiquid banks at penalty rates on good collateral. Ideally, the mere announcement of its commitment, by assuaging people's fears of inability to obtain cash, would be sufficient to still panics without the need for making loans.

Banking scholars agree that the Bank of England in the last third of the nineteenth century was the lender of last resort par excellence. More than any central bank before or since, it adhered to the strict classical or Thornton-Bagehot version of the LLR concept. That version, named for its principal framers Henry Thornton and Walter Bagehot, stressed (1) protecting the aggregate money stock, not individual institutions, (2) letting insolvent institutions fail, (3) accommodating sound institutions only, (4) charging penalty rates, (5) requiring good collateral, and (6) preannouncing these conditions well in advance of any crisis so that the market would know exactly what to expect. These precepts served the Bank well. So well, in fact, that the U.K. suffered no banking crises after 1866. Even today, the Thornton-Bagehot version of the LLR concept provides a useful benchmark or standard for central bank policy. It is time to document the evolution and logic of that concept in some detail.

Henry Thornton's contribution

The term 'lender of last resort' owes its origin to Sir Francis Baring, who in his *Observations on the Establishment of the Bank of England* (1797) referred to the Bank as 'the dernier resort' from which all banks could obtain liquidity in times of crisis. But the concept itself received its first – and in many respects still its most rigorous, complete, and systematic – treatment in the hands of Henry Thornton. It was Thornton who, in his testimony before

[*] This paper draws from my contribution to the article, coauthored with Robert E. Keleher, 'The Lender of Last Resort: A Historical Perspective,' *Cato Journal* 4 (Spring/Summer 1984): 275–318.

Parliament, in his speeches on the Bullion Report, and in his classic *An Enquiry Into the Nature and Effects of the Paper Credit of Great Britain* (1802), identified the Bank of England's distinguishing characteristics as an LLR. It was he who also specified the LLR's primary function, who distinguished between the micro and macroeconomic aspects of this function, and who analyzed the LLR's relationship with the monetary control function of the central bank. Finally, it was he who first enunciated the so-called 'moral hazard' problem confronting the LLR.

Distinctive features

Thornton identified three distinguishing characteristics of the LLR. First was its unique position as the ultimate source of liquidity for the financial system. The LLR, he pointed out, maintained and created a strategic stock of high-powered money (gold and Bank of England notes) that could be used to satisfy demands for liquidity at critical times. More precisely, it held the central gold reserve from which all banks could draw. Equally important, it supplied the non-gold component of the monetary base in the form of its own notes – notes which, by virtue of their unquestioned soundness and universal acceptability, were considered the equivalent of gold and therefore constituted money of ultimate redemption. The Bank's effective monopolistic power to issue these notes gave it sole control over an inexhaustible source of outside money – the first requisite of an LLR.

Arresting internal drains

The second hallmark of the LLR was its special responsibilities as custodian of the central gold reserve. It must hold sufficient reserves to inspire full confidence in their ready availability in times of stress. Also it must rely on its own resources (since as the last resort, it can turn to no other source) to protect the reserve from gold-depleting specie drains. Specifically, it must stand ready to freely issue its own paper to stem the panics that produce internal drains as cashholders seek to switch from country bank notes to gold or its equivalent. And, while relying on the Bank's monetary control function to prevent external drains caused by persistent inflationary overissue of paper, it must hold so large a gold reserve as to withstand those temporary and self-reversing external drains caused by real shocks to the balance of payments. Should the Bank nevertheless find its gold reserve depleted by an extraordinary succession of such shocks (Thornton mentions three successive crop failures), it must take steps to ensure that the eventual return flow of gold is not delayed by domestic monetary contractions that depress aggregate production and reduce output available for export. For, according to Thornton (1939, p. 118), given downward inflexibility of wages and prices in the face of a money-stock collapse:

the manufacturer, on account of the unusual scarcity of money, may even ... be absolutely compelled by necessity to slacken, if not suspend, his operations. To inflict such a pressure on the mercantile world as necessarily causes an intermission of manufacturing labor, is obviously not the way to increase that exportable produce, by the excess of which, above the imported articles, gold is to be brought into the country.

In short, the central bank must ensure that secondary monetary shocks do not prolong temporary external drains originating in real disturbances. To do so, it must sterilize or neutralize those drains with temporary increases in its own note issue. In so doing, it maintains the base of high-powered money and prevents sharp contractions in the money stock, contractions which, by depressing manufacturing activity and thus reducing output available for export, would prolong the trade deficit and hinder the return flow of gold. By judicious expansion of its own paper, the Bank of England arrests and reverses these specie drains that imperil its gold reserve.

Public duties

The third characteristic of the LLR was that it was not just like any other bank; it had public responsibilities. Unlike an ordinary commercial banker, whose responsibilities extend only to his stockholders, an LLR's responsibility extends to the entire economy. The LLR's duties include preserving the aggregate quantity and hence purchasing power of the circulating medium during bank runs and panics, and assisting the entire financial system in times of crisis. This responsibility, Thornton argued, dictates that the LLR behave precisely the opposite of a commercial banker in times of general distress, expanding its note issue and loans at the very time the banker is contracting his. For whereas the individual banker can justify his loan and note contraction on the grounds that it will enhance his own liquidity and safety while not materially worsening that of the whole economy, the LLR can make no such assumption. On the contrary, the LLR must assume that, because of its influence over the total money supply, any contractionary policy on its part would adversely affect the economy. Consequently, the LLR must expand its note issue and loans at a time when the prudent commercial banker is contracting his.

Policy issues

Having outlined the distinctive features of the LLR, Thornton next expounded on four policy issues pertaining to the LLR. The first concerns a possible conflict between the central bank's responsibility as controller of the paper component of the monetary stock and its function as lender of last resort. Since the central bank bears the responsibility for providing a stable framework of monetary growth, it must exercise a moderate and continued restraint on the rate of expansion of its own note issue. It must do so either to protect its gold reserves from displacement by excess paper so that it can maintain the convertibility of its currency under fixed exchange rates or to prevent domestic inflation under floating exchange rates. But coping with unusual liquidity strains or panics through exercise of the LLR function calls for abandonment of this restraint and relinquishing control over the growth rate of the Bank note component of the monetary base. Hence, some banking specialists have noted an apparent conflict between these two central banking objectives.

Monetary control and the LLR

Thornton, however, saw no inconsistency between a policy of stable monetary growth and the actions required to deal with liquidity crises. In the following passage, which Joseph Schumpeter called the 'Magna Carta of central banking,' Thornton distinguishes between the long-run target growth path of paper money and temporary emergency deviations from the path. The proper policy of the Bank of England, Thornton (1939, p. 259) said, is

> [T]o limit the total amount of paper issued, and to resort for this purpose, whenever the temptation to borrow is strong, to some effectual principle of restriction; in no case, however, materially to diminish the sum in circulation, but to let it vibrate only within certain limits; to afford a slow and cautious extension of it, as the general trade of the kingdom enlarges itself; to allow of some special, though temporary, increase in the event of any extraordinary alarm or difficulty, as the best means of preventing a great demand at home for guineas;[1] and to lean to the side of diminution, in the case of gold going abroad, and of the general exchanges continuing long unfavourable; this seems to be the true policy of the directors of an institution circumstanced like that of the Bank of England. To suffer either the solicitations of merchants, or the wishes of government, to determine the measure of the bank issues, is unquestionably to adopt a very false principle of conduct.

Remedies for external drains

Thus, to Thornton, the main responsibility of the central bank was to regulate paper money so that it expands at a steady noninflationary pace roughly comparable to the long-term growth rate of output. The bank must also counter those specie drains that periodically threatened to deplete its gold reserve and force suspension of convertibility. As previously mentioned, these

---

1   Thornton is here referring to the public's demand for gold coin, the guinea being the name of a standard gold coin in use in England at the time.

drains were of two types: external (or foreign), composed of exports of gold to cover an adverse balance of payments, and internal, consisting of panic-induced increases in the quantity of gold held by domestic residents. Now temporary (self-reversing) external drains arising from transitory real shocks to the balance of payments can normally be met from the large buffer stock of gold reserves held precisely for that purpose, the temporary runoff of gold being off-set by a reverse flow later on. But an extraordinary succession of such drains, if sufficient to exhaust the metallic reserve and deplete the gold in circulation, may require expansionary policy. Such policy, Thornton argued, would neutralize (sterilize) the gold outflow, prevent needless monetary contraction and the resulting disruption of the export industries ('those sources of our returning wealth'), and thereby contribute to the prompt correction of the trade deficit and the speedy return of gold. By contrast, *persistent* external drains arising from inflationary over-issue of paper call for restrictive policy. Either by reducing inflated British prices relative to foreign prices or by creating an excess demand for money which domestic residents attempt to satisfy by selling more goods and buying less, such restrictive policy spurs exports, checks imports, eliminates the trade-balance deficit, and halts the outflow of gold. Clearly monetary contraction, he thought, is the correct remedy for persistent external drains.

LLR and internal drains

In the case of a panic and internal drain, however, the Bank should be prepared temporarily to expand sharply both its note issue and its loans to satisfy the public's demand for high-powered money. This means that the Bank must step off its path of stable note growth to prevent the money stock from shrinking. Indeed, Thornton argued that emergency expansions of Bank of England notes were required to keep the entire stock of paper money (Bank notes plus notes issued by country banks) on path in the face of panic-induced demands to switch out of country notes. There need be no conflict between the functions of money control and lender of last resort, however, since the first refers to the long run and the second to temporary periods of emergency that may last for only a few days. If the LLR responds promptly and vigorously to the threat of a liquidity crisis, the panic will be averted quickly. Indeed, Thornton held that the mere expectation of such a response may be sufficient to stop the panic before additional notes are issued. Thus, the deviation of the paper component of the monetary base from its long-run target path will be small, both in magnitude and duration.

Macro vs. micro responsibilities

The second issue considered by Thornton concerns the extent of the lender of last resort's responsibility to individual banks as opposed to the banking system as a whole. Suppose these individual banks are unsound. Must the

LLR act to prevent their failure; that is, are bailout operations necessary to preserve the stability of the payments mechanism? Thornton (1939 p. 188) answered in the negative.

> It is by no means intended to imply, that it would become the Bank of England to relieve every distress which the rashness of country banks may bring upon them; the bank, by doing this, might encourage their improvidence. There seems to be a medium at which a public bank should aim in granting aid to inferior establishments, and which it must often find very difficult to be observed. The relief should neither be so prompt and liberal as to exempt those who misconduct their business from all the natural consequences of their fault, nor so scanty and slow as deeply to involve the general interests. These interests, nevertheless, are sure to be pleaded by every distressed person whose affairs are large, however indifferent or even ruinous may be their state.

Thornton made four key points in this passage. First, the lender of last resort's primary responsibility is to the market ('the general interests') and not to the individual bank. The central bank has no duty to sustain particular institutions. Second, the LLR must take account of the moral hazard problem. That is, it must recognize that when it makes liberal accommodation available, it may create incentives that encourage laxity and recklessness in the lending practice of individual banks. Thornton's solution to this problem was to advise against bailout operations for banks whose distress arises from 'rashness,' 'improvidence,' or 'misconduct.' By subsidizing the risk-bearing function of poorly managed banks, such rescue operations, he asserts, would encourage other banks to take excessive speculative risks without fear of the consequences. In short, individual imprudence should be punished by losses. Only if the financial repercussions of such punishment threaten to become widespread should the lender of last resort intervene. His third point, however, was that even in this latter case, aid should be extended sparingly and on relatively unfavorable terms. Finally, he was skeptical of the claim that economic welfare is inevitably harmed when a bank fails. This argument, he noted, would provide every large bank, no matter how poorly run, with an automatic justification for aid. He was aware that the public interest may be better served by the demise of inefficient banks, because the resulting improvements in resource allocation may well outweigh any adverse spillover side effects of the failure.

Containing contagion

The third issue addressed by Thornton was whether the lender of last resort should try to prevent shocks to the financial system. Here Thornton answered in the negative. The lender of last resort exists, he said, not to prevent shocks but to neutralize their secondary repercussions. He argued that a panic could be triggered by any kind of 'alarm'; for example, rumors of a foreign invasion, an initial bank failure, and so on. The central bank has no responsibility for stopping these triggering events, but it does have a responsibility for arresting the panic, stopping it from spreading throughout the system. 'If any one bank fails,' said Thornton (1939, p. 180), 'a general run on the neighboring ones is apt to take place, which if not checked at the beginning by a pouring into the circulation a large quantity of gold, leads to very extensive mischief.'

The proper response, according to Thornton, is not to stop the initial failure, but to pump liquidity into the market. In Thornton's view, the actual occurrence of a widespread panic would be properly attributable not to the initial bank failure, but to the central bank's failure to insulate the economy from the impact of that event. He distinguished between the effect of closing an individual bank and the policy errors of the lender of last resort. Closing an individual bank, he said, contributes very little to 'general distress' or 'general commercial difficulty.' By contrast, policy errors of the lender of last resort create a 'general shock to credit' that 'produces Distress through the whole Kingdom' (Thornton, pp. 287–88, 304–5).

Protecting the money stock

Finally, Thornton identified the paramount objective or primary purpose of the lender of last resort. That objective he specified as the prevention of panic-induced declines in the money stock, declines that could produce depressions in the level of economic activity. That is, he viewed the LLR as essentially a monetary rather than a banking function. While recognizing that the LLR also functions to forestall bank runs and avert credit crises, he insisted that these functions, although undeniably important, were nevertheless ancillary and incidental to the LLR's main task of protecting the money supply. In other words, the LLR's crisisaverting and run-arresting duties were simply the means (albeit the most efficient and expeditious ones) through which it pursued its ultimate objective of preserving the quantity, and hence the purchasing power, of the money stock. The important point was to prevent sharp short-run shrinkages in the quantity of money, since hardship ensued from these rather than from bank runs or credit crises per se.

In this connection, he drew a sharp distinction between bank *credit* (loans and discounts) on the one hand and the stock of *money* on the other. He then argued that, while the two aggregates tend to rise and fall together, it is the fall of the money stock that does the damage to the real economy. More precisely, he asserted that, while credit indeed finances and supports business activity, such credit arises from money rather than vice versa. Since credit springs from money and not money from credit, it follows that monetary contractions rather than credit collapses per se are the root cause of lapses in economic activity. Regarding this point, Thornton (1939, p. 307) asserted that a run-induced contraction in bank credit is not as harmful as the corresponding decline in the money stock: 'It is not the limitation of Discounts or Loans, but ... the limitation of Bank Notes or the Means of Circulation that produces the Mischiefs [of unemployment and lost output].'

To show how such monetary contraction and the resulting fall in output and employment would occur in the absence of an LLR, Thornton traced a chain of causation running from an alarm or rumor to financial panic to the demand for high-powered money to the money stock itself and thence to aggregate spending and the level of real economic activity. Panics, he noted, trigger doubts about the solvency of country banks and the safety of their note and deposit liabilities. As a result, moneyholders seek to convert these assets into money of unquestioned soundness, namely gold or Bank of England notes. These two items, he noted, comprise the base of high-powered money, an unaccommodated increase in the demand for which in a fractional reserve banking system is capable of causing a multiple contraction of the money stock. The demand for base money, he said, is doubly augmented during panics. For at the same time that moneyholders are attempting to convert suspect country bank notes and deposits into gold or its equivalent, country banks are seeking to augment their reserves of these high-powered monetary assets, both to meet anticipated cash withdrawals and to allay public suspicion of financial weakness. The result is a massive rise in the demand for base money – a rise that, if not satisfied by increased issues, produces sharp contractions in the money stock and equally sharp contractions in spending. Since Thornton contended that wages and prices were downwardly sticky and therefore responded sluggishly to declines in spending, he thought that output and employment would bear most of the burden of adjustment; that is, the monetary contraction would fall most heavily on real activity.

To prevent this sequence of events, the LLR must stand ready to accommodate all panic-induced increases in the demand for high-powered money. And this it can readily do since it has a monopoly over its own Bank note component of the monetary base. Expressed in modern terminology, Thornton's argument was essentially this: The LLR must be prepared to offset falls in the money multiplier arising from panic-induced rises in currency and reserve ratios with compensating rises in the monetary base. By so doing, it maintains the quantity of money intact and therefore also the level of economic activity.

Walter Bagehot's contribution

After Thornton, LLR theory received its strongest and most influential exposition in the writings of Walter Bagehot. In his seminal 1873 volume, *Lombard Street*, Bagehot revived and restated many of the points made earlier by Thornton. For example, he emphasized the Bank of England's special position as the holder of the ultimate reserve. This position, he noted, rendered the central bank different from ordinary commercial banks. It also gave the Bank the power as well as the duty to lend to all solvent institutions offering good collateral in a crisis, the very time when other bankers would be contracting their loans. He also followed Thornton in advocating that the Bank of England hold large buffer stocks of gold reserves from which periodic drains could be met without adversely affecting the quantity of money in circulation. Finally, like Thornton, he distinguished between the appropriate response to internal versus external cash drains. An internal drain, he said, should be countered by a policy of lending freely and vigorously to erase all doubt about the availability of bank accommodation. An external drain, however, should be met by a sharp rise in the central bank's lending rate, the high interest rate serving to attract foreign gold and encouraging the retention of domestic gold. This rate increase, Bagehot thought, was necessary to protect the metallic component of the monetary base. According to Bagehot (1962, p. 155), 'the first duty of the Bank of England was to protect the ultimate cash of the country, and to raise the rate of interest so as to protect it.'

A sufficient gold reserve, of course, was necessary both for the preservation of the gold standard and for the maintenance of public confidence in the convertibility of paper currency into gold. On the potential fragility of public confidence, Bagehot (1962 pp. 156–57) argued that 'a panic is sure to be caused' if the gold reserve falls below 'a certain minimum which I will call the "apprehension minimum."' It follows that the lender of last resort should strive to keep its gold reserves above this critical threshold.

Bagehot's Rule

Bagehot (1962, pp. 27–28) thought that a persistent external drain would trigger an internal drain as the public, observing the diminution of the gold stock and fearing a suspension of convertibility, sought to convert deposits and country bank notes into gold. 'Unless you can stop the foreign export,' he said, 'you cannot allay the domestic alarm.' In this case, in which 'periods of internal panic and external demand for bullion commonly occur together,' the lender of the last resort must 'treat two opposite maladies at once – one requiring stringent remedies, and especially a rapid rise in the rate of interest; and the other, an alleviative treatment with large and ready loans.' Therefore, 'the best remedy . . . when a foreign drain is added to a domestic drain' is the provision of 'very large loans at very high rates.' Here is the origin of the famous Bagehot Rule: 'lend freely at a high rate.'

Like Thornton, Bagehot stressed that last-resort lending should not be a continuous practice but rather a temporary emergency measure applicable only in times of banking panics. Like Thornton, he argued that if the central bank responded promptly and vigorously, the panic would be ended in a few days, by implication an interval not long enough for the paper component of the monetary base to depart significantly from its appropriate long-run growth track.

Responsibility to the market

Bagehot also viewed the role of the lender of last resort as primarily macro-economic. The central bank, he said, bears the responsibility of guaranteeing the liquidity of the whole economy but not that of particular institutions. He prescribed last-resort lending as a remedy for emergencies affecting the entire banking system, not for isolated emergency situations affecting an individual bank or a few specific banks. Nor did he intend it to be used to prevent very large or key banks from failing as a consequence of poor management and inefficiency. As shown below, he did not think that support of such distressed key banks was necessary to forestall panics. Like Thornton, he emphasized that the task of the central banks was not to prevent initial failures of unsound institutions but rather to prevent a subsequent wave of failures spreading through the sound banks of the system.

More generally, he believed with Thornton that the lender of last resort exists not to prevent shocks but to minimize their secondary repercussions. His views on this point are contained in his analysis of panics. Panics, said Bagehot (1962, p. 61), can be triggered by a variety of exogenous events – 'a bad harvest, an apprehension of foreign invasions, a sudden failure of a great firm which everybody trusted.' But 'no cause is more capable of producing a panic, perhaps none is so capable, as the failure of a first-rate joint stock bank in London' (Bagehot 1962, p. 29). The shock of this initial failure must be contained before it gets out of hand, for 'in wild periods of alarm, one failure makes many.' The problem is how to 'arrest the primary failure' that causes 'the derivative failures.' Bagehot's solution, quoted below (1962, p. 25), stresses the liberal provisions of liquidity to the whole system rather than loans to the distressed bank:

> A panic, in a word, is a species of neuralgia, and according to the rules of science you must not starve it. The holders of the cash reserve must be ready not only to keep it for their own liabilities, but to advance it most freely for the liabilities of others. They must lend to merchants, to minor bankers, to 'this man and that man,' whenever the security is good . . . The way in which the panic of 1825 was stopped by advancing money has been described in so broad and graphic a way that the passage has become classical. 'We lent it,' said Mr Harmon, on behalf of the Bank of England, 'by every possible means and in modes we had never adopted before; we took in stock on security, we purchased Exchequer bills, we made advances on Exchequer bills, we not only discounted outright but we made advances on the deposit of bills of exchange to an immense amount, in short, by every possible means consistent with the safety of the bank, and we were not on some occasions over nice. Seeing the dreadful state in which the public were, we rendered every assistance in our power.' After a day or two of this treatment, the entire panic subsided, and the 'City' was quite calm.

Conspicuously absent is any mention of the need to channel aid to specific institutions, as would be implied by bailout operations. Bagehot's emphasis is clearly on aid to the market rather than to the initially distressed bank. He obviously did not think it necessary to prevent the initial failure at all costs.

Up to this point, Bagehot has been depicted largely as a follower or disciple of Thornton. But Bagehot did more than just elaborate, refine, and coordinate Thornton's analysis. He also contributed several original points that added substance to the lender-of-last-resort doctrine and advanced it beyond Thornton's formulation. At least five of these points deserve mention.

Preannounced assurance

First, Bagehot distinguished between the central bank's extending support to the market after a crisis began, and its giving assurance of support in advance of an impending crisis. He argued that the lender of last resort's duty did not stop with the actual provision of liquidity in times of crisis, but also involved making it clear in advance that it would lend freely in all future crises. As Bagehot (1962, p. 85) put it, 'the public have a right to know whether [the central bank] – the holders of our ultimate bank reserve – acknowledge this duty, and are ready to perform it.' This assurance alone, he thought, would dispel uncertainty about and promote confidence in the central bank's willingness to act, thus generating a pattern of stabilizing expectations that would help avert future panics.

Penalty rate

Second, he advocated that last-resort accommodation be made at a penalty rate. Borrowers should have relief in times of crises, but they should be prepared to pay a price that implied a stiff penalty. The central bank has a duty to lend, but it should extract a high price for its loans, a price that would ration scarce liquidity to its highest-valued uses just as a high price rations any scarce commodity in a free market. Moreover, a penalty rate also had the appeal of distributional equity, it being only fair that borrowers should pay handsomely for the protection and security afforded by the lender of last resort. Allocative efficiency and distributive justice aside, the penalty rate, Bagehot claimed, would produce at least four additional beneficial results. First, it would encourage the importation and prevent the exportation of specie, thus protecting the nation's gold reserve. It would achieve this result by attracting short-term capital from abroad and by exerting a deflationary influence on spending and domestic prices, thereby improving the external balance of trade by spurring exports and reducing imports. Second, consistent with the objective of maintaining stable growth of the note component of the money stock, a penalty rate would ensure the quick retirement of emergency expansions of the Bank note issue once the emergency ends. The very unprofitability of borrowing at the above-market rate would encourage the prompt repayment of loans when the panic subsides, and the resulting loan repayment would extinguish the emergency issue so that the Bank note component of the money stock would return to its noninflationary path. Third, the high rate of interest would reduce the quantity of precautionary cash balances that overcautious wealth-holders would want to hold. Without the high rate to deter them, these cash-holders might deplete the central gold reserve. As Bagehot put it, the penalty rate would serve as 'a heavy fine on unreasonable timidity,' prompting potential cashholders to economize on the nation's scarce gold reserve. In this connection, he advocated that the penalty rate be established 'early in the panic, so that the fine may be paid early; that no one may borrow out of idle precaution without paying well for it; that the Banking reserve may be protected as far as possible' (Bagehot 1962, p. 97).

Last and most important, the penalty rate would, in addition to rationing the scarce gold reserve, provide an incentive for banks to exhaust all market sources of liquidity and even develop new sources before coming to the central bank. By encouraging individual banks to develop better techniques of money management and the capital market to develop new channels to mobilize existing liquidity, the penalty rate would promote allocative efficiency in the financial system. In short, the penalty rate would protect the gold reserve, minimize deviations of the Bank note component of the money stock from its stable path, allocate resources by market price, discourage reliance on the central bank, and ensure that recourse to the latter's lending facilities was truly a last resort.

Bagehot's analysis, it should be noted, implies still another use for the penalty rate: providing a test of the soundness of distressed borrowers. A penalty rate set a couple of percentage points above the market rate on alternative sources of funds would encourage illiquid banks to turn to the market first. Success in obtaining accommodation at the market rate – defined here as the going rate on default-free short-term credit instruments – would indicate that lenders judge these borrowers to be sound risks, for the borrowers and their assets would pass the market test. On the other hand, resort to the central bank at the penalty rate would tend to indicate weakness in the borrowing institutions, suggesting that they may be unable to borrow in the market at the lower rate. Fearing default, private lenders may demand a risk premium in excess of the differential between the risk-free market rate and the penalty rate, forcing the banks to resort to the central bank's lending facility. Thus, the penalty rate will have provided a test of the banks' soundness.

Eligible borrowers and collateral

Bagehot's third contribution was his specification of the types of borrowers the lender of last resort should accommodate, the kinds of assets it should lend on, and the criteria it should use to determine the acceptability of those assets. Regarding the types of borrowers, he stated that the Bank of England should be willing to accommodate anyone with good security. Last-resort loans, said Bagehot (1962, p. 25), should be available 'to merchants, to minor bankers, to this man and that man.' The objective of the central bank in time of panic is to satisfy the market's demand for liquidity. It makes little difference, he said, whether this objective is accomplished via loans to merchants, to bankers, or to any other sound borrowers.

Concerning the type of collateral on which the central bank should lend, Bagehot's answer was clear. The bank should stand ready to lend on any and all sound assets, or, as he put it, 'on every kind of current security, or every sort on which money is ordinarily and usually lent' (Bagehot 1962, p. 97). Besides the conventionally eligible bills and government securities, acceptable collateral should include 'all good banking securities,' and perhaps even 'railway debenture stock' (pp. 97, 101). In another passage he makes the point that the '*amount* of the advance is the main consideration . . . not the nature of the security on which the advance is made, always assuming the security to be good' (p. 101). The basic criterion was that the paper be indisputably good in *ordinary or normal times*. The latter qualification is important. It implies that the lender of last resort should not be afraid to extend loans on normally sound assets whose current market value is temporarily below book value owing to depression in the securities market.

To summarize, Bagehot felt that few restrictions should be placed on the types of assets on which the central bank might lend, or the kinds of borrowers it might accommodate. This position was consistent with his advocacy of price as opposed to non-price rationing mechanisms. He recommended that the central bank eschew qualitative restraints – eligibility rules, moral suasion, administrative discretion and the like – and instead rely on the penalty rate to ration borrowing.

Unsound institutions

Fourth, Bagehot delineated the extent of the lender of last resort's responsibility to individual banks as distinguished from the banking system as a whole. Concerning the question of whether this responsibility included assistance to solvent banks, Bagehot's answer was an unequivocal no. The central bank's duty, he said, is not to rescue the 'unsound' people" who constitute 'a feeble minority.' Such businesses, he said, 'are afraid even to look frightened for fear their unsoundness may be detected' (Bagehot 1962, p. 97). In short, the job if the central bank is not to prevent failure at all costs but rather to confine the impact of such failure to the unsound institutions.

Bagehot meant for his strictures to apply even to those key banks whose failure, in the absence of central bank action, could shatter public confidence and start a falling-dominoes chain-reaction sequence of financial collapse. Thus, Bagehot (1962, p. 129) acknowledged that if:

owing to the defects in its government, one even of the greater London joint stock banks failed, there would be an instant suspicion of the whole system. One *terra incognita* being seen to be faulty, every other *terra incognita* would be suspected. If the real government of these banks had for years been known, and if the subsisting banks had been known not to be ruled by the bad mode of government which had ruined the bank that had fallen, then the ruin of that bank would not be hurtful. The other banks would be seen to be exempt from the cause which had destroyed it. But at present the ruin of one of these great banks would greatly impair the credit of all. Scarcely any one knows the precise government of any one; in no case has that government been described on authority; and the fall of one by grave misgovernment would be taken to show that the others might easily be misgoverned also. And a tardy disclosure even of an admirable constitution would not much help the surviving banks: as it was extracted by necessity, it would be received with suspicion. A skeptical world would say 'of course they say they are all perfect now; it would not do for them to say anything else.'

Even in this case, however, Bagehot did not think it appropriate for the central bank to extend aid to poorly managed key banks. It is, instead, 'the "sound" people, the people who have good security to offer' who constitute 'the majority to be protected.' The lender-of-last-resort function should not be interpreted to mean that unsound banks should not be permitted to fail. Instead it implies that the failure should not be allowed to spread to sound institutions. To Bagehot, the distinction is crucial. In his words, 'no advances indeed need be made' on assets on 'which the [central] Bank will ultimately lose.' Again, in another passage, he offers assurance that if the lender of last resort 'should refuse bad bills or bad securities' it 'will not make the panic really worse.' To arrest a panic, he says, it is sufficient that the bank guarantee to provide liquidity to the 'solvent merchants and bankers' who comprise the 'great majority' of the market. This policy ensures that 'the alarm of the solvent merchants and bankers will be stayed' (Bagehot 1962, p. 97).

Strengthening self-reliance

Finally, Bagehot warned against undue reliance on the lender of last resort and stressed the need to strengthen individual banks. The lender of last resort, he pointed out, was not meant to be a substitute for prudent bank practices. Consistent with his laissez-faire, free-market philosophy, he argued that the basic strength of the banking system should rest not on the availability of last-resort accommodation, but rather on the resources and soundness of the individual banks. According to Bagehot (1962, p. 36):

[W]e should look at the rest of our banking system, and try to reduce the demands on the Bank [of England] as much as we can. The central machinery being inevitably frail, we should carefully and as much as possible diminish the strain upon it.

Bagehot (1962, p. 60) described in glowing terms the self-reliant character of a hypothetical decentralized 'natural system of banking,' composed 'of many banks keeping their own cash reserve, with the penalty of failure before them if they neglect it.' Elsewhere he pointed out that 'under a good system of banking . . . a large number of banks, each feeling that their credit was at stake in keeping a good reserve, probably would keep one; if any one did not, it would be criticized constantly, and would soon lose its standing, and in the end disappear' (Bagehot 1962, p. 52). In relying on its own soundness rather than the resources of the central bank, such a system, he noted, 'reduces to a minimum the risk that is caused by the deposit. If the national money can safely be deposited in banks in any way. This is the way to make it safe' (p. 53).

Providing liquidity via open market operations

One final observation should be made concerning Bagehot's views on the central bank's most appropriate instrument to combat panics. Today many banking experts regard open market operations, rather than discount window accommodation, as the most effective way to deal with systemic liquidity crises. Bagehot likely would have agreed. Although he consistently prescribed loans, rather than open market purchases of assets, to stop panics, this was mainly because the latter weapon was not widely used in his day. Had the technique of open market operations been highly developed at that time, he probably would have approved of its use, at least in those cases where there was no danger of the gold stock being depleted by a foreign drain. On these occasions, Bagehot favored resorting to the most expeditious means of stopping an internal cash drain. Open market operations are quite consistent with his dictum 'that in time of panic' the central bank 'must advance freely and vigorously to the public . . . on all good banking securities' (Bagehot 1962 pp. 96–97). Moreover, open market operations would have appealed to his preference for market-oriented allocation mechanisms. He would have approved of this particular policy instrument, which regulates the total amount of money but not its allocation among users or uses.[2]

Conclusion

Thornton and Bagehot believed the LLR had the duty (1) to protect the money stock, (2) to support the whole financial system rather than individual

---

2   Note that open market operations would render Bagehot's penalty rate inoperative. With such operations, however, penalty rates are in any case unnecessary since the market itself rations or allocates newly-created money among cashholders.

institutions, (3) to behave consistently with the longer-run objective of stable money growth, and (4) to preannounce its policy in advance of crises so as to remove uncertainty. They also advised the LLR to let insolvent institutions fail, to lend to creditworthy institutions only, to charge penalty rates, and to require good collateral. Such rules they thought would minimize problems of moral hazard and remove bankers' incentives to take undue risks. These precepts, though honored in the breach as well as in the observance, continue to serve as a bench-mark and model for central bank policy today.

References

Bagehot, Walter. *Lombard Street*. 1873. Reprint. Homewood, Ill.: Richard D. Irwin, 1962.

Thornton, Henry. *An Enquiry Into the Nature and Effects of the Paper Credit of Great Britain*. 1802. Edited with an Introduction by F.A. von Hayek. New York: Rinehart and Co., 1939.

11 The lender of last resort

Alternative views and historical experience

Michael D. Bordo *

I. Introduction

Recent liquidity assistance to failing savings and loans and banks (some insolvent and some large) in the U.S. and similar rescues abroad have prompted renewed interest in the topic of the lender of last resort. Under the classical doctrine, the need for a lender of last resort arises in a fractional reserve banking system when a banking panic, defined as a massive scramble for high-powered money, threatens the money stock and, hence, the level of economic activity. The lender of last resort can allay an incipient panic by timely assurance that it will provide whatever high-powered money is required to satisfy the demand, either by offering liberal access to the discount window at a penalty rate or by open market purchases.

Henry Thornton (1802) and Walter Bagehot (1873) developed the key elements of the classical doctrine of the lender of last resort (LLR) in England. This doctrine holds that monetary authorities in the face of panic should lend unsparingly but at a penalty rate to illiquid but solvent banks. Monetarist writers in recent years have reiterated and extended the classical notion of the LLR. By contrast, Charles Goodhart and others have recently posited an alternative view, broadening the power of LLR to include aid to insolvent financial institutions. Finally, modern proponents of free banking have made the case against a need for any public LLR.

The remainder of this paper is organized as follows:

II. The LLR's role in preventing banking panics
III. Four views of the LLR: central propositions
IV. Historical evidence:
    Incidence of banking panics and LLR actions, U.S. and elsewhere

* Research for this article began while the author was a Visiting Scholar at the Federal Reserve Bank of Richmond in Summer, 1988. Thanks go to the following for help on this paper and on an earlier draft: George Benston, Marvin Goodfriend, Bob Hetzel, Tom Humphrey, Allan Meltzer, Anna Schwartz, and Bob Graboyes. Paulino Texeira provided valuable research assistance. The views expressed are those of the author and not necessarily those of the Federal Reserve Bank of Richmond or the Federal Reserve System.

II. Banking panics and the lender of last resort

The need for a monetary authority to act as LLR arises in the case of a banking panic – a widespread attempt by the public to convert deposits into currency and, in response, an attempt by commercial banks to raise their desired reserve-deposit ratios. Banking panics can occur in a fractional reserve banking system when a bank failure or series of failures produces bank runs which in turn become contagious, threatening the solvency of otherwise sound banks.

Two sets of factors, some internal and some external to banks, can lead to bank failures. Internal factors, which affect both financial and nonfinancial enterprises, include poor management, poor judgment, and dishonesty. External factors include adverse changes in relative prices (e.g., land or oil prices) and in the overall price level.

Of the external factors, changes in relative prices can drastically alter the value of a bank's portfolio and render it insolvent. Banking structure can mitigate the effects of relative price changes. A nationwide branch banking system that permits portfolio diversification across regions enables a bank to absorb the effects of relative price changes. A unit banking system, even with correspondents, is considerably less effective. The nearly 6000 bank failures that occurred during the decade of the 1920s in the U.S. were mostly small unit banks in agricultural regions. Canada, in contrast, had nationwide branch banking. Consequently, many bank branches in those regions closed, but no banks failed (with the exception of one, in 1923, due to fraud).

A second external factor that can lead to bank failures is changes in the overall price level (Schwartz, 1988). Price level instability (in a nonindexed system) can produce unexpected changes in banks' net worth and convert *ex ante* sound investments into *ex post* mistakes. Instability means sharp changes from rising to falling prices or from inflation to disinflation. It was caused by gold movements under the pre-1914 gold standard, and, more recently, by the discretionary actions of monetary authorities.

Given that bank liabilities are convertible on demand, a run on an insolvent bank is a rational response by depositors concerned about their ability to convert their own deposits into currency. In normal circumstances, according to one writer, bank runs serve as a form of market discipline, reallocating funds from weak to strong banks and constraining bank managers from adopting risky port-folio strategies (Kaufman, 1988). Bank runs can also lead to a 'flight to quality' (Benston and Kaufman et al., 1986). Instead of shifting funds from weak banks to those they regard to be sound, depositors may convert their deposits into high-quality securities. The seller of the securities, however, ultimately will deposit his receipts at other banks, leaving bank reserves unchanged.

When there is an external shock to the banking system, incomplete and costly information may sometimes make it difficult for depositors to distinguish sound from unsound banks. In that case, runs on insolvent banks can produce contagious runs on solvent banks, leading to panic. A panic, in turn, can lead to massive bank failures. Sound banks are rendered insolvent by the fall in the value of their assets resulting from a scramble for liquidity. By intervening at the point when the liquidity of solvent banks is threatened – that is, by supplying whatever funds are needed to meet the demand for cash – the monetary authority can allay the panic.

Private arrangements can also reduce the likelihood of panics. Branch banking allows funds to be transferred from branches with surplus funds to those in need of cash (e.g., from branches in a prosperous region to those in a depressed region). By pooling the resources of its members, commercial bank clearing houses, in the past, provided emergency reserves to meet the heightened liquidity demand. A clearing house also represented a signal to the public that help would be available to member banks in time of panic. Neither branch banking nor clearing houses, however, can stem a nationwide demand for currency occasioned by a major aggregate shock, like a world war. Only the monetary authority – the ultimate supplies of high-powered money – could succeed. Of course, government deposit insurance can prevent panics by removing the reason for the public to run to currency.[1] Ultimately, however, a LLR is required to back up any deposit scheme.

III. Alternative views on the LLR function

Four alternative views on the lender of last resort function are outlined below, including:

- The Classical View: the LLR should provide whatever funds are needed to allay a panic;
- Goodfriend and King: an open market operation is the only policy required to stem a liquidity crisis;
- Goodhart (and others): the LLR should assist illiquid and insolvent banks;
- Free Banking: no government authority is needed to serve as LLR.

---

1 In theory private deposit insurance could also be used. In practice, to succeed in the U.S., such arrangements would require the private authority to have the power, currently possessed by the FDIC, to monitor, supervise, and declare insolvent its members. Also the capacity of the private insurance industry is too limited to underwrite the stock of government-insured deposits. (Benston et al., 1986, ch. 3). Alternatives to deposit insurance include requiring banks to hold safe assets (treasury bills), charging fees for service, and one hundred percent reserves.

The classical position

Both Henry Thornton's *An Enquiry into the Effects of the Paper Credit of Great Britain* (1802) and Walter Bagehot's *Lombard Street* (1873) were concerned with the role of the Bank of England in stemming periodic banking panics. In Thornton's time, the Bank of England – a private institution which served as the government's bank – had a monopoly of the note issue within a 26-mile radius of London, and Bank of England notes served as high-powered money for the English banking system.[2] For Thornton, the Bank's responsibility in time of panic was to serve as LLR, providing liquidity to the market and discounting freely the paper of all solvent banks, but denying aid to insolvent banks no matter how large or important (Humphrey, 1975, 1989).

Bagehot accepted and broadened Thornton's view. Writing at a time when the Bank had considerably enhanced its power in the British financial system, he stated four principles for the Bank to observe as lender of last resort to the monetary system:

- Lend, but at a penalty rate[3]: 'Very large loans at very high rates are the best remedy for the worst malady of the money market when a foreign drain is added to a domestic drain.' (Bagehot, 1873, p.56);
- Make clear in advance the Bank's readiness to lend freely;
- Accomodate anyone with good collateral (valued at pre-panic prices);
- Prevent illiquid but solvent banks from failing.[4,5]

---

2   Bank of England notes served as currency and reserves for the London banks. Country banks issued bank notes but kept correspondent balances in the London banks. From 1797 to 1821, Bank of England notes were inconvertible into gold.

3   Bagehot distinguished between the response to an external gold drain induced by a balance of payment deficit (raising the Bank rate) and the response to an internal drain (lending freely).

4   Bagehot has been criticized for not stating clearly when the central bank should intervene (Rockoff, 1986), for not giving specific guidelines to distinguish between sound and unsound banks (Humphrey, 1975), and for not realizing that provision of the LLR facility to individual banks would encourage them to take greater risks than otherwise (Hirsch, 1977).

5   In part, Humphrey's summary of the Classical position is:

'. . . The lender of last resort's responsibility is to the entire financial system and not to specific institutions.'

'The lender of last resort exists not to prevent the occurrence but rather to neutralize the impact of financial shocks.'

'The lender's duty is a twofold one consisting first, of lending without stint during actual panics and second, of acknowledging beforehand its duty to lend freely in all future panics.'

'The lender should be willing to advance indiscriminately to any and all sound borrowing on all sound assets no matter what the type.'

'In no case should the central bank accommodate unsound borrowers. The lender's duty lay in preventing panics from spreading to the sound institutions, and not in rescuing unsound ones.'

'All accommodations would occur at a penalty rate, i.e., the central bank should rely on price rather than non-price mechanisms to ration use of its last resort lending facility.'

'The overriding objective of the lender of last resort was to prevent panic-induced declines in the money stock. . . .' (Humphrey, 1975 p.9)

Recent monetarist economists have restated the classical position. Friedman and Schwartz (1963), in *A Monetary History*, devote considerable attention to the role of banking panics in producing monetary stability in the United States (also see Cagan, 1965). According to them, the peculiarities of the nineteenth century U.S. banking system (unit banks, fractional reserves, and pyramiding of reserves in New York) made it highly susceptible to banking panics. Federal deposit insurance in 1934 provided a remedy to this vulnerability. It served to assure the public that their insured deposits would not be lost, but would remain readily available.

Friedman and Schwartz highlight the importance in the pre-FDIC system of timely judgment by strong and responsible leadership in intervening to allay the public's fear. Before the advent of the Fed, the New York Clearing House issued clearing house certificates and suspended convertibility, and, on occasion, the Treasury conducted open market operations. In two episodes, these interventions were successful; in three others, they were not effective in preventing severe monetary contraction. The Federal Reserve System, established in part to provide such leadership, failed dismally in the 1929–33 contraction. According to Friedman and Schwartz, had the Fed conducted open market operations in 1930 and 1931 to provide the reserves needed by the banking system, the series of bank failures that produced the unprecedented decline in the money stock could have been prevented.

Schwartz (1986) argues that all the important financial crises in the United Kingdom and the United States occurred when the monetary authorities failed to demonstrate at the beginning of a disturbance their readiness to meet all demands of sound debtors for loans and of depositors for cash. Finally, she views deposit insurance as not necessary to prevent banking panics. It was successful after 1934 in the U.S. because the lender of last resort was undependable. Had the Fed acted on Bagehot's principles, federal deposit insurance would not have been necessary, as the record of other countries with stable banking systems but no federal deposit insurance attests.

Meltzer (1986) argues that a central bank should allow insolvent banks to fail, for not to do so would encourage financial institutions to take greater risks. Following such an approach would 'separate the risk of individual financial failures from aggregate risk by establishing principles that prevent banks' liquidity problems from generating an epidemic of insolvencies' (p. 85). The worst cases of financial panics, according to Meltzer, 'arose because the central bank did not follow Bagehotian principles.'[6]

---

6 Meltzer (1986) succinctly restates Bagehot's four principles:

> 'The central bank is the only lender of last resort in a monetary system such as ours.'
>
> 'To prevent illiquid banks from closing, the central bank should lend on any collateral that is marketable in the ordinary course of business when there is a panic . . .'
>
> 'Central bank loans, or advances, should be made in large amounts, on demand, at a rate of interest above the market rate.'
>
> 'The above three principles of central bank behaviour should be stated in advance and followed in a crisis.' (Meltzer, 1986, p. 83)

Goodfriend-King and the case for open market operations

Goodfriend and King (1988) argue strongly for the exercise of the LLR
function solely by the use of open market operations to augment the stock of
high-powered money; they define this as monetary policy. Sterilized discount
window lending to particular banks, which they refer to as banking policy,
does not involve a change in high-powered money. They regard banking
policy as redundant because they see sterilized discount window lending as
similar to private provision of line-of-credit services; both require monitoring
and supervision, and neither affects the stock of high-powered money.[7]
Moreover, they argue that it is not clear that the Fed can provide such services
at a lower cost than can the private sector. Goodfriend (1989) suggests that
one reason the Fed may currently be able to extend credit at a lower cost is
that it can make fully collateralized loans to banks, whereas private lenders
cannot do so under current regulations. On the other hand, the availability
of these fully collateralized discount window loans to offset funds withdrawals by uninsured depositors and others may on occasion permit delays in
the closing of insolvent banks.[8] Goodfriend regards government-provided
deposit insurance as basically a substitute for the portfolio diversification of a
nationwide branch banking system. By itself, however, deposit insurance
without a LLR commitment to provide high-powered money in times of
stress is insufficient to protect the banking system as a whole from aggregate
shock.

The case for Central Bank assistance to insolvent banks

Charles Goodhart (1985, 1987) advocates temporary central bank assistance
to insolvent banks. He argues that the distinction between illiquidity and
insolvency is a myth, since banks requiring LLR support because of 'illiquidity will in most cases already be under suspicion about . . . solvency.' Furthermore 'because of the difficulty of valuing [the distressed bank's] assets, a
Central Bank will usually have to take a decision on last resort support to
meet an immediate liquidity problem when it knows that there is a doubt
about solvency, but does not know just how bad the latter position actually is'
(Goodhart, 1985, p. 35).

---

7 Like Goodfriend and King, Friedman (1960) earlier argued for use of open market operations exclusively and against the use of the discount window as an unnecessary form of
   discretion which 'involves special governmental assistance to a particular group of financial
   institutions' (p. 38). Also see Hirsch (1977) and Goodhart (1985) for the argument that
   Bagehot's rule was really designed for a closely knit/cartelized banking system such as the
   London clearing banks.
8 Cagan (1988) in his comment on Goodfriend and King makes the case for retention of
   discount window lending in the case of 'a flight to quality'. In that case, the discount window
   can be used to provide support to particular sectors of the economy which have had banking
   services temporarily curtailed.

He also argues that by withdrawing deposits from an insolvent bank in a flight to quality, a borrower severs the valuable relationship with his banker. Loss of this relationship, based both on trust and agent-specific information, adds to the cost of flight, making it less likely to occur. Replacing such a connection requires costly search, a process which imposes losses (and possible bankruptcy) on the borrowers. To protect borrowers, Goodhart would have the central bank recycle funds back to the troubled bank.

Solow (1982) also is sympathetic to assisting insolvent banks. According to him, the Fed is responsible for the stability of the whole financial system. He argues that any bank failure, especially a large one, reduces confidence in the whole system. To prevent a loss of confidence caused by a major bank failure from spreading to the rest of the banking system, the central bank should provide assistance to insolvent banks. However, such a policy creates a moral hazard, as banks respond with greater risk-taking and the public loses its incentive to monitor them.

Free banking: the case against any public LLR

Proponents of free banking have denied the need for any government authority to serve as lender of last resort. They argue that the only reason for banking panics is legal restrictions on the banking system. In the absence of such restrictions, the free market would produce a panic-proof banking system.

According to Selgin (1988, 1990) two of the most important restrictions are the prohibtion of nationwide branch banking in the U.S. and the prohibition everywhere of free currency issue by the commercial banking system. Nationwide branch banking would allow sufficient portfolio diversification to prevent relative price shocks from causing banks to fail. Free note issue would allow banks to supply whatever currency individuals may demand.

Free banking proponents also contend that contagious runs because of incomplete information would not occur because secondary markets in bank notes (note brokers, note detectors) would provide adequate information to note holders about the condition of all banks. True, such markets do not arise for demand deposits because of the agent-specific information involved in the demand deposit contract – it is costly to verify whether the depositor has funds backing his check. But, free banking advocates insist that clearing house associations can offset the information asymmetry involved in deposit banking.

According to Gorton (1985), and Gorton and Mullineaux (1987), clearing houses in the nineteenth century, by quickly organizing all member banks into a cartel-like structure, established a coinsurance scheme that made it difficult for the public to discern the weakness of an individual member bank. The clearing house could also allay a panic by issuing loan certificates which served as a close substitute for gold (assuming that the clearing house itself was financially sound). Finally, a restriction on convertibility of deposits into currency could end a panic. Dowd (1988) regards restrictions as a form of option clause.[9] In an alternative option (used in pre-1765 Scotland) banks had the legal right to defer redemption till a later date, with interest paid to compensate for the delay.

For Selgin and Dowd, the public LLR evolved because of a monopoly in the issue of currency. The Bank of England's currency monopoly within a 26-mile radius of London until 1826 and its extension to the whole country in 1844 made it more difficult than otherwise for depositors to satisfy their demand for currency in times of stress. This, in turn, created a need for the Bank, as sole provider of high-powered money, to serve as LLR.[10] In the U.S., bond-collateral restrictions on state banks before 1863 and on the national banks thereafter were responsible for the well-known problem of currency inelasticity. Selgin and Dowd do not discuss the case of a major aggregate shock that produces a widespread demand for high-powered money. In that situation, only the monetary authority will suffice.

In sum, the four views – classical, Goodfriend/King, Goodhart, and free banking – have considerably different implications for the role of a LLR. With these views as backdrop, the remaining paragraphs now examine evidence on banking panics and their resolution in the past.

IV. The historical record

In this section, I present historical evidence for a number of countries on the incidence of banking panics, their likely causes, and the role of a LLR in their resolution. I then consider alternative institutional arrangements that served as surrogate LLRs in diverse countries at different times. Finally, I compare the historical experience with the more recent assistance to insolvent banks in the U.S., Great Britain, and Canada. This evidence is then used to shed light on the alternative views of the lender of last resort discussed in section III.

Banking panics and their resolution

The record for the past 200 years for at least 17 countries shows a large number of bank failures, fewer bank runs (but still a considerable number) and a relatively small number of banking panics. According to a chronology

---

9 A restriction of convertibility itself could exacerbate a panic because the public, in anticipating such restriction, demands currency sooner.

10 Selgin (1990) argues that the Bank Charter Act of 1844 exacerbated the problem of panics because it imposed tight constraints on the issue of bank notes by the Issue Department. However, the Banking Department surely could have discounted commerical paper from correspondent banks without requiring further note issue. That is one of Bagehot's main points in *Lombard Street*.

compiled by Anna Schwartz (1988), for the U.S. between 1790 and 1930, bank panics occurred in 14 years; Great Britain had the next highest number with panics occurring in eight years between 1790 and 1866. France and Italy followed with four each.

An alternative chronology that I prepared (Bordo, 1986, Table 1) for 6 countries (the U.S., Great Britain, France, Germany, Sweden, and Canada) over the period 1870–1933 lists 16 banking crises (defined as bank runs and/or failures), and 4 banking panics (runs, failures, and suspensions of payments), all of which occurred in the U.S. It also lists 30 such crises, based on Kindleberger's definition of financial crises as comprising manias, panics, and crashes and 71 stock market crises, based on Morgenstern's (1959) definition.

The similar failure rates for banks and nonfinancial firms in many countries largely reflect that individual banks, like other firms, are susceptible to market vagaries and to mismanagement. Internal factors were important, as were the external factors of relative price changes, banking structure, and changes in the overall price level. The relatively few instances of banking panics in the past two centuries suggests that either (1) monetary authorities in time developed the procedures and expertise to supply the funds needed to meet depositors' demands for cash or (2) the problem of banking panics is exaggerated.

A comparison of the performances of Great Britain and the U.S. in the past century serves to illustrate the importance of the lender of last resort in preventing banking panics. In the first half of the nineteenth century, Great Britain experienced banking panics when the insolvency of an important financial institution precipitated runs on other banks, and a scramble for high-powered money ensued. In a number of instances, the reaction of the Bank of England to protect its own gold reserves worsened the panic. Eventually, the Bank supplied funds to the market, but often too late to prevent many unnecessary bank failures. The last such panic followed the failure of the Overend Gurney Company in 1866. Thereafter, the Bank accepted its responsibility as lender of last resort, observing Bagehot's Rule 'to lend freely but at a penalty rate'. It prevented incipient financial crises in 1878, 1890, and 1914 from developing into full-blown panics by timely announcements and action.

The United States in the antebellum period experienced 11 banking panics (according to Schwartz's chronology) of which the panics of 1837, 1839, and 1857 were most notable.[11] The First and Second Banks of the United States possessed some central banking powers in part of the period; some states

---

11 Selgin (1990), based on evidence by Rolnick and Weber (1986), argues that the episodes designated as panics in the antebellum Free Banking era are not comparable to these in the National Banking era because they did not involve contagion effects. Evidence to the contrary, however, is presented by Hasan and Dwyer (1988).

developed early deposit insurance schemes (see Benston, 1983; Calomiris, 1989), and the New York Clearing House Association began issuing clearing house loan certificates in 1857. None of these arrangements sufficed to prevent the panics.

In the national banking era, the U.S. experienced three serious banking panics – 1873, 1893, and 1907–08. In these episodes, the Clearing Houses of New York, Chicago, and other central reserve cities issued emergency reserve currency in the form of clearing house loan certificates collateralized by member banks' assets and even issued small denomination hand-to-hand currency. But these lender of last resort actions were ineffective. In contrast to successful intervention in 1884 and 1890, the issue of emergency currency was too little and too late to prevent panic from spreading. The panics ended upon the suspension of convertibility of deposits into currency. During suspension, both currency and deposits circulated freely at flexible exchange rates, thereby relieving the pressure on bank reserves. The panics of 1893 and especially 1907 precipitated a movement to establish an agency to satisfy the public's demand for currency in times of distrust of deposit convertibility. The interim Aldrich-Vreeland Act of 1908 allowed ten or more national banks to form national currency associations and issue emergency currency; it was successful in preventing a panic in 1914.

The Federal Reserve System was created in 1914 to serve as a lender of last resort. The U.S. did not experience a banking panic until 1930, but as Friedman and Schwartz point out, during the ensuing three years, a succession of nationwide banking panics accounted for the destruction of one-third of the money stock and the permanent closing of 40 percent of the nation's banks. Only with the establishment of federal deposit insurance in 1934 did the threat of banking panics recede.

Table I compares American and British evidence on factors commonly believed to be related to banking panics, as well as a chronology of banking panics and banking crises for severe NBER business cycle recessions (peak to trough) in the period 1870–1933.[12] The variables isolated include: deviations from trend of the average annual growth rate of real output; the absolute difference of the average annual rate of change in the price level during the preceding trough to peak and the current peak to trough as a measure of the effect of changes in the overall price level; deviations from trend of the average annual rate of monetary growth; and the percentage change in the money stock due to changes in the deposit-currency ratio.[13]

---

12 For similar evidence for the remaining cyclical downturns in this period, see Bordo (1986, Table 6, 1A).

13 In relating the changes in the money stock to changes in the deposit-currency ratio, we hold constant the influence of the other two proximate determinants of the money supply: the deposit-reserve ratio and the stock of high-powered money. It is calculated using the formula developed in Friedman and Schwartz (1963), Appendix B.

Table 1 Banking Panics (1870–1933): Related Factors, Incidence, and Resolution

Reference Cycle		Deviations from Trend of Average Annual Real Output Growth[a] (peak to trough)**	Absolute Difference of Average Annual Rate of Price Level Change (trough to peak minus peak to trough)*	Deviations from Trend of Average Annual Monetary Growth[b] (specific cycle peak to trough)**	Change in Money due to Change in Deposit-Currency Ratio (specific cycle peak to trough)***	Banking Crisis[c]***	Banking Panic[d]***	Existence of Clear and Credible LLR Policy***		
Peak	Trough								Resolution***	Agency***
United States										
1873	1879	0.5%	−7.1%	−4.7%	2.7%		8/73	No	Restriction of Payments	Clearing Houses/Treasury
1882	1885	−3.2%	−12.2%	2.6%	5.2%	5/84		Yes	Successful LLR	Clearing Houses/Treasury
1893	1894	−9.5%	−9.0%	−9.3%	−4.3%		7/93	No	Restriction of Payments	Clearing Houses/Treasury
1907	1908	−14.7%	−6.1%	−1.7%	−2.7%		10/07	No	Restriction of Payments	Clearing Houses/Treasury
1920	1921	−7.6%	−56.7%	−2.5%	2.8%			(?)		
1929	1932	−16.7%	−12.5%	−11.7%	−27.4%	1930,1931, 1932	1933	No	Unsuccessful LLR	Federal Reserve
Great Britain										
1873	1879	0.9%	−7.1%	−3.1%	5.2%			Yes		
1883	1886	−1.2%	−5.4%	−2.8%	2.3%			Yes		
1890	1894	−0.2%	−4.4%	−2.5%	−2.2%	Baring Crisis 11/90		Yes	Successful	Bank of England
1907	1908	−4.7%	−13.6%	−1.6%	−1.0%			Yes		
1920	1921	−6.9%	−68.0%	−5.1%	4.5%			Yes		
1929	1932	−3.7%	−7.9%	−4.3%	−1.3%			Yes		

Data sources:

* See Data Appendix in Bordo (1981).

** See Data Appendix in Bordo (1986).

*** Judgmental, based on this paper and other research.

Notes:

(a) The trend growth rates of real output were 3.22% for the U.S. (1870–1941) and 1.48% for Great Britain (1870–1939). Each was calculated as the difference between the natural logs of real output in terminal and initial years divided by the number of years.

(b) The trend monetary growth rates were 5.40% for the U.S. (1870–1941) and 2.71% for Great Britain (1870–1939). Each was calculated as in footnote (a).

(c) Banking crisis – runs and/or failures. Source Bordo (1986).

(d) Banking panic – runs, failures, suspension of payments. Ibid.

The table reveals some striking similarities in the behavior of variables often related to panics but a remarkable difference between the two countries in the incidence of panics. Virtually all six business cycle downturns designated by the NBER as severe were marked in both countries by significant declines in output, large price level reversals, and large declines in money-growth. Also, in both countries, falls in the deposit-currency ratio produced declines in the money stock in the three most severe downturns: 1893–94 (U.S.); 1890–1894 (G.B.); 1907–08; and 1929–32.

However, the difference in the incidence of panics is striking – the U.S. had four while Britain had none. Both countries experienced frequent stock market crashes (see Bordo, 1986, Table 6.1). They were buffeted by the same international financial crises. Although Britain faced threats to the banking system in 1878, 1890, and 1914, the key difference between the two countries (see the last three columns of Table 1) was successful LLR action by the British authorities in defusing incipient crises.

Similar evidence over the 1870–1933 period for France, Germany, Sweden, and Canada is available in Bordo (1986). In all four countries, the quantitative variables move similarly during severe recessions to those displayed here for the U.S. and Great Britain, yet there were no banking panics. In France, appropriate actions by the Bank of France in 1882, 1889, and 1930 prevented incipient banking crises from developing into panics. Similar behavior occurred in Germany in 1901 and 1931 and in Canada in 1907 and 1914.

One other key difference was that all five countries had nationwide branch banking whereas the U.S. had unit banking. That difference likely goes a long way to explain the larger number of bank failures in the U.S.

Alternative LLR arrangements

In the traditional view, the LLR role is synonymous with that of a central bank. Goodhart's explanation for the evolution of central banking in England and other European countries is that the first central banks evolved from commercial banks which had the special privilege of being their governments' banks. Because of its sound reputation, position as holder of its nation's gold reserves, ability to obtain economies by pooling reserves through a correspondent banking system, and ability to provide extra cash by rediscounting, such a bank would evolve into a bankers' bank and lender of last resort in liquidity crises. Once such banks began to act as lenders of last resort, 'moral hazard' on the part of member banks (following riskier strategies than they would otherwise) provided a rationale for some form of supervision or legislation. Further, Goodhart argues that the conflict between the public duties of such an institution and its responsibilities to its shareholders made the transition from a competitive bank to a central bank lengthy and painful.

Though Goodhart (1985 Annex B) demonstrates that a number of central banks evolved in this fashion, the experiences of other countries suggests that alternative arrangements were possible. In the U.S. before the advent of the Fed, a variety of institutional arrangements were used on occasion in hopes of allaying banking panics, including:

- Deposit insurance schemes: relatively successful in a number of states before the Civil War (Benston, 1983; Calomiris, 1989);
- A variety of early twentieth century deposit insurance arrangements which were not successful (White, 1981);
- Clearing houses and the issue of clearing house loan certificates (Timberlake, 1984; Gorton, 1985);
- Restriction of convertibility of deposits into currency by the clearing house associations in the national banking era;
- Various U.S. Treasury operations between 1890 and 1907 (Timberlake, 1978);
- The Aldrich-Vreeland Act of 1908.

Two countries which managed successfully for long periods without central banks were Scotland and Canada. Scotland had a system of free banking from 1727 to 1844. The key features of this system were a) free entry into banking and free issue of bank notes, b) bank notes that were fully convertible into full-bodied coin, and c) unlimited liability of bank shareholders.

Scotland's record under such a system was one of remarkable monetary stability. That country experienced very few bank failures and very few financial crises. One reason, according to White (1984), was the unlimited liability of bank stockholders and strict bankruptcy laws that instilled a sense of confidence in noteholders.[14] Indeed, the Scottish banks would take over at par the issue of failed banks (e.g., the Ayr bank, 1772) to increase their own business. A second reason was the absence of restrictions on bank capital and of other impediments to the development of extensive branching systems that allowed banks to diversify risk and withstand shocks.[15] Faced with a nationwide scramble for liquidity, however, Scottish banks were always able to turn to the Bank of England as a lender of last resort (Goodhart 1985).

Although Canada had a competitive fractional reserve banking system throughout the nineteenth century, no central bank evolved (Bordo and Redish, 1987). By the beginning of the twentieth century, though, virtually all the elements of traditional central banking were being undertaken either by private institutions or directly by the government.

By 1890, the chartered banks, with the compliance of the Government,

---

14 Sweden from 1830 to 1902 had a system of competitive note issue and unlimited liability. According to Jonung (1985), there is evidence neither of overissue nor of bank runs.

15 Switzerland also had a successful experience with free banks 1826–1850 (Weber, 1988) but like Scotland's dependence on the Bank of England, she depended on the Bank of France as lender of last resort (Goodhart, 1985).

had established an effective self-policing agency, the Canadian Bankers Association. Acting in the absence of a central bank, it succeeded in insulating the Canadian banks from the deleterious effects of the U.S. banking panics of 1893 and 1907. It did so by quickly arranging mergers between sound and failing banks, by encouraging co-operation between strong and weaker banks in times of stringency, and by establishing a reserve fund to be used to compensate note holders in the event of failure.

In addition, the nationwide branch system over-came the problem of seasonal liquidity crises that characterized the United States after the Civil War, thus lessening the need for a lender of last resort. However, the Bank of Montreal (founded in 1817) very early became the government's bank and performed many central bank functions.

Because Canadian banks kept most of their reserves on 'call' in the New York money market, they were able in this way to satisfy the public's demand for liquidity, again precluding the need for a central bank. On two occasions, 1907 and 1914, however, these reserves proved inadequate to prevent a liquidity crisis and the Government of Canada had to step in to supplement the reserves.

The Finance Act, passed in 1914 to facilitate wartime finance, provided the chartered banks with a liberal rediscounting facility. By pledging appropriate collateral (this was broadly defined) banks could borrow Dominion notes from the Treasury Board. The Finance Act clause, which was extended after the wartime emergency by the Amendment of 1923, provided a discount window/lender of last resort for the Canadian banking system.

In sum, though Canada, Scotland, and several other countries did not have formal central banks serving as LLRs, all had access to a governmental authority which could provide high-powered money in the event of such a crisis.

LLR assistance to insolvent banks

The classical prescription for LLR action is to lend freely but at a penalty rate to illiquid but solvent banks. Both Thornton and Bagehot advised strongly against assistance to insolvent financial institutions. They opposed them because they would encourage future risk-taking without even eradicating the threat of runs on other sound financial institutions. Bagehot also advocated lending at a penalty rate to discourage all but those truly in need from applying and to limit the expansion in liquidity to the minimum necessary to end the panic.

Between 1870 and 1970, European countries generally observed the classical strictures. In the Baring Crisis of 1890, the Bank of England successfully prevented panic. It arranged (with the Bank of France and the leading Clearing Banks) to advance the necessary sums to meet the Barings' immediate maturing liability. These other institutions effectively became part of a joint LLR by guaranteeing to cover losses sustained by the Bank of England in the process (Schwartz, 1986, p. 19). The German Reichs-bank in 1901 prevented panic by purchasing prime bills on the open market and expanding its excess note issue, but it did not intervene to prevent the failure of the Leipziger and other banks (Goodhart, 1985, p. 96). The Bank of France also followed classical precepts in crises in 1881 and 1889.

The Austrian National Bank, however, ignored the classical advice during the Credit Anstalt crisis of 1931 by providing liberal assistance to the Credit Anstalt at low interest rates (Schubert, 1987). Then, a run on the Credit Anstalt and other Viennese banks in May 1931 followed the disclosure of the Credit Anstalt's insolvency and a government financial rescue package. The run degenerated into a speculative attack on the fixed price of gold of the Austrian Schilling.

The U.S. record over the same period is less favorable than that of the major European countries. Before the advent of the Federal Reserve System and during the banking panics of the early 1930s, LLR action was insufficient to prevent panics. By contrast, over the past two decades, panics may have been prevented, but LLR assistance has been provided on a temporary basis to insolvent banks and, prior to the Continental Illinois crisis in 1984, no penalty rate was charged. In the U.S. on three notable occasions, the Fed (along with the FDIC) provided liberal assistance to major banks whose solvency was doubtful at the time of the assistance: Franklin National in 1974, First Pennsylvania in 1980, and Continental Illinois in 1984. Further, in the first case, loans were advanced at below-market rates (Garcia and Plautz, 1988). This Federal Reserve policy toward large banks of doubtful solvency differs significantly from the classical doctrine.

The Bank of England followed similar policies in the 1974 Fringe Bank rescue and the 1982 Johnson Matthey affair. In 1985, the Bank of Canada arranged for the major chartered banks to purchase the assets of two small insolvent Alberta banks and fully compensate all depositors. In contrast to the Anglo-Saxon experience, the German Bundesbank allowed the Herstatt Bank to be liquidated in 1974 but provided LLR assistance to the market. Thus, although the classical doctrine has been long understood and success-fully applied, recent experience suggests that its basic message is no longer always adhered to.

V. Conclusion: some lessons from history

One can draw a number of conclusions from the historical record.

(1) Banking panics are rare events. They occurred more often in the U.S. than in other countries. They usually occurred during serious recessions associated with declines in the money supply and sharp price level reversals. The likelihood of their occurrence would be greatly diminished in a diversified nationwide branch banking system.

(2) Successful LLR actions prevented panics on numerous occasions. On

those occasions when panics were not prevented, either the requisite institutions did not exist or the authorities did not understand the proper actions to take. Most countries developed an effective LLR mechanism by the last one-third of the nineteenth century. The U.S. was the principal exception.

(3) Some public authority must provide the lender of last resort function. The incidence of major international financial crises in 1837, 1857, 1873, 1890–93, 1907, 1914, 1930–33 suggests that in such episodes aggregate shocks can set in train a series of events leading to a nationwide scramble for high-powered money.

(4) Such an authority does not have to be a central bank. This is evident from the experience of Canada and other countries (including the U.S. experience under the Aldrich-Vreeland Act in 1914). In these cases, lender of last resort functions were provided by other forms of monetary authority, including the U.S. Treasury, Canadian Department of Finance, and foreign monetary authorities.

(5) The advent of federal deposit insurance in 1934 solved the problem of banking panics in the U.S. The absence of government deposit insurance in other countries that were panic-free before the 1960s and 1970s, however, suggests that such insurance is not required to prevent banking panics.

(6) Assistance to insolvent banks was the exception rather than the rule until the 1970s.[16] The monetary authorities in earlier times erred on the side of deficiency rather than excess. Goodhart's view is certainly not a description of past practice. The recent experience with assistance to insolvent banks is inconsistent with the classical prescription. Liberal assistance to insolvent banks, combined with deposit insurance which is not priced according to risk, encourages excessive risk-taking, creating the conditions for even greater assistance to insolvent banks in the future.

In sum, the historical record for a number of countries suggests that monetary authorities following the classical precepts of Thornton and Bagehot can prevent banking panics. Against the free banking view, the record suggests that such a role must be provided by a public authority. Moreover, contrary to Goodhart's view, successful LLR actions in the past did not require assistance to insolvent banks. Finally, the record suggests that the monetary authority's task would be eased considerably by allowing nationwide branch banking and by following a policy geared towards price level stability. Under such a regime, as Goodfriend and King argue, open market operations would be sufficient to offset unexpected scrambles for liquidity.

---

16 Although in the U.S., the policy of purchase and assumption carried out by the FDIC and FSLIC before that date incorporated elements of public subsidy.

References

Bagehot, W. (1873). *Lombard Street: A Description of the Money Market*. London: H.S. King.

Benston, G. J. (1983). 'Deposit Insurance and Bank Failures.' Federal Reserve Bank of Atlanta *Economic Review*. (March), pp. 4–17.

Benston, G. J., R. A. Eisenbeis, P. M. Horvitz, E. J. Kane and G. J. Kaufman (1986). *Perspectives on Safe and Sound Banking: Past, Present, and Future*. Cambridge: MIT Press.

Bordo, M. D. (1981). 'The Classical Gold Standard: Some Lessons for Today.' Federal Reserve Bank of St. Louis *Review*. (May), 63: 2–17.

—— (1986). 'Financial Crises, Banking Crises, Stock Market Crashes and the Money Supply: Some International Evidence, 1870–1933.' In F. Capie and G. E. Wood (eds.), *Financial Crises and the World Banking System*. London: MacMillan.

Bordo, M. D. and A. Redish (1987). 'Why did the Bank of Canada Emerge in 1935?' *Journal of Economic History*. (June), 47(2): 401–17.

Cagan, P. (1965). *Determinants and Effects of Changes in the Stock of Money, 1875–1960*. New York: Columbia University Press.

—— (1988). 'Commentary.' In W. S. Haraf and R. M. Kushmeider, (eds.) *Restructuring Banking and Financial Services in America*. Washington: American Enterprise Institute.

Calomiris, C. (1989). 'Deposit Insurance: Lessons from the Record.' Federal Reserve Bank of Chicago *Economic Perspectives*. (May-June), pp. 10–30.

Cowen, T. and R. Kroszner (1989). 'Scottish Banking Before 1845: A Model for Laissez-Faire.' *Journal of Money, Credit and Banking*. (May), 21(2): 221–31.

Dowd, K. (1988). *Private Money: The Path to Monetary Stability*. Institute of Economic Affairs Hobart Paper 112. London.

Friedman, M. (1960). *A Program for Monetary Stability*. New York: Fordham University Press.

Friedman, M. and A. J. Schwartz (1963). *A Monetary History of the United States*. Princeton: Princeton University Press.

Garcia, G. and E. Plautz (1988). *The Federal Reserve: Lender of Last Resort*. Cambridge: Ballinger Publishing Company.

Goodfriend, M. (1989). 'Money, Credit, Banking, and Payments System Policy.' In D. B. Humphrey (ed.), *The U.S. Payments Systems: Efficiency, Risk and the Role of the Federal Reserve*. Boston: Kluwer Academic Publishers.

Goodfriend, M. and R. A. King, (1988). 'Financial Deregulation, Monetary Policy, and Central Banking.' In W. S. Haraf and R. M. Kushmeider (eds.), *Restructuring Banking and Financial Services in America*. Washington: American Enterprise Institute.

Goodhart, C. A. E. (1985). *The Evolution of Central Banks*. London: London School of Economics and Political Science.

—— (1987). 'Why Do Banks Need a Central Bank?' *Oxford Economic Papers*. (March), 39:75–89.

Gorton, G. (1985). 'Clearing houses and the Origins of Central Banking in the U.S.' *Journal of Economic History*. (June), 45: 277–84.

Gorton, G. and D. J. Mullineaux (1987). 'Joint Production of Confidence: Endogenous Regulation and 19th Century Commercial Bank Clearinghouses.' *Journal of Money, Credit and Banking*. (November), 19(4): 457–68.

Hasan, I. and G. P. Dwyer, Jr. (1988). 'Contagious Bank Runs in the Free Banking Period.' (mimeo). Cliometrics Conference, Oxford, Ohio.

Hirsch, F. (1977). 'The Bagehot Problem.' *Manchester School of Economics and Social Studies*. (September), 45(3): 241–57.

Humphrey, T. (1975). 'The Classical Concept of the Lender of Last Resort.' Federal Reserve Bank of Richmond *Economic Review*. (January/February), 61:2–9.

—— (1989). 'Lender of Last Resort: The Concept in History.' Federal Reserve Bank of Richmond *Economic Review*. (March/April), 75: 8–16.

Jonung, L. (1985). 'The Economics of Private Money: the Experience of Private Notes in Sweden, 1831–1902.' (mimeo) Lund University.

Kaufman, G. G. (1988). 'The Truth about Bank Runs.' In C. England and T. Huertas (eds.), *The Financial Services Revolution*. Boston: Kluwer Academic Publishers.

Kindleberger, C. (1978). *Manias, Panics and Crashes*. London: MacMillan.

Meltzer, A. (1986). 'Financial Failures and Financial Policies.' In G. G. Kaufman and R. C. Kormendi (eds.), *Deregulating Financial Service: Public Policy in Flux*. Cambridge: Ballinger Publishing Company.

Morgenstern, O. (1959). *International Financial Transactions and Business Cycles*. Princeton: Princeton University Press.

Rockoff, H. (1986). 'Walter Bagehot and the Theory of Central Banking.' In F. Capie and G. E. Wood (eds.), *Financial Crises and the World Banking System*. London: MacMillan.

Rolnick, A. and W. Weber. (1986). 'Inherent Instability in Banking: The Free Banking Experience.' *Cato Journal*, 5(3): 877–890.

Schubert, A. (1987). 'The Creditanstalt Crisis of 1931 – A Financial Crisis Revisited.' *Journal of Economic History*. (June), 47(2).

Schwartz, A. J. (1986). 'Real and Pseudo – Financial Crises.' In F. Capie and G. E. Wood (eds.), *Financial Crises and the World Banking System*. London: MacMillan.

—— (1988). 'Financial Stability and the Federal Safety Act.' In W. S. Haraf and R. M. Kushmeider (eds.), *Restructuring Banking and Financial Services in America*. Washington: American Enterprise Institute.

Selgin, G. A. (1988). *The Theory of Free Banking: Money Supply Under Competitive Note Issue*. Totowa, N. J.: Rowman and Littlefield.

—— (1990). 'Legal Restrictions, Financial Weakening, and the Lender of Last Resort.' *Cato Journal*. forthcoming.

Solow, R. M. (1982). 'On the Lender of Last Resort.' In C. P. Kindleberger and J. P. Laffargue (eds.), *Financial Crises: Theory, History and Policy*. Cambridge: Cambridge University Press.

—— *An Enquiry into the Nature and Effects of the Paper Credit of Great Britain*. Edited by F. A. Hayek. Fairfield: Augustus M. Kelley.

Thornton, H. (1802). (1978). *The Origins of Central Banking in the United States*. Cambridge: Harvard University Press.

Timberlake, R., Jr. (1984). 'The Central Banking Role of Clearing House Associations.' *Journal of Money, Credit and Banking*. (February), 16:1–5.

Weber, E. J. (1988). 'Currency Competition in Switzerland, 1826–1850.' *Kyklos*. 41.4 (3):459–78.

White, E. N. (1981). 'State Sponsored Insurance of Bank Deposits in the United States, 1907–20.' *Journal of Economic History*. (March), 13(1): 33–42.

White, L. H. (1984). *Free Banking in Britain: Theory, Experience, and Debate 1800–1945*. Cambridge: Cambridge University Press.

12 The emergence of the Bank of England as a mature central bank [1]

Forrest H. Capie

I

England in the seventeenth and eighteenth centuries can be regarded as a developing economy. It had a fragile financial system that was subject to frequent banking panics and financial crises which recurred well into the nineteenth century. But over a long period this economy found its way towards a large measure of monetary and macroeconomic stability. Over the course of more than a century lessons were learned and the system was adapted. The banking system became less regulated, largely found its own way to prudence, and became more concentrated, with a portfolio that was well diversified both geographically and by activity. At the same time a central bank emerged as a lender of last resort. With these dispositions and institutions in place there followed more than a hundred years of remarkable stability, with no bank runs and no financial crises. The first part of the period lasts from around 1700 to about 1870; the stability followed from the 1870s.

The emphasis in this essay is on the practical business of learning lessons in an ever-changing institutional environment. But it should be remembered that the learning process took place against a background of wider intellectual debate, some of which involved the development of economic theory centring on the nature of money and the role of banking in the economy. Some of the debate was more political or philosophical, concerned with the relative merits of laissez-faire as compared with a role for the state. In many ways the debate on money and banking is intimately bound up with that on free trade. In money and banking it took place in a context of rules versus discretion over monetary policy, with the slightly paradoxical outcome that rules were thought to be more necessary when the dominant policy was one of laissez-faire.

As indicated, however, the principal concern of this essay will be with how the Bank of England emerged as a modern central bank. At the centre of this

1 This paper was prepared for a British Academy meeting held in Cambridge in March 2001. The paper has benefited from comments made on earlier versions presented at the Bank of England and the IMF, and by participants at the Cambridge seminar.

concern is the question of how acceptance of the concept of lender of last resort was established and made part of banking practice. The concept is a useful one when clearly defined, but it is also one that invites interpretation and is sometimes misunderstood and on occasion distorted. In its most useful form it connotes the ability to provide funds on any scale and to do this quickly and decisively. It is the fact that central banks have the power to create high-powered money that allows them to be the lender of last resort. The purpose of a lender of last resort is to ensure stability in the financial system, and possibly to avert panic by taking appropriate action. Over a long period, this function evolved in England and helped to transform a financial system of considerable fragility into one of the utmost robustness. It is not something that can be achieved overnight – reputation and credibility take time to acquire.

This essay will show how the issues of solvency/insolvency, moral hazard (less cautious behaviour being encouraged as with insurance cover), and 'too-big-to-fail' were handled in English circumstances. Scotland's free-banking arrangements did not require a lender of last resort; the system there relied on competition delivering a stable outcome. Ireland was slightly different again. There were a number of private banks in Dublin and the Bank of Ireland was founded in the 1780s, modelled on the Bank of England. But the Irish system was much less developed than its English counterpart and experienced a major collapse in 1820.

II

There are three principal components to the institutional setting that are of central importance in any discussion of the lender of last resort: the Bank of England, the commercial banking system, and the discount houses. The Bank was founded during the financial upheavals of the 1690s. At that time it was not a central bank, merely a large prestigious bank and the only joint-stock bank then allowed, and it continued as such until the second quarter of the nineteenth century. However, in the great debate that broke out in the last decade of the eighteenth century the Bank came under intense scrutiny. During the Napoleonic wars and following the suspension of convertibility in 1797, all the elements that made for a great debate came together: inflation, exchange-rate depreciation, poor harvests, support for continental allies, balance-of-payments deficits, and so on – a mixture of real and monetary factors that made it more difficult than usual to separate causes and effects. But the role of the Bank (and of the rest of the monetary system) was at the centre of the debate. Was it overissuing and causing inflation (and thereby exploiting its powerful monopoly to make profits in a time of war)? *Could* it overissue? The Bank claimed, via the 'real-bills doctrine', that overissue was not possible. The argument was that if the bills were 'real' this meant that they were based on the genuine needs of traders and that meeting such needs could never be inflationary. However, as Henry

Thornton and others showed at the time, many bills could cover the same goods, and there were other ways too in which abuses could occur. The debate remained unresolved, even if the bullionists (those maintaining that all currency should be backed by equivalent amounts of bullion) are usually seen to have been triumphant when the restoration of convertibility was accepted (the legislation was approved in 1819). The Bank's monopoly joint-stock position was eroded by two pieces of legislation in the 1820s and 1830s (see below), but it remained the dominant force in the monetary system.

There was still a question running through the 1820s and 1830s (where the debate was conducted as between two schools, 'currency' and 'banking') as to what the gold standard meant. Although the eighteenth century is usually described as a period in which a *de facto* gold standard operated, the prevailing mercantilist philosophy resulted in rules forbidding the export of gold and the melting of gold. This, then, differed greatly from what became accepted as the rules of the international gold standard during the nineteenth century. More than this, however, no clear view existed as to what the standard meant. In the 1830s, for example, there was the view of Horsley Palmer, Governor of the Bank of England, 1830–3 (Deputy Governor 1828–30), and leader of the 'banking school', who wanted the Bank to have discretionary control over the volume of currency. 'Palmer evolved his own currency principle, by which note circulation would fluctuate in relation to the Bank's holding of specie.'[2] Palmer first explained his ideas to the Bank Charter Committee of 1832: 'when exchanges are at their best ... the Bank should have a specie reserve equal to *about* one-third of notes and deposits' (my italics).[3] Starting from here, all fluctuations in the Bank's notes and deposits should be equal to changes in the Bank's holding of specie. An alternative scheme was propounded by the economic commentator James Pennington: changes in the Bank's notes should move in relation to specie. But since Pennington advocated the suppression of private issue the entire circulation would have been covered.

This long-running debate was essentially resolved in the 1844 Bank Charter Act, which is seen by some as a triumph for the 'currency school'. This act divided the Bank in two – an issue department and a banking department. The former could easily have been a separate institution. The act provided for a fiduciary note issue of £14 million and thereafter a one-for-one issue against gold reserves. It also gave the Bank the monopoly of note issue, though banks already issuing could continue at the existing level. No new note-issuing rights were permitted and when banks merged their issuing

---

2 H. V. Bowen, 'The Bank of England during the long eighteenth century', in R. Roberts and D. Kynaston, eds., *The Bank of England: money, power and influence, 1694–1994* (Oxford, 1995), p. 22.

3 Ibid.

rights were forfeited. This was the one significant reversal in the trend towards less regulation and it was deeply resented by the country banks.

Running through the discussions and debate on monetary policy in the first half of the nineteenth century was a concern over the precise behaviour of an institution such as the Bank of England: should it be subject to a set of rules or left free to act at its own discretion and according to the vagaries of the seasons, the markets, and other random elements? This too was part of the larger debate on the appropriate extent of government intervention in the economy. There had long been two views on the rules/discretion issue and these continue to the present day. For example, Richard Sayers believed that the essence of central banking was discretionary control of the monetary system. On the other side was the view that policy should be bound by some rules: it was seen as undesirable to leave it in the hands of individuals who either did not understand it or were liable to manipulate it for the wrong reasons. Nor could it be left entirely to the market. For example, on this last-mentioned aspect Milton Friedman, carrying on a Chicago tradition, wrote that 'monetary arrangements have seldom been left entirely to the market, even in societies following thoroughly liberal policies in other respects, and there are good reasons why this should be the case.'[4] The reasons included the technical-monopoly character of a pure fiduciary currency which required setting an external limit on its amount.

Nineteenth-century classical economists inclined strongly towards laissez-faire in banking matters; they favoured a basic rule because of 'their distrust of discretion by a government dominated by an aristocracy and by a bank run by a company of traders'.[5] The Bullion Committee in 1810 was explicit in repudiating the ability of the monetary authorities to regulate the money supply: in their view, it could not be done. Later, Bagehot felt that it was the discretion of commercial bankers that was open to question. The monetary rules adopted in the nineteenth century represented a victory for the 'currency school'. In particular, the 1844 Bank Charter Act laid down a firm rule for the operation of the gold standard. After 1844, then, the Bank operated essentially under a strict and well-defined rule of the gold standard. There remained the problem of the relative importance of its private interests (its obligation to its shareholders) as against its public responsibility. But from the mid-century onwards it was clear that the latter was rising to dominance. The monetary debate died away and the only serious remaining issue unresolved was that of lender of last resort. This was finally settled in the 1870s.

It is the argument of this essay that by the 1870s the Bank of England had emerged as a fully-fledged central bank and mature lender of last resort. But there was some way to go before this was achieved. The second element in the

4   Milton Friedman, *A program for monetary stability* (New York, 1968), p. 4.
5   F.W. Fetter, *The development of British monetary orthodoxy* (Cambridge, Mass., 1965), p. 143.

institutional setting was the commercial banking sector. In England, banks had been limited to partnerships of no more than six persons from the end of the seventeenth century. Failures were frequent and many, and by the 1820s it was being argued that the banks were too small and undercapitalized; they needed to be allowed joint-stock formation. This was granted in 1826, even if some of the Bank of England's monopoly was retained by not allowing new banks to encroach within 65 miles of London.[6] This restriction was lifted in 1833, when such banks were allowed in London. At this stage they were still unlimited-liability companies. A private clearinghouse had emerged in the eighteenth century and by 1819 40 banks belonged to it. In 1854 the joint-stock banks were admitted, and finally in 1860 the Bank of England was admitted.

Ever since the origins of banks in the late seventeenth century there had been frequent bank failures. Joint-stock formation did not remove that danger, even if unlimited liability helped to ensure caution. The debate on the corporate status of banks continued throughout the second quarter of the nineteenth century and legislation enabling the introduction of or conversion to limited liability came in two acts in 1858 and 1862.

The banks groped their own way towards a reputation for good practice. In a rapidly changing world this was not easy. But a concern for prudent behaviour entered at an early stage, and in this the Scottish contribution should not be discounted. For example, George Rae, an Aberdonian, made a major contribution both as a banker in Liverpool from the 1830s to the 1870s and as the author of the most durable textbook for bankers in the nineteenth century. Rae offered wisdom on a range of subjects but was particularly keen on caution: 'There is . . . a possibility of being over cautious; but in banking that is one of the cardinal virtues, compared with the opposite evil and mischief of being over credulous.'[7] The banks found their own way to the appropriate capital/asset and reserve/deposit ratios, overall liquidity ratio, and reserve and loan/asset ratios. These often began high but gradually came down to levels that were more profitable without endangering the bank.

The banks also improved the diversification of their portfolios by spreading their activities across the country. Mergers took place throughout the century but accelerated in the closing decades, so that by the end of the century there was a highly concentrated system with the five largest banks holding around 70 per cent of deposits. In 1914 there were 56 banks, but the big five dominated and there were close to 8,000 branch offices in total.

6   For a recent examination of the politics of money and banking and the liberalizing of the system in the second quarter of the nineteenth century, see P. Cottrell and L. Newton, 'Banking liberalization in England and Wales, 1826–1841', in G. Tortella *et al.*, eds., *The state, the financial system, and economic modernization* (Cambridge, 2000), pp. 75–117.

7   G. Rae, *The country banker: his clients, cares and work* (1885).

There are many ways of measuring concentration. Using a Herfindahl-Hirschman index on a numbers-equivalent basis, there were 74 banks in England and Wales in 1870, 61 in 1880, 58 in 1890, and 45 in 1900. This number had fallen to 27 in 1910, and to just 11 in 1920.[8] Thus what had emerged was a system where prudence was important and was supported by a well-branched network. Heavily concentrated as it was, the industry gave the appearance of an oligopoly, but it is not clear how far it deviated from a competitive system. This institutional factor played some part in making the system enormously stable. Entry was free, though access to the clearing-house was not always straightforward. The system was free of bank runs and crises.[9] Even in the great depression of 1929–32 there were no bank failures. Profitability in banking remained almost undisturbed. The downside to all this is that the banks have long been criticized for their conservatism and particularly for failing to lend to industry. These attacks have seldom gone away and to some extent, while never entirely accurate, they were not discouraged by the banks themselves, who have always been keen to foster an image of prudence.

The third element in the institutional setting was the discount houses. In the course of the industrial revolution in the eighteenth century financial intermediation in all forms developed apace and the bill of exchange became an important financial instrument. There grew up bill brokers who brought together those with funds and those seeking funds. At the same time as this was happening country bankers were developing links with London banks – correspondent banks. It is helpful to remember at this stage that the banks in the eighteenth and early nineteenth centuries felt considerable animosity towards the Bank of England on account of the privileged joint-stock monopoly that the Bank held. This was particularly true of the provincial banks and had become acute by the time joint-stock formation was allowed. The new joint-stock banks therefore preferred to place their surplus funds with the bill brokers rather than the Bank. These brokers made such progress that they soon developed a sufficiently large capital base to run their own portfolios, and at that point became discount houses. One of these, Overend Gurney (about which there is more to say later) grew so large in the first half of the nineteenth century that it came to rival the Bank of England itself. These discount houses had ready access to the Bank's discount window and provided the perfect buffer between the commercial banks and the Bank of England.

---

8   For details, see F. Capie and G. Rodrik-Bali, 'Concentration in British banking, 1880–1914', *Business History*, XXIV (1982), pp. 107–25.

9   See A. J. Schwartz, 'Real and pseudo financial crises', in F. Capie and G. E. Wood, eds., *Financial crises and the world banking system* (1986), pp. 11–31.

III

If we turn now to financial crises, there are different schools of thought. Some commentators take a narrow view that emphasizes the banking system, while at the other end of the spectrum there are those who are prepared to consider extreme price movements in almost any asset as evidence of a crisis. Anna Schwartz has made a useful distinction here between what she calls 'real' as opposed to 'pseudo' crises:

> A financial crisis is fuelled by fears that the means of payment will be unobtainable at any price and, in a fractional reserve banking system, leads to a scramble for high-powered money. It is precipitated by actions of the public that suddenly squeeze the reserves of the banking system. . . . The essence of a financial crisis is that it is short-lived, ending with a slackening of the public's demand for additional currency.[10]

In other words a financial crisis is quite different from the failure of one financial institution, and Schwartz's approach helps to distinguish between financial crises and exchange-rate crises. A financial crisis also contrasts with a disinflation (the reversal of policies that have produced inflation), which is likely to be long and drawn out.

Thus many of the phenomena of recent times that have been called financial crises have in fact been pseudo-crises: stock-market collapse, property-price collapse, Britain's departure from the ERM and the slump in the price of sterling, and the failure of Barings Bank in 1995 – to name a few at random. A real financial crisis occurs when the stability of the banking system is threatened. It is only in that circumstance that the use of money threatens to contract and the financial structure is threatened. This distinction between real and pseudo-crises helps to direct attention at what actually happens, and what the ramifications might be. It is also useful in concentrating attention on the appropriate solution, which is for the lender of last resort to provide the *system* with immediate and sufficient liquidity to allay the panic. When that is done and the panic is over, the next step is to extract the excess liquidity from the system.

A useful way of approaching the subject of the action required of a central bank in a financial crisis is by means of the money-multiplier framework. One way of expressing this is as follows:

$$M = mB$$

This states that the money stock is equal to high-powered money, or the

---

10   Schwartz, 'Real and pseudo financial crises' in F. Capie and G. E. Wood, eds., *Financial Crises and the world banking system* (1986), pp. 11–31.

monetary base times the money multiplier. The multiplier can be written as follows:

$$M = \left[\frac{1 + \frac{C}{D}}{\frac{C}{D} + \frac{R}{D}} \right] B$$

where $\frac{C}{D}$ is the currency/deposit ratio of the public, and $\frac{R}{D}$ is the cash/deposit ratio of the banks. In times of panic, or of events that people might believe might lead to panic, whatever their origins, the public will take the precaution of holding higher amounts of currency than deposits. They do this for fear that the financial system will fail, that their institution will be part of this failure, and that they will therefore lose their deposits. The currency ratio will therefore rise sharply. In the same way, banks that see problems ahead will try to safeguard themselves from prospective difficulties by holding higher cash reserves to satisfy the potential demand of their customers. The reserve ratio should therefore rise noticeably. The combined effect of the change in the two ratios is to diminish the money multiplier greatly and so produce a collapse in the money stock. When the authorities see such a pattern evolving they can supply all the monetary base necessary to keep the money stock on an even keel. Knowing that they will do this also helps to allay the panic.

Throughout the eighteenth century and into the nineteenth there were frequent banking crises. The argument of this essay is that the lessons from these crises were gradually learned and changes were made to the institutions that ultimately brought about a system that was free from such crises. During the Napoleonic wars Pitt wanted to avoid the failure of banking houses and pushed the Bank of England to formulate stabilization policies. In the aftermath of the wars there was a concern with inflation and a desire to find the means of avoiding it. The chronology of crises in the nineteenth century is as follows: 1825, 1836–9, 1847, 1857, 1866. There were in addition some events that would be called pseudo-crises under Schwartz's categorization, such as those occurring in 1878 and 1890. To these can be added two others: in 1914, associated with the outbreak of war; and in 1931, when there was an exchange-rate crisis that was not a banking crisis.

The pattern in these *real* financial crises was usually very similar: a boom would develop, perhaps including stock market mania, commodity prices would rise, and so on. At some point the Bank of England would attempt to curtail the excess or protect its own reserves, the boom would come to a halt, and there would be a rush to cash. In 1825 South American stocks were at the root of the crisis: the Bank was slow to act but did so eventually, quelling the panic. This crisis prompted the legislation to allow joint-stock banking. To some extent the Bank was limited in what it could do while the usury

laws were still in force. While these, like most regulations, could always be circumvented, such action was not possible for the Bank. But it was at this point that the usury laws began to be relaxed.

In 1836–7 and 1839 it was European bank promotion that was at the core of the boom, but the pattern was similar. In 1839 the Bank raised its rate above 5 per cent for the first time and it became clear that this was a useful device. 1847 is said to have been the last great harvest crisis, but the mid-1840s was also a boom period, with banks, insurance companies, and railways leading the way. Then there was the potato famine of 1845–6 and other poor harvests. Again, when Bank reserves fell to dangerous levels Bank Rate was raised, the boom ended, and a banking panic ensued. On this occasion the Bank appealed to the Chancellor of the Exchequer, who signed a letter suspending the recently enacted Bank Charter Act of 1844 and allowed the Bank to print as many unbacked notes as were needed.

In the next crisis, in 1857, the source of the problem was the United States, where there had been feverish activity in the mid-1850s. Bad news filtered through from the west, banks failed, convertibility was suspended in the USA, and this was transmitted to Liverpool – the most exposed city. Again, Bank of England reserves fell, Bank Rate was raised, and panic followed. Once more, too, the provisions of Peel's act had to be broken and the Bank of England printed more notes without gold cover. Following this crisis an investigation was held and it was clear from the hearings that the Bank of England still did not accept that it had the role of lender of last resort: it had acted as such a lender but had felt that it should not. The Bank also asserted that part of the problem lay in the access that the discount houses had to the Bank's discounting facilities and withdrew the privileged access. Bagehot later pointed out the futility of this, and in any case the access was soon restored.

The crisis of 1866 was in some ways different. As has been noted, after 1825 London bankers increasingly placed their funds with bill brokers and stopped discounting with the Bank of England. In March 1858 the Bank announced that bill brokers and the emerging discount houses were to be barred from the right to take bills to the Bank for discount, save only during the 'shuttings' (the period when the Bank's stock registers were closed for the preparation of interest payments). This was an impediment to the operation of the system that was then evolving, but the ruling was gradually relaxed and discount houses were granted access again. Eventually, this became privileged access. Incidentally, in 1858 limited liability of banks was allowed, and in 1862 Overend Gurney, the major discount house, took advantage of this new freedom.

Overend Gurney's origins were Quaker: the company had been highly respected in the financial sector from at least as early as the late seventeenth century. Few, it was said, were as wise in the ways of the City or more judicious than Samuel Gurney. The decade of the 1860s was the high point of the mid-Victorian boom. In 1866 the Chancellor of the Exchequer, Gladstone, was decidedly upbeat about the economy. In May Bank of

England reserves were in good shape. Then, on 10 May, Overend Gurney & Co. failed. Overend's was a giant financial institution, dominating the discount market. But it had become involved in bad asset management and found itself grossly overcommitted to risky enterprises: 'the most celebrated of old houses had misused money,' as Clapham put it.[11] Many of the booming firms of the 1860s failed and this led to Overend's failure. Panic set in immediately, the worst since 1825, at 'this ruin of its most famous neighbour and sometime rival, "the Corner House", the greatest private firm in England'.[12]

Overend's epitaph was written by Bagehot: in six years, from 1860 to 1866, the immensely rich partners 'lost all their own wealth, sold the business to the company, and then lost a large part of the company's capital. And these losses were made in a manner so reckless and so foolish that one would think a child who had lent money in the City of London would have lent it better.'[13] Samuel Gurney's old, sound business had called for 'great care with every bill, great knowledge of the "standing of parties", and considered use of that knowledge. The younger men now in charge held bills of doubtful subordinate. Portfolios were filled with all sorts of flimsy paper, including the so-called "finance securities".'[14] These latter were 'issued in advance by company promoters, perhaps before the public had even subscribed, to contracting firms, and by them discounted. And Overend had gone far beyond dealings in bills, good or bad. They were mixed up in all sorts of financing, were partners in almost every kind of speculative and lock-up business.'[15]

On 11 May 1866 there was an unprecedented fall in Bank of England reserves. Deputations to Gladstone called for and received a suspension of the Bank Charter Act. Bank Rate went to 10 per cent and stayed there for three months. More banks failed. Bagehot criticized the Bank for lending 'hesitatingly, reluctantly, and with misgiving. In fact to make large advances in this faltering way is to incur the evil of making them without obtaining the advantage.'[16]

It is worth pausing here to consider the 'too-big-to-fail doctrine' as it might have applied to Overend Gurney. Overend's had become banker to the London and country banks and on the day it failed *The Times* said that it 'could rightly claim to be the greatest instrument of credit in the Kingdom'.[17] Its balance sheet was roughly ten times the size of those of the Midland Bank and the Westminster Bank, two of the biggest banks in the country; and while they operated with capital/asset ratios of about 9–11 per cent, Overend's was 2 per cent. (Discount houses do have lower ratios, but Overend was conducting banking business.)

---

11 Sir John Clapham, *The Bank of England*, 2: *1797–1914* (Cambridge, 1970), p. 261.
12 Ibid., p. 261.   13 Walter Bagehot, *Lombard street* (1873), p. 19.
14 Clapham, *Bank of England*, II, p. 261.   15 Ibid., p. 262.
16 Bagehot, *Lombard street*, pp. 64–5.   17 *The Times*, 30 Sept. 1866.

Overend's appeal to the Bank of England for help was refused: 'The Governor took the view that the Bank could not assist one concern unless it was prepared to assist the many others which were known to be in a similar plight.'[18] There was considerable animosity between the two institutions. Nevertheless, this decision can clearly be seen as a further step on the road by which the Bank came to see its function as one of coming to the aid of the market as a whole rather one of than bailing out imprudent and insolvent institutions. The panic of 1866 was huge. But in spite of Overend's size and apparent centrality to the system the panic passed and the system went on to become strong and stable. The Bank's refusal to support Overend Gurney, then, can be regarded as a signal that was an important step on the road towards a sound policy towards financial crises in Schwarz's sense of the term.

'Too big to fail' is a cost/benefit concept. Generally speaking, for banks of a certain size the benefits, to the rest of the system and to the economy as a whole, of saving them are reckoned to outweigh the costs of them failing. The costs of failing are relatively short-term and susceptible to some calculation. But the benefits to the system of a salutary lesson in allowing them to fail must be seen as so long-term as almost impossible to measure. Take Overend Gurney: the cost of refusing assistance was high, but the benefit of making it clear to all institutions that they could not count on the Bank of England saving them must have run over of a very long period. When it becomes clear that the lender of last resort will not rescue an individual institution, moral hazard is removed from the discussion.

In 1878 there was a similar episode when the City of Glasgow Bank failed. It, too, was a very large institution in Scotland, with 133 branches. But in spite of (or perhaps because of) the fact that it was an unlimited-liability company it took great risks and hid these from its shareholders. Its failure undoubtedly caused great misery and some shock waves in the system. That it did not constitute a financial crisis, however, is readily seen from an examination of the reserve/deposit and currency/deposit ratios (Figure 1), where hardly a flicker is registered.[19] When it seemed that there might be a panic, the Bank did prepare for another suspension of the 1844 act. Rothschild approached the Chancellor of the Exchequer, asking him to sign the necessary letter in advance of his leaving London over Christmas.[20] In the event it was not used.

In 1914 London suffered its first financial crisis for a very long time – possibly for as long as half a century. This crisis, however, was different. It arose as a direct result of the war; there was no preceding boom, and it was

18 W.T. C. King, *A history of the London discount market* (1936, new edn. 1972), p. 242.
19 F. Capie and A. Webber, *A monetary history of the United Kingdom, 1870–1982* (1985).
20 L. S. Pressnell, 'Gold reserves, banking reserves, and the Baring crisis of 1890', in C. R. Whittlesey and J. S. G. Wilson, eds., *Essays in money and banking: in honour of R. S. Sayers* (Oxford, 1968).

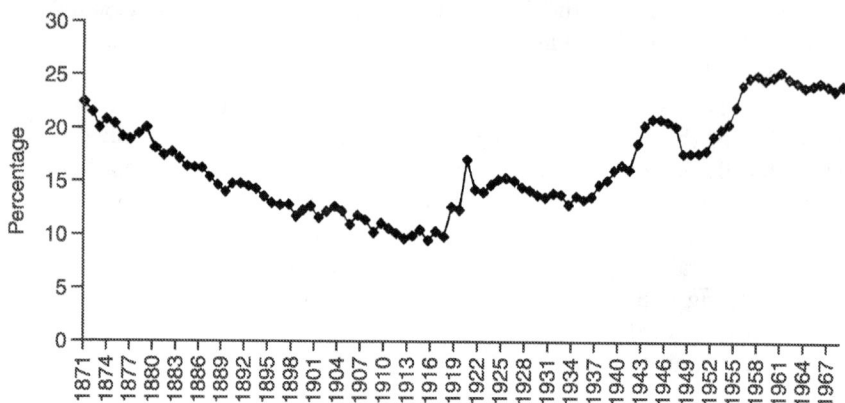

Figure 1. Ratio of currency to net bank deposits.

Source: Capie and Webber, *Monetary History*, tab. 1.3 (III), pp. 76–7.

comparatively short-lived. When war became a probability in late July selling speeded up on the Stock Exchange, exchange rates became more volatile, and foreigners were unable to make remittances to the London acceptance houses. Banks in London started calling in loans they had made to the stock market. The root cause of the crisis was a failure of remittance. London was a massive creditor of most of the rest of the world, and that included the enemy. British stockbrokers were owed money by foreigners, but by late July foreign stock exchanges were closing, moratoria were being declared, and debts became irrecoverable, at least for the foreseeable future. The London banks had lent money to the brokers 'on the margin': that is, they had called for securities as collateral for the loans to an amount 10 to 20 per cent greater in value than the loan. When security prices began to fall that margin was eroded and the banks, not unreasonably, began to call in the loans. The brokers sold more securities in order to repay the loans and in the process drove security prices down further – a familiar pattern in such circumstances.

A variety of measures was taken in response to these events, and together they must be judged largely successful in containing the crisis. These measures included the suspension of the 1844 act (the provisions had been legally met on the 1 August but had served no useful purpose), the suspension of specie payments, a general moratorium, and the issue of Treasury notes of £1 and £10 denomination – an injection of base money. The response to the crisis was entirely appropriate to the needs of the time. But once a crisis is over some plan for extracting the extra cash injected should be implemented. There was no such plan in 1914. Nor was there in the subsequent years, and this in part explains the extent of the inflation experienced in the course of the next few years.

There were, however, occasions when the Bank organized the rescue of an ailing institution. The classic case here is Barings in 1890. There had been a boom in Argentina in the mid-1880s which had improved that country's credit rating. Capital flowed in. Poor harvests in 1889 and problems in servicing debt contributed to the resulting coup in July 1890. There was some default. Barings had underwritten large bond issues to Argentina and it became clear that they were liable for large amounts. Barings was a huge financial institution and the government pressed the Bank of England, along with other leading banks, to provide support for Barings. The Bank in turn asked the government for a guarantee. Suspension of the 1844 act was discussed but William Lidderdale, the Governor, rejected the idea, lending further weight to the view that this was not a general liquidity crisis but rather an individual firm in difficulty.[21] Although the Bank arranged a 'lifeboat operation', this does not qualify it as being regarded as a lender of last resort.

It is also instructive to consider the case of the Manchester-based bank, William Deacon and Co., with 173 branches, mostly in the northwest, which got into difficulty in 1930. This was a case of a poorly-run bank: its assets were heavily tied up with the cotton industry and when that industry suffered in the 1920s so too did the bank. The governor of the Bank of England, Montagu Norman, was in aggressive mode at the time, trying all manner of schemes to improve the image of the Bank and of the banking system and their respective contributions to the economy. In many ways, however, the Bank could be held responsible for some of Deacon's problems: it had encouraged Deacon's to participate in the rationalization of the cotton industry, which meant lending to some doubtful firms. A failure of this bank (even though it had less than 5 per cent of total deposits in the financial system) may not have led to greatly damaging effects for the system, but it would have reflected badly on it, and perhaps on the governor. Norman, not wanting to see any further concentration in English (as opposed to British) banking, encouraged the Royal Bank of Scotland rather than an English bank to take over Deacon's. Again, this is surely not the action of a lender of last resort; at most it might be described as an aspect of crisis management – keeping the system on an even keel and preventing anything that threatened to disturb the calm that had long prevailed in the system. This was no doubt seen as especially necessary at a time when signs of distress were being detected in continental Europe. But no lending took place. There may have been other isolated examples of this kind of action between 1870 and 1970, but none of them can be viewed as constituting the action of a lender of last resort.

Some mention should be made at this stage of the views on the functions of the Bank of England of two outstanding contemporaries, Henry Thornton and Walter Bagehot. This short summary inevitably passes over the many other distinguished contributions to the debate in the 1820s, 1830s, and

---

21 Ibid.

1840s, notably those of Thomas Joplin.[22] Henry Thornton has been described as the father of the modern central bank. His classic monograph *Paper credit* (1802) presents his principal ideas: Joseph Schumpeter called it the 'Magna Carta of central banking'. In it Thornton stated clearly the operating principles for the bank[23] and outlined the nature of a crisis and its solutions.[24] Bagehot was the great developer and expounder of these views later in the nineteenth century. His first treatment of the subject was in 1848 in the first article he published, at the age of 21.[25] Bagehot was writing about the previous year's financial crisis and commenting inevitably on the act of 1844. The article contains one of the clearest statements of the need for liquidity and the form its provision should take. The English banking system was continuing to evolve, sometimes in ways that Bagehot did not entirely approve of: he would have preferred there to be no central bank and for free competition to prevail. Nevertheless, he accepted that the system that had emerged was something with which people had to live.

In the course of the nineteenth century it was not always possible to predict the behaviour of the Bank. Sometimes it came to the rescue of the market and sometimes it did not. Sometimes it helped out institutions and at others it did not. In the context of these developments, Bagehot presented his views first in the pages of *The Economist*, of which he was editor in the middle decades of the century, and then in *Lombard street* in 1873. It was in the latter article that Bagehot set out what is now taken to be his definitive position. When Thornton was writing there were no joint-stock banks, but by 1870 when Bagehot published his article in *Lombard street* there were many such banks and they were beginning to dominate the system. The risk of panic was clearly increased if a large joint-stock bank collapsed: 'No cause is more capable of producing a panic, perhaps none is so capable, as the failure of a first-rate joint-stock bank in London.'[26] Bagehot's solution was essentially the same as that proposed by Thornton, though with refinements that allowed for the changed and changing institutional setting.

IV

What emerges from this discussion is that the lender of last resort exists first and foremost because it is the ultimate source of cash: it can provide the

22 See D. O'Brien, *Thomas Joplin and classical macroeconomics: a reappraisal of classical monetary thought* (Aldershot, 1993).
23 H. Thornton, *An enquiry into the nature and effects of the paper credit of Great Britain* (Fairfield, 1802).
24 Ibid., p. 188.
25 Walter Bagehot, 'The currency problem', *Prospective Review*, (1848), pp. 297–337. Reprinted in N. St. J. Stevas, ed., *Complete works*, 9.
26 Ibid., p. 251.

required liquidity. The liquidity should be provided to the market as a whole and the lender should not bail out individuals. The ideal way to do this is to act anonymously.[27] There should be no commercial rivalry that might deflect the Bank from its task. It is also important to stress that it is the peculiar position of the monopoly note issuer and holder and provider of the ultimate means of payment that allows, almost obliges, a central bank to behave as the lender of last resort. (The phrase seems to have its origins in French legal history: the 'dernier resort' was the ultimate legal authority beyond which there was no appeal.) The central bank is the only institution that can supply *without limit* (but at an increasing price) the ultimate means of payment. It is the knowledge in the markets that supply cannot run out which serves to assure the market and allay the panic. And if this position is made known in advance the picture is complete.

The money-multiplier model outlined above does not imply causality. It is irrelevant that the model was not set out formally until the 1930s. Nor does it matter that central banks did not see themselves as behaving as if they were conscious of this framework. It is simply a useful way of sorting out the issues. For example, the model shows how the public have a role to play in determining the money stock by virtue of the way in which they hold cash and deposits. The banks too have a role to play in the way they hold their cash reserves in relation to deposits. The monetary authorities either control the monetary base or it is determined via the balance of payments. In a financial crisis the public moves into cash, and the banks try to cope with this by raising their cash reserves. Both of these actions reduce the money multiplier, and unless the monetary authorities take counter-measures there will be a collapse in the money stock. In such circumstances the monetary authorities need to raise the supply of monetary base, sometimes dramatically so. This is the purpose of the lender of last resort. But there is disagreement on the method of operation, with one persisting view being that it entails the rescue of individual institutions and the other holding that it should entail only the rescue of the market as a whole – the provision of liquidity to allay widespread panic.

Any commercial bank may, from time to time, extend loans to customers who are illiquid or even insolvent. They may do so even when the present expected return from the new loan itself is zero or negative, if this is warranted by the wider effects on their own reputation for commitment or the potential knock-on effects of the failure of the first customer on others. By the same token, a nascent central bank – an institution still some way short of maturity as a central bank – may 'rescue' some client or correspondent bank, just as the commercial bank may support its business customer. But we would not want to describe such *ad hoc* exercises as involving a conscious assumption of a systematic function of a lender of last resort. Nor would we

---

27 Schwartz, 'Real and pseudo'.

want to see a mature central bank endeavouring to rescue individual banks: there is simply too much moral hazard involved.

No central bank would want to precommit itself to giving special support to *any* individual bank that was running into liquidity problems. Especially with the development of efficient, broad, inter-bank and other short-term money markets, a bank-liquidity problem that is not caused by some technical factor is likely to be a reflection of some deeper suspicions about solvency. Consequently, an unqualified precommitment to provide assistance to an individual firm would involve too much moral hazard.

Besides, it is worth pausing to consider what can reasonably be meant by 'bail out'. Central banks in general do not have the capital resources to salvage single-handedly an institution of any significant size – significant in the sense that its failure could have damaging consequences for the rest of the system. If the central bank discounted at face value the inferior assets of an individual institution in difficulty, then, if these assets were subsequently marked to market their values would appear much lower on the bank's balance sheet. Thus the central bank would be seen to be damaging its own balance sheet, since it would have parted with cash in exchange for assets of lower value. If this in turn required government assistance in raising more capital, the central bank would in effect have taken a fiscal decision. Thus, all the central bank can really do is to oversee or organize a rescue operation, perhaps putting pressure on others to subscribe new capital.

How can the ideal operation be achieved? Anonymity is highly desirable in the proper execution of the lender-of-last-resort function. The lender of last resort supplies funds to the market in times of need; it does not supply individual institutions. In its proper form it should not engage in bailing out firms of any kind, be they banks or anything else. Therefore it would be best if the operation could be carried out such that the identity of those seeking funds was not known to the bank. Anna Schwartz has proposed such anonymity as a policy to be adopted within the United States.[28]

The mechanism can be envisaged as the central bank having a discount window made of frosted glass and raised just a few inches. Representatives of institutions could appear at the window and push through the paper they wanted discounted. The central banker would return the appropriate amount of cash, reflecting the going rate of interest. The central banker does not know, nor does he care, who is on the other side of the window. He simply discounts good quality paper or lends on the basis of good collateral. In this way institutions holding good-quality assets will have no difficulty in obtaining the funds they need. Institutions with poor-quality assets are likely to suffer. In times of panic, the interest rate would rise.

By something of a happy accident this was in effect the system that developed in England. At the beginning of the nineteenth century the Bank

---

28 Schwartz, 'Real and pseudo'.

of England's monopoly aroused the ire of the banking community. Such was the antipathy between the bank and the new joint-stock banks that they preferred to keep each other at a distance. Discount brokers conveniently emerged to transact business between them. These discount brokers gradually acquired the capital base to finance their own portfolios and by the third quarter of the nineteenth century had developed into the modern form of the discount house.

When the commercial banks were under pressure in a liquidity squeeze their first line of defence was to call in their loans to the discount houses; this in turn sent the discount houses off to the Bank of England, where they had special access. If the commercial banks had to cash in bills they would do this at the discount houses and the latter would in turn take them to the Bank. In this way the central bank never needed to know where the great bulk of the demand was coming from. The precise source of the demand is largely an irrelevance – good bills get discounted. In practice, of course, we know that individual institutions did take bills directly to the Bank, and borrowed on good security from the Bank when pressure developed. These were in the main its own customers.

Some confusion in the discussion of the nature of the lender-of-last-resort function may have arisen from too cavalier a treatment of this model. Central banking was more advanced in Britain than in other countries and so the British model of central banking was often adopted elsewhere. But the actual mechanism did not always exist in places where the model was adopted. Thus a key feature of the British system, its in-built protective device for anonymity, was overlooked. As a result, in most other countries the institutions went themselves to the central bank, forfeiting their anonymity by so doing. Difficulties were exacerbated when a government's bank and commercial banks were in competition for commercial business. This problem seems to have been ignored in much of the literature, and it may be this that accounts for the way in which bailing out has been treated.

In addition to the constituents outlined above, the lender-of-last-resort function should require that the Bank declare its position to the market in advance – what is called precommitment. It is in this aspect alone that the Bank of England failed to meet the criteria. Other than this, by the 1870s it had become a *de facto*, fully-fledged lender of last resort, coming to the rescue of the market in an appropriate fashion through the buffer of the discount houses. By extension, it could be argued that the Bank's continental European counterparts did not and could not act in this way until at least the end of the nineteenth century, and in most cases probably not until the beginning of the twentieth century. This had serious implications for the comparative stability of the respective systems.

Before the latter part of the nineteenth century central banks were generally expected to carry out commercial banking functions. In some cases, when they were first established they offered the only source of commercial banking services and they were often the largest and most important commercial bank in their countries. Consequently, the early relationship between central banks and commercial banks was often one of business rivalry and competition. This adversarial relationship was in most cases resolved around the beginning of the twentieth century by a largely uncodified concordat whereby, in return for the central bank's withdrawal from commercial banking, the commercial banks voluntarily accepted the central bank's leadership. (There were a few exceptions to this, such as Australia.[29]) A central bank assumes the function of lender of last resort when it accepts responsibility for the banking system as a whole, and when this responsibility overrides any residual concern for its own profitability. It is the appreciation of how such an institution should behave in a crisis, rather than any individual act of rescue, that signals its acceptance of the role.

V

This essay has argued that the evolution of the Bank of England as a lender of last resort was a slow learning process accompanied by changes in the surrounding institutional environment that facilitated the Bank's operations. If we ask how exactly the Bank of England managed to reach the position it had attained in the 1870s, the answer would need to take in many factors. The political environment was as important as developments in monetary thinking. From the time of Ricardo's *Letters to the Morning Chronicle* on the Bullion Report of 1809, which were addressed to the public, through to Bagehot, who was a brilliant journalist with a powerful influence, there were a number of clear forces acting on public opinion. People such as Thomas Joplin wrote persuasively in a variety of media. And there were other important influences. In the end, what decided matters was probably the advent of a new generation of officials at the Bank itself, replacing the older generation that had constantly complained about Bagehot's attacks. It is also worth stressing the uniqueness of the path taken in Britain: there were no models to follow. The Bank of England was clearly the first of its kind, operating in the most sophisticated financial markets of the time. The emergence of the modern central bank took place in the leading industrial country – a country that was beginning to export capital on a considerable scale and to manage the international gold standard.

There had been many crises in the eighteenth century, and these were followed by an intense examination of the monetary system during the Napoleonic wars. As further crises arose a number of regulations were relaxed and certain rules established. First, the usury laws went. Then joint-stock banking was allowed outside London, and then within London. The gold standard was more clearly defined, and the access of the discount houses to the Bank

---

29 For a fuller discussion, see F. Capie, C. Goodhart, S. Fischer, and N. Schadt, eds., *The future of central banking* (Cambridge, 1994).

sorted out. Alongside this there developed a prudent, diversified, limited-liability banking structure. Within this institutional context the Bank became a true lender of last resort. It was able to act quickly and decisively once the accepted arrangement with government was established – a letter suspending the 1844 act was always available, and indeed was rejected by the Bank in 1878 and 1890.

For the hundred years following 1870 there seems to be ample evidence that the British financial system, and more especially its banking system, was enormously stable and that this stability was due in good part to the operations of the Bank of England. The value of the currency was maintained, apart from wartime fluctuations, for most of this period. More significantly, there were no financial crises: whereas crises had been periodic before 1870, they now became a thing of the past. There were occasions when banks failed, just like other firms, but such occurrences do not constitute financial crises. On occasions there were crises around the world which were generally transmitted to other countries by means of the fixed exchange-rate system, but they failed to have significant impacts in Britain: 1907 is a good example. By this time, of course, it was accepted in Britain that the Bank knew how to behave; signs of panic abroad did not spark panic in Britain, even if some precautionary action was deemed necessary. The same is true of the interwar years, when again British banking was enormously stable. There was a crisis in 1931, but this was an exchangerate crisis; no banks failed, even if there was some fudging of the issue. And, generally speaking, bank profits were not badly dented. This stability contrasts starkly with what occurred in most of the rest of the world, with one or two exceptions such as Canada and the Netherlands.

Furthermore, after 1870 the Bank of England was willing to act to avoid panics, and seems to have done so very successfully. Of course, there were other factors in the British experience that contributed to stability, the most important being the structure of the banking system itself. Britain came increasingly to possess a thoroughly branched system that allowed banks considerable diversification. At least in the years before 1914, this stability did not depend on the banking cartel, which had barely come into being at that date. Weighing up the respective contributions of these factors is a task yet to be tackled: the structure of the banking system will no doubt turn out to have been of prime importance, but the stabilizing presence of a trusted central bank must have made its own highly significant contribution.

Select bibliography

Still the best general history of the Bank of England in the nineteenth century is Sir John Clapham, *The Bank of England*, 2: *1797–1914* (Cambridge, 1970). To put this in its eighteenth-century context his volume 1 is useful, as is H.V. Bowen, 'The Bank of England during the long eighteenth century', in R. Roberts and D. Kynaston, eds., *The Bank of England: money, power and influence, 1694–1994* (Oxford, 1995), pp. 1–18.

The Bank's development is put in more general context – the emergence of other central banks – in F. Capie, C. Goodhart, and N. Schnadt, 'The development of central banking', in F. Capie, C. Goodhart, S. Fischer, and N. Schnadt, eds., *The future of central banking* (Cambridge, 1994). Further needed institutional detail is found in W. T. C. King, *A history of the London discount market* (1935, new edn. 1972); and G. Rae, *The country banker: his clients, cares and work* (1930).

The most useful general study of monetary history and thought in the period that matters is, F. W. Fetter, *The development of British monetary orthodoxy 1797–1875* (Cambridge, Mass., 1965).

The monetary thought that was current and of some influence is found in the first place in H. Thornton, *An enquiry into the nature and effects of the paper credit of Great Britain* (Fairfield, 1802). Also important at an early stage was Thomas Joplin as shown by D. O'Brien, *Thomas Joplin and classical macroeconomics: a reappraisal of classical monetary thought* (Aldershot, 1993). And the classic treatment of how the Bank should behave is, W. Bagehot, 'The currency problem', *Prospective Review* (1848), 297–337, reprinted in N. St. J. Stevas, ed., *Collected works*, vol. IX (1986); and more importantly, W. Bagehot, *Lombard Street* (1873). Modern interpretations and assessments of the contributions to the fundamental theory of the lender of last resort can be found in Thomas Humphrey, 'The classic concept of the lender of last resort', *Federal Reserve Bank of Richmond Economic Review* (1975), 1–7; and in Michael Bordo, 'The lender of last resort, alternative views and historical experience' *Federal Reserve Bank of Richmond Economic Review* (1990), 18–29.

On what a financial crisis is and how it should be handled there is no better article than A. J. S. Schwartz, 'Real and pseudo financial crises', in F. Capie and G. E. Wood, eds., *Financial crises and the world banking system* (1986), pp. 11–31.

On the financial crises of the nineteenth century there is a considerable output but on three key crises the following are useful: 1847, J. Frenkel and R. Dornbusch, 'The gold standard and the Bank of England in the crisis of 1847' in Michael Bordo and A. J. S. Schwartz, eds., *A retrospective on the classical gold standard, 1821–1931* (Chicago 1984); 1857, J. R. T. Hughes, 'The commercial crisis of 1857', *Oxford Economic Papers* (1956) 194–222; and on 1866 for a slightly different perspective, R. Batchelor, 'The avoidance of catastrophe: two nineteenth-century banking crises' and L. S. Pressnell's comment on that in Capie and Wood *op. cit.* For the fullest treatment of the events of 1890 see L. S. Pressnell, 'Gold reserves, banking reserves, and the Baring crisis of 1890', in C. R. Whittlesey and J. S. G. Wilson, eds., *Essays in money and banking: in honour of R. S. Sayers* (Oxford, 1968), pp. 1–62.

Supplementary data can be found in F. Capie and A. Webber, *A monetary history of the United Kingdom, 1870–1982* (1985).

13 Myths about the lender of last resort *

C. A. E. Goodhart**

Abstract

This topic has been prone to the accretion of myths that sometimes obscure the key issues. As a start, Bagehot is often treated as the first to write on the subject, ignoring Thornton's contribution. Next, Bagehot's proposal that such lending be at 'high' rates is incorrectly translated into 'penalty' rates. This paper, however, concentrates on and criticizes four further myths: that it is generally possible to distinguish between illiquidity and insolvency; that national LOLR capacities are unlimited, whereas international bodies, such as the IMF, cannot function as an ILOLR; that moral hazard is everywhere and at all times a major consideration; and that it might be possible to dispense with LOLR altogether.

I. Introduction

There are few issues so subject to myth, sometimes unhelpful myths that tend to obscure rather than to illuminate real issues, as is the subject of whether a central bank (or an international financial institution (IFI) such as the International Monetary Fund (IMF)), should act as a lender of last resort (LOLR).

Perhaps the very first myth is that the fount of all wisdom, the *fons et origo*, on this subject is to be found in Bagehot's great book *Lombard Street* (1873). In fact, most of the key policy proposals set out there were anticipated by Henry Thornton in his outstanding study *The Paper Credit of Great Britain*,

* My thanks are due to Forrest Capie, David Clementi, Kevin Dowd, Xavier Freixas, Max Fry, Henry Gillett, Rosa Lastra, Ronald McKinnon, Adam Posen, Benn Steil, Paul Tucker, Geoffrey Wood and Paul Volcker, and several anonymous referees. Nevertheless, the views expressed here are the sole responsibility of the author, and do not represent those of the Bank of England, or anyone else. This work was sponsored by the Financial Markets Group, LSE, and the ESRC Research Centre. A revised and shortened version of this paper was also given as the Henry Thornton Lecture of the City University Business School on 17 November 1999.

** Financial Markets Group, London School of Economics.

the greatest treatise on the conduct of monetary operations ever written, though Bagehot gave little credit to any prior writers on the subject in his own book. The main proposals outlined by Bagehot (1873, pp. 196–7) are:

1. Lend freely.
2. At a high rate of interest.
3. On good banking securities.

Let me demonstrate how Thornton dealt with these same questions. First, he wrote on lending freely, as follows:

> The directors [of the Bank], therefore, must seem to themselves to act with extraordinary liberality towards those who apply to them for discounts, [during a season of consternation]. . . . The liberality in lending which they must exercise, if, when the gold is low, they even augment their paper, must be very extended indeed.
>
> (Thornton 1802, p. 116)

On Bagehot's second two principles of lending on good security at a high rate of interest Thornton wrote:

> It is by no means intended to imply, that it would become the Bank of England to relieve every distress which the rashness of country banks may bring upon them: the bank, by doing this, might encourage their improvidence. . . . The relief should neither be so prompt and liberal as to exempt those who misconduct their business from all the natural consequences of their fault, nor so scanty and slow as deeply to involve the general interest.
>
> (Thornton 1802, p. 121)

And again:

> That the bills which the bank discounts, are, generally speaking, so safe, that the security either of goods, or stocks, or land. . . . may be considered as nearly superfluous. A very small proportion of the five per cent discount, gained upon the bills turned into ready money at the bank, has compensated, as I believe, for the whole of the loss upon them, even in the years of the greatest commercial failures which have yet been known.
>
> (Thornton 1802, pp. 119–20)

Bagehot only goes further than Thornton in placing more emphasis on the need to raise interest rates to deter unnecessary domestic borrowing, for both Thornton and Bagehot were aware of the need to raise interest rates to check a foreign drain of gold from the bank. But Thornton's lack of emphasis on this point may well have been due to the continuing effect of the usury laws, in force until the 1830s, capping (formal) interest rates at 5% and preventing the bank from using this instrument aggressively in a crisis.

But this emphasis in Bagehot on the need for 'high' interest rates for LOLR has led some commentators (e.g. Humphrey and Keleher 1984)[1] to go further and claim that Bagehot proposed that LOLR should always be at a 'penalty' rate; that is, at a rate *higher* than that available in the market place. This is not so.[2] Certainly the rate should be above that in effect in the market prior to the panic, but not necessarily above the contemporaneous market rate.[3] Bagehot was very concerned that, unless the Bank of England was prepared to lend on the basis of what was normally regarded as good security, no one else would do so at all. The penalty rate would then be infinite. Bagehot wrote:

> If it is known that the Bank of England is freely advancing on what in ordinary times is reckoned a good security – on what is then commonly pledged and easily convertible – the alarm of the solvent merchants and bankers will be stayed. But if securities, really good and usually convertible, are refused by the Bank, the alarm will not abate, the other loans made will fail in obtaining their end, and the panic will become worse and worse.
>
> (Bagehot 1873, pp. 198–9)

The levels to which bank rates were raised during the period of the Gold Standard were mild[4] by the standards of our current age, with its bouts of

---

1 They describe the policy prescription for simultaneously meeting external and internal drains as being to 'lend freely at a high (penalty) rate' (p. 200), with those words in quotes, as presumably coming from a separate authority, e.g. Thornton or Bagehot. But no source, or page numbers, are given, and I have not been able to find such a reference, or indeed *any* reference to a 'penalty' rate in either Thornton or Bagehot.

2 I asked a research assistant to check for any references in *Lombard Street* to 'penalty' or 'penal'. There are four. One, at the start of Chapter 13 (p. 329), notes that the Bank of England is 'under no effectual penalty of failure'. A second (Chapter 7, p. 175), commends the Bank for not over-issuing during the suspension of the Gold Standard when there was 'no present penalty on it'. The other two references are in Chapter 4, describing the penalty individual banks might suffer for over-lending in a 'natural' system without a central bank.

3 The key reference in Bagehot (p. 197) reads as follows: 'The end is to stay the panic; and the advances should, if possible, stay the panic. And for this purpose there are two rules: – First. That these loans should only be made at a very high rate of interest. This will operate as a heavy fine on unreasonable timidity, and will prevent the greatest number of applications by persons who do not require it. The rate should be raised early in the panic, so that the fine may be paid early; that no one may borrow out of idle precaution without paying well for it; then the banking reserve may be protected as far as possible. Secondly. That at this rate these advances should be made on all good banking securities, and as largely as the public ask for them. The reason is plain. The object is to stay alarm, and nothing therefore should be done to cause alarm.'

4 They were certainly so in nominal terms in comparison to today. Given medium-term expectations of price stability, 7% nominal is quite high in real terms, but it was not expected to last long, as can be inferred by the remarkable stability (again as compared to today) of

inflation and currency crises. When Bagehot remarked that LOLR 'loans should only be made at a very high rate of interest', he would have it in mind that a bank rate of 6 or 7% was very high, and 10% extraordinarily high. It was then said that '7% would draw gold from the moon'.[5]

An even more pervasive interpretation of the teaching of these early scholars is that they advocated that LOLR lending could, and should, be adjusted to distinguish between the illiquid and the insolvent. Indeed, the first of the main myths that I shall discuss is that it is generally possible for a central bank to distinguish between illiquidity and insolvency, and should then confine its LOLR loans solely to the former. Thereafter I want to deal with three other views, which I also hold to be mistaken. These are:

1. That national central bank LOLR capacities are unrestricted, whereas international bodies, or IFIs such as the IMF, cannot function as an ILOLR.
2. That moral hazard is everywhere and at all times a predominant consideration.
3. That it might be possible to dispense with an LOLR altogether.

II. Myth 1

The first myth is that it is generally possible to distinguish between illiquidity and insolvency.

The possibility of large shocks – for example, large jumps in asset prices, especially crises when such a jump is downwards – means that there may be multiple equilibria, to use the current jargon. Panic conditions can lead to circumstances where firms that would be viable during normal times become insolvent, though perhaps only temporarily. This syndrome may be especially serious in commercial banks, because of their interconnectedness (Allen and

Consol prices. It is difficult to compare these real rates with those applied in modern crises, since the forward-looking expectations of future inflation are less well anchored. Even so, the rates introduced in Sweden, and the 15% bank rate briefly attempted in the UK during the EMS crisis, and several occasions of official rates during the East Asian crisis, e.g. in Korea and Hong Kong, produced real rates well above those in nineteenth-century crises. Moreover, these latter real rates failed to restore confidence and bring in foreign exchange inflows from abroad, perhaps because they were perceived as 'too high'.

5   David Kynaston quotes this in his history of the City of London (1995, Volume II, p. 453), where he writes, 'It was probably at this time [1907] that the tag was coined in the London money market that "7% brings gold from the moon".' The problem nowadays is that, with less of a firm anchor for exchange rate expectations, during crises the minimum level of interest rates necessary to maintain or restore foreign confidence may be perilously close to the maximum that the domestic economy can meet without instigating a financial collapse.

Gale 1998, 1999). Bagehot[6] and Thornton[7] were well aware of this; Bagehot remarked approvingly of the bank's operations in 1825 when the bank made advances 'by every possible means consistent with the safety of the Bank, and we were not on some occasions over-nice' (p. 52).

In Bagehot's time, the money market operated almost entirely through the discount of bills of exchange. If the bill was 'good' in the sense that the initial drawer of the bill would certainly pay on maturity, a central bank that rediscounted the bill would be repaid in due course, whatever happened to the (bank) intermediary from which it had rediscounted in the meantime.

Bagehot's test of whether a central bank should lend during a crisis did not depend on the individual borrower, but on the security; thus 'advances should be made on all good banking securities and as largely as the public ask for them' (p. 197). But this test has really nothing to do with the question of whether (on best mark-to-market accounting principles) the applicant borrower (commercial bank) had a capital value below some lower limit (e.g. zero or insolvency). Indeed, then as now, a central bank faced with an application for LOLR had, and has, no quick or accurate way of ascertaining this. Instead Bagehot's proposal related simply to the collateral that the applicant could offer, and the effect of this rule in practice was to distinguish, in part, between those loans on which the central bank might expect with some considerable probability to make a loss (bad bills and collateral) and those on which little, or no, loss should eventuate.

Such discounting of bills was simultaneously the standard way in Bagehot's time both for injecting cash into the market as a whole and for lending to individual banks. This changed thereafter in the UK towards the end of the nineteenth century, because the Bank of England became increasingly unhappy about regular direct bilateral negotiations with the joint stock commercial banks, since the amalgamation process was causing the latter to become much larger in size than the Bank itself. Instead, from the latter part of the nineteenth century right through to the final decade of the twentieth century, the bank would carry out its general liquidity operations through the discount houses, a group of small intra-market subsidiaries which the Bank actively fostered. Meanwhile direct, last resort support for individual commercial banks, as in the Baring crisis (1890), was separately organized, as we shall discuss below.

6 'A panic, in a word, is a species of neuralgia, and according to the rules of science you must not starve it. The holders of the cash reserve must be ready not only to keep it for their own liabilities, but to advance it most freely for the liabilities of others. They must lend to merchants, to minor bankers, to "this man and that man", wherever the security is good. In wild periods of alarm, one failure makes many, and the best way to prevent the derivative failures is to arrest the primary failure which caused them' (Bagehot 1873, pp. 51–2).

7 'If any one bank fails, a general run upon the neighbouring ones is apt to take place, which, if not checked in the beginning by pouring into the circulation a large quantity of gold leads to very extensive mischief' (Thornton 1802, p. 113).

This distinction between generalized control of systemic liquidity via open market operations, determining the rate of growth of the monetary base, and LOLR transactions with individual financial institutions, (normally banks) has been taken further today. With the development of broad and deep money markets, e.g. repo markets, the CB operates to determine interest rates (and by those same actions to adjust the monetary base) by open market operation (OMO), undertaken through general market operations, and not in bilateral negotiation with any individual institution.

Among the factors influencing the CB in its conduct of OMO will be issues such as the degree of confidence/risk aversion in markets (e.g. as measured by the pattern of spreads), the demand for cash or measures of public confidence in the banking system. Some writers on this subject have described injections of high-powered money, open market purchases, undertaken to calm actual, or potential, losses of confidence in the financial system as a whole (that is, systemic problems), as LOLR operations. In my view it is wrong to do so. One main reason is that it is practically impossible then to distinguish LOLR-OMO from non-LOLR-OMO. For example, the Bank of Japan has at times in recent years aggressively increased the monetary base. Which actions, and how much of this increase, could be designated as LOLR? It is not possible, except in rare circumstances,[8] to make such a distinction. Hence the concept is effectively non-operational. By contrast, the distinction between lending by the CB to an individual institution and OMO dealing with the market as a whole is simple, practical and self-evidently justifiable. In my view only the former should be described as LOLR, and that is what will be done henceforth.

Individual banks nowadays adjust their own liquidity through these same wholesale money markets. Banks will much prefer, under normal conditions, to do so than to borrow directly, and bilaterally, from the CB, whether collateralized or not. There is a potential reputational cost from being observed to borrow directly from the CB (at least this is so in most countries). Again in most countries, bilateral direct borrowing from the CB will be more expensive (a penalty rate) than the market rate. There will be times when the wholesale market rate is driven up to the CB's penalty (Lombard) rate, or when the CB's discount rate is commonly below the market rate (as in the US), when lending to individual banks becomes both commonplace and constrained by other (reputational) factors.

Except in such instances, an individual bank will only go to a CB for direct bilateral LOLR assistance when it *cannot* meet its liquidity needs on the wholesale interbank money markets. Almost by definition this must be because it is running out of good security for collateralized loans *and* other

8   One such occasion was the announcement by the Federal Reserve after the 1987 stock market crash that it would make additional liquidity available to the financial system both via OMO and through easy access to the discount window.

(bank) lenders will not lend to it on an unsecured basis in the quantities required (at acceptable rates). Again almost by definition this latter must be because there is some question about its ultimate solvency. The greater the insistence of the CB on charging a 'penalty' rate on its own LOLR loans, the greater the endeavour of commercial banks to use their existing good collateral to borrow in the market place first.

There are some exceptions to this rule, that nowadays illiquidity implies at least a *suspicion* of insolvency. But such exceptions tend to prove the rule. One of the most famous LOLR occasions of recent decades was the massive lending on one overnight occasion (20 November 1985) by the Federal Reserve Bank of New York to the Bank of New York. The Bank of New York had had a computer malfunction. It was a leading participant in the US Treasury bond market; the computer had paid out good funds for Treasury bonds bought, but would not accept cash in-payments for Treasury bonds sold. As a major player in the market with a huge gross turnover, this rapidly led to a ballooning cash deficit. The bank was still, of course, patently solvent; moreover its cash deficit was matched by surpluses spread amongst the other banks, mostly in New York. Nevertheless the private market could not cope with recycling the money back to the Bank of New York, at least not quickly enough. The size of the liquidity deficit was so huge that no one single bank could possibly have been the counterpart lender, since it would have both exhausted its own liquidity and broken through its various (internal) controls on large exposures. Thus a coordinated, syndicated response would have been necessary, and the arrangement of such coordination is time-consuming, somewhat expensive and subject to free rider problems. It was just far easier to let the FRBNY manage the temporary problem.

So, as a generality, whenever an individual commercial bank approaches the CB for direct bilateral loans (LOLR) (unless interest rate relativities make that profitable for the commercial bank), the CB must/should suspect that the failure of the bank to adjust its liquidity on the open market means that there is at least a whiff of suspicion of insolvency. It is not, however, possible for the CB, at least within the relevant timescale, to ascertain whether such suspicions are valid or not; and if valid, what the extent of the solvency problem is.[9] Of course, a CB, or the associated bank supervisory agency, will, or should, have a good knowledge of the prior reputation of a bank seeking assistance, and *may* be able to obtain a quick reading of the market value of its trading book. I emphasize 'may' because in a crisis situation liquidity can disappear and values become very volatile; moreover, the true value of a complex position in derivatives markets can be far from easy to ascertain.

---

9 Moreover, as Freixas (1999) has noted, the franchise value of a bank as a going concern may often exceed its mark-to-market accounting value, so the franchise value may be positive while at the same time the accounting value is negative; that is, the bank is insolvent.

There certainly will be cases where the CB has such concern about the solvency, and prior inappropriate banking behaviour of a suppliant bank borrower, that the request for LOLR can, and should, be turned down flat. The fact that there is often a murky area where illiquidity and insolvency cannot be distinguished does not mean that this is so in every case of requests for LOLR.

For many 'liberal' commentators the argument that bilateral LOLR generally occurs only when there is a suspicion of insolvency is a good reason why a CB should eschew any such LOLR actions, but confine itself only to OMO. They claim (e.g. Humphrey and Keleher 1984) that this course of action is consistent with the Bagehot principles.[10] I do not believe that this is so. The rules proposed by Bagehot were intended both to prevent the CB suffering any significant loss on its LOLR loans and to prevent an excessive expansion of the money stock. When the CB discounted 'good bills' for a financial intermediary, it did not and could not at the same time estimate the borrower's solvency. It had no good measure of the borrower's balance sheet.

An LOLR loan by a CB is like any other loan, in that it may be repaid (plus interest) or alternatively will be subject to default and some potential loss. That loss would impair the capital of the CB. When the CB was private, as in most cases in the nineteenth century, the capital strength of the CB was as important and relevant an issue as it was to any other private institution. From a CB's viewpoint, Bagehot's concern that no CB should lend in a manner that might expose it to undue loss resonated with good sense.

How far does this concern alter, if at all, when the CB becomes explicitly a public sector body, via outright nationalization or otherwise? Not necessarily that much. For example, in the case of the Bank of England there used to be an implicit distinction between those aspects of its business that were the affairs of the Bank and those that were the affairs of the government.[11] The Bank of England's own retained capital still gave it some leeway and freedom to act at its own independent volition, and it prized that margin of freedom. Most crisis management continued to be done under the aegis of the Bank, *qua* Bank, with its independent capacity for action. This capacity remained, in some large part though not entirely, bounded by its capital. In Japan, for example, Okina (1999) has noted that the Bank of Japan is concerned whether further purchases of assets, in order to increase the monetary base, might bring about losses. This could be so even for purchases of government

---

10 Thus they write: 'Conspicuously absent is any mention of the need to channel aid to specific institution, as would be implied by bail-out operations. Bagehot's emphasis is clearly on aid to the market rather than to the initially distressed bank. He obviously did not think it necessary to prevent the initial failure at all costs' (Humphrey and Keleher 1984, p. 300).

11 See the Radcliffe Committee's (1959) discussion of 'The Bank's Relationship with the Central Government' (paragraphs 760–75), and the associated Minutes of the session of the Committee with C. F. Cobbold (Governor), H. C. B. Mynors (Deputy Governor) and A. W. C. Dascombe (Secretary of the Bank) (pp. 892–900).

bonds, JGBs (see Okina 1999, pp. 18–21). In so far as a CB acts independently but subsequently is forced by events to go directly to the government for financial support in one guise or another, it will lose reputation and independence, as in the case of the Bank of England and Johnson Matthey Bankers in 1984.

Under the Gold Standard, CB loans, whether to maintain market liquidity, to protect the financial system or to support the government's wartime aims, could lead to a drastic reduction of its gold reserves (and in some cases also to an impairment of its capital strength). In such cases the government would step in to declare the Bank's liabilities to be legal tender. Such '*cours forcé*,' as this was known in the nineteenth century, was always perceived as a sign of the fundamental weakness of the CB. Such weakness, of course, became generalized in the First World War, and thereafter with the breakdown of the Gold Standard in the inter-war period. Although usually emitted notionally by the CB,[12] flat money depended not on the (capital) strength of the CB, but on the strength and taxing power of the government behind it. Does this mean that Bagehot's limits for the potential capital loss to the CB no longer had much, or any, force?

The answer, to some extent and in some countries, is 'yes', as Max Fry (1997) has shown. CBs in some countries, mainly in Latin America, have actually become technically insolvent (using generally accepted accounting principles) as a result of losses incurred on loans in support of the domestic financial system. But such insolvency does not make much difference because what stands behind the liabilities of the CB is *not* the capital of the CB but the strength and taxing power of the State.[13]

What does this tell us about the handling of systemic problems within a country? Unless such problems involve only a small potentiality for loss, so that the CB can handle it on its own books, such systemic problems will nowadays require joint management and resolution by the supervisory body, the CB and the government. As emphasized in Goodhart and Schoenmaker

12 Usually but not always. The ten shilling and one pound notes issued in the UK in 1914 after the start of the First World War were the liabilities of H. M. Treasury.

13 Both Thornton and Bagehot were well aware of this. Thornton, for example, noted (pp. 31–3) that the 1793 financial crisis was resolved, absent sufficient resolve by the Bank of England, by direct LOLR support from Parliament. Bagehot noted that the experience of 1797, and the subsequent suspension of the 1844 Bank of England Act, 'confirmed the public conviction that the Government is close behind the Bank, and will help it when wanted'. The complete passage reads as follows: 'But no one in London ever dreams of questioning the credit of the Bank, and the Bank never dreams that its own credit is in danger. Somehow everybody feels the Bank is sure to come right. In 1797, when it had scarcely any money left, the Government said not only that it need not pay away what remained, but that it *must* not. The 'effect of letters of licence' to break Peel's Act has confirmed the popular conviction that the Government is close behind the Bank, and will help it when wanted. Neither the Bank nor the Banking Department have ever had an idea of being put 'into liquidation'; most men would think as soon of "winding up" the English nation' (p. 40).

(1993), he who pays the piper calls the tunes. In large-scale, systemic domestic cases the government pays the piper, so it will be the government which ultimately will decide how the crisis is handled and who bears the losses.

III. Myth 2

The second myth is that a national CB's LOLR capacities are unrestricted (even without support from its own government), whereas international bodies, or IFIs such as the IMF, cannot function as an ILOLR.

The gist of my thesis so far has been that the key factor determining the scope and scale of a CB's LOLR functions has been its ability to absorb losses. As this has waned, relative to the scale of financial losses involved in systemic problems, as in Japan and Scandinavia recently, the responsibility for handling such crises has, willy-nilly, passed to the governments involved.

But such governments only have domestic, not (almost by definition) international powers. They can require domestic taxes be paid, and internal debts be settled, in their own fiat money. But they cannot create foreign currency,[14] and they cannot force foreign creditors to accept payment in domestic liabilities, if the contract specifies otherwise. Moreover, if the domestic authorities create additional domestic fiat money to buy the requisite foreign currency in the open market, this would usually be largely or entirely offset by depreciation in the international value of the domestic currency.

So, just as commercial banks will turn to their CB when they cannot borrow additional high-powered money on acceptable terms in money markets, these national governments and CBs will want to turn to an international LOLR when they, or their private sector, cannot borrow foreign currency on acceptable terms in the international money market. Step forward the IMF. How does the IMF's position as an ILOLR compare with that of a domestic CB's position as an LOLR? In several respects the IMF is much *better* able to act as ILOLR than a CB to act as LOLR within the domestic context. The IMF has more capital, and could sustain larger losses. Moreover, the IMF always has the most senior ranking as creditor, so losses are perhaps even less likely than in the case of a domestic CB. Historically the IMF has suffered very little actual loss on its loans, although quite a large number of countries, almost all heavily indebted poor countries, such as the Sudan, have been in arrears in repayment. Few countries, other than 'basket cases', are likely voluntarily to remain in 'arrears to the IMF', since it carries such a high penalty. Such a country cannot get access to private funds or other public

---

14 Kevin Dowd has raised the question with me, in personal correspondence, of whether governments could not also require taxes to be paid in foreign currency. This would happen naturally in a country that 'dollarized'. Even in the absence of dollarization, in certain emerging countries where access to the international capital market is restricted, serious thought has been given to the possibility of requiring multinationals operating in that country to make (tax) payments in US dollars to the government.

funds (other than concessional funds, e.g. from the World Bank), no matter how desperate it may be.

Nevetheless, as is well known, the IMF's resources and capital are limited, exactly as those of a domestic CB are limited.[15] As a result CBs have eked out their own scarce resources by involving the private sector and by acting as crisis manager in arranging the disposition of funds from a much wider range of private sector institutions. The Fund has done exactly the same. CBs have often sought to resolve crises by acting as guarantors, rather than putting up their own money up front, and by giving their seal of approval to the affairs of the distressed borrower. The Fund does so even more. In these respects, as Fischer (1999) has noted in his paper on the IMF as an ILOLR, the IMF acts in exactly the same way as a CB.

The IMF differs from national CBs in two main respects. First it cannot buy/sell assets in open financial markets using its own currency liability (the Special Drawing Right, or SDR). Indeed, the conditions under which, and how, the issue of SDRs may be made are strictly controlled and constrained; consequently no issue has been made since 1981; and the issues actually made between the first issues, at the start of the 1970s, and then had relatively little impact on world liquidity. Without the ability to issue its own liabilities at will, the IMF has virtually no capacity to undertake open market operations,[16] e.g. in order to influence world liquidity conditions. Of course, given free international capital mobility, no domestic CB, apart from the US Federal Reserve Board, can do much to influence the level of real interest rates, and/or the risk spreads, in its own country.[17] So in that sense the IMF is not at such a disadvantage in comparison to the capacities of most national CBs.

15 Moreover, the class of recipient of both the IMF's and domestic CBs' LOLR loans are limited. The IMF can only lend to member governments; the CB (by convention) to domestic commercial banks. In both cases this is primarily because the key reserves, foreign currency in the case of the IMF, high-powered money in the case of the CBs, are centralized in the recipient bodies. But there are subsidiary reasons in both cases, relating to trying to economize on monitoring efforts, to limit the scale and scope of 'safety nets', to concerns about the use of power etc. The dividing lines between commercial banks and other financial intermediaries and between domestic and multinational banks are becoming blurred, and this may cause some difficulties on this front to domestic CBs. There may be some analogues for the IMF; for example, if there were, as an unlikely event, a foreign currency crisis in Euroland, to whom would the IMF lend? Again, could the IMF lend to a subsidiary government with a different currency from the federal government, as in the case of Hong Kong. No doubt Fund lawyers have thought about all such cases.

16 For some economists writing on this subject (e.g. Capie 1998; Keleher 1999), the central, possibly sole, function of a proper, effective LOLR is to use OMO to offset generalized liquidity crises. For them, no OMO capacity implies, virtually by definition, no LOLR capacity. I have been trying to explain throughout this paper why I disagree.

17 Robert Keleher, in his role of Chief Macroeconomist to the Joint Economic Committee, has seized on this difference to argue that the Federal Reserve, rather than the IMF, could, and perhaps should, act as an ILOLR. Thus his conclusions (Keleher 1999, p. 10) are: 'Under existing institutional arrangements, the IMF cannot serve as a genuine LOLR. Specifically,

Nevertheless, it is generally the level of nominal, rather than real, interest rates that is important for the resolution of (systemic) financial difficulties.[18] Indeed, it is the fear that national CBs may lower short-term interest rates too far, for the maintenance of price stability, in the pursuit of systemic stability, that lies behind the argument that a CB with both price and stability objectives could occasionally face a conflict of interest (see Goodhart and Schoenmaker 1993). Whether, or not, such conflicts may be common and problematical, this is clearly a power which the IMF cannot use *directly*. In practice, however, the IMF can influence borrowing governments to vary interest rates as part of 'conditionality'. In the Asian crisis the main criticism of the IMF was that it put pressure on the countries involved to raise interest rates *too much*.

Where the IMF is, however, at a crucial disadvantage compared with national CBs is that it does not have a single (world?) government standing behind it, with international powers and taxing authority (note also that the first difference above, the inability freely to issue its own fiat liabilities, follows logically from this second and much more fundamental difference). Consequently the IMF can neither issue fiat money freely nor – and this is vastly more important for ILOLR concerns – expect any loss that impairs its available capital resources to be absorbed by its member governments, or not at least without such a row as would imperil the IMF's own position. The fundamental issue is about decision-taking and burden-sharing in national and international government forums. No CB can cope with a large financial crisis on its own, but it can usually expect to obtain a clear and reasonably quick decision on how to proceed and how the burdens are to be shared from its own national government. As, I would hope, the exception that proves the rule, the failure of the Japanese government to reach any such clear, quick decisions has been a major cause of the long drawn-out difficulties in the financial system there. By contrast, the problems that the IMF would face in getting its disparate governing body to agree to a clear, quick decision on crisis handling and burden sharing are obvious.[19]

---

the IMF cannot create reserves, cannot make quick decisions, and does not act in a transparent manner in order to qualify as an authentic international LOLR. The Federal Reserve, however, does meet the essential requirements of an international LOLR. It can quickly create international reserves and money, although it has not openly embraced international LOLR responsibilities. The Federal Reserve can easily implement this function by employing several readily available market price indicators and global measures.'

18 It is sometimes argued that the Federal Reserve helped to relieve US financial difficulties at the end of the 1980s and outset of the 1990s by keeping short rates low, relative to long rates.

19 Keleher (1999, p. 6) emphasizes this point as follows: '*The IMF cannot act quickly enough to serve as a LOLR*. Genuine LOLR decisions often must be made very quickly, sometimes within hours (as in a banking liquidity crisis). Under current practices, however, IMF decision-making is ordinarily quite slow and cumbersome. For example, in providing money to a borrowing country, the IMF conducts lengthy negotiations involving reform programs

This view of LOLR emphasizes the potentiality for loss involved, and hence the need for decisions on burden sharing. After all, if there was no such prospective loss, why could not the market handle any such problem on its own? If such losses may be large, the ability of a CB to absorb them on its own will be stretched beyond its limit; hence the need to involve government. A national CB has one national government with which to cooperate and jointly to come to a decision. This process *should* be much easier than that facing an international body, such as the IMF, with many national representatives on its governing body.

What this analysis also indicates is that the crucial features of the organization of Euroland are such that the European Central Bank (ECB) has much more in common with the IMF, effectively operating as an ILOLR, than with national CBs operating as domestic LOLRs. The central EU government is weak, with strictly limited taxing powers. If the ESCB should find that a rescue operation stretched its own capital position unduly, it could not look for executive action, financial support and decisions on burden sharing from the Commission, the European Parliament and the EU Budget. It would have to appeal for support to the European Council and the Parliaments and budgets of the member states. The 'political' difficulties of that course are all too clear.

Since national governments still maintain the bulk of fiscal power in Europe, the retention of LOLR activities within the euro zone in the hands of NCBs and national governments would seem the best course for the time being. The problem is that, once financial systems across the euro zone become more integrated, NCBs and national Parliaments will become increasingly unwilling to resolve, and pick up the tab for, problems that may have largely originated elsewhere within the EU.

For the time being the considerable (and even surprising) extent of segmentation in national financial systems within Europe will enable the present system of crisis resolution being centred on national institutions to continue (with the ECB playing a consultative, overseeing and advisory role). Once the European financial system becomes more integrated, the disjunction between a centralized, federal monetary system and decentralized national fiscal powers will become more difficult to reconcile. It will be interesting to observe how this disjunction will be resolved in future.

IV. Myth 3

The third myth is that moral hazard is everywhere and at all times a major consideration.

and related conditionalities. Letters of intent and memoranda of understandings are drawn up. IMF executive board decisions are subject to the votes of executive directors who often consult their national authorities. All of this takes a good deal of time.'

The market can be expected to provide loans on its own to banks short of liquidity when no loss is to be expected. So LOLR is, almost always, only sought, or needed, when there is some potentiality for loss, in some cases a very large potential loss. If LOLR is then provided, this raises the possibility, often the likelihood, that such losses will fall on those providing the support funds (with CBs nowadays being public sector bodies, this effectively means the tax-payer, whether the loss is absorbed on the books of the CB or not).

This means that some part of the loss will generally fall on those who have had no responsibility for the decisions that led to the loss. This shifting of the burden from those closer to the source of the loss-making decisions to those further away, tax-payers, may cause the decision-makers to take riskier decisions for well known reasons – that is, moral hazard. Many liberal economists and commentators claim that moral hazard is so serious and pervasive that LOLR, as contrasted with standard OMO for liquidity control reasons, should be eschewed altogether.

Even if moral hazard is so pervasive, there remains the question of the possible extent of loss, should there be a (contagious) systemic panic, if the CB refuses LOLR. The CB has to weigh the benefits of preventing panic now against the costs of inducing riskier activity later. Liberal economists claim that any such panic can be checked and prevented by OMO rather than LOLR. But Goodhart and Huang (1999) reply that the uncertainty, dismay and panic engendered by the newsworthy failure of a (large) bank make it that much more difficult to calibrate the necessary extent of LOLR with any accuracy. Again, Okina (1999, pp. 23–4) argues against base money targetry on the grounds that financial instability made the public's demand for currency unstable and unpredictable.

The danger of moral hazard affecting those *closest* to decision-making has always been recognized. There is an apocryphal story of the CEO of a large money-centre bank in the US coming to the then Chairman of the Federal Reserve, Paul Volcker, and asking how he, Volcker, would react if the CEO was to come to him with a request for a rescue injection of liquid funds. Volcker is reputed[20] to have replied that he would be happy to discuss the issue with the CEO's successor. The need to ensure that those whose actual executive decisions have led the commercial bank, or financial institution, into a mess do not benefit from CB LOLR, or rescue, operations is well known and widely understood. It was the failure to remove the executives of LTCM from their positions that caused much of the public disquiet about that episode, even given that no public Federal Reserve money was at stake in this rescue.

While the principle is clear, it is sometimes honoured in the breach. In particular, the current executives have a certain monopoly of inside

---

20 Alas the story *is* apocryphal. When I checked with him, he wrote back, 'I wish the story were true. In spirit, it is true.' Private correspondence.

information, and at times of crisis that information may have particular value. For such reasons some of the executives of Barings (1995), and the top management of LTCM (1998), were allowed to continue in post.

In the case of ILOLR operations carried out by the IMF, the policy measures required to be implemented under the conditionality agreements have been so severely restrictive in recent cases that no one can regard calling in the Fund as a 'soft option'. Indeed, the reverse is probably the greater danger – that is, that the Fund's required terms are perceived as likely to be so onerous that calling for Fund assistance is delayed too long,[21] by which time foreign exchange reserves are depleted, the financial system is weakened, wealth eroded, foreign capital in full flight etc. (see, for example, Lissakers 1999).[22]

Besides the decision-taking executives, the terms and nature of the equity contract imply that shareholders should also be required to face the responsibility and the adverse consequences of failure, loss and insolvency until their positive asset valuation is eliminated. Shareholders, with their downside protected by limited liability, and being the recipients of any upside potential, have some incentive to encourage (bank) executives into riskier action. (Note that the question of whether shareholders, whether in banks, financial intermediaries or elsewhere, should *not* enjoy the full protection of limited liability is too complex to discuss here.) One proposal recently put forward at a joint meeting of Shadow Regulatory Committees (June 1999) is to require banks also to hold a tranche of subordinated debt as part of their capital. Without any share in upside profit potential, and unprotected from loss of their stake following insolvency, such debt holders could be expected to be acutely sensitive to risk. One benefit could be that the yield on such debt might be a good measure of perceived risk. If so, it would need to be understood that support by the authorities, whether resulting from LOLR activities or otherwise, did not temper any losses to such debt-holders associated with a fall in the distressed bank's capital values.

The problem of where the burden of loss should fall becomes more difficult and complex the further away one moves from the central locus of decision-making. How far, if at all, should a failing bank's losses, beyond

---

21 Dr Lastra has reminded me that, in order to counter this syndrome, conditionality has been relaxed in certain respects over recent years, through new facilities (with 'softer' conditions) and through accelerated procedures to disburse money.

22 McKinnon, in personal correspondence, has, however, pointed out that the two-step procedure whereby the IMF lends to a government, and then the domestic monetary authorities lend to commercial banks can lead to a double jeopardy in moral hazard. 'Because the IMF must lend through national governments who in turn bail out national banks, limiting moral hazard involved faces double jeopardy. To be effective, IMF conditionality imposed on governments must sanction them from misbehaving in the future. But this is only effective if the government receiving the loans is not undermined by (undetected) undue risk taking by its own banks.'

those already absorbed by equity and bond holders, fall on its other creditors, especially but not only its interbank creditors? The principle has been broadly accepted that it would be socially wasteful to require ordinary small depositors to monitor their bank, and that some considerable (though preferably *not* 100%) deposit insurance for such depositors is justified. There is no need to re-open that issue here. One hundred per cent deposit insurance may, indeed at times certainly does, lead to moral hazard in the sense that depositors do not monitor their bankers, and instead shift their funds to institutions offering the highest interest rates irrespective of reputation or apparent probity. This can be contained by partial insurance, or co-insurance. Meanwhile, the polar opposite of zero insurance is just too inequitable and socially wasteful to be acceptable. The absence of any (partial) deposit insurance is, therefore, likely to enhance the implicit guarantee of full protection to all depositors, since the political alternative is just too horrible to contemplate.

The more immediate question is what to do about the nexus of interbank connections, both domestically and internationally. It is above all such connections that are feared to lead to contagion and systemic problems, as was demonstrated in the Continental Illinois case and has been modelled theoretically by Allen and Gale (1999) and by Aghion et al. (1999). On the other hand, banks ought to be in a better position to monitor their fellow-banks than anyone else, (apart from the official supervisors). Moreover, interest rate terms and spreads are set in bank-dominated wholesale financial markets. If interbank lenders are (thought to be) protected from loss by the operation of domestic and international LOLRs, will not then the pattern of relative interest rates fail properly to reflect true risk, and hence the allocation of capital become distorted?

This is, perhaps, now the focus of most concern, certainly internationally, to a rather lesser extent nationally. How far does LOLR primarily benefit other bank creditors? If so, should this be allowed to continue? When banks have lent to financial intermediaries, such as the Juzen in Japan, what should be the balance of burden absorption between the banks and the tax-payers? On the one hand, placing the burden on the banks would weaken them further at a time of fragility and hence cause more danger of contagion. On the other hand, the banks *should* have known the risks, and it is unfair (besides incurring moral hazard) to shift the burden to the tax-payer.

The same argument runs in the international sphere. There are several schemes for 'bailing-in' the international bank lenders. The 'U-drop' proposal by Buiter and Sibert (1999) is one, among several other, such. As in the domestic arena, a response of the banks is that any such prospective restriction/penalty would make contagion (between countries) more likely and more immediate, and that it could further worsen the volatility of both spreads and flows, as well as raising the average level of spreads faced by emerging countries.

Any supportive action by the authorities represents a form of insurance, and any form of insurance involves moral hazard. But that does not mean that insurance must never be undertaken. There is a need to be careful about the resulting incentive structure. Within this field of LOLR, and financial support actions more generally, the main need – though often not honoured – is to avoid any protection of the position of the main executive decision-makers. Thereafter there is a consensus that equity and bond holders should suffer the full 'hit', up to the extent implied by limited liability at least, but that ordinary (retail) depositors should be largely (though not necessarily) protected. The current battle-ground, both domestically and internationally – but especially the latter – is what should be the status of interbank creditors of failing institutions. That will no doubt continue to be a main focus for discussion.

V. Myth 4

The fourth myth is that it is possible to dispense with LOLR altogether.

Being caught in a financial crisis is highly unpleasant. The history of capitalism is littered with such episodes. If the public sector authorities are not in a position to help to prevent the worst effects of such crises, those involved will try to establish private sector alternatives.

Of course, central banking was not the only model, and more oligopolistic systems, as in the US and Canada, had other self-help mechanisms, concentrating in the US around the institution of the clearing house. In the American crises of the late nineteenth century, the (New York) clearing house provided LOLR after a fashion to its members (Timberlake 1978, 1984). But both this mechanism and the underlying problems of moderating (seasonal) fluctuations in liquidity in a system without a central bank were perceived as inherently unsatisfactory after the 1907 crisis. A mammoth official comparative study, the National Monetary Commission (1910–11), indicated that the alternative central bank model was superior; hence the advent of the Federal Reserve.

Given our history, it is unthinkable that any government or central bank would now stand idly by and watch the closure of any of its major banks, the realization of large-scale losses on the bank deposits of its citizens and the collapse of its financial markets, if the authorities could avoid such events. And they could avoid them by judicious LOLR. It is all very well for academic liberals to claim that the best long-term course for the economy would be for the authorities to allow *any* bank to close its doors, while restricting their assistance to generalized OMO. Even if the externalities generated by the resultant panic were not so severe as to make this line of action socially wasteful, it would not be politically acceptable, in the sense that a government doing so would suffer extreme unpopularity.

There is an important question of what *exactly* we mean when we talk about a bank 'failing', and/or about a bank being 'rescued' or 'bailed out'. If the current management of a bank is removed, and the shareholders lose their equity, but the bank is allowed to continue in operation, does that count as a 'rescue' or a 'bail-out'? If we mean by 'failure' the removal of ownership from existing shareholders and of control from existing management, then this can be done, effectively by (temporary) nationalization. This has happened in Japan and Scandinavia, for example. If we mean by failure the closure and liquidation of all positions, then the economic, social and political consequences would become much more extreme.

There *may* be other ways of providing mutual insurance within the banking system with a much larger role for the private sector e.g. the cross-guarantee scheme advocated by Bert Ely (for example, 1995). There are certainly ways of trying to lessen the potential burden on the tax-payer, e.g. via prompt corrective action, otherwise known as Structured Early Intervention and Resolution, suggested by Benston and Kaufman (1994a, b), and partially incorporated in the Federal Deposit Insurance Corporation Improvement Act, or FDICIA, (1991). The approach taken by New Zealand of requiring all directors, each year as a condition of continued appointment, to sign a letter indicating that they have personally checked, and are happy with, internal risk control mechanisms, thereby leaving themselves open to legal suit if something goes badly wrong, is another highly promising innovation (see Mayes 1997; Shirakawa 1997).

There is much that can be done around the edges, e.g. to improve the incentives facing bank executives and to encourage bank supervisors to intervene earlier. But such measures, highly desirable though they may be, do not lessen the crucial economic verity, that the domestic monetary authorities, the government and central bank, will be held responsible by the electorate for the maintenance of systemic financial stability. This cannot be abrogated in a fit of extreme *laissez-faire*, and any attempt to pre-commit to do so would run into the most patent time-inconsistency.

The domestic monetary authorities have many powers. They can create fiat money, force errant bank managers to step down, recapitalize, merge or nationalize financial intermediaries etc. But, by definition, they cannot create foreign currency, and they cannot by their own actions normally relieve foreign currency indebtedness within their own countries, except by encouraging or facilitating various forms of default (the pros and cons of which take us beyond the range of this paper).

Since a shortage of foreign currency, and an associated potential shortfall in imports and trade finance for exports (in its other guise a collapsing foreign value of the domestic currency), will disrupt the domestic economy, weak countries in such crises will seek financial support from their stronger neighbours. Just as weaker, smaller banks sought financial help from a larger, more central bank within a country, so smaller countries will seek out a larger protector in case of need.

If the IMF should be abolished, it would *not* lead to a cessation of inter-country support actions and 'bail-outs'. Instead of an international financial intermediary, we could then expect arrangements to develop whereby certain groupings of states attempt to arrange their own mutual insurance, perhaps around a hegemon, perhaps not. In Latin America, the abolition of the IMF would simply transfer more responsibility and involvement to the US Treasury. It is arguable that the main moral hazard in international lending came from the view that friends of the US would always be bailed out, rather than anything that the IMF, in so far as it could act independently of the US, would do. Circumscribing the role of the IMF in such circumstances would be akin to shooting the messenger, but failing to understand the message. In Asia, perceived limitations of the IMF in dealing with the recent crisis have led to proposals for an Asian Monetary Fund under Japanese leadership. In the absence of effective IMF ILOLR, the euro zone would play a similar role in Eastern Europe and Africa (and possibly elsewhere).

If the IMF were abolished, or so circumscribed in its resources and functions that it could not play an effective ILOLR role, the alternative would not be the restoration of a perfectly free market, in which each country stood, or fell, on the basis of its own individual failures or successes. There would, instead, develop an *ad hoc* system of regional (self-help) systems centred on a major currency, and a major power. The implications of that are not, on this view, welcome. Dividing the world into regional spheres of major powers would not be an advance on a truly international solution. Proponents of pure international *laissez-faire* should be aware that the political realities suggest that the result of curtailing the IMF would be a descent into a murkier world of regional major-power groupings, and not a system of pure free markets.

Financial crises are all too common, painful and potentially contagious. Faced with such dangers, all agents will try to insure against it. The weak will look to the strong for support. The question is not whether to have a lender of last resort, either nationally or internationally, because it is vain to think that such a mechanism can be abolished on the altar of free-market doctrine. The more relevant and interesting question is how best to organize the LOLR function that will continue to exist both nationally and internationally.

Charles Goodhart
Financial Markets Group
Centre for Economic Performance
London School of Economics
Houghton Street
London WC2A 2AE
UK

References

Aghion, P., P. Bolton and M. Dewatripont (1999), 'Contagious Bank Failures', preliminary draft paper (March).
Allen, F., and D. Gale (1998), 'Optimal Financial Crises', *Journal of Finance*, 53, 1245–84.
—— (1999), 'Financial Contagion', draft paper (March).

Bagehot, W. (1873), *Lombard Street: A Description of the Money Market*, revised edition with a foreword by Peter Bernstein. New York: Wiley (1999).

Benston, G. J., and G. G. Kaufman (1994a), 'The Intellectual History of the Federal Deposit Insurance Corporation Improvement Act of 1991', in G. G. Kaufman ed., *Reforming Financial Institutions and Markets in the United States*. Dordrecht: Kluwer Academic Publishers.

—— (1994b), 'Improving the FDIC Improvement Act: What Was Done and What Still Needs to Be Done to Fix the Deposit Insurance Problem', in G. G. Kaufman ed., *Reforming Financial Institutions and Markets in the United States*. Dordrecht: Kluwer Academic Publishers.

Buiter W., and A. Sibert (1999), 'UDROP: A Contribution to the New International Financial Architecture', *International Finance*, 2(2), 227–48.

Calomiris, D. (1999), 'Moral Hazard Is Avoidable', in W. L. Hunter, G. G. Kaufman and T. H. Krueger, eds, *The Asian Financial Crisis: Origins, Implications and Solutions*. Dordrecht: Kluwer Academic Publishers.

Capie, F. M. (1998), 'Can There Be an International Lender-of-last-resort?', *International Finance*, 1(2), 311–25.

Ely, B. (1995), 'Bringing Market-driven Regulation to European Banking: A Proposal for 100 Per Cent Cross-guarantees', Centre for the Study of Financial Innovation, Paper 16, July.

Fischer, S. (1999), 'On the Need for an International Lender of Last Resort', paper presented at CFS Research Conference, Frankfurt, 11 June.

Freixas, X. (1999), 'Optimal Bail Out Policy, Conditionality and Creative Ambiguity', paper presented at the Financial Markets Group conference on 'The Lender of Last Resort', London School of Economics, 13 July.

Fry, M. J. (1997), 'The Fiscal Abuse of Central Banks', in M. I. Blejer and T. Ter-Minassian, eds, *Macroeconomic Dimensions of Public Finance: Essays in Honour of Vito Tanzi*. London: Routledge, pp. 337–59.

Goodfriend, M., and R. G. King (1988), 'Financial Deregulation, Monetary Policy, and Central Banking', *Federal Reserve Bank of Richmond Economic Review*, May/June, 3–22.

Goodhart, C. A. E., and H. Huang (1999), 'A Model of the Lender of Last Resort', IMF Working Paper, WP/99/39, March.

Goodhart, C. A. E., and D. Schoenmaker (1993), 'Institutional Separation between Supervisory and Monetary Agencies', in F. Bruni, ed., *Prudential Regulation, Supervision and Monetary Policy*. Centro di Economia Monetaria e Finanziaria 'Paolo Baffi', Università Commerciale Luigi Bocconi.

Humphrey, T. M., and R. E. Keleher (1984), 'The Lender of Last Resort: A Historical Perspective', *Cato Journal*, 4(1), 275–317.

Keleher, R. (1999), 'An International Lender of Last Resort, the IMF, and the Federal Reserve', Joint Economic Committee Report of the US Congress, February.

Kynaston, D. (1995), *The City of London. Volume 2, Golden Years, 1890–1914*. London: Chatto & Windus.

Lissakers, K. (1999), 'The IMF and the Asian Crisis: A View from the Executive Board', in W. L. Hunter, G. G. Kaufman and T. H. Krueger, eds, *The Asian Financial Crisis: Origins, Implications and Solutions*. Dordrecht: Kluwer Academic Publishers.

Lindgren, C.-J. (1999), 'Commentary on "What's Wrong with the IMF" and "Containing the Risk" ', in W. L. Hunter, G. G. Kaufman and T. H. Krueger, eds,

The Asian Financial Crisis: Origins, Implications and Solutions. Dordrecht: Kluwer Academic Publishers.

Mayes, D. G. (1997), 'Incentives for Bank Directors and Management: The New Zealand Approach', paper presented at the Bank of England Conference on 'Regulatory Incentives', 13–14 November.

National Monetary Commission (1910–11), *Series of Volumes Presented to the US 61st Congress as Senate Documents*. Washington, DC.

Okina, K. (1999), 'Monetary Policy under Zero Inflation: A Response to Criticisms and Questions Regarding Monetary Policy', Institute for Monetary and Economic Studies, Bank of Japan, IMES Discussion Paper Series, no. 99-E-20.

Radcliffe Committee (1959), *Committee on the Working of the Monetary System: Report*, Cmnd 827, and *Minutes of Evidence to the Committee* (1960). London: HMSO.

Shirakawa, M. (1997), 'Reflections on the "New Zealand Approach" to Banking Supervision', paper presented at the Bank of England Conference on 'Regulatory Incentives', 13–14 November.

Thornton, H. (1802), *An Enquiry into the Nature and Effects of the Paper Credit of Great Britain*. London: Hatchard.

Timberlake, R. H. Jr (1978), *The Origins of Central Banking in the United States*. Cambridge, MA: Harvard University Press.

—— (1984), 'The Central Banking Role of Clearinghouse Associations', *Journal of Money, Credit and Banking*, 16(1), 1–15.

14 The lender of last resort: Pushing the doctrine too far? *

Charles P. Kindleberger

I perhaps owe my readers an apology for referring once again to the doctrine of lender of last resort. The late Fred Hirsch brought the subject to the forefront of discussion with a brilliant paper half a generation ago (Hirsch, 1977). Hugh Rockoff discussed it earlier in this series honouring Henry Thornton (1986). Governor Carlo Ciampi of the Bank of Italy lectured on the subject in his own country in February of this year (Ciampi, 1992). The issue has been pursued in at least two of my books (1973 [1986], Chs. ix, x; 1984 [1993], *passim*, but especially pp. 277–83 of the 1984 edition). On this occasion, however, my purpose is not to defend the doctrine in the face of monetarists who believe that the money supply should be fixed, or grow at a fixed rate, rather than be allowed to expand in periods of widespread illiquidity and distress. That issue, to my mind, has been settled in favour of a lender of last resort in financial crisis. Rather, I suggest that the world may have pushed the doctrine too far with deposit insurance for commercial banks and thrifts, the rescue from bankruptcy of such bodies as New York City, some corporations such as Penn Central, Lockheed and Chrysler Corporation, banks 'too big to fail' even though their deposits exceed insured limits by wide margins, brokerage houses that loaned to such a commodity speculator as Bunker Hunt, who tried to corner the world silver market in the early 1980s. Even now in Japan, government money is called upon to make whole an institution owned by a rich bank, the troubles of which were caused by fraud rather than mistakes (*The Economist*, 1992, p. 105). Many high-minded principles suffer from entropy or decay over time, and the lender of last resort may be one of them.

The doctrine was first enunciated by Sir Francis Baring and Henry Thornton at the end of the eighteenth century apropos of a series of recent financial crises, especially that of 1793. It was formulated more precisely by Walter Bagehot, at age 22 in 1848, written following the 1847 suspension of the Bank Act of 1844. To quote that paper:

---

* This lecture was delivered on 11 November 1992 at City University, London.

It can be a great defect of a purely metallic circulation that the quantity of it cannot be readily suited to any sudden demand . . . Now as paper money can be supplied in unlimited quantities, however sudden the demand may be, it does not appear to us that there is any objection on principle to sudden issues of paper money to meet sudden and large extensions of demand . . . This power of issuing notes is one excessively liable to abuse . . . It should only be used in rare and exceptional cases . . . when the fact of an extensive *sudden* demand is proved.

(Bagehot, 1848 [1978], IX, p. 267, emphasis in original)

The constant repetition of the word 'sudden', and its emphasis in one instance, makes clear that Bagehot at an early age was thinking in terms of what is now known as rational expectations which makes special allowance for 'unanticipated events'. It is also of some mild interest that Bagehot in *Lombard Street* ascribes the origin of the idea of a lender of last resort to David Ricardo. However modest on his part, the notion seems far-fetched (1873 [1978], p. 75).

I should perhaps mention in passing T.S. Ashton's view that the Bank of England and the Exchequer recognized well before economists laid down rules for treatment of crises that the remedy was for an emergency issue of some form of paper which bankers, merchants and the general public would accept 'until men regained trust in one another', and that the Bank of England was already a lender of last resort in the eighteenth century (1959, pp. 110–2). In *Lombard Street*, written in response to the Overend, Gurney failure of 1866, Bagehot refined the concept of a lender of last resort, calling for the central bank to lend freely at a penalty rate, freely since limited lending on earlier occasions in the eighteenth century had increased the panic, and at a penalty rate to fend off merely precautionary borrowers who were not in dire straits.

In 1793, the Bank of England stated its invariable practice of discounting only two-months commercial paper on two first-class London names (Clapham, 1945, I, p. 261). Crisis by crisis the rules were breached as loans were made on important but not first-class names, on mortgages, a coal mine, a West Indian plantation, copper works, to three American banks in Liverpool whose initial requests had been refused (Clapham, 1945, I, II, *passim*). As panic and bank runs built up because of an absence of rescuers on the horizon, central banks and governments everywhere found it necessary to rescue themselves and provide the sought-for cash, or make ready to do so, which usually relieved the situation by itself. Often when one institution promised not to save banks from the consequences of imprudent speculation or lending, when the crash arrived it preserved its dignity by finding another means, for example the Bank of England in 1826 when Lord Liverpool at the Treasury had sworn not to relieve a liquidity crisis through issuing Exchequer bills, and banking guarantees of Barings liabilities in 1890 when Lord Lidderdale of the Bank of England judged that rescues by the Bank were becoming so usual that the market counted on them.

As an aside, I may mention that in writing *Manias, Panics and Crashes*, I came across a remark that in some crisis the Bank's lending had not been 'over nice'. I seemed to have lost the reference, and so gave none (1978 [1989], p. 196). For some purpose undisclosed to me, my colleague, Stanley Fischer, asked where I had gotten the statement, and I diligently searched my notebooks but to no avail. He then turned to his friend Mervyn King, Executive Director of the Bank of England, where research revealed that the characterization had been cited by W.C.T. King in his *History of the London Discount Market* (1936) I had accurately remembered the phrase, but failed to note its provenance. Its origin was from the testimony of Jeremiah Harman, director of the Bank between 1794 and 1827, governor in 1817 and 1818, before the 1832 Parliamentary Committee of Secrecy on the Bank of England. The evidence dealt with the Bank's response to the crisis of 1825, with the expression furnished in an answer to the question in para. 2217 – in case any of you share Professor Fischer's curiosity.

In an episode foreshadowing the United States troubles of the 1980s and 1990s, the Bank of England yielded to the pleas of the three American 'W' banks – Wiggins, Wildes and Wilson – but failed in the effort to save them, and succeeded in liquidating the assets taken over only 14 years later (Clapham, 1945, II, p. 157).

After World War I, the Bank of England undertook a wider policy of intervention in industry, along with banking, that Sayers called 'out of character' (1978, I, p. 314). The problems lay particularly in steel, which had experienced a boom immediately after the war, when it appeared that German industry would be out of action for a time. The Bank started with a private customer of the Newcastle branch, Armstrong Whitworth, the overdraft for which had been increased in 1918. The company then plunged. By 1925 it was clear that it had made a great many bad investments, and the Bank of England loaned it £2.7 million on the construction of a newsprint plant in Newfoundland. In the end, the Bank lost only £200 000 capital, and £300 000 in foregone interest on these operations. In 1928 Vickers Armstrong was formed and received a five-year guarantee of its profit, which cost the bank £1 million over five years. Further complex operations in steel took more and more of the Bank's and Governor Norman's time, especially after the Hatry crisis of September 1929. In this, and in its dealings in cotton textiles, the Bank tried to keep its activities secret, partly so as not to encourage the Labour Party to involve the rescue operations in politics (Tolliday, 1987, esp. ch. viii).

Rescue in cotton textiles was necessitated by the troubles of the Williams Deacon Bank, a London clearing institution with its head office in Manchester, and with, at the end of 1928, advances of £3 770 000 to 40 cotton companies. The Bank first guaranteed these advances up to £1 million. In an interesting exercise in what is now called 'conditionality', to preserve secrecy, the Bank allowed Williams Deacon to maintain its dividend, but not to raise it, and required it to reduce its dividend if any other clearing bank were to do so (Sayers, 1976, I, p. 285). When in 1929 the Royal Bank of Scotland took

Williams Deacon over, the Bank of England added a sweetener to the deal by throwing in its own Burlington Gardens branch in west London. Sayers explains that the Bank had, on the one hand, lost interest in its own profits from private business, and sought to divert public attention away from the real reason for the merger (ibid., pp. 285–6). All in all, the Bank's net loss was £3.2 million, most of which was written off early.

I shift from London to Italy by an easy transition without getting into the 1974 'life boat' operation in favour of the fringe banks. Along with steel and cotton, the Bank in 1929 led a rescue of the Banca-Italo Britannica, owned and controlled by a British holding company, in which London clearing banks and a British insurance company were involved, along with some Roman and Milanese banks. Banca-Italo Britannica was operated in Italy where it suffered from the 1926 deflation, some bad investments, a certain amoung of malfeasance in the accounts, plus the tightening of interest rates in the Wall Street boom that started in March 1928. Sayers said that the Banca-Italo was widely regarded as a British responsibility, despite its Italian management. As it began to fail, the Bank of England and the three London clearing banks put up most of the funds to keep it going for a while before it was ultimately wound up. The Bank of England's loss of £250 000 – its entire contribution to the rescue – is stated to have been 'the cost of saving London from threatened shame' (ibid., pp. 259–62).

Secret rescue, or as the Italians call them 'salvage', operations, had been under way for a quarter century as the Bank of Italy took over bad assets of leading banks in financial crises of 1907, 1921, 1926 and 1930. When the full fury of the 1929 depression broke, the Italian government formed the Istituto Riconstruzione Italiana (IRI), to take over these assets from the Bank of Italy in exchange for government bonds, with the thought that they would be worked off over time. IRI was patterned to some extent after the 1931 Reconstruction Finance Corporation (RFC) in the United States, established to make advances to banks and business with liquidity problems, but handicapped by a Democratic party requirement in subsequent legislation that loans to banks be made public. This last requirement effectively barred its use for banks which would, by borrowing, announce that their condition was shaky. Substantial loans were made to industry. When the war came, the RFC was converted into the Defense Plant Corporation (DPC) to simplify the provision of credit to the defence industry as compared to reliance on the capital market or commercial banks. In due course, with strong recovery during and after the war, the RFC/DPC were able to liquidate all these investments, as companies with profits paid off their loans or bought plant to enable debtors to do so. This was a successful workout without a trace of scandal. IRI on the other hand was reorganized. The collection of financial and industrial assets was converted into ownership, and IRI operated the companies concerned, largely because of the difficulty of privatization – to use a current neologism – given a weak Italian capital market and the absence of large wartime corporate profits.

Success in working out bad loans and investments, in contrast to writing them off, depends on one or more of several felicitous circumstances: rapid and strong recovery of the economy and asset prices; a buoyant capital market such as that prevailing in the United States in the postwar 'golden years'; buyers willing to take over failed banks, minus government write-offs. In this last connection, valuations placed on 'good' and 'bad' assets in a financial crisis may not hold up over the long run. The cautionary tale is that of the 1929 threatened failure of the Bodencreditanstalt in Austria, rescued by being taken over by the Creditanstalt, which itself collapsed in May 1931, largely as a consequence of the turning bad of the good assets it had acquired from the Bodencredit.

A conservative view of banking is that assets should always be 'market to market', and that a bank should be closed down and liquidated if its capital is impaired. I confess I do not understand the reasoning of young Henry Thornton, the nephew, in closing down Pole, Thornton & Company in the crisis of 1825 because while solvent he was concerned that if he borrowed a second time to gain liquidity, as all the directors of the Bank of England were willing that he should, he feared that it would be taken from him by the country banks for which Pole, Thornton served as London correspondent (Ashton and Sayers, eds, 1953, ch. vii, esp. pp. 102–4). The doctrine of marking to market, however, leaves little room for work-outs. It fails, moreover, to recognize the distinction between a mutual fund and a bank, or the functions of banks in issuing liabilities that are used as money. If all loans and investments were traded in efficient markets, assets could be marked to market at appropriate intervals, but unless there were a very large amount of capital, liabilities would have to change correspondingly and could no longer serve as money, which has a fixed price. On the asset side, moreover, cash and investments can be valued regularly, but loans cannot. Securitization of mortgages, credit-card liabilities, and in Britain export credits, changes the balance between assets that can be valued regularly, and those – loans – that cannot.

One must be careful, too, to insist that the markets in which assets are priced are efficient. At the outbreak of the crisis in Third World debt, a few economists insisted that there were market valuations for some of these loans, such as Mexican bonds. But these quotations were largely nominal, and an attempt to sell a substantial quantity would have quickly disclosed their illiquidity. The same is true of many assets which bulk large in balance sheets, even of central banks. Gold is the classic example. Once the United States closed the gold window in 1968, the metal became a commodity and no longer represented money. The liquidity of asset markets is infinitely graded from short-term government bills at one extreme – although in some financial crises, it has been claimed that even they cannot be sold at any, meaning any normal, price – and the junkiest of junk bonds at the other. But as Charles Goodhart (1972 [1986]) and Albert Wojnilower (1992) assert, there is a difference in kind, as well as in degree, between investments saleable in a market, and loans based upon a relationship with a borrower. The latter are not marked to market except in the doleful circumstances of bankruptcy proceedings that have advanced some distance.

Perhaps the largest step in the progressive breakdown of the pure doctrine of the lender of last resort came with the adoption in the United States of deposit insurance. Its origin in the 1933 depression was in what is now called, somewhat ponderously, asymmetric information, the difference in sophistication between individuals of wealth and substantial corporations, and the ordinary householder and small business. The former were thought to be able to judge the solvency of a bank, the latter unable. A limit initially set at $5000 per depositor was thought adequate to divide the two groups. With inflation after World War II, rather than any extension of financial ignorance, the figure was progressively raised, first to $10 000, then $20 000, $40 000 and finally to $100 000. I am told that the $100 000 limit was agreed upon in a Congressional conference committee as a compromise between the House and Senate conferees, one set of which had brought in a bill raising the limit from $40 000 to $50 000, the other from $40 000 to $60 000.

All was quiet during the golden years to 1973, with deposit insurance coming to the rescue of the few banks in trouble. Difficulties were still minimal in the middle 1970s until the second sharp rise in the price of oil in 1979 that threatened inflation. Banks had been forbidden to pay more than 5 1/2 per cent on time deposits under Federal Reserve regulation Q. When interest rates rose sharply in 1979 to 1981 widespread disintermediation took place as sophisticated depositors withdrew time and saving deposits from banks to redeposit them in new money funds which paid higher returns because they were unburdened by ceilings. It is a matter of some cynical interest that savings banks in poor parts of cities or poor regions of the country were not disintermediated because their depositors were not conscious of the opportunity to increase their return on idle cash from $5\frac{1}{2}$ per cent to 10 per cent or more.

Disintermediation was particularly hurtful to the thrift institutions – savings banks, saving and loan associations and credit unions – which were limited to a few assets, largely long-term fixed-interest mortages. Squeezed between the high rates they had to pay to replace the withdrawn deposits and low fixed-interest income, the industry pleaded with the Congress to remove limits on which they could pay depositors, and for permission to make wider and riskier investments. There was also a shift to the adjustable-rate mortgage, but too late to produce substantial change. Deregulation, however, occurred simultaneously with the development of the so-called 'junk bond', one below investment grade because of the lesser coverage of interest paid by normal income. The consequence was that a wide number of thrift institutions started to pay high rates of interest to attract deposits, and to invest in high-paying risky investments to earn the necessary returns. A further development which increased the ultimate burden to be borne by the Federal Deposit Insurance Corporation (FDIC) and its thrift analogue, the Federal Savings and Loan Corporation (FSLIC, pronounced like a patent medicine, Fislick) was the spontaneous development of a new business of deposit brokering. Substantial deposit amounts would be broken up by these brokers into amounts of less than $100 000, and parcelled out among a number of high-interest paying banks, almost certainly weak, in order to qualify for deposit insurance. This was adverse selection with a vengeance. In retrospect, raising the insurance limit from $10 000 or $20 000 per deposit was a mistake as the transactions cost of placing, say, $5 million among 500 or 250 banks might not have been worth while as compared with 50.

As interest rates paid on deposits rose, and investments became riskier, the ethics of old-fashioned banking wore thin, and a number of bankers slipped into unseemly ways, buying Rembrandts with bank money to decorate their offices, yachts to entertain their boards of directors, and possibly their deposit brokers, hiring salesmen to persuade unsophisticated depositors to switch out of insured deposits into the bank's uninsured (junk) debentures, this to bolster the banks' capital/deposit ratios. Hundreds of such bankers are currently on trial or in jail in the United States.

The ostensible purpose of deposit insurance was to protect the unsophisticated depositor from the odd failure of an individual bank. At a deeper level, the rationale was to prevent bank runs that might spread to other banks and other localities and thus threaten the safety of the banking system as a whole. It was this purpose, in my judgement, that led to the progressive raising of the insured-deposit limit. It was clearly the motive for saving the Continental Illinois which had bought a great many oil loans from the high-flying Penn Square Bank of Oklahoma, close to the top of the oil market. With its high interest rates, the Continental Illinois had attracted a lot of Japanese depositors, with large amounts of money, who may or may not have been sophisticated. To avoid a precipitous run and a foreign-exchange crisis, the Continental Illinois was rescued without limit with respect to deposit size, and the doctrine that some banks are too big to fail was born or resurrected. In the same vein, the Federal Reserve System urged the New York banks to rescue J.S. Bache and Company, a brokerage house, not a bank, which had advanced hundreds of millions of dollars to Bunker Hunt when he was trying, unsuccessfully, to corner the world silver market, loans which he was unable to repay on schedule.

There are two types of bank runs, one by public depositors, the outsiders, the second by other banks which become suspicious of an adventurous bank, perhaps a newcomer trying to push its way into the market; after a time they refuse to accept its paper, or exchange contracts, or to lend it federal funds. This was the fate of the Franklin National Bank in 1974, when other New York banks first approached the Federal Reserve Bank of New York to warn it that the Franklin National was on a dangerous course, and, when the Federal Reserve seemed to take no steps to correct the situation, finally stopped dealing with it (Spero, 1980).

A recent book on financial crises has some curious remarks about depositor runs. It suggests that the depositors who lead such a movement – called 'sequentially-served depositors' – are helpful insofar as they monitor the performance of banks (Calomiris and Gorton, 1991, p. 120). One wonders whether they would say the same of those who start panics in theatre fires. The authors call this source of bank runs 'asymmetric information' – some depositors and presumably bank officials know more than others and contrast it with a separate theory based on 'random withdrawals', such as used to occur in the United States in the nineteenth century when bank credit was strained each fall by the necessity to finance the seasonal movement of crops off the farm. Asymmetric information is measured in another paper in the same volume (Mishkin, 1991) by the spread in yields between high-quality assets like treasury bills and commercial paper of equal maturity, or between government or triple A bonds and B bonds, both of which spreads widened in financial crisis. Another term for this phenomenon is a 'flight to quality', as sophisticated investors shift assets to higher grade (and lower yield) assets as the banking system moves into distress as it approaches crisis.

In the United States monitoring of bank performance may have been left to a limited extent to sequentially-served depositors, but legally was assigned to government regulators whose performance in the 1980s left much to be desired. In one view the problem lay in the duplication of bank examinations by the staffs of the Comptroller of the Currency in the US Treasury, the Federal Reserve System, and state bank commissions, plus to some extent the personnel of the FDIC and FSLIC, 'Shared responsibility', said Ludwig Bamberger, a prominent German banker a century ago, 'is no responsibility'. Edward Kane, who is more cynical than I deem is warranted, believes that the multiple layers of examination led to bureaucratic competition in deregulation (Kane, 1989). Nor have the legal and accounting professions covered themselves with glory in a number of isolated cases where representatives of each have blessed transactions that later have proved to be some distance below the standards of professional probity. Lenders of last resort in my country have brought suit against lawyers and accountants in these circumstances, but have no chance of recovering any sizeable part of the losses from malfeasance. The same problem cropped up last spring in Japan when Toyo Shinkin, an Osaka-based credit union, forged certificates of deposit and ended up with bad debts of ¥252 billion. After trying first to push the loss on the creditors, and then on the Sanwa Bank group that owned Toyo Shinkin, both of which resisted, the Ministry of Finance laid the burden on the official Industrial Bank of Japan, an instance of public money used to make good losses from criminal fraud rather than imprudent lending, although the line between the two, in this age, is sometimes hard to draw (*The Economist*, 1992, p. 105).

Choosing between work-out or write-off presents an agonizing problem for banks in distress, but equally so for the lender of last resort. Sometimes, of course, a bank will embark on one course, and then choose or be obliged to change, as Citicorp did in the spring of 1987 after five years of attempted workout, when it wrote off more than $1\frac{1}{2}$ billions of its Third World sovereign debt. Even more perplexing is the task of the Resolution Trust Corporation (RTC), charged with disposing of the assets taken over by the FDIC and FSLIC from banks that are closed, merged, or bailed out. Substantial cyclical recovery might float some of the boats that look wrecked. On the other hand, the longer the RTC waits the more its losses mount because of accumulating interest. Other questions are whether to sell off the odds and sods of hotels, office buildings, shopping malls, banking quarters, residential housing, golf courses and the like, at wholesale or retail, and if retail, through regular market channels of brokers or by auction. A decision has been made that the government, that is, the taxpayer, bears the loss, now or in the future as debt is paid off, rather than the bank depositor and the holder of bank shares, as in 1930 to 1933.

I came late to at least a partial understanding of the issues through reading a short time ago Homer Hoyt's book, *One Hundred Years of Land Values in Chicago*, written in 1933. Hoyt has more detail on the separate sections of that city that grew at various rates during the century in question than interests me, but he is superb on the question of real-estate bubbles and their bursting. (Parenthetically I learned about the book when I made up a list of 50 books to be read for enjoyment and instruction by retired bankers, only to have Moses Abramovitz ask why I left off Hoyt.) Hoyt pointed out that stock-market booms often spread to real estate, especially in growing cities, but that their respective down-side behaviour differs. In a stock-market collapse, the shakeout of leveraged speculators is wound up in a matter of months. At the time of the crash speculators in real estate who had been infected by the euphoria in shares congratulate themselves that they are financed by term loans, rather than day-to-day money, and have real instead of paper assets. In the five crashes in Chicago to 1933, and again in 1987, however, it was not possible to evade the liquidation process in real estate. Interest on real-estate loans stayed high, along with taxes on the property. Lenders became shy about renewing or extending loans. Buyers suddenly saw the advantage of waiting, rather than carrying out previous intentions. Rents fell as new speculative buildings came on the market, and their owners had difficulty in selling them or finding tenants. When old leases in existing buildings ran out existing tenants bargained rents down. Instead of liquidation coming to completion in less than a year, it stretched to four, five or even more years with devastating effects on owners and lenders, especially banks. It was this experience that produced the FDIC and later FSLIC. Those of you who watched the Olympia and York story unfold in Canada, New York and Canary Wharf will understand the prescience of Homer Hoyt, writing sixty years ago.

Despite widespread opinion to the contrary, it was not the decline in the money supply that produced the depression of 1929 to 1933, but the reverse. Ben Bernanke was correct when he wrote in 1983 that tight money could lead to depression otherwise than through the money supply. The analysis applied well to the stock-market crash of 1987 which made banks leery of lending, and produced a delayed but sharp collapse in real estate, bursting the bubble of the 1980s. In 1929, however – at least in my opinion – the effect was felt immediately on commodity prices, as banks in trouble because of illiquid brokers' loans rationed credit to commodity brokers, who were thus unable to clear commodity markets of goods shipped to New York on commission at anything close to prevailing prices. This effect could not recur in 1987 because imported commodities in the United States are bought in the exporting country, not sold on arrival in New York. The major impact in the 1929 depression of falling commodity prices in the first few weeks after the stock-market crash has been questioned lately by Barry Eichengreen who observes that the same mechanism did not operate in London where brokers' loans were much less substantial than in New York. The reasoning seems not to take into account that if prices of internationally traded goods fall in one market they fall in all (1992, p. 230).

As lender of last resort, the Resolution Trust Corporation seems still, at the time of writing, to be experimenting with how to handle the disposal of its ragbag of assets. With only a few assets of modest value, at any one time, the Bank of England could work off its acquisitions slowly and secretly, covering losses by annual modest charges against profits. In the United States today, the problem is far too substantial to admit of such a relatively happy solution. To sell in large batches runs the risk of awarding profits to wealthy capitalists so large as to give rise to an echo of the scandals that contributed to the lamentable problem.

A precedent exists in Italian history when, just after unification in 1860 in which the new kingdom acquired substantial debts from the constituent kingdoms, duchies and principalities, it seized church lands and a number of large estates. To convert these into cash, it created a private concern, the *Società Anonina per la Vendita dei Beni del Regno* (Corporation for the Sale of Assets of the Kingdom) to sell the collection of 'church properties, iron mines on the island of Elba, forests, mineral springs, arsenals, some irrigation canals and common lands, especially sea swamps and mountain tops', administered from 1860 to 1882, with an estimated total value of 1928 million lire (then approximately $400 million [Clough, 1964, pp. 47–54, quotation from p. 49]). Similar disposal problems for which I lack sources with details, were the seizure of church lands and buildings by Henry VIII in Britain, of church and noble lands in France in the revolution, and another large-scale confiscation in Spain in the early nineteenth century. In no case, I gather, was the operation accomplished neatly and without steps forward and back. The problem forcibly dumped in the lap of the RTC will equally become, in the inelegant American expression, 'a can of worms'.

The central question is who bears the burden of this ill-advised investment and thievery. The list of candidates is substantial:

– the investors and malefactors themselves;
– their creditors;

- bank owners, through the decline in their shares, or their worthlessness, assuming limited liability, leaving aside double liability, such as obtained in many states before 1929, or the unlimited liability, that afflicted the Glasgow tobacco lords who lost their estates in 1772 in the failure of the Ayr bank;
- depositors when banks failed without deposit insurance, or were covered only to a limit, except in those cases where the limit was ignored to prevent a run;
- the central bank, although where central-bank profits above statutory amounts accrue to the government, and the losses do not reduce profits below this amount, the loss falls on the state;
- the state through many possible channels: directly in the case of institutions like the RTC, either the original write-off, or an ultimate one; through tax losses where the losses of depositors, investors, banks and others are written off against other taxable income; through the forgiveness of foreign loans through such arrangements as the Paris club.
- the country as a whole if bad investments lead to bank runs, collapse and depression;
- debt holders of all kinds if the debts acquired by the state in fending off financial crisis are shrugged off through inflation.

Inflation is an unlikely indirect effect of bad investments, though it could occur if a lender of last resort operated with such a lavish hand, failing to shrink the money supply after first enlarging it, that spending got out of hand.

Now that the lender-of-last-resort function has shifted from a rare and infrequent expedient, held under tight control, to one undertaken readily, perhaps too readily, and even light-heartedly, it is well to bear in mind that it has strong features of redistributing income and wealth. Ambiguity as to whether investors or their banks will be saved or not has much to recommend it in order to reduce moral hazard and make nominal caretakers take real care. As in *Candide*, it is well from time to time to cut off the head of a general (let a substantial bank collapse) to 'encourage the others'.

One appropriate set of losers when a bank fails through ineptitude or worse is the officers, who should lose not only their jobs and the value of their shares but also any options to buy more at low prices, should the bank and its shares ultimately recover. At the time of the salvage of the Continental Illinois, I was offended that while the responsible officers were sacked, they left by the terms of their employment contracts with golden parachutes in amounts which, in a few cases, exceeded one or two million dollars. When on one occasion at a meeting I expressed this indignation, a lawyer present said that such amounts were inconsequential solace for the lawsuits to which the officers would submit for years ahead. Even so.

The redistribution effects evoke an aspect of last-resort lending and its entropy that I have not stressed, that is, the political dimensions. Recall that

Governor Norman wanted to keep his activities in steel and textiles secret so as not to let the Labour Party become involved in the decision-making. Lender-of-last-resort help for Austria and Germany in May and June 1931 aborted when France made them conditional on Austria giving up the Zoll-Union with Germany, and on Germany abandoning the construction of the *Panzerkreuzer* (pocket battleship). Japan is holding back in efforts to carry the Commonwealth of Independent States through the current crisis because of the Kurile Islands. In the United States, voting new funds for the FDIC, the FSLIC and RTC is embroiled in party politics, which is why the money is voted in spoonful rather than in an effective dollop, evoking a reminder of Bagehot's 'freely'. There are strong political arguments against entrusting last-resort operations to independent bodies which might play favourites, and discriminate against outsiders in favour of the Establishment. But financial crises often call for decisive and immediate action that central banks are capable of producing, and deliberative political bodies, including such international organizations as the International Monetary Fund, may not be able to deliver.

A sharp observer of financial economics in the United States, Albert M. Wojnilower, senior advisor of First Boston Asset Management, suggested some years ago, at the start of the banking crises, that since the United States government had to make good in one way or another most of the losses from exuberant and misguided investment in booms and/or bubbles, there might be merit in converting parts of the government into a monopoly bank, making loans and investments, and issuing money, hoping for positive returns and/or seigniorage, but ready to absorb unpreventable losses. Ricardo in 1824 proposed a similar idea that all bank notes be issued by the government (Fetter, 1980, p. 109). It is remotely possible that this was the origin of Bagehot's view in *Lombard Street* that Ricardo, rather than Henry Thornton and Sir Francis Baring, first formulated the last-resort doctrine (1873 [1978], p. 75).

Rather than move to having government take over the financial system, including banking, I would prefer to try to stuff the genie back in the bottle, reduce the last-resort function to a weapon of rare and occasional use, buttressed by better and more responsible bankers, lawyers and accountants, stricter bank examinations and occasional isolated bank failure. I fear this is a counsel of perfection. Communication today is so far-ranging and instantaneous, innovation so institutionalized, emulation so dominant and independence of thought so rare, that booms and busts are a continuous threat and require that government maintain constant alert to damp down the first and fend off the second. This may be merely the pessimism of advanced years. I fervently hope so.

References

Ashton, T.S. (1959) *Economic Fluctuations in England, 1700–1800* (Oxford: Clarendon Press).

Ashton, T. S., and R. S. Sayers (1953) *Papers in English Monetary History* (Oxford: Clarendon).

Bagehot, Walter (1848 [1978]) 'The Currency Monopoly', in Norman St. John-Stevas (ed.) *The Collected Works of Walter Bagehot* (London: *The Economist*) Vol. ix, pp. 235–75.

Bagehot, Walter (1873 [1978]) *Lombard Street*, in Norman St. John-Stevas (ed.) *The Collected Works of Walter Bagehot* (London: *The Economist*) Vol. ix, pp. 48–233.

Calomiris, Charles W., and Gary Gordon (1991) 'The Origins of Banking Panics: Models, Facts and Bank Regulations', in R. Glenn Hubbard (ed.) *Financial Markets and Financial History* (Chicago: University of Chicago Press) pp. 109–73.

Ciampi, Carlo A. (1992) 'Lending of Last Resort', in Banca d'Italia, *Economic Bulletin*, No. 14 (February) pp. 63–9.

Clapham, Sir John (1945) *The Bank of England: A History* (Cambridge: Cambridge University Press) 2 vols.

Clough, Shepherd B. (1964) *The Economic History of Modern Italy* (New York: Columbia University Press).

(The) Economist (1992), Vol. 323, no. 7758, May 9 to 15.

Eichengreen, Barry (1992) *Golden Fetters: The Gold Standard and the Great Depression, 1919–1939* (New York and Oxford: Oxford University Press).

Fetter, Frank W. (1980) *The Economist in Parliament: 1780–1868* (Durham, N.C.: Duke University Press).

Goodhart, Charles (1972 [1986]) *The Business of Banking, 1891–1914*, 2nd ed. (Aldershot: Gower).

Hirsch, Fred (1977) 'The Bagehot Problem', *The Manchester School of Economics and Social Studies*, Vol. 45 (September) pp. 241–57.

Hoyt, Homer (1933) *A Hundred Years of Land Values in Chicago: The Relationship of the Growth of Chicago to the Rise in Its Land Values, 1830–1933* (Chicago: University of Chicago Press).

Kane, Edward J. (1989) *The S&L Insurance Mess: How Did it Happen?* (Washington, D.C.: Urban Institute Press).

Kindleberger, Charles P. (1973 [1986]) *The World in Depression, 1929–1939*, rev. ed. (Berkeley: University of California Press).

Kindleberger, Charles P. (1978 [1989]) *Manias, Panics and Crashes: A History of Financial Crises*, rev. ed. (New York: Basic Books).

Kindleberger, Charles P. (1984 [1993]) *A Financial History of Western Europe* (New York: Oxford University Press).

King, W.C.T. (1936) *A History of the London Discount Market* (London: Routledge).

Mishkin, Frederic S. (1991) 'Asymmetric Information and Financial Crises', in R. Glenn Hubbard (ed.) *Financial Markets and Financial Crises* (Chicago and London: University of Chicago Press) pp. 69–108.

Rockoff, Hugh (1986) 'Walter Bagehot and the Theory of Central Banking', in Forrest Capie and Geoffrey Wood (eds) *Financial Crises and the World Banking System* (London: Macmillan) pp. 160–80.

Sayers, Richard S. (1976) *The Bank of England, 1891–1914*, 3 vols (Cambridge: Cambridge University Press).

Spero, Joan Edelman (1980) *The Failure of the Franklin National Bank: Challenge to the International Banking System* (New York: Columbia University Press).

Thornton, Marianne (1825 [1953]) 'The Crisis of 1825: Letters from a Young Lady', in T.S. Ashton and R.S. Sayers (eds.) *Papers in English Monetary History* (Oxford: Clarendon Press) pp. 96–108.

Tolliday, Steven (1987) *Business, Banking and Politics: The Case of British Steel, 1918–1939* (Cambridge, Mass.: Harvard University Press).

Wojnilower, Albert M. (1990) 'Financial Institutions Cannot Compete', pamphlet (New York: First Boston Management Corporation).

Wojnilower, Albert M. (1992) 'Markets and Relationships', pamphlet (New York: First Boston Management Corporation).

15 The Bagehot problem *

Fred Hirsch †

I

Under the lead of Friedman and Johnson, monetary analysis in the past two decades has been largely transformed. The previous institutional approach has been replaced by the application of microeconomic analysis; banking has been treated as an industry in which the size and pattern of output, and the remuneration of factor inputs, are determined by the standard market influences. Normatively, particular characteristics of banking have been recognised as justifying some minimum of official regulation. But such regulation is itself to be exercised with the minimum administrative discretion and the minimum social control. Thus the major normative implication of the analysis is that competition in banking is to be maximised, and administrative intervention minimised, subject only to the constraints stomming from the technical monopoly characteristics embodied in banking.[1]

The application of standard microeconomic analysis to banking has yielded obvious and now well known insights. But an important limitation of the approach has been the neglect of one general characteristic of banking: the prevalence of imperfection of information, and of associated asymmetries in information. This omission, which is part of a more general neglect by financial analysts of the implications of imperfect information for the working of financial markets, suggests the need to extend the standard microeconomic analysis to embrace the wider set of factors, including externalities, that determine social optima in market conditions of this kind.

This article focuses on one consequence of informational imperfection, on the relationship between the banks and the regulatory authorities, and

* Manuscript received 28.3.77.
† [Deceased] An earlier draft of this paper was read to meetings of the Royal Economic Society and the Money Study Group. The author was grateful for comment and criticism from Michael Artis, Charles Goodhart and Marcus Miller.
1 The characteristics of banking that modern monetary theorists have regarded as justifying official regulation have been (1) the position of currency issue and supply of aggregate money as a technical monopoly if infinite inflationary escalation is to be avoided, (2) the need to prevent fraud and the reneging on promises to pay, i.e. to enforce contracts, (3) the externalities endemic in the destruction and creation of money, and (4) general banking economies of scale. See Friedman (1959, pp. 4–8) and Johnson (1968).

the resulting influence on banking stability.[2] This approach qualifies the Friedman-Johnson normative prescription of maximum competition combined with minimum administrative discretion, although it yields no dominant alternative prescription.

The problem of banking stability came into sudden prominence in 1974 as an international phenomenon. A succession of failures of medium-sized banks in Germany, the United States and Switzerland, following the collapse of the 'fringe' banks in the United Kingdom, threatened the international credit structure with repercussive effects on the illiquidity or insolvency of banks with important connections in the international system. The problem was indeed an old one – it was what the nineteenth century knew as a financial crisis; but many analysts, the present author included, had assumed this class of problem to have been left behind with the Credit-Anstalt in 1931. Thus, the issue found no place in the extensive academic literature and official documentation of the previous fifteen years; it is absent from the literature comprehensively surveyed by Williamson (1973).[3]

This omission reflected the belief that banking stability had been ensured by the greater responsibilities and improved regulations adopted by central banks in the wake of the Great Depression. The doctrine expounded by Walter Bagehot in *Lombard Street*, in 1873, that the bankers' bank had a duty to lend freely when no other lenders would, had become the orthodoxy, even among those who resisted active counter cyclical policy of the Keynesian type. But the form in which this Bagehot function of lender of last resort is to be performed, and reconciled with operation of the economy according to anonymous market forces, has remained curiously vague and ambiguous. The join between macrostability and micro-efficiency here is an awkward corner, to use the terminology of Joan Robinson. When central banks lend, they need to take a specific view about the quality of the assets they are acquiring. Moreover, at a time of banking panic, the need is to prevent the failure of specific banks. How can these things be done consistently with maintaining the normal market incentives for prudence and good management?

This article suggests that these issues are related to a more general problem of a market economy. This is the dependence of well functioning markets on certain individual behavioural characteristics, such as telling the truth and keeping one's word, which because of limitations and asymmetries of

---

2 The need to invoke asymmetries of information to justify government intervention in the supply of money is also discussed by Klein (1974). Klein points out that if future divergences in the supply of different private currencies could be perfectly anticipated, along with the likelihood of fulfilment of contractual obligations, the private incentive for over-issue of such currencies would disappear. The crucial role of the informational assumptions, and their obvious non-fulfilment in any conceivable real world, is ignored by Hayek (1976) in his advocacy of *Choice in Currency*.

3 I refer here to official documentation in the context of international monetary reform, as distinct from particular operational or policy issues.

information, can be regarded as collective intermediate goods. That is to say, these goods and the final output dependent upon them, will not be 'produced' in socially optimal quantity by maximisation of individual welfare without implicit or explicit co-operation (see Arrow, 1972; Sen, 1973a; Hirsch, 1977, chapter 10). But such co-operation is technically easier to organise in a small group of like-minded individuals and institutions than in an open group.

Competition and free entry in themselves tend to impede the supply of intermediate collective goods. In industries or markets where these factors are significant, there will therefore be some offset to the beneficial effects of competition and free entry on optimality of final output and on internal or X-efficiency (see Leibenstein, 1966). Restriction of competition will still involve allocative distortions in the mix of output, e.g. providing bank buildings rather than bank services. But the standard depressive effect on total output then runs together with an expansionary effect from the support given to collective intermediate goods. This article suggests that banking can fruitfully be regarded as an industry subject to such ambivalence in the net impact of competition. This view suggests a positive explanation for the worldwide phenomenon of cartelisation and/or oligopoly in commercial banking, and for the exercise of central banking functions by public agencies making use of administrative discretion and informal influence.

II

Central banking was pioneered in the British banking system, and in that system it embodied an informal control mechanism. The Bank of England grew into its responsibility for the stability of the London money market as a natural outcome of its position as the dominant bank, and as the bank endowed with privileges of note issue and banker to the government. Acceptance by the Bank of England of the function of lender of last resort gave it leverage over the institutions that enjoyed direct or indirect access to this facility, and enabled it to influence their normal operation and management. Exertion of this leverage was helped by the closely knit social connections between the leading City institutions.[4] But the influence also ran the other way, with the Bank's paternalism reinforcing the existing club and keeping newcomers out. The closely knit social pattern of the British financial system was traditionally seen as a factor of stability and strength, e.g. in the 1931 crisis (see, for example, Truptil, 1936).[5]

---

4 Leading merchant banking families such as the Barings and the Normans participated in the management of the Bank of England as directors and as governors; professional management was introduced only in the 1930's and became dominant only in the 1960's.
5 Truptil emphasised the importance of Oxbridge connections as well as family ties in the development of trust and the exchange of information, and the collective concern felt for

In the 1950's and 1960's the growth ethos turned attention to the nether side of institutional stability, now seen as a potential impediment to efficiency and innovation. The social connections permeating the British financial system were exposed to prominent public view in the evidence of the Parker Tribunal (1957) and the Radcliffe Committee (1959), and became a target of criticism (see in particular Lupton and Wilson, 1959; Devons, 1959; Artis, 1965). A growing chorus called for British banking to be opened to competition by downgrading informal and administrative controls, which were seen as protecting existing institutions. Academic analysts in Britain, less concerned than their predecessors with institutional arrangements, increasingly argued that the basis of official regulation should be switched to a general and in principle anonymous control over the supply of money and/or credit. They were backed part of the way by official agencies concerned with competition rather than financial regulation (see Griffiths, 1970; NBPI, 1967; Johnson, 1967; Monopolies Commission, 1968; Artis, 1968). The new approach was partially accepted by the British authorities in 1971,[6] when the political pendulum as well as economic fashion had swung in favour. In conjunction with an expansionary monetary policy, the liberalisation of banking regulation produced a major credit boom, and ensuing inflation of stock exchange and property values. The subsequent collapse of this boom in turn brought illiquidity, and in a number of cases consequential insolvency, to the new banks that had played a big part in fuelling it.

To check the contagion, the Bank of England reverted to traditional habits. The established 'primary' banks were organised to mount a collective rescue operation, ensuring that no depositors in British banks lost money. Foreign parent companies of subsidiaries and consortium banks in London were obliged to take responsibility for any losses incurred by their British offshoots. The significant characteristic of a bank again became its standing with the Bank of England. Banking stability was preserved at its core, but only by closing the ring. The Bagehot function was again associated with paternalism and informal control within a close knit group.

safeguarding the reputation of the City. He cites with approval an encomium in the *Financial News* that 'A city which for six months on end can obey a sanctionless ordinance to refrain from issuing foreign loans . . . is no mere agglomeration of banks and brokers, but an organism knit together by bonds of a finer fibre than the common desire to make money'. *Op. cit.*, page 197.

6   As enunciated in 'Competition and Credit Control', *Bank of England Quarterly Bulletin*, 1971, pages 189–93, and address by Governor of the Bank of England, *ibid*, pages 195–98. Continued concern with protection of the existing institutional structure, and notably of the discount houses, was evident in the selection of bank assets eligible for the reserve base; by including commercial bills and call loans to the London money market which could be backed by government securities, the authorities weakened their control over the money supply. See the critique by Lomax (1971).

III

The question arises: are there any general factors, unconnected with the historical legacy of particular institutional arrangements and habits, that impede the efficient exercise of a comprehensive backstop function for commercial banking on the basis of arm's length operations, such as would leave the banks to pursue their own direct profit-oriented interests, as constrained only by formalised statutory regulations? One such important general factor can be derived from the economics of imperfect information. The insurance element in central banking – i.e. the insurance provided to both commercial banks and the economy as a whole against illiquidity – can be seen as part of a more general class of problems that has been associated by economic theorists in recent years with imperfect information: and more specifically with unequal information in the possession of the two parties to a market transaction.

A pioneering exposition of the effect of asymmetrical information on commercial transactions was provided by Akerlof (1970) in his analysis of the used car market as 'The Market for "Lemons"'. Because I know more about the true condition of the car I have been using than you as a potential buyer can expect to know about it, the price you will be prudently willing to pay will be what it seems to be worth to your eye *less* some discount estimated to represent the deficiencies in quality you may have missed. Obviously, therefore, if my car really is as good as it looks, I will gain by not selling it but continuing to use it myself. Because the market must assume used cars to be lemons, they mostly are: the market for used cars is sub-optimal, and the market for good used cars may be non-existent.

The insurance literature has long recognised the phenomena of adverse selection based on unequal information between buyer and seller (disproportionately many sick people try to get insurance and disproportionately many healthy people self-insure) and of moral hazard (when the insurance pays the bill, you let it run up more than if you paid outright) (see Grubel, 1971). Arrow (1963) has shown that the health insurance market is sub-optimal in total size, and non-existent for those most in need of it.[7] This produces a case for public health insurance on allocational as well as on equity grounds. Yet institutions of public insurance established as a corrective must be expected, as long as moral hazard is present, to overshoot in the

---

7   Pauly has contested the appellation 'moral hazard' in this context, on the grounds that an increase in consumption stimulated by a zero price implies individual economic rationality, with no moral connotations. Arrow points out that moral standards of behaviour to reinforce trust (in this case, trust that individuals who seek to insure risks associated with a particular pattern of behaviour will not change that behaviour when they get the insurance), is one means to an efficient solution that may otherwise be unattainable. See Pauly (1968, pages 531–7) and Arrow (*ibid*, pages 537–8). In the same vein, Sen (1973a, *op. cit.*) has argued that individualistic preferences, in 'prisoners' dilemma' situations, can be most efficiently met only by non-individualistic behaviour.

other direction, by the standard criterion of equating consumers' marginal rates of substitution with producers' marginal rates of transformation; as well as needing to find a substitute for the stimulus given by competition to internal or X-efficiency.

This is the economic dilemma in the health industry. But in the case of health, the problem is somewhat mitigated by the existence of time costs and other consumption deterrents (having operations is not pleasant in itself, for most of us); in addition, availability of health services at normal or zero cost to those in greatest physical need (i.e. the unhealthy) can be counted as a distributional benefit in itself,[8] as can substitution of time costs for money costs which encourages consumption by the worse off (see Nichols *et al*, 1971). These considerations probably explain why in practice we have a state health service, but not a state used car exchange. But we do have a state central bank.

Imperfections in capital and credit markets have long been noted, being most apparent in the phenomenon of credit rationing, but they have usually been attributed to institutional imperfections. A different interpretation has recently been put forward by Arrow (1974). He suggests that imperfections are inherent in the characteristics of loan transactions, because they necessitate enforcement of a contract in the uncertain future, which weakens the self-enforcing element. This element of uncertainty makes it especially desirable for the lender to have as much information about the borrower as possible, which can be obtained only by a 'very individualised information-seeking relation which is quite far removed from the arm's length impersonal model of a market.' People who are known and trusted can buy all the banking services they are prepared to pay for; others cannot. Banking and other forms of financial intermediation, we may infer, are less extensively developed than they would be if the information and unenforceability problems did not exist. This leads to familiar gaps and discontinuities in the capital market, some of which are countered by public intervention (small loan agencies, etc.).[9]

The absence of banking services involves associated welfare losses, but no obvious external diseconomies. But the same is not true at the higher level of

---

8   This is strongly argued by Sen (1973b, p. 79): 'The national health service has a built-in system of attempting to match payments to needs . . .'.

9   The non-existence of markets in future contingencies, including markets in forward exchange for more than six or twelve months, is a more familiar example of the influence discussed in this paragraph. For Friedman and his school, the failure of such markets to develop is explained by the intrusion of arbitrary intervention of governments and central banks, and anticipation of such intervention. The Arrow approach suggests rather that only government can be expected to create or under-write such markets, either because the social risks involved are less than the sum of individual risks, or because government decides to shoulder uncertainty that market institutions shun. The same line of thought gives a rationale for official exchange market intervention in general (Fred Hirsch, *Comment*, IMF conference on The New International Monetary System, 1977, forthcoming).

banking for bankers, as embodied in the lender of last resort function of central banks. A deficiency of 'output' here, in the form of denial of facilities to the risky borrower, may threaten national output as a whole, if it leads to panic and general collapse.

The commercial market institutions that performed some of the functions of a bankers' bank before the emergence of the fully fledged central banking function were inclined to essentially the same dysfunctional selectiveness that has been diagnosed for the purely commercial health insurance agency. That is to say, they preferred to avoid the risks that most needed to be covered and to withdraw altogether in the face of a threatened crisis in the system, involving uncertainty of a kind that commercial insurance cannot allow for.[10] Hence Bagehot's behest to the Bank of England to reverse the banker's normal instinct in a crisis and to lend more freely rather than less. But provision of banking reinsurance beyond the scope forthcoming on a commercial basis would itself tend to induce distortions of the kind noted in the case of public health insurance – viz. encouraging extravagance or carelessness (moral hazard) and consequential excess 'output' of banking services for the public.

A familiar example of this phenomenon on the international plane is the granting of commercial credits and other short term loans to governments and other borrowers beyond their prospective capacity to repay, in the expectation that the commercial lenders will be baled out by their own authorities, whether through specific credit insurance cover or in the context of a negotiated debt re-scheduling. Moral hazard virtually rules out insurance of loans on a commercial basis.

The extra-market facility accordingly demands an extra-market control mechanism. In England this developed in a natural way, and completely consistently with Bagehot's pragmatic and eclectic approach, as informal control exercised through paternalistic and moral leadership within a small-numbers group.[11]

---

10 This inclination towards a *sauve qui peut* strategy – i.e. action that is individually optimal but collectively second best and perhaps disastrous – admittedly tends to be checked in an oligopolistic structure, in which the small-numbers characteristic allows the collective good of mutual credit support to be produced on a voluntary basis. However, this basis is inherently uncertain, and thereby lacking in assurance. Moreover, oligopolies may choose to renounce possible short term gains from stabilising action in the expectation of strengthening or protecting their market dominance over a longer term, i.e. they may let outside or otherwise disfavoured competition go to the wall and reckon on riding out the consequences themselves. The collapse of the Bank of the United States in 1930 may be interpreted in this light (see footnote 12).

11 Bagehot, as one of his few hostile critics has indelicately pointed out, was through his family bank of Stuckey's a not uninterested party: 'He was recommending *other people* to lend freely, in time of panic, as a way of saving Bagehot.' (Sisson, 1972, page 97.) Bagehot made clear that he would have preferred the responsibility for maintaining the 'ultimate banking reserve' to have been spread among a number of comparably sized leading banks, and was

A striking recent manifestation of this tendency was seen in Britain in 1973–74 with the virtual collapse of the 'fringe banks' (i.e. banking new-comers: the appellation exactly captures the implicit presumption of an established banking fraternity). This new sector of British banking was laid low by a panic of pre-Bagehotian severity. When the first such banks ran into difficulties in December 1973, and it became clear that the fire break was to be drawn around the newcomer banks rather than among them, new deposits were immediately switched to established banks; and all banks outside the protected circle experienced large attempted withdrawals of deposits, so that their fate was sealed. The underlying cause was an erosion of asset values through the collapse of the property market in which these banks had been heavily involved. The resulting threat to solvency set off a consequential liquidity drain in deposit withdrawals.

A banking name in Britain has always had a special cash value deriving from rules of access to facilities at the Bank of England, notably the require-ment that commercial bills eligible for re-discount at the Bank must bear two approved British names, normally of members of the Accepting Houses Association. In the past this made the most practicable means of breaking into British banking the acquisition of an existing but tired merchant bank as a 'shell'. This route has never been available for injection of competition into deposit banking, which has now become largely divided between a four mem-ber oligopoly. The established banks were effectively required, through the informal network, to commit their resources through the 'lifeboat committee' to avoiding losses to depositors of the fringe banks. Some banks indicated their displeasure at the imposition. The complaint detracted attention from the main significance of the episode for the British banking structure. For individual banks, the tying up of funds in a joint support operation is an irritant. For the established banks collectively, the rescue operation marks the removal of a source of competition, at least compared with the *status quo ante* and a situation in which central bank support was available to all banks.

The informal controls and established patterns of behaviour which under-pin official regulation of the banking structure in Britain constitute a mech-anism closer to the understanding of the sociologist than of the modern neo-classical economist thinking in terms of optimisation subject to a budget,

---

merely recognising the accomplished fact of the Bank of England's dominance (*Op. cit.*, pages 65–70). This passage has sometimes been regarded as an aberration in which Bagehot failed to understand Bagehot, since the concept of a spontaneous joint effort to fulfil the reserve function misses the potential conflict between private and collective interest in reserve banking for a bank other than one dominant in size. But the anomaly appears rather less if the banks are assumed to be not pure individual profit maximisers but institutions imbued with a felt responsibility for doing their part to preserve order in the system. Bagehot, like John Stuart Mill, took it for granted that private behaviour was substantially permeated by collective norms, so it is not surprising that the collective good 'problem' seen by modern economists was less obtrusive.

but not social, constraint. It is significant that while Friedman cites Bagehot with approval, he strongly favours the downgrading of re-discounting and its substitution by the more impersonal mechanism of open market operations. In this approach, controls against abuse of central bank facilities would be limited to explicit statutory regulations, such as reserve requirements – possibly at 100 per cent – which might eliminate the need for compulsory deposit insurance (see Friedman, 1959, *op. cit.*; Friedman and Schwartz, 1963, especially chapter 7; also the review of the former work by Lerner, 1962).

But appropriate general regulations are notoriously difficult to lay down. Balance sheet ratios have well known weaknesses as a control device. In Revell's (1974) recent assessment: 'What the supervisory authorities must aim at is being able to put themselves in the position of the management of each bank . . . no set rule-of-thumb ratios can substitute for this vicarious participation in the management process.' The various overlapping banking authorities in the United States attempt in principle a comprehensive and detached review which fits the category of Revell's vicarious management (see Pesek and Saving, 1968, chapter II, and Kaufman, 1973, pp. 86–88).

IV

Resistance to this degree of intervention by public authorities requires a readiness to endure the failure of particular banks, relying on the support given to the aggregate money supply through open market operations to maintain stability. The adequacy of this approach has never been tested, and Friedman himself does not push it to its limits.[12] The Federal Reserve in 1969 gave serious consideration to supporting the paper of Penn Central (see Maisel, 1973, pp. 41–45 and 122). In 1974 the New York Federal Reserve Bank gave massive support to the Franklin National Bank, in the view that failure of the bank would have serious adverse consequences for its depositors and creditors and would have 'jeopardised the stability of the United States banking system, with further serious repercussions for domestic and international financial markets in general' (see Federal Reserve Bank of New York, 1974). To be sure, the Federal Reserve like other central banks attempts to draw lines between depositors, other creditors, management and equity shareholders. Maximum protection for depositors,[13] combined with

12 Witness Friedman's emphasis on the especial importance of the failure of the Bank of the United States in December 1930. The refusal by the leading New York banks to respond to appeals from the New York Federal Reserve to rescue this bank with predominantly Jewish connections, a refusal which Friedman has associated with anti-Semitism, illustrates how dependent any private substitute for the Bagehot function is on social affinity and eventual solidarity (Friedman and Schwartz, *op. cit.*, pages 308–311).
13 Deposit insurance in the United States by the Federal Deposit Insurance Corporation is limited to small deposits up to a limit recently raised from $20,000 to $40,000; this still leaves one third of deposit volume uncovered.

full exposure for the equity and risk of dismissal for management, would serve the insurance function while retaining some restraints against moral hazard in the form of excessive risk taking by bank managements. But a distinction of this kind, even if successfully applied, is not sufficient to prevent contingent support for depositors from encouraging banking concentration. To maintain the balance between banks of different size, it would be necessary in addition for the public to be persuaded that the central bank is prepared to allow the largest banks to go under as readily as smaller banks.

In the nervous atmosphere caused by a small crop of bank failures in the third quarter of 1974, placements of large money market deposits both nationally and internationally immediately became more selective; and the dominating principle of selection was a bank that was sure of having its central bank behind it. Marked differentials developed in rates on certificates of deposits of different banks, with size and pre-eminence being taken as the main general criterion. The largest international banks such as the Chase Manhattan and the First National City were widely believed to be overwhelmed with offers of very large deposits in this period, and consequently shaded down their offered rates on such deposits – a reversal of the normal premium on deposit size.[14]

This tendency exposed a continuing dilemma faced by central banks anxious to prevent their support of banking stability from weakening banking competition and long term banking efficiency. The central bank has to find a means of checking moral hazard. It can take the 'English' route of informal controls and inculcation of a club spirit among the commercial banks to play the game according to the established conventions which are seen to be in the interests of all participants.[15] In return for the insurance premium of responsible behaviour, insurance cover is comprehensive and assured. Participation in such an arrangement must obviously be limited to those who can be trusted to be responsible – call them gentlemen. This will mean excluding those not known to be gentlemen; and they will be those not known to

---

14 In the London market for dollar certificates of deposits, the list of issuer names acceptable to the majority of institutional buyers was described by a market participant as having become very narrow indeed – 'perhaps as few as seven names being universally acceptable' (Clark, 1975, page 43). Between end-April and July 1974, banks with total deposits of $500 million or more accounted for nearly 90 per cent of the increase in large time deposits issued to individuals, partnerships and corporations, increasing their share of the total from 74.2 to 75.9 per cent. The Federal Reserve Board had earlier referred to 'an increased preference by some investors for the liabilities of a small number of the largest commercial banks' in an atmosphere of 'heightened public concern about the stability of financial institutions' in the third quarter of 1974 (*Federal Reserve Bulletin*, January 1975, page 13, and November 1974, page 748).

15 Informal controls play an important role also in a number of continental European countries, notably Switzerland.

existing gentlemen. So entry will be socially controlled, and competition discouraged.[16]

The alternative strategy is for the central bank to attempt to exert its counterforce to moral hazard through a continued market discipline which makes no demands on commercial banks to depart from their individual profit orientation but confronts them with a contingent risk of failure. Insurance here is less than comprehensive and available only along with significant self insurance (e.g. of the equity and of large deposits, which are in effect 'deductibles' from the insured risk).[17] This may be categorised as the German and to the lesser extent the American approach to the lender of last resort function. The difficulty with this approach is that it appears unlikely in practice to be applied evenly to banks of different size, because failure of big banks is generally, and surely correctly, regarded as more disruptive to the financial system than failure of small ones. Consequently, the greater the perceived risk of particular banks being allowed to go under, the greater will be the tendency for bank depositors to seek shelter in the banks considered too large for the authorities to subject to such therapy, and the greater the tendency towards banking concentration. It is significant in this context that the country in which the Bagehot function is perhaps least entrenched, Germany, is also the country in which the large banks are especially dominant, not only within banking but in ownership and control of industry.

The general point can be put as follows. In principle, the regulatory authorities may aim to preserve the sanctions against bank equity and management to maintain solvency, while relieving the mass of bank depositors and the banking system as a whole of the risk of illiquidity. In practice, solvency and liquidity are not fully separable, since insolvency is often exposed only under liquidity stress. Enforced liquidation itself usually depresses the value of assets. Large banks that can count on the confidence of the public, based ultimately on the unwillingness of the authorities to face the repercussions of the bank's default to even large depositors and perhaps also other creditors, thereby enjoy a cushion against careless bank management that is denied to smaller banks.

Thus informal controls lead to cartelisation; 'market' controls to oligopoly. Whichever strategy the central banking authorities choose, their ultimate support for banking stability tends to discourage banking competition. Neither strategy, therefore, is dominant as a means of promoting internal efficiency. In addition, non-market controls are needed to attain the allocation

---

16 Entry of new participants will tend to be further restricted by the general tendency for informal agreements to become more difficult to enforce as the size of the group increases. This is well established in the literature on collective goods. See for example Olson (1965).

17 Henry C. Wallich, a governor of the Federal Reserve Board, has referred to bank capital as self-insurance and deposit insurance as pooled insurance. ('Some Thoughts on Capital Adequacy', Speech at a Management Seminar, Washington, D.C., February 28, 1975, mimeograph.)

that a market with perfect information would reach, and to give individuals the benefit of the transactions they will relinquish if they take advantage of their opportunity to 'cheat' (i.e. alter their behaviour) in response to market opportunity (see also footnote 7 above). As Arrow (1968, *op. cit.*) has emphasised, truth and trust are preconditions of well functioning markets; yet the habits of truth and trust cannot be expected to result from individual optimisation, except perhaps in small and immobile communities where any benefit from transgressions is relinquished by the future costs imposed by the damage to reputation. Therefore: 'Non-market controls, whether internalised as moral principles or externally imposed, are to some extent essential for efficiency.' The non-market controls that permeate banking systems underpin efficient banking, as well as often undermining it.

V

An unresolved question hovering over the international financial system is how the huge continuing surpluses of most of the oil exporting countries will be channelled through that system: and, specifically, whether it will continue to be sound and feasible for the bulk of the funds to be channelled, as they have been since 1974, through the private sector and predominantly through the banks in unmanaged market processes. In a continuing refrain, what is so special about this problem that the market, left to itself, cannot handle it? The answer to this refrain should probably be: that it is a banking problem, which the market left to itself has never been able to handle, for solid but neglected reasons of economic theory.

The difficulty is that the means of public intervention that can themselves make good the market deficiency involve unwanted side effects that can bring new distortions. Domestically, in the development of the stabilising and insurance functions of central banking and bank supervision, these object-ives have conflicted in some part with the objective of maximum competition and arm's length controls free of paternalism and of subjective official judg-ments about banking business. It remains uncertain whether the full Bagehot function can be fulfilled in a system in which the key banks extend further than the length of a Lombard Street, in social space as distinct from geo-graphical space. This poses an obvious obstacle to the international extension of the Bagehot function. But the pressure for such extension has undoubtedly been increased by the large additions to the funds seeking placement through the international banking system as disposition of the oil surpluses. This suggests that some of the same side effects of central banking that have encouraged banking concentration at the national level may now be extended internationally.

Nor is it fanciful to envisage as a concomitant the international extension of informal controls and élite groups. The arena for such socialisation has existed for some time in the growing contact between top commercial bankers and financial officials of other countries, contacts that are formalised at annual gatherings such as those of the American Bankers' Association, and at the inner core of the annual meetings of the International Monetary Fund. The chairman of the Federal Reserve Board, Dr. Arthur Burns, has recently proposed more formal coordination, under which commercial banks would align their loan terms with the IMF and would be given partial access to its information.[18]

The support in financial circles for a wider role for international official financing has stemmed in large part from the over-exposure of commercial banks operating in a competitive environment. Yet it is difficult to foresee on the international plane more than a minimal degree of cohesion and informal controls by the standards prevailing in the parish of the Bank of England. To this extent the potentiality for international extension of the Bagehot function remains ambiguous, reflecting the same ambiguity as exists in the scope for a lender of last resort in a domestic banking system regulated only at arm's length.

References

Akerlof, G. A. (1970). 'The Market for "Lemons": Qualitative Uncertainty and the Market Mechanism', *Quarterly Journal of Economics*, Vol. LXXXIV, No. 3, pp. 488–500.

Arrow, K. J. (1963). 'Uncertainty and the Welfare Economics of Medical Care', *American Economic Review*, Vol. LIII, No. 5, pp. 941–973.

—— (1968). 'The Economics of Moral Hazard: Further Comment', *American Economic Review*, Vol. LVIII, No. 3, Part 1, pp. 537–80.

—— (1972). 'Gifts and Exchanges', *Philosophy & Public Affairs*, Vol. 1, No. 4, pp. 343–363.

—— (1974). 'Limited Knowledge and Economic Analysis', *American Economic Review*, Vol. LXIV, No. 1, pp. 1–10.

Artis, M. J. (1965). *Foundations of British Monetary Policy*, Oxford, Oxford University Institute of Economics and Statistics Monograph 9.

Artis, M. J. (1968). 'The Monopolies Commission Report', *Bankers' Magazine*, Vol. 206, No. 1494, pp. 128–135; reprinted in Johnson, H. G. (ed.), *Readings in British Monetary Economics*, Oxford, Clarendon Press, 1972.

Bagehot, W. (1915). *Lombard Street* (14th edition), London, John Murray.

Bank of England (1971). 'Competition and Credit Control', *Bank of England Quarterly Bulletin*, Vol. 11, No. 2.

Clark, J. B. (1975). 'Top Seven Only Please', *Euromoney*, February, p. 43.

Devons, E. (1959). 'An Economist's View of the Bank Rate Tribunal Evidence', *The Manchester School*, Vol. XXVII, No. 1, pp. 1–16.

Federal Reserve Bank of New York (1974). *Annual Report*, New York, Federal Reserve Bank.

Federal Reserve Board (1974). 'Financial Developments in the Third Quarter of 1974', *Federal Reserve Bulletin*, Vol. 60, No. 11, p. 748.

---

18 Speech in New York reported in the *Financial Times*, April 14, 1977.

—— (1975). 'Changes in Time and Savings Deposits at Commercial Banks, April-July 1974', *Federal Reserve Bulletin*, Vol. 61, No. 1, p. 13.

Friedman, M. (1959). *A Program for Monetary Stability*, New York, Fordham University Press.

—— & Schwartz, A. (1963). *A Monetary History of the U.S., 1867–1960*, Princeton, Princeton University Press.

Griffiths, B. (1970). *Competition in Banking* (Hobart Paper 51), London, The Institute of Economic Affairs.

Grubel, H. G. (1971). 'Risk, Uncertainty and Moral Hazard', *Journal of Risk and Insurance*, Vol. 38, No. 1, pp. 99–106.

Hayek, F. A. (1976). *Choice in Currency* (Occasional Paper 48), London, The Institute of Economic Affairs.

Hirsch, F. (1977). *Social Limits to Growth*, London, Routledge & Kegan Paul.

Johnson, H. G. (1967). 'The Report on Bank Charges', *Bankers' Magazine*, Vol. 204, No. 1481, pp. 64–68; reprinted in Johnson, H. G. (ed.), *Readings in British Monetary Economics*, Oxford, Clarendon Press, 1972.

Johnson, H. G. (1968). 'Problems of Efficiency in Monetary Management', *Journal of Political Economy*, Vol. 76, No. 5, pp. 971–990; reprinted in Johnson, H. G. (ed.), *op. cit.*

Kaufman, G. F. (1973). *Money, the Financial System and the Economy*, London, Rand McNally.

Klein, B. (1974). 'The Competitive Supply of Money', *Journal of Money, Credit and Banking*, Vol. VI, No. 4, pp. 423–453.

Leibenstein, H. (1966). 'Allocative Efficiency Versus X-Efficiency', *American Economic Review*, Vol. LVI, No. 3, pp. 392–415.

Lerner, A. P. (1962). 'Review of Milton Friedman, *A Program for Monetary Stability*', *American Statistical Association Journal*, Vol. 57, pp. 211–220; reprinted in Mittra, S. (ed.), *Money and Banking*, New York, Random House, 1970.

Lomax, D. F. (1971). 'The New Credit Controls', *The Banker*, Vol. 121, No. 548, pp. 1160–1165.

Lupton, T. & Wilson, C. S. (1959). 'The Social Background and Connections of "Top Decision Makers" ', *The Manchester School*, Vol. XXVII, No. 1, pp. 30–51.

Maisel, S. J. (1973). *Managing the Dollar*, New York, Norton.

Monopolies Commission (1968). *Report on Proposed Bank Merger*, London, H.M.S.O.

NBPI (National Board for Prices & Incomes) (1967). *Bank Charges*, Report No. 34, Cmnd. 3292, London, H.M.S.O.

Nichols, D., Smolensky, E. & Tideman, T. N. (1971). 'Discrimination in Waiting Time by Merit Goods', *American Economic Review*, Vol. LXI, No. 3, Part 1, pp. 312–323.

Olson, M. (1965). *The Logic of Collective Action*, Cambridge, Mass., Harvard University Press.

Parker Tribunal (1957). *Tribunal to Inquire into Allegations of Improper Disclosure of Information Relating to the Raising of Bank Rate, Report and Proceedings*, London, H.M.S.O.

Pauly, M. V. (1968). 'The Economics of Moral Hazard: Comment', *American Economic Review*, Vol. LVIII, No. 3, Part 1, pp. 531–7.

Pesek, B. & Saving, T. R. (1968). *The Foundations of Money and Banking*, New York, Macmillan & Co.

Radcliffe Committee (1959). *Committee on the Working of the Monetary System, Report*, Cmnd. 827, and *Minutes of Evidence* (1960), London, H.M.S.O.

Revell, J. (1974). 'The Solvency of Banks', *The Banker*, Vol. 124, No. 575, pp. 29–31.

Sen, A. (1973a). 'Behaviour and the Concept of Preference', *Economica*, Vol. XL, No. 159, pp. 241–259.

—— (1973b). *On Economic Inequality*, Oxford, Clarendon Press.

Sisson, C. H. (1972). *The Case of Walter Bagehot*, London, Faber & Faber.

Truptil, R. J. (1936). *British Banks and the London Money Market*, London, Jonathan Cape.

Williamson, J. (1973). 'International Liquidity: A Survey', *Economic Journal*, Vol. 83, No. 331, pp. 685–746.

16 The lender of last resort reconsidered

Geoffrey E. Wood*

The Central Bank's lender of last resort role was developed by a series of authors in the very late eighteenth and through the nineteenth centuries. It was tested in practice in a number of countries and was found to be effective in providing monetary stability in the face of adverse shocks. There have recently been attempts to broaden the role – to make the central bank responsible for the stability of asset markets, or for protecting individual banks – and there have recently also been claims that an international lender of last resort is necessary. This article considers and rejects these proposed extensions to the classic lender of last resort role.

1. Introduction

In 1793, war was declared between France and Britain.

> That dreadful calamity is usually preceded by some indication which enables the commerical and monied men to make preparation. On this occasion the short notice rendered the least degree of general preparation impossible. The foreign market was either shut, or rendered more difficult of access to the merchant. Of course he would not purchase from the manufacturers; ... the manufacturers in their distress applied to the Bankers in the country for relief; but as the want of money became general, and that want increased gradually by a general alarm, the country Banks required the payment of old debts. ... In this predicament the country at large could have no other resource but London; and after having exhausted the bankers, that resource finally terminated in the Bank of England. In such cases the Bank are not an intermediary body, or power; there is no resource on their refusal, for they are the *dernier resort*.[1]

Thus did Francis Baring, writing in 1797 of the dramatic events of 1793,

* Cass Business School, City University.

introduce the notion of the Bank of England as the 'last resort' of the banking system. The concept was soon thereafter developed very substantially by Henry Thornton (1802). Throughout the nineteenth century, the Bank of England's practice in the task gradually evolved. Further refinements to the concept were introduced by Walter Bagehot (most notably in *Lombard Street* (1873), but also in his writings in *The Economist* and elsewhere). By 1910 the practice had spread to some other countries, and its efficacy in stabilizing a country's banking system was clearly demonstrated. In view of all this, why does the concept require reexamination? There are at least three reasons.

First, there are regularly repeated attempts to broaden the central bank's responsibilities to encompass supporting not just the banking system but the financial system more generally, including financial markets. In her classic 'Real and Pseudo Financial Crises' (1986), Anna Schwartz considered and rejected this recommendation. But it recurs, so further examination is worthwhile. Second, it has become fashionable to argue that the central bank's responsibility for the banking system may from time to time require the rescue of individual banks – because they are 'too big,' or at least too important, to be allowed to fail. As with taking responsibility for financial markets, such rescue would be a dramatic broadening of traditional lender of last resort responsibilities, so this, too should be considered. The third reason is in part semantic. Various activities carried out not just by central banks but also by international agencies have started to be described as 'lender of last resort' actions. This may simply be the result of terminological confusion; but it may also represent an attempt to borrow respectability for otherwise hard-to-defend actions. Either way, bringing more clarity to the area should facilitate discussion and help understanding.

Addressing these three matters, then, is the objective of this article. The structure of the article is as follows.

The next section (section 2) briefly reviews the development of lender of last resort theory and practice from Francis Baring to the beginning of the twentieth century. That section also shows how the success of the activity in achieving a particular goal was demonstrated. Section 3 considers the arguments and evidence for broadening the role beyond its early twentieth century scope and adding to it responsibility for financial markets. Next, the complex set of arguments for from time to time supporting an individual bank are considered. The penultimate section of the article examines some attempts to broaden the meaning of the term *lender of last resort*. The article concludes with consideration of whether any of the arguments reviewed justifies significant changes to the lender of last resort role as it was viewed in the early years of the twentieth century.

2. The development of the lender of last resort[2]

Very soon after Francis Baring's 1797 use of the term *dernier resort*, Henry Thornton (1802) provided a statement of what it was, why it was necessary, and how it should operate. Quite remarkably, this statement was essentially a complete description of the lender of last resort role as it worked up to the beginning of this century. His statement was made in a particular institutional context, and it is as well for the sake of subsequent clarity to consider what this context was.[3]

There were many banks in England, all (except the Bank of England) constrained to being partnerships of six or fewer. The joint stock form was not generally allowed until 1826, and limited liability not until 1858. Even with the care that unlimited liability surely brought, failures were common. It is here that the Bank of England comes in.

> If any bank fails, a general run upon the neighbouring banks is apt to take place, which if not checked in the beginning by a pouring into the circulation of a very large quantity of gold, leads to very extensive mischief.
>
> (Thornton, 1802, p. 182)

And who was to 'pour in' this gold? The Bank of England.

> . . . if the Bank of England, in future seasons of alarm, should be disposed to extend its discounts in a greater degree than heretofore, then the threatened calamity may be averted.
>
> (Thornton, 1802, p. 188)

This approach was not incompatible with allowing some individual institutions to fail:

> It is by no means intended to imply that it would become the Bank of England to relieve every distress which the rashness of country banks may bring upon them: the Bank by doing this, might encourage their improvidence. . . . The relief should neither be so prompt and liberal as to exempt those who misconduct their business from all the natural consequences of their fault, nor so scanty and slow as deeply to involve the general interests.
>
> (Thornton, 1802, p. 188)

Concern should be with the system as a whole.

And the reason a 'pouring into the circulation' (to use Thornton's phrase) would stop a panic and thus protect the system was described with great clarity by Bagehot in 1873:

> What is wanted and what is necessary to stop a panic is to diffuse the impression that though money may be dear, still money is to be had. If

people could really be convinced that they would have money. . . . Most likely they would cease to run in such a herd-like way for money.

(Bagehot, 1873, pp. 64–65)

In the kind of banking system that Britain had by the mid- to late nineteenth century, a system based on gold but with the central bank the monopoly supplier of notes, the responsibility for diffusing '. . . the impression that . . . Money is to be had' clearly rested with the central bank.

Exactly why was elegantly articulated by Bagehot in 1848:

It is a great defect of a purely metallic circulation that the quantity of it cannot be readily suited to any sudden demand; it takes time to get new supplies of gold and silver, and, in the meantime, a temporary rise in the value of bullion takes place. Now as paper money can be supplied in unlimited quantities, however sudden the demand may be, it does not appear to us that there is any objection on principle of sudden issues of paper money to meet sudden and large extensions of demand. It gives to a purely metallic circulation that greater constancy of purchasing power possessed by articles whose quantity can be quickly suited to demand. It will be evident from what we have said before that this power of issuing notes is one excessively liable to abuse because, as before shown, it may depreciate the currency; and on that account such a power ought only to be lodged in the hands of government. . . . It should only be used in rare and exceptional circumstances. But when the fact of a *sudden* demand is proved, we see no objection, but decided advantage, in introducing this new element into a metallic circulation.

(Bagehot, 1848, p. 300)

That, then, summarizes nineteenth century theory on the subject. Because the central bank was the monopoly note issuer, it was the ultimate source of cash. If it did not, by acting as lender of last resort, supply that cash in a panic, the panic would continue, get worse, and a widespread banking collapse ensue, bringing along with it a sharp monetary contraction.

What was nineteenth century practice? It is useful to describe here another institutional feature. Setting it out facilitates understanding that while the feature affected the details of how the Bank of England operated, it was in no way essential to lender of last resort operations. The feature was the existence of a set of institutions, now essentially gone, called discount houses. These originated as bill brokers who brought together those who wished to issue bills of exchange (an important means of trade finance) and investors who wished to purchase such bills. These brokers grew, built up their capital base, and ceased to be pure brokers, instead holding some bills on their own account. They then became discount houses.

In part because of a degree of animosity between the banks and the Bank of England (due to the latter's privileges), the banks preferred to place their surplus liquidity with the discount houses. These in turn had access to borrowing facilities at the Bank of England, by discounting bills there. Both the commercial banks and the Bank of England were happy to have the discount houses as a buffer. The commercial banks' original motivation for this has been mentioned. As for the Bank, the commercial banks grew rapidly and the Bank did not, so it was happy to have an intermediary between itself and its large customers.

Within that setting, how did practice develop? It has to be said that it developed with remarkable rapidity. Sterling returned to its prewar gold parity in 1821. The first subsequent occasion for emergency assistance from the Bank was in 1825. There had been a substantial external drain of gold, and there was a shortage of currency. A panic developed, and there were runs on banks. The type of bills the Bank would normally discount soon ran out, and the panic continued. If a wave of bank failures were to be prevented, the banks would have had to borrow on the security of other types of assets. On December 14, the Bank of England suddenly deviated from its normal practice and made advances on government securities offered to it by the banks, instead of limiting itself to discounting commercial bills. Of that change of policy Jeremiah Harman, a Director of the Bank, spoke as follows when giving evidence before a Parliamentary Committee in 1832. The Bank had lent money

> . . . by every possible means and in modes we had never adopted before; we took in stock on security, we purchased Exchequer bills, we made advances in Exchequer bills, we not only discounted outright but we made advances on the deposit of bills of exchange to an immense amount, in short by every means consistent with the safety of the Bank, and we were not on some occasions over nice.
>
> (Harman, 1832, p. 689)

As Hawtrey wrote of these now famous remarks, 'In reality the advances he describes were of a highly conservative character' (1932, p. 122). But to continue that quotation from Hawtrey,

> The importance of the change in practice was that it admitted a class of borrowers on irreproachable security, who had nevertheless been barred by the previous limitations. The concession was a real one, and it stayed the panic (p. 122).

The next step was taken in 1866, with the Overend and Gurney Crisis.

Overend, Gurney, and Co. originated with two eighteenth century firms, the Gurney Bank (of Norwich) and the London firm of Richardson, Overend and company. By the 1850s, the combined firm was very large; its annual turnover of bills of exchange was in value equal to about half the national debt, and its balance sheet was 10 times the size of the next largest bank. It was floated during the stock market boom of 1865. By early 1866 the boom had ended. A good number of firms were failing. The bank rate had been raised from 3% in July 1865 to 7% in January 1866. After February, bank rate started to ease, but on May 11 Gurney's was declared insolvent.

To quote the *Bankers' Magazine* for June 1866, 'a terror and anxiety took possession of men's minds for the remainder of that and the whole following day' (p. 15). The Bank of England for a brief time made matters worse by hesitating to lend even on government debt. The Bank Charter Act (which among other things, restricted the note issue to the extent of the gold reserve plus a small fiduciary issue) was then suspended, and the panic gradually subsided.[4]

The failure in 1878 of the City of Glasgow Bank was much less dramatic. It had started respectably, was managed fraudulently, and failed. There was fear that the Bank Charter Act would have to be suspended again (see Pressnell, 1968), but no major problems appeared: 'There was no run, or any semblance of a run; there was no local discredit' (Gregory, 1929, p. 164). Other Scottish banks took up all the notes of the bank; Gregory conjectures that they acted in that way to preserve confidence in their own note issues.

Then in 1890 came the (first) 'Barings Crisis'. Barings was a large bank of great reputation; in 1877, when Treasury bills were introduced, Bagehot praised them as being 'as good as Barings '.' Barings nevertheless became involved in a financial crisis in Argentina. The Argentinean government found difficulty in paying the interest on its debt in April 1890; then the national Bank suspended interest payments on *its* debt. This precipitated a run on the Argentinean banking system, and there was revolution on July 26. Barings had lent heavily to Argentina. On November 8 it revealed the resulting difficulties to the Bank of England. The Bank and the government were horrified, fearing a run on London should Barings default. A hurried inspection of Barings suggested that the situation could be saved, but that £10 mn was needed to finance current and imminent obligations. A consortium was organized, initially with £17 mn of capital. By November 15, the news had leaked, and there was some switching of bills of exchange into cash. But there was no major panic and no run on London or on sterling. The impact on financial markets was small. Barings was liquidated and refloated as a limited company with additional capital and new (but still family) management.

Why the great difference between the first, second, and third of these episodes? The Bank of England had both learned to act as lender of last resort (LOLR) and had made clear that it stood ready so to act. What the Bank had done wrong in 1866 was to lend . . . 'hesitatingly, reluctantly, and with misgiving . . . In fact, to make large advances in this faltering way is to incur the evil of making them without obtaining the advantage' (Bagehot, 1873, p. 66)

The Bank learned the appropriate action quickly; H.H. Gibb, Governor of the Bank from 1875 to 1877[5] described the 1866 crisis as 'the Bank's only real blunder in his experience' (p. 66), but he did not criticize the then Governor, for '. . . the matter was not as well-understood then as it is now . . .' (p. 67).[6]

So the lesson that was learned in Britain was that a banking crisis could be stopped by prompt lender of last resort action. As will be seen in a moment from the brief review of French and Italian crises, absence of such action can prove disastrous. But it is not quite so clear as Bagehot maintained that the Bank of England's taking on the LOLR role was what brought stability to Britain after 1866. For branch banking was starting to spread rapidly. By the fourth quarter of the nineteenth century, mergers among banks, leading to banks with wide geographical diversification and diversification by type of customer, were well advanced.[7] Branched banks are more robust, at any rate to localized shocks, than unit banks; note that of the 9036 banks that failed in the U.S. during the Great Depression, only 10 were branched (Benston, 1990). (This may of course reflect the effect not just of branching but also of other factors such as scale.)

The British experience thus provides somewhat contaminated evidence of the success of lender of last resort action. A brief glance at some developments in France and in Italy, however, provides supporting evidence free of such contamination.

The Banque de France can trace its origins to a bank founded in 1800 by a group of Parisian banks. Early in its history it was willing to discount commercial paper very freely in the face of liquidity crises. It did so in 1810, 1818, and 1826. But on other occasions it did not, and here the demonstration of the importance of LOLR is clear. In 1848 it allowed the failure of all provincial banks of issue. This allowed the Banque de France to turn them into branches of itself – the origin of the Banque de France's present day extensive branch network. Gille (1970) claims it deliberately allowed the failures so as to eliminate rival note-issuing banks. Cameron (1961) says that the failure to act in 1868, with the consequent failure of Credit Mobilier, and in 1882 when Union-Generale failed was also deliberate, again with the aim of eliminating potential note-issuing competitors. That interpretation is disputed (Levy-Leboyer, 1976).[8] Be that as it may, the French experience supports the view that LOLR action contains a crisis, while absence of such action allows a localized panic to turn into a widespread banking crisis.

Italy confirms that lesson. The Kingdom of Italy was established in 1861, a result of the steady expansion of Kingdom of Sardinia. After the new State was founded, the currency was unified, but there remained several banks of issue. In the 1880s there was a series of crises.[9] Banks had rapidly expanded their loans to industry and to real estate speculation. Following a rapid expansion in construction, prices collapsed and numerous real-estate companies and banks failed. The banks of issue, themselves involved in this situation, were pressed by government to rescue other banks and in consequence got into severe problems. In 1893 the Banca d'Italia was founded, and the number of banks of issue was reduced from six to three. By 1907 the

Banca d'Italia had adopted the Bagehot principle of lending freely in a crisis (it referred to Bagehot in its 1907 Report and Accounts), and in 1910 acted in accordance with his principles. In its report of that year, the Bank of Italy wrote:

> At that particular time, what was important to the Italian business community was not so much to obtain funds at reasonable conditions, but to know that credit was still available for good risk transactions. And the Bank did not fail to provide this type of credit (p. 12).

In contrast to the 1880s – despite there still being a system of many banks, each with at most a few branches – there was no crisis in the sense of a run on the banking system. Problems were contained by LOLR action. It thus seems reasonable to conclude that such action is sufficient to prevent localized panic leading to general crisis.

This conclusion, based on nineteenth and early twentieth century episodes, was reemphasized recently, first in Argentina and more recently still in East Asia. Argentina had adopted what was in all essential features a currency board, fixing the peso against the U.S. dollar, in April 1991. Inflation fell, fiscal discipline was restored, and private capital started to flow in. But there had been no reforms to the banking system. It was undercapitalized, and, while the central bank had regulatory powers, because of the currency board arrangement it could not act as lender of last resort. The banking system was thus both fragile and without access to central bank liquidity provision in a panic.

Seeing the fall of the Mexican's peso (in 1995), depositors at Argentinian banks had the similarities between Mexico's and Argentina's circumstances thrust before them. They withdrew pesos and converted them to U.S. dollars. Inevitably, in the absence of a lender of last resort, there was a sharp monetary contraction. The GDP fell by over 5% in 1995, and unemployment rose from 10% to 17%.

The still more recent Southeast Asian experience is similar. In the wake of the collapse of the Thai baht, attention turned to Indonesia, Malaysia, and the Philippines. Banks had been lending extensively in domestic currency while borrowing in foreign currency. When depositors started to withdraw their funds, no liquidity could be provided by the central bank. Again, consequent upon lack of lender of last resort action, severe problems followed.

3. Responsibility for financial markets?

3.1. Crisis prevention?

It was implicit in the preceding discussion that a crisis that called for LOLR action was exclusively a banking system problem. The failure of any other type of firm, however large, might well prove disruptive, but unless it spread to the banking system and thus threatened the money supply, no LOLR action was called for. Nor did problems in financial markets call for such action. An asset price collapse, whether or not it followed a 'bubble' and whatever kind of assets were involved, called for LOLR action only if the banking system were threatened.

This latter view is implied in the title of McKay's 1854 classic, *Extraordinary Popular Delusions and the Madness of Crowds*; bubbles were 'manias,' worthy of study but requiring no policy action. Later, Palgrave (1894) emphasized the distinction between business failures in general and banking crises in particular: 'Commercial crises may take place without any reference to the circulating medium as has been exemplified in Hamburg and elsewhere.'

In more recent years, this view of the kind of problem requiring LOLR action has been criticized as too narrow. The first version of this criticism was decisively rejected by Anna Schwartz in 1986:

> A widely held belief in the United States and the world financial community is that the default of major debtors – whether companies or municipalities or sovereign countries – could lead to bank failures that would precipitate a financial crisis. The remedy proposed by those propagating this view is that major debtors therefore must be rescued from the threat of bankruptcy to avert the projected dire consequences for banks and for the stability of the financial system. I shall argue that (a) the debtor whose affairs have been mismanaged should be liquidated or reorganised under new management; (b) default by major debtors need not result in bank failures; (c) if defaults do result in bank failures, so long as the security of the private sector's deposits is assured, no financial crisis will ensue.
>
> (Schwartz, 1986, p. 11)

Her argument was in three parts. First there is a brief comparative history of crises in England and of episodes when they did not occur in England but did in the United States, and an explanation for the contrast in the records. This comparison is followed by an examination of the frequently expressed views of Charles Kindleberger (e.g., 1978) that 'manias' and crises are inextricable. And third, she argues that the belief that 'financial distress' triggers financial crises is based on a misunderstanding of history.

The individual episodes she considers took place in 1866, 1873, 1890, 1907, 1914 and 1931. The events of 1866 have already been discussed. What of the others? In 1873 there were, consequent upon a sharp fall in stock prices in Vienna, a series of such declines across Europe. But Britain experienced only a series of increases in Bank rate over four weeks, followed by their reversal over the subsequent ten weeks. In contrast, the U.S. experienced a 'real' crisis: 'By 22 October, the currency was virtually unobtainable at par' (Schwartz, 1986, p. 4). In 1890 there were stock price falls in the U.S., and in London the failure of Barings, but no financial crisis occurred in either country. In 1907 there were serious problems in New York; there was a restriction of payments by banks, and currency went to a premium over deposits. But in London there was no panic, but only three increases in bank rate, intended and sufficient to restore gold stocks after shipments to New York. The year 1914 saw panic in both countries, and a severe liquidity squeeze with the outbreak of war, but crisis in neither. And finally, 1931: Britain's abandoning of gold is often said to have been a crisis, but internally there was no crisis; indeed, all the consequences were benign. Schumpeter's description is characteristically vivid:

> In England there was neither panic nor – precisely owing to the way in which the thing had been done or, if the reader prefer, had come about – loss of 'confidence' but rather a sigh of relief.

> (1939, p. 956)

Why the contrasts between these various episodes? Schwartz explains as follows:

> The reasons may now be summarised, accounting for financial crises that did or did not occur in the past. In both cases the setting is one in which the financial distress of certain firms became known to market participants, raising alarm as creditors became concerned about the value of their claims not only on those firms but also firms previously in sound condition. Banks that were creditors of the firms in distress became targets of suspicion by the depositors. *When monetary authorities failed to demonstrate readiness at the beginning of such a disturbance to meet all demands of sound debtors for loans and of depositors for cash, a financial crisis occurred. A financial crisis per contra could be averted by timely predictable signals to market participants of institutional readiness to make available an augmented supply of funds* [emphasis added]. The sources of the funds supplied might have been inflows from abroad – attracted by higher domestic than foreign interest rates – or emergency issues of domestic currency. The readiness was all. Knowledge of the availability of the supply was sufficient to allay alarm, so that the funds were never drawn on.

> (Schwartz, 1986, p. 21)

Does this account fit 1931? Here, surely, a crash did produce a crisis and a recession. Certainly one followed the other. The 'Great Crash' (Galbraith, 1955) of 1929 preceded the 'Great Contraction' (Friedman and Schwartz, 1963).

Whether there was an inescapable causal connection is, however, not so clear. Stock prices (as measured by the S&P90) reached their peak of 254 on September 7, 1929. There were then four weeks of uneventful decline to 228 on October 4, after which the index climbed to 245 on October 10. Decline turned into panic on October 23. On October 24, the index fell to 162, and about 16.5 mn shares were traded – compared to a September daily average of just over 4 mn. (After a brief recovery, the index continued down, reaching its low in 1931.) It is hard to claim that the crash *caused* the downturn, for a cyclical peak occurred in August, before the peak of the market and well before the dramatic market fall. Can the crash be blamed for the *severity* of the 1930s Depression? Some authors have claimed that it did, at the least, contribute to that severity, changing the atmosphere to gloom and making consumers and business cautious and reluctant to spend[10] (Hansen, 1932; Schumpeter, 1939; Gordon, 1952; Romer, 1990).

Consistent with this claim, there was a decline in velocity (of M2). The velocity fall (of 13%, in 1929–1930) was, however, in size only second among the seven velocity falls between 1907–1908 and 1929–1930. The fall in 1913–1914 was of the same size, and that of 1920–1921 was 15%. A 13% fall in velocity, unless offset by a sustained monetary expansion, is bound to be associated with a fall in nominal income. There was no sustained monetary expansion, and by October 1930 industrial production had fallen 26%, prices 14%, and personal income 16% from the cyclical peak in Summer 1929.

This decline cannot be ascribed solely to the crash and its effect on velocity. The money stock also fell, by just over 2½% from the August 1929 cyclical peak to October 1930. This fall is larger than in all but four previous contractions, and these four were also severe contractions. Nevertheless, the large velocity fall, together with the speed of slowdown increasing with the crash, do suggest that the crash may well have contributed to the severity of the 1929–1930 recession.[11]

But 1929–1930 was not the 'Great Contraction.' There were a further three years of decline, until by 1933 money income had fallen by 53% and real income by 36% from the 1929 peak. The pace of bank failures accelerated sharply from November 1930, when Caldwell and Company of Nashville failed. This was the largest investment banking firm in the South. That failure undoubtedly affected confidence, and bank failures became widespread in agricultural areas. The pace of failures accelerated yet again in December, and on December 11 the Bank of the United States failed. This New York bank was the largest (by value of deposits) ever to fail up to that time in the United States. There followed the first of a series of liquidity crises that did not end until March 1933.

The initial crisis was short lived. Bank deposits rose from January to March 1931, and in 1931 there were some signs that the downturn in activity was approaching an end. Industrial production rose from January to April, and the rate of decline of factory employment slowed sharply. But a second banking crisis broke in March. The public converted deposits to currency, and banks sold assets to increase their liquidity. This action put downward pressure on the money stock, which was only partly offset by inflows from abroad. The Federal Reserve did not act to offset the squeeze. There was a resumption of drain abroad when Britain's leaving the gold standard in September 1931 caused fears that the U.S. would do likewise. Domestic depositors started to withdraw currency from the banks. The Federal Reserve raised its discount rate sharply. While ending the external drain, this intensified domestic difficulties, for the Federal Reserve had raised the rate – half of Bagehot's prescription – but it neglected the other half and did not lend freely. Its net holdings of U.S. government securities actually fell.

A large-scale bond purchase program was eventually started in April 1932, but yet again, relief proved temporary. In reaction to a further wave of bank failures and fears of a foreign drain – there were rumors (subsequently justified) that the incoming administration would devalue – the Federal Reserve acted as it had in September 1931. It raised its discount rate but took no action to offset the effects of either the external or internal drains from the banks. President Roosevelt closed all banks and suspended gold redemption shipments abroad on March 6, 1933. The banks did not reopen until Congress authorized emergency issues of Federal Reserve Notes, and banks then gradually reopened over March 13, 14, and 15.

Why were there these successive waves of bank failures? Two explanations have been advanced – banking practices of previous years, with banks getting into securities dealing through affiliates; and the behavior of the Fed.[12]

What is the evidence? White (1986) found that the presence of securities affiliates reduced the risk of bank failure, that affiliates dampened rather than increased fluctuations in combined bank-affiliate earnings, and that neither capitalization nor liquidity was adversely affected by the presence of an affiliate. Peach (1941) examined the behavior of affiliates. He found the following: while some gave misleading information on high-risk securities, this was not common; affiliates were used for the personal profit of bank directors, but on a scale trivial in comparison to the economy; and occasionally, a parent bank was drawn into losses on a security floated by an affiliate, but also on a scale sufficient to threaten only a few institutions. Benston (1990) largely sustained these conclusions; and Kroszner and Rajan (1994) concluded that, in general, banks underwrote high-quality securities. Losses on government bonds greatly exceeded losses through securities affiliates. Interest rate mismatching may have contributed to the problems, but the scale of the bond price collapse was such that the primary responsibility must rest with the Fed. There was a substantial and unrelieved pressure on bank liquidity, resulting from the conversion of deposits to cash and subsequent (and resulting) forced sales of bonds at deep discount, which the Federal Reserve did not relieve.[13]

The Federal Reserve had failed to act adequately as lender of last resort. Rather it acted exactly as the Bank of England had in 1866: it lent '. . . hesitantly, reluctantly, and with misgiving.' That 1866 behavior incurred the following criticism from Bagehot: '. . . to make large advances in this faltering way is to incur the evil of making them without obtaining the advantage . . . [that] is the worst of all policies . . .'

It was that 'worst of all policies' that caused the worst of all depressions in the United States, not the stock market crash in itself.

To summarize this section of the discussion, then, the argument that the central bank needs to stabilize asset markets so as to prevent recession is inconsistent with the facts.[14] Should asset price collapses affect the banking system, *then* LOLR action may prove necessary.

At this point an objection may be raised that the world has changed since these above-discussed episodes. There is no longer a clear boundary between banks and other types of financial institution.[15] This point is undeniable, but it in no way weakens the above conclusion. The reason is as follows. Concern in the past was with the banking system not for its own sake but because a banking system collapse inevitably produced a severe monetary contraction, and such a contraction produced in turn a sharp and possibly prolonged contraction in economic activity. Accordingly, then, LOLR action should be taken when an asset price collapse threatens the stock of whichever measure of money is most closely associated with economic activity, regardless of the kinds of institutions whose liabilities predominantly make up that measure of money. This was *always* the objective of classic LOLR action. In the past, this objective was stated as 'stabilizing the banking system' because it was the banking system whose liabilities were money; but it was always recognized that it was the money, not the system, that mattered.[16]

That is not, however, the end of the argument that central banks need be concerned with asset prices. Two other strands of argument remain.

3.2. A measure of prices?

Many central banks currently target inflation – either explicitly or implicitly, sometimes as part of a range of objectives, and sometimes as a sole objective. Whatever the nature of the target, a particular proposal about the nature of the price index used would, although not prompted by LOLR concerns, lead to central banks stabilizing asset prices, just as those (such as Kindleberger, 1978) who argue for stabilization on LOLR grounds would wish. The proposal is that asset prices should figure in the price index targeted for inflation control purposes.

Of course, not all asset prices are proposed for this role; many financial assets (bank loans, for example) do not have observable prices. The proposal is that the prices of *traded* assets be included. What is the argument? The following draws on Alchian and Klein (1973); Goodhart (1999a), the most recent proponent of this position, essentially relies on the same basic arguments.

Current utility depends on current consumption (including the consumption of services currently yielded by assets.) Thus movements in an index (such as the UK's RPI and RPIX, the targeted inflation measure, or the USA's CPI), which measures changes in the money cost of a bundle of goods and services used for current consumption, measure changes in the money cost of achieving a particular level of utility.

But, the argument runs, lifetime utility depends on *future* as well as on current consumption. Hence movements in price indices reflecting current consumption mismeasure changes in the money cost of a given level of lifetime utility unless the price of current relative to future consumption does not change. Hence, Alchian and Klein (1973) argue, a 'correct' measure of inflation should include asset prices – for these show the current money prices of claims on future consumption.

If we were to argue that the task of monetary policy was to stabilize or otherwise control the money price of *current* consumption, then the Alchian and Klein argument could simply be ignored. This approach, however, would be somewhat unsatisfactory, for it is indisputable that lifetime utility depends on lifetime consumption, that current utility is seldom a good proxy for average utility over a lifetime, and that inflation control is not an end in itself but a means of increasing utility. Hence measuring inflation by a measure little related to utility would seem to lack point.

But there is another argument. Goods now cannot be directly exchanged for goods later; there is no such market (at least of any significance). But goods can be exchanged *indirectly*. Cash can be exchanged for bonds, which in due course secure cash later. Hence the value of goods now relative to goods later can be stabilized if two conditions are satisfied: first, if the price of goods now in terms of money now is stable across time periods; and second, if the return on exchanging money now for money later through the bond market is constant.

Satisfying the first condition is equivalent to stabilizing a 'normal' consumer price index (such as the RPI or the CPI). Doing that would also eliminate the inflation expectations component for the nominal bond yield. This step would not leave the nominal yield constant, but it would eliminate all sources of disturbance that the *monetary authorities* could eliminate. The forces of productivity and thrift could still interact to produce a changed real rate, but monetary policy can do nothing systematic about that. Further, as a matter of history, eliminating the inflation expectations component would eliminate the most variable component, and often by far the biggest component, of nominal bond yields (see Schwartz, 1989; Friedman and Schwartz, 1982).

Accordingly, then, one must conclude on this issue as follows: As good an approximation as monetary policy can deliver to stabilizing the money cost of a given lifetime level of utility is produced by stabilizing the money cost of a level of current utility. Once that is done, any attempt to go further and stabilize asset markets on these grounds is at best useless and can well be harmful. The policy is useless if asset prices have moved as a result of a bubble; if they are detached from 'fundamentals,' then it is difficult to see what monetary policy, which affects one of the fundamentals, can do. Alternatively if asset prices have changed because of a

change in the desire to save or the desire to invest, any attempt to interfere by changing monetary policy would impede the efficient intertemporal
allocation of resources.

Thus, it is wrong to assign responsibility for asset market stabilization to
the monetary authorities on the grounds that asset prices should be in the
price index for the stability of which they are responsible.[17]

3.3. A lead indicator?

A third reason for a central bank being concerned with asset prices is that
these prices may give information about future inflation. If this were the case,
then the central bank might well in effect stabilize asset markets by tightening
policy when they rose and easing when they fell. This approach would, of
course, in one way be quite different from traditional LOLR action: such
action is aimed at keeping monetary conditions unchanged, whereas what is
now being discussed uses asset markets as an indicator of when to change
monetary conditions. That difference aside, is there a case on inflation control
grounds for central banks to respond to asset price movements?

It is possible to extract information about inflation expectations from bond
markets. Can anything be done with this information? The difficulty is with
interpreting it. Suppose expectations are in line with the policymaker's target.
What does that mean – that policy is appropriate, that the policymaker's
credibility is high, or that both policymakers and markets are wrong? Similar
problems arise if expectations are 'off target': is the market wrong, or policy?
The signals are not unambiguous.

The exchange rate presents similar problems. If the rate is moving, what
does that tell us? Among the range of possibilities are real changes, changes
in monetary policy abroad, changes in monetary policy at home, or, of
course, expectations about any or all of these three. Interpretation is not easy,
and mistakes are readily made, because the 'noise to signal' ratio is high. An
example from recent British economic history confirms this. When the first
Thatcher government came to office in 1979, it was determined to reduce
inflation. Policy was for a time guided by monetary targets, but these became
misleading, in part at least because of changes in the U.K. banking system.
Various other means of guiding policy were tried, including for a time
(March 1987 to September 1990) 'shadowing the Deutschemark' – that is to
say, keeping the exchange rate stable against the DM without committing
publicity to doing so. The result was that continual attempts by sterling to
appreciate led to an excessive easing of policy, and an acceleration of inflation from 3.6% pa in March 1987 to 10.9% pa in September 1990 (12 month
on 12 month% changes).

What, finally, of equity (common stock) markets? As with bond markets,
they can move for real as well as for nominal reasons. Accordingly, one would
not expect them to be a good and reliable predictor. And so, indeed, the
evidence confirms.

The relationship between U.K. stock market prices (as measured by the *Financial Times Actuaries 500* index) and the retail price index was investigated using Granger causality tests. On the basis of monthly data for the period 1952 to 1998, monthly stock returns were found strongly to Granger-cause monthly retail price inflation. There was also little evidence of feedback, particularly when a small but pervasive seasonal component in retail prices was removed by seasonal differencing.[18]

When subperiods of the data were investigated, however, a pattern of varying causality was discovered. For subperiods beginning in 1952 and ending in 1969 or 1972, causality running from retail price inflation to stock returns was found, while for subperiods beginning in the early 1970s and ending in 1998, the direction was reversed and the full-sample result of stock returns causing inflation reestablished itself. However, further investigations revealed a much greater variability in causal direction, with subperiods beginning in 1979 or 1980 showing that stock returns and inflation were independent of each other. Indeed, if attention is focused solely on data from the 1970s, then only when the early years are included is there strong evidence of a causal link running from stock returns to inflation. Otherwise, there is little evidence against the two being independent of each other![19]

Accordingly, one could not justify central bank action to stabilize asset markets on the grounds that such action would help stabilize inflation.[20]

To conclude on asset prices, none of the arguments for central bank action to stabilize them – whether they be LOLR arguments or any other considered here – stands up.

4. Too big to fail?

Can any bank be too big or too important to fail? Certainly in the nineteenth century, the answer would have been no, as is well illustrated by the failure of Overend and Gurney. That episode has already been described, along with how the consequences of that bank's failure were contained by classic LOLR action. At this point it is necessary only to note again the vast (relative) size of that bank – ten times bigger than the next biggest. That historical episode does not help the 'too big to fail' doctrine.

What of Barings? Perhaps not too big to fail, but too important? Here, too, however, the 'too big to fail' doctrine does not get support. For before assistance was organized for Barings, efforts were made to ensure that the bank was solvent and that its crisis was purely liquidity. This was established by a rapid inspection of Barings' books. So an *insolvent* bank was not assisted. Now, since Barings was not insolvent, why could it not get assistance in the market? The answer to this is in two parts. Its assets were not sufficiently liquid to be discountable; and its shortage too great for any one bank to help by a nonsecured loan. For the latter reason, a 'consortium' or 'lifeboat' was organized. It is undeniable that the Bank of England acted as crisis manager. But that role was different from the classic LOLR. Not only was it different: while *only* the central bank can act as a classic LOLR, *any* bank of appropriate standing can act as a crisis manager. This issue is discussed further below.

Setting out fully why the Bank of England got involved in helping Barings would involve too long a digression. But the following points should be noted. Even then, the Bank, by being the bankers' bank, was seen as a custodian of the system. One of the Bank's responsibilities was keeping Britain on gold, and there were fears that the failure of Barings would trigger a foreign drain of gold. And finally, it should not be forgotten that the Bank was then still privately owned, had a commercial business, and was concerned that a major failure in London would damage this business.

In summary, history provides no support for 'too big to fail.'

A second argument for bailing out insolvent banks is that in a time of crisis it is hard, perhaps impossible, to tell an illiquid from an insolvent bank. Accordingly, a central bank should simply decide whether or not it wishes to lend to a bank, and not concern itself with the bank's solvency. Charles Goodhart (1999b) sets out two arguments that lead to the above conclusion. First, Bagehot's (1873) advice was that in a crisis, 'advances should be made on all good banking securities and as largely as the public ask for them' (p. 70).

This advice, Goodhart continued, was '. . . to distinguish, in part, between those loans on which the central bank might expect, with some considerable probability to make a loss (bad bills and collateral) and those on which little, or no, loss should eventuate' (1999b, p. 351). That interpretation is surely right. But Bagehot's advice also served another purpose. Showing that there is nothing new in the insolvency/illiquidity argument, one finds it tackled with his characteristic lucidity by Ralph Hawtrey (1932):

> In the evolution of the Bank of England as the lender of last resort, we have seen how at the beginning it was inclined to ration credit by refusing all applications in excess of a quota, but later on its restriction took the form of limiting the kind of security it would take. It is not ordinarily possible to examine in detail the entire assets of an applicant for a loan. Demonstration of solvency therefore cannot be made an express condition of the loan, at any rate at a time when the need for cash has become urgent. But the furnishing of security makes scrutiny of the general solvency of the borrower unnecessary. The secured debt being covered by assets more than equivalent to it, there is less need to enquire whether the remainder of the borrower's assets will be sufficient to cover the remainder of his debts (pp. 126–127).

Hawtrey goes on to elaborate how the type of security accepted should be broadened in a crisis, and, while doing so, again implies that the purpose of taking security is to make irrelevant the solvency of the institution that seeks to borrow:

> The right course is rather to accept any security representing a sufficient amount of wealth to cover the loan with adequate margin, without being too particular in defining the form of the security or even in insisting on its immediate marketability (p. 130).

In her 1992 paper, 'The Misuse of the Fed's Discount Window,' Anna Schwartz adds her opposition to the claim that individual, possibly insolvent, banks should be assisted by the central bank. She deploys two arguments; first, that there is a substantial cost to the taxpayer; and second, an essential complement to the first, that such support is unnecessary.

The cost to the taxpayer arises because Federal Reserve lending to individual institutions (rather than 'to the market' – a phrase whose interpretation is considered below) has delayed the closure of insolvent institutions. This delay '. . . encourages risk taking and invites moral hazard problems' (Schwartz, 1992, p. 66). Now, that price could be acceptable were it necessary to prevent banking system collapses. But, as Schwartz goes on to argue, it is not necessary. Her argument is based on both a specific example and a general observation. The example is the failure of Continental Illinois in 1984. Had that bank been closed promptly. 'The market would have known that the claimants on Continental were not in jeopardy' (p. 66). There might have been liquidity problems, but these could have been solved by the generalized supply of liquidity.

To quote Schwartz again,

> . . . contagion need not arise if open market purchases are made adequate both to reassure the market and to prevent a collapse in the quantity of money. Examples are the Fed's provision of liquidity to cushion the economy from the effects of the 1987 stock market crash and the collapse of Drexel Burnham.
>
> (1992, p. 66)[21]

It thus would seem to follow that the argument Goodhart (1999b) develops is slightly off the point.

> . . . an individual bank will only go to a central bank for direct bilateral LOLR assistance when it *cannot* meet its liquidity needs on the wholesale interbank money markets. Almost by definition this must be because it is running out of good security for collateralised loans *and* other (bank) lenders will not lend to it on an unsecured basis in the quantities required (at acceptable rates). Again almost by definition this latter must be because there is some question about its ultimate solvency (p. 350).

It may well be, as this statement suggests, that direct lending would probably be to an insolvent bank; but that likelihood does not address the argument that bailouts are in general unnecessary so long as there is ample general provision of liquidity.[22,23]

Can any case for bailouts be constructed? One case immediately has to be conceded. If an entire banking system were to become insolvent, then allowing it to fail would be worse than the alternative. The consequence of such mass failure would be the Great Depression writ large. Of course, the terms on which the banking system is helped should be such as to provide the minimum possible incentive to future imprudence. Indeed, it would be desirable to look for willing, possibly overseas, buyers to take over the constituents of the system. But this process could take too long.

A case for bailing out an individual bank, a part (albeit a large one) of a country's system, has been constructed in an imaginative paper by Goodhart and Huang (1999). Since that paper is one of the few to face this issue directly, an examination of it is required.

But it is useful first to think a little more about the 'too big to fail' (hereafter TBtoF) doctrine. The term was coined by the U.S. Comptroller of the Currency to describe the 11 largest banks in the U.S. after the Continental Illinois failure of 1984 (Soussa, 1999). The rationale for the doctrine is that some banks are so large relative to the rest of the system that a major shock to the financial system is caused by their failure. This rationale would seem to leave unspecified what else is going on at the time; for example, is the central bank supplying abundant liquidity? Setting that issue aside, what are the channels through which an individual bank's failure may be disruptive? Four have been suggested. First, other banks may be affected through their bilateral exposures. Second, financial markets may be disrupted if the failing institution is significant in a particular market. Third, the 'private information' a bank has about its borrowers may be destroyed, thus reducing the efficiency of financial intermediation. And fourth, the failure may cause uncertainty about the soundness of other, quite unrelated, banks and lead to runs on them.

These are considered in turn.

Interbank exposures are undeniable. But these are already being limited (at a cost) by increasing use of real-time gross settlement, a procedure that while not reducing risk, does transfer some of it from the banking system. Further, banks are exposed to large *nonbank firms*. Why are such firms not TBtoF? Presumably because it is accepted that such risks are regarded as ones that banks should monitor and control. Interbank exposures may be more variable and larger, but there is little evidence on these.

What of disruption to financial markets? This is an old argument in a new guise. Indeed, it is close to what happened in the U.S. in 1931. Banks scrambled for liquidity, the Fed did not supply liquidity on security, and the Great Depression followed. Here the conclusion is clear. The risk of such disruption is real, and classic LOLR can prevent it. There is no need for TbtoF. (Of course, if it is costless, that does not matter; but evidence is presented below to suggest that it does have costs.)

Next we come to the drying up of credit channels. This outcome too, would certainly be important if in fact it actually happened. But, as Benston (e.g.,

1990) has documented, certainly in the United States a failing bank does not just disappear. In most cases, it is taken over and run by new management with new shareholders or at least with new and additional capital; so the 'private information' does not vanish.[24] The same holds true in the U.K.

What, finally, of doubts about the stability of other banks? According to the record, bank runs on unconnected sound banks are rare (Kaufmann, 1991).[25] This is not, of course, to say that such bank runs never happen. Goodhart and Huang (1999) cite the example of the so-called 'Asian banks' in the U.K. after the collapse of BCCI. After the collapse, there were withdrawals from these banks, which were largely run by Asians and which took deposits from and served their local Asian communities. These banks were (essentially unjustly) tainted by BCCI. They could not get liquidity from the wholesale markets because their names were not known as regular borrowers and lenders in good times. The Bank of England decided to give liquidity support. That was, in a sense, the central bank dealing with a case of market failure. The market did not provide liquidity because it had not been given the information that would justify such provision. The Bank, relying on supervisory information, did act. That was not generalized LOLR action, but it *was* rational exploitation of an informational advantage. It was not the propping up of an insolvent group.[26]

Finally, can the propping up of a large bank be justified? Here we come to Goodhart and Huang (1999). As they observe, '. . . LOLR has been primarily driven by macro, rather than micro, concerns' (p. 9). The macro concern they identify is that bank failures create 'extra uncertainty' about the desired 'level of deposits in the system' (p. 10).[27] The reason is that in the wake of the failure of a bank, particularly a major one, demands for liquidity by both the bank and nonbank private sectors became unpredictable, or at any rate more unpredictable than in more stable times. This point is indisputable.

Goodhart and Huang (1999) then test the importance of this observation in practice and find that, in three of the five countries they examine, H/M (the ratio of monetary base to broad money) became much more unpredictable after a panic. These countries were the U.S.A (twice, 1872–1914 and 1921–1940), Australia (1861–1913), and Mexico, (1980–1987). The two countries that did not yield their expected result were Japan and South Korea (1988–1998); but these were countries with close to 100% deposit insurance (thus reinforcing the point made in footnote 27).

Now, the evidence of Goodhart and Huang (1999) is interesting about the significance of deposit insurance. But, as Friedman and Schwartz (1963) demonstrated, what matters is not H/M, but M/Y (the ratio of a broader aggregate to income). It is the latter that affects the economy. The criticism of the Fed in the Great Depression was not that it let the monetary base fall but that it did not inject enough monetary base to stabilize a broader aggregate. Central banks in the past have focused on a broad aggregate and stabilized the economy in the face of the failure of a large bank. Consider (yet again!)

the failure of Overend and Gurney. In the wake of that failure, the Bank of England sought suspension of the Bank Charter Act. Why? Under the Gold Standard, the focus of policy was implicitly M/Y. When there was a flight to cash from deposits, the constraints of the Gold Standard had to be relaxed to allow the focus on M/Y to continue. The behaviour of H/M is interesting, but it is M/Y that matters for the present discussion.

When that point is borne in mind, the problems caused by the bank failures noted by Goodhart and Huang are seen in a different light. The examples they cite are the Great Depression in the U.S., the inflation that in some countries followed the post-1987 cash injection of liquidity, and the growth of high-powered money in Japan having no effect on that economy's recession. The first point has been discussed. As to the second, inflation did not follow everywhere, but only in those countries (such as the U.K.) that allowed M/Y to stay up for some time. There were no problems in countries (such as the U.S.) where the liquidity was withdrawn.[28] And the third? Banks in Japan were short of capital. However much liquidity they had, they could not lend and thus expand broad measures of money. (See Hoggarth and Thomas, 1999, for an examination of this episode and a discussion of why the Japanese banks did not raise additional capital.)

Accordingly, one is driven to conclude that TBtoF has to rest on one support only – the danger posed by interbank connections. These are of course, regime dependent. In other words, TBtoF by its very existence makes the need for TBtoF more likely. The defence that it is costless is not available; Soussa (1999) shows that it is seen by the markets and provides a subsidy to the cost of capital for larger banks.

On balance, it has to be concluded that justification for unsecured lending to individual institutions rather than secured lending 'to the market' (the meaning of which is described below) can rest only on the informational superiority of the central bank over the market. That superiority is at best transitory. The informational advantage from supervisory information decays quickly, and appears to be gone within three to six months of the last supervisory visit (Soussa, 1999).

4.1. What does 'fail' mean?

The meaning of *fail* is usually taken to be self-evident. It is not. It can mean overnight collapse; or, at the other extreme, it can mean failure to grow with the rest of the industry. Overnight collapse in the absence of procedures for prompt and orderly liquidation is troublesome in any industry. But there is no reason for it to happen. Indeed, steps have been taken in the U.S. to ensure prompt closure before calls on the deposit insurance fund become substantial (Benston et al., 1986). If procedures are in place for orderly liquidation and prompt valuation of assets, then liquidity provision by the Central Bank (classic LOLR) would be sufficient to smooth over market disturbances. Further, large banks do not usually 'fail' without warning. Rather they decline gradually, and are taken over by some other banks. Continental Illinois was the exception, and even then only to the second part of the story. The bank had been in decline, and other banks had been reducing their exposure to it for at least two years before closure.[29]

4.2. Lend to the market?

An argument now sometimes heard is that it is impossible nowadays to 'lend to the market' as a last resort lender, and that such lending will inevitably be to individual institutions (e.g., Goodhart, 1999b). Hence some insolvent institutions inevitably end up being supported. It is far from clear who would do such lending and bear such losses. No central bank could bear such loss – central banks are simply too small. They could only engage in such activities as agents of the government.

But is it impossible to 'lend to the market'? Examination of the origin of the phrase is useful both in clarification of what it means and in answering that question. *The market* is not a disembodied entity. When in the nineteenth century the Bank of England lent *to the market*, it was lending to the discount houses, which were discounting at the Bank bills that they had previously discounted for their customers. The Bank of England did not know from which bank or banks the demand was originating. It knew only that the demand was of such a scale that the discount houses required assistance to meet it. The Bank simply provided cash on security. So the phrase *lend to the market*, then, means to lend to any institution that offers acceptable security.[30]

Interpreted thus, it is obvious that there is a modern counterpart to the old system. This is (in the U.K.) supplying funds via the gilt repo market. That is to say, by engaging in sale and repurchase agreements for government stock (gilts, in U.K. terminology) with financial institutions, the Bank would be providing cash on security, just as it did in the nineteenth century. The procedure would to the superficial observer be different, but the essence of the transaction would be the same. There are analogous markets in most other countries. Accordingly, the claim that central banks cannot 'lend to the market,' when last resort lending, is mistaken.[31]

5. Expansion of meaning?

Last in this examination of proposed changes to the classic LOLR role come changes to the meaning of *LOLR*. A complete collection of these changes – or extensions – to the term is to be found in Fischer (1999) Fischer starts by distinguishing between *crisis lender* and *crisis manager*.

The former is what has been described earlier as the classic LOLR.

What is a *crisis manager*? It is '. . . the institution that takes upon itself the responsibility for dealing with a crisis or potential crisis whether or not it itself lends for that purpose' (Fischer, 1999, p. 87). That two-part definition is not helpful. A crisis manager need not lend at all: JP Morgan (whom Fischer cites) sometimes acted thus. A good account can be found in Chernow (1990). Sometimes a crisis manager does lend, but this action need not be with the aim of providing liquidity. A good example here is the Bank of England in the Barings crisis. There was no panic run requiring an injection of liquidity. But the Bank did contribute to the supply of capital to Barings. So a crisis manager can manage without lending; that is not LOLR. Or it can supply capital; well or ill judged, that too is not LOLR. Both acts can be done by the central bank or by some other institution. But classic LOLR, in the sense we have traced the term from Francis Baring, is the provision of liquidity, and that can only be done by the central bank.

Both functions are useful, albeit in different circumstances, but it is hard to see what is gained by calling them the same thing. An analogous practice might be to use the phrase *put on a band-aid* to mean either *put on a band-aid* or *insert some stitches in the wound*. It is hard to imagine such a usage being recommended. Fischer (1999) also observes that '... taxpayer or deposit insurance money was used in over half the 120 banking rescue packages' (p. 91) studied by Goodhart and Schoenmaker (1993). The central bank may well have organized that activity, but it is quite different from classic LOLR and has to be justified in entirely different terms. Using the same name for the activity obscures the necessity for different justifying arguments.

Fischer (1999) also considers the case for an international LOLR. This, he suggests, is necessary to facilitate the smooth functioning of the international capital market. There is, he says, such a need:

> ... it arises both because international capital flows are not only extremely volatile but also contagious, exhibiting the classic signs of financial panics, and because an international lender of last resort can help mitigate the effects of this instability, and perhaps the instability itself (p. 100).

Now in the classic sense, neither the IMF nor any other international body can fulfill that role; what body except a nation's central bank can print a nation's currency? But Fischer actually does not mean classic LOLR; he means crisis manager. This manager can give advice, or it can (if it is the IMF) lend from a pool of reserves provided by IMF members. The latter would be closely parallel to the Bank of England's activities in the Barings crisis (of 1890), an event where it is generally acknowledged that the Bank did *not* act as LOLR.

In conclusion, then, the role of crisis manager is an important one. Sometimes it has been taken in the past by a central bank, and sometimes by some other body. That last observation reveals that, important as it is, it is different from classic LOLR. It is not clear what is gained by combining the two activities under one name.

6. Conclusion

When the term *dernier resort* was introduced into English usage in 1797, it very plainly dealt with the injection of liquidity into a banking system so as to stave off a panic. After being Anglicized to *Lender of Last Resort*, the same activity was still what was meant. Analysis of various historical episodes – analysis in which the work of Anna Schwartz is prominent – shows that such activity is sufficient to stabilize the stock of money.

Despite that, there have been attempts in recent years to make the central bank responsible for financial market stability, not just for money stock stability. Similarly, it has been argued that the central bank should from time to time bail out individual institutions, should they be big enough. And various activities such as crisis manager have by some authors been gathered under the term *LOLR*.

The present article has argued that all three of these attempted changes to the classic LOLR role are misconceived. The first is not necessary. The second can generally not be carried out by a central bank, and it is hard in any case to find empirical justification for it, apart from the occasional special case when advantage is being taken of supervisory information confidential to the central bank. The attempts to broaden the term combine so many disparate activities under it as to make the term unhelpful.

The classic LOLR – the one analyzed and advanced by a long line of distinguished scholars from the early nineteenth century to the present day – is still important, still useful, and still sufficient to maintain monetary stability in the face of an adverse shock. Reconsideration of the role of lender of last resort shows revision of it to be unnecessary.

Acknowledgments

I am indebted to George Benston, Dick Brealey, Forrest Capie, Franklin Edwards, Donald Hodgman, George Kaufman, and Anna J. Schwartz for their most helpful comments on a draft.

Notes

1 This quotation comes from pages 19–23 of the 1967 facsimile reprint by Augustus Kelly of the 1797 edition of Francis Baring's *Observations on the Establishment of the Bank of England and on the Paper circulation of the Country*. Baring, as well as importing the term, used it in a new, metaphorical, way. In France it referred to the final court of appeal.
2 A brief and very clear account of the development of the Bank of England as a Lender of Resort can be found in chapter IV ('The Lender of Last Resort') of Ralph Hawtrey's *The Art of Central Banking* (1932). Capie (forthcoming) also deals well with the matter, and in more detail than the present article.
3 His writing in *Paper Credit* continually interwove analysis with factual examples. In an early essay on the book, Francis Horner (writing in the *Edinburgh Review*), observed that this made *Paper Credit* hard to read and to understand, and

accordingly, as well as praising the book's insights very highly, he summarized its analytical framework.

4 Suspension of the Act freed the note issue from the constraint of the Bank's gold reserves. This action has parallels in Italy later in the nineteenth century, and again in East Asia in 1998. (For a brief discussion of that 1998 episode, see Wood, 1999.) There was also a parallel in the U.S. in 1932 when the Banking Act of 1932 (the Glass-Steagall Act) broadened the collateral the Fed could hold against Federal Reserve notes. While the gold requirement was left unchanged at 40%, the act added government bonds to the list of eligible paper that could take up the remaining 60% (see Benston, 1990).

5 It is worth noting that until the tenure of Montagu Norman (Governor of the Bank from 1920 to 1944), the Governor usually served only a two-year term.

6 Even after the matter was 'well understood,' a problem remained. In a pure fiat system with a floating exchange rate, such as the U.K. and the U.S. have today, the lender of last resort has an unlimited capacity to act. But under the Gold Standard (except in a period of temporary suspension) or in the recent East Asian crisis, there was always the possibility lurking in the background that the LOLR itself might run short of reserves. This, of course, is likely to make the LOLR hesitant and perhaps prone to mistakes. Bagehot worried about the problem but did not come up with a clear-cut rule for its solution. A good discussion of the relationship between the gold standard (and, by implication, fixed exchange rates) and LOLR can be found in Eichengreen (1992).

7 See, e.g., Capie and Rodrick-Bali (1982).

8 Claims that the central bank deliberately acted so as to cause a rival to fail are made of more than one central bank. De Cecco (1975) argues that the defective action of the Bank of England in 1866 was policy, not indecision, and had been with the intention of destroying Overend and Gurney. There was certainly rivalry between Overend and Gurney and the Bank, but the general view (see, e.g., Pressnell, 1986) is that De Cecco makes too much of this.

9 In the course of these, Italy left the gold standard.

10 A good bit of any effect must have been indirect; investment in stocks and shares was much less widespread than now.

11 It is well worth observing at this point that the London market fell by about the same amount as New York in 1929, but Britain experienced no subsequent depression. (A brief account of the behavior of the British economy and stock market from 1928 to the outbreak of the Second World War can be found in Capie, Mills, and Wood, 1986.)

12 The first was the justification for the Glass-Steagall Act.

13 The problem was shortage of liquidity, a problem lender of last resort action can cure, rather than shortage of capital, which such action cannot help. The similarity of symptoms between the U.S. in the 1930s and Japan in the 1990s should therefore not disguise a fundamental difference in cause – in the U.S. a shortage of bank liquidity, and in Japan a shortage of bank capital.

14 A comparatively recent British episode reinforces this conclusion. The British stock market had its biggest fall to date in 1974. The banking system was not shaken, and the economy did not experience a recession.

15 It should be remembered that it was equally true at times in the past that the line between banks and other types of organizations was not clear. Both shops and lawyers took deposits and made loans.

16 I am indebted to Franklin Edwards and George Kaufman for the close questioning that led me to clarify this point.

17 If they were, then of course the central bank would have to change policy should, for example, there be a tax change that affected stock prices. Such action can surely not be desirable.

18 Monthly returns and inflation rates (i.e., first differences of logarithms) were used to ensure stationarity (there was no evidence of cointegration between the levels of the logarithms of the two series). Tests were also calculated with inflation seasonally differenced in order to remove a small but pervasive seasonal component in the retail price index. Granger causality tests were calculated using 12 and 24 lags of returns and inflation, and the results were robust to the choice of lag. When Granger causality was found, it was typically at very low levels of significance (0.03 or less), i.e., these were strong rejections of the null hypothesis of Granger *noncausality*.

19 The popular idea in the U.K. that there is some connection may originate from 1975 – a year of high inflation – when the stock market index rose 50% in one month, January.

20 I am indebted to my long-time coauthor, Terry Mills, for this work on the indicator properties of the U.K. stock market.

21 She could also have pointed to the fact that a quarter (by number) of the U.S. banking system failed between 1921 and 1927, but the money stock continued to grow and the U.S. economy experienced one of the greatest booms in its history.

22 One might argue that now and again an institution solvent with hindsight fails because of a mistake by the market, and that central bank action can prevent such mistakes. This does, however, imply accepting that central bank and governments are infallible. See Demsetz (1969) for an examination of this often implicit but seldom plausible assumption.

23 It is also plain that when Goodhart (1999b) describes as a 'myth' (about the lender of last resort) that 'It is generally possible to distinguish between illiquidity and insolvency,' he is misleading in two ways. First, as is made absolutely clear in Hawtrey (1932), the distinction is irrelevant for classic LOLR lending on security. Second, as the description of the problems of Pole, Thornton, Free, Down, and Scott in 1825 (given in Chapter 3 of Forster, 1956) makes clear, before providing *unsecured* funds the Bank of England took pains to ensure that the firm was solvent, as it did in the better-known case of Barings in 1890.

24 This raises the question of what *fail* means. This is discussed subsequently.

25 This also seems to be true internationally. There is, for example, no evidence of the so-called Tequila Effect having existed. (See Wood, 1999, for a review.)

26 'Background information on this episode can be found in Bank of England, *Financial Stability Review* (Autumn) and in the Banks' Annual Reports for 1991–1992 and 1992–1993.

27 Traditional concern is with the money stock, not that particular component of it. If the concern is the stock of deposits, surely deposit insurance, which would remove the uncertainty by making deposit holders confident about their deposits, is sufficient. But that is subsidiary to the point pursued in the text.

28 This brings to the forefront the point that deciding when to intervene to supply liquidity and when to withdraw the liquidity continues and will continue to require judgment. It will be some time before this aspect, at least, of a central bank's responsibilities can be guided by a rule.

29 It is also worth noting that Continental Illinois, though large, was as a result of the Illinois banking laws at that time a unit bank.

30 The Bank did discount bills directly for some banks – those which were its own customers (Ogden, 1989)

31 A good description of the gilt repo market can be found in 'The Gilt Repo Market,' *Bank of England Quarterly Bulletin* (May 1996), 142–145.

32 At this point, Fischer implies in his footnote 33 that traditional financial panics and international capital flights are the same thing because both are characterized by multiple equilibria. Both may well have that characteristic, but that is hardly sufficient to show they are the same thing.

References

Alchian, A., and B. Klein. 'On a Correct Measure of Inflation.' *Journal of Money, Credit and Banking* 5, no. 1 (February 1973, part 1), 173–191.

Bagehot, Walter. 'The Currency Problem.' *Prospective Review* (1848), 297–337.

Bagehot, Walter. *Lombard Street*. London: Henry King, 1873.

Benston, G.J., Robert J. Eisenbeis, Paul M. Horvitz, Edward J. Kane, and George G. Kaufmann. *Safe and Sound Banking: Past, Present and Future*, Cambridge, Mass: MIT Press, 1986.

Benston, G.J. *The Separation of Commerical and Investment Banking. The Glass-Steagall Act Revisited and Reconsidered.* London: ONP, and New York: Macmillan, 1990.

Calomiris, Charles W., and Wilson, Barry. 'Bank Capital and Portfolio Management: the 1930s Capital Council and the Scramble to Shed Risk.' NBER Working Paper No. 6649, July 1998.

Cameron, R. *France and the Economic Development of Europe, 1800–1914*. Princeton: Princeton University Press, 1961.

Capie, F.H. 'The Evolution of the Lender of Last Resort: The Bank of England.' Forthcoming.

Capie, F.H., T.C. Mills, and G.E. Wood. 'What Happened in 1931?' In: F.H. Capie and G.E. Wood, eds., *Financial Crises and the World Banking System*. New York: St. Martin's Press, 1986.

Capie, F., and G. Rodrik-Bali. 'Concentration in British Banking 1870–1920.' *Business History* 6 (1982), 107–125.

De Cecco, M. *Money and Empire: the International Gold Standard*. Totowa NJ: Rowan and Littlefield, 1975.

Chernow, Ron. *The House of Morgan*. New York: Simon and Schuster, 1990.

Eichengreen, Barry. *Golden Fetters: The Gold Standard and the Great Depression 1919–1939*. NBER Series on Long Term Factors in Economic Development. New York and Oxford: Oxford University Press, 1992.

Fischer, S. 'On the Need for an International Lender of Last Resort.' *Journal of Economic Perspectives* 13, no. 4 (Fall 1999), 85–104

Forster, E.M. *Biography of Marianne Thornton. 1797–1887. A Domestic Biography*. London: Edward Arnold, 1956.

Friedman, M., and Anna J. Schwartz. *A Monetary History of the United States, 1867–1960*. Princeton, NJ: Princeton University Press, 1963.

Friedman, M., and A.J. Schwartz. *Monetary Trends in the United States and the United Kingdom*. Chicago: University of Chicago Press, 1982.

Galbraith, J.K. *The Great Crash, 1929*. Boston: Houghton Mifflin Company, 1955.

Gille, B. *La Banque de France au Xixeme siecle*. Geneve: Droz, 1970.

Goodhart, C.A.E. and D. Schoenmaker. 'Institutional Separation between Supervisory and Monetary Agencies' In: F. Bruno, ed., *Prudential Regulation, Supervision, and Monetary Policy*. Bruni: Centro de Economia, Monetoria & Finanziara 'Paolo Baffi', Universita Commerciale Luiigi Bocconi, 1993.

Goodhart, C.A.E. 'Time, Inflation, and Asset Prices.' Paper presented at a conference on 'The Measurement of Inflation.' Cardiff Business School, August 1999a.

Goodhart, C.A.E. 'Some Myths about the Lender of Last Resort.' *International Finance* 2, no. 3 (November 1999b) 339–360.

Goodhart, C.A.E., and H. Huang. 'A Model of the Lender of Last Resort.' *IMF Working Paper WP/99/39* March 1999.

Gordon, Robert A. *Business Fluctuations.* New York: Harper, 1952.

Gregory, T.E. *Select Statistics, Documents and Reports Relating to British Banking 1832–1928.* Oxford: Oxford University Press, 1929.

Hansen, Alvin. *Economic Stabilisation in an Unbalanced World.* New York: Harcourt Brace, 1932.

Hawtrey, R.G. *The Art of Central Banking.* London: Longmans, Green & Co., 1932.

Hoggarth, G., and Joe Thomas. 'Will Bank Recapitalisation Boost Domestic Demand in Japan?' *Bank of England Financial Stability Review* (June, 1999), 85–93.

Kaufmann, George. 'Lender of Last Resort: A Contemporary Prospective.' *Journal of Financial Services Research* 5, no. 2 (1991), 95–110.

Kindleberger, Charles P. *Manias Panics and Crashes.* New York: Basic Books, 1978.

Kroszner, Randell S., and Ragharan G. Rajan. 'Is the Glass-Steagall Act Justified? A Study of the US Experience with Universal Banking before 1933.' *American Economic Review* 84, no. 4 (September 1994), 810–832.

Levy-Leboyer, M. 'La specialisationts des establissenant bancaires.' In: F. Braundel and E. Labrousse, eds., *Histoire économique et sociale de la France*, vol. 3. Paris: Press Universitaires de France, 1976.

Ogden, E.M. 'The Bank of England as Lender of Last Resort.' *Unpublished Ph.D. dissertation.* London: City University, 1989.

Palgrave, Sir R.H.I. *Dictionary of Political Economy.* London: Macmillan, Vol. 1, 1894; Vol. 2, 1996; Vol. 3, 1998.

Peach, W. Nelson. *The Security Affiliates of National Banks.* Baltimore: Johns Hopkins Press, 1941.

Pressnell, Leslie. 'Gold Flows, Banking Reserves and the Baring crisis of 1890.' In: C.R. Whittlesey and J.S.G. Wilson, eds., *Essays in Money and Banking in Honour of RS Sayers.* Oxford: Oxford University Press, 1968.

Pressnell, Leslie. 'The Avoidance of Catastrophe: Two 19th Century Banking Crises: Comment.' In: F. Capie and G.E. Wood, eds., *Financise Crises and the World Banking System.* New York: St. Martin's, 1986.

Romer, Christina D. 'The Great Crash and the Onset of the Great Depression.' *Quarterly Journal of Economics* 105, no. 3 (August 1990), 597–624.

Schumpeter, J.A. *Business Cycles.* New York and London: McGraw Hill, 1939.

Schwartz, A.J. 'Real and Pseudo Financial Crises.' In: F.H. Capie and G.E. Wood, eds., *Financial Crises and the World Banking System.* London: Macmillan, 1986.

Schwartz, A.J. 'The Misuse of the Fed's Discount Window.' *Federal Reserve Bank of St Louis Review* (September/October 1992), 58–69.

Schwartz, A.J. 'A Century of British Market Interest Rates.' In: F. Capie and G.E. Wood, eds., *Monetary Economics in the 1980s: the Henry Thornton Lectures.* London: Macmillan, 1989.

Soussa, F. 'Too Big to Fail: Moral Hazard and Unfair Competition.' *Mimeo, Center for Central Banking Studies, Bank of England* 1999.

Temin, Peter. *Did Monetary Forces cause the Great Depression?* New York: Norton, 1976.

Thornton, Henry. *An Enquiry into the Effects of the Paper Credit of Great Britain.* Facsimile, 1802. Reprinted (with introduction by F.A. Hayek) Fairfield, NJ: Augustus Kelly, 1978.

White, Eugene N. 'Before the Glass-Steagall Act: An Analysis of the Investment Banking Activities of National Banks.' *Explorations in Economic History* 23, (1986), 36–37.

White, Eugene N. 'When the Ticker Ran Late.' In: Eugene N. White, ed., *Crashes and Panics: the Lessons from History* Homewood, IL: Dow Jones Irwin, 1990.

Wood, G.E. 'Great Crashes in History: Have They Lessons for Today?' *Oxford Review of Economic Policy* 15, no. 3 (1999), 98–109.

Section Three

International

17 Walter Bagehot and the theory of central banking[1]

Hugh Rockoff

Introduction

In the debate in monetary economics over 'rules' versus 'discretion' there is one issue that receives little attention because it appears to have been settled long ago – what to do in a crisis. Here, the textbooks tell us, Walter Bagehot proved that there is one and only one correct course of action – 'lend freely at high interest rates'.[2] The appropriate policies for non-crisis periods are debated, and the appropriate arrangements for assuring that the monetary authority has the power to act on Bagehot's principle are debated, but the rule itself and Bagehot's case for it are seldom discussed.

Part of the reason, I think, is that Bagehot dazzles us. He had in Clapham's (1944, V. 2, p. 283) words 'as good a head and as good a pen as any in England'. His works bristle with brilliant epigrams – his collected works contains an index of them, surely unique for an economist – while they display deep practical knowledge of the money market. He wrote widely on literature and politics as well as economics, and *The English Constitution* has attained a status in political science that rivals that of *Lombard Street* in economics. He was the confidant of the leading businessmen and statesmen of the day. Indeed, he was known as the 'spare chancellor', a phrase that became the title of one of his biographies (Buchan, 1959). No wonder we are tempted to accept his word on things. This, I hope to show, is unfortunate because *Lombard Street* contains a subtler analysis, and raises more questions than our memory of Bagehot's epigram suggests.

The main problem, I believe, is this. There are really two Bagehots, even though we remember only one. There is, of course, the Bagehot who tells us to 'lend freely at high rates' in a panic, but there is also the Bagehot who tells us to 'protect the reserve' when the market is merely apprehensive. Both speak authoritatively, but to whom should we listen? It is here that Bagehot fails us, for nowhere does he supply an explicit guide for recognising the state of the market that calls for one policy rather than the other.

This weakness is not obvious when we confine ourselves to the theoretical parts of *Lombard Street*, but it becomes apparent when we turn to the historical parts. Indeed, I will argue below that when we compare Bagehot's descriptions of the nineteenth-century crisis with those of other analysts, particularly those of Clapham based on the records of the Bank, the conclusion that forces itself upon us is that the problems of the Bank were seldom if ever due to an unwillingness to lend in a panic. Rather the problem was typically one of recognising the right moment for extreme actions, and of avoiding being pushed to take actions it thought were unnecessary. *Lombard Street*, in other words, for all its excellent qualities, and I will have occasion to notice many of them, did not create an exception to the general rule of monetary economics. In this area, as in others, the crucial issues are still controversial.

It is always worthwhile to take a fresh look from time to time at our economic classics. But current policy discussions make a fresh look at *Lombard Street* seem particularly worthwhile. There exists a mounting concern that the world financial system has grown fragile, while the inability of the less developed countries to meet their obligations has increased the probability of a shock to the system. Plans for reforms of the system are discussed frequently. One argument, pressed perhaps most notably by Charles Kindleberger (1978) for example, is that what is most needed is an international lender-of-last-resort with the freedom and power to follow Bagehot's formulae. At the other end of the spectrum is the school of thought that would have us return to the gold standard in order to return to a lost world of monetary stability. Bagehot wrote about a world on the gold standard in which the Bank of England was (it could be argued) in a position to perform as an international lender-of-last-resort. It makes sense, therefore, to attend closely to what he had to say about that world.

I have divided the paper as follows. In the next section I review the central themes of *Lombard Street*. In the third section I then review some of the traditional criticisms, and the weaknesses that I think have been neglected next in the fourth section. In the fifth section I examine Bagehot's use of historical evidence. In the sixth section I review the remainder of the nineteenth century to see to what extent later episodes also reveal shortcomings in Bagehot's analysis. In the seventh section I take up the role of the gold standard. And in the eighth and final section I set out my main conclusions.

The central themes of *Lombard Street*

Bagehot began writing *Lombard Street*, he tells us (1873, p. 46), in the autumn of 1870. The reason is not hard to find. The Franco-Prussian War had forced the Bank of France to suspend specie payments. Now more than ever any great demand for gold, including an indemnity, would fall on the Bank of England. The appropriate response was for the Bank of England to hold a larger reserve. But Bagehot was not convinced that this was appreciated at the Bank. The point had to be driven home to the Bank and to the world of opinion. Hence, *Lombard Street*.

The lend-freely rule was, in fact, a secondary theme of *Lombard Street*.

This was the lesson that later writers, such as Hawtrey (1933), distilled from Bagehot. But they were writing with a different financial system in mind, with different preconceptions about how the economy works, and with different social concerns. The Bank had stilled the panic that followed the failure of Overend, Gurney & Co. in 1866 by lending freely, and had even admitted its responsibility to do likewise in future crises. There had been some backsliding in the form of statements by Thomson Hankey, one of the directors of the Bank, who denied the Bank had an unequivocal duty to lend widely in panics. And Bagehot intended to set this right in *Lombard Street*. But the point at which he hammered away the most, because he thought it was the least understood, was the duty of the Bank to maintain a large reserve in all 'seasons of trouble'.

There is obviously a potential contradiction between maintaining or augmenting a reserve and lending it freely. Bagehot resolved this conflict by distinguishing between periods in which the market was merely apprehensive and periods in which it was in a panic. When the market was apprehensive the chief concern in the City was, according to Bagehot, with the level of the Bank of England's reserves. The appropriate policy was to protect and if possible augment them by raising the discount rate and restricting credit. Higher reserves would calm the market's fears and restore credit to normal. But, if the Bank failed to calm the market and if apprehension became panic, then the only plan open to the Bank was the 'brave plan', to lend freely. In a panic each man fears that the next deny him credit if he cannot show that he has money. Only when he gets cash, and sees that men in debt to him can get it, will the panic end.

It was altogether natural that Bagehot should make a psychological distinction the key to his theory. As Keynes (1915) pointed out long ago, it is Bagehot's psychological approach that provides the common thread of his seemingly diverse interests. He was best, moreover, in Keynes' view, at analysing men like himself, active self-confident men of business or politics.[3] But note that Bagehot's schema makes everything depend on the Bank's 'psychoanalysis' of the market. If the Bank mistakes apprehension for real panic and lends freely, then the reserve will fall and the level of apprehension will rise. On the other hand, if the Bank mistakes panic (significantly, Bagehot referred to it as a species of 'neuralgia') for mere apprehension, the Bank will starve the market of funds and the panic will intensify.

Although he was confident that the psychology of the market could be accurately read, and the appropriate medicine prescribed, Bagehot was not confident that the Bank of England as it was then constituted could do it. It was for this reason that he suggested his famous reforms of the Bank of England. There should be, he thought, a permanent Deputy Governor, to provide a clear head in a crisis – when the Governor and the Directors might be engaged with their own affairs. (Did he have himself or, more likely, a friend in mind?) And he thought that bankers, as well as brokers and exchange dealers, should be admitted to the 'court' – the flow of correct information to the Bank was crucial.

Bagehot's policy, it should be noted, was harder to apply than one which simply held that the Bank's reserves could be gradually augmented in 'normal' times and then used when troubles loomed. Bagehot, for example (1861, pp. 20–22), favoured a policy of augmenting the reserve in ordinary times, but it is clear from his analysis of historical episodes that this would not necessarily be enough. There were also sensitive periods when the market was close to panic, and yet when the correct policy was a further augmentation of the reserve.

The distinction between augmenting the reserve in normal times and augmenting it in periods of trouble was stressed earlier by Henry Thornton (1802, pp. 161–7), and the contrast between his analysis and Bagehot's helps to clarify the distinction.[4] Thornton, writing in the aftermath of the crisis of 1797, saw no reason to augment the reserve once the feeling was widespread that the reserve was inadequate; this was like trying to increase the supply of grain when there was already a shortage. Thornton simply had not conceived of it as a purely psychological problem in which the state of credit was closely tied to the level of reserves. There was more sense, Thornton thought, in the idea that the Bank of England should have tried to increase the reserve in more normal times. But this was ruled out, Thornton believed, by the cost to the shareholders of the Bank. The shareholders had a right to a normal return, and this would have been precluded by a build-up of reserves.

Given the crucial role of a larger reserve in Bagehot's schema, it is surprising that he did not consider some way of defraying the costs of accumulating gold. It would be natural to argue that since the economy as a whole benefits from a larger reserve at the Bank, the Treasury should subsidise the reserve. The costs of such a subsidy might be met in turn through a tax on the joint stock banks since the larger reserve is going to be of greatest benefit to them. Implicit taxes had been imposed on the joint stock banks before to the benefit of the Bank of England – the limitations on the note issue. But such a recommendation might have seemed out of place in the heyday of *laissez-faire*. In any case, Bagehot noted the profit problems of the Bank (1873, pp. 66–7). But he evidently believed that it was sufficient to point out to the Bank its appropriate duties. This decision may have been based on a close reading of the kind of men that directed the Bank. But in retrospect it appears to have been a mistake to ignore the profit problem. As we will see below, it was years before the Bank accumulated the additional reserves that Bagehot advocated.

Traditional criticisms

Bagehot is not without his critics. Perhaps the point made most frequently is that the existence of a lender-of-last-resort creates a problem of moral hazard. If the banks know that someone is there to bail them out in a crisis, they are likely to take more chances – reserve ratios will be reduced, dividend pay-outs will be increased, risky loans will be undertaken – and as a result, panics will be more frequent than they would otherwise be.[5] Charles Kindleberger (1978, pp. 215–20) has referred to it as a familiar argument, although he does not put much weight on it. He has argued, for example, that the presence of a lender-of-last-resort may actually reduce the frequency of panics by removing fears that a rapid business expansion must end in a liquidity crisis.

How would Bagehot have responded to this point? Hirsch (1977) argues that Bagehot implicitly assumed that the problem could be solved through the paternalistic leadership of the Bank within the narrow confines (social as well as physical) of Lombard Street. This seems to be a good suggestion. It fits well with Bagehot's neglect of a mechanism for providing the Bank with a financial incentive for holding more reserves. Men who had been to the right schools could be counted on to do the right thing once it was pointed out to them. But we also have some direct testimony in *Lombard Street* that shows that Bagehot thought this to be a minor point in any case. Moral hazard was the heart of Thomson Hankey's objection to the Bank committing itself to the role of lender-of-last-resort, the statement that so irritated Bagehot. Bagehot's answer was simply that the joint stock banks already acted on the principle that the Bank was there to bail them out. Their reserves were already reduced to the point where they were insufficient to meet the extra demands of a panic (1873, pp. 133–5). Any further movement of the joint stock banks in the direction of greater risk probably did not seem very important to Bagehot, especially because panics were as likely to be started by an external shock – war, a bad harvest, and so forth – as by bad banking.

A number of other reservations have been expressed. Mints (1945, p. 249) and Sayers (1957) expressed a concern that Bagehot's recommendation of a high discount rate sometimes did more harm by keeping up rates than good by slowing the loss of bullion from the Bank or by drawing fresh supplies from abroad.[6] And Kindleberger (1981, pp. 297–300) has noted that there may be a problem of mopping up excess liquidity after the panic has subsided. But despite the willingness of many economists to think critically about Bagehot's message, the literature seems to ignore a number of thorny problems that follow from a policy that grants the Bank – and more particularly the 'permanent deputy governor' – unrestricted authority to declare a crisis and to shift radically the Bank's policies.

Some neglected problems

A panic, Bagehot evidently believed, was something to be read from the furrowed brows of the brokers in Lombard Street, not something to be deduced from quantitative indicators. With only one exception, the reserve of the Bank, the variables that play such a large part in modern discussions of monetary policy – the stock of money, interest rates, the supply of credit, and so on – are ignored. Bagehot apparently assumes that it is easy (at least for the right man) to intuit the state of the market. And when it comes to a certain kind of crisis, he is probably right. If the market is sailing along smoothly, and suddenly without warning a giant bank with a reputation for soundness fails, and if there is a sudden demand for cash, there is not likely to be much disagreement with labelling the situation a panic. As it turns out, the crisis of 1866, the one that was one of the provocations for *Lombard Street*, could be described in these terms without doing very much violence to the facts; it was very much a bolt from the blue. But in earlier crises, I will try to show below, it was not so easy to decide the state of the market.

The problem with leaving the definition of a panic to the discretion of the Bank is that without objective criteria it becomes extremely difficult for the Bank to resist political pressures to define any period of distress as a panic. As a matter of political survival the Bank is likely to find itself embarking on a policy of lending freely when it doesn't want to. As we will see below, Bagehot criticised the Bank for having allowed its reserves to become dangerously low in pre-1866 crises. But he is somewhat vague on why these mistakes were made. A closer look at these episodes shows that the reason was that there were many qualitative signs of a panic, and the Bank was under strong pressure to act as if there was one.

A second difficulty with Bagehot's set of proposals, is that it assumes that the market always responds in a simple and predictable way to the policy chosen by the Bank. Thus, it ignores the likelihood that the market will learn to anticipate the sharp changes in Bank policy that Bagehot advocates. Once it is established that the Bank has adopted a Bagehotian policy, Lombard Street is likely to watch the Bank closely and react, possibly in counterproductive ways, to changes in the Bank's official perception of the market.[7] The decision to raise the discount rate in an apprehensive market may further alarm the market once it is understood that this is the Bank's standard policy in an incipient crisis.

In short, the psychological states of the market that lie at the core of Bagehot's schema appear to have been harder to diagnose, and less stable than Bagehot suggested.

Bagehot was aware that the market watched the Bank closely. But he tended to ignore the implications of this for his own proposals. This was especially true in his discussion of the Bank's reserve. Bagehot argued that the main cause of apprehension in the market in past crises, before the point of actual panic, was a concern with the level of the Bank's reserves. He believed that at the time when he was writing apprehension would become acute when the reserve in the Banking Department reached £10 000 000. This was the 'apprehension minimum'. To prevent this level from ever being approached he suggested an effective minimum of £15 000 000. The reserve had been £10 320 000 in 1869, close to the apprehension minimum, and averaged £12 259 750 in the years 1869–73. So Bagehot was advocating an increase of perhaps £3 000 000, about 25 per cent. He undoubtedly had figures of this sort in mind. A figure of £10 million was also mentioned by Thomas Tooke (1838, V.2, pp. 330–1), and Bagehot may have been influenced by him, or the figure may have simply been part of the lore of the market.

In any event, the crucial question is what would have happened if the Bank had adopted these figures as a guide to policy? The obvious answer is that once the market learned that whenever the reserve approached £15 000 000 the Bank would take restrictive actions – raising the discount rate, allowing bills to run-off, and so on – the market would react to the approach of £15 000 000 by limiting credit. The approach of the minimum would itself produce a crunch. Bagehot recognised this problem in a slightly different context. In considering the American plan of fixed legal reserve ratios he pointed out that if this plan were adopted by the Bank of England then, 'In a sensitive state of the English money market the near approach to the legal limit of reserve would be a sure incentive to panic; if one-third fixed by law, the moment the banks were close to one-third, the alarm would begin and would run like magic (1873, p. 216). Granted that a legal reserve ratio would be worse than a voluntary level of reserves, why would not this argument apply to Bagehot's proposal as well, even if on only a limited scale?

Thus Bagehot failed to solve the classic problem of defining the appropriate guide for monetary policy. In the case of panics he proposed giving the monetary authority complete discretion without giving them any bulwark against pressures to upgrade periods of stress to the status of panics. In the case of apprehensive markets he proposed a guide, the level of reserves, but one which on his own reasoning was not likely to work well.

Bagehot as economic historian

Because the state of the market, in Bagehot's schema, is something to be recognised intuitively, the ex-post definition of the state of the market can become a mere tautology. If we observe a period in which the Bank followed a policy of liberal lending, and we observe that things got worse, we can say that the market was merely apprehensive, and the Bank should have been concentrating on building up its reserve. If we observe a period in which the Bank holds on to its reserve, and we observe that things got worse, we can say that the market was in a panic, and the Bank should have been lending freely. At points Bagehot comes very close to this sort of reasoning.

He supports his case with an examination of the five crises, after the restriction, that preceded *Lombard Street*: 1825, 1939, 1847, 1857, and 1866. The crisis of 1825 was, next to 1866, his most persuasive example. His analysis of 1825 is simple. The Bank failed to protect its reserve and so produced a panic. The reserves (total bullion in the Bank) fell from £10 721 000 in December 1824 to £1 260 000 in December 1825 and, to quote Bagehot, 'the consequence was a panic so tremendous that its results are well remembered after nearly fifty years' (1873, p. 138). The Bank then took the correct action and lent freely. In a passage that has become famous he quoted Jeremiah Harman.[8]

'We lent it,' said Mr Harman, on behalf of the Bank of England, 'by every possible means and in modes we had never adopted before; we took in stock on security, we purchased Exchequer bills, we not only discounted outright, but we made advances on the deposit of bills of exchange to an immense amount, in short, by every possible means consistent with the safety of the Bank, and we were not on some occasions over nice. Seeing the dreadful state in which the public were, we rendered every assistance in our power.'

(1873, p. 73)

But what was going on in 1825? Why did the Bank's reserve decline so precipitously? Well before December of 1825, and the fall of Sir Peter Pole & Co. that is associated with the actions that Harman mentions, there were signs of strain in the banking system. Clapham (1944, V.2, p. 98) writes of abnormal bankrupticies beginning at the end of September. Tooke and Newmarch (1838+, v.2, p. 184) suggest that there were runs on the country banks by small noteholders 'after the summer' of 1825 (although the evidence they cite mentions the end of the year). Now couldn't we argue as follows, using Bagehot's own principles? The reserve had fallen from £11 787 430 in August 1824 to £3 634 320 in August 1825, and perhaps this was a mistake, perhaps the drain was an external one that could have been stopped without alarming the money market. But beginning in the fall of 1825 there was an internal drain prompted by the fears of noteholders that could only be stayed by following the policy of lending freely. I think that we could reason along these lines; the only problem is that the crisis got worse. It is only in hindsight that it is clear that the Bank was following the wrong policy by lending freely in the fall of 1825.

In recounting the crisis of 1825 Bagehot made an instructive error stressed by Frank Fetter (1967).[9] Bagehot refers to a letter from Peel to Wellington discussing the Government's quandary over whether to issue more Exchequer bills, to make borrowing from the Bank easier, or whether to force the Bank into lending directly on goods, the course ultimately followed. Bagehot suggests that this letter refers to the same moment in the crisis as the statement by Harman quoted above. In fact, Peel's letter refers to events some months later. It is a natural error, and perhaps Bagehot is not to be faulted too much for making it. But it does illustrate the problem of defining a panic. Should the Government have gone to any length to make borrowing easier, or was it right in allowing other concerns (in this case a rather dubious concern with out-of-pocket expenses) to take precedence? The heaviest demands on the Bank had passed, but failures were still high. The pressure on the Government to define the situation as one requiring extreme measures was obviously great.

To be sure, the Bank could not use the discount rate during the crisis in the manner suggested by Bagehot due to the usury law. The rate was kept at 4 throughout 1825 until it was raised to 5 per cent in December. Bagehot could have argued consistently that an earlier and more vigorous increase in Bank rate, had it been legal, might have reduced the outflow of cash from the Bank. But what would have been the effect of a rapid increase in the discount rate in 1825, and in particular what would have been the effect if the public realised that this was a sign that the Bank thought its own reserves were inadequate?

Of the crisis of 1839 all that Bagehot tells us is that 'the Bank was compelled to draw for £2 000 000 on the Bank of France; and even after that aid the directors permitted their bullion, which was still the currency reserve as well as the banking reserve, to be reduced to £2 404 000: a great alarm pervaded society' (1873, p. 138). Clapham (1944, V.2, p. 166) is more circumspect, but he also criticises the Bank for 'a rather shortsighted complacency [about reserves]' from the autumn of 1938 on.

The moment that Bagehot has in mind is July 1839. Before that date, presumably, the Bank should have been defending its reserve. But if we look at the period before the final humiliation (the loan from France!), it is easy to point to a number of similarities to a 'panic', and to show that the Bank was following the policy that Bagehot recommended for a panic. (1) There was a banking panic on the Continent in 1838 marked by a major suspension of payments by a bank in Belgium, a run on a banking house in Paris, and a collapse of credit and wave of failures throughout France (Clapham 1944, V.2, p. 166). The Bank of England was not under any obligation in Bagehot's scheme to act as an international lender-of-last-resort. But the linking of currencies under the gold standard created strong pressures on the Bank to operate in this way. (2) Two years earlier there had been significant closures in Britain and the circumstances had suggested that British firms were vulnerable to financial instability centred in other countries. It seems possible that the English market remained sensitive to any evidence of an unwillingness on the part of the Bank to lend when financial conditions in a major trading partner were deranged.

With these events in the backround, the Bank followed essentially the sort of policy Bagehot recommended for a panic. (1) It raised the discount rate from 4 to 5 per cent in May 1839 and from 5 to 5.5 in June. (2) In February it repeated its offer to lend on securities other than bills of exchange, and in general it followed a policy of 'allowing the public to act upon the bank' – as the policy was later described to Parliament (Clapham 1944, V.2, p. 166). From the outward course of events, in other words, we can argue that the Bank was behaving as an international lender-of-last-resort, and we can regard the Bank's difficulties as a failure of that policy. In retrospect, of course, we can also argue with Bagehot that there was no genuine panic in late 1838 or early 1839, and that the Bank followed the wrong policy. But the point is how was the Bank to know, and how was it to avoid the pressure for labelling this as a period when lending should be easy?

'The next trial,' according to Bagehot (1873, p. 138), 'came in 1847, and then the Bank permitted its banking reserve (which the law had now distinctly separated) to fall to £1 176 000; and so intense was the alarm, that the

executive government issued a letter of license, permitting the Bank, if necessary, to break the new law, and, if necessary, to borrow from the currency
reserve.' Again, Bagehot has the most dramatic moment in mind, the 'week
of terror', 16–23 October 1847. But there were signs of a crisis well before
October. Failures of major commercial houses, according to Clapham (1944,
V.2, p. 203), began in August, when Bank rate was raised from 5 to 5.5 On
1 October, the Bank announced a number of actions to defend its reserve – a
rate of 6 per cent for bills longer than a month, and a discontinuance of loans
on stock or Exchequer bills. And it was these actions which at the time were
blamed for producing the panic (Clapham 1944, v.2, p. 205), rather than the
fall in the Bank's reserve cited by Bagehot; a fair illustration of the potential
for Bagehot's formulae to prove counter-productive.

With hindsight we can argue that it was too late to defend the reserve at
the end of September, and that the time had come to lend freely. But again
the question is how could the Bank have divined this at the time? There is
nothing in Bagehot's schema to help the Bank to decide on which course to
follow.

The panic of 1857 was the first observed directly by the mature Bagehot; he
was then 31, and would become director of *The Economist* two years later.
But he argues in the same way about this crisis as about earlier ones. In
Lombard Street (1873, p. 138) he shows the banking reserve falling from
£4 024 000 on 10 October 1857 to £957 000 on 13 November. The result was
that 'a letter of licence like that of 1847 was not only issued, but used'. The
clear implication of this passage is that the Bank should not have 'let' the
reserve fall. At the time, incidentally, Bagehot wrote a piece for the *National
Review* (1858) in which he took a more moderate view. He then argued that
the panic was aggravated by Peel's Act, and that some regular way for relax-
ing it was needed. But he did not directly criticise the Bank for allowing
the reserve to fall, although he may have done so indirectly in one hard to
interpret passage (1858, p. 69).

But why, to return to the main point, were there such stupendous
demands on the Bank during this period? The answer, which by now should
be obvious, is that the panic was already on, and the Bank was trying to put
out the fires. The panic began, it appears, in the USA in September. Late in
October the Liverpool Borough Bank went down. The Bank of England
was clearly following Bagehot's lend-freely policy. The discount rate was
raised from 6 to 7 to 8 in October, and then to 9 and the unprecedented
figure of 10 in November. The Bank used its reserves as 'bravely' as possible, but its resources proved inadequate. The crisis dragged on even with
the help of the letter of licence to break the Act of 1844. Finally, Bank rate
was lowered from 10 to 8 on Christmas Eve, and this may be taken as a
symbol of the end of the acute phase of the crisis (Clapham 1944, V.2,
pp. 227–34).

Bagehot could have argued that the Bank was remiss in not building up its
reserves over the years after the crisis of 1847. Or he might have argued that

the letter of licence should have been issued earlier, although this course of action seems less consistent with his basic faith in the long-run usefulness of the gold standard. But it is hard to credit the argument – implicit in his discussion of the movement of reserves in October and November – that the Bank should have prevented the crisis by refusing to lend. The Bank, in other words, was listening to the Bagehot who says to lend freely in a panic; it is just that in retrospect this was the wrong Bagehot.

The panic of 1866, the one immediately preceeding *Lombard Street*, raised the fewest questions about Bagehot's schema, and one cannot help thinking that his theory was essentially a generalisation of this experience. It would be wrong to suggest that there were no signs of danger before the failure of Overend, Gurney & Co. Ltd on 11 May 1866. Yet it appears that 'panic, true panic, came with unexpected violence that day' (Clapham 1944, V.2, p. 263). Bagehot did not blame the Bank of England's reserve policy for contributing to the crisis (1873, p. 140), and he thought (1873, p. 79) the Bank's response, on the whole, was correct, although it may have erred in permitting a rumour to circulate that it was not accepting consols.

If all crises were as simple as the crisis of 1866, then Bagehot's schema might be adequate. But our review of the earlier crises shows that despite Bagehot's jamming and pushing not all of them can be made to fit into the 1866 mould. In some cases the crisis struck first in foreign countries or at the English country banks. Was this a situation that demanded action by the lender-of-last-resort? Sometimes the crisis grew slowly over months or even years. Again, when did the situation change from 'apprehension' to 'panic'? Is it any wonder that in these periods of uncertainty the Bank allowed its reserves to fall, when perhaps it should have been conserving them against a more acute demand. Without an explicit guide for defining a panic, Bagehot's analysis really helps in only a small number of cases, and may make it harder to follow an appropriate policy in others.

The remainder of the nineteenth century

What happened after *Lombard Street*? Did the Bank follow Bagehot's recommendations?[10] It is easiest to speak about the call for higher reserves. In the sixteen years between the publication of *Lombard Street* and the Baring crisis, the average yearly reserve exceeded Bagehot's minimum of £15 000 000 only four times: in 1876, 1880, 1881, and 1885. In those sixteen years, the Bank's reserves averaged £13 376 000 compared with £12 693 000 during the years *Lombard Street* was being written. Indeed, in half those years the Bank's reserves averaged less than they had when Bagehot was working on *Lombard Street*. After the early 1890s the reserve began to grow rapidly. But this was clearly due to the flood of gold from South Africa, Australia, the US, and elsewhere, and owed nothing to Bagehot. At least in the long run Bagehot's call for higher reserves went unheeded.

The reason was probably the mundane factor which Bagehot decided not to pursue in *Lombard Street*: the cost to the Bank of holding larger reserves. The sums involved do not seem large. Holding an extra £2 000 000 in gold during these years might have cost the Bank, say, £100 000 per year, and so reduced its annual dividend (about £700 000), if it were all to come out of dividends, by about 14 per cent. Not a high price for Britain to pay for a smaller chance of a financial crisis, but too high a price for the shareholders to pay.

In the years closer to *Lombard Street* there were some spells of trouble in the money market. And Bagehot was able to assimilate those that came in his time (he died in 1877) within his system. There was a crop of commercial failures in 1875 – although none of the order of Overend, Gurney & Co. – but the Bank was never faced with a panic. Bagehot (1875, 1876) claimed that this was because the Bank had maintained a large reserve. But the reserve was not really larger than it had been in the years when he was writing *Lombard Street*: the reserve averaged £10 037 000 in 1874, barely above the apprehension minimum, and £11 597 000 in 1875. Perhaps it was true that the reserve was large given the demands placed upon it.

But the plain fact was that these years, as might be said of the rest of the century, were relatively free of the sort of crisis that had repeatedly shaken the system before *Lombard Street*. The reason is not really clear, although I would lean to the view expressed by R. C. O. Matthews (Kindleberger and Laffargue 1982, p. 2) that the relative absence of major was played a part, along with perhaps the rising supply of gold at the end of the period. The next real test of the Bank came with the Baring crisis in 1890, a crisis similar to 1866 in the sense that it involved the sudden (although not completely unanticipated) failure of a giant house in London.

The reserve on the eve of the Baring crisis was only £10 815 000, close to the apprehension minimum defined by Bagehot seventeen years earlier, and well below the working minimum of £15 000 000 he had laid down. Bagehot could well have berated the Bank once again for maintaining an inadequate reserve, but further events moved along lines that Bagehot had not foreseen. Bank rate was raised from 5 to 6 per cent in November when the Bank learned of the difficulties of Barings. But Clapham (1944, v.2, p. 330) conjectures that the Bank didn't want to raise the rate further because it might alarm the City, once again illustrating the problem of unwanted announcement effects that Bagehot had ignored in *Lombard Street*. Once bills on Barings began to come in it was time for the Bank, according to Bagehot, or more properly to one of the Bagehots, to stem the crisis by lending freely. Instead, the Bank resorted to a device completely outside Bagehot's rules – a collective guarantee of the liabilities of the Barings, provided by the Bank, the government, and leading financial institutions. As it turned out this device was effective, and a panic was avoided (Clapham 1944, V.2, 326–39; Pressnell, 1968). The success of the guarantee showed one way towards greater financial stability. But it was not a triumph for Bagehot.

The gold standard and Bagehot's dilemma

The weaknesses in Bagehot's schema which I have been discussing are clearly a product of the gold standard. It is the finite limit to the stock of high-powered money that forces the Bank of England constantly to look over its shoulder at its reserves. Under a fiat standard, by way of contrast, the Bank could never run out of high-powered money. It could always lend freely in a crisis.

If the Bank could draw on some other large supply of gold besides its own reserves, then it would be in a position to act something like a central bank with fiat powers. Several possibilities have been suggested to me as ways of reconciling Bagehot's two rules, but all seem to me to miss one of the main points of *Lombard Street*, that the supply of gold was truly limited. It could be argued, for example, that Bagehot counted on Peel's Act being suspended in a panic. Indeed, Bagehot argued, as we have seen, that there should be some formalised means of suspending the Act, and in parliamentary testimony he conceded that the Act might have to be suspended. But it is clear from his remarks on the crises of 1847 and 1857, quoted above, that he regarded the suspension of the Act as a failure of policy. Nor is it clear that suspending the Act would always have the desired effect. The amount of gold in the Bank would still be limited, and the alarm of the financial community, particularly note holders, might increase. Only going off gold altogether would really help and this was clearly anathema to Bagehot.

It has also been suggested to me that Bagehot might have been assuming that an increase in the discount rate could bring in gold, allowing the Bank to follow a lend-freely policy without worrying about the level of its reserves. But attracting gold to London was not the same as attracting it to the Bank. In these years, as Cramp (1961) has shown, the participants in the market treated an increase in the discount rate as a signal that stormy weather lay ahead. Firms tried to strengthen themselves, and one result was to pull gold from abroad. But the same consideration that led firms to bring gold home led them not to deposit it with the Bank. The Bank, as Bagehot repeatedly argued, was the one great reserve of gold in the world. It could not readily augment that reserve in times of trouble because there was no place for the gold to come from.

The gold standard, by linking currencies together, tends to force any national bank that acts as a lender-of-last-resort to act as an international lender-of-last-resort. It may choose to build its reserves to the point where it can act alone, or it may choose to act in concert with other central banks, but it cannot remain aloof from crisis in other countries. Bagehot was not comfortable, I believe, with this aspect of the gold standard. Consider, for example, his evident disgust when the Bank of England was forced to borrow from the Bank of France during the crisis of 1839. It would be fair, I think, to infer that Bagehot believed that as long as panic was confined to foreign countries, or even to the British countryside, the Bank of England should look towards its reserves; only when the panic spread to Lombard Street should the Bank begin to lend freely. But that this is the best course of action is, of course, an empirical proposition. By then it might be too late. And it is clear that the Bank would be under strong political pressures to abandon its defensive posture long before the panic hit the City itself.

Under a fiat standard, it might be thought, Bagehot's two rules (1) lend freely and (2) defend the reserve are effectively reduced to one, and the problem of deciding which to apply disappears. Undoubtedly, the eclipse of the gold standard explains why modern students of banking tend to remember only one of Bagehot's rules. But even under a fiat system a central bank is likely to have goals, such as maintaining the trend growth of the money supply, that conflict with its lender-of-last-resort duties when the latter are broadly defined. Typically, the central bank will find itself under heavy pressure to upgrade each period of stress to the status of panic. But if this is done repeatedly the long-run goal may be lost.

Thus, the dilemma posed by Bagehot's policy is in great measure a function of the attempt to formulate an adequate policy under a gold standard. In a world of fiat monies and flexible exchange rates it would be easier to play the role of lender-of-last-resort. The immediate relevance, then, of a closer look at Bagehot is to the case for returning to a gold standard. Advocates of a return might argue that the nineteenth-century gold standard was plagued by crises, but that modern theories of central banking derived from Bagehot provide an adequate means for managing such crises. My point here is that Bagehot provides a clear guide only to the most obvious situations. Ambiguous cases will remain so even after they are examined in the light of *Lombard Street*. We cannot rely on central banks to prevent crises under a new gold standard.

Conclusions

The problem I have been discussing may be put this way. In Bagehot's day the Bank of England had to be concerned with its own liquidity as well as that of the rest of the financial system. Bagehot's advice was for the Bank to protect its reserve when the state of the reserve was the major source of alarm on Lombard Street (a period of apprehension), and to lend freely when the main source of alarm was each firm's fear that its own reserve would soon prove inadequate (a panic). But how was the Bank to distinguish between these two delicate states of the market? And how could it be sure that actions taken to cure an apprehensive market wouldn't produce a panic? The most one can derive from *Lombard Street* is the implicit assumption that the right course of action would be obvious once the facts were examined.

In a few cases this appears to have been true. In the crisis of 1866, one that hit almost without warning, few would dissent from Bagehot's prescription of 'lending freely'. But other cases were ambiguous. Sometimes the crisis evolved slowly (1837–9), and sometimes it was centred initially in foreign countries (1857) or outlying regions of the UK (1825). It was not clear which Bagehot the Bank should have listened to, and the pressure was to listen to the one who advised 'lend freely'. As it turns out, *Lombard Street* argues that this policy was the wrong one. But it is hard to see how the Bank could have avoided the course it chose on these occasions without an explicit guide to fall back on.

One approach to try to rectify this weakness might be to attempt to frame an explicit definition of a financial panic. It would be possible, for example, to 'fit' a definition to the historical episodes that Bagehot described as panics. Such a Bagehotian definition would be extremely narrow by some modern standards. Panics requiring free lending would be brief moments, not long periods. They would be domestic, rather than international; indeed it would not be a true panic until the crisis hit the financial centre itself. And they would be moments when the payments mechanism itself would be in danger, when the demand was for the means of exchange. But even such an explicit definition leaves considerable room for discretion and promises difficulties as the moment for switching policies approaches.

There is much to be said, therefore, for relying on a quantitative guide such as the stock of money even during a financial crisis. This would provide the central bank with some defence against the pressure to redefine the crisis as a panic. ('Our monetary aggregates remain within their targeted range despite the unfortunate recent events on the continent!') And it would provide for the automatic increase in the means of payment as the demand for it increased. But the main point is simply that when we begin to think about the practical problems in applying Bagehot's formulae, we are led back to the standard debates on monetary policy.

The gold standard, I should reiterate, is at the heart of Bagehot's dilemma. In his day the Bank of England could run out of base money. In an emergency Peel's Act could be suspended. But even this would not eliminate the strait-jacket imposed by the gold standard. That could be achieved only by eliminating convertibility, but Bagehot evidently believed that the gold standard was such an integral part of the system of credit that had grown up in England that any abridgement of it would impose serious costs on the financial system. Today, a central bank can adopt the 'lend freely' policy more frequently and with greater vigour than it could in Bagehot's day. But a similar problem remains. The modern central bank has goals, such as maintaining a low trend rate of growth of the stock of money, which are analogies of Bagehot's goal of maintaining the reserve.[11] Bagehot, in modern terms, advises the Bank to abandon such policies in a panic. The problem is to recognise when an apprehensive market has degenerated into a panic, and to avoid announcement effects that cause the very transformation of the market the Bank seeks to prevent. The solutions to these problems, unfortunately, are not to be found in *Lombard Street*.

I have been rather critical of *Lombard Street*. I have argued that Bagehot should have proposed a system of taxes and subsidies to assure that the Bank would accumulate the additional reserves he thought necessary. I have argued that he should have proposed better guides for recognising the states of the market that were crucial to his theory. And I have argued that he should have proposed ways of preventing the potentially destabilising announcement effects that might have been created by adopting his policies. But I do not mean to disparage Bagehot's achievement. By asking the central questions – what is the Bank of England, and what should it do – and by providing a clearly stated answer, Bagehot made one of the most important contributions to the development of the theory of monetary policy in the nineteenth century. Rather, my point is that *Lombard Street* is a far more subtle book, a harder book to use Keynes' (1915) term, than the one suggested by the epigram 'lend freely at high rates'. After all, what better praise can there be for an author than to say that people are still thinking about his work more than a century after it was written?

Notes

1 I would like to thank Anna Jacobson Schwartz, Richard Sylla and Eugene White for a number of thought-provoking comments on an earlier draft. They are not responsible, of course, for any remaining errors.
2 I first learned to pronounce Bagehot's name correctly in a class given by Professor Stigler. He explained that despite the spelling, the name was not pronounced, as most Americans supposed, as Baggy-hot.
3 Bagehot came from a banking family (indeed, he was literally born in a bank), and he maintained an active interest in the firm. So his adult observations of the money market, made from his post at *The Economist*, were joined by personal observations, some possibly from far back in his childhood. See the biography by Norman St John-Stevas (1959) for a brief well-written account of his life.
4 Thornton and Bagehot were treated by Humphrey (1975) as co-founders of the concept of the lender-of-last-resort. How much, if anything, Bagehot owed to the earlier writer, however, is unclear. In this and similar cases it should be remembered that Bagehot was not an academic, and was not concerned with intellectual precedence.
5 Roger Hinderliter and I (1976) once tried to examine the effects of the Bank of England behaviour on reserve ratios in a comparative context.
6 The high discount rate that Bagehot recommended for panics probably played several roles in his thinking. But the most important was simply that of providing some protection for the reserve (1873, p. 187). Gold or notes would be given to those who were truly desperate.
7 The argument that participants in the market form expectations and base their behaviour in part on what they perceive the policies of the Government to be has, of course, become a central issue in modern macroeconomics. The classical reference is perhaps Lucas (1976). Intuitively, central banking seems to be a clear case where considerations of this sort appear to be highly plausible.
8 This passage is quoted, for example, by Friedman and Schwartz (1963, p. 395).
9 This error was also noticed by Hawtrey (1933, p. 122), but he did not draw any conclusions from it.
10 See Fetter (1965, chapter 9) for a more positive view of Bagehot's impact.
11 In the draft of the paper presented at the conference I went a bit further in pressing this analogy than was warranted, and this was the basis of some of the comments.

References

I have listed the references to Bagehot's writings separately so that I could cite them by their original date in the text. All are available in his *Collected Works*.

Bagehot, W. (1858) 'The monetary crisis of 1857'. Originally published in the *National Review*, reprinted in the *Collected Works of Walter Bagehot*, edited by Norman St John-Stevas, vol. 10 (London: *The Economist*, 1978): 49–76.

Bagehot, W. (1861) 'The duty of the Bank of England in times of quietude', reprinted in the *Collected Works of Walter Bagehol*, vol. 10: 20–2.

Bagehot, W. (1873) *Lombard Street: A Description of the Money Market* (London: H. S. King) Reprinted in the *Collected Works of Walter Bagehot*, vol. 9: 45–233.

Bagehot, W. (1875) 'The lesson of recent events in the money market', reprinted in the *Collected Works of Walter Bagehot*, vol. 11: 48–53.

Bagehot, W. (1876) 'The use of a large bank reserve', reprinted in the *Collected Works of Walter Bagehot*, vol. 11: 54–6.

Buchan, A. (1959) *The Spare Chancellor: The Life of Walter Bagehot* (London: Chatto & Windus).

Clapham, Sir J. (1944) *The Bank of England: A History*. 2 vols. (Cambridge: Cambridge University Press).

Cramp, A. B. (1961) *Opinion on Bank Rate, 1822–60* (London: The London School of Economics and Political Science).

Fetter, F. W. (1965) *Development of British Monetary Orthodoxy, 1797–1875*. (Cambridge, Mass.: Harvard University Press).

Fetter, F. W. (1967) 'An historical confusion in Bagehot's *Lombard Street*', *Economica*, New Series, 34 (February 1967): 80–3.

Friedman, M. and Schwartz, A. J. (1963) *A Monetary History of the United States* (Princeton: Princeton University Press).

Hawtrey, R. G. (1933) *The Art of Central Banking* (London: Longmans, Greene).

Hinderliter, R. and Rockoff, H. (1976) 'Banking under the gold standard: an analysis of liquidity management in the leading financial centres', *The Journal of Economic History* 36 (June 1976): 379–98.

Hirsch, F. (1977) 'The Bagehot problem', *The Manchester School of Economics and Social Studies* 45 (September 1977): 241–57.

Humphrey, T. M. (1975) 'The classical concept of the lender of last resort', Federal Reserve Bank of Richmond, *Economic Review* 61 (January/February, 1975): 1–7.

Keynes, J. M. (1915) 'The Works of Bagehot', *The Economic Journal* 25 (September 1915): 369–75.

Kindleberger, C. P. (1978) *Manias, Panics, and Crashes* (New York: Basic Books).

Kindleberger, C. P. (1981) *International Money: A Collection of Essays*. (London: George Allen & Unwin).

Kindleberger, C. P. and Laffargue, J. P. (eds) (1982) *Financial Crises: Theory, History, and Policy* (Cambridge: Cambridge University Press).

Lucas, R. E., Jr. (1976) 'Econometric policy evaluation: a critique', in *The Phillips Curve and Labor Markets*, edited by K. Brunner and A. H. Meltzer. Carnegie-Rochester Conference Series on Public Policy, vol. 1: 19–46.

Mints, L. W. (1945) *A History of Banking Theory in Great Britain and the United States* (Chicago: University of Chicago Press).

Pressnell, L. S. (1968) 'Gold reserves, banking reserves, and the banking crisis of

1890', in *Essays in Money and Banking in Honour of R. S. Sayers*, edited by C. R. Whittlesey and J. S. G. Wilson (Oxford: Clarendon Press).

St John-Stevas, N. (1959) *Walter Bagehot* (London: Eyre & Spottiswoode).

Sayers, R. S. (1957) *Central Banking after Bagehot.* (Oxford: Clarendon Press).

Thornton, H. (1802) *An Enquiry into the Nature and Effects of the Paper Credit of Great Britain*, edited by F. A. Hayek. (New York: Farrar & Rinehart, 1939).

Tooke, T. and Newmarch, W. (1838+) *A History of Prices, and the State of the Circulation from 1792 to 1856* (London: Longman, Orme, Brown, Green, and Longman) Reprinted with an introduction by T. E. Gregory (New York: Adelphi, 1928).

COMMENT – KURT SCHILTKNECHT

In his paper, Hugh Rockoff shows very clearly the weakness of Bagehot's proposal 'to lend freely at high interest rates'. I share Rockhoff's view that Bagehot failed to solve the problem of defining the appropriate guide for monetary policy before and during a panic. But is this problem solved today? Does a central bank really know how to respond to a financial crisis? Hugh Rockhoff seems to have some doubts, at least his remark that 'even under a fiat system a central bank is likely to have goals that conflict with its lender-of-last-resort duties' gives the impression that monetary authorities have plenty of discretion to play the role of a lender-of-last-resort.

In my view there is no conflict between the ultimate goal of a central bank, namely price stability, and its lender-of-last-resort duties. In the following I would like to elaborate on this point a bit. In addition – and I think this is the main reason for my being invited to contribute to this discussion – I shall comment on the position of the Swiss National Bank with respect to its role as a lender-of-last-resort.

To begin with, I would like to define the monetary characteristics of a panic. In principle a panic in the monetary sector is characterised by a sharp increase in the demand of the public and the banks for base money. The public withdraw deposits from banks and transform them into currency. In order to prepare for such operations, banks increase the demand for reserves. Such an increase is, however, only possible for banks with no solvency problems and no credibility gap. For all the others it is extremely difficult to improve their reserve positions even if they offer interest rates above the market levels. Both developments, the transformation of deposits into currency and the increase in the demand for bank reserves, have a contractionary effect on the money stock. A shrinking money stock certainly does not serve the ultimate goal of a central bank. Therefore, a central bank has to supply more base money in order to offset the deflationary effect of the exogenous increase in the demand for base money. Given the difficulties in estimating the size of the shift in the demand for base money, the best solution for a central bank is temporarily to abandon the money stock target and to shift to an interest rate target. After a while, however, the central bank has to focus on the monetary aggregates again. The target for a narrow aggregate has to be revised upwards in order to satisfy the higher liquidity preference during a crisis. When the crisis is over, the increase has to be offset. Of course, such an approach leaves some room for discretion. But in my view such a strategy minimises the risk with respect to both the deflationary impact of a panic and the inflationary impact of the increase in the monetary base.

The specific nature of the crisis determines how the monetary base is increased during a panic. As a first step, a central bank has to supply liquidity for banks in trouble. The Swiss National Bank has made it clear to the banks that it would be in their own interest to hold assets that allow them to use the rediscount and lombard facilities offered by the National Bank. On average, the Swiss banks are very well equipped with such assets. Deposits of the Government with banks short of liquidity are another way to solve liquidity problems of individual banks. This approach was quite often and successfully applied during the crisis in the thirties. The Government can either raise the liquidity in the market, if the supply of base money is already high enough, or it can borrow from the Swiss National Bank.

Much better, and this is fully in line with the idea of Bagehot, is to prevent a panic. This can be done if a central bank immediately responds to the first signs of a crisis. The recognition of these first signs of a monetary crisis is much easier for the central bank if it follows a monetary base approach and if banks have under normal conditions no access to the rediscount and lombard facilities. In a country where commercial banks have virtually unlimited access to the rediscount and lombard facilities, the actual demand for reserves corresponds more or less to the amount of required reserves. Excess reserves are then quite low, because the holding of excess reserves is not attractive for the banks, as long as they can borrow base money from the central bank at a rate close to the current official rates. Even if a bank expects some difficulties, it will not increase its reserve holdings. Therefore, a central bank has no possibility of recognising the first signs of a crisis. In Switzerland, where the Swiss National Bank does not serve as a lender-of-first-resort, the response of a bank is different. If a bank expects problems, it would first try to improve its reserve position, in order to be prepared for the monetary impact of the crisis. Since the only possibility for a bank to increase its reserves is to attract base money from other banks, a shift in the demand for reserves is immediately transmitted into higher interest rates in the money market. For a central bank, a sudden, unexpected and large rise of interest rates signals that some kind of a crisis in the monetary sector may have developed. An analysis of the individual reserve positions of each bank may help to locate the problem in the banking system. In addition, a comparison between the actual and the predicted demand for reserves may enable the central bank to distinguish between random fluctuations in the demand for reserves and systematic shifts. If the change in demand is identified as systematic, the central bank has to make offsetting operations.

Of course, the most natural behaviour of a bank facing a liquidity problem is to inform the central bank about its difficulties. Then it is up to the central bank to decide whether an increase in the monetary base is necessary. During the so-called Chiasso fiasco of Credit Suisse the Swiss National Bank was faced with such a situation. Since that episode sheds some light on the practical problems of monetary management, I shall briefly discuss it.

As a result of the difficulties faced by Credit Suisse in May 1977, the Swiss financial community became concerned that the public would lose confidence in the banking system and that large-scale withdrawals of deposits would ensue. These concerns prompted the commercial banks to augment their demand for precautionary reserves. If the Swiss National Bank had refused to supply additional base money to the banking system, the scramble for reserves would have caused a sharp contraction in the money supply. In order to forestall this, the Bank decided to increase the monetary base at a rate faster than originally planned. Despite this flexibility of the Swiss National Bank, however, the expansion in bank reserves was, as we realised later, not sufficient to accommodate fully the shift in demand. For this reason, short-term and medium-term interest rates rose markedly. This rise induced a slower growth of M_1. Later in the year, it became known that the Credit Suisse would be able to absorb the losses of its Chiasso branch without much difficulty. Since the commercial banks no longer faced the prospect of large-scale deposit withdrawals, they gradually restored their normal levels of reserves and the National Bank could reduce the growth of the monetary base to its planned level.

This episode shows that targets for the money stock and monetary base must be handled in a flexible manner if a central bank is to prevent unexpected shifts in the demand for base money from exerting harmful effects on the economy.

To conclude my remarks I would like to comment briefly on one of the traditional criticisms of Bagehot's proposal. Hugh Rockhoff writes that 'perhaps the point made most frequently is that the existence of a lender-of-last-resort creates a problem of moral hazard. If the banks know that someone is there to bail them out in a crisis, they are likely to take more chances – reserve ratios will be reduced . . . risky loans will be undertaken – and as a result, panics will be more frequent than they would otherwise be'. This traditional criticism is misplaced. The role of a lender-of-last-resort only implies that a central bank may provide liquidity during a crisis in order to prevent a shrinking of deposits. In general, a central bank supplies liquidity against sound assets. The provision of base money against bad assets takes place in extreme situations only. But in such a case the risk of the bad assets remains with the bank. As long as the losses on the assets of the banking system are not taken over by the central bank, it is wrong to consider lender-of-last-resort activities as bailing out operations. The possibility of making a loss in fulfilling the role of a lender-of-last-resort has in any case to be weighed against the possibility of a contraction in the money supply. In the short run, priority has to be given to the protection of the money stock under all circumstances, while in the longer run the central bank has to take care that losses are covered by the banking system.

If a central bank does not leave any doubt that the banks have to cover the losses, it is hard to understand why banks should grant riskier loans when it is known that the central bank will serve as a lender-of-last-resort. Especially under a strict monetary base approach an over-extension of loans is not very profitable.

I would like to summarise my comments in three points:

1. Within an explicit money supply framework it is possible to develop a lender-of-last-resort strategy which is in line with the ultimate goal of a central bank.
2. A monetary base approach, contrary to the gold standard, facilitates the prevention or solution of a financial crisis.
3. Central banks must distinguish explicitly between solving a liquidity crisis and bailing out the banking system.

COMMENT – J. S. FFORDE

I have read Hugh Rockoff's paper with considerable interest. It invites questions about how central banks should best respond in today's monetary policy environment, with today's institutional framework, either to the onset of conditions which threaten a financial crisis or to the actual occurrence of such a crisis. I would like to attempt some comment on one or two of those questions, from the viewpoint of one who was an operational central banker from 1966 to 1982.

Bagehot's propositions, put forward some 100 years ago, were conditioned by the existence of a privately owned central bank, subject to the statutory restraints of the gold standard and operating in what we would now call a broadly deregulated banking system. In that environment, occasional conflicts were likely to arise between the statutory obligation to maintain the gold convertibility of Bank notes and the implied duty of the central bank to afford the community some substantial degree of protection from disorderly collapse in the banking system. These conflicts could partly be resolved by a prudent build-up or husbanding of gold reserves, despite the expense, and despite the high degree of monetary stringency that could ensue, and partly, if the worst came to the worst, by backing-off from the letter of the gold standard in the interests of averting or dispelling a panic. Pursuit of these activities clearly needed the use of judgement and discretion by the central bank and clearly opened up the risk of misjudgement and error. Accordingly, as I understand it, Bagehot was concerned that the Bank should be equipped both with adequate rationale and adequate expertise; and he made suggestions about both.

All this has some rather special interest today because in many countries, following the monetary disturbance of the past decade or more, there is now a considerably greater emphasis on rules as opposed to discretion in the conduct of monetary policy, and, at least in some countries, a considerably greater emphasis on competitive freedom in banking as opposed to the restrictive regulation and supervision which in many cases resulted from past failure of central banks to avert financial disorder. So there follows some presumption that the nineteenth-century conflicts of objective can again come to the fore, perhaps particularly during a transition to much lower levels of inflation and a concurrent steep reduction in inflationary expectations. This may lead some people, including some economists, to worry lest central banks are so concerned to avert disorder that they back off too readily, and thereby seriously weaken the force of their counter-inflation strategy. The same people worry further lest these risks are made the more serious by the vulnerability of central banks in many countries to transitory pressures of public opinion which could cause long-term objectives to be sacrificed to short-term needs. Associated with these worries is a concern about moral hazard, namely, that central banks, together with the governments with which they are associated, may over the past decades of regulation have come to assume, or be thought to have assumed, such a degree of de facto responsibility to bail out banks in a crisis as positively to encourage or promote imprudent behaviour both by banks and by depositors in a newly deregulated system.

It is not for me to pronounce on whether these worries are well founded in respect of the UK and of the British monetary authorities. But we certainly recognise the problems to which they draw attention and are probably content to be judged by our behaviour in meeting them. By way of illustration let me draw on an at times defective memory, combined with the published record, of some of the events of recent years.

First, let me refer to the secondary banking crisis of 1973–4 and its treatment by the device known as the Lifeboat. As you know, what happened was that deposits of the general public with the so-called secondary banks were indeed all met on maturity, with funds provided as required by the Bank and by the clearing banks. The proprietors of the secondary banks, and depositors directly connected with those banks, were, of course, not similarly rescued and lost a lot of money, though they may in some cases have benefited from the careful management put in by the Lifeboat banks. So being 'bailed out', as the phrase goes, is far from painless and it would be surprising if anyone in the business of banking in the UK now thought it was.

But we did indeed realise the awkward precedent created by our appearing, with the clearing banks, to be prepared to stand behind the ordinary depositors at some rather extraordinary institutions. Isolated episodes in the fifties and sixties had in fact *not* met with a similar response. The upshot of the awkward precedent was the provision made in the subsequent Banking Act for a Deposit Protection Fund financed by the banking system (broadly defined) and guaranteeing 75 per cent of deposits up to £10 000. In the view of the Government and of Parliament this, together with the licensing and supervisory provisions in the Act, provided an adequate degree of guaranteed consumer protection: without encouraging the belief that *all* deposits with all licensed institutions were de facto riskless.

The message would therefore seem to be that bailing out of depositors is not guaranteed but that if it occurs, in the interests of the stability of the whole system, it will not be painless for the proprietors of the institution concerned. I suggest that this may have got the balance about right for the present; and that the solution to the problem of moral hazard lies in a proper balance of partial guarantee of deposits, pain for proprietors where bailing out does occur, and special supervision.

But what about monetary policy 'backing off' too soon, out of undue or exaggerated concern for the health of financial institutions whose ill health would damage the economy more generally? Here, the episode that comes to my mind is the conduct of policy during the winter of 1974–5 when inflation was accelerating to 20 per cent. The broad money supply ($M3$) was only growing at around half that rate but the narrow money supply ($M1$) was growing considerably faster. Yet we exploited an opportunity provided in the main by a fall in US interest rates very early in 1975 and we backed off. Short-term interest rates were allowed to fall by some 2 percentage points and, rather more importantly, the emphasis of debt management was sharply altered so as to encourage a fall in long-term rates and a recovery in long-term asset values. The yield on long-dated Government bonds had reached a peak of around 18 per cent late in 1974 and fell to 13½ per cent by the end of March 1975. Our *Quarterly Bulletin* of March 1975, in referring to this adjustment of policy said, 'Private industry had in many cases become over-dependent on short-term borrowing at high rates of interest, and the fall in the capital value of assets, resulting in part from the earlier sharp rise in rates, threatened to create balance sheet problems for some financial institutions; high interest rates and low equity prices had also severely hampered the new issue market.' Somewhat later our Annual Report for the year ending February 1975 remarked, 'The pressing need in the closing months of 1974 seemed to be the restoration of confidence to financial markets, and this underlay the official response to the revival in the gilt-edged market which began early in the New Year.'

In Bagehot's terminology, we had by the end of 1974 reached a condition of generalised apprehension with some flavour of incipient panic. Using a somewhat free adaptation of Anna Schwartz's illuminating terminology, I think we had at least run into a real pseudo-crisis. But I do not recall it being thought subsequently, by any notable body of opinion, that we were mis-informed, that our response was wrong, or that we backed off too soon, or that we had fallen victim to transient or myopic political pressures. Rather we had been criticised earlier, in the summer of 1974, for not backing off sooner.

However, it could be argued that steering a successful course through episodes like the one I have just described places altogether too heavy a burden of judgement on a small band of fallible central bankers dealing with infrequent situations, each of which may well be outside the experience of the ruling generation of officials. So I would agree that any means of lightening that burden would be useful. Since 1974, and especially during the difficult period of 1980–2, I believe one way of reducing the burden has been further developed. I am referring to the work of the Industrial Finance Division of the Bank as developed in the first instance by Lord Benson, who became our Industrial Adviser in 1975. This work has not involved the Bank in lending money to anybody; but it has facilitated a process whereby the various bankers, managements, and sometimes also the principal shareholders, of large companies facing severe difficulties, can effect in collaboration such necessary changes of management, asset realisations, and liability-reconstructions as are required to overcome such difficulties without resort, in most cases, to the procedures of sudden bankruptcy with their associated financial alarms and apprehensions. Perhaps there is some echo here, but an industrial echo, of the Bank's approach to the Baring crisis. Be that as it may, it seems that this industrial finance activity can help very considerably, in periods of stress, to reduce the level of apprehensiveness, to avert the onset of incipient panic, and therefore reduce both the chances of having to back off and the associated burden on central banking judgement.

So I am suggesting that both in respect of the moral hazard problem and of the main Bagehot dilemma, of which Hugh Rockoff reminds us, some ways have been developed through which their practical importance can be effectively diminished, or limited. Perhaps this is the most one should expect.

18 On the need for an international lender of last resort

Stanley Fischer *

The frequency, virulence, and global spread of financial crises in emerging market countries in the last five years – Mexico in 1994, with the subsequent tequila contagion in Latin America and for a day or two in east Asia; east Asia in 1997 and 1998, with contagion spreading crisis within the region; Russia in 1998, itself affected by Asian contagion, with the Russian contagion spreading to Latin America in addition to eastern Europe and the rest of the former Soviet Union – has led to the most serious rethinking of the structure of the international financial system since the breakdown of the Bretton Woods system in 1971. In the coming months and years, governments and international institutions will be putting in place a series of changes designed to strengthen the international financial system.

The vision that underlies most proposals for reform of the international financial system is that the international capital markets should operate as well as the better domestic capital markets. To express the goal in this way is to drive home the point that volatility and contagion cannot be banished, for asset prices inevitably move sharply, and in ways that are significantly inter-correlated. But while volatility and contagion will always be with us, we can surely do better in reducing the frequency and intensity of emerging market financial crises, and the extent of contagion, than we have in the last five years.

As we consider how to make the global capital markets operate better and how to reduce the frequency and virulence of financial crises, I would like to revisit a literature that emerged out of the financial crises of the last century, that on the lender of last resort. The best-known classic writing on the lender of last resort is Walter Bagehot's (1873) *Lombard Street*.[1] The most famous lesson from Bagehot is that *in a crisis, the lender of last resort should lend*

* Stanley Fischer is First Deputy Managing Director, International Monetary Fund, Washington, D.C.

1 Henry Thornton's (1802) analysis of the role of lender of last resort is also remarkably sophisticated. For an historical discussion of the lender of last resort, see Humphrey and Keleher (1984).

freely, at a penalty rate, on the basis of collateral that is marketable in the ordinary course of business when there is no panic.

I will start by reviewing the case for a lender of last resort in the domestic economy, and the set of rules that the lender of last resort is supposed to follow. I will then discuss the moral hazard problem that is created by the existence of a lender of last resort – that is, the problem that the existence of a lender of last resort may create incentives for risky behavior which raise the chances of financial crises – and measures to mitigate it. I then turn to the international system and will argue that it too needs a lender of last resort. I will argue that the International Monetary Fund, although it is not an international central bank, has undertaken certain important lender of last resort functions in the current system, generally acting in concert with other official agencies – and that its role can be made more effective in a reformed international financial system.[2]

The domestic lender of last resort

The role of lender of last resort for the central bank is associated with the prevention and mitigation of financial crises. Financial crises and panics have been taking place for centuries (Kindleberger, 1996; MacKay, 1841). They are typically associated with a sudden loss of confidence in the standing of some financial institutions or assets. Because the chain of credit is based on tightly interlinked expectations of the ability of many different debtors to meet payments, a sense of panic can spread rapidly, contagiously, through the financial system, and if unchecked, have significant effects on the behavior of the real economy. The role of the lender of last resort is to offer an assurance of credit, given under certain limited conditions, which will stop a financial panic from spreading – or better still, stop it from even getting started.[3]

While there is considerable agreement on the need for a domestic lender of last resort, some disagreements persist about what the lender of last resort

---

2   Among those who have sought to build on and develop the analysis of the role of lender of last resort in recent years, see Benston et al. (1986), Freixas (1999), Garcia and Plautz (1988), Goodhart (1995), Goodhart and Huang (1998), Goodfriend and Lacker (1999), Holmstrom and Tirole (1998), Kindleberger (1996, first edition 1978), Meltzer (1986), Mundell (1983), Schwartz (1988), Solow (1982), and Wijnholds and Kapteyn (1999). Claassen (1985) provides an interesting discussion of the role of an international and domestic lenders of last resort in an international context. Recent discussions of the potential role of the IMF as an international lender of last resort include Calomiris (1998), Calomiris and Meltzer (1998), Capie (1998), Chari and Kehoe (1999), Giannini (1998), Jeanne (1998), and Meltzer (1998). Mishkin (1999) and Radelet and Sachs (1998) take up lender of last resort issues in the context of the Asian crisis.

3   In economic theory panics can be modeled as cases of multiple equilibria, possibly dependent on herd behavior. The classic reference is Diamond and Dybvig (1983). For a related model in the international context, see Chang and Velasco (1998).

should do. I will start with the traditional Bagehot (1873) conception, as summarized and developed by Meltzer (1986, pp. 83):

> The central bank is called the lender of last resort because it is capable of lending – and to prevent failures of solvent banks must lend – in periods when no other lender is either capable of lending or willing to lend in sufficient volume to prevent or end a financial panic.

Meltzer lists (pp. 83–4) five main points concerning a lender of last resort, the first four derived from Bagehot:

> The central bank is the only lender of last resort in a monetary system such as [that of the United States].
>
> To prevent illiquid banks from closing, the central bank should lend on any collateral that is marketable *in the ordinary course of business when there is no panic* [emphasis added]. It should not restrict lending to paper eligible for discount at the central bank in normal periods.
>
> Central bank loans, or advances, should be made in large amounts, on demand, at a rate of interest above the market rate. This discourages borrowing by those who can obtain accommodation in the market.
>
> The above three principles should be stated in advance and followed in a crisis.
>
> Insolvent financial institutions should be sold at the market price or liquidated if there are no bids for the firm as an integral unit. The losses should be borne by owners of equity, subordinated debentures, and debt, uninsured depositors, and the deposit insurance corporations, as in any bankruptcy proceeding.

Meltzer's (1986) statement for the most part agrees with other formulations, but does not emphasize the view, summarized for instance by Humphrey (1975) and attributed to Thornton (1802), that the overriding objective of the lender of last resort should be to prevent panic-induced declines in the aggregate money stock, and thus that the lender of last resort role can be viewed as part of a central bank's overall task of monetary control. In some more recent formulations, this view has been extended to what could be considered a sixth precept, which could be added to the above list: 'In the event of a panic, the central bank should assure liquidity to the market, but not necessarily to individual institutions.'[4]

With this notion of the lender of last resort in mind, I will take up six questions about the role of the domestic lender of last resort.

---

4   In private conversation, Meltzer has indicated that he sees no advantage to the rule that the central bank should lend only to the market rather than on occasion if necessary also to individual institutions.

Is the central bank the only lender of last resort?

Lenders of last resort have generally undertaken two roles: *crisis lender* and *crisis manager*. The crisis lender provides financing to deal with a crisis. The crisis manager takes responsibility for dealing with a crisis or potential crisis, whether or not the institution itself lends for that purpose. In the midst of a financial crisis, there is often a potential managerial (or facilitating or coordinating) role in which other agents or institutions may be encouraged to act in the right way, for instance by extending a loan to an institution whose failure could have systemic consequences.

While historically the central bank has generally been both the crisis manager and the crisis lender, neither role has to be carried out by the central bank. If a certain authority, and access to resources, are necessary for taking this coordinating role, then a Treasury may be able to do it as well as a central bank. At various times in U.S. history, institutions other than the central bank have played one or both of these roles, including: the U.S. Treasury; private institutions, such as clearing-houses; and in 1907, J.P. Morgan (Kindleberger, 1996, pp. 133–35).[5] Indeed, the separation of the roles of crisis lender and crisis manager could become more frequent as the task of supervision of the financial sector is separated from the central bank, as it has been in the United Kingdom and elsewhere.

Does the lender of last resort need the ability to create money?

There is no question that a lender of last resort will often find it useful to have the power to create money. The clearest example is when a panic takes the form of a run from bank deposits into currency. Then the central bank is well-positioned to create quickly the currency needed to deal with the panic, and at no first-round cost to the taxpayer.[6]

However, panics caused by a demand for currency are rare (Kaufman, 1988; Schwartz, 1988). More generally, a panic may take the form of a run, possibly enhanced by contagion, in which deposits shift from those banks and financial institutions deemed unsound to those thought to be healthy. In these cases, creating additional money may be unnecessary. At least in principle, the liquidity can simply recirculate from the institutions gaining money back to those losing it. Again in principle, the market can accomplish this

---

5   Although some have pointed with approval to the role of clearinghouses in financial panics, note Kindleberger's quotation (1996, p. 134) from Jacob Schiff in 1907: 'The one lesson we should learn from recent experience is that the issuing of clearinghouse certificates in the different bank centers has also worked considerable harm. It has broken down domestic exchange and paralyzed to a large extent the business of the country.'

6   Accordingly, Schwartz (1988) argues that the central bank should act as lender of last resort only in the event of a run from banks into currency.

shift, if it is able to distinguish the merely illiquid from the insolvent companies.

But – and this is the critical point – *the line between solvency and liquidity is not determinate during a crisis.* If a crisis is well-managed, the number of bankruptcies may remain small; if it is badly managed, it may end in general illiquidity and insolvency. A skilled lender of last resort, able to assure the markets that credit can and will be made available to institutions that would be solvent in normal times, can help stem a panic and reduce the extent of the crisis.

All this is straightforward, provided the central bank is free to create money. However, at the time that Bagehot (1873) wrote *Lombard Street*, the Bank of England was bound by gold standard rules; that is, money could only be created in accordance with the amount of gold held by the Bank, and the Bank did not have the ability to create gold. Nonetheless, Bagehot enjoined the Bank to act as lender of last resort. In the three financial crises preceding the writing of *Lombard Street*, the Bank of England was given permission to break the gold standard rule, and since Bank of England credit was accepted as being as good as gold, it managed to stay the panics. The key was not the legal right to create money, but the effective ability to provide liquidity to the market.

A similar question, of whether there can be a lender of last resort when the central bank is constrained in the creation of money, arises today in countries with currency boards, where foreign exchange holdings constrain the domestic money supply. If the question is how to deal with domestic financial institutions that may suffer liquidity problems, one solution adopted in Bulgaria, where the banking department of the central bank is assigned the task of (limited) lender of last resort, is to set up an agency that is endowed with sufficient resources to lend in the event of a panic or banking sector problems. If the problem is how to deal with a potential external shock that puts pressure on the domestic banking system, then the country may either hold excess foreign exchange reserves, or as in the case of Argentina, borrow from the markets and the official sector and put in place international lines of credit. In these cases, the private and public sector lenders to the central bank are acting as the crisis lender, while the central bank is acting as crisis manager.[7]

These examples make the point that lender of last resort need not have the power to create money, as long as it can provide credit to the market or to institutions in trouble. It is possible to set up an agency to deal with potential banking sector problems and endow it with sufficient funds – perhaps from the Treasury – to cover the anticipated costs of normal crises. In dealing with banking crises, the lender of last resort has more often acted as crisis

---

7 Of course, the question arises why any external financing is needed in response to a currency shock if the rules of the currency board are strictly applied. The answer is that the monetary authority may want to mitigate the adverse effects of an external shock on the banking system and the economy.

manager, as coordinator, without putting up its own funds, than as outright lender. In the 20-year period ending in 1993, taxpayer or deposit insurance money was used in over half the 120 banking rescue packages studied by Goodhart and Schoenmaker (1995), in part because the central bank simply did not have the real resources that were required to deal with the banking problem. In any case, the costs of major financial system difficulties will one way or another be borne by the fiscal authority, either explicitly or implicitly, in the form of lower central bank profits over an extended period of time.[8]

This point – that while it is advantageous for the lender of last resort to be able to create money, it is not an essential attribute of the lender of last resort – is both central to the argument of this paper, and controversial. I make the argument on logical and historical grounds, namely, that it is possible to conceive of an institution that does not have the ability to create money acting usefully as both crisis manager and crisis lender and that as a historical matter, such institutions have usefully undertaken such roles. Others would argue that without the ability to create unlimited amounts of money, the would-be lender of last resort lacks credibility and thus cannot stabilize a panic. Those who take the latter view should interpret the argument of this paper as being that there is a useful role to be played by an institution that can be both crisis manager and crisis lender, even if – according to their own definition – it cannot be a lender of last resort.

Why should a lender of last resort lend only against collateral, especially collateral evaluated at its value in noncrisis times?

By basing the decision to lend on the availability of acceptable collateral, the lender of last resort applies a rough but robust test of whether the institution is in trouble because of the immediate panic, or because of an insolvency that will persist even after the panic. Moreover, when financial institutions know that the lender of last resort will demand collateral, they have an incentive to reduce risks in their portfolios by holding assets that would be accepted as collateral.

The requirement that the collateral be good in normal times is the critical insight. The implicit view behind the requirement that the lender of last resort require collateral, and that the collateral be valued at noncrisis levels, is that there is a good equilibrium towards which the lender of last resort is trying to steer the system. By lending on the basis of the value of collateral in normal times, the lender of last resort helps prevent the panic in the market from becoming self-fulfilling.

---

8   Not all financial crises need ultimately to be costly to the public sector; indeed, if the lender of last resort intervenes in a pure panic and manages to stabilize the situation, it should expect to come out ahead when its lending is repaid. Apparently both the Swedish and Norwegian bank restructuring agencies that were set up in the crises of the early 1990s have come close to meeting this criterion. (I am indebted to my colleague Stefan Ingves for this information.)

More broadly, this rule also suggests that the lender of last resort should apply the rules of collateral generously. In a famous passage bearing on this point, Bagehot (1873 [1924 edition, p. 52]) quotes the Bank of England in 1825: 'We lent it by every possible means and in modes we had never adopted before; we took in stock on security, we purchased Exchequer bills, we made advances on Exchequer bills, we not only discounted outright but we made advances on the deposit of bills of exchange to an immense amount, in short by every possible means consistent with the safety of the bank, and we were not on some occasions over-nice.' In a similar spirit, the Governor of the Bank of England described the Bank's reaction to the Overend financial crisis in May 1866 (as quoted in Clapham, 1944, Volume II, pp. 283–4): 'We did not flinch from our post . . . we made advances which would hardly have been credited . . . before the Chancellor of the Exchequer was perhaps out of his bed we had advanced one-half of our reserves . . . I am not aware that any legitimate application for assistance made to this house was refused.'

Why should the lender of last resort charge a penalty interest rate?

The penalty interest rate serves several functions. It limits the demand for credit by institutions that are not in trouble. It reduces the risk that financial institutions will take excessive risks in normal times, secure in the knowledge that they will be able to borrow cheaply in tough times. It encourages institutions to repay the lender of last resort as soon as possible after the crisis, in preference to other outstanding loans.[9]

But just as the requirement for collateral is not intended to stifle the lender of last resort, neither is the application of penalty interest rates. The penalty rate need not be defined relative to the rate at which institutions would lend to each other in the market during a panic. Instead, the penalty must be relative to the interest rate during normal times. In practice, the lender of last resort has frequently lent at a nonpenalty rate (Giannini, 1998).

Should the lender of last resort lend only to the market, and not to individual institutions?

This view holds that, given the provision of sufficient liquidity to the markets, the private sector will be able to decide which institutions should be saved.

---

9   Mints (1945, pp. 191) attributes Bagehot's advocacy of a high lending rate to his view that internal and external drains typically accompany each other; that is, an internal financial panic under a gold standard was often accompanied by gold leaving the country. The high interest rate was designed to stop the external drain of gold, and lending freely would stop the internal drain – a reading that is consistent with Bagehot.

Moreover, by providing liquidity to the market, the lender of last resort avoids the political hazards of lending to individual institutions.

This idea is a worthy one that should be followed when possible. But given the uncertainties in the midst of a panic over what market conditions will exist in the future, and thus over which institutions should survive, the precept cannot be accepted as a general rule of conduct for the lender of last resort. Almost by definition of a financial panic, a market in the throes of a panic will not do a sound job of allocating credit across institutions. Indeed, Goodhart and Huang (1998) argue that adopting the view that the lender of last resort should lend only to the market is to reject the notion of the lender of last resort.

Should the principles on which the lender of last resort would lend be clearly stated in advance?

During a crisis, the knowledge that there is an effective lender of last resort should tend to reduce the incentive for runs on otherwise healthy institutions. However some, who fear that market participants will have an incentive to take excessive risks if they believe a lender of last resort will always be available to stem panics, argue for *constructive ambiguity* about the circumstances in which a lender of last resort will step in to seek to stabilize a crisis. The uncertainty generated by such ambiguity should encourage market participants to take fewer risks.[10]

Some ambiguity is simply unavoidable: no central bank or lender of last resort will ever be able to spell out precisely in advance the circumstances under which it would act as either a crisis lender or crisis manager and the conditions it will lay down at that time. But unnecessary ambiguity is not constructive, for it implies that occasions will occur when the putative lender of last resort is expected to deliver, but does not – for example in the Russian crisis of August 1998, when many market participants expected the official sector to prevent a Russian devaluation. In such a setting, ambiguity makes the economic costs of a given financial crisis worse; indeed, Guttentag and Herring (1983, pp. 24) describe as the worst possible system as one in which a lender of last resort is expected to take action, but the relevant institution cannot or does not provide the function.

There are three reasons for a lender of last resort to spell out its rules to the extent possible. First, by specifying a good set of rules, the central bank reduces the likelihood of unnecessary self-justifying crises. This was Bagehot's (1873) justification. Second, by announcing and implementing a particular set of rules, the lender of last resort provides incentives for other stabilizing private sector behavior; for instance, in the holding of assets good for

10 Freixas (1999) develops a theoretical case for constructive ambiguity by the lender of last resort.

collateral. Third, by spelling out the rules in advance, the lender of last resort somewhat limits its own freedom of action after the event, which reduces risks of politically motivated or spur-of-the-moment actions. Of course, *in extremis* the rules could be broken as they were by the Bank of England when it violated the gold standard rules to provide additional credit during crises in the 19th century. Spelling out the rules would nonetheless serve a useful purpose, since the lender of last resort would hesitate before incurring the cost of breaking them.

Much of the discussion of these six questions revolves around a common topic, the issue of moral hazard, to which I will now turn.

Moral hazard

'Moral hazard,' notes Guesnerie (1987, pp. 646), 'refers to the adverse effects, from the insurance company's point of view, that insurance may have on the insuree's behaviour.' The standard but extreme example is that of an individual with fire insurance who burns down the property; the less extreme example is of a fire insurance holder who, after becoming insured, takes less care to prevent a fire. More generally, the idea of moral hazard applies to any situation where a perceived reduction in the risk it faces leads a party to take riskier actions, or to neglect precautionary measures.

In the case of the domestic lender of last resort, moral hazard problems could arise with respect to both the actions of managers of financial institutions who believe they are better protected against risk because they would receive loans from the lender of last resort during a crisis, and the actions of investors in those financial institutions (Hirsch, 1977). If the lender of last resort was able to intervene only to stop unwarranted panics, leaving institutions that would be insolvent in normal times to fail, the managers of these institutions and their investors would face the right incentives and there would be no moral hazard created by the existence of the lender of last resort. But the lender of last resort is unlikely to be able to distinguish perfectly between warranted and unwarranted crises. Moreover, financial institutions already know that because of the existence of deposit insurance and the too-big-to-fail doctrine that the government has an incentive to prevent them from failing and thus already have a moral hazard motivation to believe that a government rescue of some sort will be forthcoming. For all these reasons, measures to offset the moral hazard of both managers of financial institutions and investors would be helpful.

In considering how to reduce moral hazard, it is important to recognize that the problem has no perfect solution. Instead, appropriate policies will generally combine the provision of insurance with measures to limit moral hazard. In the case of moral hazard resulting from the existence of a lender of last resort (as well as resulting from deposit insurance and too-big-to-fail provisions), there are three categories of measures to limit moral hazard: official regulation; encouragement for private sector monitoring and self-regulation;

and the imposition of costs on those who make mistakes, including enforcement of bankruptcy procedures when appropriate (Stern, 1999). I consider these in turn.

First, to be eligible for loans from a lender of last resort, banks' portfolio activities are regulated. The regulations are intended to limit the likelihood of panics and the need for a lender of last resort, while not preventing well-informed risk taking by investors.

Second, the system seeks to encourage private sector monitoring of financial institutions, particularly by sophisticated investors. Requirements for the provision of information to investors are helpful in this regard. The limit on the size of bank accounts covered by deposit insurance is intended to provide an incentive for large depositors to monitor banks (along with limiting government liability in the case of a bank failure); however, because of concerns that large institutions are too big to fail without threatening financial contagion, these limits rarely operate when large institutions get into trouble. In addition, when the lender of last resort, acting as crisis manager, arranges a bank rescue package financed by the private sector, it encourages more careful monitoring by such institutions in the future.

Third, the lender of last resort should seek to limit moral hazard by imposing costs on those who have made mistakes. Lending at a penalty rate is one way to impose such costs. Changes in management of an institution that is being helped should typically occur, and, as specified in Meltzer's fifth law stated above, equity-holders and holders of subordinated claims on the firm should suffer losses. In the case of insolvency, institutions should be sold or liquidated under the provisions of well-defined bankruptcy laws, which help ensure that workouts for insolvent firms are carried out in an orderly way.

How well do these devices work to limit moral hazard work? A first judgment, based on the frequency of financial crises around the world during the last two decades, is this: Not very well. But this answer is too sweeping. Moral hazard is something to be lived with and controlled, rather than fully eliminated; some crises are bound to happen in any system that provides appropriate scope for private sector risk taking; and many financial crises have been caused by waves of euphoria and depression, not by the existence of a lender of last resort – for after all, the long history of financial crises predates lenders of last resort and deposit insurance. The right comparison is not between the real world and a hypothetical world with no financial crises, but rather between the operation of a system with a lender of last resort (and deposit insurance) and one without them. I am not aware of careful studies that have attempted to make this more sophisticated judgment. However, I suspect that such a study, while likely to absolve the presence of various official forms of financial insurance, including the assumption that there is a lender of last resort, from blame for much financial instability, would conclude that it is important to do a better job of controlling moral hazard in the domestic financial system.

An international lender of last resort?

The case for a domestic lender of last resort is broadly accepted. In the aftermath of the global financial turmoil of the last five years, the question arises of whether the international financial system needs a lender of last resort.

The issue is whether there is a useful role for an institution that takes responsibility for dealing with potential and actual crises, either as a crisis lender, or as a crisis manager, or both. This differs from the question that is sometimes asked as to whether leading central banks should accept some responsibility for the performance of the global economy, along with their national economy. For instance, when Kindleberger (1986) blames the Great Depression on the absence of an international lender of last resort, he means that no agency – and the natural candidates were the Bank of England, the Banque de France, and the U.S. Federal Reserve – pursued a monetary policy that took account of the international dimensions of the crisis in which it found itself. Kindleberger would probably say, approvingly, that in the late 1990s, the Fed *has* acted as international lender of last resort in that sense, even though it was taking actions in the interests of the United States.

I will focus specifically on the case for an international agency to act as lender of last resort for countries facing an external financing crisis. In such a crisis, a country – and by this I mean both the official and private sectors within the country – faces a typically massive demand for foreign exchange. The domestic central bank cannot produce this currency. Thus, the fact that the country may have its own central bank capable of creating the domestic currency is typically irrelevant to the solution of an external financing problem.

There is a potential need for such assistance to a country both because international capital flows are not only extremely volatile but also contagious, exhibiting the classic signs of financial panics,[11] and because an international lender of last resort can help mitigate the effects of this instability and perhaps the instability itself. At the macroeconomic level, a country faced with a sudden demand for foreign exchange can permit its exchange rate to adjust and/or can restrict domestic demand to generate a current account surplus. At the microeconomic level, foreign creditors can attempt to collect on obligations and financial institutions and corporations can – if necessary, and if the domestic legal system is adequate – be put into bankruptcy. However, all such measures are likely in a panic to result in a considerable overshooting of the needed adjustment, and there is accordingly a case for the public sector both to provide emergency foreign exchange loans and to assist the domestic authorities in attempting to manage the crisis.

---

11 For models with multiple equilibria in an international context, see Chang and Velasco (1998) and Zettelmeyer (1998).

The argument rests also on the view that international capital mobility is potentially beneficial for the world economy, including for the emerging market and developing countries. Critics of this view argue that neither the theoretical nor empirical evidence supports a positive link between openness to international capital markets and growth. Indeed, both China and India have grown rapidly during the 1990s with only limited openness to international capital markets and appeared relatively immune from the east Asian financial crisis. It is true that there is as yet little convincing econometric evidence bearing on the benefits or costs of open capital markets. However, all the economically most advanced countries are open to international flows of capital, which suggests that this should be the eventual goal for other countries. In addition, countries that close themselves off to international flows of capital also thereby protect the financial sector from foreign competition, which reduces the efficiency of this important industry. Finally, I suspect, but cannot of course establish, that with regard to empirical work on the benefits of capital account liberalization, the economics profession is a little behind where we were a decade ago on trade liberalization, when empirical work showing its benefits was widely regarded as highly suspect, too.

But the critics of international capital mobility are correct to this extent: its potential for economic benefit can only be realized if the frequency and scale of financial crises can be reduced. The founders of the Bretton Woods system provided for the use of controls on international capital flows to reduce the likelihood of such crises. Some controls – particularly controls that seek to limit short-term capital *inflows* – can be envisaged as a useful part of a transitional regime while the macroeconomic framework and financial structure of an economy are strengthened. The use of controls to limit capital *outflows* has been advocated in the recent crises by several academics and adopted by Malaysia. But it is surprising and impressive how few countries have enacted capital controls in recent years. Indeed, policymakers in Latin American countries that often had such controls in the 1980s have rejected them this time around, emphasizing that the controls were inefficient, widely avoided, and had cost them dearly in terms of capital market access. It remains an open question whether more countries will turn to capital controls in the next few years, either in normal times or in the midst of crises. The answer will depend to an important extent on the success of other financial reforms that are implemented in the next few years.

I will argue not only that the international system needs a lender of last resort, so that the global economy can reap greater net benefits from international capital mobility, but also that the IMF has increasingly been playing the role of crisis manager for the last two decades (Boughton, 1998). Changes in the international system now under consideration – particularly those relating to efforts to bail in the private sector – should make it possible for the IMF to exercise the lender of last resort function more effectively.

In focusing on the Fund's potential role as lender of last resort, I leave aside its other important functions. For example, Article I(i) of the Articles of Agreement, as enacted in 1944, describes the first of its fundamental purposes as being: '[t]o promote international monetary cooperation through a permanent institution which provides the machinery for consultation and collaboration on international monetary problems.' Other functions of the Fund include lending for current account purposes to countries that lack market access; surveillance and the associated provision of information; and technical assistance, including policy advice and monitoring.

Let me immediately turn to the argument that the IMF cannot act as a lender of last resort because it is not an international central bank and cannot freely create international money. As discussed earlier, even the domestic lender of last resort – whether as crisis lender or as crisis manager – is not necessarily the central bank. The IMF has resources to act as a crisis lender, because its financial structure, close to that of a credit union,[12] gives it access to a pool of resources which it can lend to member countries. The IMF also has been assigned the lead as crisis manager in negotiating with member countries in a crisis and helping to arrange financing packages. Finally, as will be discussed below, it also has the ability – not so far used – to create international reserves in a crisis.

The question arises whether the IMF, as crisis lender, has sufficient resources to do the job. The Fund has reached its present size as a result of a series of increases in countries' quotas – that is, the amount which members of the IMF agree to deposit in the Fund in their own currencies. Relative to the size of the world economy, the IMF has shrunk significantly since 1945. If the Fund were today the same size relative to the output of its member states as it was in 1945, it would be more than three times larger.[13] If the quota formula applied in 1945 were used to calculate actual quotas today, the Fund would be five times its present size. If the size of the Fund had been maintained relative to the volume of world trade, it would be more than nine times larger; that is, the size of the Fund would be over $2.5 trillion. Since the Fund was set up at a time when private capital flows were very small, its scale relative to private capital flows has declined even more than its size relative to trade flows.

Despite this significant shrinkage relative to the original conception, the Fund as lender of last resort is still able to assemble a sizeable financial package in response to a crisis. In case of systemic problems, the Fund can augment the use of its own resources by borrowing. Further, as demonstrated in the recent Brazilian and east Asian financial rescue packages, member governments and other international financial institutions may add significantly to these packages in cases they deem to be of particular importance. Whether the Fund will in future be large enough relative to the scale of

---

12 The analogy is due to Kenen (1986).
13 Total quotas are approximately $300 billion. The effective availability of resources to lend is smaller, since the weaker currencies held by the Fund are not in practice usable for lending.

problems will depend on the future scale and volatility of international capital flows, which will in turn depend on the effectiveness of reforms, including measures to deal with problems of moral hazard.

The earlier discussion noted in the domestic case that while it is not essential that the lender of last resort be the central bank, it is helpful. Would it be useful for the IMF to be able to create reserves? Under Article XVIII of the Articles of Agreement, the Executive Board of the Fund can by an 85 percent majority allocate Special Drawing Rights (SDRs) 'to meet the long-term global need, as and when it arises, to supplement existing reserve assets.' These SDRs would augment the reserves of member countries. It is easy to envisage circumstances under which a targeted increase in reserves would be useful to prevent a seizing up of flows of credit in the world economy; indeed, for a short period that seemed to be the case in the fall of 1998. However, a general allocation of SDRs has to be made in proportion to quota holdings and so this mechanism would not in its current form be well-suited to dealing with a problem that affects a specific group of countries.

The IMF thus has the capacity to act as crisis lender to individual countries, and in specified circumstances, through an issue of Special Drawing Rights, could lend more broadly. It also acts as crisis manager. Kindleberger (1996, p. 188) complains that the Fund is too slow in emergencies, but in Korea in late 1997 the IMF has demonstrated an ability to move very rapidly, using the Emergency Financing Mechanism introduced after the Mexican crisis in 1994. The main constraint on the IMF's ability to react speedily in a crisis is that governments suffering a financial crisis delay too long in approaching it, in part because excessive delay is a common characteristic of governments that experience financial crises, but also because they hope to avoid taking the actions that would be needed in a Fund program.

The evolving context of the international financial system

The IMF already acts in important respects as international lender of last resort, but the job can surely be done better. However, before addressing that issue directly, I will discuss four central elements in the ongoing evolution of the international financial system: exchange rate systems; reserve holdings; measures to bail in the private sector; and international standards.

In regard to the first subject, over a century of controversy has produced no clear answer to the question of which exchange rate system or monetary regime is best. The best exchange rate for a country seems to depend on the country's economic history, particularly its history of inflation. Nonetheless, it is striking that the major external financial crises of the last three years – in Thailand, Korea, Indonesia, Russia and Brazil – have affected countries with more or less pegged exchange rates. Further, the assumption within these countries that the exchange rate was stable profoundly affected economic behavior and certain kinds of risk taking, especially in the banking system, and contributed to the severity of the post-devaluation crises.

The link between pegged exchange rates and susceptibility to crisis is far from ironclad, however. Several countries with very hard pegs, particularly Argentina and Hong Kong, have succeeded with fixed exchange rates. Some countries with flexible rates, among them Mexico, South Africa and Turkey, have been severely affected by the global economic crisis. Nor should we forget that many countries benefitted from using a pegged or fixed exchange rate as a nominal anchor in disinflation efforts and that the fear of devaluation is often a vital discipline for weak governments. Nonetheless, the virulence of the recent crises is likely to shift the balance towards the choice of more flexible exchange rate systems, including crawling exchange rate pegs with wide bands.

But while the number of nominal exchange rate pegs may decline in the coming years, the world is unlikely to move to a system in which exchange rates for all countries float freely. If countries desire to fix their exchange rates, they may well want to do so definitively, through a currency board. In the longer run, if Europe's move to a single currency succeeds, the result may be additional currency unions and fewer currencies. Because sharp shifts in international investor sentiment regarding even a country with a floating rate can set off a panic and contagion, and because some countries will continue to peg their rates, the need will still exist for an international lender of last resort.

Second, regarding the issue of reserves, there has been surprisingly little emphasis on the fact that countries with very large foreign exchange reserves have generally fared better in the recent economic crises than those with small reserves. However, a number of countries, particularly Korea, have recognized that ratio of reserves to short-term external liabilities is an important factor determining the likelihood of a financial crisis (Calvo, 1995), and are accumulating reserves accordingly.[14]

Foreign exchange reserves can be built up in several ways. The most obvious approach is to run a current account surplus; indeed, it is likely that a general desire by emerging market countries to built up reserves by running current account surpluses will impart a deflationary impact to the world economy in the next few years. Reserves can be borrowed, although the interest costs are typically well above the return on reserves. Argentina and a few other countries have put into place a variation on the idea of borrowing reserves, which is to arrange for precautionary or contingent lines of credit, which can be drawn on at short notice if needed. International reserves might also be increased by international agreement on, for example, an issue of Special Drawing Rights. It is not possible without a more detailed analysis to decide which approach is preferable: the approaches differ in terms of effects

---

14 The focus in the text is on the numerator of the ratio of reserves to short-term debt; however, countries need also to ensure that the denominator stays under control. This element plays an important role in the evolving international architecture, but I shall not pursue it here.

on aggregate demand, the distribution of seigniorage and other variables. However, I expect that one way or another, the recent experience of crises will lead to larger holdings of reserves.

Third, no topic in the new international financial architecture has received as much public attention as the need to involve the private sector in the resolution of financial crises. The arguments are simple and compelling. At the economic level, as the role of private capital flows in the international economy increases, the public sector should not take upon itself the full responsibility for financing countries from which the private sector is withdrawing, for to do so is to court moral hazard on a major scale, to set the wrong incentives for private sector investors and to accept an impossible task – since the public sector will not in the end have enough resources to carry out such a commitment. At the political level, elected officials are unwilling to make public money available for unlimited bailouts of previously incautious private investors.

One approach, just mentioned, is to put in place precautionary lines of credit from private sector lenders. Such lines of credit can serve as a useful supplement to the holding of reserves, and might well be cheaper than actually increasing reserves. A second approach, suggested in a report by the C-10 deputies after the Mexican crisis, is the proposal that bond contracts should be modified to facilitate the rescheduling of payments in the event of a crisis, including by permitting creditors to make decisions by majority rather than unanimity.[15] Yet another suggestion, associated with Jeffrey Sachs, is the possibility of a mechanism which would formally impose or allow a stay on payments by a country in financial crisis, a proposal which is sometimes referred to as international bankruptcy. Some developing countries object that such measures would make it more expensive for them to borrow, but most likely that would reflect a more appropriate pricing of risks.

Private sector involvement in external financing crises needs to be approached carefully, lest proposed solutions increase the frequency of crises. For instance, it is sometimes proposed that banks (or other creditors) should always be forced to share in the financing of IMF programs. But if such a condition were insisted on, the creditors would have a greater incentive to rush for the exits at the mere hint of a crisis. This problem suggests that even with private sector involvement, a lender of last resort will continue to be necessary. It also suggests that the involvement of the private sector should differ according to the circumstances of each country: sometimes a formal approach may be necessary, as in Korea at the end of 1997; at other times less formal discussions could serve better; and on occasion, if a country enters an IMF program sufficiently early, perhaps private creditors need not be approached at all.

---

15 This possibility is developed in the report of the [G-22] Working Group on *International Financial Crises*. See also the speech by Gordon Brown (1998).

Fourth, because weaknesses in financial sectors and in the provision of information were such an important factor in the recent crises, a major effort is now underway to encourage emerging market countries to meet agreed international standards of financial and corporate sector behavior, as well as the provision of information. The best-known standards are those for banking, defined by the Basel Committee on Banking Supervision. The IMF's Special Data Dissemination Standard has just gone into full operation. Codes of fiscal practice and monetary and financial transparency are also being prepared by the IMF in cooperation with other institutions. A major international effort will be undertaken to improve banking standards, in part through international monitoring and IMF surveillance in cooperation with the World Bank. Among other important international standards already developed or in the process of development are international accounting standards, International Organization of Securities Commissions (IOSCO) standards for the operation of securities markets, and an international standard for bankruptcy regulations.

The main incentives for a country to adopt any of these standards are the expectation that the economy would operate more efficiently and the hope that international investors would treat the economy more favorably. In fact, most leading emerging market countries have subscribed to the IMF's Special Data Dissemination Standard, which suggests that these incentives may suffice to encourage participation in international standards. Nonetheless, further incentives may prove useful; for instance, the risk weights assigned by regulators in creditor countries could reflect the recipient country's observance of the standards. Further incentives can be provided by the appropriate design of official lending facilities.

Improving the functioning of the international lender of last resort

At the end of 1997, the IMF introduced the Supplemental Reserve Facility (SRF), which can make short-term loans in large amounts at penalty rates to countries in crisis. SRF loans have been made to Korea, Russia, and Brazil, subject to conditions that certain economic policies be followed. In addition, in April 1999, the Executive Board of the IMF established the Contingent Credit Line (CCL) facility, designed to provide countries with a line of credit that can be drawn on in the event they are struck by contagion from an external crisis. To qualify for a CCL, a country must be pursuing good macroeconomic policies, have a strong financial sector and either meet or be moving towards meeting international standards in a variety of areas. The CCL is thus intended to provide an element of insurance and reassurance for countries with good policies, and incentives for others to pursue good policies, rather than to come to the assistance of countries that are already in trouble. The lending terms for the CCL are similar to those for the SRF. No CCLs have yet been arranged.

Calomiris (1998) and Calomiris and Meltzer (1998) recommend that the IMF act only as lender of last resort, under Bagehot rules, and only to countries that meet a stiff set of requirements, most importantly on the banking system. Among these conditions is the requirement that foreign banks be allowed to operate in the country, a reform that countries should adopt in any case. Loans would be made to qualifying countries on the basis of collateral, and without policy conditionality. Without going into the overall merits of their analysis,[16] I would like to note that the CCL goes some way towards meeting their proposals. It would further be desirable if the rate charged for access to the CCL and the SRF depended on the extent to which countries meet the relevant international standards. For example, a nonqualifying country might pay a higher penalty interest rate, or be subject to tougher policy conditionality, or in extreme cases, be denied access to the lender of last resort funds.

IMF lending under the Supplemental Reserve Facility incorporates the classic Bagehot (1873) prescription that crisis lending should be at a penalty rate. Policy conditionality can be interpreted as a further element of the penalty, as seen from the viewpoint of the borrower country's policymakers. But what about the Bagehot prescriptions that lending should take place on good collateral, and that institutions that would be bankrupt in normal times should not be saved?

The Articles of Agreement permit the Fund to ask for collateral, but it has rarely done so. The Fund and the World Bank are regarded as preferred creditors, who have a first claim on payments made by countries in debt to them, and their collateral is thus the threat of denying access to global capital markets to countries that default. That is the main, and a powerful and effective, incentive for countries to repay – which is almost always done, in full and on time. While collateralized lending should remain a possibility for the Fund, it does not seem to be essential given the Fund's preferred creditor status.

The more general Bagehot prescription that institutions which are truly bankrupt should not be saved by a lender of last resort is difficult to apply in the international context. To the extent that foreign creditors have claims on private sector corporations in a debtor country, the bankruptcy rules for the debtor country should apply and the Bagehot prescription would be relevant. But it has to be recognized that bankruptcy regulations in many emerging market countries have been ineffective, which is why an effort is now underway to develop an international standard for a domestic bankruptcy code. For a sovereign debtor, the ability to generate repayments is more a matter of political than of economic feasibility. There is no bankruptcy status for a

16 I note for the record that the suggestion that the IMF should operate only as lender of last resort either overlooks or grossly undervalues the other functions carried out by the IMF, which were noted earlier in this discussion.

sovereign, but workout procedures, including those of the Paris and London Clubs, and possibly those to be developed as private sector bail-ins are considered further, play a similar role.

The one Bagehot prescription that does not apply in an international crisis is that of lending freely, if by freely is meant without limit. As already discussed, such a policy would create too much moral hazard.[17] How can an international crisis lender and manager deal with moral hazard problems? Charging a penalty rate of interest should help discourage borrower moral hazard, but moral hazard for borrowers is of much less concern than for investors. Borrower moral hazard is already deterred by the requirements of policy conditionality. Governments try to avoid going to the IMF – indeed they frequently delay too long – and policymakers who preside over a crisis and then have to turn to the IMF generally lose office, as witness the Asian crisis countries and Russia.

Investor moral hazard – that a lender of last resort would encourage investors to loan unwisely – is a more serious concern. In considering this issue, it is important to distinguish the hazards associated with different types of international capital flows.[18] In the case of equity investment, for example, the investor needs to be held responsible – and they have been, for equity investors have taken large losses in the recent crises. In the case of interbank lines of credit, however, the responsibility for addressing the risk of unwise lending because of moral hazard lies as much with the government of the lender as with the borrower government, for it is the former which supervises and tends to protect its banks. Lender supervisory authorities will have to recognize the responsibilities of their institutions to participate in workout procedures and private sector bail-ins when necessary.

The single most important change in the international system that will tend to limit moral hazard by encouraging better monitoring and self-regulation by capital market participants is the adoption of better methods of involving the private sector in financing the resolution of crises. As discussed above, the issues here are immensely difficult; they are also immensely important. Unless better ways of involving the private sector are found, the IMF will not be able to perform its proper function as international lender of last resort, both as crisis lender and crisis manager. At present, the official sector is seeking to involve private sector lenders in several countries in crisis; as this experience is analyzed within the coming months, some general principles for how to involve the private sector should be distilled and begun to be implemented in cases of crisis lending by the IMF and other official institutions.

The crises of the last five years have revealed major weaknesses in the structure of the international economy. It is urgent to start developing and implementing the constructive solutions that have been proposed, among

---

17 To say this does not, however, determine the optimal size of crisis loans.
18 I am grateful to Mervyn King for emphasizing this point.

them improvements in transparency, the adoption of appropriate exchange rate systems, the development and monitoring of international standards, including a bankruptcy standard, the development of precautionary lines of credit, and methods to involve the private sector in financing the resolution of emerging market crises. Important progress has been made during the last twelve months. As these changes continue to be implemented, the role of the international lender of last resort will become both better defined and more effective.

■ *This is a revised version of a paper prepared for delivery at the joint luncheon of the American Economic Association and the American Finance Association, New York, January 3, 1999. A longer version of the paper will be published in the Princeton Series in International Finance. I am grateful to my MIT colleague Charles Kindleberger for sparking my interest in this question many years ago, for his support and for the pleasure provided by a fresh reading of* Manias, Panics, and Crashes; *to Mervyn King for helpful discussions during the writing of the paper; to Allan Meltzer, Olivier Blanchard, Jack Boorman, Guillermo Calvo, J. Bradford De Long, Peter Diamond, Eduardo Fernandez-Arias, Curzio Giannini, Charles Goodhart, Stephen Grenville, Bengt Holmstrom, Alexandre Kafka, Arend Kapteyn, Peter Kenen, Martin Mayer, Frederic Mishkin, Jacques Polak, Andrei Shleifer, Robert Solow, John Spraos, Onno Wijnholds, and David Williams for helpful comments and discussions; to Timothy Taylor for his editing; and to Claire Adams for excellent research assistance. The views expressed in this paper are those of the author, and are not necessarily those of the International Monetary Fund; indeed, it may safely be said that they are not the views of some members of the International Monetary Fund.*

References

Bagehot, Walter. 1873. *Lombard Street: A Description of the Money Market*. London: William Clowes and Sons.

Benston, George, Robert Eisenbeis, Paul Horvitz, Edward Kane and George Kaufman. 1986. *Perspectives on Safe and Sound Banking: Past, Present, and Future*. Cambridge, Massachusetts: MIT Press.

Boughton, James. 1998. 'From Suez to Tequila: The IMF as Crisis Manager.' Unpublished; Washington: International Monetary Fund.

Brown, Gordon. 1998. 'Rediscovering Public Purpose in the Global Economy.' Speech delivered at the Kennedy School, December 15.

Calomiris, Charles. 1998. 'Blueprints for a New Global Financial Architecture.' Unpublished; New York: Columbia Business School.

Calomiris, Charles and Allan H. Meltzer. 1998. 'Reforming the IMF.' Unpublished; New York: Columbia Business School.

Calvo, Guillermo. 1995. 'Varieties of Capital Market Crises.' University of Maryland Center for International Economics, Working Paper 15.

Capie, Forrest. 1998. 'Can there be an International Lender of Last Resort?' Unpublished; London: City University Business School.

Chang, Roberto and Andres Velasco. 1998. 'The Asian Liquidity Crisis.' NBER Working Paper 6796, November.

Chari, V.V. and Patrick J. Kehoe. 1999. 'Asking the Right Questions about the IMF,' in *The Region*, 1998 Annual Report of the Federal Reserve Bank of Minneapolis, pp. 3–26.

Claassen, Emil-Maria. 1985. 'The Lender-of-Last-Resort Function in the Context of National and International Financial Crises.' *Weltwirtschaftliches Archiv.* 121:2, pp. 217–37.

Clapham, Sir John. 1944. *The Bank of England.* Cambridge: Cambridge University Press.

Diamond, Douglas and Philip Dybvig. 1983. 'Bank Runs, Deposit Insurance, and Liquidity.' *Journal of Political Economy.* June, 91:3, pp. 401–19.

Freixas, Xavier. 1999. 'Optimal Bail Out Policy, Conditionality ad Creative Ambiguity.' Unpublished; Bank of England.

Garcia, Gillian and Elizabeth Plautz. 1988. *The Federal Reserve: Lender of Last Resort.* Cambridge, Massachusetts: Ballinger.

Giannini, Curzio. 1998. 'Enemy of None but a Common Friend to All? An International Perspective on the Lender-of-Last-Resort Function.' Unpublished; Washington: International Monetary Fund.

Goodfriend, Marvin and Jeffrey M. Lacker. 1999. 'Limited Commitment and Central Bank Lending.' Federal Reserve Bank of Richmond, Working Paper January, 99:2.

Goodhart, Charles A. E. 1995. *The Central Bank and the Financial System.* Cambridge, Massachusetts: MIT Press.

Goodhart, Charles A. E. and Haizhou Huang. 1998. 'A Model of the Lender of Last Resort.' Unpublished; Washington: International Monetary Fund.

Goodhart, Charles A. E. and Dirk Schoenmaker. 1995. 'Should the Functions of Monetary Policy and Bank Supervision Be Separated?' *Oxford Economic Papers.* 47, pp. 539–60.

Guesnerie, Roger. 1987. 'Hidden Actions, Moral Hazard and Contract Theory,' in *The New Palgrave: A Dictionary of Economics.* Eatwell, John, Murray Milgate and Peter Newman, eds. Volume II, pp. 646–51. London: The Macmillan Press.

Guttentag, Jack and Richard Herring. 1983. 'The Lender-of-Last-Resort Function in an International Context.' *Princeton University Essay in International Finance.* No. 151, May.

Hirsch, Fred. 1977. 'The Bagehot Problem.' *The Manchester School.* September, 45:3, pp. 241–57.

Holmstrom, Bengt and Jean Tirole. 1998. 'Private and Public Supply of Liquidity.' *Journal of Political Economy.* February, 106:1, pp. 1–40.

Humphrey, Thomas. 1975. 'The Classical Concept of the Lender of Last Resort.' *Federal Reserve Bank of Richmond Economic Review.* February, 61, pp. 2–9.

Humphrey, Thomas and Robert Keleher. 1984. 'Lender of Last Resort: An Historical Perspective.' *Cato Journal.* 4:1, pp. 275–321.

Jeanne, Olivier. 1998. 'The International Liquidity Mismatch and the New Architecture.' Unpublished; Washington: International Monetary Fund.

Kaufman, George. 1988. 'The Truth about Bank Runs,' in *The Financial Services Revolution: Policy Directions for the Future.* England, C. and T. Huertas, eds. Boston: Kluwer Academic Publishers.

Kenen, Peter. 1986. *Financing, Adjustment, and the International Monetary Fund.* Washington: Brookings Institution.

Kindleberger, Charles. 1996. *Manias, Panics, and Crashes: A History of Financial Crisis (Wiley Investment Classics Series)*. New York: John Wiley & Sons, 3rd edition. (First edition, 1978).

Kindleberger, Charles. 1986. *The World in Depression, 1929–1939*. Revised and enlarged edition. Berkeley: University of California Press.

MacKay, Charles. 1841. *Extraordinary Popular Delusions and the Madness of Crowds*. New York: Farrar, Straus and Giroux (reprint, 1932).

Meltzer, Allan. 1986. 'Financial Failures and Financial Policies,' in *Deregulating Financial Services: Public Policy in Flux*. Kaufman, G. G. and R. C. Kormendi, eds. Cambridge, Massachusetts: Ballinger.

Meltzer, Allan. 1998. 'What's Wrong with the IMF? What Would be Better?' Paper prepared for Federal Reserve Bank of Chicago Conference: *Asia: An Analysis of Financial Crisis*, October 8–10.

Mints, Lloyd W. 1945. *A History of Banking Theory*. Chicago: University of Chicago Press.

Mishkin, Frederic S. 1999. 'Lessons from the Asian Crisis.' National Bureau of Economic Research Working Paper 7102, April.

Mundell, Robert. 1983. 'International Monetary Options.' *Cato Journal* 3:1, pp. 189–210.

Radelet, Steven and Jeffrey D. Sachs. 1998. 'The East Asian Financial Crisis: Diagnosis, Remedies, Prospects.' *Brookings Papers on Economic Activity*. 1, pp. 1–74.

Schwartz, Anna. 1988. 'Financial Stability and the Federal Safety Net,' in *Restructuring Banking and Financial Services in America*. Haraf, W. S. and G. E. Kushmeider, eds. Washington: American Enterprise Institute.

Solow, Robert. 1982. 'On the Lender of Last Resort,' in Kindleberger, C. P. and J. P. Laffargue, eds. Cambridge: Cambridge University Press.

Stern, Gary. 1999. 'Managing Moral Hazard.' *The Region*. Federal Reserve Bank of Minneapolis, June, 13:2.

Thornton, Henry. 1802. *An Enquiry into the Nature and Effects of the Paper Credit of Great Britain*, Hayek, F. A., ed. Fairfield: Augustus M. Kelley Publishers (reprint, 1978).

Wijnholds, Onno and Arend Kapteyn. 1999. 'The IMF: Lender of Last Resort or Indispensable Lender.' Unpublished; International Monetary Fund, June.

Zettelmeyer, Jeromin. 1998. 'International Financial Crises and Last Resort Lending: Some Issues.' Unpublished; Washington: International Monetary Fund.

19 The IMF's imprudent role as lender of last resort*

*Charles W. Calomiris***

Throughout history, financial collapses have been defining moments for public policy. Crises promote action, embodied in new financial institutions or policy doctrines. The motives that underlie such policies are sometimes short-sighted – driven by short-run pressures rather than long-run principles – and it is easier to enact unwise policy in the midst of crisis than to reverse coures after the crisis has passed, after policies become embodied in institutions or statutes.

The responses by the IMF and the U.S. government to the Mexican crisis of 1994–1995 and the recent Asian crises are examples of dangerous short-sightedness. In the wake of those crises, the Clinton Administration is promoting a new doctrine of global financial bailouts, administered through IMF largesse and conditions. If the IMF and U.S. Treasury are permitted to prevail, the efficiency of global capital markets will suffer, and the incidence and severity of financial crises will grow.

The Mexican and Asian collapses follow a pattern dating back to 1982, and are the byproduct of fundamental flaws in the incentives facing bankers in developing countries. Incentives to assume excessive risk result from the unhealthy partnerships between government and business in many countries, which manifest themselves in taxpayer bailouts of insolvent banks. International support for bank bailouts will deepen that unhealthy partnership, and thus make the preexisting problems in these countries even worse.

The uses of IMF assistance and the U.S. Treasury Department's Exchange Stabilization Fund to bail out insolvent emerging market banks and international bank lenders are not only improper (in the sense that these sources of funds were not designed to be used in this way); such assistance and the doctrine that underlies it are a threat to the stability of the world financial system.

The suggestion that the IMF's capital and facilities should be expanded to permit it to engage in more such activity in the future is troubling. The principal lesson of the recent bailout programs managed by the IMF and the U.S. government (and the longer history of generous domestic bailouts of

* *Cato Journal*, Vol. 17, No. 3, pp. 275–94. Copyright © Cato Institute. All rights reserved.
** Professor of Economics, Columbia University.

banks in developing economies) is the vital need for all parties (including host governments, the IMF and the U.S. government) to find a credible way to commit not to sponsor such counterproductive bailouts.

Why are bailouts misguided?

A guiding principle of a well-functioning market economy is that those who undertake risks should either lose or gain according to the outcomes produced by those decisions. The idea that government, or governments acting through the IMF, should absorb losses when risky decisions turn out badly is fundamentally contrary to this guiding principle of a free-market economy. This is, regrettably, precisely what the IMF and the U.S. government are doing. While assistance is often couched as 'liquidity' assistance to resolve 'balance of payments' problems, in fact assistance is designed to absorb the losses of insolvent banks and their borrowers in developing economies, and to insulate international lenders from the losses that they would otherwise suffer.

What have been the costs of government absorption of financial losses? Three kinds of costs figure prominently: (1) undesirable redistributions of wealth from taxpayers to politically influential oligarchs in developing economies; (2) the promotion of excessive risk taking and inefficient investment; and (3) the undermining of the natural process of deregulation and economic and political reform which global competition would otherwise promote. I will explain each of the three categories of cost in turn.

Bailouts benefit the politically powerful at the expense of others

The first undesirable consequence of these bailouts is the massive redistribution of wealth away from taxpayers in emerging economies, and toward the wealthy political cronies who control their countries' industries and financial institutions, and whose imprudence precipitates financial collapse.

While bailouts entail loans from the IMF and foreign governments at subsidized interest rates to developing country governments, taxpayers in the United States and other developed economies who pay the subsidies associated with these loans are not the biggest losers from the bailouts. The IMF and the U.S. Treasury in most cases are repaid. Loans from the IMF and the U.S. Treasury, however, provide powerful justification for increased taxation to repay the loans. When the crisis has passed, the big winners are the wealthy, politically influential risk takers, and the biggest losers are the taxpayers in countries like Mexico or Indonesia.

Mexico's financial crisis of 1994–95–often seen as a 'success story' by the Clinton Administration – provides a case in point. During the resolution of the Mexican banking collapse, the Mexican government (through its deposit insurance agency) purchased more than $45 billion of bad debts from Mexican banks, half of which are the debts of bank-related conglomerates. The government promised (at the time) that it would not absorb those debts permanently, and that it would hold debtors responsible for paying their obligations. So far, it has done virtually nothing to retrieve funds from borrowers liable for the debts (Financial Times 1997: 2). Together with the nonperforming loans remaining in Mexican banks, the total taxpayer exposure to loss from the bailout of insolvent Mexican banks is estimated at 16 percent of GDP. Thus, in addition to bailing out foreign and domestic bankers who had lent funds to Mexican firms prior to the crisis, the likely result of the Mexican bailout will be the transfer of billions of dollars from Mexican taxpayers collectively to the country's wealthiest and most politically powerful enterprises and individuals. The economic result of these taxes is more than a pure transfer to the rich; taxation has also slowed recovery from the recession.

The bailout and redistribution of wealth in Mexico – like those currently underway in Asia – was blessed by the IMF and the U.S. government. In addition to lending money, the IMF and the U.S. Treasury effectively lend respectability and external political imperatives to tax-and-transfer schemes to benefit the rich.

Some proponents of IMF bailouts argue, however, that by intervening the IMF is able to promote fundamental structural reforms (in particular, reforms to domestic banking systems) that reduce the likelihood of future bailouts. The 1994–95 intervention in Mexico, however, provides contrary evidence. In 1995, I was a member of a World Bank team that provided advice to the Mexican government to assist it in implementing its promised reform of the deposit insurance system, which was part of the package of proposed IMF-U.S. Treasury-World Bank reforms. All deposits are 100 percent insured in Mexico, and this complete insurance has effectively subsidized high-risk bank lending to powerful risk-taking conglomerates. (Insured depositors have little incentive to question the use of their funds, which leaves bankers free to make whatever use of the funds they please.) In November 1995, we presented a detailed plan for reform to the Mexican government that would have introduced a small element of market discipline into the system and thus would have partially removed some of the government subsidies enjoyed by the Mexican banks.

Ostensibly, as a vaguely worded condition for the World Bank to release $500 million in funds to the Mexican government, the government had to agree to consider some version of the reforms we were advocating. After a day of lip service (and the release of the funds), one of the Mexican officials in charge took me aside and expressed his appreciation for my efforts, and then told me that 'of course, the banks won't let us do any of this.' That was not a surprise; why would anyone want to give up a subsidy if they have the political influence to maintain it?

So far, little has been done to introduce market discipline into the Mexican banking system, and there is no reason to believe that anything will be done to limit the current system of subsidizing the risks of the industrial conglomerates and the banks they control. According to unofficial estimates, the overwhelming majority of domestically owned Mexican banks are insolvent.

On average, 40 percent of the loans of domestic Mexican banks are not performing (even after having shed large amounts of their non-performing loans via government subsidized purchases).

The Mexican experience has made me suspicious of IMF financial sector 'conditionality.' I expect similar results from the current conditions being attached to IMF assistance in Asia, where backsliding on conditions has begun even earlier than in Mexico. It is very hard to undermine the corrupt partnership between powerful industrialist-bankers and governments by giving them both money in exchange for promises to reform in the future. It is even harder to do so when those conditions are specified in secret agreements – such secrecy makes it impossible for any outside observer to evaluate the wisdom of the conditions, or gauge a country's eventual compliance with them, which further weakens the incentives of recipient countries to comply.

Indonesia is now working on its third IMF bailout agreement, after staring down the IMF on its two previous 'agreements.' The Economist (1998: 37) noted that 'In January, Mr Suharto promised to dismantle many of the monopolies and cartels which control trade in some products. But he seems to have forgotten to tell the monopolists: the plywood cartel, run by his former golf partner . . . continues to issue instructions to its members. Restructuring of the financial system, awash with red ink, has barely begun.' By mid-March, Suharto had become openly defiant of the IMF. His insistence on a currency board and his announced intention to appoint Mohamad Hasan, 'the biggest of the cronies,' as industry and trade minister, make it hard even for the IMF to argue that conditions will be respected (Borsuk 1998: A12).

Korea's leadership has been much more cooperative with the IMF, but here appearances may be deceiving. As Moon Ilhwan (1998: 54–55) noted in Business Week, President Kim 'wants the banks to stop lending to big companies at preferential rates. But just in the past six weeks, banks have provided nearly $1 billion in "emergency relief loans" to sickly chaebol . . . "The loans are offered at far below market interest rates, and this is a distorted distribution of limited resources," laments Lee Chae Kwang, head of research at Daiwa Securities in Seoul.' IMF aid is being channeled to the banks, which pass it along with impunity to the conglomerates that own them. Thus in Korea, the IMF has not even been able to prevent the immediate misuse of its funds, much less reform the long-term structure of bank-industry relationships.

That is not to say that IMF conditions of all kinds always fail. The IMF has been somewhat successful in getting countries to change tax or expenditure policies, foreign trade policies, and monetary policies. Banking policy is fundamentally different, however, for two reasons. First, real reform in the banking system takes years to accomplish because it entails new ways of measuring and managing risk, new regulations, and new supervisory procedures. These changes are both politically difficult (because the politically powerful must forego subsidies) and technically challenging. The time horizon necessary to implement successful reform is at least five years (judging from the successful examples of Argentina and Chile, which did so very aggressively and voluntarily). Building effective financial institutions, and reforming the legal and regulatory environment in which they operate, is a protracted and difficult learning process, even when countries have the political will to do so.

The horizon of IMF crisis assistance and conditionality (typically two years or so) is simply not suited to achieve true reform in the banking system.

Second, banks are controlled by powerful and concentrated vested interests who are willing to fight hard to maintain their access to subsidized credit and block those reforms. A basic principle of political economy is that powerful minorities (in this case, a handful of conglomerate-controlled banks) generally will be successful in obtaining political favors paid for by fragmented majorities (the average taxpayer).

Thus in practice, crisis countries will always find it easy to promise (but never deliver) true banking reform. Instead, they will tax quickly and deeply, pay back their loans to the IMF, replenish the poker chips of their risk-loving conglomerates, and return to business as usual.

Another criticism of IMF conditions in Asia, as put forth by Martin Feldstein (1998), is that they are inappropriately detailed and microeconomic. Feldstein argues that it is inappropriate for an international agency to intrude so deeply into domestic economic policy, especially since its charter provides no mandate to do so. I agree with that view, but I would hasten to add that the lesson is not that the IMF should provide bailouts with fewer conditions. Rather, I would characterize the new tendency of the IMF to intervene too deeply into the structure of borrowing country economies as the natural result of overstepping the agency's original limits of providing assistance. The new intrusiveness reflects an unwise new goal (providing massive bailouts for insolvent financial institutions and international lenders), a noble hope (to restructure the economies of recipients to prevent future dependence on bailouts), and an unrealistic belief in the ability of such conditions to succeed.

The expectation of bailouts increases the fragility of the world financial system

The predictable failure of government to allow losses to fall on risk takers after financial crises not only produces a one-time wealth transfer, but encourages behavior that will lead to a repeat of the same problem in the future, which brings us to the second category of costs resulting from bailouts.

If the risk-taking bankers know that future gains from taking on risk will be private, but losses will be borne by taxpayers (again), that amounts to a government subsidy for risk, which thereby encourages excessive risk taking (the so-called moral-hazard problem).

In the United States, we learned during our Savings and Loan debacle that subsidies for risk taking could lead to large losses from unwise, high-risk investments. The losses to taxpayers from that experience (roughly 3 percent of 1990 GDP), however, were small compared to what has been happening in developing economies over the past 15 years – an era that has seen an unprecedented epidemic of high-cost bank insolvency. Studies by the World Bank and the IMF have documented some 90 episodes of severe banking crisis since 1982. In more than 20 of those cases, the bailout costs to developing country governments have exceeded 10 percent of GDP. In roughly half of those cases (including the estimated losses of some of the current Asian-crisis countries) losses have been in the range of 25 percent of their GDP (see Caprio and Klingabiel, 1996a, 1996b; and Lindgren, Garcia, and Saal 1996).

These facts warrant emphasis. This string of enormous losses is unprecedented, and is occurring during a relatively stable period of positive global economic growth. Losses to depositors in the United States during the Great Depression, for example, were comparatively small. National banks (the only banks for which depositor loss data are readily available) issued 47 percent of U.S. bank deposits (FDIC 1940: 66). Losses to national bank depositors from bank failures during the worst four years of the Depression (1930, 1931, 1932, and 1933) together amounted to only 1.9 percent of average U.S. GNP over those years (GNP data are from Economic Report of the President 1968: 218). Assuming similar loss rates to deposits of national and state-chartered banks would imply an estimated loss on all deposits of roughly 4 percent of GDP. Losses during other historical periods of the most severe economic crises – the 1830s, the 1850s, and the 1890s – also pale by comparison to the experience of the last 15 years. Indeed, in many countries historically, severe recessions have not been associated with any significant losses to depositors (Bordo 1985, Calomiris 1993).

What can explain the enormity of loss since 1982? Surely not 'shocks' of unprecedented magnitude (like oil price hikes, wars, or global downturns in demand), since such influences have been absent during this period. The explanation for the new epidemic of worldwide banking instability is the roller coaster of risk produced by the choices of banks in developing economies – choices that are the byproduct of government subsidies for risk-taking.

Why are banks behaving so differently now from the way they behaved previously? The answer is simple. Prior to the 1980s, banking systems did not subsidize risk nearly as much as they do now. The wave of partial economic and financial liberalization that swept through the developing world in the 1980s and 1990s has been enormously beneficial in many ways, but it should not be confused with true economic liberalization. While many countries have opened themselves to world trade, have privatized many important sectors of their economies (including their financial sectors), and have moved away from direct governmental control of domestic credit, a key flaw in the new era of liberalization has been an expanded, and unhealthy, partnership between government and private business.

Private business in many developing economies is dominated by oligopolistic conglomerates, often controlled by a small minority of wealthy, politically influential families or corporations. At the center of the unhealthy partnership between government and business in many developing countries is a new kind of bank – What I call the quasi-public bank. Quasi-public banks (typically owned and controlled by conglomerates) are private institutions with an implicit claim to public resources (which pay for their losses). They are a key instrument of domestic economic control for conglomerates, and a key vehicle for the transfer of political patronage from the government to these conglomerates.

Prior to the 1980s, banks in developing countries were often state-owned institutions, or private banks subject to strict controls that limited private allocation of credit. That system was highly inefficient and limited private sector access to funds. It was replaced by a 'privatized' banking system with a different set of inefficiencies – an unnaturally risky form of bank 'privatization' that brought freedom without responsibility. When quasi-public banks (and their parent conglomerates) make profits, they keep them; when they suffer losses, the public pays for them (through bank bailouts). That is a formula for encouraging banks to take on extreme risk.

Quasi-public banks don't always choose to take extreme risk, however, and that explains why they sometimes can survive successfully for years before imposing such large costs on taxpayers. But they are extremely fragile institutions, and they magnify risk for the rest of the economy, particularly during recessions. These banks turn normal economies into a house of cards – one which collapses in the face of even moderate-sized adverse shocks.

The key to understanding how quasi-public institutions magnify economic risk is to consider how they respond to initial losses produced by adverse shocks to their borrowers. Normal private banks experiencing loan losses tend to reduce their portfolio risk to restore the confidence of their depositors and limit the risk of bank failure. But quasi-public institutions need not concern themselves with the risk of failure, since bank depositors and stockholders are all insured against loss by taxpayers. In the wake of losses, these banks face opposite incentives – to channel ever riskier loans to their conglomerates.

Financial crises in these economies tend to go through three stages: (1) initial losses, followed by purposeful increases in bank lending risk; (2) consequent increases in the probability of devaluation, followed by purposeful increases by banks in their currency risk; and (3) large devaluation, followed by enormous losses to banks and taxpayers. The consistency of this pattern is uncanny. It was first visible in the Chilean collapse of 1982–83 (that experience has been described in detail by the former Chilean minister of finance in de la Cuadra and Valdes 1992). The same pattern was followed in Mexico in 1994–95, and in Thailand, Indonesia, and Korea in the recent crisis.

The sequence is disturbingly predictable. First, as initial losses of borrowers and their banks mount, banks and their borrower-owners increase credit and thus pursue higher-risk resurrection strategies. The initial recessionary shock that hits these economies raises the probability of devaluation (slightly, initially). The resultant increase in bank risk makes devaluation more likely because of the link between expected bank losses and future government money supply increases.

Second, increased risk of banking collapse means a greater chance of a government bailout of bank losses. Since those losses are often in the range of 10 or 20 percent of GDP, the implications of these potential losses for government expenditure and money supply increases make drastic devaluation a real possibility.

The high probability of devaluation provides banks and their borrower-owners a new opportunity for profitable risk taking in the form of currency risk. As the risk of devaluation grows, the interest rate difference between local currency-denominated debt and dollar-denominated debt rises (reflecting the expectation of a devaluation). Now banks and their borrower-owners face the choice between domestic-denominated borrowing – which has a high current cost, but no currency risk – and foreign-denominated borrowing – which has a low current cost, but a risk of loss following a devaluation (when the value of hard-currency debts can rise astronomically). Because the banks and their owner-borrowers know they will be bailed out by the government if a devaluation occurs, they prefer to borrow via low-interest rate, dollar-denominated debt, and need not worry about the enormous losses they will suffer from a devaluation.

Third, the more the economy increases its dollar-denominated borrowing, the more likely it will be unable to meet those hard-currency obligations. Thus devaluation becomes more and more likely over time.

That, in short, is how quasi-public banks have turned many developing economies into the riskiest financial systems the world has ever seen. Indeed, several former government officials in these economies have issued what amount to 'public confessions' that document exactly this pattern (notably the central bank president of Venezuela, Ruth de Krivoy [1995], and the finance minister of Chile, Sergio de la Cuadra). Consider de la Cuadra's discussion of the Chilean collapse.

As in many other countries, the adverse macroeconomic consequences of the initial exogenous shocks to the Chilean economy made it politically difficult to impose the necessary discipline on banks. As de la Cuadra and Valdes (1992: 75) argue, 'The superintendency could not include in its loan classification procedure a truly independent assessment of the exposure of bank debtors to foreign exchange and interest rate risk because such an assessment would have interfered with official macroeconomic policies.'

De la Cuadra and Valdes go on to trace how excessive risk taking by banks and firms, and eventual losses from those risks, produced economic devastation by 1982 and increasingly perverse incentives for lenders. Their discussion warrants recounting in detail:

In 1981 most banks saw their effective capital plummet further as soon as optimistic debtors became less willing to pay when the net worth of their corporations fell. This reluctance reinforced the previous perverse incentives to banks, so that banks became even more willing to assume credit risks derived from exchange rate and interest rate risks.

By 1981 financing decisions by Chilean firms and banks reflected a de facto government guarantee to the private sector for foreign exchange risk. Our analysis has identified the superintendancy's lack of penalization of credit risk in its loan classification criteria as the channel for the guarantee.

The outcome of this structural contingent subsidy was that many small and medium-sized businesses got deeply into debt in 1981. Debts to banks increased during 1981 from 37.6 percent to 50.4 percent of GDP in response to the rise in real interest rates. . .

By mid-1982 the fall in GDP was so steep that it took on the character of a depression. In June 1982 the government finally decided to devalue the exchange rate by 14 percent. By the end of 1982 the losses that the devaluations had inflicted on the holders of dollar-denominated debts had created insolvency among firms of all sizes.

The sorry state of most debtors caused delinquent loans to rise from 2.34 percent of loans in December 1981 to 3.83 percent in February 1982 and 6.31 percent in May. Most delinquent loans turned out to be 100 percent losses, so they reduced the net worth of banks.

On July 12, 1982, the central bank decided to allow banks to defer their losses over several years, so it began to buy the banks' delinquent loan portfolios at face value. The banks, however, had to promise to repurchase the portfolios at face value over time with 100 percent of their profits, so the scheme did not improve bank solvency by itself. It solved a liquidity problem but also set the stage for making good the implicit contingent subsidy that the government had offered to speculators in 1981 [De la Cuadra and Valdes 1992: 79–80].

De la Cuadra and Valdes emphasize that loans to industrial firms that were linked to banks via conglomerates were especially forthcoming from banks as a consequence of the government subsidization of risk. Thus despite its free-market orientation and stated commitment to private discipline in banking, Chile ended up insuring 'uninsured' claims on banks, subsidizing high-risk resurrection strategies on the part of its banks, and passing on enormous risk-encouraging credit subsidies to industrial firms with close links to banks.

The Chilean pattern was repeated in Mexico in 1994–95. Initial bank loan losses were aggravated by currency devaluation's effects on Mexican firms that had undertaken dollar-denominated debts. Furthermore, Mexican banks, like those in Chile in 1982, had bet heavily against devaluation. Despite the fact that Mexican banking regulations prohibited banks from assuming currency risk, as the peso devalued Mexican banks suffered large losses from illegal 'structured note' agreements they had entered into with American banks (discussed in Garber 1997).

In the recent Asian crises, Thailand, Korea, and Indonesia also have seen enormous increases in their dollar-denominated debts over the past year – after recessionary shocks and bank losses were widely known. In the case of

Korea, as early as the end of 1996, its chaebols had averaged debt-equity ratios of 400 percent. As exports fell in 1997, debt rose even further (Woodall 1998: 6).

By June 1997, foreign bank debt had grown to 45 percent of GDP in Thailand, 35 percent of GDP in Indonesia, and 25 percent of GDP in Korea, most of which was short-term debt. By June 1997, South Korea's short-term debt was three times its foreign reserves (ibid.: 6). The devaluations of recent months (in combination with the prior pursuit of low-interest dollar-denominated funds) have produced an enormous burden on the taxpayers of these countries who now must repay the dollar-denominated debts at inflated exchange rates.

Ironically, some supporters of international bailouts – notably, Jeffrey Sachs et al. (1995) – see the high dollar-denominated short-term debt burdens of developing market economies as the 'cause' of 'unwarranted' runs on their currencies which they claim produce financial crises. According to that view, large amounts of short-term foreign debt expose countries to the fickle preferences of foreign speculators. That view is misleading for at least three reasons.

First, the run-up in short-term foreign debt is a symptom of weakness (a characteristic of an economy that cannot attract long-term debt) and indicative of the perverse risk-taking incentives of banks and conglomerates that are willing to absorb massive amounts of foreign currency risk at taxpayers' expense.

Second, fickle foreign speculators are not the source of devaluation pressure. Developing economies in which government and business are too closely linked tend to suffer two kinds of fundamental problems which underlie devaluation pressures: low productivity growth, and off-balance-sheet fiscal pressures resulting from weak banking systems. Because crony capitalism is highly inefficient, it produces low long-term factor productivity growth, which can threaten the long-term maintenance of a fixed exchange rate against the dollar. As Paul Krugman (1994) and Alwyn Young (1995) noted of the 'Asian tigers' years ago, their impressive growth resulted from combining large amounts of savings with inexpensive unskilled labor, not high factor productivity growth.

Fiscal pressures are also important. The off-balance-sheet liabilities associated with costly bank bailouts imply the need to monetize government debts. Because these potential costs and their monetary implications are anticipated by markets, they can undermine the credibility of the fixed exchange rate. A common error of many macroeconomic analyses of exchange rate collapses in Asia and Mexico is the tendency to focus only on the official government deficit, ignoring the enormous costs of bank bailouts.

The Sachs view is also wrong to identify foreign funds as the primary sources of balance-of-payments outflows. In many cases (as the IMF's report on the Mexican crisis made clear) foreigners are not the ones who initiate the run on the currency. Well-informed domestic market participants often are the first to flee once it becomes clear that devaluation is imminent.

To what extent are the IMF and the U.S. Government magnifying moral hazard?

My review of the moral-hazard consequences of bailouts over the past 15 years has emphasized that domestic governments have often been the most important source of perverse incentives for their banks. Where does the IMF fit in? The main influences of the IMF and the U.S. government in the 1990s have been to aggravate the problem in two ways: (1) to lend legitimacy to (and thus facilitate) domestic bailouts by providing conditions that call for taxation of the domestic middle class to repay the bridge loans from the IMF and the U.S. government; and (2) to insulate foreign creditors (especially banks) from losses during these crises.

Of the two influences, the second is the more pernicious. Insulating foreign banks from loss (by ensuring that bailout packages also rescue them) removes the incentive for foreign banks to avoid lending to high-risk countries. That aggravates the moral-hazard problem by promoting the flow of dollar-denominated 'hot money' during the second and third stages of the financial crises outlined above.

In this regard, consider the contrast between what creditors learned from the Mexican crises of 1982 and 1994. In 1982 (in the wake of a decline in oil prices and the rise in U.S. interest rates) foreign lenders to Mexican firms suffered enormous losses as the peso depreciated to $1/3$ of its pre-crisis value, making foreign-denominated debt unsustainable for many firms. For example, the workout of one of the largest Mexican conglomerates, Grupo Alfa, entailed eventual losses to some of its creditors in excess of 50 percent. Painful lessons were learned by some of these creditors. Citibank in particular learned important lessons about managing risk on its commercial lending in Mexico, and managed its exchange and credit risk much better during the 1980s and 1990s. During and after the crisis of 1994–1995, its losses were far smaller than in 1982.

What will foreign banks learn from the 1994–95 Mexican crisis, or the recent Asian crisis? I fear they are learning that they can lend without fear of default because of the implicit protection of the IMF and the U.S. Treasury. And it does not help matters that the IMF and the Treasury are signaling their intent to provide future bailouts by calling for ever-increasing amounts of IMF capital and new IMF lending facilities. That, of course, will add fuel to the fire of risk-taking in developing economies.

Undermining the process of economic reform in developing economies

The cost of insuring foreign lenders against loss runs even deeper, however, which brings me to the third category of costs from bailouts. By insuring foreign creditors who fuel developing economy risk taking, the IMF and U.S. government are undermining the natural process of reform in many emerging economies.

For developing economies true reform is a big step – one that requires the fundamental political transformation from a domestically oriented, rent-seeking society to one willing and able to participate in the competitive global economy. Powerful local oligarchs often can successfully block liberalization if they choose to do so. But the oligarchs may prefer true liberalization if they profit from it. The attraction of participating in the competitive global economy is that globalization offers greater access to foreign markets and foreign sources of capital. That may lead powerful special interests to permit true liberalization if it is the necessary path to globalization. Entrenched oligarchs may choose to liberalize in order to trade a large slice of a small pie for a small slice of a much larger pie.

The incentives for oligarchs to liberalize can be strong if foreign sources of capital are only willing to provide funds to economies with appropriate capitalist infrastructures – that is, those which are based on the rule of law, the protection of creditors and stockholders rights, a predictable means of laying claim to title, an orderly bankruptcy procedure, an intelligible system of accounting principles, a non-confiscatory tax system, and fair competition in markets.

But IMF and U.S. government assistance can undermine the incentives that encourage the liberalization process. If oligarchs can avoid true liberalization but still maintain access to foreign capital, where is the incentive for them to relinquish the rule of man in favor of the rule of law, or to allow competition and democracy to flourish? If foreign investors are protected by the IMF and the U.S. government, foreigners will be less discriminating about where they place their funds, and thus provide less of an incentive for reform in developing economies.

Thus, bailouts undermine the natural process of reform that global competition would otherwise promote. They do so not only by taxing (and thus weakening) the emerging middle classes in developing countries (the segment of society most likely to push for real reform), but by undermining the incentives of the existing oligarchs to permit liberalization.

From some quarters one hears praise for IMF bailouts as a means to political 'stability' in developing economies. If the pursuit of stability means tilting the balance to preserve corrupt rulers and undermine democratic forces within developing economies, it becomes harder to defend policies solely on the basis of the political stability that accompanies them. I for one am very thankful that stability was not the overriding objective of Americans in 1776.

Distinguishing liquidity crises from solvency crises

Supporters of the IMF sometimes refer to its assistance as an infusion of 'liquidity.' While liquidity has nothing to do with financing bank bailouts, liquidity assistance was the motive that gave rise to the IMF as part of the Bretton Woods system. Traditionally (under the pre-1973 Bretton Woods system) IMF intervention was supposed to help bolster central bank reserves to preserve a fundamentally sound exchange rate regime buffeted by 'destabilizing speculation.'

After the collapse of the Bretton Woods system and throughout the 1980s, the IMF's role changed. It assumed the role of helping mainly developing countries devalue in an orderly way, and establish credibility in private markets. The IMF offered technical advice, and monitored compliance with macroeconomic policy objectives. During that period, one could argue that the IMF provided 'liquidity' assistance (rather than simply wealth transfers) in the sense that its policies sometimes helped to restore credibility by reversing adverse trends in the fundamental macroeconomic determinants that drove exchange rate depreciation.

In the 1990s, the IMF has stretched the notion of 'liquidity' assistance beyond any reasonable definition. IMF programs in Mexico and Asia are now microeconomic bailouts that restore the solvency of clearly insolvent financial institutions. That objective has nothing to do with bank or government liquidity, or with temporary imbalances in the balance of payments.

These bank bailouts also have nothing to do with 'panic prevention.' In particular, there is no connection between current IMF programs and the historical interventions by central banks or private coalitions of banks to stem banking crises. (The history and theory of banking panics, and the proper role of the lender of last resort, are reviewed in Gorton 1985, Bordo 1990, Kaufman 1991, 1994, Calomiris 1990, 1993, 1994, 1997, Calomiris and Gorton 1991, Calomiris and Schweikart 1991, and Calomiris and Mason 1997.) The current IMF bailout policies are bridge loans in support of the large wealth transfers from domestic taxpayers to recapitalize clearly insolvent financial institutions and related parties. Historical lender-of-last-resort assistance during banking panics, in contrast, was geared to prevent the failure of solvent banks which were temporarily in need of cash to prevent their unwarranted failure.

Given some of the recent concerns of a threat from 'irrational financial contagion' voiced by policy makers in the popular press, it is worth emphasizing that the literature on the history and theory of banking panics (cited above) demonstrates that panics have been 'rational' phenomena. Bank panics result from reasonable concerns on the part of bank depositors, and are predictable historical phenomena. Random, irrational attacks on financial systems are not evident in financial history. Thus concerns of 'irrational contagion' spreading from one country to another without any fundamental explanatory link connecting the countries are unwarranted. Such concerns should not be used to justify financial bailouts. For example, there are clear fundamental economic connections (notably export product competition) that have produced 'spillover' effects across countries within Asia during the recent crisis. As during the Mexican crisis, not all countries suffer from the fallout; the spillovers can be traced to economic and financial linkages, not irrational contagion.

IMF bailouts cannot be justified by panic prevention, as that term is properly defined. Nor could the IMF serve as an effective lender of last resort to the banking systems of developing economies. A lender of last resort (whether private or public) must be in the position to observe and control the uses of the funds it provides. Historically, bank clearinghouse coalitions or central banks have been the lenders of last resort.

There is no reason to believe that legitimate lender of last resort protection to stem financial panics would be best achieved via IMF or U.S. government intervention. Runs on banks are either the consequence of fears of impending devaluation (which central banks control via monetary policy), or the consequence of confusion about default risks within the banking system. In both cases, local authorities are the proper institutions to deal with the problem (by resolving the exchange rate uncertainty in the former case, or by deciding on the appropriate lender-of-last-resort policy in the latter case).

In cases where lender-of-last-resort assistance is warranted, the local central bank (unlike the IMF) has the information and legal authority to enforce the necessary conditions on the behavior of banks receiving such lending. Furthermore, those conditions may involve long-run reforms of banking practices. As I argued before, the brief time horizon of IMF involvement makes any attempt by the IMF to achieve meaningful reform of the financial sector, as a condition for assistance, virtually impossible. Financial sector reform is a process that requires many years to design and implement. Countries that have achieved successful banking reform have done so over many years and as the result of a strong domestic commitment to improve banks' incentives, not in response to IMF conditions (Calomiris 1997).

The current Asian crisis and the proposed increase in IMF capital

If there is no respectable intellectual justification for the current direction of IMF policy (as illustrated in Mexico and Asia), then why are so many people coming out in support of expanding the IMF's capital and lending facilities? If IMF-sponsored bailouts are weakening democracy, strengthening corruption, aggravating inequality and poverty, and fostering systemic financial instability and industrial inefficiency, why are they so popular?

I think part of the answer lies in the short-run fears of American banks and businesses, which have led them to equate support for expansion of the IMF with support for its programs in Asia. Many U.S. banks and businesses would stand to lose if the current IMF Asian bailouts were undermined. For many, the 'long-run' appropriateness of IMF policy is not the issue; their current exposure in Asia is their overarching concern.

Of course, deciding not to expand the IMF's capital would not in any way undermine the IMF's existing commitments in Asia. Rather, it would only limit the IMF's ability to expand such commitments in the future, in Asia and elsewhere. Thus, I think much of the support demonstrated for the IMF on the part of U.S. banks and businesses is not only myopic, but misguided.

There is no immediate threat to Asia from limiting the ability of the IMF to expand in the future.

Policy recommendations

The following are four specific recommendations that follow from my analysis.

First, policymakers should recognize that IMF bailouts like those provided in Mexico and Asia are counterproductive. The IMF can best contribute to global financial stability by committing not to insulate foreign or domestic creditors from loss. The more that developing countries are forced to handle their own financial insolvencies, and the more foreign investors are forced to bear the costs of their investment decisions, the more developing countries will be attracted by the benefits of true liberalization. International 'coordination' of assistance to insolvent creditors is counterproductive to the stability and efficiency of the global financial system.

Second, consequently, there is no reason to expand the IMF's capital or to develop the new proposed lending facility to provide bailouts to financial systems in distress. Indeed, an expansion of IMF capital or facilities would do real harm by signaling an intention to strengthen and expand the IMF's commitment to provide bailouts in the future. The U.S. government should at the very least try to limit the IMF to its pre-1994 goals of advising countries on their macroeconomic policies (to improve exchange rate stability) and serving as an international delegated monitor charged with tracking those policies and providing credible information to global capital markets. The IMF has more than enough capital to achieve those ends. It currently has $45 billion to allocate, and within three years (after its Asian loans have been repaid), it will have much more.

The IMF and World Bank sometimes have been successful in helping to identify and give credibility to regimes that are honestly pursuing the path of reform. In my view, their expressions of support for these regimes have been more important than the funds they have contributed in support of those reforms. The IMF does not need to use funds to bribe countries to restore balance to their macroeconomic accounts or proper incentives to their banks. The IMF should place its trust in global competition, which gives the most reliable encouragement to true liberalization. Wise economic policies will be rewarded by prosperity, and by global inflows of 'unprotected' capital. In the case of banking reform, bribery is not only unnecessary but ineffectual. The IMF should recognize that it cannot control (and should not try to control) the banking regulations of developing economies.

Third, denying the IMF its desired increases in capital and facilities, and working to restrict its purview, are not enough to stop the trend toward unwise expansion of global bank bailouts. Other means of promoting bailouts must also be forsworn. Along with refusing to expand the IMF's capital, Congress should abolish the Exchange Stabilization Fund – a legacy of the

Great Depression which has no legitimate role in U.S. monetary policy today. The Exchange Stabilization Fund – originally created to 'stabilize the exchange value of the dollar' (Schwartz 1997: 135) – was the source of a $12 billion loan to Mexico in January 1995. No one could plausibly argue that the loan to Mexico was a form of exchange intervention in support of the dollar. This was not the first time the Exchange Stabilization Fund was used inappropriately. Indeed, as Anna Schwartz (1997) documents, the history of the Exchange Stabilization Fund – contrary to its stated purpose – is rife with similar examples of abuse by previous administrations.

The World Bank – which has been partially successful in providing advice and support for long-term financial sector reform – should also be prevented from serving as a substitute vehicle for bailouts. Whatever assistance the World Bank provides should be limited to gradual support promoting long-run reform of the financial sector. For that purpose, sudden large flows of credit subsidies are unnecessary and counterproductive. Subsidizing privatization of banks requires only small annual flows of credit. Such funds should be distributed only in response to credible government reforms – that is, only after reforms have been initiated, not before.

Fourth, IMF secrecy is contrary to its proper role as a source of independent, objective, and informed opinion about the economic performance and financial risks of member countries. In pursuit of its appropriate mission, any policies or conditions for assistance advocated by the IMF should be revealed publicly. That will encourage a lively debate about their merits, and permit critical evaluation of their effectiveness.

References

Bordo, M.D. (1985) 'The Impact and International Transmission of Financial Crises: Some Historical Evidence, 1870–1933.' Revista di Storia Economica 2: 41–78.

Bordo, M.D. (1990) 'The Lender of Last Resort: Alternative Views and Historical Experience.' Federal Reserve Bank of Richmond Economic Review (January/February): 18–29.

Borsuk, R. (1998) 'Likely Suharto Nominee Called Rebuff to IMF.' Wall Street Journal, 12 March: A12.

Calomiris, C.W. (1990) 'Is Deposit Insurance Necessary? A Historical Perspective.' Journal of Economic History 50 (June): 283–95.

Calomiris, C.W. (1993) 'Regulation, Industrial Structure, and Instability in U.S. Banking: An Historical Perspective.' In M. Klausner and L.J. White (eds.) Structural Change in Banking, 19–116. Homewood, Ill.: Business One-Irwin.

Calomiris, C.W. (1994) 'Is the Discount Window Necessary?' Federal Reserve Bank of St. Louis Economic Review (May/June): 31–55.

Calomiris, C.W. (1997) The Postmodern Bank Safety Net: Lessons from Developed and Developing Economies. Washington, D.C.: American Enterprise Institute.

Calomiris, C.W., and Gorton, G. (1991) 'The Origins of Banking Panics: Models, Facts, and Bank Regulation.' In R.G. Hubbard (ed.) Financial Markets and Financial Crises, 109–73. Chicago: University of Chicago Press.

Calomiris, C.W., and Schweikart, L. (1991) 'The Panic of 1857: Origins, Transmission, and Containment.' Journal of Economic History 51 (December): 807–34.

Calomiris, C.W., and Mason, J.R. (1997) 'Contagion and Bank Failures During the Great Depression: The June 1932 Chicago Banking Panic.' American Economic Review 87 (December): 863–83.

Caprio, G., and Klingabiel, D. (1996a) 'Bank Insolvency: Bad Luck, Bad Policy, or Bad Banking?' In M. Bruno and B. Pleskovic (eds.) Annual World Bank Conference on Development Economics, 1996. Washington, D.C.: World Bank.

Caprio, G., and Klingabiel, D. (1996b) 'Bank Insolvency: Cross-Country Experience.' World Bank Policy Research Working Paper, No. 1620. Washington, D.C., July.

De la Cuadra, S., and Valdes, S. (1992) 'Myths and Facts about Financial Liberalization in Chile: 1974–1983.' In P. Brock (ed.) If Texas Were Chile: A Primer on Banking Reform, 11–101. San Francisco: ICS Press.

Economic Report of the President (1968) Washington, D.C.: Government Printing Office.

The Economist (1998) 'Once Again, Indonesia Starts Living Dangerously.' 21 February: 37–38.

Federal Deposit Insurance Corporation (1940) Annual Report. Washington, D.C.: Government Printing Office.

Feldstein, M. (1998) 'Refocusing the IMF.' Foreign Affairs (March/April): 20–33.

Financial Times (1997) 'Debt Burden Drags on Economy.' 16 December: 2.

Garber, P. (1997) 'Managing Risks to Financial Markets from Volatile Capital Flows: The Role of Prudential Regulation.' Brown University Working Paper. Providence, R.I.

Gorton, G. (1985) 'Clearing Houses and the Origin of Central Banking in the U.S.' Journal of Economic History (June): 277–83.

Ihlwan, M. (1998) 'Kim's War on Two Fronts.' Business Week, 2 March: 54–55.

Kaufman, G. (1991) 'Lender of Last Resort, Too Large to Fail, and Deposit-Insurance Reform.' In J.R. Barth and R.D. Brumbaugh Jr. (eds.) The Reform of Federal Deposit Insurance: Disciplining the Government and Protecting the Taxpayer, 246–58. New York: Harper Business.

Kaufman, G. (1994) 'Bank Contagion: A Review of the Theory and Evidence.' Journal of Financial Services Research 8 (April): 123–50.

De Krivoy, R. (1995) 'Lessons from Financial Crises: Evidence from Venezuela.' In Proceedings of the 31st Annual Conference on Bank Structure and Competition. Chicago: Federal Reserve Bank of Chicago.

Krugman, P. (1994) 'The Myth of Asia's Miracle.' Foreign Affairs (November/December): 62–78.

Lindgren, C.J., Garcia, G., and Saal, M.I. (1996) Bank Soundness and Macroeconomic Policy. Washington, D.C.: International Monetary Fund.

Sachs, J., Tornell, A., and Velasco, A. (1995) 'Lessons from Mexico.' Mimeo. Harvard University, March.

Schwartz, A.J. (1997) 'From Obscurity to Notoriety: A Biography of the Exchange Stabilization Fund.' Journal of Money, Credit and Banking 29 (May): 135–53.

Woodall, P. (1998) 'Frozen Miracle: A Survey of East Asian Economies.' The Economist, 7 March: 1–18.

Young, A. (1995) 'The Tyranny of Numbers: Confronting the Statistical Realities of the East Asian Growth Experience.' Quarterly Journal of Economics. 110 (3) (August): 641–80.

The Cato Journal is published in the spring/summer, fall, and winter by the Cato Institute, 1000 Massachusetts Ave., NW, Washington, D.C. 20001–5403. The Views expressed by the authors of the articles are their own and are not attributable to the editor, editorial board, or the Cato Institute. Printed copies of the Cato Journal may be ordered by calling 1–800–767–1241. Back issues are also available on the Cato Institute Web site: http://www.cato.org. Email comments or suggestions to cato@cato.org.

20 Is there a need for an international lender of last resort? *

Anna J. Schwartz [†]

In a luncheon speech at the American Economic Association meeting on January 3, 1999, Stanley Fischer, first deputy managing director of the International Monetary Fund, argued the case, in a reformed international financial system, for 'an agency that will act as lender of last resort for countries facing a crisis.' He asserts that there is a need for such an agency and 'that the IMF is increasingly playing that role, and that changes in the international system now under consideration will make it possible for it to exercise that function more effectively' (Fischer 1999: 8–9). One would never know from Fischer's remarks that the IMF has been subject to serious charges by critics of its performance – not only with respect to its policy recommendations but also with respect to the basic loan agenda as creating moral hazard for country borrowers and foreign lenders. His lengthy discussion of moral hazard never implicates the IMF. He offered nothing more than a public relations effort to promote an expansive role for the IMF.

The speech raises at least three questions. First, is it true that the IMF possesses the attributes of a lender of last resort (LOLR)? Second, one should ask whether the countries that were recipients of IMF loans have benefited or been harmed by the Fund's operations. Would they have been worse off had they had to manage without the IMF? Third, Fischer discusses the possibility of countries prequalifying for IMF loans. Is that a workable scheme?

Attributes of a lender of last resort

A financial panic occurs in the money market. It can be quickly ended by a LOLR. A financial crisis occurs when asset prices plunge, whether of equity, real estate, or commodities, when the exchange value of a national currency

---

* *Cato Journal*, Vol. 19, No. 1 (Spring/Summer 1999). Copyright © Cato Institute. All rights reserved.
† Anna J. Schwartz is a Research Associate at the National Bureau of Economic Research. This paper is based on her report at the March 1999 meeting of the Shadow Open market Committee.

experiences substantial depreciation, when a large nonfinancial firm, a large municipality, a financial industry, or a sovereign debtor defaults. A financial crisis is a prolonged disturbance that is resolved by government agencies other than the central bank, although at some stage it may provide liquidity to the market through the discount window or open market purchases. The collapse of the U.S. savings and loan industry is an example of a financial crisis that initially involved the deposit insurance agency and subsequently a new agency – the Resolution Trust Corporation – to deal with the problem. Resolving the savings and loan crisis was not a lender of last resort responsibility.

According to Fischer, the IMF now sees itself as a financial crisis manager and a financial panic lender, and seeks the status of an international lender of last resort (ILOLR). It is a confusion of two roles in a domestic setting, and betrays a faulty resetting of a domestic LOLR as an ILOLR.

Which attributes of a domestic LOLR must an ILOLR have? A domestic LOLR can create high-powered money without limit. Can the IMF create international reserves? Fischer's answer is that the IMF 'has access to a pool of resources, which it can onlend to member countries.' He notes that its resources, if they bore the same size relative to output, to the quota formula, and to the volume of world trade as in 1945, would be three, five, or more than nine times larger than they are today (Fischer 1999: 9). Is there an implication that quota increases that have been sought every five years since the IMF founding will in the future be sought more often? Fischer also counts on the IMF's use of authorization to create Special Drawing Rights as a supplement to its resources, and its ability to borrow. Therefore, according to Fischer, the IMF has the capacity to act as crisis lender to individual countries. One wonders, what happened to the idea that the IMF was a revolving fund of relatively small short-term loans that countries repaid so others could borrow?

One major difference between a central bank LOLR and the IMF, to which Fischer does not allude, is that the IMF needs a vote of its Executive Board to take any action. It has no independent authority, such as a central bank has, even one subject to the consent of the minister of finance. Fischer refers to a complaint that the Fund is too slow in emergencies, but counters that the Emergency Financing Mechanism, introduced after the 1994–95 Mexican peso crisis, enables it to move very rapidly. Very rapidly means after weeks or months, while an agreement with the distressed country is produced. A central bank has the freedom to act with dispatch within days.

The IMF, it is clear, is only a simulacrum of a LOLR. It is not the real thing. What will its function be? There will be changes in the international financial system that Fischer describes – a shift to floating exchange rates, larger holdings of international reserves by emerging market countries, private sector involvement in financial crises, international standards – but he does not enumerate any changes in the way the IMF operates. The IMF will still provide loans to pay off a country's foreign debts, although since 1998 no longer at subsidized interest rates, and will impose fiscal and monetary conditions and micromanage institutional behavior. Are these IMF activities that should be perpetuated?

Emerging market countries without the IMF

Every country that has been a recipient of IMF loans has suffered a severe decline in output, punishing high interest rates, and accelerating inflation, despite the loans. The loans are massive, but the IMF has never revealed how it determines their magnitude, nor how the recipient has expended them. It may not even know how the money was spent. In the Mexican case, it seems that the money was given to local and foreign *tesobono* investors. In the absence of the IMF loans, investors would have taken a hit but economic conditions in Mexico would have been no worse than they were with the loan, and Mexico would not have had the burden of repaying the loan.

The IMF is a paternalistic institution whose staff assumes that it possesses wisdom superior to that of the officialdom of the countries to whom it is lending. It acknowledges mistakes ex post. An emerging market country that gets into trouble does not need the ministrations of the IMF to overcome its difficulties.

The problem may be a financial panic or financial crisis or both. If the banking system is short of liquidity, the domestic central bank, not the IMF, must create high-powered money to calm depositor fears. If the monetary and fiscal situations indicate lax policies, if the current account deficit is growing as a percent of GDP, foreign investors will be seized by doubts about the economy's viability. A government or the private sector that has borrowed abroad will be faced with sudden investor flight. Asset markets in which the investments were made will plunge, and the exchange rate of the domestic currency will depreciate. Correction of the conditions that produced this setback must fall on the troubled country, not the IMF.

If it cannot service and amortize its foreign borrowings, the country, not the IMF, has to negotiate a workout with the foreign lenders. If individual banks or other financial institutions are insolvent, domestic agencies either exist or must be established to recapitalize or shut them down. The same solutions apply to corporate and nonfinancial businesses that are in trouble. Financial crises, unlike panics, are not quickly ended. They may require fiscal infusions and the resolution may not be attained for months or years. Compensating for the loss of wealth that a financial crisis imposes may exact a reduction in personal consumption and increased national saving over an extended period. This is what troubled countries have to endure. The presence of the IMF does not spare them from these bleak consequences.

It is hard to see why Fischer proposes lending freely by the IMF on Bagehot's rules through the Supplementary Reserve Facility. Given global capital markets that will be ready to lend to countries that are willing to pay a penalty rate of interest and to offer good collateral, why is the IMF needed?

Fischer (1999: 13) parses 'lending freely' as meaning 'ready to lend early and in sufficient amounts to other countries that might be affected by contagion from the crisis.' He nowhere defines contagion or justifies the assumption that it occurs.

Contagion, if the term is used accurately, occurs only in circumstances in which other countries are free of the problems of the country that first experienced trouble and yet suffered unwarranted investor disaffection. It has become a dogma since the 1995 Mexican bailout that there was a tequila effect. The evidence of contagion that has been offered since then is that the currencies and stock markets of countries (other than the original one to surface with problems) have declined. What is overlooked or deliberately omitted is that the countries said to be victims of contagion had the same problems as were present in the country that was supposedly the source of contagion. Proponents of the contagion dogma do not explain the absence of contagion from the New York stock market crash of 1987 or from the 1990 crash of the Tokyo stock market and property bubbles.

A final point is that a country that cannot meet the conditions for borrowing that the private market sets may require financial aid. Outright gifts from an international agency may be the right solution for such a country.

Is prequalification for a loan a workable scheme?

At the 1998 annual IMF meetings, President Clinton proposed to give the IMF the right to arrange precautionary credit lines for member countries on which they could draw to supplement their reserves before they are engulfed in a financial crisis. If substantial numbers of 182 member countries would prequalify, the IMF would clearly require a big increase in its supply of funds. Fischer expressed belief that this was a proposal worthy of consideration. Secretary of the Treasury Rubin, however, questioned its practicality on grounds that lenders would assume that they would be bailed out if countries were assured of IMF assistance in the event of a crisis because they prequalified. Nevertheless, the IMF subsequently approved such a scheme, known as Contingent Credit Lines. But what if a country that prequalified because it met certain criteria subsequently did not live up to the criteria? Brazil might have been such a prequalifier, yet once it had access to IMF funds could not satisfy any of the conditions on which the loan had been granted. The loan furthermore did not restore investor confidence. The program also assumes that the IMF can know in advance when a crisis will occur, when there is no record that it has acted on early warning signs. True, it has claimed that it warned East Asian countries in advance of the crises that befell them but its warnings were disregarded. This is an additional reason to doubt that the world will be the worse if the IMF is stripped of its illusions that it is an ILOLR.

Conclusion

Countries need a central bank to fill the limited role of a LOLR in a financial panic. Central banks have no special function when a financial crisis occurs. Other agencies must then take charge. The IMF has neither attribute of a LOLR – power to create unlimited amounts of high-powered money and independent authority to exercise that power. It is not needed if many countries experience a financial panic – each of them has a central bank. If many countries face financial crises, each of them has to reconstruct the broken elements of its financial system, whether domestic institutions or negotiations with foreign lenders. If they need to borrow abroad, they will find private sector lenders in international capital markets if they will pay a penalty rate and offer good collateral. These are the terms on which the IMF now says it will lend. The IMF may then be a lender in competition with private capital markets, but that does not make it an ILOLR. The IMF was established in 1944 to serve as a lender to countries when private international capital markets were limited and repressed. In the 1990s private international capital markets are deregulated and flush with funds. Is the existence of the IMF in this decade a statement that the market is a failure?

Reference

Fischer, S. (1999) 'On the Need for an International Lender of Last Resort.' Paper presented at the joint luncheon of the American Economic Association and the American Finance Association, New York, 3 January. (Page references are to the online version of the paper: http://www.imf.org/ external/np/speeches/1999/010399.HTM.)

21 Earmarks of a lender of last resort

Anna J. Schwartz

Some observers of the financial distress of countries in Asia and Latin America in recent years have suggested that what the world needs is an international lender of last resort. The institution that could serve this purpose, it is claimed, is the International Monetary Fund (IMF), either as presently constituted, or perhaps with some minor adjustments of its mandate.

In the first part of this lecture, I define the role of a lender of last resort in a domestic setting, give the historical context of the origin of the institution and cite examples of a lender of last resort that performed well and examples of a lender of last resort that performed poorly. I then describe modifications in this century of the time-honoured rules for a lender of last resort, and sum up the discussion by listing the attributes of a lender of last resort in a domestic context. In the second part of the paper, I examine the changing role of the International Monetary Fund since its creation in 1944. I then ask whether it is possible for an international institution like the IMF to possess the attributes of a lender of last resort. The answer, I believe, is negative. In the third part of the paper I conclude that world capital markets are prepared to hasten the recovery of countries in financial distress by lending to them on appropriate terms, putting in question the need for IMF lending.

1. The domestic context

Definition of a lender of last resort

A responsibility of a central bank, the institution that occupies a central position within a country's financial system, is to serve as a lender of last resort in order to maintain an unimpaired payments system. Let me first note what the term 'payments system' refers to, and then how a payments system becomes impaired and what a lender of last resort does to prevent it from happening. A payments system refers to the procedures used to arrange transfers and advances of money between individuals and firms in an economy.

To answer the question about how a payments system becomes impaired, it is necessary to describe a modern banking system. It is a fractional reserve requirements banking system. In such a system, ordinary banks meet their reserve requirements – a fraction of the deposits on their books – by holding as vault cash the notes of the central bank and maintaining reserve balances with the central bank. Central banks control both the issue of bank notes and bank reserves – the sum of which is known as high-powered money.

One way a payments system may become impaired is when depositors fear for the safety of their deposits and run on banks. By withdrawing their deposits in cash, they squeeze the reserves of the banking system, threatening continued convertibility of deposits into cash. The fear that demands of depositors for cash cannot be met leads to a scramble for high-powered money. In a futile attempt to restore reserves, banks may call loans, refuse to roll over existing loans, or resort to selling assets. This is the sequence of events that impairs the payments system. It can also happen when fears prevail that funds are unavailable at any price to enable sound debtors to make payments that are due. The entire financial system is then at risk, as financial services are disrupted, and economic activity is reduced.

Central banks as lenders of last resort

During the nineteenth century, central banks had to learn the role of lender of last resort. They learned initially to provide the banks with additional reserves to cut short a panic once it had begun, but eventually learned to act in advance to avert its occurrence. The traditional way to discharge the responsibility was to extend loans of high-powered money to all solvent banks and all solvent borrowers that were temporarily illiquid. The only institution that had the resources to provide such loans in a crisis was the central bank, which could create high-powered money without limit, and hence was the lender of last resort.

The prescription for the exercise of lender of last resort responsibility was developed by Henry Thornton in 1802 and by Walter Bagehot in 1873. They advised that eligibility for loans be limited to solvent banks, that the banks pay a penalty rate for the loan, that is, a rate higher than the prevailing market interest rate, and that the banks offer good collateral. The offer of good collateral was one indication that the bank requesting the loan was indeed solvent. It was also important for the central bank to give timely and predictable signals to market participants of institutional readiness to make available an augmented supply of funds. The signal in and of itself was often sufficient to allay alarm, so that the funds were never drawn on.

The British model of a lender of last resort

The Bank of England was a slow learner of the need for lender of last resort assistance. A series of financial panics in 1825, 1847, 1857, and 1866 occurred before it developed the appropriate response to restore public confidence in the financial system. It was ineffective in quelling each of these four panics. It provided some assistance but not enough, and it did so hesitantly, so financial markets were not reassured. The panic of 1866, however, was the last one that the British experienced. After that date, the Bank of England was alert to the threat of panic and took actions that prevented the effects of individual bank failures from spreading to the entire financial system.

Evolution of the concept of the lender of last resort in the US

In this country the First Bank (1791–1811) and the Second Bank (1818–36) of the United States were precursors of a central bank, but it was not until 1913 with the founding of the Federal Reserve System that the idea of a lender of last resort was given substance. The immediate cause for the implementation of the concept was the panic of 1907, the last of a series after the Civil War (1873, 1884, 1890, 1893) that had destabilized US financial markets, though, as I have noted, there were no comparable British panics after 1866. This difference in the experience of panics in the two countries was explained in part by the unit banking system and undiversified asset portfolios of US banks and the highly concentrated British banking system with well-diversified asset portfolios. Hence US banks were more prone to fail than were British banks. The other part of the explanation was the absence in this country of a lender of last resort comparable to the Bank of England.

The institution that had been corralled into service during panics before 1914 in the absence of a US lender of last resort was the regional clearinghouse association of banks in selected cities (New York, St. Louis, New Orleans, Baltimore, and Atlanta). During panics, the clearinghouses issued loan certificates that banks used as if they were legal reserves. Loan certificates have been described as 'quasi-high-powered money.'

The most usual feature of a panic, when depositors sought to convert deposits into cash, was the decision by banks to restrict cash payments, that is, the banks restricted the amount a depositor could withdraw as cash, say, to $10 a week, when the deposit account was a large multiple of that amount. The issue of loan certificates by the clearinghouses for which the banks were charged interest halted the impairment of the payments system. Clearinghouses during panic times enabled banks to continue lending without having to pay out their reserves, and firms and households had the means to pay their debts.

It was dissatisfaction with this ad hoc arrangement to cope with panics that led to the creation of the Federal Reserve System. During the 1920s many banks failed but no panic developed. The first test of the Federal Reserve as a lender of last resort came in November 1930, when a run started on a large investment banking firm in the South, and in December 1930, when a run on a large New York City bank led to panic conditions. The Federal Reserve failed that test as well as subsequent ones during panics in 1931, 1932, and 1933. The toll of bank failures and the one-third reduction in the quantity of money that it entailed over this period resulted in the adoption of deposit insurance, when an effective lender of last resort would have obviated the need for such an agency.

Lenders of last resort since the great depression

Neither the Bank of England nor the Federal Reserve has conducted lender of last resort operations in recent years according to the principles established by Thornton and Bagehot. The injunction to lend freely has been modified by involving other commercial institutions in addition to the central bank in rescuing troubled institutions. In the case of the Bank of England, this modification started as early as 1890, when the Bank arranged for other banks to join in the rescue of Baring Bros. This practice also occurs in France and Germany. In the US, the recent rescue of Long Term Capital Management was organized by the Federal Reserve Bank of New York in 1998, but only with private contributions.[1] In addition, banking problems are often resolved by the deposit insurance agency, not the central bank.

A second modification has characterized the injunction to lend only to temporarily illiquid but solvent banks. The justification for this change is the allegation, first, that during a crisis, the lender of last resort cannot distinguish between an illiquid and an insolvent bank and, second, that it may be desirable to rescue an insolvent bank because of contagion effects on sound banks. Neither of these allegations is convincing to me.[2] The practice of central banks, however, has been to prop up banks 'too big to fail,' and, if insolvent banks are shut, to do so only in the case of small banks. The Federal Reserve in 1989–90 gave discount window assistance to insolvent banks until the deposit insurance agency was in a position to resolve their future.[3]

Finally, the injunction to lend at penalty rates on good collateral has not been observed. Central banks have given assistance at market rates or below market rates. In addition, far from signaling in advance their intention to

---

1 See Edwards (1999), who believes that 'traditional lender-of-last-resort approach' would probably not have failed in the case of LTCM's collapse, it was 'almost certainly not' 'the most efficient way for the Federal Reserve to provide assistance.'

2 See Chari and Kehoe (1999), who explain: 'The prospect of receiving funds from the lender of last resort, even if the bank is insolvent, reduces the extent to which interest rates on deposits vary with the riskiness of the bank's portfolio. Thus, the lender of last resort implicitly subsidizes the risk taking by banks. The subsidy leads banks to take on excessive risk and paradoxically can make financial panics more frequent and more severe when they occur. One way the lender of last resort could avoid moral hazard is to lend only to illiquid but solvent banks' (p. 14).

3 See Anna J. Schwartz, 'The Misuse of the Fed's Discount Window,' *Federal Reserve Bank of St. Louis Review* 74(5). September/October 1992, pp. 58–69. The FDIC Improvement Act of 1991 limits the use of the discount window for long-term loans to troubled banks. It also curtails the regulator's discretion regarding when to intervene in the case of an undercapitalized bank.

provide the financial markets with assistance, central banks have preferred to be ambiguous, so banks would not presume that they would be bailed out in case of difficulties. 'Constructive ambiguity' supposedly constrains excessive risk taking by banks.

These modifications of the time-honoured rules, it seems to me, replace them with discretion and, contrary to the briefs by central banks in their defense, invite forbearance on their part.

Lender of last resort problem in an emerging market country

Central banks in emerging market countries can serve as lenders of last resort for domestic borrowers with domestic-currency-denominated liabilities. They can always print any amount of domestic currency to accommodate a sudden surge in demand. In emerging market countries, however, ordinary banks may borrow foreign currency and make domestic loans not only in domestic currency but also in foreign currency. If there is a surge in demand for foreign currencies, central banks can provide only the available foreign exchange reserves they hold; they cannot create more. I mention a possible solution to this problem at a later point.

A summary of the domestic context

A domestic lender of last resort can create high-powered money denominated in its own national currency. It can exercise its own discretion in allocating the resources it commands. Time-honoured rules for the decisions it makes about how much to lend to which institutions on what conditions have been bent over the years since the rules were formulated. Nineteenth and twentieth century-type panics are no longer observed. Instead, lenders of last resort intervene whenever they believe there is a risk of contagion. I defer consideration of the validity of the idea of contagion until I deal with the claims of the International Monetary Fund that it can serve as an international lender of last resort.

2. The international context

The changing mission of the International Monetary Fund

I shall first describe the evolution of the IMF's mission from what it was originally conceived to be. It was created in 1944 by the framers of the Bretton Woods Articles of Agreement. They believed that international capital flows had destabilized the 1930s, and that floating exchange rates had encouraged competitive devaluation of national currencies. Therefore, the Bretton Woods design for the postwar world permitted government controls to limit international capital flows and provided for exchange rates pegged in terms of the US dollar or gold to achieve exchange rate stability.

In this set-up, the IMF's role was to enforce the rules in the pegged exchange rate system about when fundamental disequilibrium justified changing the peg, and to provide temporary loans to countries with a balance-of-payments deficit. The source of IMF resources was initially $8.8 billion in quotas that members contributed (25 per cent in gold, 75 per cent in currencies) – quotas that could be raised every five years – plus in 1961, up to $6 billion in their currencies that 10 industrial countries agreed to lend the Fund. A further addition to IMF resources was the creation of Special Drawing Rights (SDRs) by a 1967 amendment to the Articles of Agreement – so-called paper gold – and their first allocation in 1970. SDRs allowed the IMF to provide credit to member countries in excess of their quota subscriptions. Central banks, when allocated SDRs, can monetize them by issuing their equivalent value in national currencies.

The Bretton Woods system broke down in 1971, for reasons that do not need to be reviewed here. What is pertinent to this discussion is that the collapse destroyed the IMF's purpose. Floating exchange rates, the successor to the Bretton Woods pegged exchange rates, eliminated the IMF's exchange rate regulatory role, and changed the character of balance-of-payments problems. Since 1971, the IMF has been seeking a redefinition of its role.

In the international context, one important change in the environment in which the IMF operated under the Bretton Woods system is that since its demise, a highly liquid international financial system has arisen, and the world capital market has become increasingly mobile. The significance of this change is the basis for the view that I present in the third part of this lecture.

During the 1970s and 1980s, the direction the IMF pursued for itself was the provision of advice and information to its members numbering over 180 countries. The Mexican bailout in 1995 that the Clinton administration engineered, however pointed the IMF in a new direction. After some false starts, the administration orchestrated a $50 billion rescue package – Mexico did not in fact obtain the full amount – to be provided by the Federal Reserve, the Treasury's Exchange Stabilization Fund, the IMF, and the Bank for International Settlements. This experience planted the idea that the IMF could function as an international lender of last resort.

Why the IMF cannot be a lender of last resort

In a luncheon speech at the American Economic Association meeting on January 3, 1999, Stanley Fischer, the first deputy managing director of the IMF, argued the case, in a reformed international financial system, for 'an agency that will act as lender of last resort for countries facing a crisis.' He asserted that there was a need for such an agency and 'that the IMF is increasingly playing that role, and that changes in the international system now under consideration will make it possible for it to exercise that function more effectively.'[4] The speech raises the question whether it is true that the IMF possesses the attributes of a lender of last resort.

I have shown that central banks have the capacity to serve as their banks' and, more generally, their financial system's lender of last resort. They can create high-powered base money in their own national currency, they can act quickly, and they need the consent of no other agency to act. The IMF lacks each of these attributes. It cannot create high-powered money in any national currency, so it cannot create international reserves. Fischer's answer is that the IMF 'has access to a pool of resources, which it can onlend to member countries.' He notes that, if the IMF's resources bore the same size relative to output, to the quota formula, to the volume of world trade, as in 1945, its resources would be three, five, or more than nine times larger than they will be in 1999. Is there an implication that quota increases that have been sought every five years since the IMF's founding will in future be sought more often?

Fischer also counts on the IMF's use of authorization to create SDRs as a supplement to its resources as well as its ability to borrow. One major difference between a central bank lender of last resort and the IMF, to which Fischer does not allude, is that the IMF needs a vote of its Executive Board to take any action. It has no independent authority, such as a central bank has, even one subject to the consent of the minister of finance. The IMF cannot issue SDRs and cannot borrow except if authorized by vote of the member countries.

The IMF cannot act quickly. Before the IMF provides money to a borrowing country, it first engages in lengthy negotiations to introduce a reform program. If it abides by time-honoured principles, a national lender of last resort rescues solvent banks temporarily short of liquidity. It does not rescue insolvent institutions. The IMF has no such inhibitions.

Fischer refers to a complaint that the Fund is too slow in emergencies, but counters that the Emergency Financing Mechanism, introduced after the Mexican crisis, enables it to move very rapidly. Very rapidly means after weeks or months, while an agreement with the distressed country is produced. Lending with conditionality and providing money only in tranches do not meet the requirements for overcoming a shortage of liquidity. A national central bank can promptly provide liquidity to the money market without administrative complications.

The IMF, it is clear, is only a simulacrum of a lender of last resort. It is not the real thing. What will its function be? There will be changes in the international financial system that Fischer describes – a shift to floating exchange

---

4   See Stanley Fischer, 'On the Need for an International Lender of Last Resort,' revised version of a paper delivered at the American Economic Association and the American Finance Association. New York, January 3, 1999. Available at: http://www.imf.org/external/np/speeches/1999/010399.HTM. Fisher is not the only one to propose a lender of last resort role for the IMF. See also Steven Radelet and Jeffrey Sachs (1997) and George Soros (1998).

rates by emerging market countries, their holdings of international reserves will be larger, private sector institutions will be involved in rescues of countries in distress, and those countries will adopt international standards – but he does not enumerate any changes in the way the IMF operates. It will still provide loans to pay off a country's foreign debts, although since 1998 no longer at subsidized interest rates, and will impose fiscal and monetary conditions and micromanage institutional behaviour.

Fischer proposes that in the future the IMF will lend on Bagehot's rules through the Supplementary Reserve Facility. Given global capital markets that will be ready to lend to countries that are willing to pay a penalty rate of interest and to offer good collateral, is there a need for an IMF? Fischer parses lending freely as meaning 'ready to lend early and in sufficient amounts to other countries that might be affected by contagion from the crisis.' He nowhere defines contagion or justifies the assumption that it occurs.

The myth of contagion

Will an individual country that has mismanaged its affairs precipitate an international financial crisis? One myth is that the loss of creditworthiness by the country in question has a tequila effect. The supposed tequila effect is that other countries without the problems of the troubled country are unfairly tarnished as also subject to those problems. In this way, it is said, contagion spreads the crisis from its initial source to other innocent victims. The second myth is that a bailout of the troubled country is essential. The rationale is again the idea of contagion. Failure to organize a bailout will create an international financial crisis by a domino effect. Rescuing the troubled country saves the rest of the world from unwarranted financial collapse.

Contagion, if the term is used accurately, occurs only in circumstances in which other countries are free of the problems of the country that first experienced trouble and yet suffered capital flight. It has become a dogma since the 1995 Mexican bailout that there was a tequila effect as a result of its distress. The evidence that has been offered since then is that the currencies and stock markets of countries (other than the original one to surface with problems) have declined. What is overlooked or deliberately omitted is that the countries said to be victims of contagion had the same problems as were present in the country that was supposedly the source of contagion.

Glib references to spillovers from disturbances that originate elsewhere are common in the current literature on international financial crises. The truth is that it is not necessary to invoke spillovers to account for multi-country financial disturbances. Capital flight from countries with similar unsustainable policies is not evidence of contagion. Proponents of the contagion dogma do not explain the absence of contagion from the New York stock market crash of 1987 nor from the 1990 Tokyo stock market and property bubble crashes.

It is ironic that the Mexican bailout of 1995 has inspired the model of what needs to be done. The emphasis by the IMF is on a standing procedure and faster access to funds. It thinks of itself as a financial panic lender. Lending by the IMF and the other rescuers, however, was not directed to the Mexican money market. The question that should be asked is, for whose benefit was the Mexican rescue arranged? Is there any doubt that the loan package was designed to pay dollars to Mexicans and nationals of other countries who invested in government tesobonos and cetes as well as dollar-denominated loans to Mexican nonfinancial firms? Is that the reason emergency loans are needed? To eliminate risk from investment in high-yielding foreign assets?

People in countries that pursue unsound economic policies pay a heavy price for those mistakes – slower if not negative growth, government austerity, and unemployment. But US-backed bailouts protect investors who lent money to governments or private sector institutions, not the people who suffer the consequences of unsound policies. In the absence of the IMF loans, investors would have taken a hit, but economic conditions in Mexico would have been no worse than they were with the loan, and Mexico would not have had the burden of repaying the loan. The East Asian countries and Brazil that were recipients of IMF loans are further examples of bailouts that limit wealth losses by investors in advanced countries, without benefit to the local populations.

Moreover, the Mexican bailout may well have fostered the belief among foreign investors in the East Asian countries that they were extending riskless loans because the IMF would provide the funds to pay them off. That in itself is enough reason to question the ground for the IMF's intervention. And there are surely other reasons related to the IMF's policy recommendations as conditions for its loans that could be challenged.

In my view, an emerging country that gets into trouble does not need the ministrations of the IMF to overcome its difficulties. Instead of bailouts that create conditions that promote the spread of financial crisis, the country can travel a different road to recovery.

3. Recovery without the IMF

It is important to distinguish between a financial panic and a financial crisis. A financial panic occurs in the money market and is a threat to the economy's payments system. A panic can be quickly ended by a lender of last resort. The recent difficulties of emerging market countries have involved financial crises rather than financial panics. A financial crisis occurs when asset prices plunge, whether prices of equities, real estate, or commodities, when the exchange value of a national currency experiences substantial depreciation, when a large nonfinancial firm or a financial industry faces bankruptcy, or a sovereign debtor defaults. A financial crisis is a prolonged disturbance that is resolved by government agencies other than the lender of last resort, although at some stage it may provide liquidity to the market through the discount window or open market purchases.

In this country, the collapse of the savings and loan industry was an example of a financial crisis that initially involved the deposit insurance agency and subsequently a new agency – the Resolution Trust Corporation – to deal with the problem. Resolving the savings and loan crisis was not a lender of last resort responsibility.

The IMF thinks of itself not only as a financial panic lender but also as a crisis manager. It can fill neither role. Only the emerging market country can do so. If the banking system is short of liquidity, the domestic central bank, not the IMF, must create high-powered domestic money to calm depositor fears. If the problem is a shortage of foreign money, the answer again is not the IMF. Some emerging market countries have devised schemes to deal with a sudden demand for foreign currency. The Argentine central bank has an option that cost it 33 basis points, under a repurchase agreement with 14 international banks to swap Argentine government securities for up to $7 billion US dollars, for which it will pay LIBOR plus 205 basis points. The length of the loan varies from two to five years, depending on the counter-party bank. Mexico has an arrangement with 31 commercial banks for a $2.5 billion foreign currency credit line. These are emerging market country, not IMF initiatives.

Correction of the conditions that produced a financial crisis must fall on the troubled country, not the IMF. If the country cannot service or amortize its foreign borrowings, the country, not the IMF has to negotiate a workout with the foreign lenders. The same applies to firms or banks that cannot repay on due dates what they have borrowed. If individual banks, other financial institutions, corporate and nonfinancial businesses are insolvent, domestic agencies either exist or must be established to recapitalize them or shut them down.

Currency crises and severe banking problems have accompanied recent financial crises. Emerging market countries that peg the exchange rate of their currencies to the currency of a developed country are prone to currency crises. When foreign investors believe that the nominal parity of the currencies is inconsistent with economic fundamentals, they sell off the currencies. Efforts by the emerging market countries to support the pegged value by deploying foreign exchange reserves ultimately collapse, and they have no alternative but to allow the exchange value to float. Domestic entities with debts denominated in foreign currencies suffer. A depreciated exchange value of a national currency will recover when reformed internal policies signal to the market that the economy's health is improving.

Flaws in the operation of the banking systems of emerging market countries have been uncovered in the course of financial crises. Bad loans are a pervasive problem of their portfolios. The best hope to remedy a shortage of bank capital is for foreign banks to acquire an interest in the banks of emerging market countries.

Financial crises, unlike panics, are not quickly ended. They may require fiscal support, and the resolution may not be attained for months or years.

Compensating for the loss of wealth that a financial crisis imposes may exact a reduction in personal consumption and increased national saving over an extended period. This is what troubled countries have to endure. The IMF does not spare them these bleak consequences. Every country that has been a recipient of IMF loans has suffered a severe decline in output, punishing high interest rates, and accelerating inflation, despite IMF loans.[5]

The IMF was established in 1944 to serve as a lender to countries when private international capital markets were limited and repressed. IMF lending had a proper role in that regime but it no longer exists. Nowadays, private international capital markets are deregulated and flush with funds. IMF lending in the regime that now exists is a carryover for which there is no proper role. Every day brings news of the success of emerging market countries in raising funds from pension, mutual, and hedge funds, even countries barely over a financial crisis. South Korea, five months after its crisis in November 1997, sold a bond offering of $4 billion to international investors. Colombia sold $500 million in bonds in March 1999 six months after its crisis. Thailand, Mexico, and Argentina in the past year also had similar success in raising funds. Peru sought a loan but rejected the offer because it was unwilling to pay the credit risk interest premium.

What is the secret of access to capital markets? Countries that need to borrow abroad can count on finding private sector lenders if they will pay a penalty rate and offer good collateral. These are the terms, according to Fischer, on which the IMF in the future will lend. Does the IMF see itself as a lender in competition with capital markets?

Some countries that cannot meet the conditions for borrowing that the private market sets may require financial aid. Outright gifts to them from an international agency may be the right solution. A case can be made for such gifts to countries that have endured earthquakes, hurricanes, monsoons, plagues.

For economic development, however, emerging market countries that are reforming their banking structures, creating the proper mix of regulation, oversight, and market discipline to enforce acceptable rules of conduct in lending and investing, pursuing sound monetary and fiscal policies, and encouraging open capital markets will be well on the way to recovery from recent financial crises.

Concluding comments

To create a more stable international financial system, each country should have in place a lender of last resort. A lender of last resort can forestall

---

5 Thus far, Brazil has not experienced high inflation in the aftermath of its financial crisis. The delinking of wages and the exchange rate before the onset of crisis conditions appears to be the explanation for this result.

threats to the payments system associated with bank runs and stock market crashes. Despite references to the IMF as an international lender of last resort, it lacks the attributes of such an authority either in a domestic or global setting.

Financial crises differ from financial panics. Crises require the involvement of domestic agencies other than the lender of last resort. The IMF is no substitute for these crisis resolvers.

Crises and panics differ from currency crises, depreciation of the exchange value of a national currency as the result of a loss of confidence by investors in the currency of a country pursuing unsustainable policies, encompassing large current account deficits, excessive credit growth and misallocation of investment funds, excessive monetary expansion, and fiscal laxness. Currency crises occur when the nominal exchange rates at which countries peg their currencies are inconsistent with the economic fundamentals.

The widening and deepening of world capital markets in recent decades have established them as providers of loans to creditworthy countries, putting in question the need for IMF lending.

References

Bagehot, Walter (1873). *Lombard Street: A description of the money market*, London: Henry S. King and Company.

Chari, V. V. and Patrick J. Kehoe (1999). Asking the Right Questions About the IMF. *The Region* 13 (May); 2–26. Federal Reserve Bank of Minneapolis.

Edwards, Franklin R. (1999). Hedge Funds and the Collapse of Long-Term Capital Management. *Journal of Economic Perspectives*, 13(2) Spring: 189–210.

Fischer, Stanley (1999). On the Need for an International Lender of Last Resort. Available at http:/www.imf.org/external/np/speeches/1999/010399.HTM.

Radelet, Steven and Jeffrey Sachs (1997). What have we learned, so far, from the Asian financial crisis? mimeo, Harvard Institute for International Development. Available at; www.hiid.harvard.edu.

Schwartz, Anna J. (1992). The Misuse of the Fed's Discount Window. *Federal Reserve Bank of St. Louis Review*, 74(5): September/October, pp. 58–69.

Soros, George (1998). The Crisis of Global Capitalism. *Wall Street Journal*, September 15, 1998.

Thornton, Henry (1802[1965]), *An inquiry into the nature and effects of the paper credit of Great Britain*. Edited with an Introduction by F. A v. Hayek. New York: Augustus M. Kelley.

Index

Abel, John 54
Abramovitz, Moses 346
acceptance/s 225, 25
acceptance houses 231, 249, 308
Accepting Houses Association 359
accountants 345, 349
accounting principles 456
advance/s 74, 97, 98, 101, 102, 108, 109, 111, 113, 118, 119, 121, 122, 124, 185, 186, 187, 189, 190, 191, 192, 195, 202, 235, 239, 240, 250, 275, 276, 340, 341, 371, 383, 468
Africa 335
alarm 98, 99, 100, 101, 108, 114, 116, 117, 121, 122, 124, 131, 144, 209 n.12, 248, 253, 254, 269, 270, 271, 272, 367, 369, 376, 407, 410, 411, 412
Alchian, A. and Klein, B. 379–80
Aldrich-Vreeland Act 288, 291, 294
America *see under* United States
American Bankers' Association 364
American Economic Association 463, 473
Amsterdam 8, 9, 19, 57
anonymity 312, 313
'apprehension' 409, 412, 421
'apprehension minimum' 271, 404, 410
Argentina/the Argentine 248, 309, 372, 374, 427, 437, 448, 478
Armstrong Whitworth 340
Arrow, K.J. 356, 357, 363
Ashton, T.S. 339
Asia 335, 441, 447, 448, 449, 450, 454, 457, 458, 459, 468
Asian Monetary Fund 335
asset/s xix, 110, 183, 186, 191, 192, 193, 206, 235, 245, 247, 249, 254, 256, 274, 275, 276, 277, 281, 306, 312, 324, 342, 345, 346, 353, 371, 377, 379, 417, 418, 428, 430
  bad 341, 342, 418
  disposal 346, 347
  high-yielding foreign 476
  liquidating 340
  portfolios 470

  price collapse 374, 378
  valuation 342, 387
  values 359, 362, 421
Atlanta 470
assignats 22, 23
Australia 260 n.7, 314, 386, 409
Austria 349
  Banking Act 1862 260 n.5
  treasury certificates 260 n.5
  National Bank 293
Ayr (Air) bank 6, 7, 11, 13, 291, 348

Bache and Company, J.S. 344
Bagehot, Walter xiii, xvii, xx, xxi, xxiii, 85–125, 131, 132, 151, 159, 187 n.2, 189, 201, 223, 227, 228, 229, 230–31, 250, 263, 270–78, 279, 282, 294, 300, 305, 306, 309, 310, 314, 316, 317, 318, 319, 320, 321, 325, 338–9, 349, 352–66, 368, 369, 370, 372, 373, 378, 383, 399–422, 423, 425, 429, 430, 469
  function 362
  Lombard Street xx, 152, 183, 189, 222, 223, 229, 231, 233, 270, 282, 286 n.10, 310, 339, 349, 353, 368, 378, 399, 400–14, 423, 427
  prescription 441
  principle/s 324, 373, 471
  Rule/s 271, 287, 440, 465, 475
  The English Constitution 399
'bail-in' 332, 434, 436, 441
bail-out/s 257, 258, 259, 268, 273, 307, 310, 312, 313, 317, 333, 334, 335, 346, 383–5, 402, 403, 418, 419, 420, 421, 438, 445–62, 465, 466, 472, 473, 475, 476
balance of payments 264, 267, 311, 446, 454, 457
  deficit/s 282 n.3, 298, 473
  disequilibrium 224
  French 232
balance of trade 9, 10, 15, 16, 45, 207, 208, 225, 253, 273
balance sheet ratios 360

For Product Safety Concerns and Information please contact our EU
representative GPSR@taylorandfrancis.com
Taylor & Francis Verlag GmbH, Kaufingerstraße 24, 80331 München, Germany